THE WOODWORKER'S FURNITURE CONSTRUCTION/REPAIR BIBLE

THE WOODWORKER'S FURNITURE CONSTRUCTION/REPAIR BIBLE

BY V. M. MacKERCHER

TAB BOOKS

BLUE RIDGE SUMMIT, PA. 17214

FIRST EDITION

FIRST PRINTING—DECEMBER 1979

Printed in the United States of America

Library of Congress Cataloging in Publication Data

MacKercher, V. M.
The woodworker's furniture construction/repair bible.

Includes index.
1. Furniture making. 2. Furniture—Repairing. I. Title.
TT194.M32 684.1'04 79-22975
ISBN 0-8306-9716-6
ISBN 0-8306-1134-7 pbk.

Preface

Those persons who appreciate beauty and cherish its every manifestation necessarily regard the acquisition of fine furniture as essential to the enhancement of their homes. Whether the pieces they treasure were carefully culled from swap meets and garage sales at little cost, or purchased from prestigious showrooms at great expense, their preservation is of paramount concern. And because the activites of daily living—the usual happy complement of hospitable parties, playful children and romping pets—take their inevitable toll in scratches, gouges, stains and burns, fine furniture owners find themselves in the position of having to learn something about repair and restoration if they are to preserve their precious pieces.

This book was conceived as an aid to those persons. Its pages are packed with suggestions on the creation and maintenance of beautiful furniture. Its readers will include those who elect to build their own furniture from raw lumber, collectors who restore antiques for pleasure and profit, and handy men and women interested in home repairs.

Even the reader who does not intend to undertake any of these tasks himself will find this volume illuminating. It describes successful methods of construction and repair so that the reader who prefers to direct these projects, rather than perform them himself, will be informed as to how they should be accomplished and, thus, be better able to supervise the work.

This volume cannot presume to contain all the answers. Furniture construction and restoration is a highly complex art about which no one can profess to know everything. The continuous invention and discovery of new building materials and finishing products, the introduction of fresh design concepts, and the changing demands of constantly evolving life styles are always opening unexplored vistas to furniture craftsmen. Those for whom this work is a labor of love rejoice in its infinite variety; they welcome the challenge of each new project, deriving their greatest satisfactions from doing a difficult job well.

Fortunately for the novice, woodworking is an art in which even the inexperienced need not meet with failure. Wood itself is a marvelously resilient material. Like the tree from which it comes (which even to the ancients was a reassuring symbol of eternal life) wood is capable of withstanding the rigors of climactic change, insufficient moisture and mishandling. Notwithstanding these blights, wood, like the parent tree itself, demonstrates a springtime resurgence of beauty once it is given a kinder exposure and gentler treatment.

This book outlines the maintenance necessary to keep this versatile, durable natural product at its beautiful best. Considering that wood fashions many of humanity's most useful and exquisite artifacts and is representative of significant handcraft achievements, it richly deserves our tender loving care.

V. M. MacKercher

Contents

Introduction

The art of working in wood is almost as old as Man himself. From the moment when the first savage used a sharp stone to whittle a point on his staff, rather than searching for a fallen tree bough with a natural point, human beings have been working in wood to fashion the tools, weapons, household utensils, furnishings and shelters which are the revealing artifacts of his life style. His developing skill and creativity in crafting woods are regarded as significant gauges of his evolutionary advances and his degree of civilization. Later generations judge his intelligence quotient by his works. His concepts, the functions for which they are designed, and the finesse with which they are executed, attest to his broadening mental horizons. Every novice woodworker who undertakes to learn this challenging craft follows in the footsteps of this first woodworker, experiencing anew the wonder and satisfaction of hitherto-unrealized, ever-burgeoning creativity.

For the modern woodworker, as for his savage antecedents, tools provide the means by which he imparts his creative vision to the raw lumber. Therefore, discussions of all kinds of hand-manipulated and power-driven tools are given paramount importance in this text. Basic hand tools—because they most sensitively interpret the woodworker's designs, yet are versatile implements for other construction endeavors—represent a valid investment for every householder. Their functional significance merits the elaborately detailed description given them in this text. Because hand tools demand much less operational and storage space and are relatively less costly than power tools, they are much more practical for the home workshop than are their mechanized counterparts.

However, power tools—particularly portable models capable of performing multiple operations—are fully covered as well. These are recommended for the serious artisan for whom woodworking and furniture construction are more than casual hobbies.

The information on tools given in this text serves to guide the woodworker in making the proper selection for his particular projects. It teaches him how to recognize top quality tools, discusses the greater versatility of certain models, describes the usage and operation of all basic tools, and suggests best methods of repairing and maintaining them. Using this information, the hobbyist will be better informed as to which hand and power tools to acquire and will limit his choice to those which are truly useful, durable and designed for ease of handling.

To realize the fullest potential of a craft, whatever its challenges, the artisan must fully understand the nature of the material in which he works. The sculptor must utilize the malleable plasticity of the clay, the mason must overcome the obdurate resistance of the granite, the painter must become adept at tempering colors in infinite tonal gradations. The woodworker, in his turn, must become familiar with the attributes of all species of woods. He must acquaint himself with the essential differences between so-called "hardwoods" and "softwoods," study the distinctive grain patterns which different ways of cutting lumber produce, understand the relative strengths and weaknesses of various woods, and learn how to use them to his own advantage or overcome them by careful structuring.

To this purpose, a section of this book is devoted to describing how wood grows, how lumber is cut and dressed, how wood is marketed and purchased, and the best ways of storing it for future use.

One of the major concerns of this text is that of furniture construction. This important section describes the ways in which individual pieces of wood are joined—with nails and screws, with hardware fasteners, and with wooden jointing reinforced with glue. The latter method—because it represents the strongest and most satisfactory way of joining wood—is explored in comprehensive detail. All the principal types of wood joinery are covered in respect to design, construction and relative strengths. Diagrams are given of all types of wood joints, along with explicit instructions on how to fashion them and suggestions as to where they are most advantageously employed in making furniture. Also included is a comparative study of adhesives which describes their relative merits and makes recommendations as to the use of specific glues for certain jobs.

Every woodworker, even though his interest is primarily that of repair and refinishing furniture, should be thoroughly knowledgeable of the basic principles of furniture construction. Therefore, in this text, we study in comprehensive detail the various operations commonly performed in making furniture. How to construct surfaces (such as table tops, desk tops and counters), how to attach legs, how to build cabinet frames, how to make and fit drawers, how to install shelving, best ways of fashioning and hanging drawers—these and other essential construction procedures are explained in graphic, easy-to-understand, step-by-step instructions. Thus, when the reader undertakes to execute any of the furniture repairs described in the next section, he already understands the original construction which must be rebuilt if the piece is to be restored.

Whether or not the reader is an antique collector, he will make good use of the section on furniture repair. Even recently purchased contemporary furniture suffers some damage with constant use and occasionally requires some repair. This section explains how to repair such structural defects as warped tops, balky drawers, out-of-alignment frames and carcases. Numbers of tested methods for removing surface blemishes, renewing worn finishes, restoring color and repairing chipped veneer are covered, as well as ways of eradicating scratches, gouges, dents, stains, burns and other disfiguring damage.

The *finish* given wood is of extreme important, both to the preservation of the wood and to its appearance. In this text, *transparent* finishes, which dramatically reveal and enhance the color and pattern of the grain, are described in wide variety. *Opaque* finishes, which conceal woods of unattractive or indifferent grain and camouflage with vibrant color the many structurally strong but plain looking wood products commonly in use today, are given full coverage. *Appliqued surfacing*—such as veneers, wood-grained plastics, tile, carved wooden moldings and medallions, decoupage and gold and silver leafing—are time-honored methods of enhancing furniture made of ugly or badly worn wood whose defects would be even more noticeable if given a revealing transparent finish. The applied surfacings which camouflage unattractive wood so satisfactorily are described in painstaking detail in these chapters. Each process is fully explained in easy-to-follow, step-by-step instructions so that even an amateur who has never before laid tile, glued veneer or appliqued decoupage can obtain professional results.

As regards the techniques of applying paint and stain, the woodworker has an exhaustively comprehensive manual in this text. Contained herein are thorough instructions for transparent finishes using all of the following media: wax, oil, stain, varnish, shellac and lacquer. Included are descriptions of the famous French polish finish, the always-successful varnish-and-oil finish, several interesting pickled finishes and bleached finishes. The always-charming antiqued finish, which adds such patina to either transparent finishes or enamel finishes, is fully covered in all of its interesting variations. Also included are many novelty finishes—such as the marbleized enamel finish which simulates the genuine stone, the flame finish which produces such dramatic effects on nude wood, and the antiqued gold leafing which adds such richness to fine furniture.

In addition, this book contains a wealth of general information of pertinent interest to professional and amateur woodworkers. It affords a quick and comprehensive reference on any and every aspect of wood working—from ordering the correct lumber and driving the proper nail to correctly cleaning the paint brushes. Every hobbyist will gain greater insight into a project by reading the simple explanations and examining the helpful sketches in this book. So well-delineated and detailed is its approach to the seemingly insurmountable tasks of furniture construction, repair and refinishing that even the first-time amateur gains confidence. With this manual, discovering and exploring one's own creativity becomes a truly enjoyable adventure, resulting in personally crafted furniture of which one can be justly proud.

Chapter 1

The Home Workshop

When planning a home workshop, the first consideration should be the amount of space designated to it because the amount of space available determines the size and number of tools with which the workshop may be outfitted. Perhaps there is room in the basement which could be adapted to woodworking. A shop area might be partitioned off at one end of the carport. Attics are ideal if they are heated. Perhaps the garage provides space. Sometimes the only feasible solution is the erection of a building specially constructed as a woodshop. Whatever the space selected, a sketch to scale of the area, designating the placement of the various pieces of equipment, will help in making realistic, workable plans.

The work area should contain three different categories of tools: (1) the hand tools most often needed in woodworking and home repairs (this category of tools may require constant expansion as new tools are added for new projects), (2) power tools, both stationary and portable, needed to expedite certain woodworking chores, and (3) the tools necessary for the repair, sharpening and maintenance of the shop equipment itself.

In furnishing the home woodworking shop, the primary requirement is a workbench. This necessary item is the very nucleus of the shop. It is the hub of all activity, the production center for every task. At one end of the workbench, the vise is mounted on which all work is secured. At the other end, if space permits, another cabinet unit the same height as the woodwork bench is placed at right angles to the workbench to double the counter-top working space (see Fig. 1-1).

The workbench and the cabinet are both fitted with drawers and open shelves. The drawers provide excellent storage for small, flat hand tools, such as measuring rules and gauges, files, rasps, cabinet scrapers, spokeshaves, burnishers, nail sets, drill and brace bits, as well as for such materials as abrasive papers, boxes of steel wool, packages of cheesecloth, sponges, and similar items.

Shelves are excellent places to keep the large hand tools too big and bulky to be hung on the wall, portable power tools, hand sanders, oil stone and oil can and other tools necessary for the maintenance of the equipment itself.

Every wall in the workshop should be surfaced in pegboard, on which frequently-used hand tools such as saws, hammers, mallets, scissors, chisels, gouges, braces, drills, clamps, and cramps can be mounted for quick accessibility. Painting a silhouette of every tool on the pegboard indicating where that tool is hung makes for the easy replacement of all tools.

In addition to the two counter cabinets, the workshop should contain at least one sturdy, free-standing worktable which would act as an island work space for projects which need to be worked on "in the round"—on all four sides simultaneously. Also, such a worktable offers a safer, less congested space in which to operate portable power tools, which operate at high speeds and require greater caution and attention while they are in use.

For screws, nails, tacks, bolts and nuts and similar small hardware, see-through cannisters or apothecary jars similar to those used in kitchens are ideal. In these, screws and nails in graded size lots can be kept on a shelf above a section of the counter top where, for reasons of lighting or access to the tools for such jobs, most of the nail driving and screw setting is done.

Several wall-mounted cupboards are necessary for storing sharp tools which might be dangerous in the hands of children or which are less frequently used; and a closed container like a cupboard and a coating of paste wax or light grease are necessary to prevent them from rusting, particularly if the workshop is damp.

At least one good-sized metal cabinet is necessary to hold such inflammables as paint, varnish, sealer, turpentine, paint remover, shellac, lacquer, and alcohol.

Several vertical cabinets are useful for storing lumber and plywood, as well as for housing the pushbroom, utility vacuum cleaner and scrub pails necessary for cleaning the shop itself. If the floor space is insufficient to allow for all the lumber needing storage, the walls can be hung with bracketed shelving which would hold stacked planks up near the ceiling line. Open ceiling beams provide

Fig. 1-1. Example of a well-organized workshop.

excellent storage for doweling, two-by-fours and light planking. Small strips of lumber are nailed every foot or so between two parallel beams, and the lumber is stored across them, between the beams and parallel with them, resting on the wooden strips.

Such facilities as sufficient light and air must be considered. The electrical wiring itself is of vital importance. For safety and efficiency, the circuits must be adequate to supply the demands for light and power made of them without being overloaded. Wherever possible, each power tool should be wired individually, instead of relying on a multiple outlet cord which plugs into a wall receptacle.

Each work area and electric tool area should be brightly lighted and the entire shop adequately illuminated, for safety's sake and to provide the visibility necessary for efficiency.

The shop should be well ventilated, otherwise harmful solvent vapors will be present during the finishing and restoring processes. An exhaust fan on the outside wall, as well as sufficient windows to open, will allow bad air to escape and fresh air to constantly circulate.

Another consideration vital to the efficient functioning of the workshop is the positioning and handling given the various power tools. Every power tool should be accorded sufficient space for best operation and safety. The operator should learn exactly how to use the tool and what are the tool's strengths and weaknesses. All guards and safety devices provided with the tool should be used every time it is operated. A central cut-out switch, which turns off all tool machines when the master switch is pulled, is an excellent precautionary device. Magnetic switches installed on each machine are wise safety features, as is the use of push sticks, rather than fingers, near high-speed cutters. A safety feature of paramount importance is a fire extinguisher hanging near every exit door.

Although hand tools are the most generally used and, therefore, the most essential kinds of tools to own, power tools are great time and labor savers and are almost indispensable in the construction of large projects. The speed, accuracy and ease with which they perform many humdrum routine jobs is remarkable.

PORTABLE POWER TOOLS

Generally, portable power tools are better than stationary ones for the home workshop. Portable power tools have four virtues which the larger machine tools do not have:

1. They do not take up as much space as the large stationary models.
2. They can be carried to the work, rather than carrying the heavy lumber to them.
3. They can be stored when not in use.
4. They are much more economical to purchase, operate and maintain than larger, more complex tool machines which frequently require the installation of additional wiring before they can be used.

In essence, unless the workshop's productivity is such that the cost of large tool machines is warranted, portable power tools are the wiser choice.

To select the best power tools for home workshop projects, consideration should be given to the following attributes:

1. Capacity of the tool
2. Type of beatings
3. Availability of parts and service
4. Revolutions per minute (rpm) of the motor
5. Efficiency of the safety guards and electric cord groundings
6. Cost to purchase

The question of which power tools to acquire should be regulated by the operations which the woodworker wishes expedited and which such tools could handle. Suggestions would include a ¼-inch portable drill, a 3-inch portable saber saw, a 3-inch portable belt sander, a ¼-inch portable router, and a 6-inch portable band saw. We will discuss the merits of each in turn.

The Portable Drill

This portable motorized tool was among the first pieces of electrical equipment to be adopted by the woodwork hobbyist, and it is still one of the first power tools he buys. Its versatility is the reason for its continuing popularity. Although drilling holes in wood, metal and many other materials is its primary function, it can be converted by various attachments into ripping saw, saber saw, grinder and buffer. It can mix paint, act as a sander, buff, polish and when outfitted with a circular wire brush, do a good job of rust removal.

The capacity of an electric drill is established by the size of the largest drill bit it will hold. One-half-inch or ⅜-inch drills are the most generally useful. Larger drills have a geared key which locks the chuck at the desired bit size; smaller drills have an allen-key wrench for tightening the bit in the chuck.

The main parts of a portable electric drill are motor, chuck, handle and switch (see Fig. 1-2).

The following safety precautions must be observed in operating a power drill:

1. Make certain that the machine is equipped with a ground lug.
2. Always unplug the drill before inserting or removing the drill bit.
3. Make sure that the lumber being drilled is securely held in the vise before beginning.

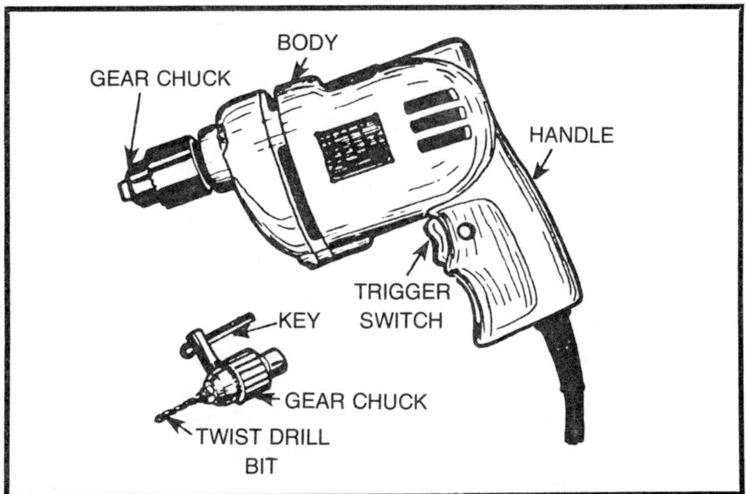

Fig. 1-2. Portable electric drill, showing its parts.

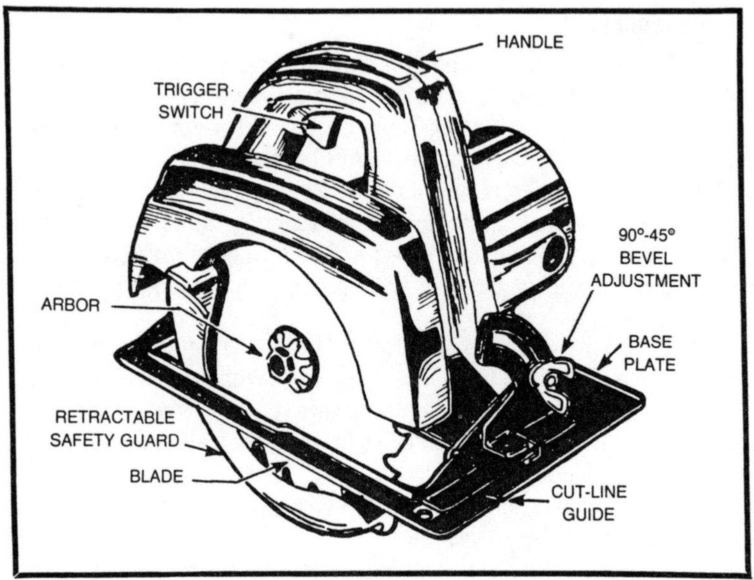

Fig. 1-3. Portable electric circular saw, with parts indicated.

4. When drilling large holes, use a waste wood block to back up the stock to avoid a gaping, ragged hole where the drill emerges.
5. Hold the drill firmly while it is in operation.

The method of operating an electric drill is not too dissimilar from that used in operating a hand drill:

1. With a bradawl, mark the place where the hole is to be drilled.
2. Place the bit drill on the center point and start the motor.
3. Withdraw the bit while the motor is still running.

The Portable Electric Circular Saw

The portable saw is a real labor saver, especially in construction work where it saves moving long, heavy stock to the workbench or stationary saw. This versatile machine performs all sorts of sawing chores, crosscutting, ripping, beveling, rabbeting, cutting dadoes, grooves, miters and compound miters. With the use of an abrasive disc in addition to the saw blade, it can be used to saw materials other than wood such as marble, concrete block, and tile. Portable power saws range in size from 4-inches to 12-inches. A 6-inch to 8-inch size, fitted with a combination blade, is the most practical for a workshop.

Primary parts of this tool are the motor, blade, handle, base plate, retractable safety guard, bevel adjustment and rip fence attachment (see Fig. 1-3).

Because of the circular power saw's speed and power, it is probably the most dangerous tool in a woodworking shop. Certain safety precautions should be consistently observed in operating it:

1. The retractable safety guard should be kept operable at all times.
2. All adjustments should be tightened and the saw allowed to attain its full speed before cutting is commenced.
3. Care should be taken to keep the blade sharp, pointing in the right direction, set correctly, and projecting the required amount (see Fig. 1-4). An ordinary circular saw blade (not tungsten tipped) needs sharpening after every four hours it is in use.
4. Disconnect the plug when the circular power saw is not in use.
5. Use a fence or guide line when sawing a long straight cut.
6. Hold the saw firmly in both hands and avoid careless handling of the wood or the blade. Use a push stick when working near the saw teeth.
7. One (not both) end of the board being cut should be supported; otherwise, the blade will bind.
8. Learning to operate the circular power saw can save hours of manual labor. However, the woodworker *must concentrate* on the careful performance of his task, for this speedy, powerful tool can easily get out of hand.

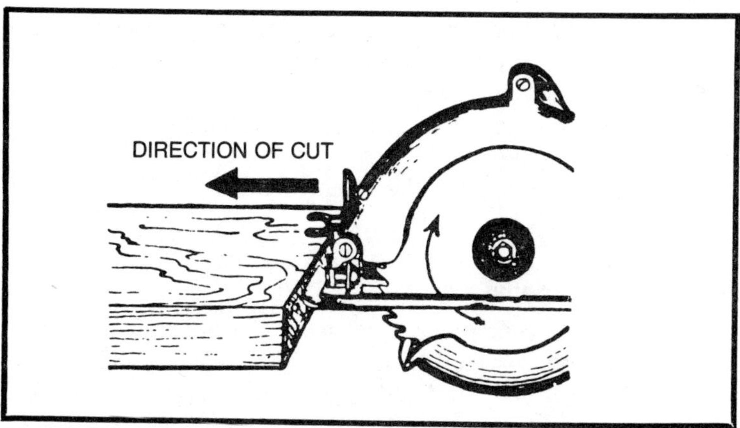

Fig. 1-4. Close-up of saw blade, showing degree of projection and direction of teeth.

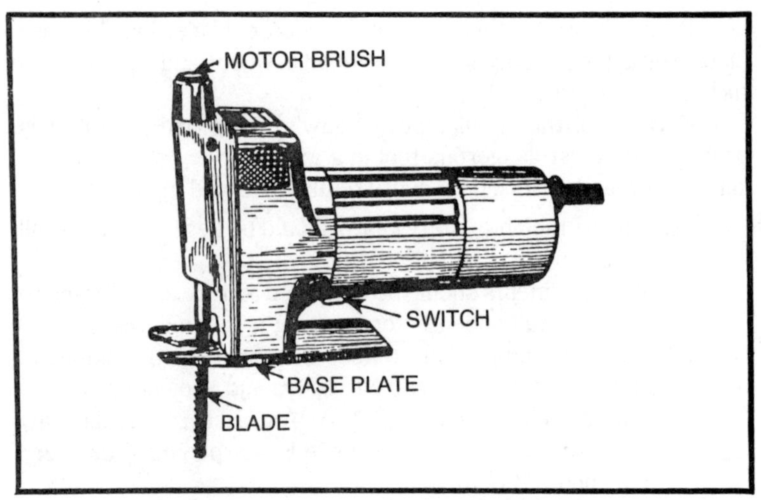

Fig. 1-5. Portable electric saber saw, showing principal parts.

To operate the circular power saw easily and efficiently, follow these eight procedural steps:

1. Mark the line to be sawed with a sharp pencil.
2. Select the proper blade and secure it tightly in the saw at the desired depth. Remember that the blade teeth cut upward.
3. Secure the work on the bench or on a saw horse.
4. Start the saw, allowing it to attain full speed before beginning to cut.
5. Guide the saw slowly along the waste side of the marked line.
6. To insure the accuracy of the cut when ripsawing plywood panels, clamp a steel straightedge to the stock instead of using the ripping guide.
7. When sawing bevels, be sure to tilt the base plate to the angle desired.
8. Always disconnect the machine when you have finished using it.

Portable Electric Saber Saw

For furniture construction, the saber saw is a truly invaluable tool. It is primarily designed to perform like a jigsaw, with the added advantages of (1) being portable and, therefore, able to perform wherever needed, (2) having a capacity which will accept any diameter bit, and (3) being able to cut just about any type of material and perform intricate curving cuts as well as accurate straight cuts. Special interchangeable blades are available which can incise such materials as arborite, composition board, rubber, leather and plastic. Portable saber saws are available in 3½-inches to 6-inches (see Fig. 1-5). The variable speed model is recommended for ultimate versatility.

As with any tool, certain safety precautions must be observed:

1. Always disconnect the plug before replacing the blade.
2. Secure the work to the bench or table with a vise or cramp.
3. Always hold the saw steady, with a firm grip, keeping your fingers well back from the cutting line.
4. Position the saw on the stock before turning on the switch, and permit the saw to fully stop before removing it from the work.
5. When sawing internal patterns, drill a starter hole the width of the blade on the waste side of the wood being cut out from the center (see Fig. 1-6).
6. While the saw is operating, give it your undivided attention.

The saber saw is capable of cutting out intricately curved designs. The pattern desired is laid on the stock to act as a guide, and the proper blade is secured in the machine following the manufacturer's instructions. Then the saber saw is operated as follows:

1. The forward edge of the saw base is placed on the stock and the saw turned on.
2. Holding the saw firmly, the operator exerts a downward and forward pressure.

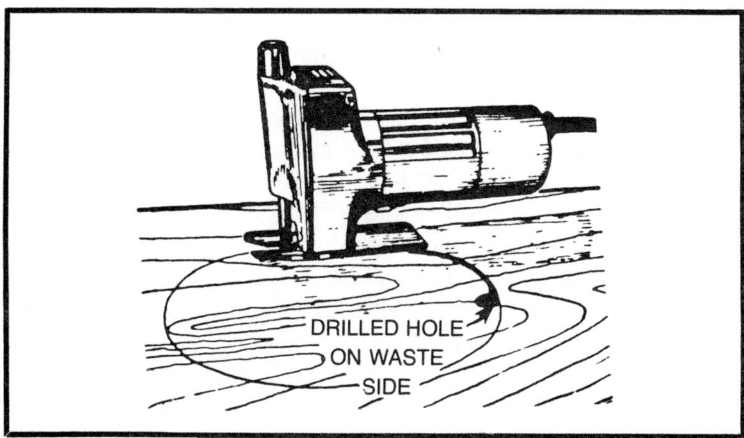

Fig. 1-6. Making internal cut with saber saw.

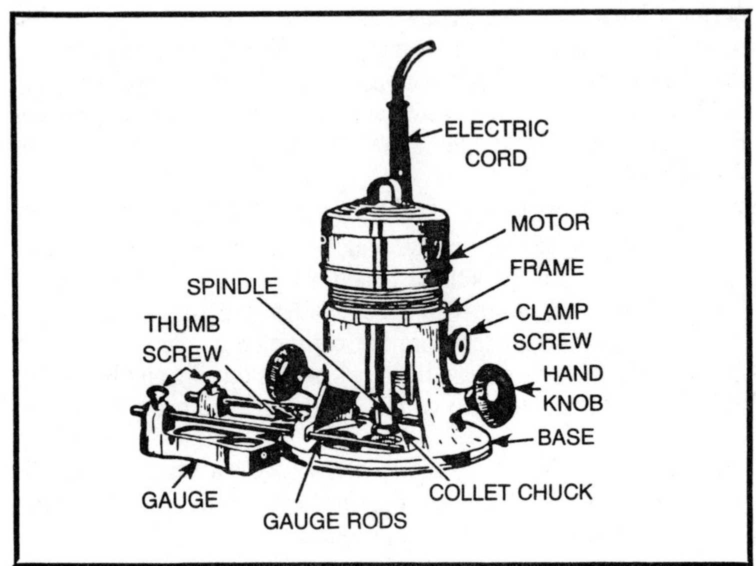

Fig. 1-7. Parts of a portable electric router.

3. The saw is carefully guided along the marked line, always cutting on the waste side.
4. A straightedge is cramped to the stock to serve as a ripping guide.
5. When the cutting is completed, the switch is turned off and the saw allowed to come to a complete stop before it is removed from the work.

Portable Electric Router

The electric router is capable of performing many more jobs than the hand-operated router. In effect, it is an inverted spindle molder, able to produce all manner of moldings and housing (dadoes). The motor is enclosed in a casing fitted with two side handles for guiding the tool (see Fig. 1-7). The router's principal parts are motor, chuck, base, handles and switch. The entire tool weighs about 12 pounds, is quiet and easy to handle. The router comes with a number of attachments which enable it to cut moldings, carve, cut spiral flutes and make joints (such as dove tail, tongue-and-groove, and dado); as well as shape and plane wood. Using a cutter with a carbide tip, the router can saw Formica, arborite and composition woods; make recesses for door hinges; and aid in constructing stairways. The router operates at a very high speed—20,000 revolutions per minute and is available in a variety of sizes. The one-half horsepower and the one-quarter horsepower are the sizes generally used in woodworking (see Fig. 1-8).

Because of the speed of this power tool, the operator must be doubly careful to use every safety precaution in operating it. Here are some important measures to consider:

1. Disconnect machine before changing cutter bits or attachments.
2. Insert the bit directly into the spindle of the motor and be sure it is really secured in the collect-type chuck.
3. Keep the cutter bits sharp.
4. Move the router from left to right when cutting straight or making convex curves. When making concave curves, move the router from right to left, feeding the work in counter-clockwise.
5. *Wear goggles to protect the eyes from flying chips and splinters.*

Operational procedures are as follows:

1. Select the proper cutter for the result desired—straight, cove, chamfer, core box, dove tail, rounding over, beading, Roman ogee or rabbeting.

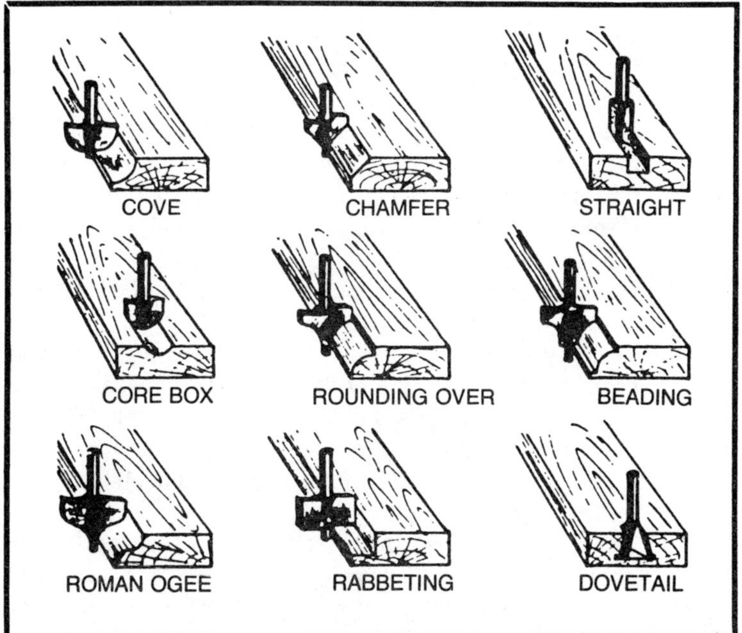

Fig. 1-8. Router bits, showing cuts each makes.

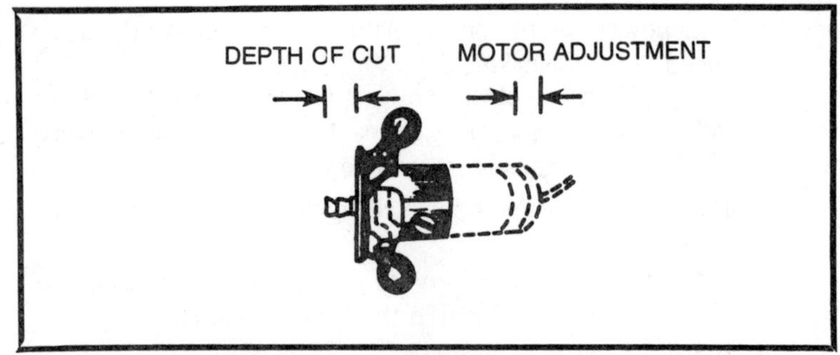

Fig. 1-9. Adjusting for depth and swath of cut.

2. Insert the cutter in the chuck and make certain that it is securely tightened.
3 Adjust the depth of the cutter by moving the motor vertically in the depth sleeve(as the motor housing is sometimes called). This adjustment extends or retracts the cutter bit to predetermined settings which are accurate to 0.004-inch. The lower the motor is set, the farther the bit will be extended and the deeper will be the saw cut. The higher the motor is set, the less the bit will protrude and the shallower will be the cutting (see Fig. 1-9).
4. Secure the wing nut which positions the motor in the depth sleeve.
5. Using a piece of waste wood, try the cutting to be produced on the work. Readjust the motor setting as required.
6. With those bits not having a pilot tip, use a fence cramped to the edge of the work. The fence will control the swath (or width) of the cutting. Alternatively, a batten can be cramped down to the work, and the edge of the machine will follow the batten (see Fig. 1-10).
7. Be sure to adjust the guide on the parallel fence rods to the desired swath (see Fig. 1-11).
8. Cramp the stock and pass the router over it toward you several times, making a shallow cut each time. Keep the router flat on the surface of the work, guiding it firmly with the hand knobs.
9. Continue cutting until the entire edge has been fashioned on the stock.
10. To keep from chipping the edge when shaping the end grain, cramp a piece of waste wood to the end nearest you to provide a cutting margin for the final cut as the router moves toward you.

Fig. 1-10. Regulating width of cut by adjustment of fence.

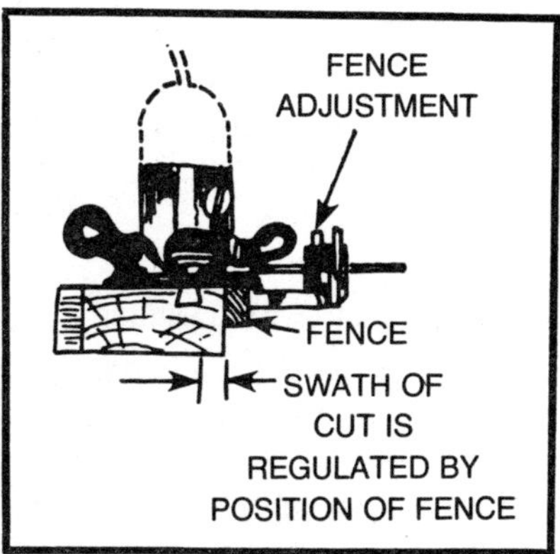

The procedure for cutting dadoes, plows and grooves is slightly different from the method used for shaping edges:

1. First the proper cutter bit is selected and fastened securely into the chuck of the machine.
2. The bit is then adjusted to the desired depth.
3. The guide is fastened to the base and adjusted to the width required.
4. Using a piece of wood scrap, a trial cut is made.
5. The stock is securely fastened and the router switched on to begin the cut.

Fig. 1-11. Adjustment of fence for parallel cuts.

6. The desired groove is reached by making several light cuts.
7. Should a wider groove be desired, the gauge is reset by moving it slightly along the parallel bars, and the surface is re-plowed.

Portable Electric Belt Sander

This is one of the most frequently used power tools and is available in three different styles: the belt sander, the orbital sander and the disc sander. The belt sander is probably the type most popular with woodworkers. This sander operates on an abrasive belt which continuously runs over pulleys—one at each end. When speaking of the size of a belt sander, one uses the dimensions of the sanding belt with which the sander is fitted. A 3 in. × 24 in. and a 4 in. × 27 in. sander are the preferred sizes. Larger belt sanders are primarily used to sand large areas such as floors or wall paneling. Most belt sanders are equipped with a dust-retention system which collects the dust from the belt into a bag for emptying, thus rendering the sanding operation relatively dust-free. The chief parts of the belt sander are the motor, drive pulley, tighter pulley, tension mechanism, sanding belt and dust bag (see Fig. 1-12).

Certain operating precautions should be observed, as with all highpowered tools:

1. Disconnect the belt sander before replacing or removing the sanding belt.
2. Always lift the sander or turn it on its side before turning it on.
3. Take care not to sand over the electric cord.
4. Hold the sander firmly, particularly when a new coarse abrasive belt with good traction has just been installed.
5. Keep hands away from the right-hand side of the blade because if the blade should break, it will fly to that side.

As when using other power tools, the work should first be secured before the sanding is begun. Then a sanding belt of the proper abrasive material and grit should be selected, and the new abrasive belt installed as follows:

1. Pull back the tension lever, which will pull back the idler pulley.
2. Making sure that the arrow indication inside the belt is pointing in the right direction, slip the new belt over the pulleys and release the tension lever.

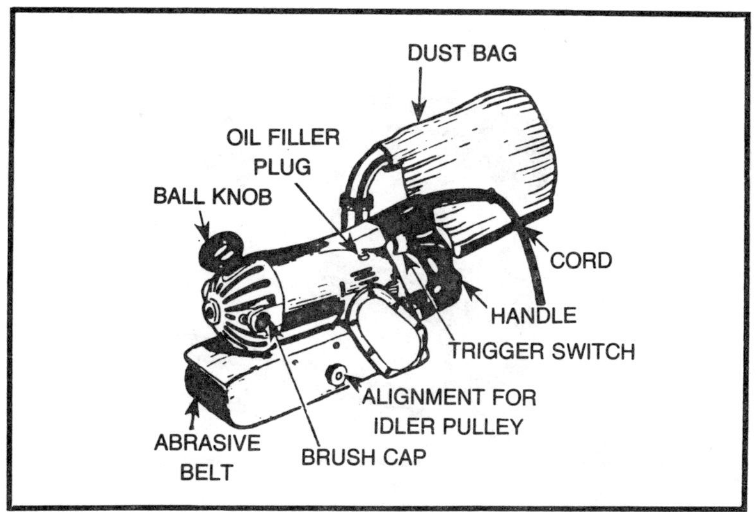

Fig. 1-12. The portable belt sander, indicating main parts.

3. To make sure that the belt will track properly on the pulleys, tighten the alignment on the idler pulley.
4. Lift the machine and switch it on; then lower it to the surface of the work and begin sanding with the grain.
5. Move the sander back and forth steadily, without pausing long enough for the sander to grind off excessive surface leaving it uneven and wavy.
6. Keep replacing the belt with belts of finer and finer grits until a smooth surface is achieved.

Portable Orbital Sander

The original sander gets its name from the orbital movement of the sanding pad. This sander is a very useful one for fine sanding and finishing because it cuts very slowly and produces a very smooth finish. Because of the slight movement of its rubber sole, which either oscillates or moves in very small orbits, it is suitable for extremely fine sanding and polishing. This machine would not be suitable for finishing a rough-sawn surface; its specialty is removing ripples and slight indents left by the plane (see Fig. 1-13).

Some orbital sanders have a combination straightline sanding mechanism as well. These are more versatile. Also, many models come equipped with a dust collector or an adapter which allows them to be attached to a vacuum cleaner hose.

The orbital sander is one power tool which is relatively safe to operate. It requires almost no pressure. The operating procedure is

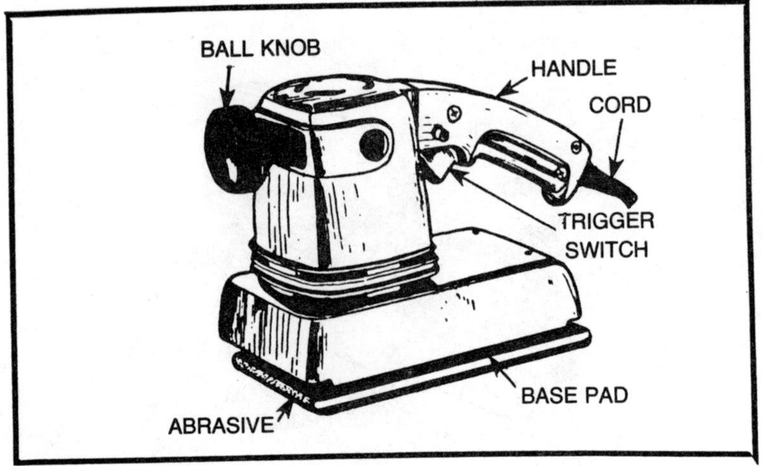

Fig. 1-13. The portable orbital sander.

much like that of ironing a sheet—merely passing the sander smoothly and fairly slowly over the surface (see Fig. 1-14).

The operational steps are as follows:

1. Fasten the work securely.
2. Disconnect the electric cord.
3. Select the proper grit of adhesive paper and fasten a rectangular piece of it across the rubber sole pad, attaching it in place with the spring cramps provided.
4. Plug in the sander and sand with a finer and finer grit until a beautifully smooth surface is acquired, always disconnecting the sander when replacing one abrasive sheet with another.

Disc Sander

This sander is available in both stationary bench and portable models, the latter being more difficult to operate successfully (See Fig. 1-15).

As a bench machine, the disc sander is a very handy accessory. A circular steel plate (the disc from which this sander derives its name) is glued to a circle of garnet paper. Usually, the disc cement used to glue on the paper is in stick form and melts under the friction generated by the rotating disc. Therefore, it is applied to the disc while the disc is in motion. When the disc has been coated with sufficient glue, the machine is turned off and disconnected while the circle of abrasive paper is pressed firmly and smoothly into position on the disc. Then the machine is plugged in and turned on and the sawing is accomplished through the following procedural steps:

1. The work is fed steadily into the sander.
2. Only minimum pressure is applied.
3. If a rather wide thickness of material has to be removed, the work is fed through several times until the cut is completed.
4. A tilting mechanism on the machine adjusts the attack of the disc to an angle (rather than straight on, which would clog the machine and burn the wood).

Because this sander works best at a slight angle, the *portable* disc sander is harder to control. The disc must not be placed flat on the work, but must be held at an angle with only the trailing edge working. The operator must take care not to exert pressure, but to allow the speeding disc to do the cutting. Pressure will only slow the motor and cause rings to appear in the stock.

The *portable* disc sander design affords a slightly easier method, however, of replacing abrasive paper. A rubber backing pad is attached to the chuck of the tool; and the sanding discs, all of which have a central hole, are bolted onto the pad with a recessed nut.

STATIONARY POWER TOOLS

The first mechanized tools were powered manually. Then steam activated them. Today they are driven by electric motors. Most of the larger woodworking machine tools are designed to perform a single task; however, the fact that space is limited in the usual home workworking shop motivates the woodworker to acquire

Fig. 1-14. Operating the orbital sander.

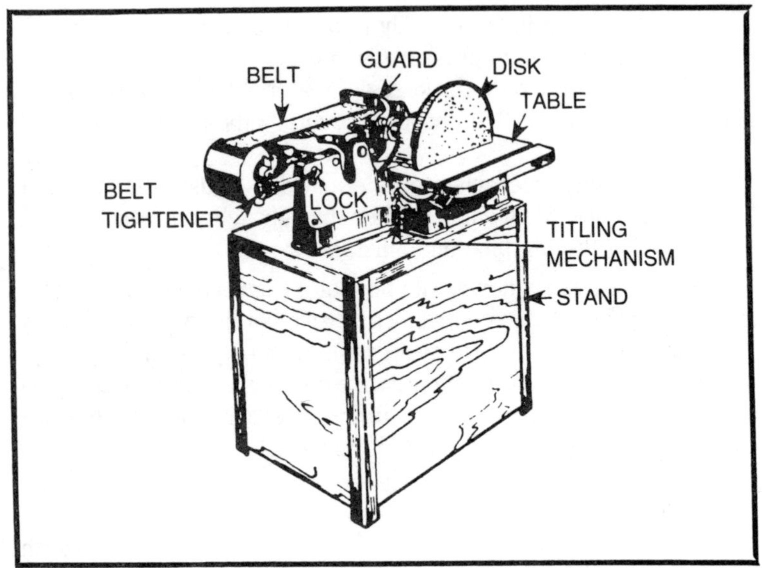

Fig. 1-15. Parts of the stationary disc sander.

only those machine tools capable of performing a series of operations with only a few minor adjustments. The single performance machines have a definite place in the industrial workshop, but they are not flexible enough for home use. Therefore, because this book is primarily directed toward the home hobbyist, we will limit our discussion of power machine tools to those few which are most frequently useful in woodworking; the band saw, the scroll (or jig) saw, the circular (or table) saw and the woodturning lathe. We have already discussed the stationary belt sander machine. Should more stationary machine tools be required, the drill press, radial saw, jointer, shaper, mortising machine and thickness planed might be considered. Or, if space is limited, a multi-use machine tool like the shopsmith would be an excellent choice because its production capabilities are so numerous and diversified.

Electrical Scroll Saw Machine

With this compact machine took, internal and external curves may be cut precisely on thin stock and beautiful inlays and marquetry produced. Also, accurate angle cuts may be sawed by tilting the table of the tool to a given angle.

The principal parts of this machine tool are the base, arm, table, upper and lower chucks, tension sleeve, and the guide assembly (which retains the wood in the correct position for sawing). (See Fig.

1-16). The capacity of the jigsaw is ascertained by the distance from the saw blade to the arm in line with the table and the maximum thickness of the wood which the saw will cut.

To ready the jigsaw machine for cutting, the procedure is as follows:

1. Insert the blade in the lower chuck with the teeth pointing down. Secure the blade carefully.
2. Release the tension on the sleeve and allow the upper chuck to come down. Fasten the upper end of the blade to the top chuck.
3. Using the suggestions in the operator's manual for your particular machine, adjust the tension on the upper sleeve.
4. Place the work on the table and lower the guide assembly to rest on the work being cut.
5. To do internal cutting, make a hole large enough to clear the blade in the waste area (see Fig. 1-17). Then insert the blade through the hole and secure it in both the upper and lower chucks. Adjust the sleeve tension.

To cut crisp-edged curves in the wood, use the following method:

1. Mark the pattern carefully on the stock.
2. Feed the stock into the saw blade slowly and carefully, faithfully following the pattern outline.

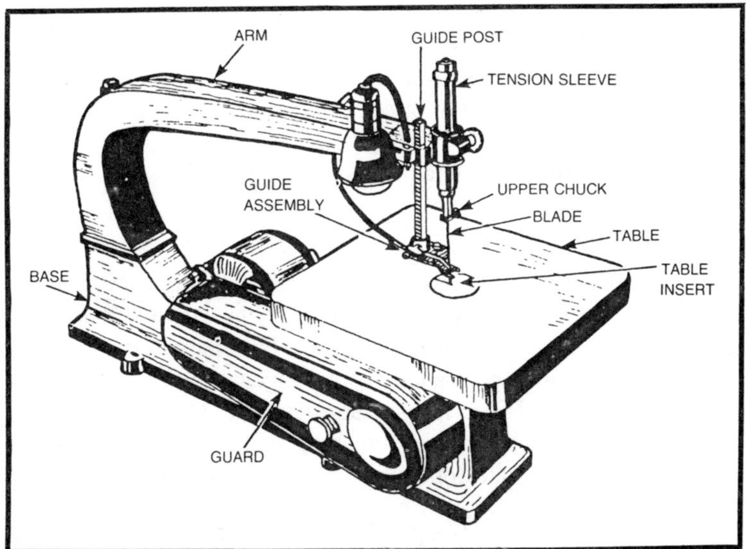

Fig. 1-16. The stationary jig (or scroll) saw, indicating chief parts.

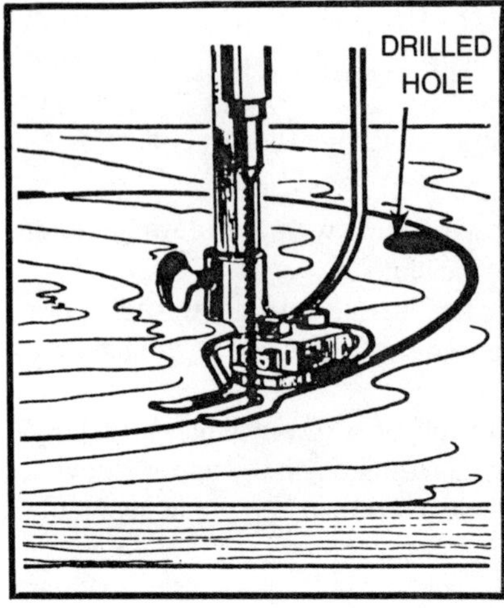

Fig. 1-17. Internal pattern sawing with jigsaw.

3. If repetitive patterns are desired, saw two duplicate cutouts at once by nailing two thin strips of veneer together, driving the nails through the waste side of the wood. Saw the double-ply veneer very slowly, as though it were only one ply.

Always observe the following safety measures:

1. Check all adjustments before starting the machine.
2. Adjust the guide assembly to rest on the work.
3. Use both hands to manipulate the saw.
4. Keep your hands at a safe distance from the blade.
5. Never walk away from the machine while it is running; wait until it has come to a complete stop.
6. Lubricate all moving parts periodically.
7. Keep the blade under tension at all times.

Band Saw Machine

We include the band saw in our coverage of stationary machine tools for the hobbyist's workshop because, in woodworking, it is undoubtedly one of the most indispensible. First patented in England in 1808, this saw is made in a variety of designs. Some band saws cut logs; others recut planks; and smaller ones cut stock, incising both curved and straight lines. The tilting table feature, available in some models, allows the operator to cut angles and compound angles, as well.

The band saw blade is endless ribbon of steel with shaped teeth on the leading edge. The band saw can be as narrow as ⅛-inch, but a

⅜-inch blade is best for the home workshop. The narrower the blade used, the tighter the curve which the band saw is capable of cutting.

To make the cutting operation, the blade revolves around two large pulleys. The bottom pulley is powered by an electric motor, but the top pulley is free-wheeling. Consequently, the top pulley is the one where the tension adjustments are made and where the tracking of the blade is checked and re-aligned with the tracking screw.

These pulley wheels may be as large as 60 inches in diameter. Some smaller machines, however, have 10-inch wheels. On a two-wheel band saw machine, the incision made by the saw blade into the board (sometimes referred to as the "throat size") can never be deeper than the diameter of the wheel. Some small machines have three wheels; the addition of the third wheel increases the throat size without increasing the size of the wheel.

The pulley wheels of the band saw are usually fitted with rubber tires; the tires themselves are crowned, so that the force of rotation will cause the blade to climb to the highest point of the camber. The tracking screw adjusts the tilt of the top pulley so that the blade will move correctly over the exact center of the wheel (see Fig. 1-18).

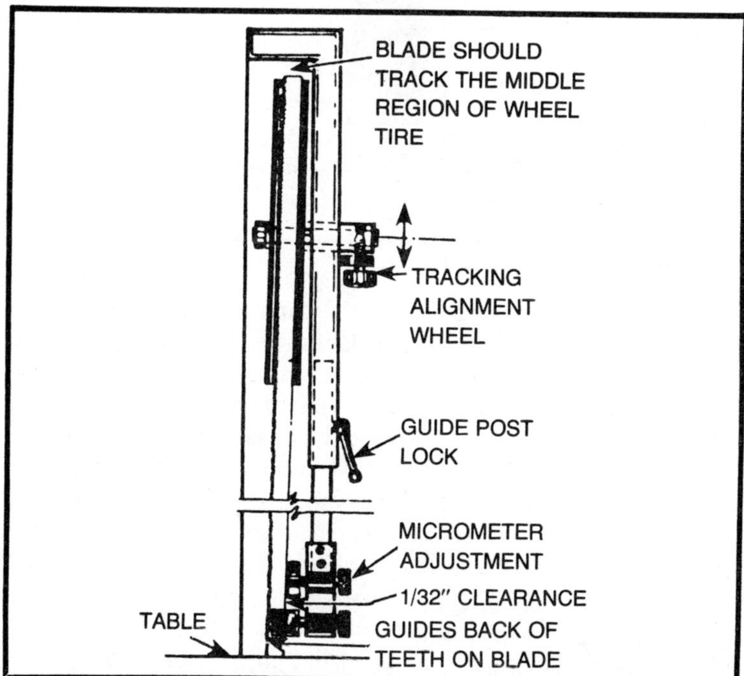

Fig. 1-18. Alignment of band saw blade over rubber tires of upper pulley wheel.

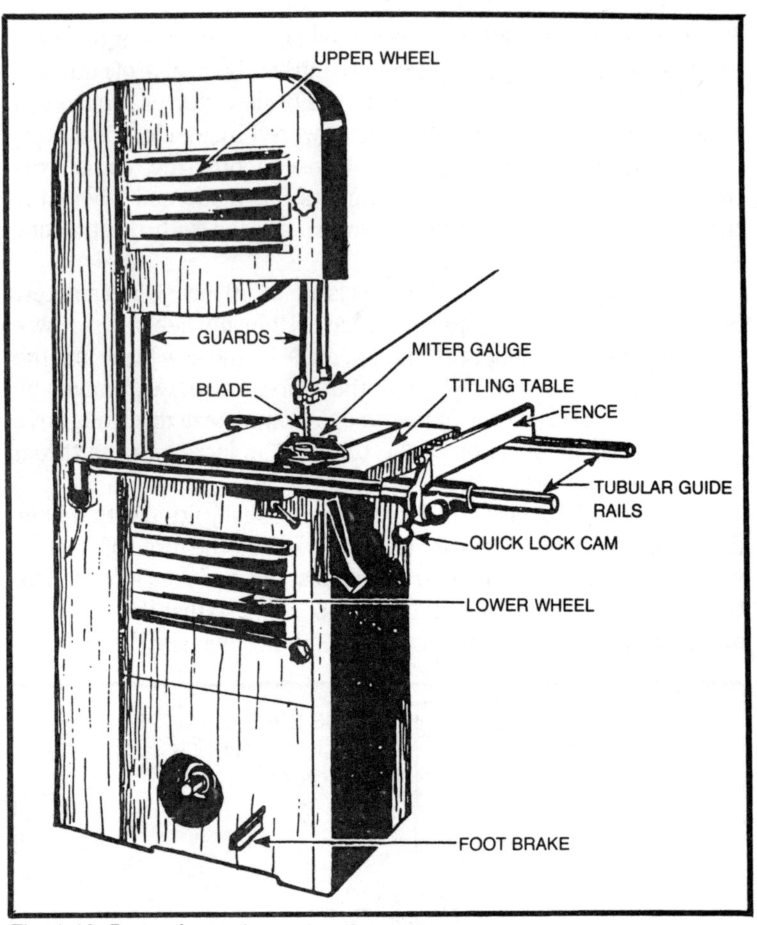

Fig. 1-19. Parts of a stationary band saw.

The adjustable saw guide on the band saw should always be adjusted so that it just clears the surface of the work to give the blade maximum two-fold support. A bronze thrust wheel supports the blade from the back, and a fiber pad affords lateral support.

The capacity of the two-wheel band saw is indicated by the diameter of the wheels. Band saws are available in 12-inch to 42-inch capacities; the most practical capacity for a woodworking shop is the 20-inch. Machines with smaller wheels impose undue flexibility on the blade which results in the steel (of which the blade is made) eventually crystallizing and becoming too brittle to operate.

Principal parts of a band saw machine are the frame, upper and lower wheels, tilting table, band, blade, guards, adjustable guides and adjusting levers (see Fig. 1-19).

Preparational steps for sawing on the band saw machine are:

1. Select a suitable blade for the job to be done—a narrow blade for sawing small areas, a wider blade for cutting or resawing sections of wood.
2. Open the wheelguards and lower the upper wheel. Position the blade with the teeth pointing down on the cutting side.
3. Tighten the tension on the upper wheel. Turn the wheel by hand to make sure that the blade is reasonably tight.
4. Check the tracking of the blade on both wheels to make sure that the blade runs over the *middle* region of the wheel tire. If it does not, tilt the upper wheel as necessary to insure the proper tracking.
5. Adjust the guide mechanism at the back edge of the blade to within 1/32-inch of the blade itself (see Fig. 1-20).
6. The guides supporting the sides of the blade should be in line with the blade with a clearance of about 1/64-inch (see Fig. 1-21). Adjust the top guide to within ¼-inch of the work.
7. Examine the machine for major adjustments. Make sure the guards are in position. Start the saw and wait until it reaches its load speed before commencing work.
8. Slowly move the work into the blade, making cuts on the waste side of the layout line.
9. Make all short cuts first, saving lengthy cuts for later.
10. Use the rip fence and meter gauge wherever these accessory tools facilitate safer, more accurate cutting.

Safety Precautions. Generally speaking, the band saw is considered one of the safest machine tools in the shop. If the following rules are observed, there is minimal danger of accident:

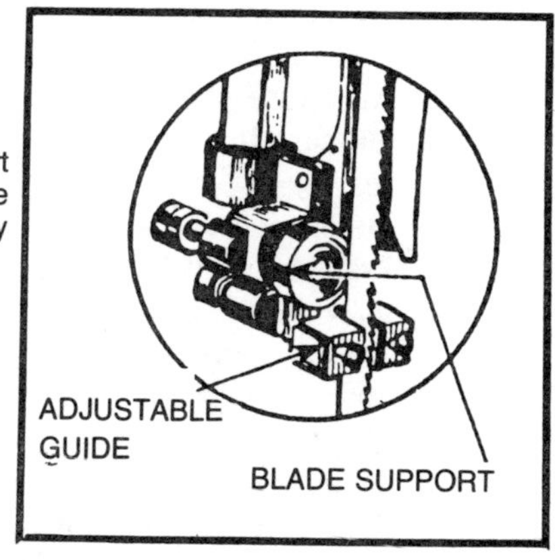

Fig. 1-20. Close-up of blade support assembly, showing adjustable guide which must be set to clear blade by 1/32-inch.

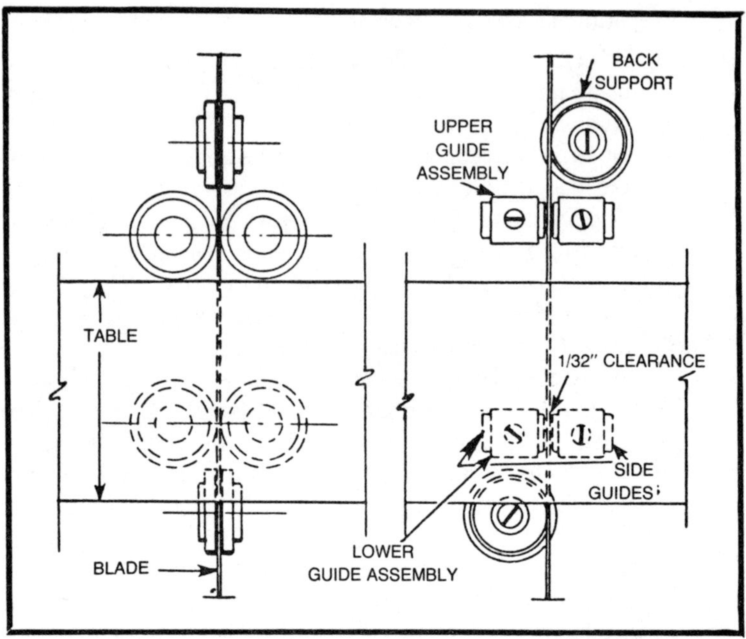

Fig. 1-21. Setting clearance on guides, showing both upper and lower guide assemblies.

1. Check all major adjustments on the machine before switching it on.
2. Cramp the guide post about ¼-inch above the stock to be cut.
3. Use push sticks to hold and position the work, particularly if the stock is small.
4. Keep your hands a safe distance from the blade.
5. Be sure that the blade is the proper type for the job and that it is sharp.
6. Make use of all guards provided with the machine.
7. Be sure that the machine has come to a full stop before leaving it.
8. Before incising a sharp curve, make relief cuts to avoid cramping and clogging the blade (see Figs. 1-22, 1-23, and 1-24 on laying out and cutting a cabriole leg— note relief cuts at curves).
9. Always use a stick or brush—not your hand—to clear the saw table.
10. Keep the machine clean and well lubricated. Coil the saw blade for storage to prevent injury to the teeth.

Fig. 1-22. Relief cuts made before cutting curve.

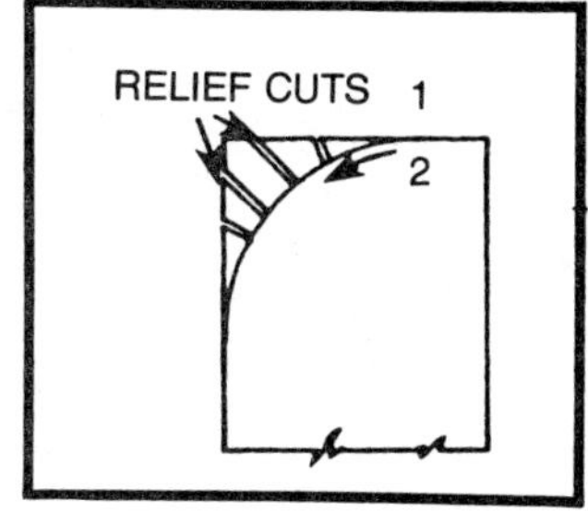

Circular or Table Saw

Holland is credited with the invention of this saw in 1777. Since then it has become one of the most useful and versatile saws for all manner of woodworking. Originally, it was simply a tempered steel blade mounted on a shaft which was attached to a wooden frame. Today, its uses have been greatly extended by new interchangeable blade designs which have so multiplied its functions that it merits the name by which it is generally known—the variety saw.

The variety model table saw has one arbor on which the blades are interchangeable, while the universal model table saw has two arbors which may be adjusted independently to make different cuts. The universal model saves time in changing blades.

Since table saw machines operate on direct drive, the blade is mounted on an arbor which is an extension of the motor rotor. Other table saw machines operate on the gear-and-belt system, or a combination of direct drive and gear-and-belt.

The types of cuts possible on a table saw machine are many. Besides ripping and crosscutting, the machine can perform such cuts as tapering, mitering, compound mitering, chamfering, beveling, splining, grooving, dadoing, tenoning, and other specialized work.

Different manufacturers produce table saws to different specifications of table size, part sizes and depth of cut. However, all table saw machines have the same principal parts: the base, table,

Fig. 1-23. Diagram of cuts showing order in which they should be made.

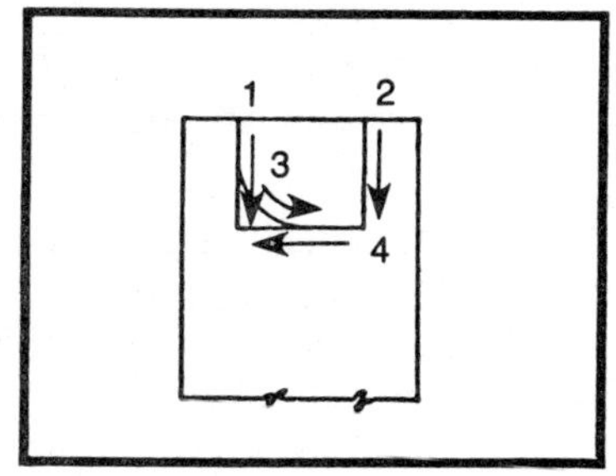

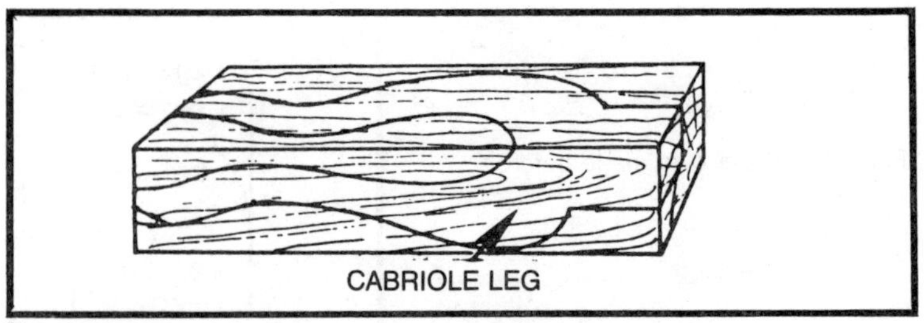

Fig. 1-24. Layout of cabriole leg outlined on stock for sawing.

arbor, fence, blade, guard and cut-off guide (see Fig. 1-25). The capacity of the table saw is determined by the diameter of the blade.

Blades vary in size from 6 inches to 18 inches, each blade differing as to the shape of the teeth. The blades most frequently used are the ripping blade, the crosscut blade and the combination blade. Other special blades include the safe-feed blade, dado blade and molding blade (see Fig. 1-26).

New steel blades will cut up to 10,000 feet per minute. Tungsten carbide-tipped blades last longer and are able to saw plastics, laminates, arborites, transitiles and other very hard, difficult-to-cut materials.

As with all other power tool machines, the table saw requires certain adjusting before any specific job of sawing is undertaken.

Necessary adjustments before sawing:

1. Choose a suitable blade for the job and fasten it on the arbor with the teeth pointing in the right direction.
2. Raise the blade to the height desired with the hand wheel which elevates and lowers the arbor. When cross-cutting or ripping, the bottom of the gullet of the teeth should clear the top surface of the work being sawed.
3. Check the angle of the cut-off gauge, if one is being used.
4. Use the blade guard whenever possible. When working without the guard, use every caution.
5. If the arbor and fences require tilting, make all adjustments now and be sure they are locked in before turning on the machine.

Some recommended safety precautions to take when using the table saw are:

1. The best safety precaution with any machine tool is thorough knowledge of the mechanism. Only after you are thoroughly familiar with the necessary adjustments and operational procedures should you attempt to use the machine.

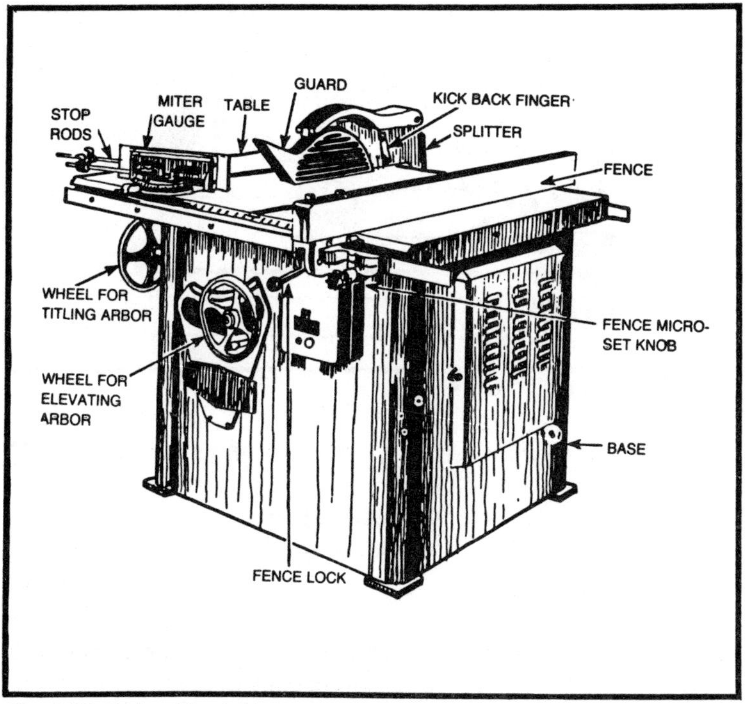

Fig. 1-25. Parts of the table saw.

2. When using the table saw, always stand to one side of the blade to avoid being hit by the kickback.
3. Use push sticks—never your hands—to feed the work to the blade.

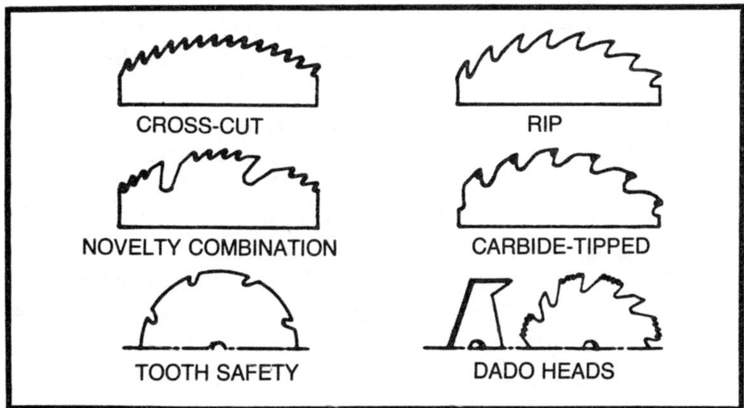

Fig. 1-26. Various saw blades used on the circular saw.

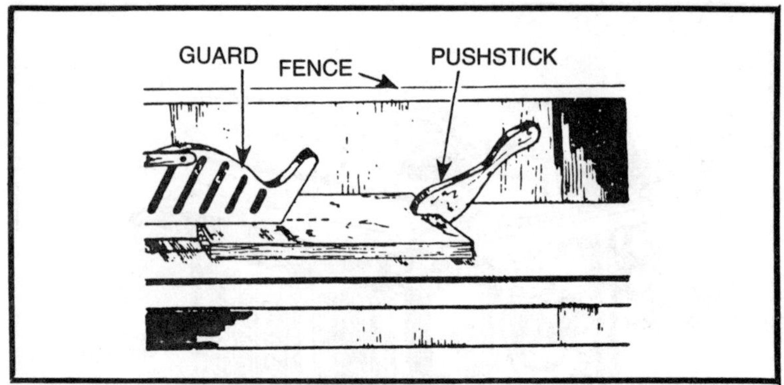

Fig. 1-27. Ripping with the grain.

4. Hold the work securely and restrain it further with the rip fence, the cut-off guide or even an improvised jig.
5. Wait until the machine fully stops before leaving it. Disconnect the machine before adjusting, cleaning or lubricating it.

Every type of cutting which the table saw so creditably performs requires a slightly different operational procedure. We shall discuss the cutting operations most frequently engaged in, beginning with rip-sawing.

Ripping

1. Select either the rip or combination blade for the job, fasten it securely on the arbor, and adjust the arbor so that the bottom of the gullet on the teeth projects above the wood being sawed.
2. Set the ripping fence to the width desired, checking with a scale the distance from the face of the fence to the tooth of the blade which sets toward the fence. Lock the fence in position.
3. Place the board on the table, making sure it lies flat and does not rock. If it rocks, turn it over and see if it lies steadier.
4. Holding the work firmly against the fence, push it into the blade with a push stick (see Fig. 1-27).
5. Take care not to stand directly behind the sawing line.
6. When ripping narrow stock, use a push stick to feed the wood into the saw.
7. When ripping large or lengthy sheets of plywood, have someone help by supporting the end of the stock farthest from the saw.

Crosscutting

1. Adjust the blade to the proper height for the thickness of the stock—allowing it to project about ½-inch above the lumber.
2. Place the cut-off guide into the slot in the table and check it for the required angle. (The angle to be checked is that from the saw blade to the face of the guide.)
3. Mark the board to indicate the saw line and place it on the table top, holding it firmly against the face of the guide.
4. Move the fence out of the way and start the machine. Allow it to reach full load speed before commencing to saw (see Fig. 1-28).
5. Push the guide and the work slowly into the blade.
6. Never do freehand sawing on a table saw.
7. To duplicate sections, mark on the table to indicate the saw lines, and set stop rods or clamp a waste piece of stock to the fence to allow for clearance (see Fig. 1-29).
8. To cut bevels, chamfers or miters, the saw arbor may be tilted or the guide set at a given angle.
9. Before making any necessary adjustments, disconnect the machine.

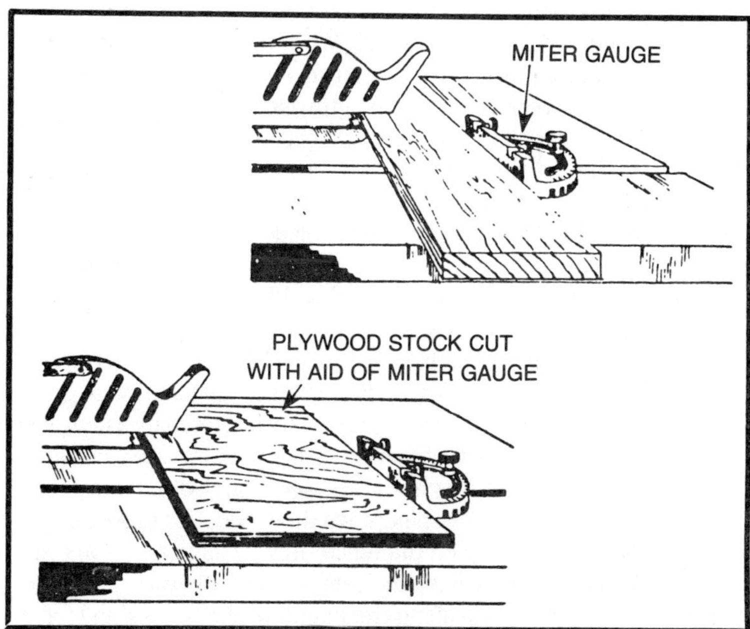

Fig. 1-28. Two views of a circular saw performing crosscutting.

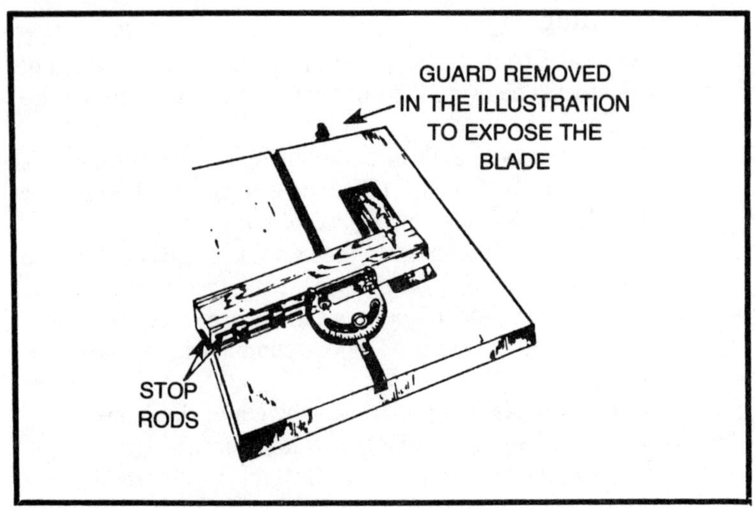

Fig. 1-29. Cutting duplicate parts, using stop rods.

Rabbeting. A rectangular longitudinal groove or recess incised by saw, plane or chisel along the corner edge of a board is called a rabbet. The method for cutting a rabbet on a table saw is as follows:

1. Square off the stock to the size desired.
2. Outline with a pencil the size of the rabbet desired on the proper edge of the stock. When a number of identical rabbeted pieces are required, make one rectangular grooved recess on the lengthwise edge of a plank long enough for all the rabbeted pieces needed. Then measure off the individual pieces and crosscut them apart at the measurement lines.
3. In sawing rabbets, remove the blade guard if necessary but practice extra caution regarding the exposed saw blade.
4. Set the fence to the required width—usually one-half the thickness of the stock.
5. Secure the dado blade on the arbor and adjust to the desired height. Make the first cut into the lengthwise edge of the board at the width previously indicated by a penciled saw line. Always test this cut on a piece of waste wood first to be sure that it is accurate (see Fig. 1-30).
6. Now unplug the machine; turn the wood; and make necessary adjustments on the fence, miter gauge and stop rods preparatory to making the center cut which will remove the corner edge strip along the length of the lumber and form the recess which is the rabbet.

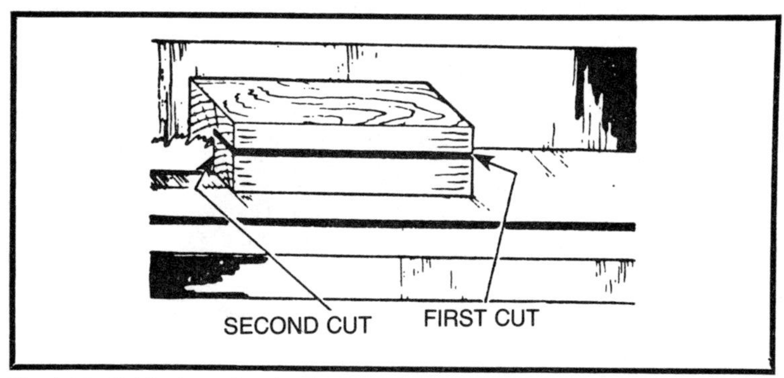

Fig. 1-30. Rabbeting, showing how the first groove is made with the grain, the second across the grain.

7. Finish by cutting the rabbeted board into individual pieces, as necessary.
8. Keep your fingers as high as possible above the blade and hold the work firmly against the fence.

Dadoing. A dado is a rectangular groove cut on the surface of a board at right angles to the grain. The operation is usually performed with a dado blade using the following steps:

1. Lay out the dado by marking the groove to be cut on the surface of the stock with a sharp pencil.
2. Adjust the depth of the cut by raising or lowering the dado blade which has been secured on the arbor. Remove the blade guard to make this cutting.
3. Hold the work very firmly against the cut-off guide.

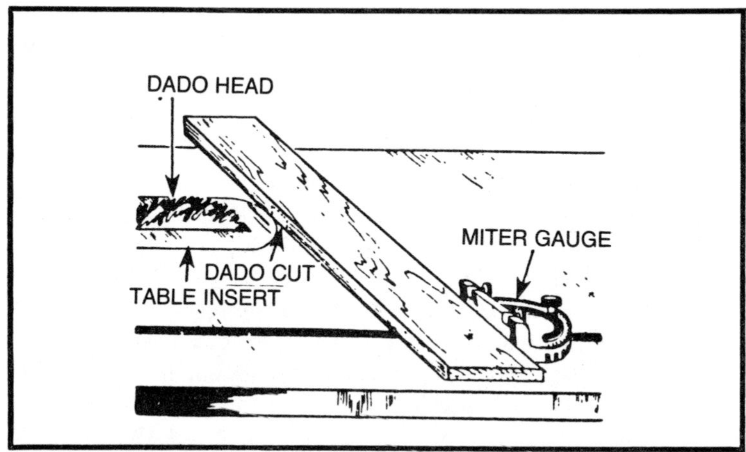

Fig. 1-31. Dadoing, showing the saw making the first cut with the grain.

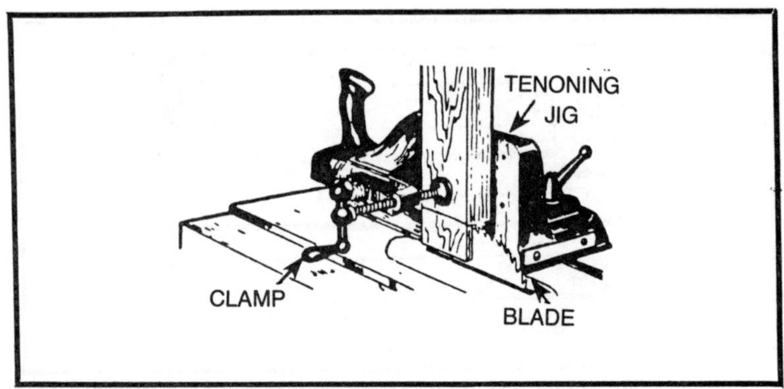

Fig. 1-32. Illustrating blade making cheek cut.

4. Turn the machine on and feed the work slowly over the blade (see Fig. 1-31).
5. To cut a wide dado to any great depth, several cuts—rather than a single cut—are advisible, particularly if the stock is hardwood.
6. Since dadoing is performed without a blade guard, additional caution must be exercised.
7. To make a stop dado, stop blocks may be clamped to the fence or table to regulate the blade's travel distance.

Note: The dado blades may also be used to cut grooves, plows and rabbets, as well as dadoes.

Cutting Tenons. A tenon is a joint which features a small tongue-like projection left remaining on the cut-away surface of stock (this projection will later be inserted and glued into another piece of wood correspondingly incised with a recess to receive the projection). (See Fig. 1-32.) In cutting tenons on a tenon saw, the following procedure should be observed:

1. Lay out the tenon to be cut by marking the saw lines on the lumber with a sharp pencil.
2. Disconnect the table saw.
3. Select a crosscut or combination blade to make the shoulder cut across the grain. Secure the blade on the arbor and adjust the height of the blade.
4. Remove the blade guard and use the fence as a guide.
5. Make the shoulder cut, using extreme caution.
6. Readjust the blade for the length of tenon, and—using the rip fence or tenoning job—make the cheek cuts next, performing the cutting cautiously because the blade is without a guard (see Fig. 1-33).

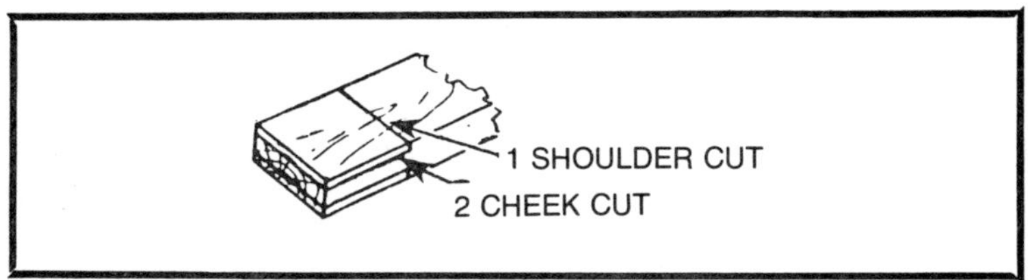

Fig. 1-33. Shoulder cut is made first, then cheek cut.

Wood-Turning Lathe

This tool is the link between machine and hand tools, combining the skill of hand-tool work with the mechanical movement of the machine—much as does a potter's wheel in shaping clay.

The first lathe used two trees far enough apart to accommodate the work being turned (or "thrown," as it was then described). The work was secured by wooden pins driven through holes bored into the two tree trunks. A rope was used to turn the work and a chisel was used to shape it (see Fig. 1-34).

Since those days, the wood-turning lathe has changed dramatically. Modern lathes feature variable speed controls and, as a recent innovation, a cutter head which turns in the opposite direction from the rotation of the spindle—an action which greatly increased the cutting speed.

The basic operations of the wood-turning lathe are two-fold: shaping spindles from lumber mounted between the live and dead

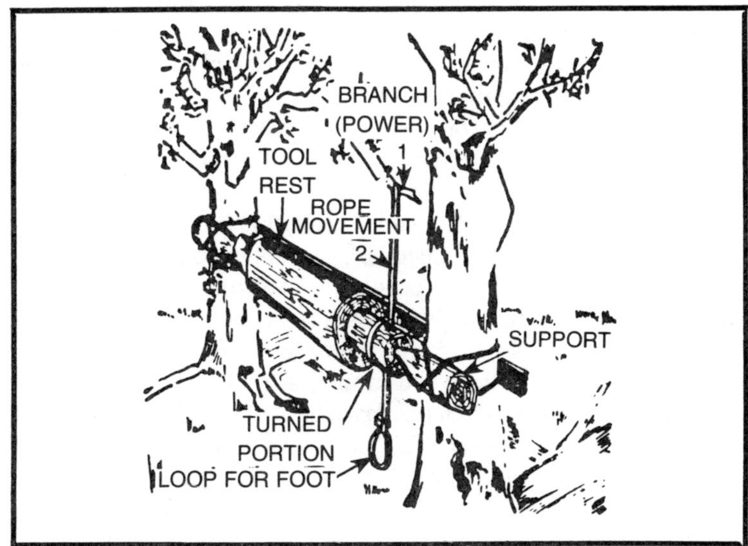

Fig. 1-34. Early version of wood-turning lathe.

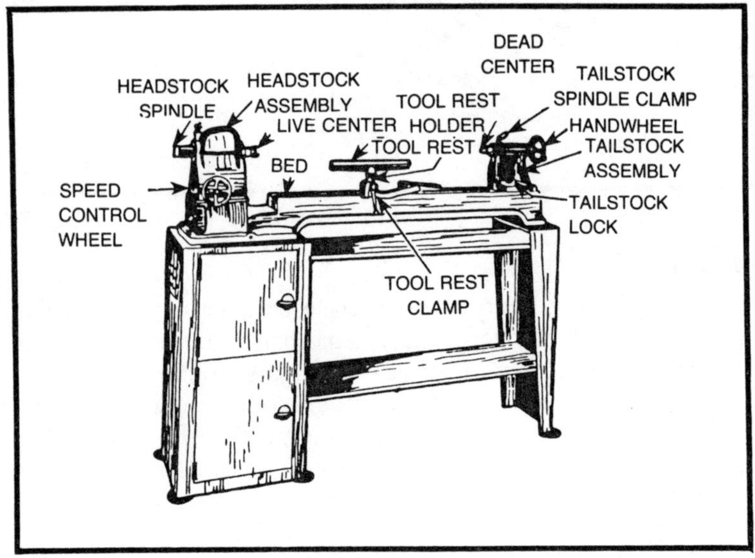

Fig. 1-35. Modern wood-turning lathe, showing chief parts.

centers of the lathe; and faceplate turning, performed by chisels on work mounted to a faceplate secured to the headstock spindle of the lathe.

The size of the lathe is determined by the maximum length of the work which can be turned on it between the live and dead centers. This length measurement is referred to as the "capacity" of the lathe and is regulated by the length of the bed. The "swing" of the lathe is the maximum diameter of stock which can be turned on the faceplate when it is mounted on the *inboard* end of the headstock spindle. (Most lathes can be used with a special, larger faceplate to perform larger turnings on the *outboard* end of the headstock spindle.)

The principal parts of the wood-turning lathe are: the headstock assembly (featuring the headstock live center spindle and speed control wheel), the tailstock assembly (featuring the dead center spindle, spindle cramp, handwheel and tailstock lock), the bed, the tool rest and the tool rest cramp (see Fig. 1-35).

The popularity of the wood-turning lathe with woodworkers is due to the wide scope which this machine tool affords the creativity of the individual craftsman. This particular power tool is favored even by that dedicated group of woodworkers who—despite present-day technological methods of producing furniture—still practice cabinet making essentially as a *hand*-craft. Certainly, the wood-turning lathe, of all power tools except perhaps the jigsaw, places demands on its operator's imagination and originality as well as his skill. Consequently, even those cabinet makers who believe fine furniture making to be a true art form—reflective of the individual artisan's impress and dependent upon his personal creativity—and who pursue their craft using the time-honored hand-fashioned methods find plenty of scope for their talents in the use of the wood-turning lathe.

Special turning tools are necessary to shape wood on the lathe. All of these tools are designed with long handles which can be easily grasped and securely held while cutting the rotating stock. Chief among these are the various gouges and chisels which actually sculpture the wood as it is turned (see Fig. 1-36).

Gouge. The serrated blade on this tool is used to rough out the spindle turning on the lathe and to cut coves wherever needed.

Skew. This tool pares and shears the lumber, smoothing the work.

Parting tool. This tool is used for cutting grooves and for establishing given diameters. It also puts a smooth face on the end of stock and cuts a length into given segments.

Roundnose chisel. This is one of three chisels used to shape contours in faceplate work.

Flatnose chisel. This is another chisel used to sculpture faceplate work.

Spearpoint chisel. A handy tool for cutting and sizing lumber on a faceplate. Makes a clean, incisive cut.

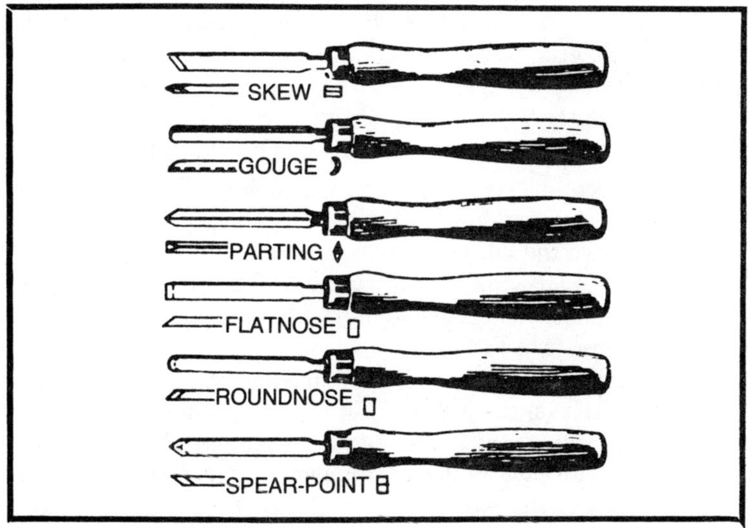

Fig. 1-36. Special chisels for wood turning.

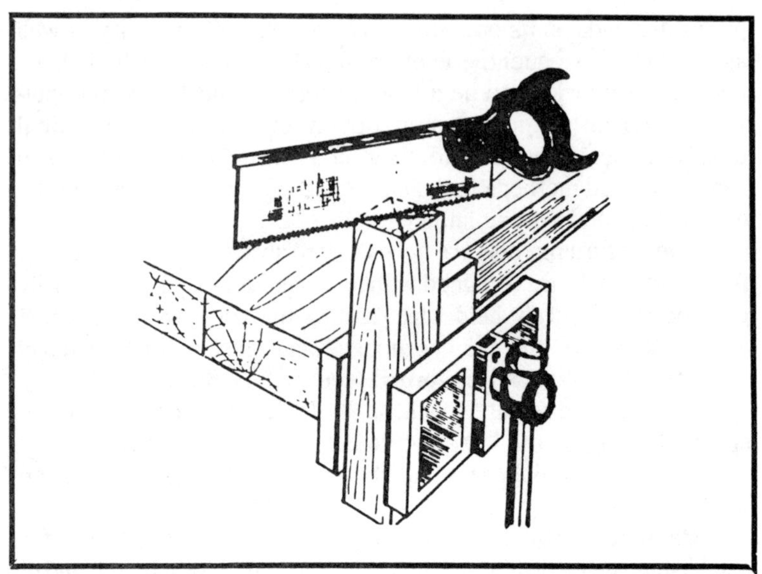

Fig. 1-37. Locating exact center of work with diagonal saw kerfs.

All lathe chisels must be correctly ground and properly held to produce smooth, well-shaped work.

Additional tools for sculpturing wood on the lathe include dividers, rulers, inside and outside calipers, and templates (patterns of proposed wood cuttings superimposed over unworked stock to act as guides).

Turning Wood Between Spindles. To get the maximum diameter from each piece of wood, the stock must be exactly centered on the two spindles. The larger the piece, the more care required to center and square the lumber. Here are some hints on establishing the exact center on a large piece of stock:

1. Select a piece of stock large enough to allow a margin of ¼-inch for turning.
2. Square the ends of the stock selected.
3. Holding the work vertically in vise, make diagonal grooves with a saw on each end of the stock to pinpoint the exact center (see Fig. 1-37)
4. Remove the live center from the headstock assembly and place it on the lumber with its center pin exactly on the place where the two saw grooves intersect. Tap the center pin with a mallet to sink the spurs slightly in the saw kerfs.
5. Remove the live center from the work and replace it in the headstock assembly.

6. Place the stock marked for the live center against the live center.
7. Bring the tailstock assembly toward the work until the cup center touches the work. Lock the tailstock assembly to the bed with the wrench provided for that purpose.
8. Now tighten the cup center of the tailstock assembly snugly against the stock and lock the spindle with the locking lever.
9. Apply a few drops of oil in the cup center. (This step may be eliminated if a ball-bearing cup center is used.)
10. Adjust the tool rest to about ⅛-inch clearance between it and the widest part of the stock.
11. Turn the work one complete revolution by hand to test for proper clearance. The project should look like Fig. 1-38.
12. Keep the turning speed at low revolutions per minute until the work is reduced to a cylinder and is well balanced.
13. Hold the gouge firmly and properly for effective cutting. As the work is reduced in diameter, move the tool rest closer.
14. For finish cutting, the skew chisel may be used and the speed may be increased. This step will produce a smoother final cutting.
15. Check the size and shape of the finished piece with calipers or with the templates you used as layouts.

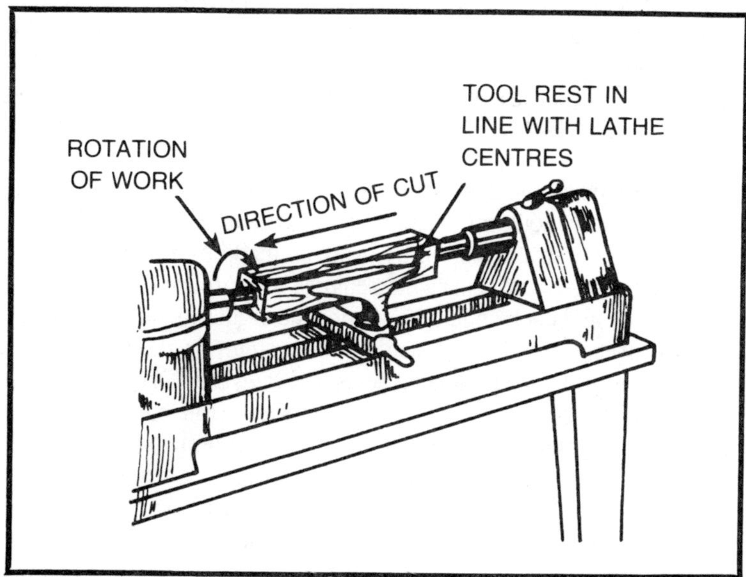

Fig. 1-38. Wood block fastened between live and dead centers on lathe, ready for turning.

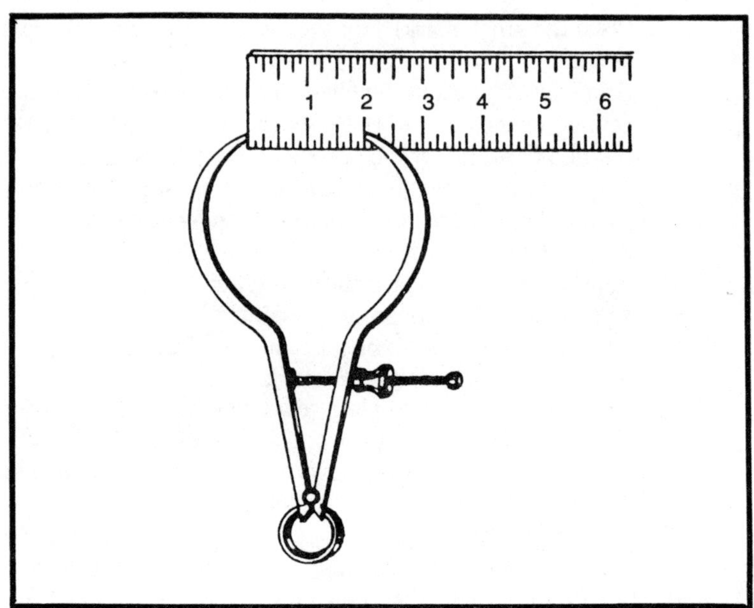

Fig. 1-39. Outside caliper being set to dimension desired.

Checking the Sizes of Stock. When turning spindles to a predetermined size, or to match other spindles exactly, measuring every gradation of curve is a must. The outside caliper is the perfect tool for this job. It may be set to a given dimension, or to the corresponding diameter on the twin spindle, and then transferred to the work on the lathe to check on the diameter developing there (see Figs. 1-39 and 1-40). The lathe should be turned off when such a check is made.

If identical spindles, stretchers or legs are desired the long piece of stock should be shaped one segment at a time—the segments being first marked off by grooves made by the parting tool. Each segment should represent a change of contouring or dimension in the work and each should be shaped individually using the parting tool to cut it to the desired size and the gouge, or skew, to whittle and contour it. If sized calipers are used during the work to check the contours being made by the gouge or skew, the contours of the individual segments will match exactly. (Incidentally, the groove made by the parting tool to indicate the changes of size must be cut wider than the blade to prevent the tool from binding.)

Safety precautions when turning wood:

1. Fasten the stock securely between live and dead centers or on the faceplate.

2. Fasten locking levers for all adjustments before turning on the machine.
3. Set the correct r.p.m. speed on the headstock assembly. Take care that the speed is slow enough for safe operation.
4. Set the tool rest as close as possible to the work, moving it closer as the size of the work diminishes.
5. Keep all turning tools sharpened and fitted with long handles.
6. *Turn off the machine to make any adjustments and wear goggles or a face shield at all times.*
7. Form-fitting clothing is less likely to become tangled in the machinery; wear such clothing to operate the lathe.

Faceplate Turning. The primary prerequisite for accurate faceplate turning is to locate the stock accurately on the faceplate. The procedure is as follows:

1. Select the stock, allowing ⅛-inch margin on the thickness, width and length dimensions.
2. True one side of the stock with a plane.
3. Locate the exact center by drawing diagonal lines on the square piece of stock.
4. Set the compass to a radius ¼-inch greater than the desired size of the work and inscribe a circle, making certain

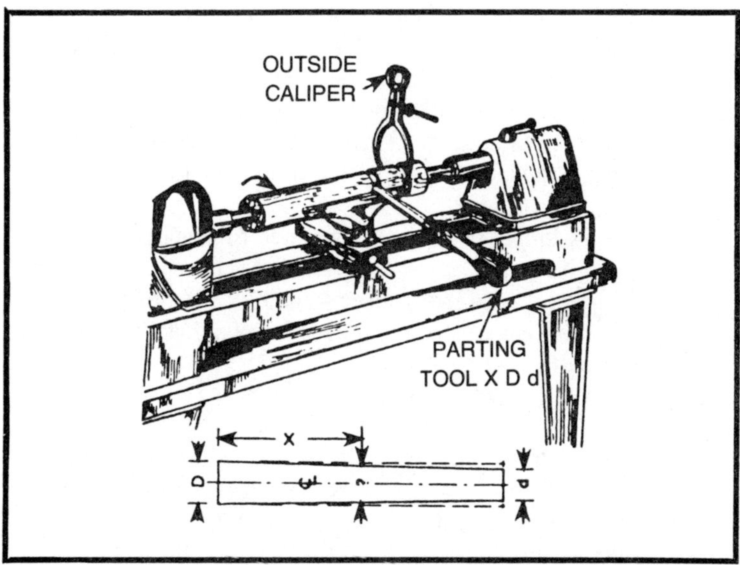

Fig. 1-40. Diameter of one section of work being tested for accuracy of measurement.

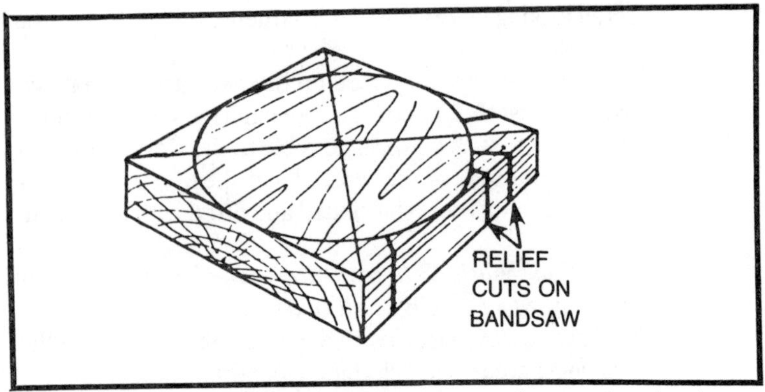

Fig. 1-41. Relief cuts are made before cutting circle from stock on bandsaw.

that the point of the compass is at all times on the exact center of the work.

5. Using the band saw, make relief cuts from the edge of the stock to the edge of the circle in the waste areas all around the pencilled compass circle. These relief cuts will prevent the band saw blade from binding when the penciled compass is cut out (see Fig. 1-41).
6. Cut out the compass-drawn circle, following the marked circumference line exactly.
7. If the stock to be turned is very thin, an auxiliary face plate covered with a glued-on circular layer of paper is necessary as a back-up to the stock. Its paper layering is glued to the stock and the regular metal faceplate mounted to the auxiliary faceplate with wood screws of sufficient length to penetrate the stock. (A circle of heavy paper toweling or scrap wallpaper is perfect for the paper layer.) See Fig. 1-42.
8. The assembly of faceplate fastened to auxiliary faceplate, glued-on paper layer and stock to be turned is then mounted on the live center spindle of the headstock.
9. The tool rest is adjusted and secured parallel to the work with ¼-inch of clearance.
10. Revolve the work by hand to check the clearance on all sides.
11. Turn on the lathe. Using the roundnose chisel, shape the *outside* of the stock according to the template or the dimensions marked on the plans.
12. Keep resetting the tool rest to maintain the ¼-inch clearance as the work progresses and the size of the stock diminishes.

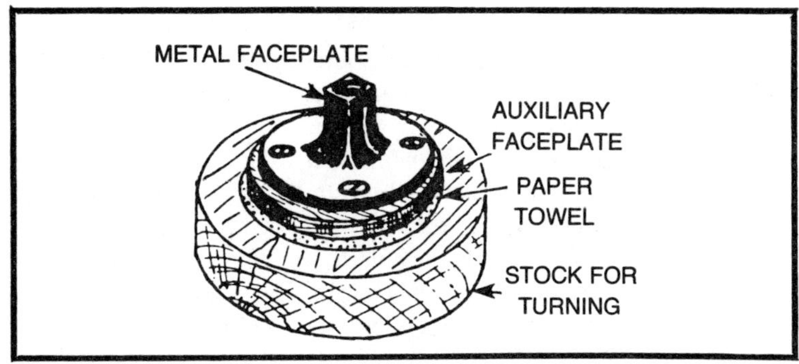

Fig. 1-42. The use of paper layer and auxiliary faceplate to back up thin stock for faceplate turning.

13. Change chisels as the contouring of the work demands.
14. Shape the inside of the object, if necessary, always working from the inside of the stock to the outside and constantly checking the progress of the project for correct proportioning against the drafted design.

Use the outside calipers to check measurements on the plan layout with the measurements of the stock on the lathe; or check the progress of the work on the lathe against the inside or outside template patterns to be sure that all dimensions are right (see Fig. 1-43).

Sanding on the Rotating Lathe

1. Remove the tool rest and slide the tool rest holder along the bed out of the way.

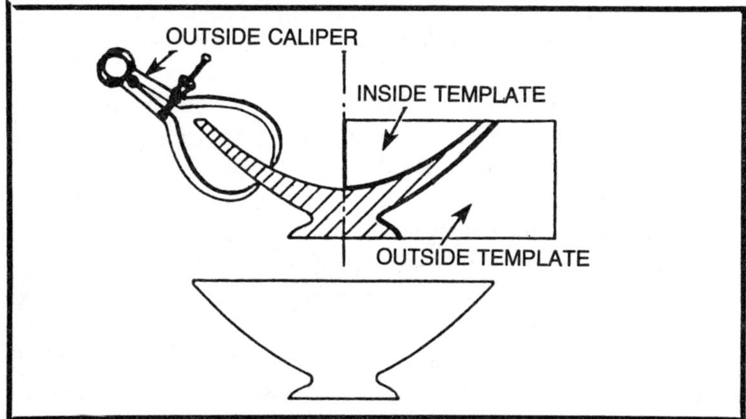

Fig. 1-43. Comparing dimensions of wood on lathe with those specified on drawing.

2. Set the speed to medium and start the lathe.
3. Select a piece of sandpaper of medium grit and move it up and down the stock being turned, working as nearly as possible with the grain.
4. Keep shifting the sandpaper as it wears thin and, applying an unused patch of the sheet to the work, keep exerting slight finger pressure.
5. Finish the lathe sanding with No. 000 sandpaper or its equivalent (see Fig. 1-44) which shows the different ways of sanding stock turned between centers and faceplate turned stock).
6. All extensive preliminary sanding can be done on the lathe. Once completed, the lathe can be stopped and the sanding finished by hand, working only with the grain and taking care to remove all circular scratches.
7. Hardwood projects will have an exceptionally smooth finish if the wood is sponged with water to raise the grain before sanding.

Applying a Shellac or Oil Finish on the Lathe

1. Remove all dust and grit from the sanded object.
2. Prepare all finishing materials: cut shellac, boiled linseed oil or a suitable vegetable oil, and several pads of soft lint-free cheesecloth.
3. Place paper over the entire bed of the lathe to protect it from drips and spills.
4. Moisten a pad with thinned shellac, sprinkling a few drops of oil on the pad. Backing the moistened pad with a dry cloth, hold the pad to the work and rotate the lathe at slow speed.
5. Keep remoistening the pad with shellac and oil as the mixture is absorbed by the wood, always keeping the pad compactly folded, so that it will not get caught in the rotating machine.
6. When a good polish has been produced on the wood (three or more applications should give the desired result), the work is ready for further finishing and may be removed from the lathe.
7. Be careful to dispose of all cloths used to apply the oil finish immediately or to store them in a self-sealed metal container. They are capable of slow combustion if improperly handled.

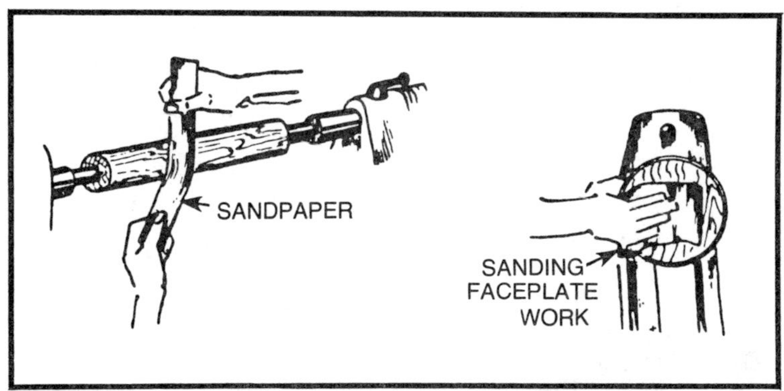

Fig. 1-44. How to do sanding on a lathe.

The machine tools described in the foregoing section are those which are most frequently employed by the hobbyist in a home woodworking shop. Professional cabinet makers might be justified by their work load, in investing in many more of these sophisticated stationary tool machines or even in more than one of each. However, machine tools are undeniably expensive to purchase, to operate and to repair. Fortunately, each machine tool has its counterpart in a portable power tool or a well-made hand tool. Therefore, the stationary machine tool may be regarded as a luxury among woodworking tools—a necessary investment only in the case of the woodworker who is building a house, a vacation cabin, a boat, or all his own furniture—or for the enthusiastic amateur craftsman who desires the further challenge which large commercial-type stationary machine tools represent.

Chapter 2
Hand Tools

Tools are a necessity. Anyone who has ever tried to hang a picture, wage a tug of war with a balky drawer, or suffered the seasick lurch of a wobbly chair has wished for a few basic tools to set matters right. This chapter will list the essential implements, those which have multiple uses and those which are more specific in function. If you are seriously engaged in woodworking and have a shop you may want to own every tool in the list. Some of the tools may be less generally useful than others, but every one of them will lighten the labor of any task to which you can employ them.

BASIC TOOLS

If you are one of those persons who believes in purchasing tools only when the need arises, you will pay dearly in frustration for procrastinating. Have you ever noticed that household emergencies have a way of happening on evenings or weekends when hardware stores are closed? Even if the situation isn't one of panic, being stuck in the middle of a job is very aggravating. With a basic tool kit, you can at least administer first aid when the repair needed is too awesome for anyone but an expert; but without tools, you are completely helpless.

Quality tools are fairly expensive, but you will save in the long run by buying them. Good tools far outperform cheap ones and are durable enough to last a lifetime. Because they are well-made and properly balance, they are easier to heft and wield. Also, they are safer. Cheap tools can be the cause of accidents when blades break,

Fig. 2-1. Bench rule.

handles come off, jaws slip or cutting edges become blunt too easily. In purchasing tools, buying less than the best is poor economy.

If the following list were to comprise all the tools which are of use in woodworking, this volume would not be large enough to contain them. Nor would the most prolific craftsman require every one of them, despite the extent of his endeavors. With these facts in mind, the list has been pared of all those items which would be used only infrequently, perform only a limited function or duplicate the function of a more versatile tool.

Measuring and Marking Tools

The first unit of measure was probably a man's forearm. This sufficed in primitive times because each man completed the job he began. Today, each man depends on the cooperative efforts of countless others around the globe. These individual efforts can be coordinated only by the science of precision measurement.

Steel Rule. A 12-inch steel rule has two uses in a workshop. Because it has no margin at the end, as many wooden rulers do, it accurately measures even such spaces as the insides of drawers and the exact boundaries of corners. Secondly, the steel rule is a test for flatness. Place it edge-down on a surface and put a light behind it. Any deviations from the true level will be instantly apparent.

Bench Rule. A 12-inch folding rule, Fig. 2-1, widely used in woodworking. Its inch dimensions are marked in eighths on one edge and sixteenths on the other.

Fig. 2-2. Tape measure.

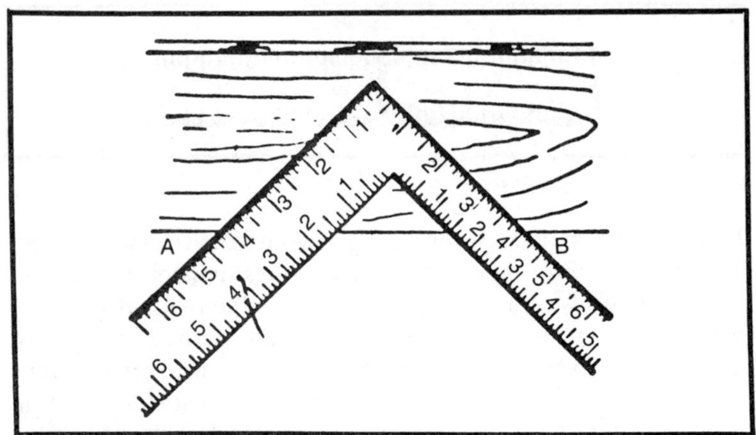

Fig. 2-3. Steel framing square.

Tape Measure. The steel tape measure with pushbutton rewind (Fig. 2-2) is very useful for long measurements.

Steel Framing Square. An all-metal, right-angle gauge (Fig. 2-3) which is permanent in shape—an indispensable aid to the carpenter and cabinetmaker in laying out square ends, rafter and stair angles and in checking the accuracy of cabinet frames. A number of helpful mesuring tables appear on its blade face.

Try-Square. The try square (Fig. 2-4) consists of two main parts—rosewood stock and steel blade. Steel rivets, each fitted with diamond-shaped brass washers, fasten the two parts together. The

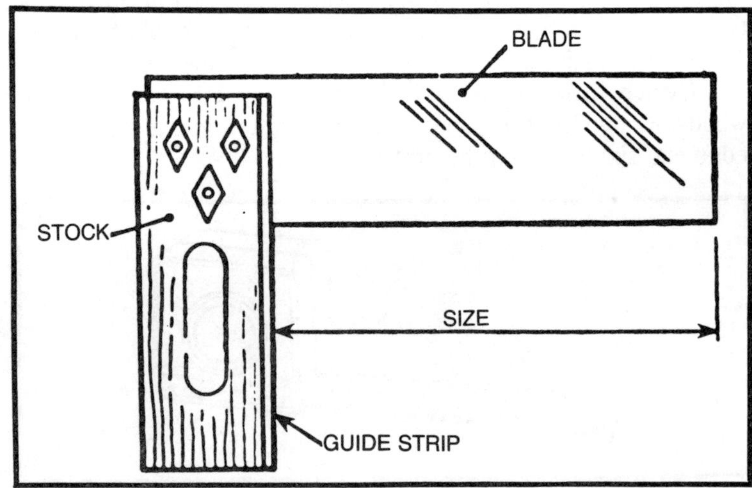

Fig. 2-4. Try-square.

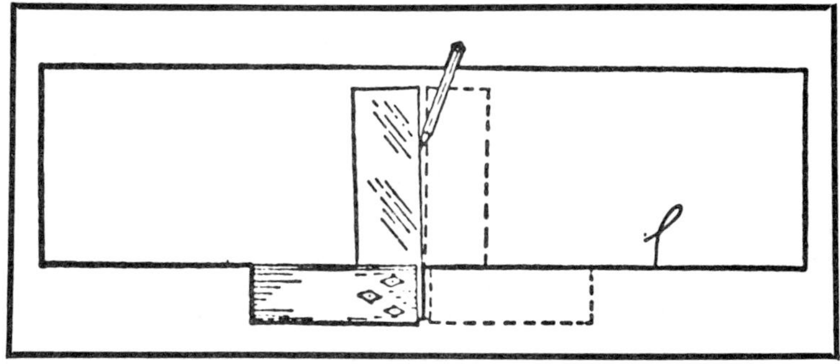

Fig. 2-5. The try-square can be checked for squareness against a straightedge, outlining it with a sharp pencil. Reverse the try-square and outline it again. The outlines will coincide only if the square is accurate.

large washers prevent the rivets from splitting the stock. A brass guide strip on the inside edge of the wooden stock keeps the stock from wearing.

The try square is used for checking and marking precise right angles. The 6-inch size is the most practical. This tool must be handled with care and never dropped if it is to retain its accuracy. The squareness of a try square may be tested in the following manner: place the square against a straightedge and mark the outline of the blade with a sharp pencil. Reverse the square and repeat (Fig. 2-5). Outlines will coincide only if square is accurate. Any discrepancy can be corrected with judicious filling. This same method of comparing outlines tests the straightness of a steel ruler, too, as shown in Fig. 2-6. Outline the ruler on all four sides. Then turn it over, placing it beside the first outline and outline it again. Any discrepancy will be doubled.

Dividers. High-precision measuring device capable of transfering spacings from a drawing to the material being worked on.

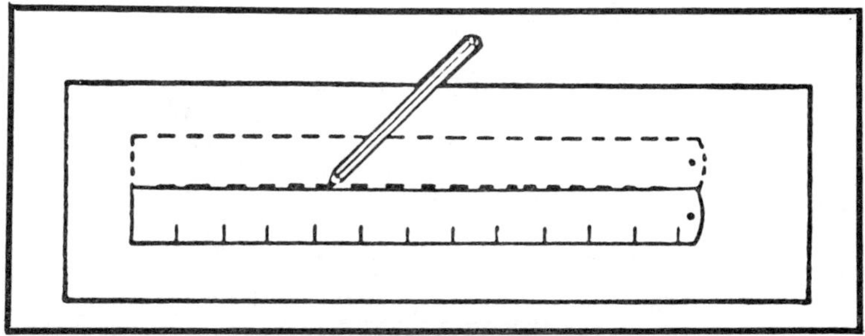

Fig. 2-6. Testing the steel rule for straightness: Outline the steel rule with a pencil; then turn the rule over and draw an outline of the opposite side beside the first outline. Any discrepancy will become doubly apparent.

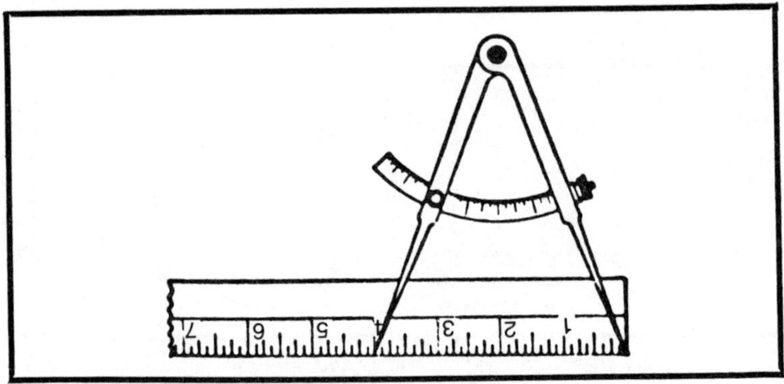

Fig. 2-7. How to set dividers to the measure required.

Dividers may be set to a desired measure with a thumb screw and used in marking off spaces which are repeated a given number of times. The sharp points of the dividers make inconspicuous pricks marking the desired segments as the space is "stepped off" by turning the divider first on one point and then on the other, as shown in Fig. 2-7.

Dividers are a convenience in laying out arcs, circles and irregular curves.

Calipers. Inside calipers can be inserted into holes, grooves, and interior spaces to determine their widths. Outside calipers check the outer dimensions of work, such as the diameter of turned wood on a lathe. Both types of calipers (Fig. 2-8) have screw type settings to hold the jaws stationary.

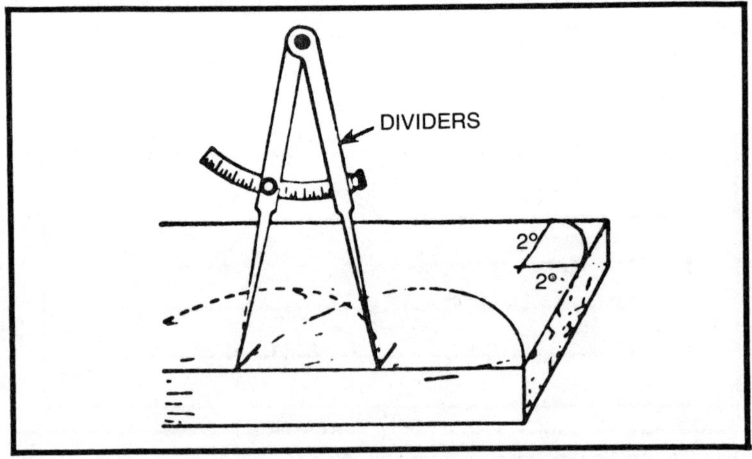

Fig. 2-8. Stepping off a repetitive measurement by turning the dividers first on one point and then on the other.

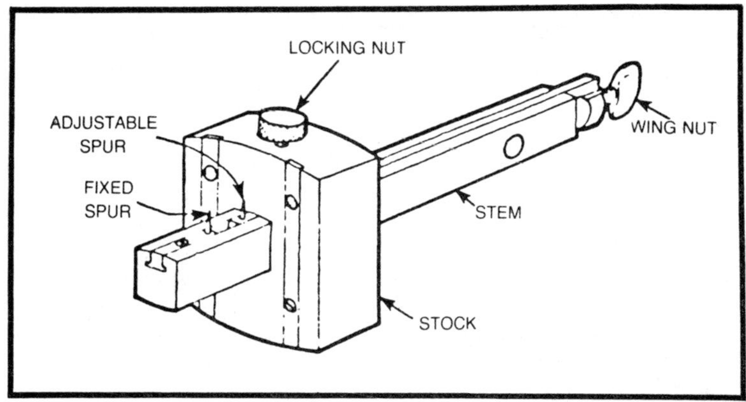

Fig. 2-9. Mortise gauge—This fine tool is usually made of rosewood with brass inlay for durability.

Mortise Gauge. The mortise gauge (Fig. 2-9) resembles the marking or measuring gauge but the chief difference is that the mortise gauge has two spurs. This gauge is used to mark two lines on wood which are parallel with one another and with the edge of the wood and always go *with* the grain. Its principal use is marking guide lines to be followed by the saw and chisel when cutting the mortise and tenon joint, hence its name.

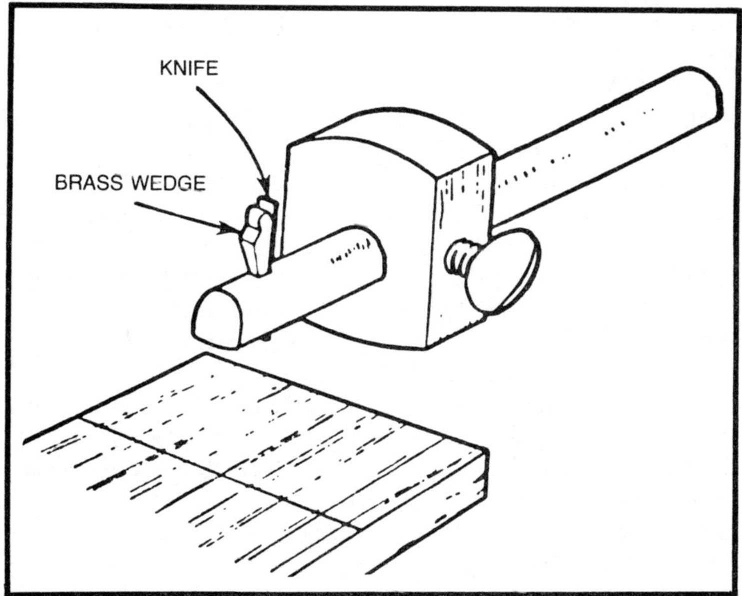

Fig. 2-10. Cutting gauge.

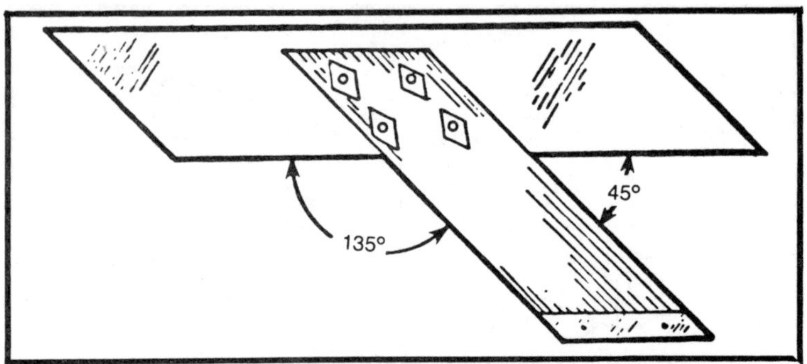

Fig. 2-11. Miter square.

The distance between the spurs may be varied by adjusting a wing nut at the end of the stem. The position of the lines from the end of the work may be adjusted by moving the stock which can be locked into position by turning the nut provided. It is usual to set the two spurs of the mortise gauge to the breadth of the chisel which will be used rather than to any given measure. The chisel should just rest between the points of the spurs when the gauge is correctly set.

The Cutting Gauge. This gauge (Fig. 2-10) marks a line on the wood *across* the grain. Here again, the tool is similar to the marking gauge, but the spur is here replaced by a small knife which is held in place by a brass wedge. As with all other gauges, the end of the wood must be square and true before the gauge can be used with accuracy.

The Miter Square. The miter square (Fig. 2-11) is similar to the try square except that the blade is inclined to a 45-degree angle to the stock. This measuring device is used for marking out and checking angles of 45 degrees and 135 degrees.

The Bevel Square. This measuring tool (Fig. 2-12) has a sliding blade which may be locked with the handle at any angle from 0 to 180 degrees. Adjust the bevel blade to the desired angle with the aid of a protractor, and tighten the blade in position with the set screw. To mark the angle required accurately on the work, the bevel must be held firmly against the surface.

Sometimes the angle required is given not in numbers of degrees, but as a ratio, in much the same manner as that used in describing to motorists the gradient of a hill. Suppose the sliding bevel is to be set to a slope of 1 to 14. To arrive at the number of degrees of the required angle in order to set the bevel square, the following steps must be taken:

1. First, choose a board with one straight edge and mark a line at right angles to the board edge with a try-square and pencil.

2. If the board is not 14 inches wide, divide the numbers in the ratio by two for greater convenience. Thus, the new ratio becomes ½ to 7. This mathematical adjustment will not alter the degree of the angle.
3. Now measure 7 inches along the line you have drawn at right angles to the edge, marking the terminus with another line at right angles to the first line.
4. Measure ½-inch along the terminus line. Join that ½-inch point with the base of the line drawn at right angles to the wood edge.
5. Set the sliding/blade of the bevel square to this line.

Trammel Points. These adjustable compass points are used for describing and laying out larger arcs and circles than those which can be marked off by dividers. They can make elipses and various geometrical figures which are multi-sided, as well. They can be adjusted along a straightedge bar and tightened into the desired position with thumb screws. They operate like dividers.

Flexible Curve. This is a designer's tool made of malleable plastic which will retain its shape with careful handling. Its flexible length (Fig. 2-13) can be used to outline any given curve and to transfer that curve exactly to a fresh, untouched piece of stock.

Dovetail Templates. The dovetail template is used as a pattern when marking out a dovetail jointure. This device can be made from a piece of steel bent and filed to the shape desired. It is a great time saver!

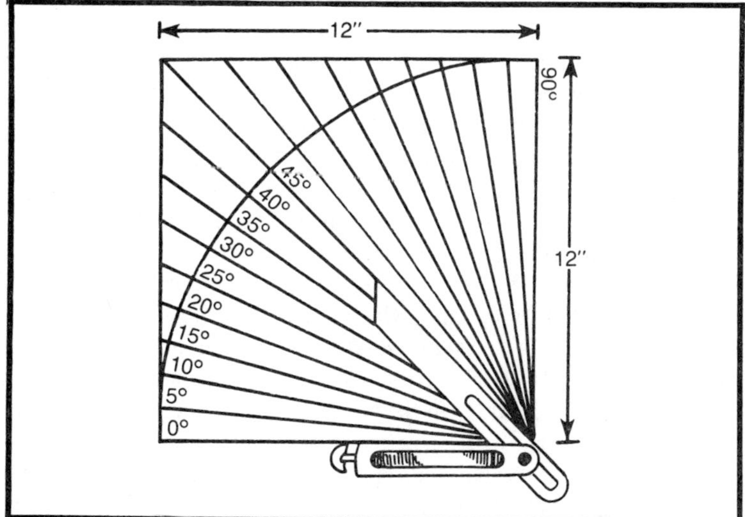

Fig. 2-12. Bevel square or T-bevel.

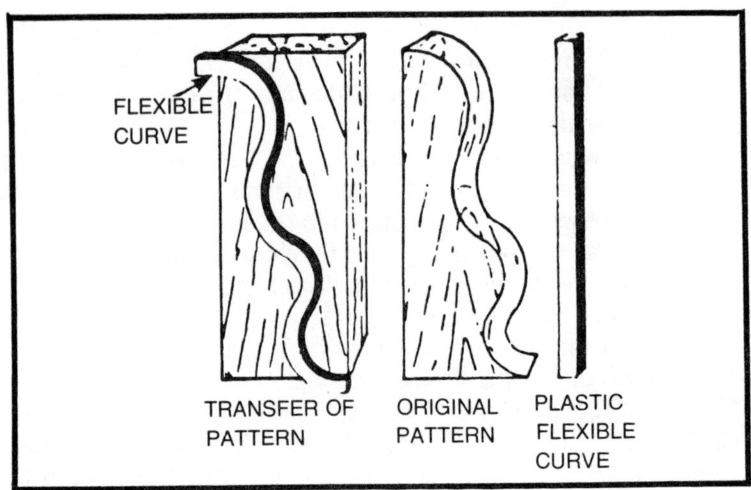

Fig. 2-13. Flexible curve.

Hammers

A hammer is still the most convenient tool for driving nails, although many tradesman—particularly plumbers and electricians—now use a special gun which fires a type of nail called a "cartridge nail'" into the material. However, hand-set nails can be more carefully and inconspicuously placed and are therefore universally used by woodworkers.

Claw Hammer. The best all-around hammer is undoubtedly the claw hammer (Fig. 2-14) which is available in two styles: curved or straight claw. The curved claw hammer demonstrates greater efficiency in withdrawing most nails because its curved head affords the best leverage. However, for removing nails from corners or restricted places, the straight claw hammer is best.

When using either hammer to pull nails (Fig. 2-15) a piece of wood should be placed under the head to prevent marring the wood.

The size of the hammer is determined by the weight of the hammer head. Hammers are available in weights of 7, 8, 9, 10, 13, 16 or 20 ounces. The head of the hammer is composed of the head itself and the handle opening which fits into the head. The handle is usually made of a resilient wood such as ash or hickory which transfers very few shocks to the hand. It has an oval grip and a shape which is waisted gently to fit the hand and to provide resilience to the hammering action.

The head of the hammer is cast of crucible steel. The striking surface is called the "face" and it is a part of a knob called the "bell," or "poll." Behind the bell is a narrower section known as the "neck".

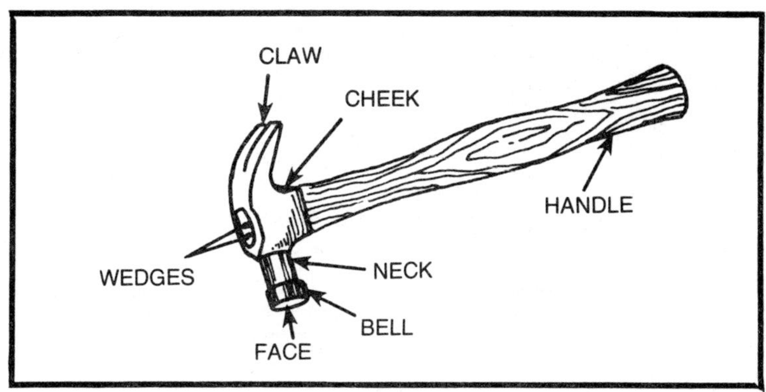

Fig. 2-14. Parts of a hammer—The waisted shape of the handle minimizes the shock of the blow to the hammering arm and makes the hammer easier to grip.

The flat-sided encasement for the handle-end is known as the "cheek" or "eye." and the double prong at the back is aptly named the "claw." The head of the hammer is fastened to the handle by a wedge of hornbeam running lengthwise on the head, and two pronged wedges of malleable iron running across the head (Fig. 2-16). Should the handle become loose, it can be tightened by driving it further into the eye encasement.

The 7-ounce hammer is convenient when driving small nails, but a 16-ounce hammer is the best weight for general carpentry.

Warrington Hammer. This hammer (Fig. 2-17) is designed with a peen end which proves extremely handy in tapping in small

Fig. 2-15. Drawing nails with a claw hammer—The work is protected by a block of waste wood.

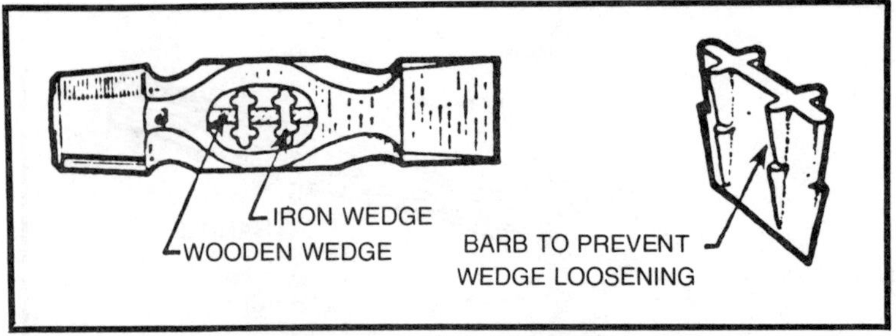

Fig. 2-16. Close-up of hammer head, showing the lengthwise wedge of hornbeam wood and the crosswise barbed iron wedges which fix the head to the shaft.

brads or nails which can be held upright between the fingers. Once these nails are set with the peen, they can then be driven into the wood with the face of the hammer.

Nail Set. This necessary tool (Fig. 2-18) is shaped like a small automatic pencil and is used to sink nail heads below the surface of the wood. Every tool assortment should contain two nail sets (or "nail punches," as they are sometimes called)—one with a wider point than the other for setting nails with larger heads. Nail sets with hollow points are best, because they are less likely to skate off the head of the nail.

To use, choose a nail punch with a smaller head than the nail you are driving. Place it on the head of the nail, which has previously been sunk flush with the wood. Holding the nail set steady on the nail head, tap the end of it with a hammer to punch the nail deeper into the wood. The depression resulting from the nail sinking deeper into

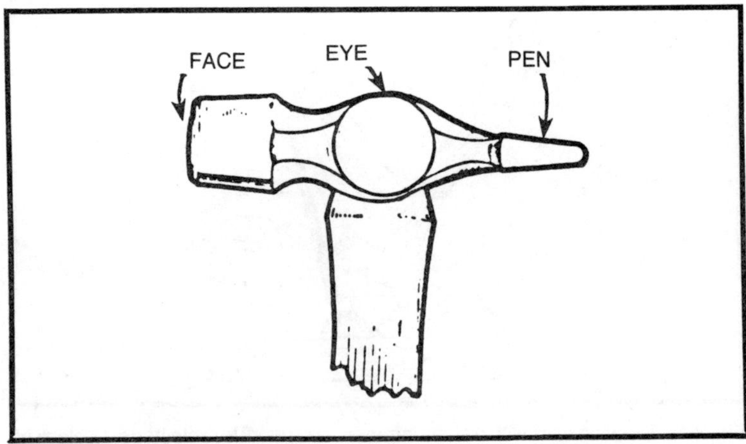

Fig. 2-17. Warrington hammer.

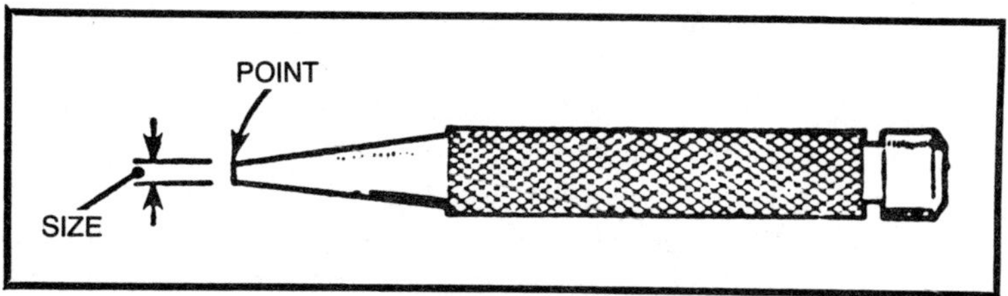

Fig. 2-18. Nail set, or nail punch as it is sometimes called.

the wood may be filled with beeswax, if the surface is to be polished, or with wood putty, if the work is to be painted.

Bradawl. This small, chisel-pointed tool (Fig. 2-19) with a bulbous, easy-grip handle is used to make the starter hole into which nails are to be placed. It is manipulated with a semi-rotary twist, by holding the blade at right angles to the wood with the cutting edge placed across the grain. An inner pin runs through the handle and the blade, sturdily reinforcing both, so that the awl may be withdrawn from the wood without losing its handle.

Screwdrivers

What the hammer is to the nail, the screwdriver is to the screw—it is the means by which the screw is put to use. For this important task, screwdrivers are made in a variety of shapes and

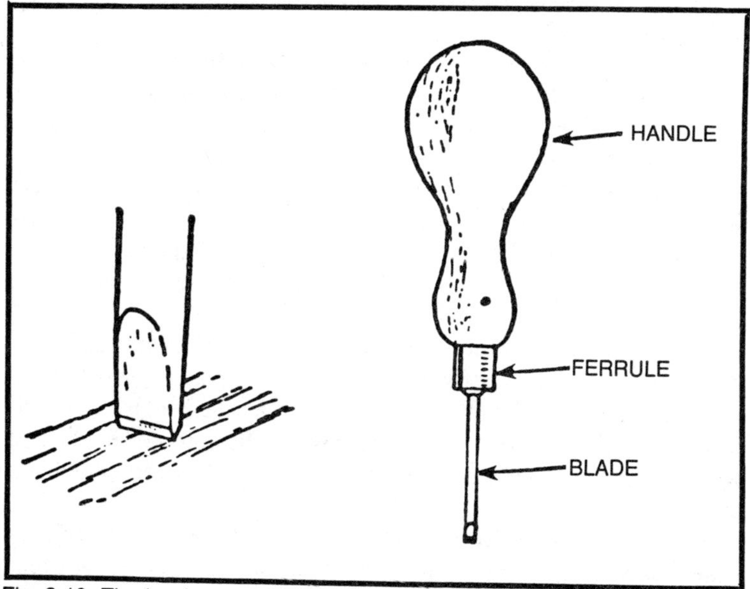

Fig. 2-19. The bradawl—showing how the blade is set across the grain and twisted to make the starter hole.

blade lengths with different widths and thickness of tip to fit properly into the slotted screw heads.

The flat tip screwdriver is the most familiar; it is designed to turn screws with single-slot heads. The Phillips screwdriver fits the screw with crisscross slotting and the Robertson screwdriver probes the center recess of the Robertson-headed screw. Both the Phillips and Robertson screwdrivers are made in three standard sizes, each size accommodating a range of screw gauges.

Screwdrivers with man-sized handles and square shanks are best. When extra leverage is necessary, the square shank can be turned with a wrench, which can make the stubbornest screw take a turn for the better.

Holding Devices

Bench Vise. Probably the single most important tool in any workshop is a vise. Both the safety of the worker and the success of the work demands that the wood being used be securely held throughout the working process. One of the best devices for holding the work stationary is a vise. Usually, this tool is permanently attached to the apron of the workbench (Fig. 2-20), although portable vises are also employed where space is limited or where more than one vise is needed. These vises can be easily fitted to a table by tightening the screw underneath. They are ideal for jobs which require a vise only temporarily, because they can be quickly dismantled and stored when the work is finished.

In choosing a vise , select one with a jaw width of 7 inches and an opening of 8 inches. This size is most useful for the type of woodworking described in this book.

To open the vise to maximum aperture, the handle must be turned in a full circle many times. Some more sophisticated models are equipped with a quick-release lever which, when pressed, allows the jaws to be pulled fully out. However, unless speed of performance is essential to the project, the expense of such a vise is not justified.

The work held in the vise should be shielded from bruising by inserting waste wood between the bite edges of the jaws on both sides and the work. Countersink bolts may be obtained which fit the two threaded holes provided in each jaw. These bolts will hold wood waste packing in place on each side, thus protecting the work from pressure dents.

Cramps. These tools—sometimes called clamps—operate on essentially the same principle as does the bench vise, except that they are highly adjustable and fully portable and, therefore, able to apply pressure or to secure work wherever necessary. Their func-

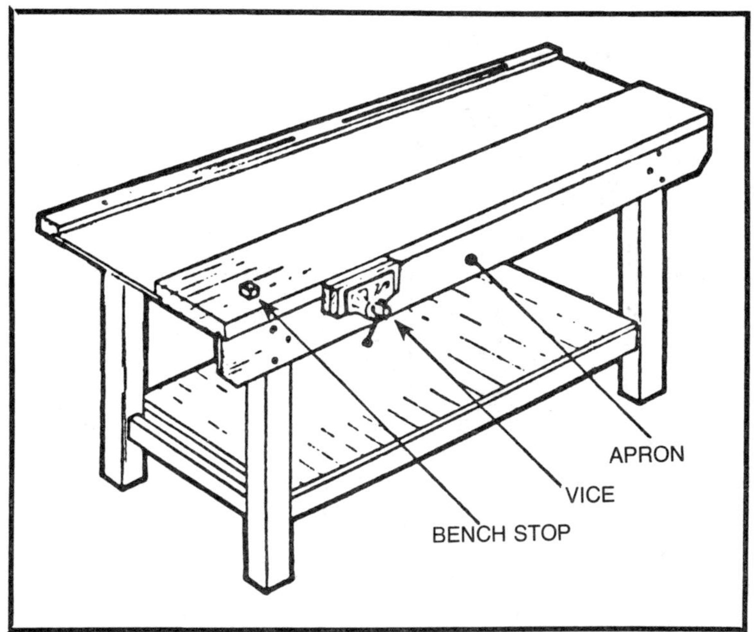

Fig. 2-20. The stationary vise is permanently attached to the workbench.

tion is two-fold: to spread the glue into a thin film between two joined surfaces, holding the two pieces firmly together until the adhesive forms a bond which will withstand the stress to which joints are subject, and to secure wood which is being curved or bent to the form of the curve.

Here is the way in which cramps are used in gluing:

1. All parts are first labeled in pencil.
2. The correct type of glue is applied to the clean, dry surfaces of both pieces being joined.
3. Cramps are applied as needed to hold the glued parts firmly together.
4. The assembly is checked to see that it is flat and square.
5. Excess glue is wiped away before it can harden.
6. Cramps are removed very slowly after glue is thoroughly dry.

Cramps are available in several varieties and sizes. Every toolchest should contain several varieties and sizes so that the proper cramp will not be found missing. The types most used, like the G-cramp described below, are often stocked in pairs since many projects require the use of two.

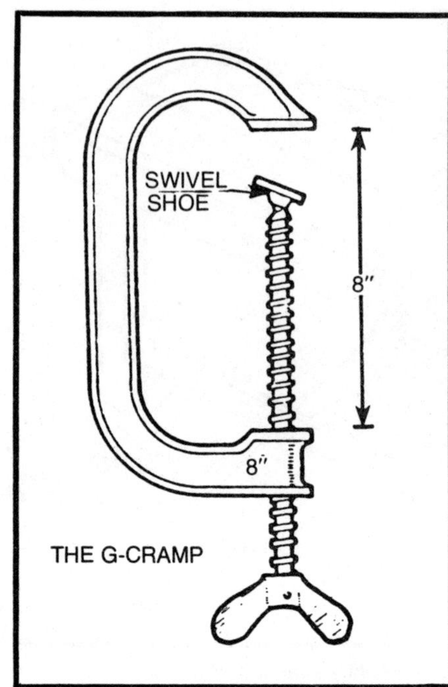

Fig. 2-21. G-cramp.

G-Cramp. The most frequently employed cramp in a woodwork shop is the G-Cramp (Fig. 2-21), so called because its shape is similar to that of the letter "G." Every woodworker will find lots of uses for it—particularly for the practical 8-inch size. It is an excellent tool for pressing the two pieces of a butt joint together while the glue dries or for holding work steady on the bench, leaving both hands free to wield tools.

Sash Cramp. Glued frame and butt jointures between two boards will be held immobile until the glue bonds them if placed between the working shoe and the tail shoe of a sash cramp. This cramp (Fig. 2-22) has a short thread on the working shoe with a handle for adjusting it to the opening desired. The tail shoe can be slid along the bar until it is snug against the work. Here, it is rigidly anchored to a bore hole while the working shoe is moved flush against the work with a few turns of the handle. Between them, the two shoes exert an enormous pressure—so much, in fact, that a buffering piece of waste wood should be placed between each shoe and the work to prevent denting. A pair of sash cramps in the 36-inch length are very practical additions to a workshop.

Handscrew Cramp. This cramp (Fig. 2-23), commonly manufactured in both wood and metal, can be purchased at any well-

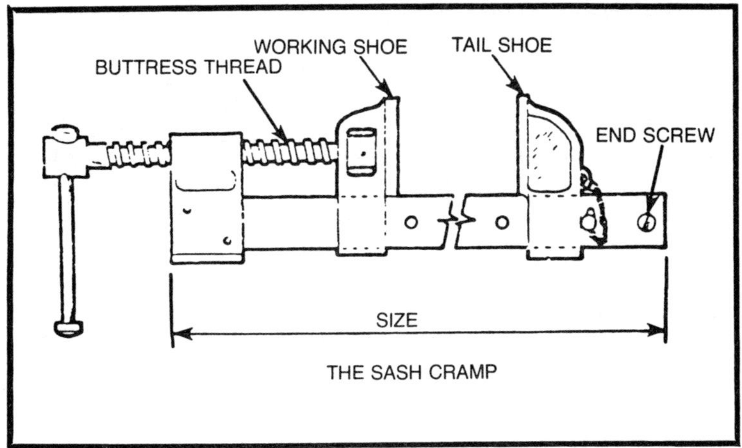

Fig. 2-22. Sash cramp.

stocked hardware store; but one is very easy to make of beech choppings and metal screws, if the woodworker wishes. To open or close the handscrew cramp, simply grab the two handles in both hands and spin the jaws head over heels. To position the cramp on

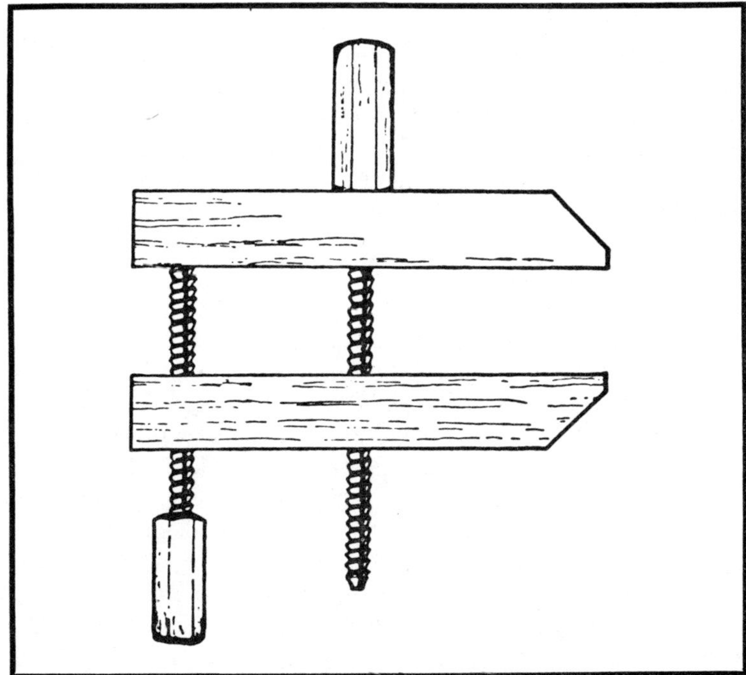
Fig. 2-23. Handscrew cramp.

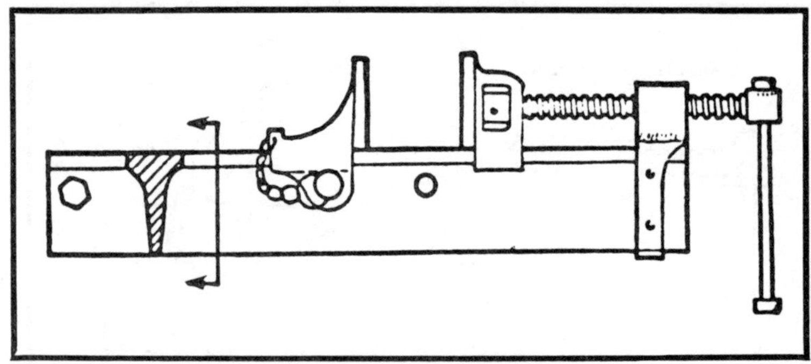

Fig. 2-24. T-bar cramp.

the work, open the jaws to the approximate width of the work. Tighten screw A, then screw B turn about until a firm pinch is established on the material between the jaws.

T-Bar Cramp. The T-shaped insert in the bar of this cramp (Fig. 2-24) gives it an even stronger grip than any of the cramps aforementioned. Care should be taken, therefore, to use this holding device only on large pieces and heavy work since it is capable of exerting too much pressure on lighter, more delicate jobs and is likely to distort them.

Tourniquets. The use of a tourniquet is often more satisfactory than a mechanical cramp especially when an evenly distributed pressure is required. The band cramp (Fig. 2-25)—a belt-like affair with a cinch-type buckling device which holds the band from slipping at the tension desired—can be purchased at any hardware store. For holding four chair legs which have been reglued, or for keeping glued stretchers in place around the four legs of a table, this type of tourniquet is excellent.

The resourceful woodworker can also devise a highly satisfactory tourniquet out of a length of soft cotton clothesline. This holding device is called the "Spanish windlass" (Fig. 2-26). The rope is wound twice around the object and firmly tied in a bow-knot. Then a stick or pipe is inserted between the doubled cords and twisted until the double-ply tourniquet is as tight as desired. The stick or pipe is then tied to the double rope or pushed behind a leg, stretcher or apron on the furniture piece to prevent its unwinding.

These flexible types of retainers are ideal for finished furniture or fine antiques because they are not so likely to mar the wood. However, because they do exert great pressure, cloth wadding should be packed under the ropes or belting at corners and points of strain to prevent damage to the finish.

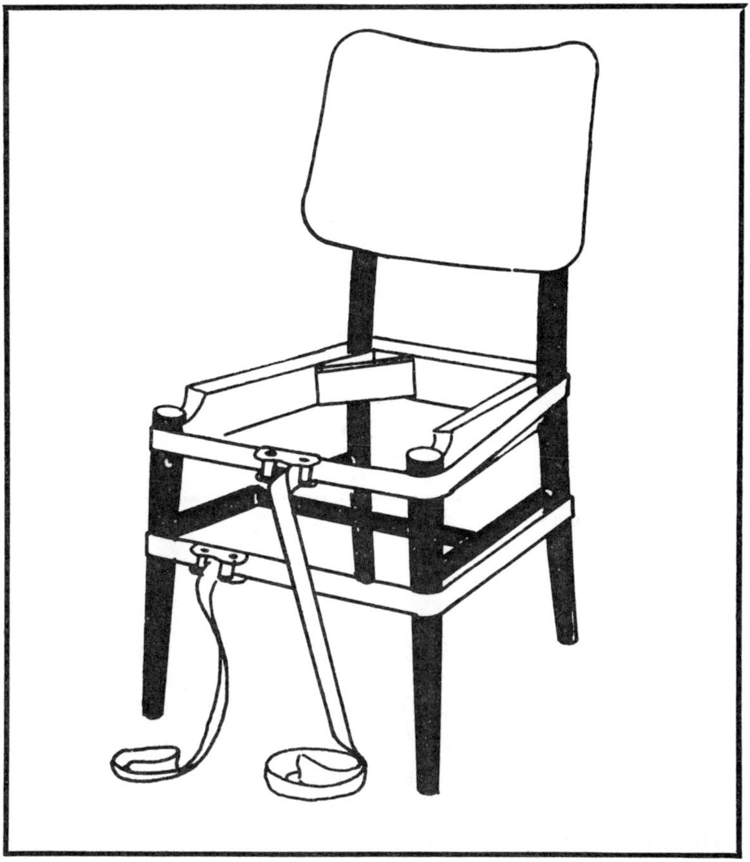

Fig. 2-25. Use of the band cramp tourniquet to hold glued legs in place until they dry.

Fig. 2-26. The Spanish Windlass is a homemade tourniquet made out of double-ply clothesline.

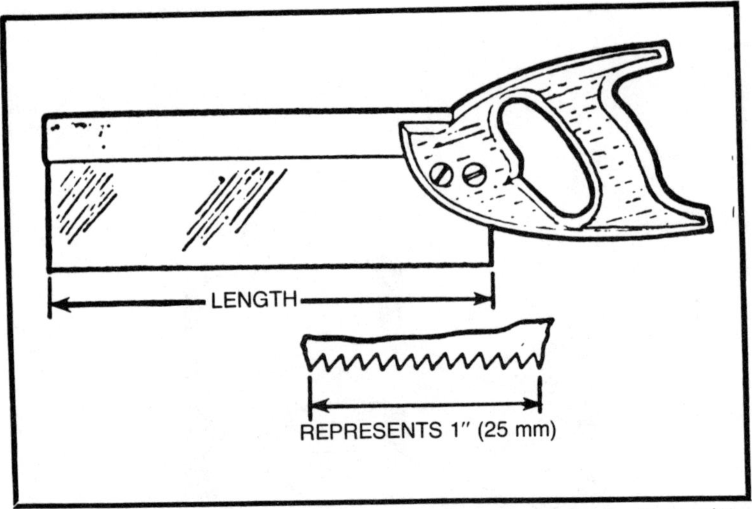

Fig. 2-27. The tenon saw, with detail showing the teeth sized to fourteen points per inch.

Cutting Tools

Stone Age Man used a jagged flintstone for cutting. From this rude beginning, the saw evolved. Ancient Egyptians were using saws similar to those of modern times as early as 3200 B.C. By 900 B.C., sawyers in Europe wielded bronze saws. Finally, the flexible, high-tensile steel blade in many shapes replaced all other metals.

The size of a saw is determined by the length of the blade in inches, the longer blades allowing for a longer stroke. The coarseness or fineness of a saw is determined by the number of points (always one less than the number of teeth) per inch. This designation is stamped on the heel of the blade.

Tenon Saw. This accurate bench saw (Fig. 2-27) is about 10 inches long. A beechwood handle is fastened by two bolts to a thin blade of cold rolled steel, stiffened and braced by an extra steel sheathing on the back of the blade. This saw is often called a "backsaw," and is one of a family of saws of similar "backed" construction. The tenon saw is especially designed for cutting mortise and tenon joints.

The work on which this saw is to be used must first be fastened securely. Place the blade on the waste side of the saw line (Fig. 2-28), raise the handle about 15 degrees and pull the saw toward you. Once the blade bites into the work, the saw may be held parallel to the surface being cut. When making angular cuts, use a miter box to guide the cutting angle.

Crosscut Saw. This saw has teeth which are sharpened like knives are sharpened and measures eight points to the inch. Because this saw is designed to cut across the grain of wood, the teeth are alternately bent outwards—one to the left of the blade, the next to the right. Were the teeth in a straight line, the saw would bind in the cut. Instead, it incises two parallel grooves in the wood. These grooves are so close together that the wood between crumbles away into sawdust.

When purchasing a crosscut saw, carefully examine the teeth for sharpness, uniform shape and outward set. Check the tension of the blade; a properly tensioned blade can be bent double.

The technique for crosscut sawing (Fig. 2-29) is as follows: first, the lumber is secured in a vise or supported on a saw horse. Then the saw is grasped by putting three fingers through the saw handle and letting the forefinger point in the direction of the cut. The blade is placed on the edge of the board on the waste side of the saw line and is drawn toward the manipulator several times until a guide groove has been cut. Then, keeping the saw at a 45-degree angle and using long strokes so as not to more quickly blunt any one section of the teeth, the workman severs the plank taking care to guide the blade during the cutting with the thumb of his free hand and

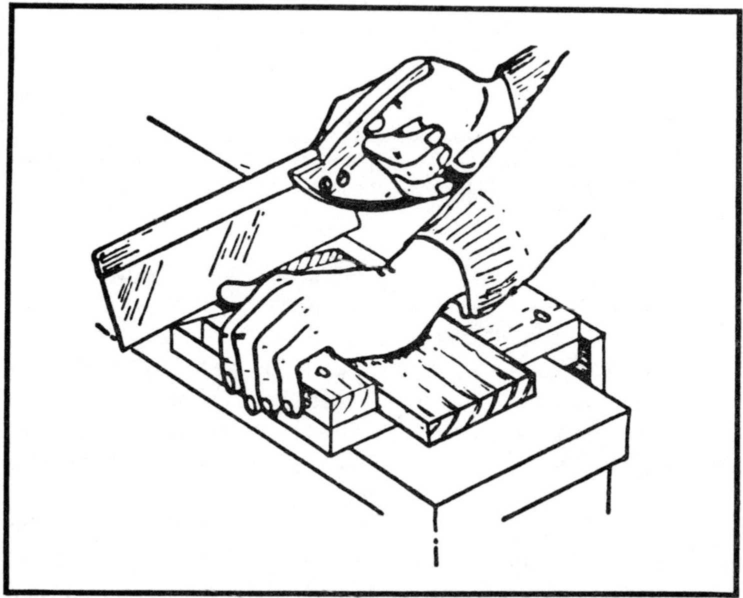

Fig. 2-28. Starting a cut with a tenon saw—the thumb on the left hand holds the blade in position while the saw is drawn toward the operator three times to make a trough at the corner of the wood as an anchor for the blade.

Fig. 2-29. Using the crosscut saw—the thumb of the left hand directs the blade, which is pictured in the act of making a starting trough by being drawn backward from the edge of the board three times.

holding the sawed-off section from falling, lest it split along the grain. The final end cut should be made more slowly, with a lowered blade, to insure a squared-off corner.

If you purchase only one saw, this is the one to buy. It performs excellently *across* the wood grain and on green lumber and performs commendably *with* the grain, if you go more slowly. The rip saw described next is much faster with the grain, but is ineffectual for crossgrain use.

Ripsaw. Saws about 26 inches long with 5½ or 6 points to the inch are best for ordinary ripping. The teeth should have chisel edges and be cut straight across. Secure the lumber vertically in a vise. Procedure for using the saw is the same as for cross-cutting, except that the blade should be held at a 60-degree angle to the stock. Figure 2-30 shows the differences between the crosscut and the ripsaw.

Coping Saw. This frame saw (Fig. 2-31) is designed to cut intricate patterns in thin stock. The narrow blade and the turning of the 6½-inch blade in the frame allows you to cut short turns. For making enclosed cuts within a piece of wood, a hole must be bored on the waste side of the cutting line and the blade threaded through the hole. The blade is then fitted to the handle, with the teeth pointing toward the handle, and is tightened by fitting the pins attached to the handle and the frame over the taper pins on the blade. Then the handle is tightened to its full extent to put tension on the blade.

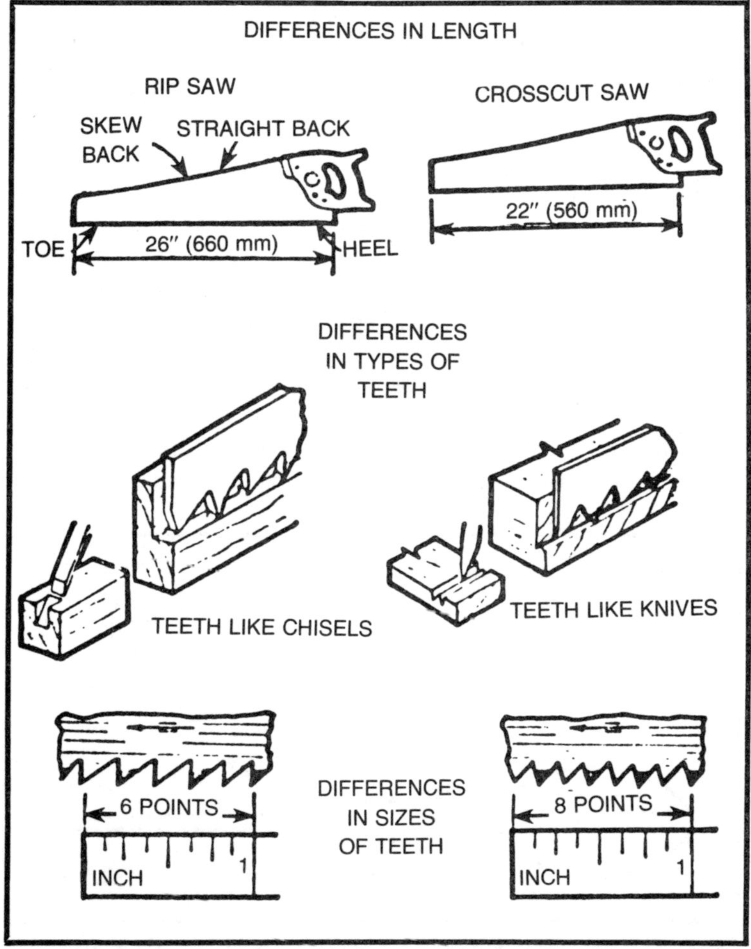

Fig. 2-30. Differences between the rip saw, which is designed to cut with the grain, and the crosscut saw, which is designed to cut against the grain.

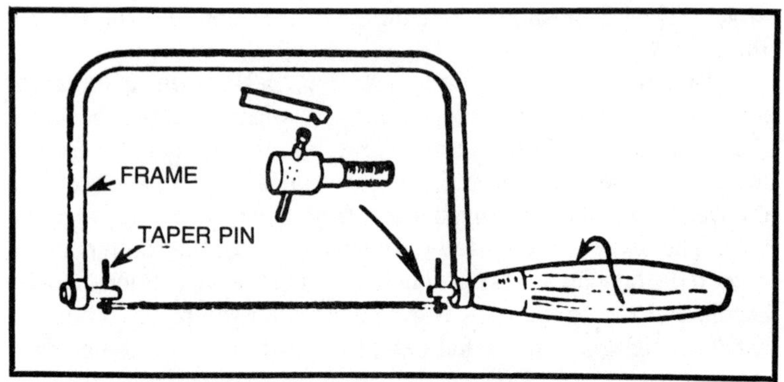

Fig. 2-31. The coping saw, with detail showing taper pin at each end of the blade. This saw is adjusted by partly unscrewing the handle and bringing the taper pins closer together to increase the spring in the steel bow frame, then fitting the frame pins over the taper pins and tighening the handle. The taut blade turns in the bow frame to cut curves.

The saw is held with both hands and is operated with an up and down motion, the cutting being done on the down stroke. The blade turns in the frame while the saw is in motion to follow the outlines of the pattern being cut.

Compass and Keyhole Saws. These saws (Fig. 2-32) are particularly useful for cutting curved holes in large panels where the coping saw cannot cut because of the limitations of the frame. First a hole, or a series of small holes, is drilled on the waste side of the cutting line. The sawing is then started in one of these holes. Keyhole saws have replaceable blades of various widths and lengths. To cut very sharp curves, use the small, tapered end of the blade.

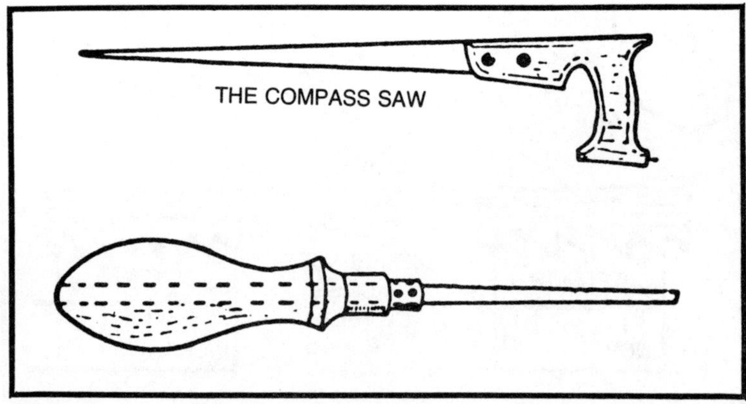

Fig. 2-32. The compass saw and the keyhole saw, with detail showing how the replaceable blade slides into the handle to expose only enough blade to do the job.

Chisels

Chisels are cutting tools used for fitting, shaping and surface decorating. They are classified as either tang or socket chisels, depending on how the handle is fastened to the blade.

The tang chisel (Fig. 2-33) has a sharp-pointed spike shank, or tang, which is inserted into, and reinforces, the wooden handle. A protruding shoulder at the base of the tang keeps the tang from further penetrating the handle when the handle is pounded with a mallet. A brass ferrule around the base of the handle above the shoulder (and sometimes around the top of the handle as well) prevents the handle from splitting. This type of chisel is used for paring.

The socket chisel (Fig. 2-34) has a tapered socket into which the tapered handle end is driven. A leather washer between the shoulder and the handle absorbs some of the shock of the mallet. Some chisels have a leather tip or metal ferrule at the handle top for the same purpose. Socket chisels include thin-bladed slicing/paring chisels, firmer chisels with thicker blades used to shape wood in a

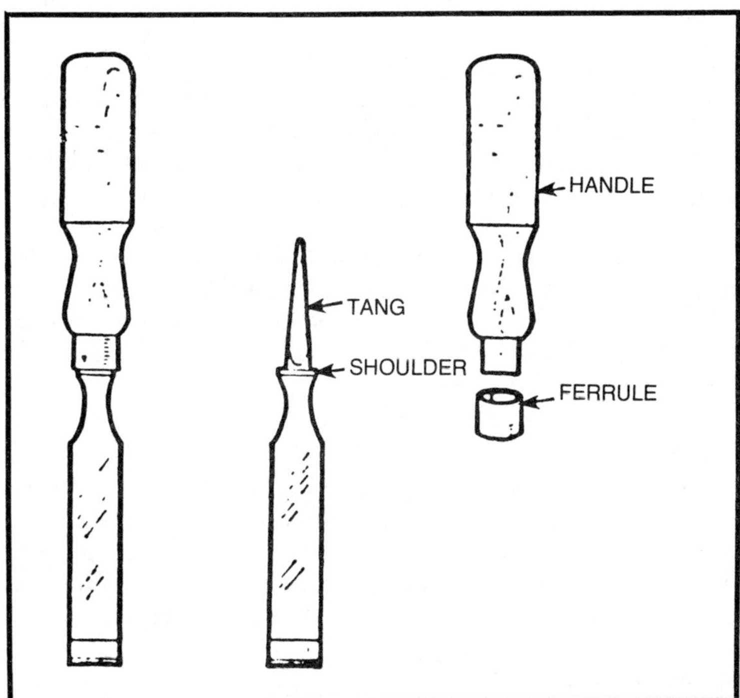

Fig. 2-33. Parts of the firmer chisel, showing the tang which inserts into the handle like a spike.

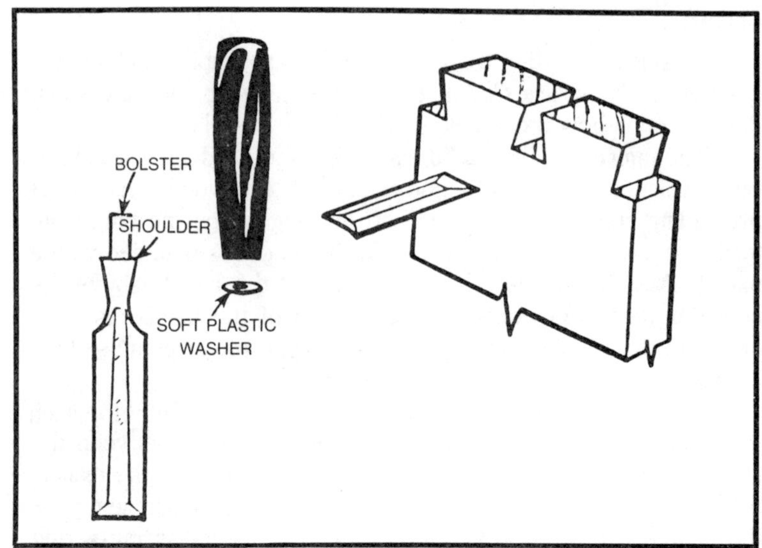

Fig. 2-34. A beveled-edge socket chisel, showing the bolster-type construction typical of all socket chisels. This chisel can slice and pare. Detail shows how the beveled-edge chisel can be used on undercut corners, such as this dovetail joint, where other chisels would not fit.

vise, and mortise chisels with a blade which is very thick toward the handle and tapered toward the bevel edge. This chisel acts as a lever for lifting and removing sections from a mortise.

Chisels are usually ⅛-inch to 2 inches in width and 3 to 6 inches in length. The cutting bevel, which is the bevel at the very bottom, must be kept sharp.

In using any chisel, secure the work with a vise or cramps and hold the chisel in both hands. Keep the sharp tip up and work with the grain or across it toward a center peak or crown, first from one side of the work, and then from the other. Finally, level off the crown to produce a flat surface.

Gouges

A gouge is similar to a chisel, except that its cutting edge is concave or convex. The scribing, or "in-cannel," gouge has the bevel on the inside and is used for vertical paring of internal curves. The firmer, or "out-cannel" gouge, has the sharpening bevel on the inside and is used for hollowing out bowl-like depressions.

Bits and Drills

The construction and repair of furniture frequently requires the boring and drilling of holes. Dowels, pegs, bolts, nails, woodscrews and some forms of ornamentation are usually anchored in bored or drilled holes.

The specific penetrating tool which makes these holes is called a "bit."Certain bits are designed to make larger holes; these fit into a brace which bores holes. Other bits are designed to make smaller holes; these are for use in a drill.

Probably the bits most useful to the woodworker are the following: the auger bit, the center bit, the Forstner bit and the expansive bit (Fig. 2-36).

Auger Bit. This spiral-flanged bit comes in various sizes from ¼-inch to 1 inch in variances of 1/16-inch. (Ships' augers come in variances of ¼-inch to 2 inches) The diameter is stamped on the tang; thus,the stamped number "6" would indicate that the bit was 6/16-inch or ⅜-inch. In length, auger bits measure 7 to 10 inches except for dowel bits which are 5½ inches.

The auger bit has six parts—each performing a specific function. The *feed screw* pulls the bit into the hole, the *spur* scores the hole, the *cutting lips* ream out a circular path through the grain of the wood, the *twist* along the shank raises and lifts out the chips, the *shank* adds length to the bit, and the *tang* fits like a tongue into the jaws of the brace.

Centre Bit. This bit is successful in drilling clean holes into thin wood. Here the *brad point* is placed on the center mark of the spot

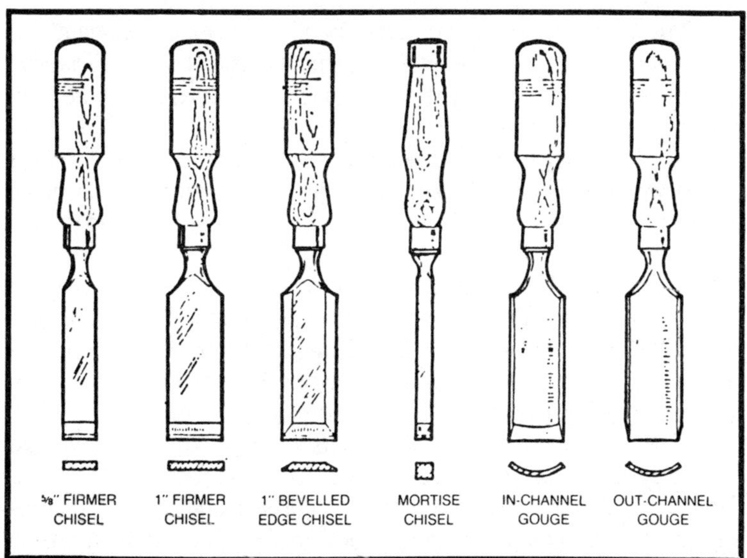

Fig. 2-35. Comparison of chisels and gouges, showing details of their respective cutting (bottom) edges.

where the hole is desired and the turn of the brace causes it to penetrate. Then the *scriber* cuts a circular path through the wood, while the *cutter* lifts the waste.

Forstner Bit. This bit is designed to bore a flat-bottomed hole, particularly into thin wood where a stop hole is required. (A "depth" or "stop" gauge is a supplementary tool which adjusts with a turn bolt to the shank of a bore bit at the depth desired. It stops the boring at that point so that whatever piece is inserted—peg, dowel, etc.—will not disappear into the bored hole. However, a block of wood cut to proper length can also serve as a stop gauge if no such tool is handy.) The Forstner bit is more specialized in its performance, but extremely helpful when needed.

Expansive Bit. This adjustable bit bores holes from ⅞-inch to 3 inches in diameter, thus producing many sizes of holes outside the common range for most bits.

Contersink Bit. To fit screws into hard wood so that the heads will be flush with the work surface is the specialized function of the countersink bit (Fig. 2-37). The hole it produces has a conical opening to accommodate the screw head. Countersink bits are made with square tangs to fit the brace and with round tangs to fit the drill. The bore bits come in two shapes: the rose head countersink and the snail countersink. The rose head has the advantage of being able to bore brass as well as wood, while the snail countersink, although only usable on wood, provides a slightly better finish.

Turnscrew Bit. As its name implies, this bit can adapt the brace for use as a screwdriver. Its only fault is one of over-efficiency. It sinks screws into wood with such rapidity that one has to take care not to snap the screw.

Bit Brace. The bit brace (Fig. 2-38) is used to hold and turn any bit with a square tang. The tang of the bit is inserted into the jaws of the chuck and the knurled outside shell is tightened by hand to hold the bit firmly.

Bits used to bore large, deep holes need considerable leverage to turn them. For this reason braces are designed with different scopes of sweep—the sweep being the diameter of the circle described by the bow. The size of the brace is determined by the number of inches sweep of which it is capable—8, 10 or 12 inches.

The ratchet brace, because of the ratchet fitted above the chuck, permits the chuck to rotate in a series of partial half-circles. Therefore, this brace can bore holes in corners and restricted areas where other braces, because they have no ratchet and must sweep full circle, would be useless.

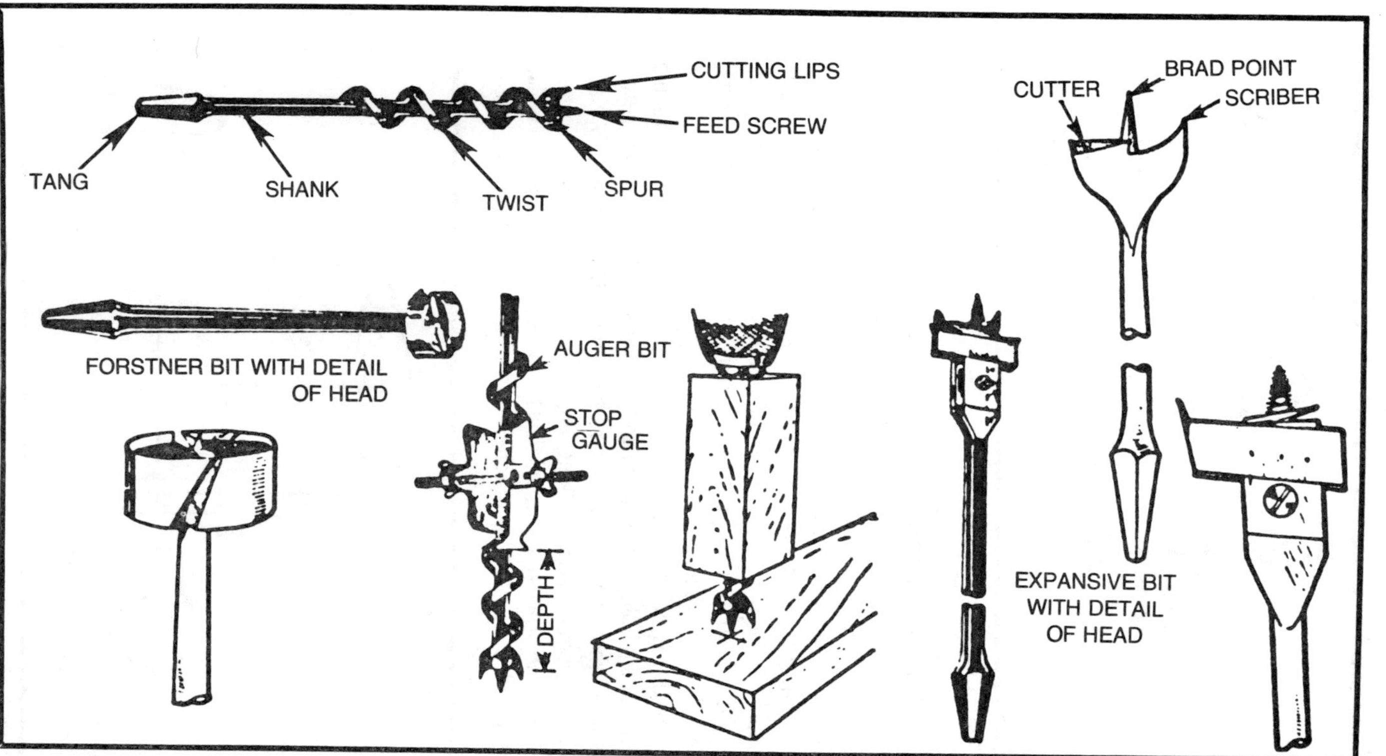

Fig. 2-36. Different types of bits.

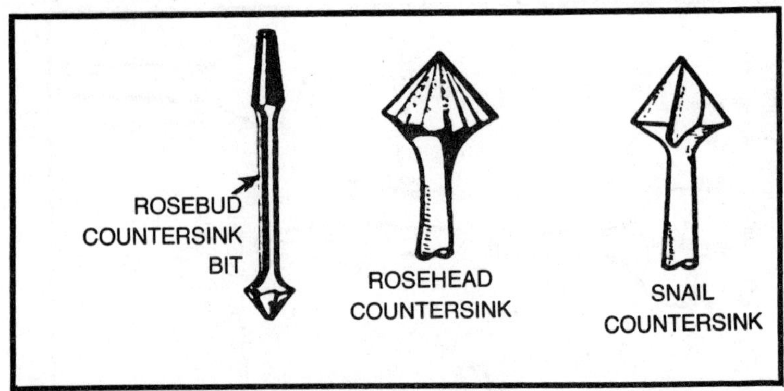

Fig. 2-37. Countersunk bits showing two head styles.

The operator uses both hands to operate a bit brace. One hand grasps the handle and revolves the bow clockwise in its sweep. The other hand exerts pressure on the head which is fitted with ball bearings to hold steady while the brace is turned. When the hole is bored almost through a board, it is wise to remove the bore from the original hole and bore a corresponding, connecting hole on the other side of the lumber. This procedure prevents the bore from splitting the stock as it emerges.

Drills. Hand drills are designed to make smaller holes than a bore makes—holes less than ¼-inch in diameter for sinking screws, bolts and other types of hardware fasteners. Drills (Fig. 2-39) are lighter and speedier at making holes than are the heavier, more cumbersome braces. The hand drill has a three-jaw chuck into which only rounded-shanked or notched bits will fit. Therefore its use is

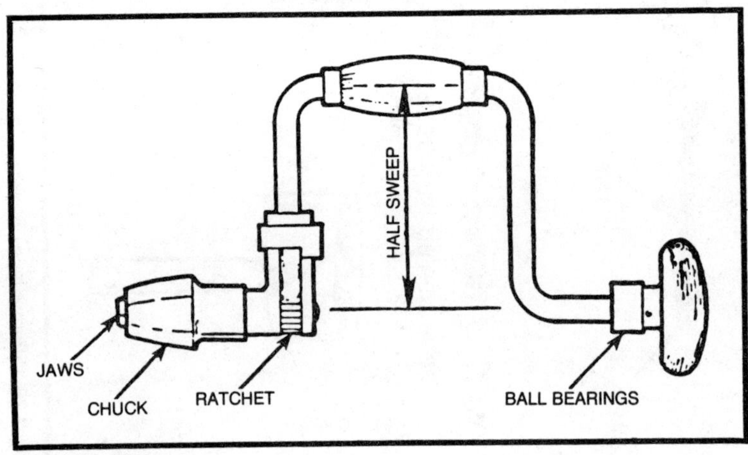

Fig. 2-38. Bit brace.

limited to the twist bit and the round-shanked countersink bit. It will grip drill bits up to ¼-inch in size.

Since the point of a drill bit is rather blunt, the careful workman will locate the center of the hole required with a center punch (Fig. 2-40). Making this starter hole prevents the blunt drill point from wandering from its correct position when the drilling begins.

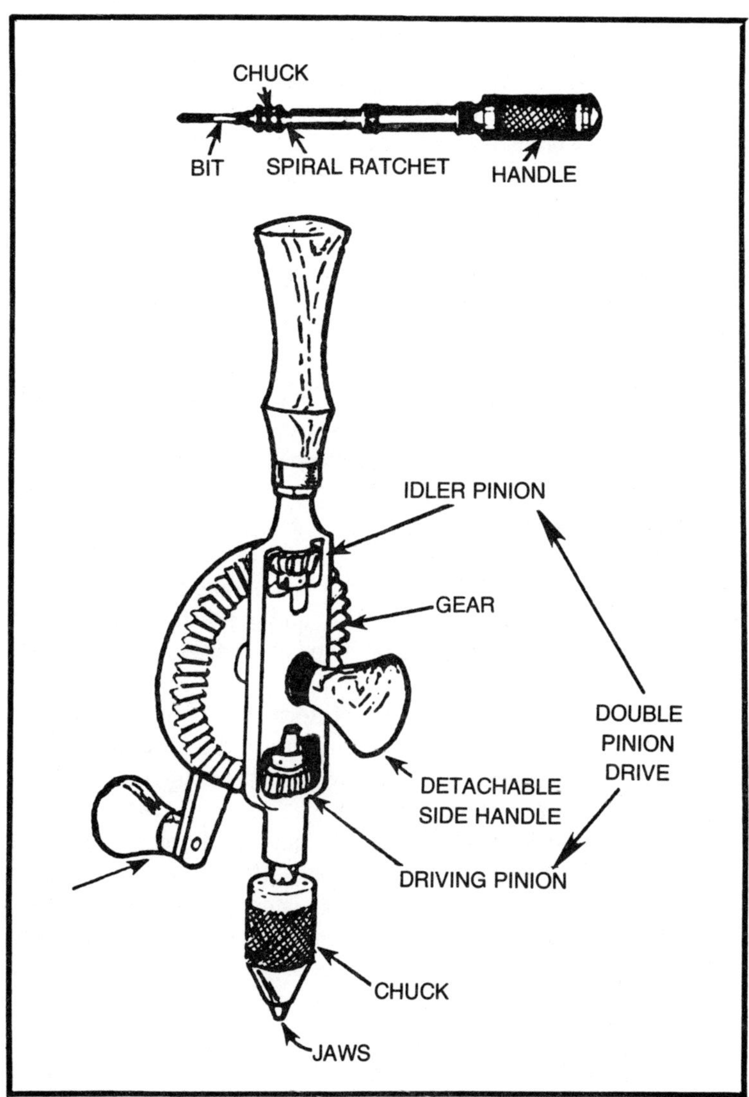

Fig. 2-39. Two popular types of drills: the spiral ratchet drill and the double pinion drill.

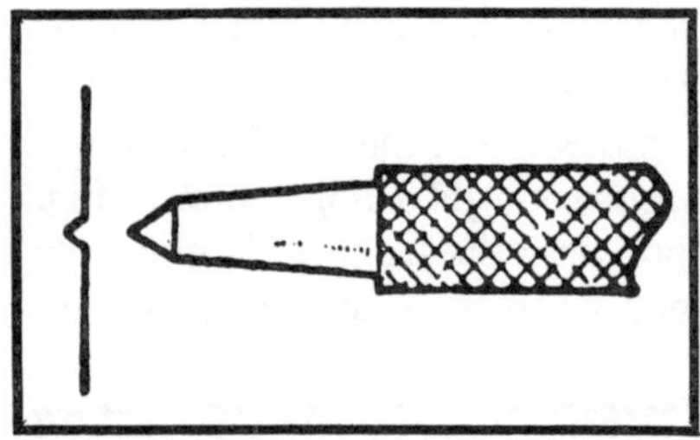

Fig. 2-40. Using the center punch to mark the location of the drill hole will provide the blunt drill bit with an anchor hole and prevent it from skating over the work.

Drills are available in two styles—the double pinion and the single pinion. Both are useful in woodworking, but the double pinion type driven by a crank and handle has a drive which is stronger and more controlled than the drive of a less expenisve single pinion drill.

In operating drills, care should be taken to exert only slight pressure on the handle and to hold the drill upright and steady to prevent it from tilting or wobbling. These precautions insure that the hole drilled will not be oversized and that the slender drill bit will not be broken.

To operate a double pinion drill, the crank is turned in a clockwise direction at a consistent, fairly slow speed. Withdrawing the drill from the hole should be done carefully to prevent snapping the drill bit. In the case of the double pinion drill, continue turning the crank clockwise as the drill is withdrawn to prevent leaving waste chips in the hole.

Drill Bits. As we mentioned before, the drill is limited in the types of bits it will accept. The countersink bit and the twist bit are the only two bits which are made with round or notched shanks to fit hand drills. Both styles may be obtained in a variety of sizes from ½-to ¼-inch.

We have already described the performance of the countersink bit as used in a brace and, since it is essentially the same when used in a drill, we will not repeat it here. However, the twist bit (Fig. 2-41) and its function merit some comment.

The Twist Drill bit is used for making small holes into which screws are to be fitted. As its name implies, this bit is fluted along its shank to ream out the hole it makes. When drilling deeply, the twist drill is liable to clog with waste, so it should be withdrawn frequently and the flutes cleaned for best operation.

Smoothing Tools

Smoothing tools are the implements that permit us to make a work of art of what otherwise would be a primitive piece of handicraft. These are the tools in which the worker takes most pride.

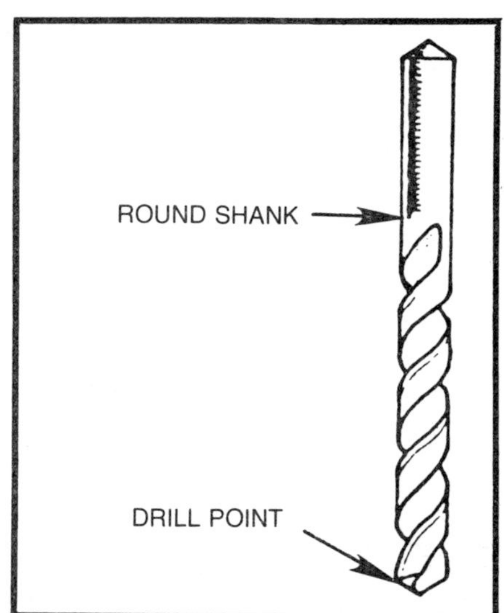

Fig. 2-41. Twist drill bit.

They must be used with skill and care as they are capable of damage as well as beauty. These tools include blade scrapers, rasps and files.

The plane is also a type of smoothing tool but because there are many types of planes, it will be covered separately.

Blade Scrapers. These flexible pieces of high-grade tool steel, about 1/16-inch in thickness, are very efficient at smoothing irregularly grained, knotty or burled timber or at removing blemishes left by the plane. A scraper (Fig. 2-42) cuts differently from a plane because its turned edge breaks shavings more often and more closely, thus producing a smoother surface than planning produces. Scrapers are available in a variety of shapes and sizes, the 3 × 5-inch rectangular and the swan-neck being the most frequently used. The former does a good job of smoothing straight pieces and

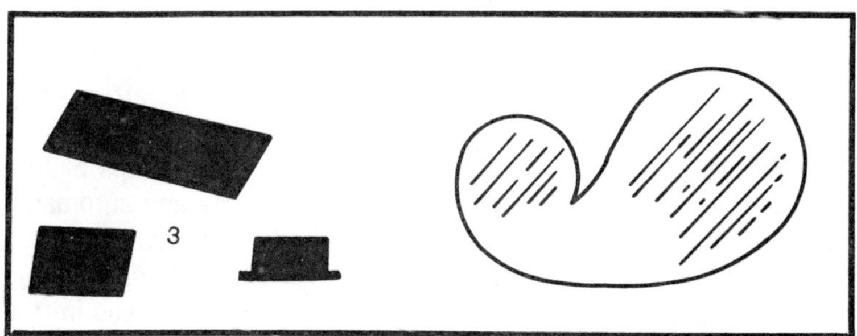

Fig. 2-42. Blade scrapers, showing a variety of rectangular scrapers and the very useful "swan neck."

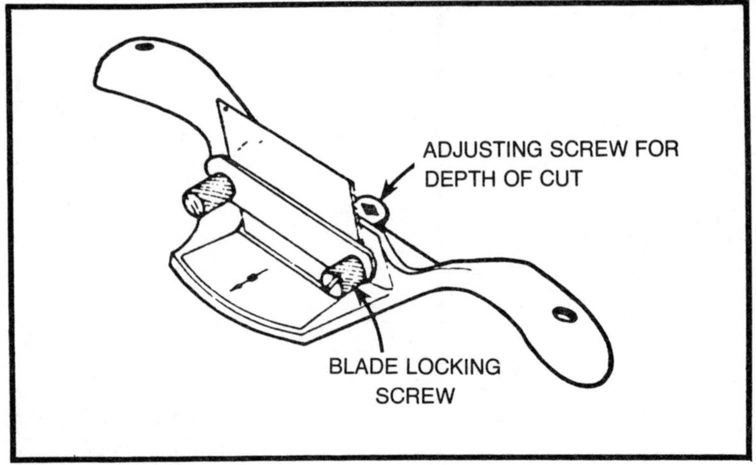

Fig. 2-43. Cabinet scraper—operates by being sprung in the hands. It is pushed away from the woodworker to smooth the work surface.

corners; the latter is best for curved and irregular shapes. All scrapers are only effective when sharp, so they must be honed frequently to be able to smooth away plane knicks and bumps and to cut through grain irregularities. To operate, hold the scraper at a 75-degree angle and pull or push it over the rough surface, producing a very thin shaving.

Cabinet Scraper. This hand-operated scraper (Fig. 2-43) is a more sophisticated version of the blade scraper. Its blade is beveled to a 45-degree angle, burnished to keen sharpness and mounted in a metal frame. The blade can be adjusted to the depth of cut desired by three thumb screws—one to adjust and two to clamp the blade. The blade is supported in the frame at a 75-degree angle.

The cabinet scraper must be operated with the utmost finesse. The operator should bear in mind that a series of extremely fine cuts is preferable to one which is too deep. Some cabinet makers do not recommend using it at all in refinishing precious antiques; instead, they employ sandpaper, steel wool and lots of elbow grease. Certainly the novice should practice with this tool before attempting anything important. One must consider that the cutting edge, unlike that of a plane or spokeshave, is operated by the thumbs of the operator. The blade is sprung by the hand, not by any automatic means. Therefore, it should always be held in both hands, at a slight angle, with the cutting edge raised a little to produce a thin, shearing cut. The cabinet scraper is manipulated by pushing it ahead in the same direction as the grain of the wood. The blade must be fairly flexible because the *center* of the convex edge is the portion of the blade which removes the thin ribbon of surface. A better smoothing job can usually be done with a plane, where the blade is sprung by a screw setting and where the sole prevents the tool from digging into the surface. But many timbers are difficult to plane and, here, a cabinet scraper comes in very handy.

Spokeshave. This handy tool derives its name from its usage in smoothing the spokes of wooden cartwheels (see Fig. 2-44). Originally, its blade was forged by the village blacksmith and its frame was wooden. Today, an all-metal version is available, as well, which comes with a choice of two blades—the flat-bottom blade for use on convex shapes, gentle hollows and horizontal cuts, and the round-bottom blade for smoothing concave shapes, such as the rounded knees of furniture legs, turned railings, and tapered hammer handles. Either blade adjusts as to depth of cut.

To operate the spokeshave, first secure the wood in a vise. Then choose the blade the work requires and adjust it in the frame to the correct cutting depth. Holding the spokeshave loosely and at a slight angle, follow the contours of the work according to the gauge lines, pulling the spokeshave toward you. Use a very fine setting for the final cuts. Care must be taken to work with the grain.

Rasps. A shoemaker's rasp is seldom found in a woodworking shop, yet it is the perfect tool for shaping and smoothing edges. This rasp is 8 inches long, one side is semi-round and the other is flat. Half the surface of each side is coarse cut, the other half is smooth cut.

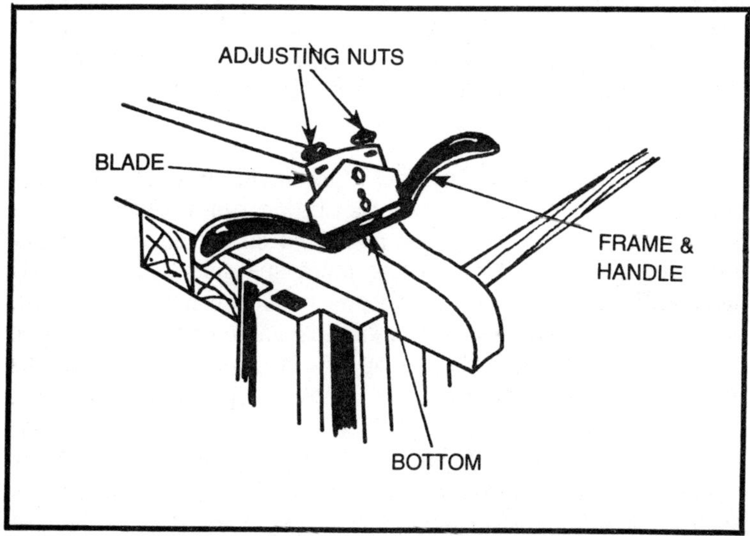

Fig. 2-44. The spokeshave smooths curved surfaces. To operate, it may be pushed or pulled over the work.

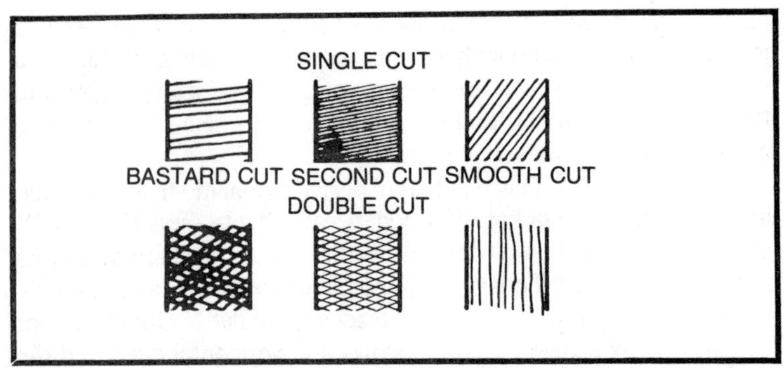

Fig. 2-45. Files come in various degrees of coarseness. The cuts shown are available in all sizes and shapes of files.

This dual cut makes changing tools unnecessary, thus speeding the work.

Files. Files (Fig. 2-45) come in a variety of shapes and degrees of coarseness. The most usual shapes are flat, square, triangular, half-round and round, in lengths ranging from 6 to 14 inches. Coarse files efficiently even off rough areas; fine files are used for finishing and for removing bumps and splinters from very hard woods or within restricted openings.

For safety's sake, all files should have handles. The teeth require an occasional cleaning with a brush and file card.

Use a coarse-cut file (preferably one with crisscross teeth) to sleek the surface in a jiffy. Then smooth away small rough spots with a fine file (one with single-row teeth). Holding the file at an angle to the side of the work prevents splintering—particularly when filing plywood, which shows a marked tendency to splinter.

Planes

Probably, the first plane was a primitive, chisel-like blade attached to a wooden block. Later, the cutting iron was held fast by a wedge. The ancient Egyptians and the Romans added their improvements and the tool became more specialized. In the early nineteenth century, mahogany became popular as a furniture wood. So exceptionally hard was this lumber that an iron cap had to be used over the cutting blade. This iron cap was designed with a curve at the throat end where it reinforced the cutting edge of the plane iron. This curved protuberance broke the chips which the cutting iron raised. Later, the American tool designer, Bailey, replaced the wedge with a lever cam; G.A. Warren added the lateral adjustment features and the separate frog. Then minute adjustments became possible between the plane iron and the plane iron cap to produce a uniform thickness of shaving.

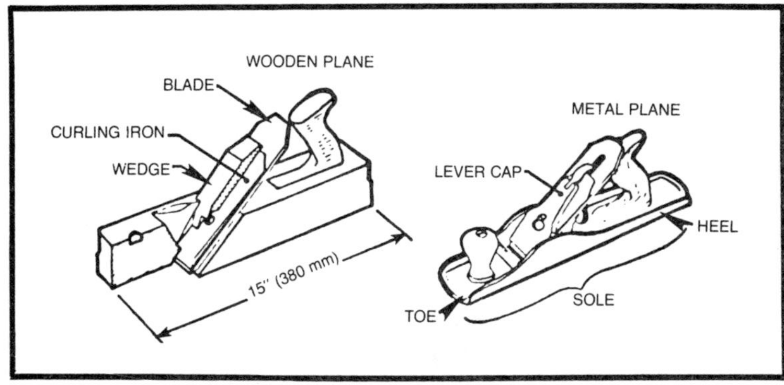

Fig. 2-46. Comparison between wooden and metal jack planes: The two planes operate on the same principle—the blade cuts the shavings from the work and the curling iron curls the shavings, preventing tears on the work surface. In both wooden and metal planes, the plane iron and the curling iron are fastened together by a large screw. The pair of irons is held to the body of the plane by a wooden wedge, in the case of the wooden plane, and by a lever cap, in the case of the metal plane.

Iron and wooden planes(Fig. 2-46) are basically alike. Each has its advantages. Wooden planes are lighter and less tiring to use over long periods. They glide more effortesssly over the surface of the work than do metal planes. Also, they are less likely than metal planes to break if dropped. On the other hand, the metal planes are

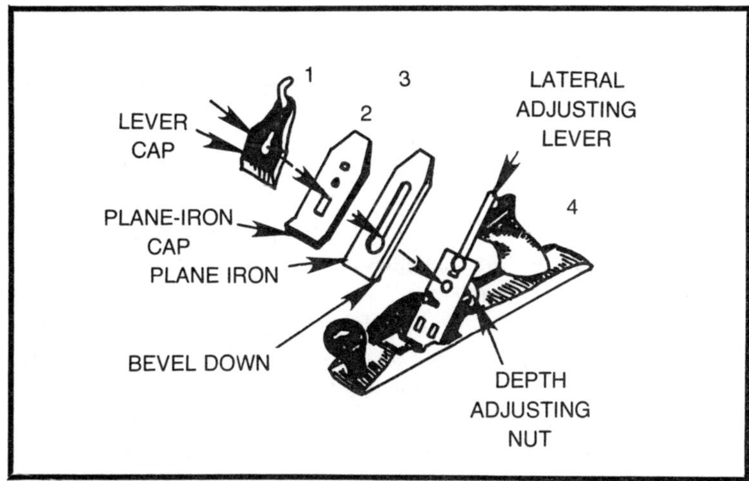

Fig. 2-47. Parts of a plane—in order to operate and repair the plane, the craftsman must learn the names of the parts, their functions and correct adjustments. Here the parts are shown in the order in which they would be disassembled for adjustment or repair. The lever cap (no. 1) is the top piece, with the plane bed (no. 4) the base of the tool.

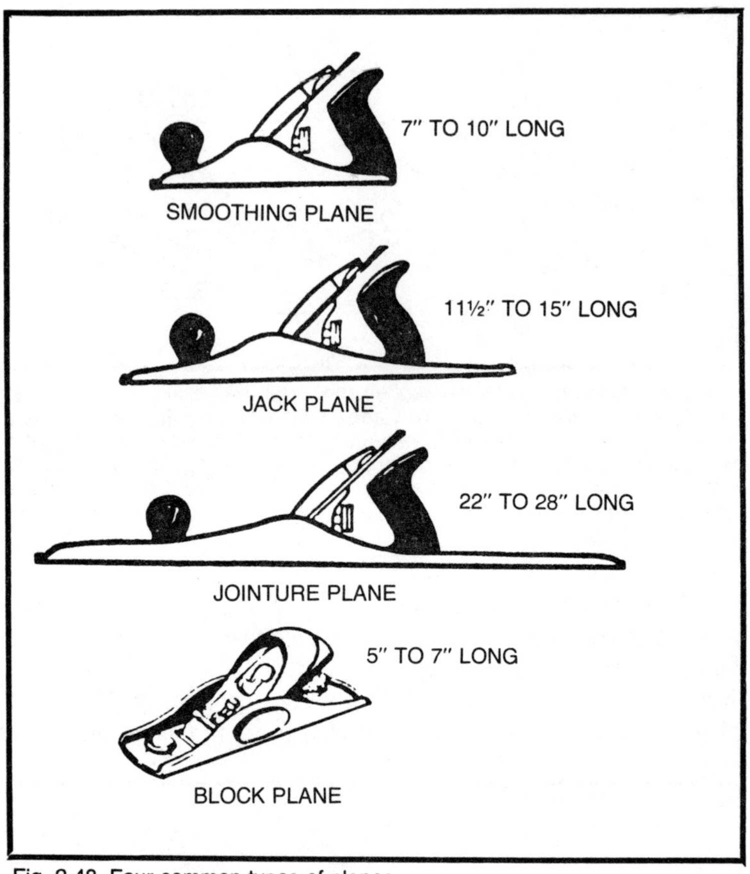

Fig. 2-48. Four common types of planes.

undeniably easier to adjust and this one advantage makes them more popular.

In both wooden and metal planes, the plane iron with its sharpened blade end cuts the shavings from the lumber while the chip breaker, with its "curling iron" curve positioned just behind the cutting blade of the plane iron, curls the shavings, thereby preventing tears (pronounced "tares") on the surface of the lumber. As Fig. 2-47 shows, blade and blade cap are fastened by a large screw and the joined pair of irons is affixed to the body of the plane either by a wooden wedge (as in the case of a wooden plane) or by a lever cap (as in the case of a metal plane).

There are four very practical models of hand planes (Fig. 2-48) differing from one another only in length and in the shape to which the cutting blades on the plane irons are honed.

Jack Plane. This plane earned its name by being a jack-of-all-trades; it is a most versatile and generally useful tool. Its length ranges from 11½ to 15 inches and its slightly convex blade edge very speedily removes rough surfaces.

Smoothing Plane. This plane (Fig. 2-49) is 7 to 10 inches shorter than the jack plane and the cutting blade is sharpened straight across with slightly rounded corners. This is an excellent plane for final smoothing where a light tool with a tissue-thin peeling action is required.

Jointer Plane. This plane is the hand version of the power jointer. Varying in length from 22 to 28 inches it produces long, straight edges and true surfaces.

Block Plane. This is a short plane measuring 5 to 7 inches, with a sliding section which can be moved after loosening the thumb screw and sliding the adjusting lever. This plane can be operated with one hand and is ideal for most small trimming jobs where frequent adjustment is not required.

Special-Purpose Hand Planes. The Bullnose, Rabbet, Router, Dado and Circular Planes—to name a few—are all planes of exact, modified function and are not useful in the general sense, as are the aforementioned planes.

The plane is possibly the most complicated of all hand tools, requiring more skill to manipulate and more care and attention to adjust and maintain than any other woodworking tool. Planes are capable of two-fold adjustment: (1) depth adjustment at the throat opening to regulate the thickness of the shaving, and (2) lateral adjustment to make the desired depth of shaving uniform.

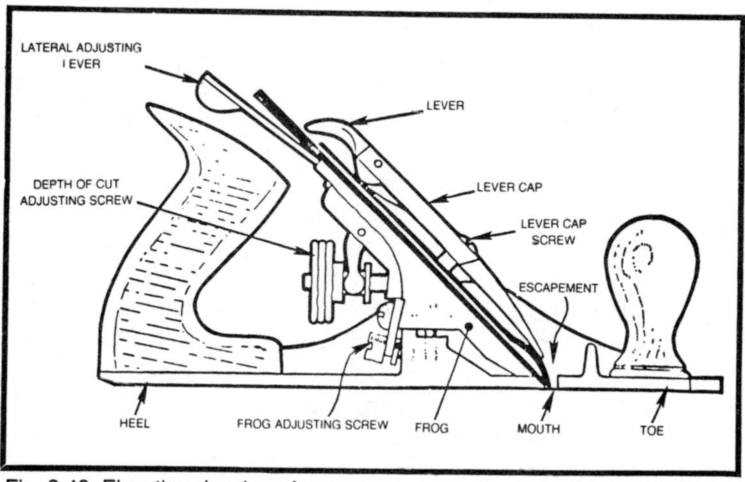

Fig. 2-49. Elevation drawing of smoothing plane with one side removed.

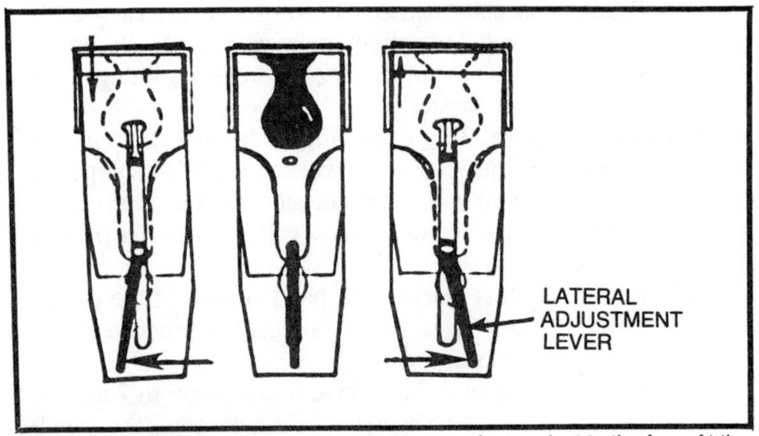

Fig. 2-50. The lateral adjustment lever is fastened on a pivot to the frog. At the pivot point, a riveted washer, which engages in the slot of the plane iron blade, permits the lateral movement of the blade when the lever is shifted.

The depth adjustment is made by means of a knurled knob on the underside of the "frog" (the piece on which the plane blade inclines at a 45-degree angle). The frog fastens to the stock with two locking screws which must be loosened one turn. Next, the frog adjusting screw (positioned on the stock just below the depth adjusting screw) must be revolved. Now the frog may be moved forward or backward to close or open the mouth of the plane. (The mouth must be closed for planing timbers inclined to tear; it must be open to take coarse shavings and for general purpose work.) Now the depth adjusting screw is turned to set the thickness of the cut. Turning it clockwise lowers the blade and makes the cut deeper.

The lateral adjustment lever (Fig. 2-50) pivots from the top of the frog. At its lower end, this lever is riveted to a washer which engages the slot in the plane iron blade. By shifting the lateral adjustment lever to one side or another, the blade is moved sideways to produce a more uniform cut.

However, this desirable uniformity is not possible if the blade does not project evenly out of the mouth with the plane iron cap, whose curved "curling iron" end acts as a chip breaker, correctly positioned about ⅛- to 1/16-inch behind the plane iron's cutting edge. Should this distance need adjustment, the plane iron cap and blade assembly must be removed from the plane. This is accomplished by lifting the lateral adjustment lever, thus loosening the plane iron cap and allowing the cutting assembly (plane iron cap and plane iron) to be lifted out.

The two parts of the cutting assembly (Fig. 2-51) are held together by a large screw which can be loosened with a broad-blade cabinet screwdriver. For safety's sake, the assembly should never be held in the hand while working on the screw. A slip could result in a bad cut.

Once the screw is loosened by one turn, the plane iron cap can be slid back from the cutting edge of the plane iron and swiveled to a 90-degree angle with the blade. From this angle, the plane iron cap can be rotated back again to lie over, and parallel to, the plane iron. Next, the plane iron cap can be slid toward the cutting edge of the plane iron blade until the cap's "curling iron" end is 1/16-inch behind the cutting edge on the plane iron blade. Finally, the large screw which holds the two parts of the cutting assembly together is securely tightened with the screwdriver and the assembly is remounted in the plane. (Fig. 2-52 shows the proper planing technique.)

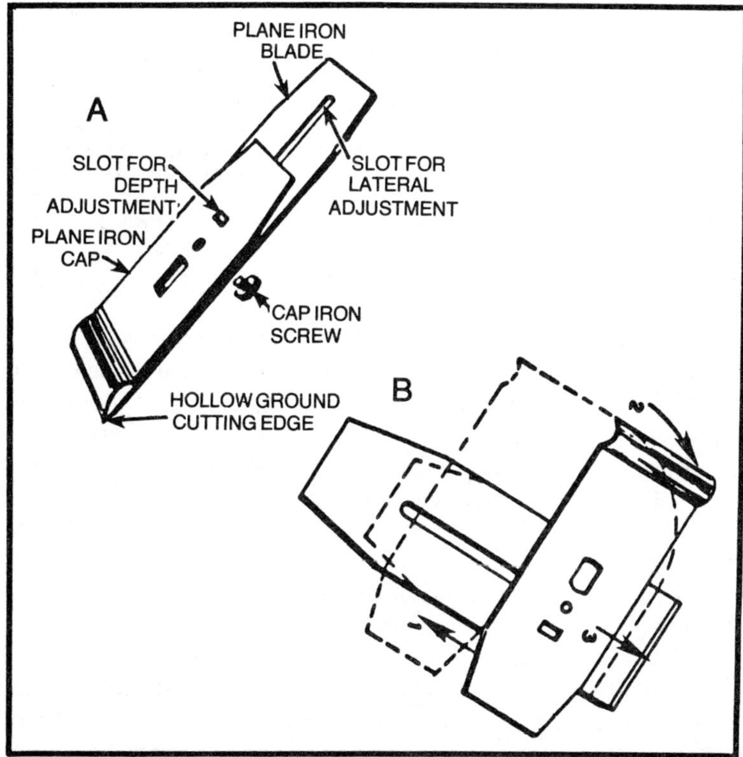

Fig. 2-51. Adjustment of the cutting blade—A) the plane cap and blade assembly must be removed from the plane bed to adjust the distance between the plane iron's cutting edge and that of the plane iron cap. B) Adjustment and reassembly of the cutting assembly—loosen the cap iron screw one turn, swivel the cap iron to a tight angle with the plane iron, slide the cap iron back from the cutting edge and rotate it back to lie on top of the plane iron, adjusting the distances between the two cutting edges as desired. Tighten the cap iron screw.

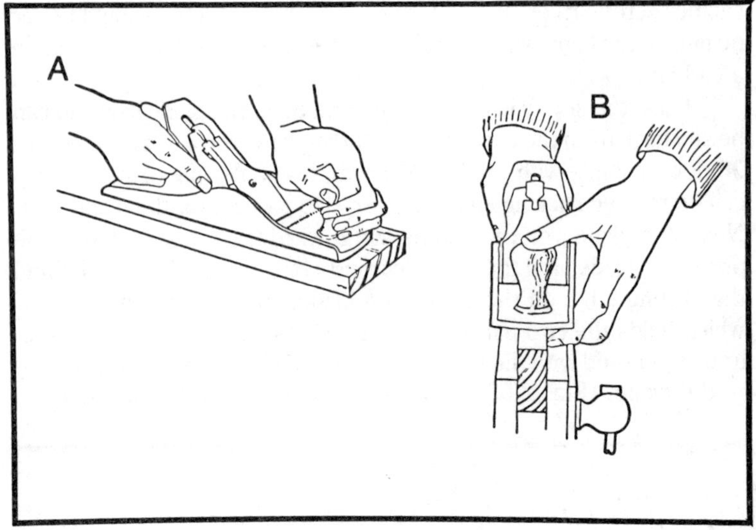

Fig. 2-52. A) How the plane is held to smooth the side of a board—the right hand propels the board forward and the left hand presses the toe of the plane to the wood. B) How the plane is held to smooth the edge of a board—on the narrow edge, the fingers of the left hand guide the work to a position directly under the center of the plane. Each stroke starts by pressing down firmly with the left hand. This pressure is released near the end to prevent splitting the wood.

MISCELLANEOUS TOOLS

The following are some generally useful tools not covered in the previous listings which should be included in every household's basic assortment. They are indispensible in almost every area of home improvement and maintainence, as well as in woodworking.

Bubble Level. This reliable measuring device registers the even flatness of surfaces, indicating immediately whether they are precisely horizontal or precisely vertical. Sometimes called a "spirit level," this tool has a window sight set into its surface which reveals a bubble centered on an indicator line when the work is exactly even and horizontal or truly plumb and vertical. It is an invaluable check on every stage of a project. The 24-inch is most practical.

Miter Box. This saw guide (Fig. 2-53) constrains the blade to an accurate 45-degree angle on either side of the work. When used to guide a fine-point tenon saw, precise miter joints can be produced and moldings can be cut for perfect corner jointing, always relegating the ragged edges of the final severance to the back of the molding. Before using the miter box, a block of waste wood large enough to cover the box bottom should be placed inside to keep the saw blade from cutting into the box itself.

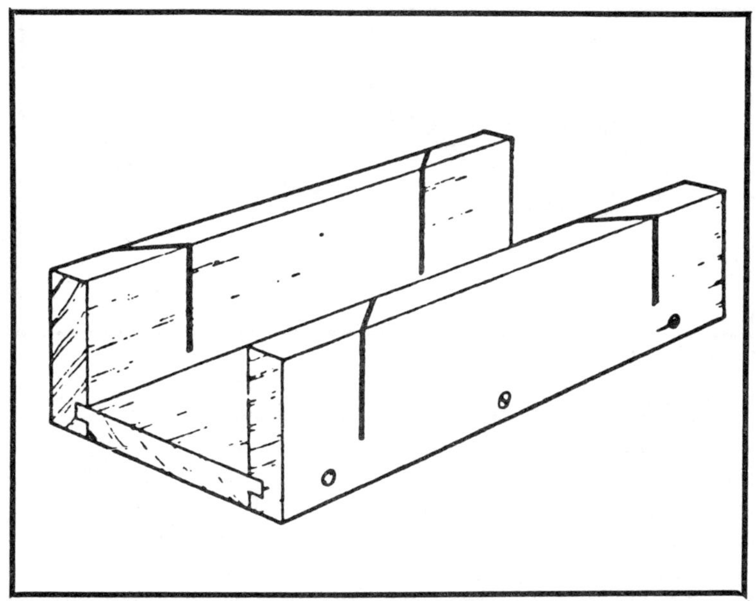

Fig. 2-53. The miter box—a sturdy accurate tool capable of handling large and small moldings.

Pincers. These grippers come in a number of styles—the so-called "tower" pattern shown in Fig. 2-54 being the most popular. The 8-inch size is very useful for withdrawing nails from tight places after first using the claw on one handle to loosen the nail. A block of waste wood must always be placed beneath the pliers to protect the wood.

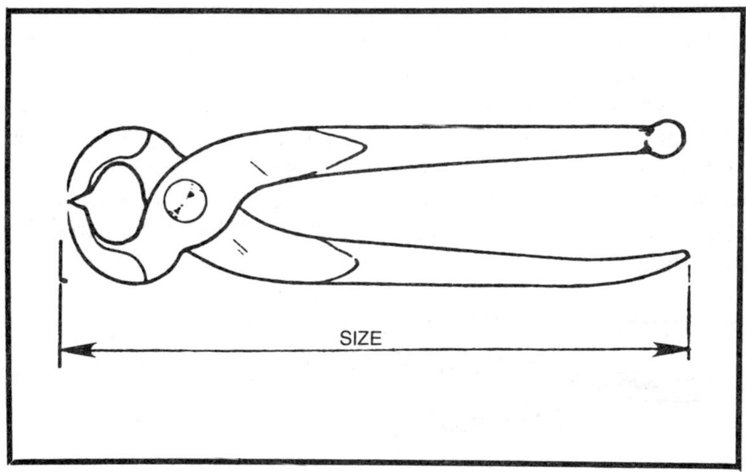

Fig. 2-54. Pincers.

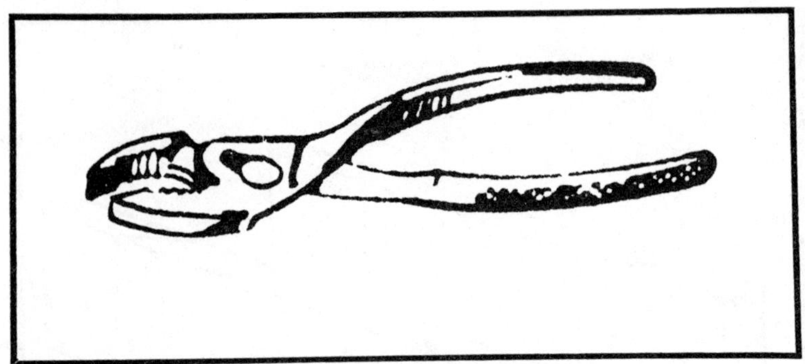

Fig. 2-55. Slip-joint pliers.

Slip-Joint Pliers. This tool (Fig. 2-55) has two smoothly meeting jaws for gripping and a slip pivot joint behind the jaws which shifts the relative positions of the handles, allowing the jaws to open more widely to grab large-diameter objects (although when the jaws are wide open, the grip is not so strong). Some slip-joint pliers have built-in wire cutters which come in handy on many jobs.

Needle-nosed Pliers. The type (Fig. 2-56) with built-in wire cutters are the best. This tool pokes its long beak into tight places, such as into intricate electrical wiring. The pointy nose can bend the ends of wires into loops and place them around terminal screws. These same slender grippers are perfect for holding small brads or nails while hammering, their reliable bite on the nail saving many a mashed finger.

Crescent Wrench. This wrench, shown in Fig. 2-57, is often still called by the brand name under which it was first produced—"Crescent"—as well as being called an "adjustable open end" wrench. It has an adjustable grip and is very adept at manipulating nuts and bolts. The 6 and 8-inch sizes are more useful.

Box Wrenches. These comparatively inexpensive wrenches (Fig. 2-58) may be purchased in sets, some with double ends (an opening at either end). The sets are inexpensive and the wrenches are capable of performing in many places where an adjustable wrench would be too bulky to fit. They can handle nuts from ¼ to ¾-inch.

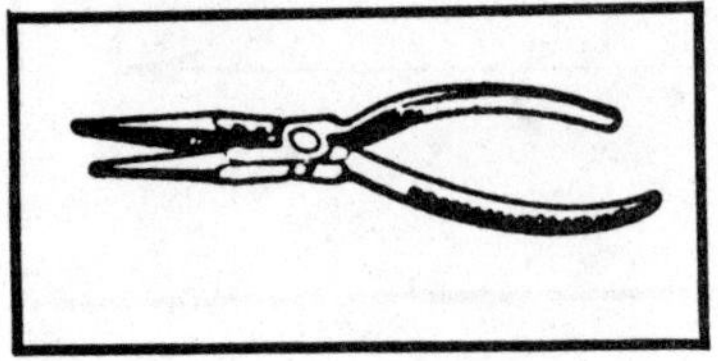

Fig. 2-56. Needle-nose pliers.

Fig. 2-57. Crescent wrench.

Locking Pliers. This highly sophisticated tool (Fig. 2-59) is a cross between a wrench and a pair of pliers, with many of the functions of both. In appearance, it looks like a complicated pair of pliers. However, a compound lever mechanism gives the jaws an infinitely more powerful grip than can be executed by hand—so powerful, in fact, that the jaws can be locked onto an object like a portable vise and can clamp, pinch or twist more effectively than either pliers or wrenches.

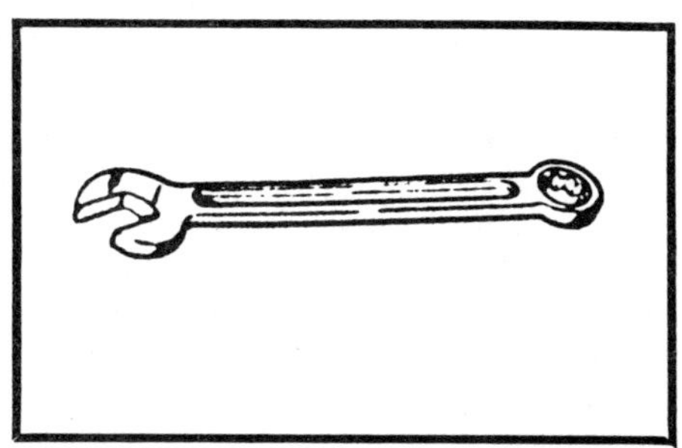

Fig. 2-58. Open end or box wrench.

Razor Blade Holder. For a few cents, at any hardware store, the woodworker can purchase a holder for a single-edged or double-edged razor blade designed so that the blade can be retracted when not in use. This cutting tool has a thousand household uses—from scraping away blistered paint to opening corrugated boxes. It should be included in every tool chest.

Scout Knife. The multi-bladed scout knife is a versatile tool for the home handyman, with the additional merit of being compactly contained. Its many blades in one handle comprise a pocket tool chest, so to speak.

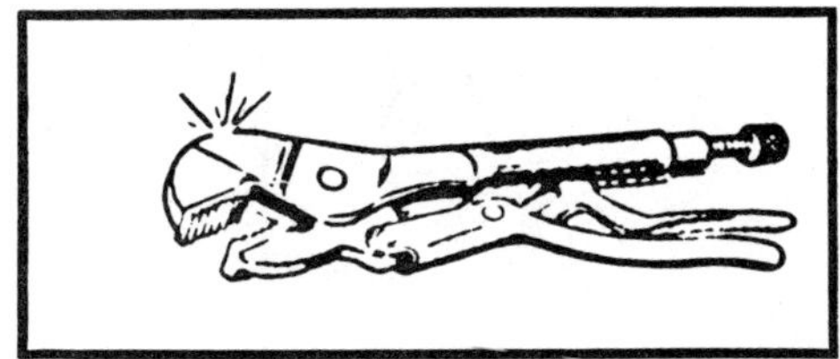

Fig. 2-59. Locking pliers.

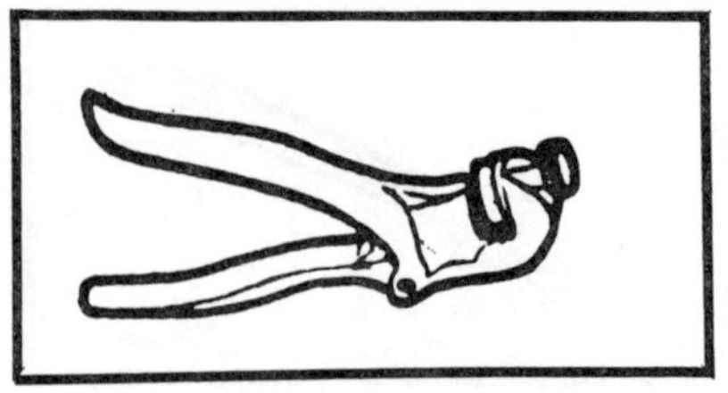

Fig. 2-60. Plier-type saw set.

Scout Axe. A small axe is a very handy tool around the house since it can be put to work chopping firewood, pruning, and making the first rough sizing on lumber in the home workshop.

Tinner's Snips. These metal shears are excellent for cutting metal. The offset jaws enable them to incise curves, leaving a crisp edge. They are efficient tool for trimming wires, fashioning pattern from thin sheet metal, etc.

Glass Cutter. Requires minimum pressure to score and sever glass cleanly and neatly. Useful for cutting the trimming window panes, mirrors, cabinet mullions and picture glass.

Plier-type Saw Set. This self-contained tool (Fig. 2-60) adjusts to sharpening handsaw from 4 to 12 points. When the handles are squeezed, the tool grips the saw and sets tooth at the required angle, bending only the top half of the tooth to prevent its cracking.

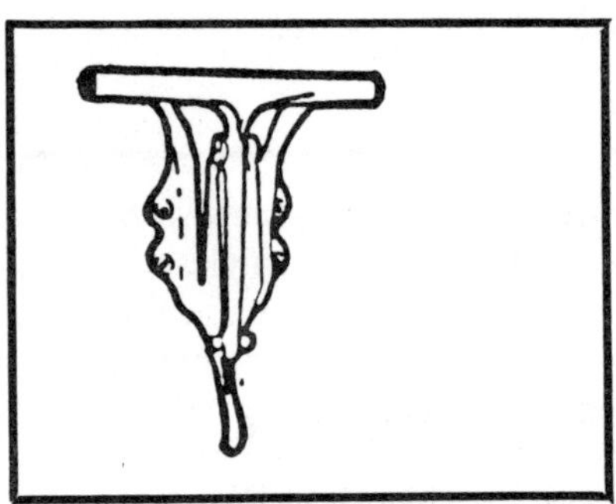

Fig. 2-61. Saw sharpening vise.

Saw-Sharpening Vise. This tool (Fig. 2-61) is invaluable for holding a blunted saw while it is being sharpened, making an exacting job much easier by freeing both hands to the task.

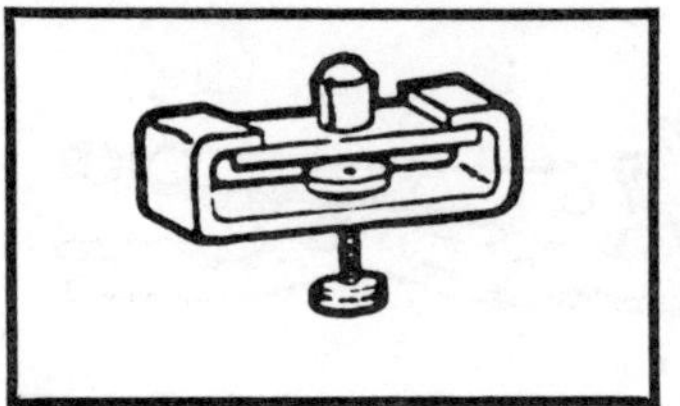

Fig. 2-62. Honing guide for plane irons.

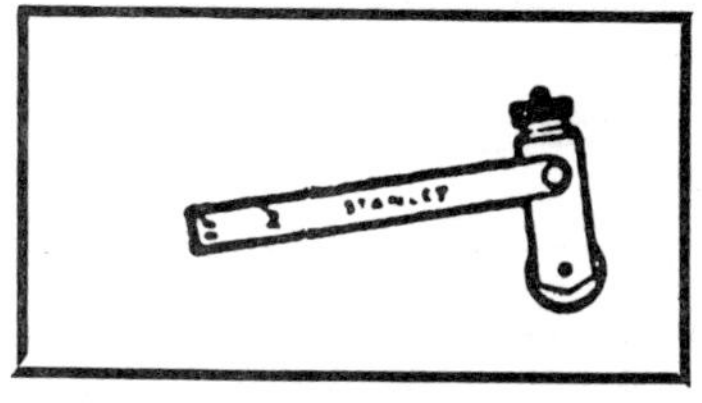

Fig. 2-63. Honing guide for chisels.

Honing Guides. Sharpening a plane iron is a difficult chore, especially for a beginner. However, a honing guide (Fig. 2-62) simplifies the task by locking onto the blade and, thus, helping the workman to maintain the proper sharpening angle. The type shown in Fig. 2-63 helps maintain the correct 30-degree angle for putting a sharp edge on a chisel.

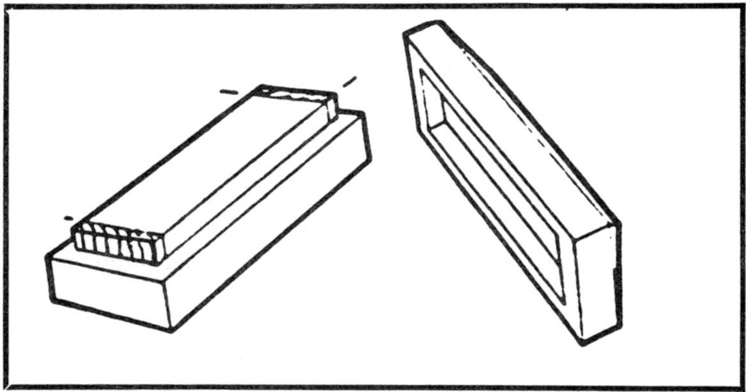

Fig. 2-64. Oilstone with cover.

Oilstone. A rectangular oilstone (Fig. 2-64) with its own storage box, to keep it from getting dusty, is the best abrasive on which to whet fine tools. A small amount of oil should be applied to the stone. Cut-oil, which is made by mixing kerosene with thin machine oil, is satisfactory; light mineral oil is acceptable; lard oil is a very good lubricant. The oil floats away the filings and prevents the glazing of the stone.

Burnisher. This tool (Fig. 2-65) looks like a thick icepick. The hardened steel blade is tapered to a point. The burnisher is used to

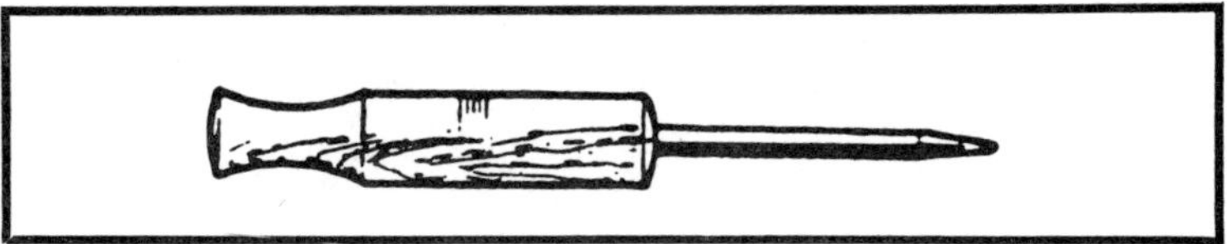

Fig. 2-65. Burnisher.

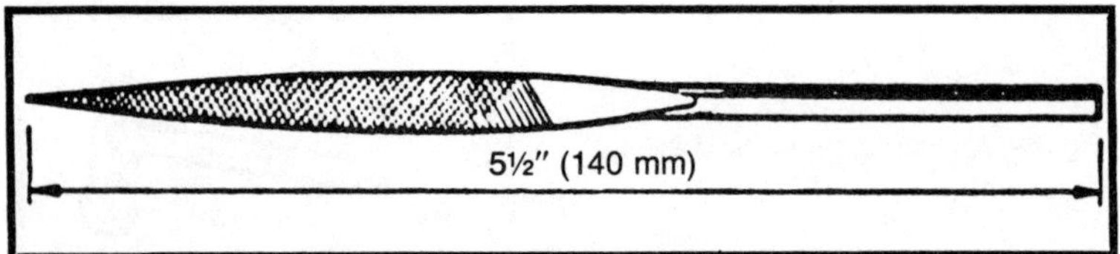

Fig. 2-66. Auger bit file.

sharpen hand scrapers, finally turning the end outward to form a burr. This out-turned edge is necessary to the efficacy of the scraper blade and the burnisher is the best and quickest way to restore such blades when they get blunted.

Auger Bit File. A specially designed file (Fig. 2-66) is used to sharpen the auger bit. To understand its use, one must consider that the auger bit performs its cutting action first with the spurs and then with the cutting lips. The spurs are sharpened by filing them on the inside, while the lips are filed on the upper side. Maintain the same uniform angle in filing both lips so that the bit will cut uniformly.

Mallets. The complete woodworking shop can use a squareheaded wooden mallet with a heavy, board head for driving heavy nails and spikes and a medium-weight mallet with a rubber head which can be used on finished pieces without harming the finish. The latter may be purchased at an automotive supply store; it was originally designed for body repair.

Chapter 3
Tool Maintenance

Tools are the agents by which man implements his creative designs on raw material. The condition of his tools, and the skill with which he wields them, determine the success he experiences in shaping raw materials to his will.

When the project he undertakes requires cutting, it is essential that the tool used for this task be kept keen. The sharpness of the cutting instrument is not only a requisite to its proper performance, it renders the tool safer, as well.

Most of the cutting edges on hand tools are made of tool steel, a material which must be ground or filed and whetted to restore its razor edge.

Because plane irons, chisels, cabinet scrapers and spokeshaves have single-edged blades, the same essential procedure may be followed in sharpening them. Generally speaking, the cutting edge should be knife sharp and the corners slightly rounded—to prevent their gouging the wood.

SHARPENING

Sharpening may require grinding or whetting of the blade edge. Since grinding wears away the blade, it should be reserved for one of the following repairs:

- To reshape a cutting edge which has been worn by excessive whetting (see Fig. 3-1);
- To reshape a cutting edge which is rounded or blunted by incorrect whetting (see Fig. 3-2); or

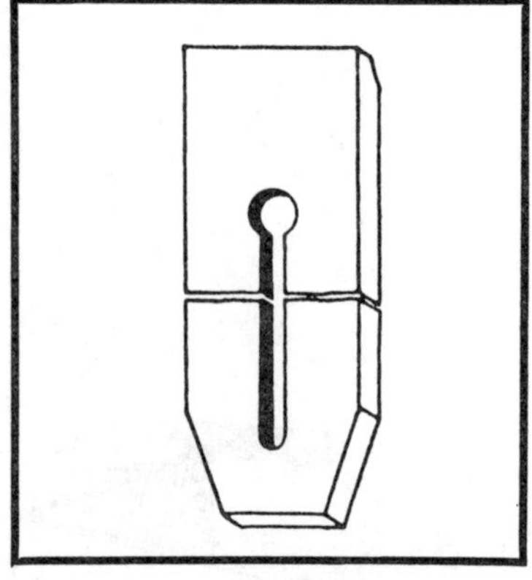

Fig. 3-1. Blade must be reground if cutting edge is blunted from excessive whetting.

- To reshape a cutting edge which has been nicked by contact with metal objects, such as nails, screws, etc. (see Fig. 3-3).

Aluminum carbide or silicon grinding wheels are best for grinding most woodworking tools. A low-speed grind setting is best, because it will not burn tool edges or alter the temper of the tool steel by overheating it. To keep it clean and true, the grinding wheel must be dressed periodically. Great varieties of grit sizes and hardnesses are available in grinding wheels so that dry grinding can be accomplished without undue overheating.

Grinding takes skill and the performance can be dangerous, so all safety precautions should be observed. The blade should be supported on a tool rest—either the one provided on the grinder or one set up by the operator (see Fig. 3-4.)

The aim of grinding is to produce a concave surface on the blade at the proper angle to result in a thin, keen edge. This cutting edge

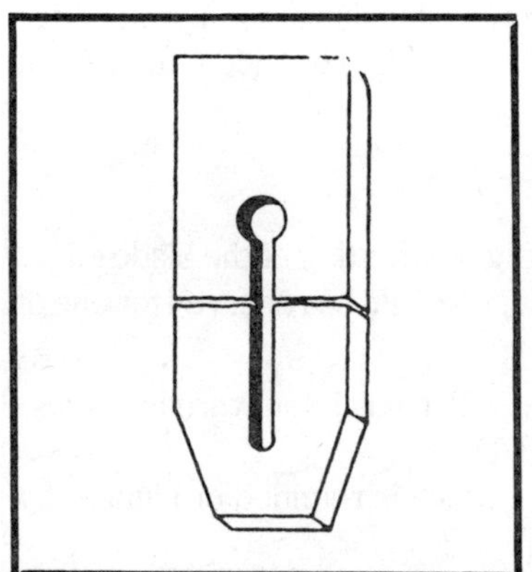

Fig. 3-2. Blade must be reground if cutting edge is out of shape from incorrect whetting.

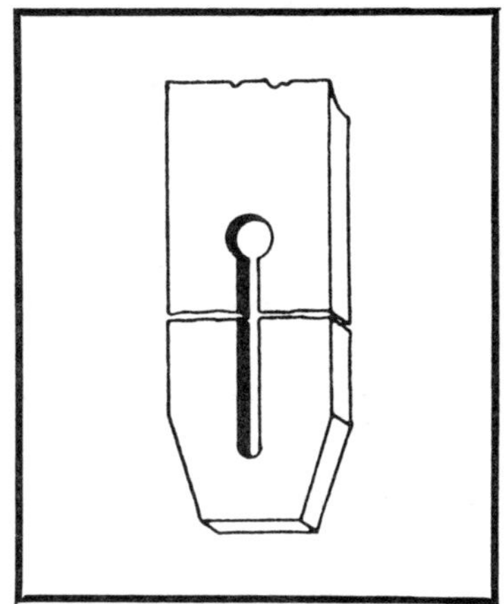

Fig. 3-3. Blade must be reground if cutting edge is nicked.

should be square with the sides and should be produced without generating such heat that the temper of the steel is actually affected. When a wire edge appears on the blade, sufficient grinding has been done. This stage is easily recognizable because sparks flow over the top surface of the blade when a wire edge has been attained. At this point, the blade should be removed from the grinder and checked for squareness with the sides. If the blade is true, it is now ready for honing.

Honing, or whetting, is the means by which the wire edge is removed and a clean razor-edged blade produced. Both natural and artificial abrasive stones in various grits are available. These may be used with either oil or water. Cut-oil—made by mixing kerosene with thin machine oil—is an excellent lubricant for oil stones. The oil floats away the filings and, thus, prevents the glazing of the stone from the abrasion of the filings themselves.

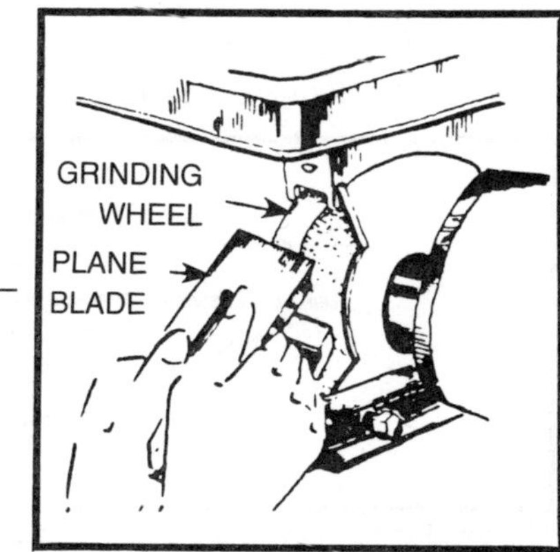

Fig. 3-4. Using the grinding wheel—tool is supported on blade rest.

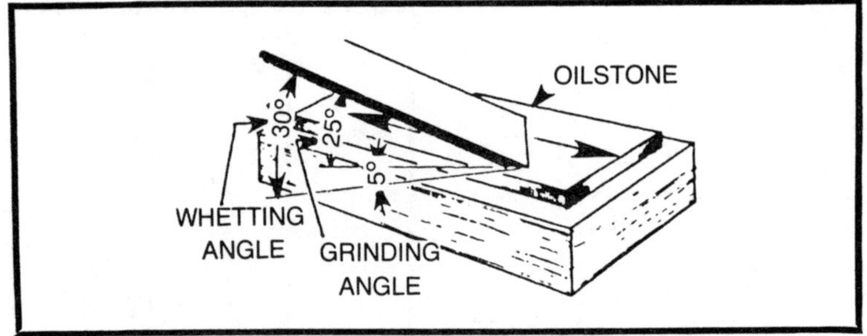

Fig. 3-5. Whetting blade on oilstone. (Note 5-degree elevation of blade heel.)

The Steps in Whetting a Blade

1. Lubricate the stone with a few drops of cut-out.
2. Place the already-ground edge of the blade on the stone and elevate the heel of the blade at a 5-degree angle.
3. Move the blade back and forth, maintaining the 5-degree angle (see Fig. 3-5).
4. Now turn the blade over and place it upside down and flat on the abrasive stone.
5. Move it back and forth until the wire edge is completely abraded away (see Fig. 3-6).
6. Test the edge on a piece of waste end-grain to ascertain its keeness. If it cuts the end-grain easily, it is sufficiently sharp for all other jobs.

Sharpening a Hand Scraper

Because a hand scraper is principally used for scraping hardwood, its edge must be kept extremely sharp. The steps in sharpening it are these:

1. Fasten the blade in the wise.
2. File off the existing burr by holding the file flat on the side of the scraper (see Fig. 3-7).

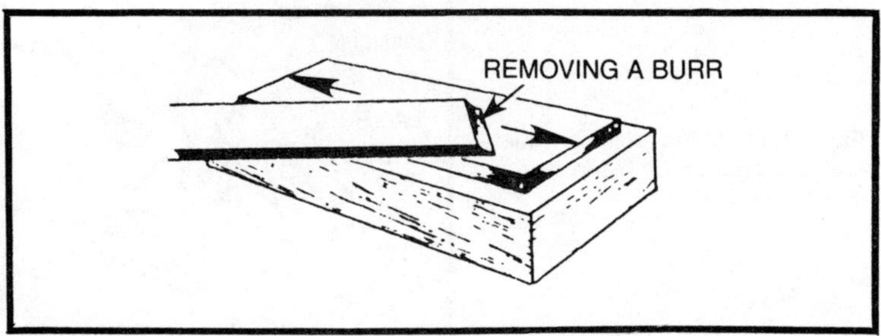

Fig. 3-6. Removing wire edge from blade on oilstone.

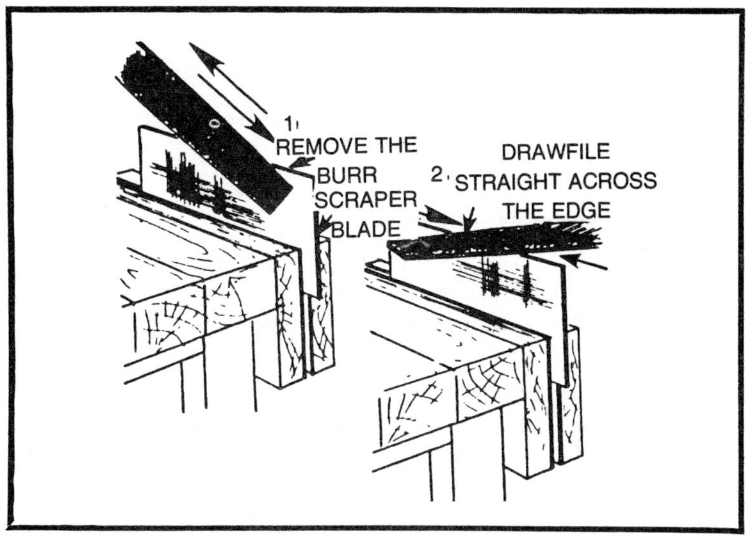

Fig. 3-7. Sharpening hand scraper blade with a file.

3. With a mill file, drawfile the edge until it is flat and square with the sides of the scraper.
4. Whet the blade on the oilstone, always holding the blade at right angles to the stone.
5. Remove the wire edges by placing the blade flat on the stone and working it back and forth.
6. To form a burr, draw a burnisher (which is a smooth, probe-shaped piece of hardened tool steel) over the edge of the scraper blade, holding the burnisher at an angle of 85-degrees to the side of the blade (see Fig. 3-8 and 3-9).

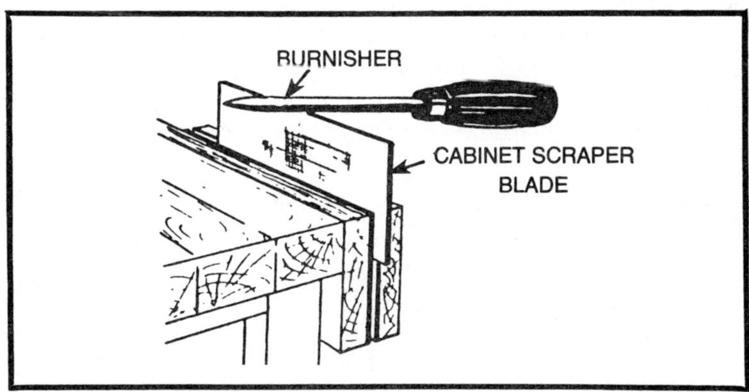

Fig. 3-8. Using burnisher to form a burr on a scraper blade, drawfiling the blade with burnisher at 85-degree angle.

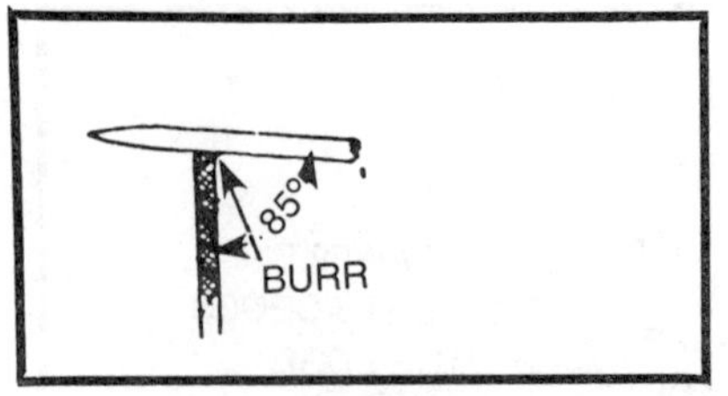

Fig. 3-9. Burr forming as filing continues.

7. Test the burnish by holding the scraper blade at a 75-degree angle to the wood surface and drawing it over the work to see if a uniform shaving is being cut.

Sharpening Auger Bits

The fluted auger drill bit must be kept sharp to do efficient work and a special tool—the auger file—has been developed for this operation. (See Chapter 2 section on miscellaneous tools.) To properly sharpen the auger drill bit, consideration must be given to its method of cutting. Before the auger bit reams out a hole with its spiral flange (or "twist," as it is sometimes called), it first penetrates the wood with the spur, which protrudes from the uppermost flute near the feed screw, and then incises the wood with the cutting lips, located on the flat top on the other side of the feed screw. The spurs are filed on the *inside* to sharpen them. (See Figs. 3-10 and 3-11.)

Fig. 3-10. The auger bit file.

Both lips are filed on the *upper* sides to give them a keen edge. The best way to get at the lips is to invert the auger drill bit, and—holding it upside-down—first file one lip and then the other with the auger drill bit. (See Fig. 3-12.) Care must be taken to maintain the same angle on both lips, in order that the bit will cut uniformly.

Auger bits should be wrapped before storing to protect their cutting edges.

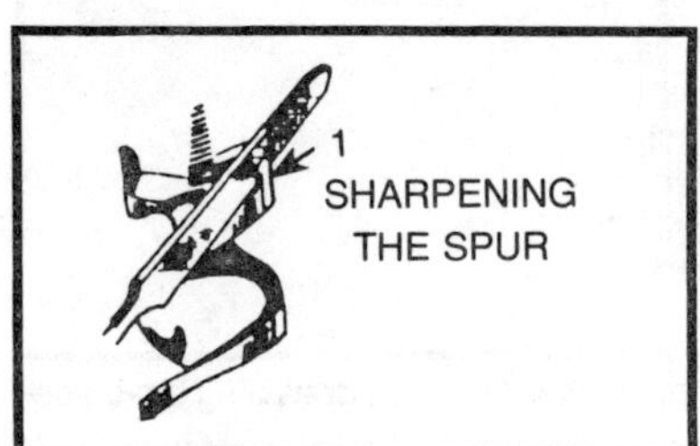

Fig. 3-11. Sharpening inside of the spur.

Fig. 3-12. Sharpening lips of the auger bit.

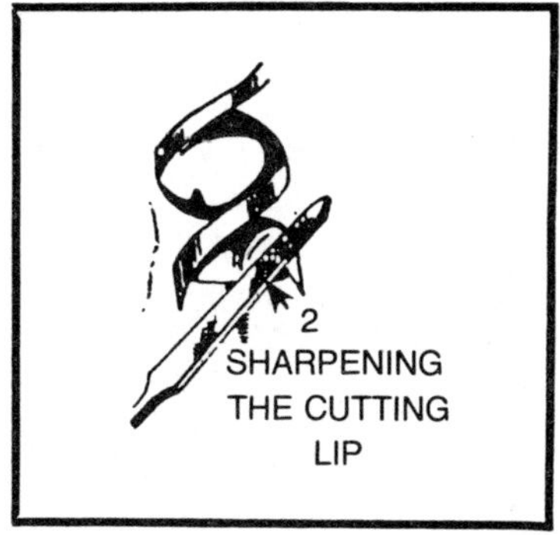

Sharpening Center Bits

Center drill bits may need sharpening from time to time with a slender needle file and an oilstone. Needle files come in various sectional shapes; but, square, triangular, flat, round and half-round are the shapes most practical for general tool sharpening and, particularly, for bit sharpening (see Fig. 3-13).

The chief consideration when sharpening the center bit is to follow the cutting angles already established by the manufacturer. Never touch the outside of a bit with the file, or the bit will bore an undersize hole or—worse still—will get stuck in the hole it drills.

The center bit is sharpened by pushing the bit point into a piece of wood to anchor and support the bit while the triangular bevel is filed until sharp on both cutting sides (see Figs. 3-14, 3-15, and 3-16).

With the center bit upturned, the inside of the scriber may be honed with the file and the brad point can be sharpened on either side, always taking care to follow the cutting angles already existing on the bit and being careful to use the non-milled surface of the file where necessary to keep from abrading adjoining parts.

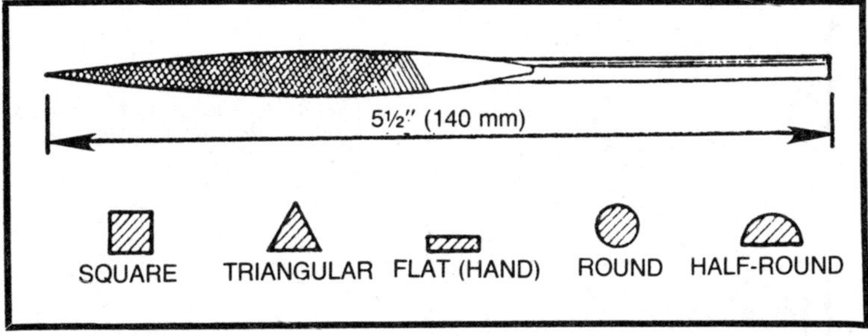

Fig. 3-13. The needle file, showing the various sectional shapes most useful in tool sharpening.

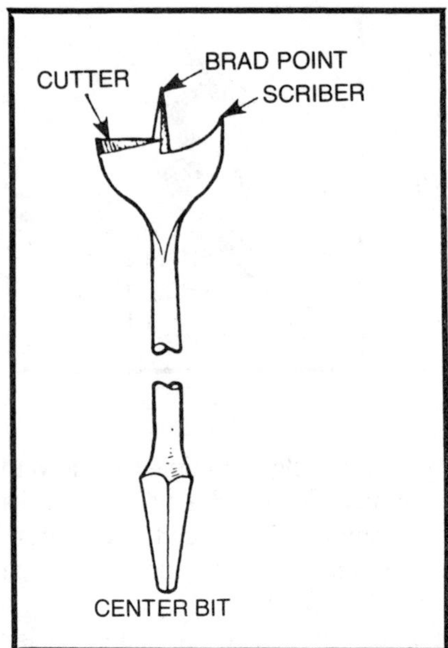

Fig. 3-14. Center bit.

Sharpening a Hand Saw

The process of sharpening a saw is three-fold: (1) Jointing and shaping, (2) setting, and (3) filing.

Jointing is only necessary when the saw teeth are no longer the same size because they have been badly abused by hard work or have been filed too many times. Jointing (or "topping") the teeth is performed by cramping the saw in a saw vise and running a file over the teeth until every tooth has been contacted. The saw vise will grip the blade near the roots of the teeth, making the leveling easy (see Fig. 3-17). The handle should be removed from the saw during sharpening. Once the teeth have been leveled to the same height,

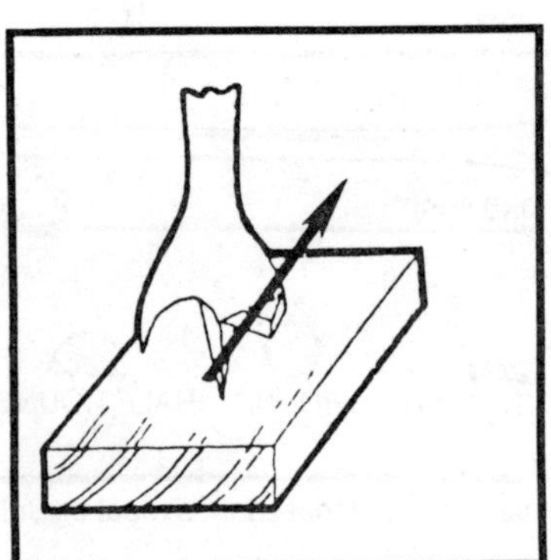

Fig. 3-15. Anchoring bit in wood to hold it firmly while filing triangular bevel on both sides.

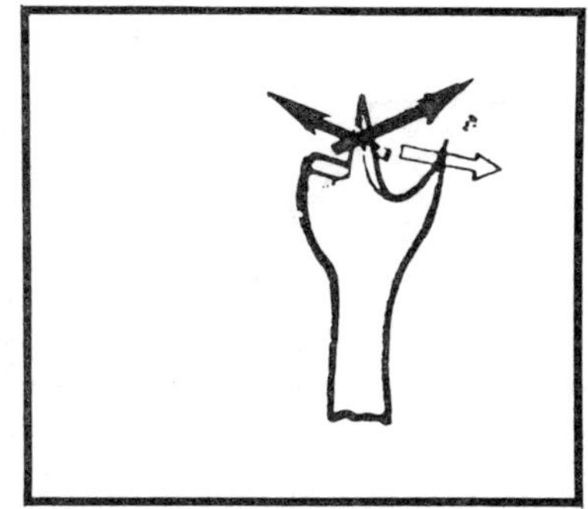
Fig. 3-16. With bit upturned, scriber and brad points are sharpened on either side.

they are then re-shaped with a slim tapered triangular needle file to the angles proper for that particular saw (see Fig. 3-18).

Setting is the process of bending each tooth alternately outward, which insures that the saw will cut a kerf that is wider than the thickness of the blade. All saws need frequent setting and the setting

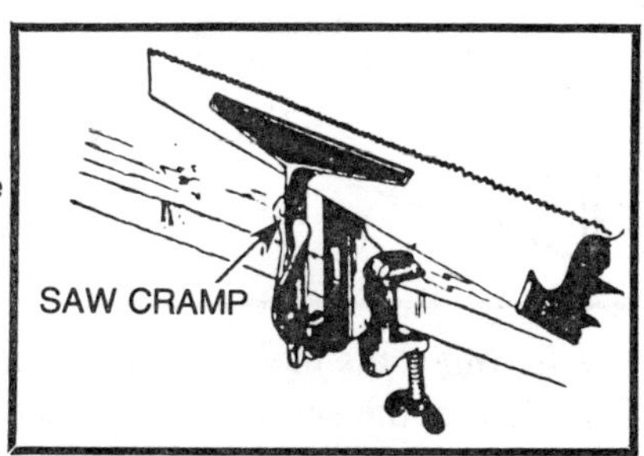

Fig. 3-17. Securing saw in saw vise for sharpening.

should be more deeply angled for green lumber than for well-seasoned stock. The number of teeth also governs the amount of set. The saw set, which is the tool used for setting the teeth, frequently has a gauge which indicates how much set is required for

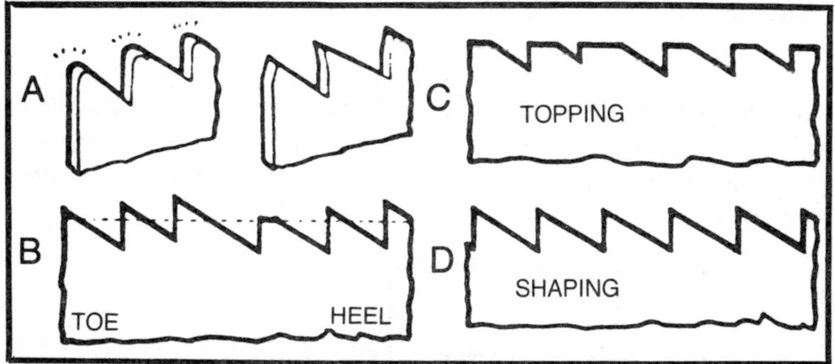

Fig. 3-18. Reasons and method for reshaping saw teeth. (a) dulled teeth and irregular teeth and (b) broken teeth are all reasons for leveling teeth off by (c) topping and then (d) shaping.

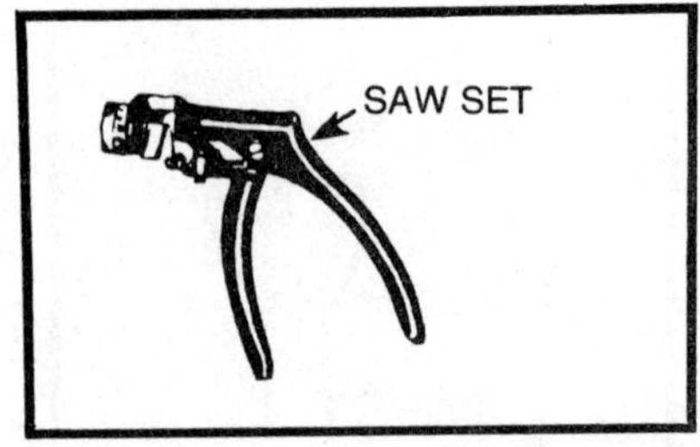

Fig. 3-19. Plier-type saw set.

saws with a given number of points. The saw-set is a plier-like tool (see Fig. 3-19,) which adjusts to the proper set for handsaws from 4 to 12 points. When the handles are squeezed together, the tool grips the saw and bends the teeth alternately outward to the required angle (see Fig. 3-20). The teeth must always be reset in the original direction.

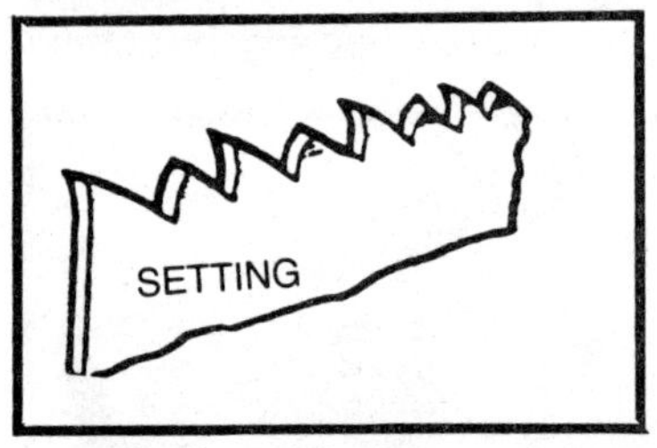

Fig. 3-20. Detail showing alternate outward set of saw teeth.

Filing is the most difficult of the three sharpening operations. The teeth of the saw are sharpened by a tapered triangular needle file held horizontally. With the rip- or dovetail saw, the teeth are filed straight across (see Fig. 3-21). With the crosscut or tenon saw, the file is held horizontally, but at an angle of 60 to 70 degrees to the blade (see Fig. 3-22). This filing angle sharpens the front of one tooth and the rear of the tooth adjoining (see Fig. 3-23). All saws are sharpened to a keen edge, but the teeth of crosscut saws are filed to knife-edge sharpness.

Nowadays, filing saws can be performed mechanically with greater speed and accuracy than by hand; but, every woodworker will want to know how to perform this tool repair himself, since it is frequently needed when the professional sharpening service is not available.

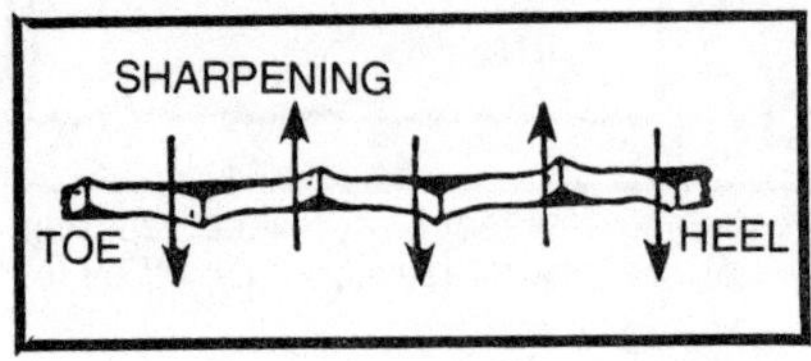

Fig. 3-21. Teeth on rip and dovetail saws are filed straight across.

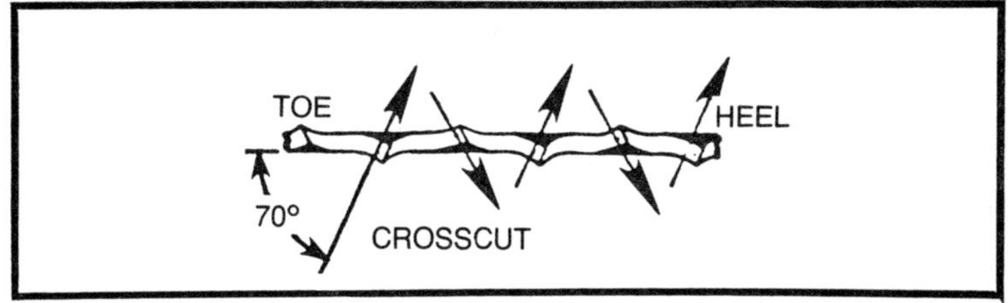

Fig. 3-22. Teeth on crosscut and tenon saws are filed at an angle of 70-degrees.

Occasionally, a backed saw will require re-tensioning. With a hammer, strike the blade-backing strip lightly with one blow at point A and one blow at point B (see Fig. 3-24). The natural reaction of the backing strip is to straighten, pulling at the blade as it does so. This pulling action tensions the blade. The best quality backed saws are backed in brass, which holds more firmly than does steel.

Sharpening the Bradawl

The gently sloping faces of the bradawl blade need to be sharp in order to sever the fibers of the wood grain and force them outwards. A small woodworking vise is very handy for holding small tools while working on the cutting edges with a file.

Sharpening Screwdrivers

When filing or grinding a screwdriver blade, do so across the blade. The resultant beveling will hold the screw more firmly (see Fig. 3-25). Always keep the thickness of the blade even at the tip and

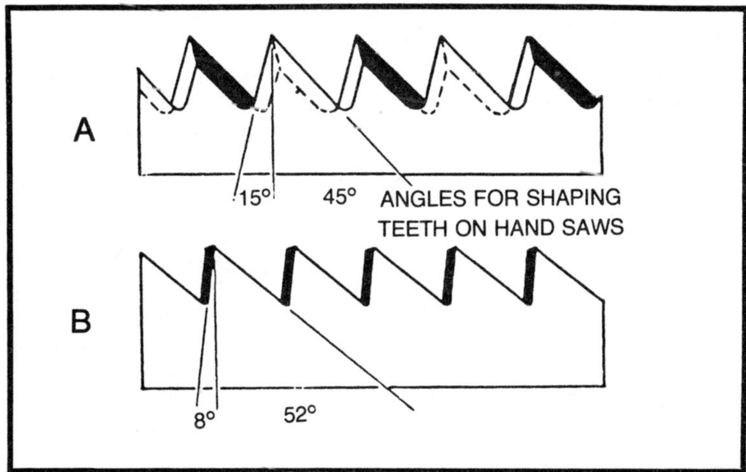

Fig. 3-23. Filing crosscut and tenon saws:angle for shaping teeth by filing front of one tooth and rear of adjoining one; filing angles for front and rear of each tooth.

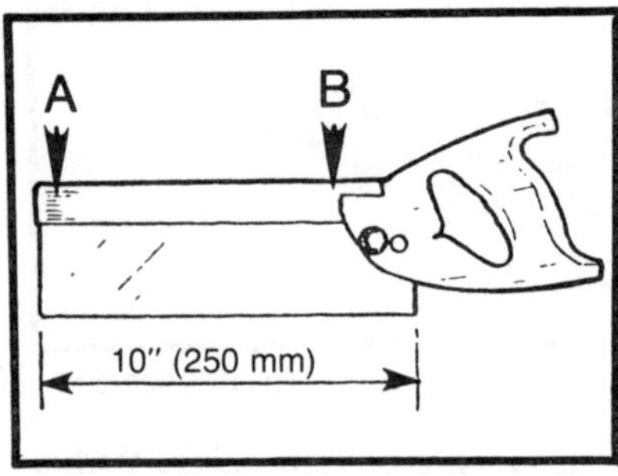

Fig. 3-24. The tenon saw, showing spots where hammer blows tension the blade.

do not file it too narrowly. Its thickness must be exactly the same as the thickness of the screw slot, otherwise the blade might jump from the slot, when pressure is applied, and score the work (see Fig. 3-26).

Sometimes it is necessary to trim a screwdriver blade to size in order to make it fit a certain sized screw exactly. Trimming may require both grinding and filing, with the filing being done carefully and horizontally across the blade to increase the blade's grip on the screw.

Sharpening the Spokeshave Blade

The problem in sharpening this tool is the small size of the blade. A block of wood with a saw cut at one end (see Fig. 3-27) makes a useful holder into which the blade can be inserted. Now the worker can get a firm grip on the blade and can hold it steady, at an angle of 30 degrees, against the oilstone to sharpen the cutting edge.

Sharpening the Cabinet Scraper

The cutter action of the cabinet scraper depends on the quality of the burr put on the edge of the blade. To produce this burr, the edge must first be honed true to a 90-degree angle with a long

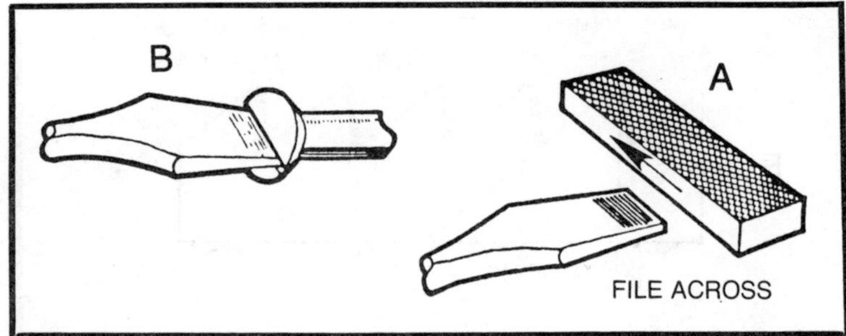

Fig. 3-25. Filing a screwdriver blade:(A) honing blade across its width with crosscut file; (B) resultant beveling holds screws more firmly.

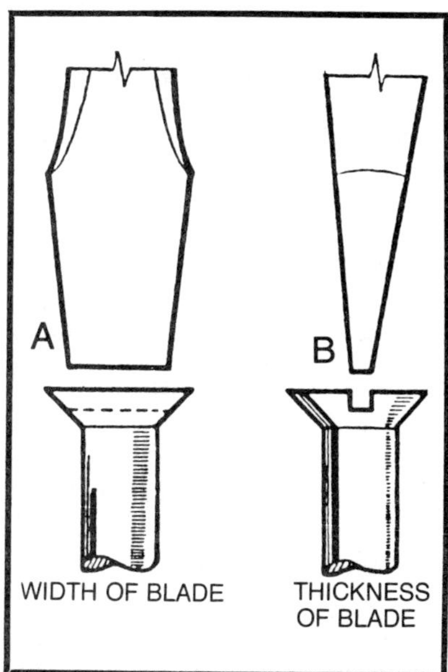

Fig. 3-26. Detail drawings of screwdriver blade showing (A) thickness which must be maintained and (B) width which must be maintained.

second-cut file. Holding the blade in a vise, apply the file lengthwise to the edge as shown (see Fig. 3-28). A few horizontal strokes will render the edge flat and square. Now, transfer the blade to an oilstone and rub both the edges and sides of the blade in turn to produce a true 90-degree corner (see Fig. 3-29). This corner must be bent outwards to form the burr. To accomplish this, replace the blade in the vise and, using either the burnisher or the back of a gouge, pass the hardened steel *firmly* along the edge of the cabinet scraper blade, keeping the burnisher at a 90-degree angle to the surface of the blade (see Fig. 3-30). Now make another firm pass

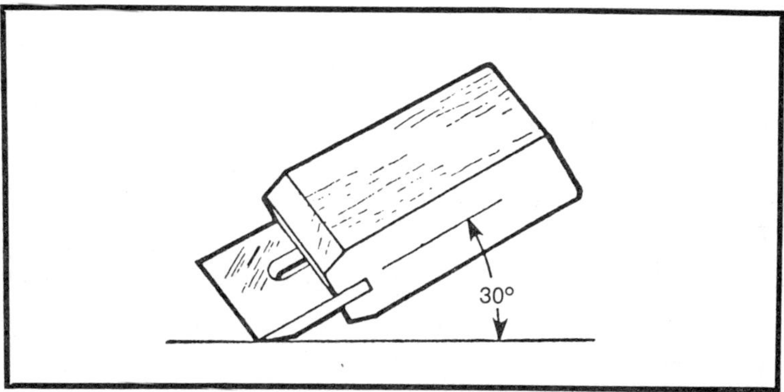

Fig. 3-27. A homemade holder for spokeshave blade makes sharpening easier.

Fig. 3-28. Filing the blade flat and square on a cabinet scraper.

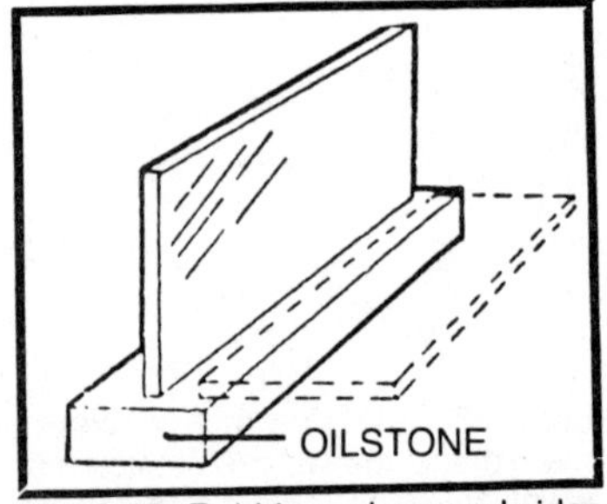

Fig. 3-29. Rubbing edges and sides of blade on oilstone to smooth and square them.

down the edge of the scraper blade with the burnisher tilted 10 degrees to an 80-degree angle with the side of the scraper blade (see Fig. 3-31). Press hard to polish the edge. Repeat the pass with the burnisher dipped to a 75-degree angle with the side of the scraper blade. (See Fig. 3-32 to better understand the three passes with the burnisher which form the burr.) The resultant burr enables the cabinet scraper to smooth wood cleanly and easily.

Sharpening the Scraper Plane

Instructions for sharpening the scraper plane are usually supplied by the manufacturer. The cutting edge is ground to 45-degrees by the manufacturer, but it must be sharpened before using. The burnisher is the best tool for this task. First burnish the flat side, holding the burnisher flat against the surface of the plane blade. This action consolidates the metal. Then, after securing the plane iron in the vise, start burnishing the 45-degree bevel. Apply steady pressure, raising the burnisher through 30 degrees until you are finally holding it firm just 15 degrees under the 90-degree horizontal (see Fig. 3-32).

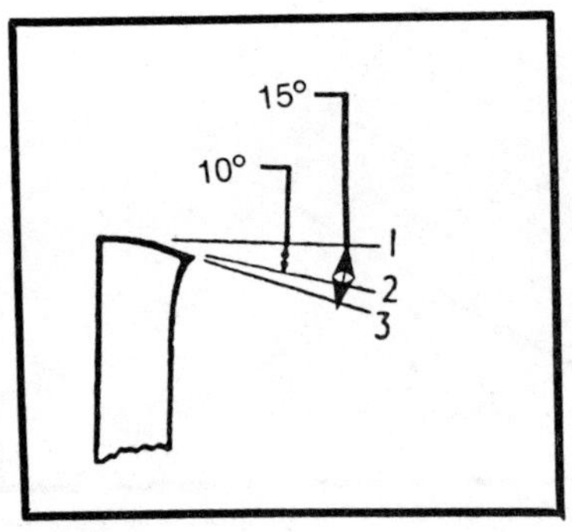

Fig. 3-30. Pressing length of edge with burnisher to form burr shown.

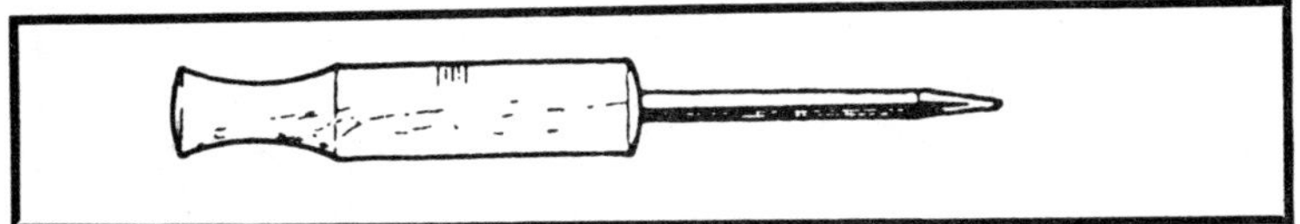

Fig. 3-31. The burnisher of hardened steel.

Sharpening Chisels

In general, the type of wood being cut regulates the frequency of sharpening the chisel. Certain timbers are so hard, or so close-grained, that the chisel needs sharpening after every six cuts. Other lumber will not blunt the chisel edge after half an hour of usage.

Fig. 3-32. The angle for burnishing a scraper plane iron—note how the burnisher is raised through 30 degrees, starting at the same 45-degree angle as the bevel, and finishing at 15 degrees below horizontal.

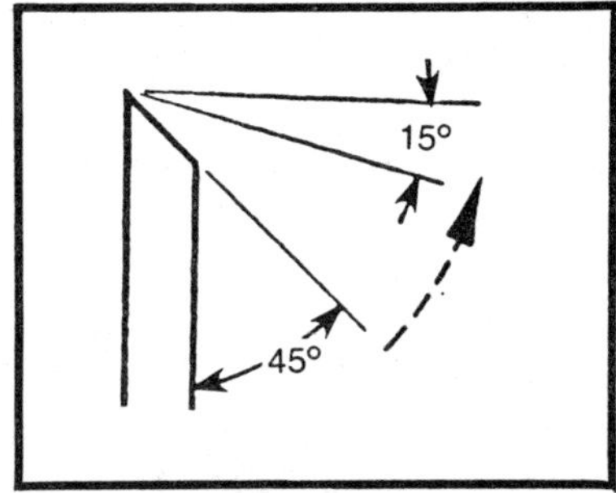

Beginners may not be sure when the chisel edge is blunt, since chiseling requires the application of force in any case. If the workman is in doubt as to the tool's dullness, the following indications will be helpful:

- Inspection of the incisions just made—are they crisp and clean?
- Recollection of the chisel's recent performance—was it easy or labored?
- Examination of the cutting edge—is it rounded and polished with hard usage so that it reflects the light from its blunted edge?
- Testing the cutting edge—does it feel sharp when the tip of a thumbnail is drawn across it?

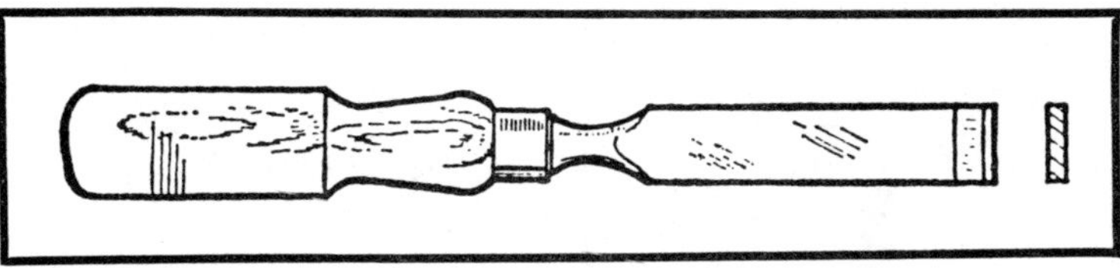

Fig. 3-33. The firmer chisel.

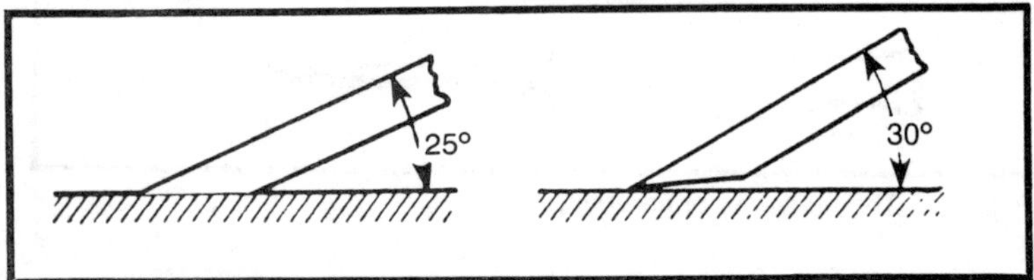

Fig. 3-34. The correct angle for sharpening chisels: (A) place 25-degree bevel of blade flat on oilstone; (B) raise blade 5 degrees to sharpening angle of 30-degrees.

New chisels have a grounding edge of 25 degrees. They are beveled to this angle at the factory; but, to prevent blunting during shipping, they are not sharpened. Therefore, the craftsman who has just purchased a new set of chisels must sharpen them before he can use them. The best of the group on which to begin is the firmer chisel (see Fig. 3-33). The other chisels are easy to handle with a little practice.

The procedure is as follows: After lubricating the oilstone with neatsfoot oil or thin lubricating oil, stand the chisel on the grinding bevel of its blade, and then lift the blade 5 degrees to the sharpening angle of 30° (see Fig. 3-34, A and B). Various guides are available to secure the blade at the proper angle for sharpening and, until the amateur craftsman has developed an instinct for the work and can dispense with such aids, these are very helpful (see Fig. 3-35).

Maintaining the 30-degree angle, *push* the blade from one end of the stone to the other. Always use a pushing motion, and avoid rocking the chisel, or the bevel will tend to be rounded rather than sharp, as desired. Keep rubbing the chisel blade against the oilstone until a wire is formed at the back of the blade (see Fig. 3-36). This wire can be felt by sliding the finger down the blade and across the edge. The wire may be removed by rubbing the back of the chisel blade flat on the oilstone (see Fig. 3-37).

During this honing, grasp the lower blade of the chisel between thumb and little finger, bunching the other fingers over the blade to exert pressure on the bevel. Rub the blade back and forth lengthwise on the oilstone, making every effort to keep the blade flat. Soon you

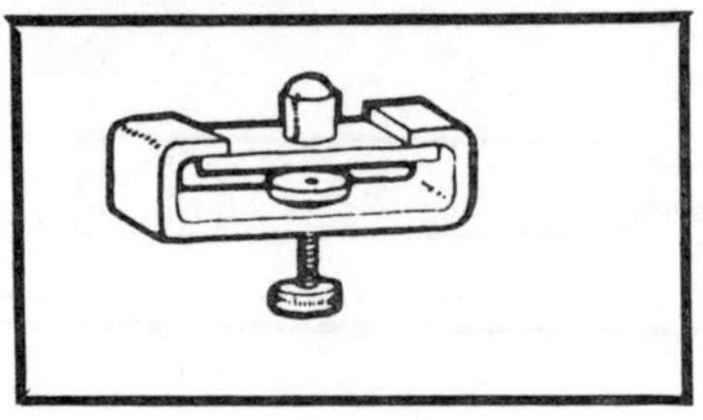
Fig. 3-35. Honing guide.

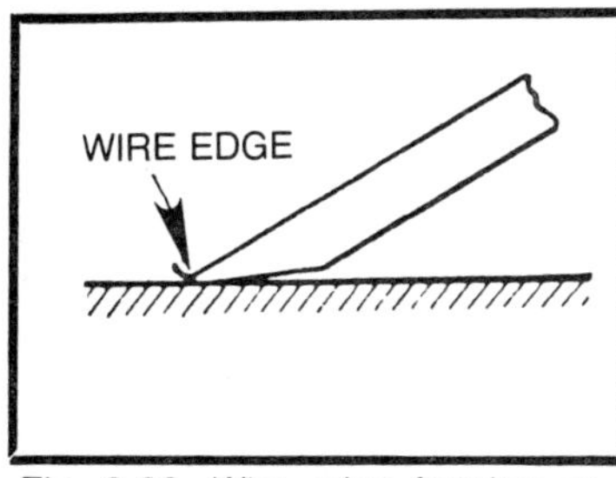

Fig. 3-36. Wire edge forming on chisel blade.

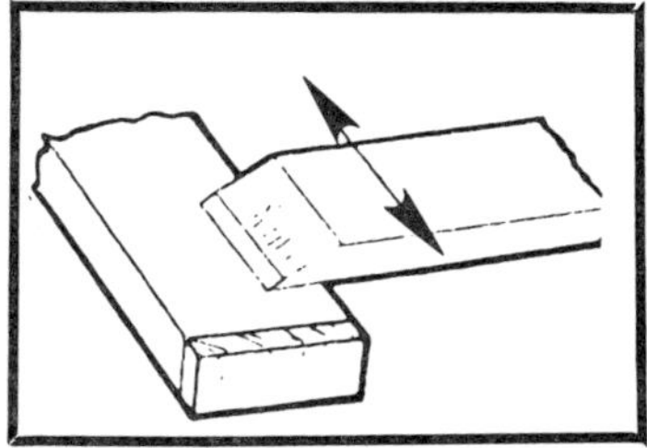
Fig. 3-37. Removing wire edge by rubbing back of blade flat on oilstone.

will note that the back of the blade is acquiring a mirror-like finish. Craftsmen who pride themselves on their tools spend time imparting this mirror-like finish to every new chisel and often put an extra-keen edge on the blade by stropping it on oiled leather dressed with jeweler's rouge. The cutting edge produced is like that on a woodcarver's tools.

Time and wear occasionally dictate the grinding of chisel blades to restore the original 25-degree bevel given the tool by the manufacturer. Note Figs. 3-38, 3-39 and 3-40 illustrating the damages to chisel blades which justify grinding. Any of these damages can be quickly repaired on a grindstone; however, grindstones are a last resort in blade sharpening. Unless a grindstone of the proper speed and the right abrasive is used, a rough edge can be left on the blade. Also, as before mentioned, the grindstone can so overheat the blade tht the heat tempering of the blade given it by the manufacturer is destroyed. Once this happens, the tool will not sharpen or retain a cutting edge and may break in use. Breakage is instantly recognizable on a blade; it manifests itself as a striated band of color indicating a cleft.

All of these accidents to the blade can occur in just a few moments on the wrong kind of grinding wheel or on a wheel set to

Fig. 3-38. Rounded edge caused by careless sharpening.

Fig. 3-39. Gashed edge caused by contact with nails and screws.

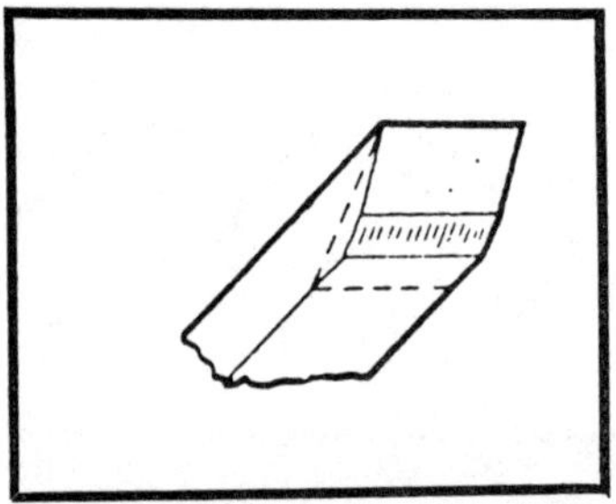

Fig. 3-40. Enlarged cutting bevel needs reshaping:(A) shows outline of cutback which will repair blade; (B) shows reshaped, re-beveled blade edge.

Fig. 3-41. Oilstone slip used to sharpen gouge.

too high a speed. The best and safest type of grinder is the one made of natural grit sandstone and powered by a slow-running electric motor. This model of grindstone is constantly cooled and cleaned by water dripping from a tank above the stone. Although few woodworking shops are outfitted with such grindstones, the craftsman may gain access to the use of one by making inquiries at tool shops, hardware stores and technical schools. The operation of such grinding tools takes some practice and skill, but the edge they give to tools is hard to come by any other way.

One must always bear in mind, however, that tools only infrequently require grinding, whereas sharpening is consistently necessary to maintain them. As a matter of fact, grinding should be avoided as much as possible since it shortens the life of the tool.

Sharpening Gouges

Gouges are sharpened, as are chisels, by using the oilstone slip (see Fig. 3-41). The scribing, or in-channel gouge (see Fig. 3-42), which has its bevel on the inside of the blade, needs the oilstone slip (moistened with neatsfoot oil) to hone its edge to sharpness, the resultant wire being removed on a flat oilstone. The firmer, or out-channel gouge (see Fig. 3-43), which has its beveled cutting edge on the outside, restores its sharpness by its beveled edge being drawn in a figure-eight movement across a flat oilstone, the

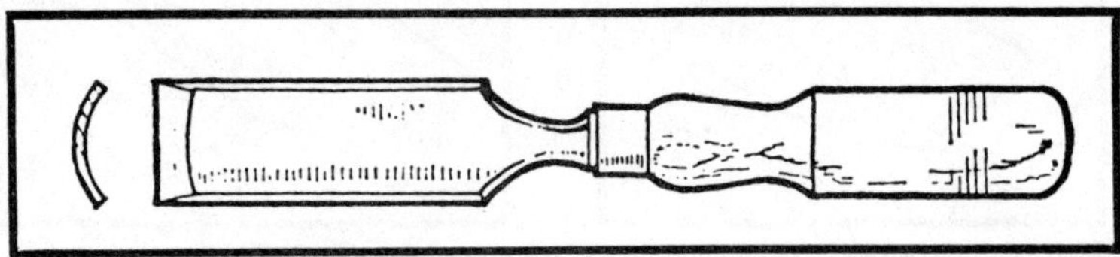

Fig. 3-42. Scribing (or in-channel) gouge.

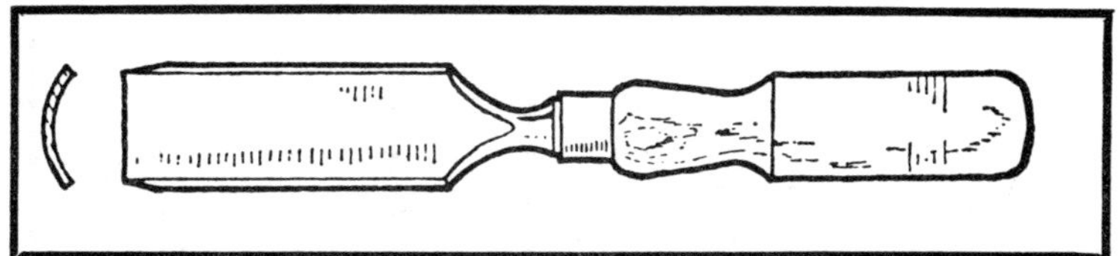
Fig. 3-43. Firmer (or out-channel) gouge.

resultant wire being removed from the inside of the gouge with the oilstone slip.

Sharpening Planes

Planes, like chisels, require frequent sharpening. The bevel pitch of most planes is 45 degrees. However, if the plane iron were sharpened at that angle (see Fig. 3-44), the friction would be excessive when the plane attempted to sheer the wood. If the blade were

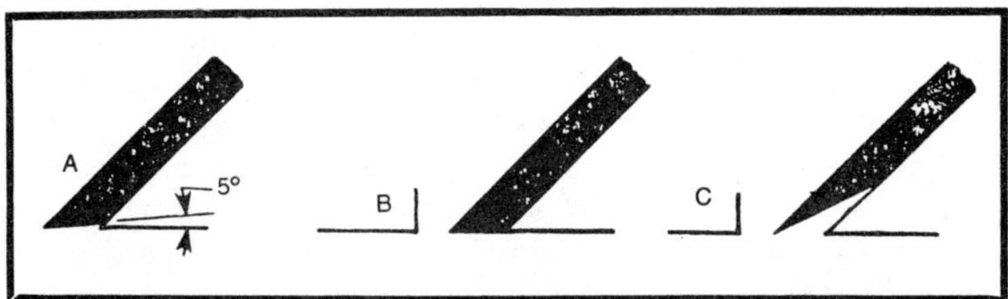

Fig. 3-44. Sharpening plane irons:(A) correct angle for sharpening plane irons; (B) if plane iron were sharpened at 45 degrees—the same angle at which it is beveled—it would generate too much friction when smoothing wood; (C) if the plane iron were sharpened to a more acute angle than 45 degrees, the planing action would bend or snap off the plane iron.

sharpened at a more acute angle than 45 degrees (see Fig. 3-45), either the edge would snap off or the blade would be bent in its effort to spring forward. The springing motion, known as "chattering," would result in a very uneven finish. Experience indicates that a 5 degrees clearance is sufficient for planes (see Fig. 3-46). At this

Fig. 3-45. The honing guide is an indispensible sharpening aid to amateur craftsmen.

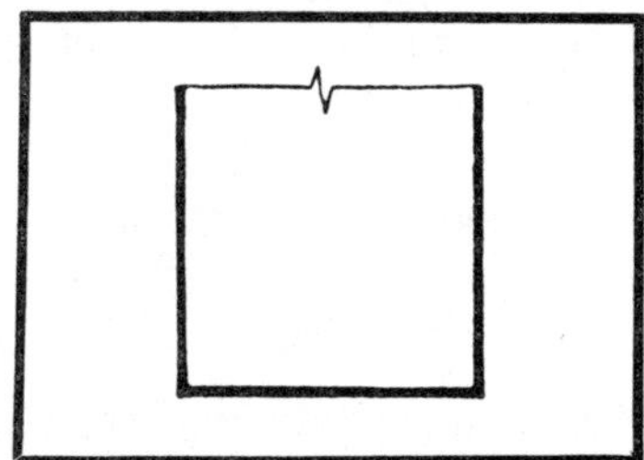
Fig. 3-46. Square cutting edges on rebate and plough plane irons.

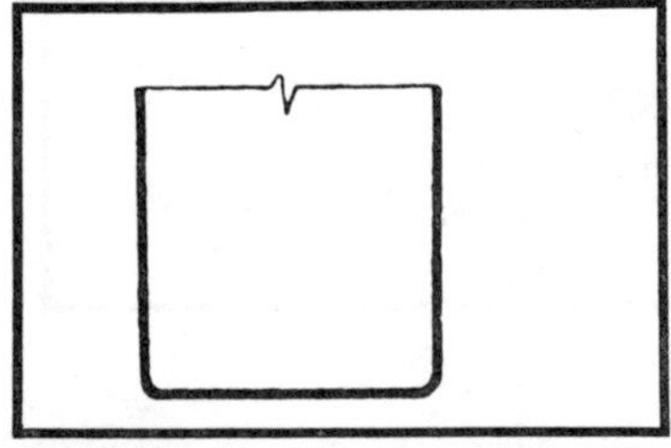

Fig. 3-47. Square cutting edges with rounded corners which plane irons for block, smoothing and trying planes require.

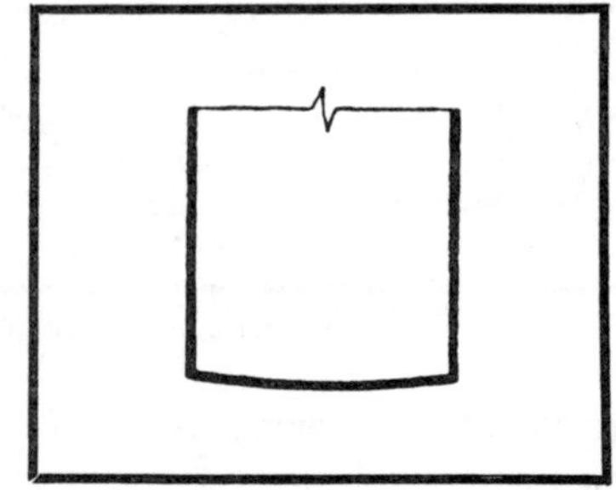

Fig. 3-48. The forward-curving plane iron of the jack plane.

bevel angle the friction of the cutting edge is reduced to a minimum, yet the blade still gets sufficient support from the frog. Plane irons are ground at an angle of 25 degrees and honed at an angle of 30 degrees. In the case of the bench plane, never sharpen the plane iron at an angle greater than the pitch of the plane.

Each plane iron—because of the varied smoothing operations for which it was designed—requires a specific sharpening operation. The plane irons of rebate and plough planes have an overall shape (or profile, if you will) which is straight and square—a difficult shape for the beginning craftsman to achieve until he has had sufficient practice (see Fig. 3-47). Cutting edges of plough planes are usually ground to a bevel of 35-degrees—a slightly more acute angle than that used for other planes—and this angle must be reproduced in sharpening.

Block, smoothing and trying planes have irons similar in shape to the squared-off shape of the plough and rebate planes, but they are rounded off at the corners on the oilstone so that they will not gouge the wood (see Fig. 3-48).

The jack plane has an iron which is rounded in profile so that it can be used to shear off coarse shavings. When planing rough lumber, this shape of plane iron is an asset; but, when working with already planed lumber (as most craftsmen do nowadays), this rounded shape may shear too deeply. Therefore, reshaping the jack plane iron to resemble that of the trying, smoothing or block plane might be more practical.

Sharpening plane irons is never an easy task for the beginner, but the job may be simplified by using a honing guide. This device locks into the plane iron and helps to establish and maintain a proper constant sharpening angle.

Sharpening the Marking Knife or Penknife

This handy tool needs frequent sharpening because it must be able to score the wood fibers neatly and cleanly in laying out saw

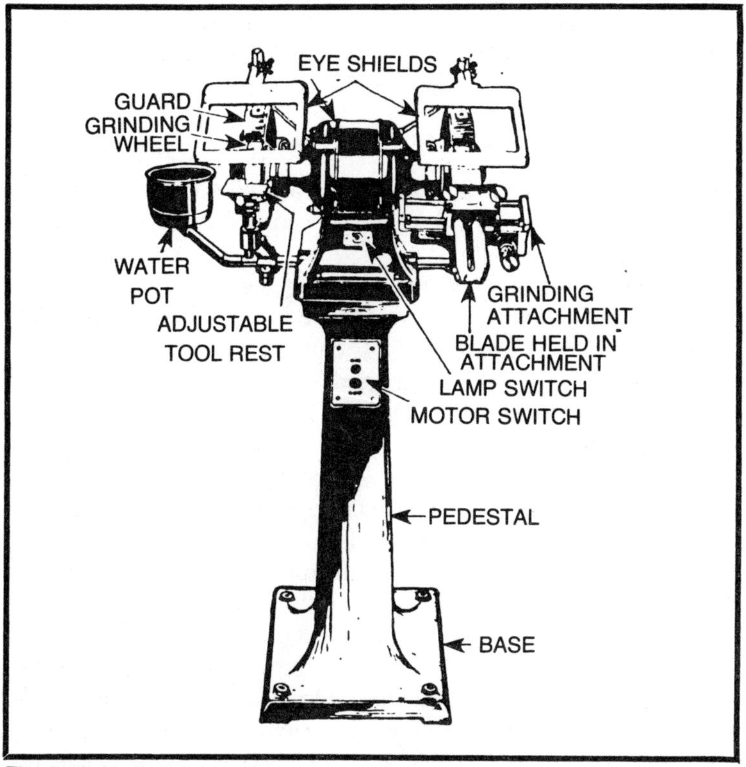

Fig. 3-49. Vertical mounted machine grindstone.

lines, outlining patterns, etc. More people prefer a penknife for this purpose, rather than the knife designed for marking. Like the marking knife, the penknife has bevels on both sides of the blade. To sharpen, use a stropping action—pushing the blade forward on the

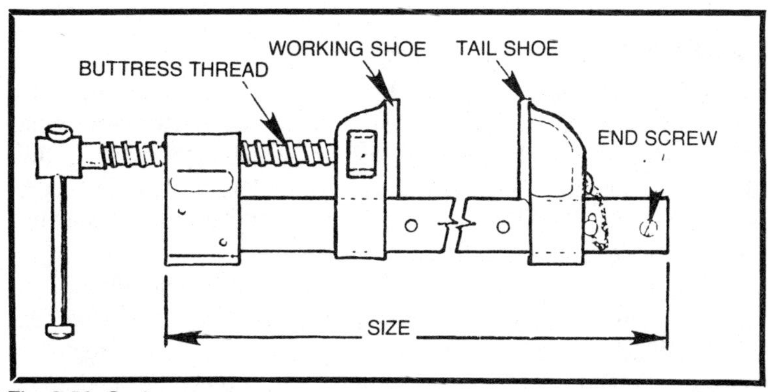

Fig. 3-50. Sash cramp.

oilstone at a slight angle, then turning the knife over and pulling it back. Check the rivets for tightness and polish the wooden or bone handle with a cloth moistened with linseed oil.

Grindstone Maintenance

Should you be so fortunate as to own a grindstone, you will want to maintain it properly so that it, in turn, can do the same for all your cutting tools.

Motorized grindstones are of two types: vertically mounted wheels washed and cooled by water (see Fig. 3-49) and horizontal wheels washed and cooled by oil. The primary servicing necessary to the vertical, water-lubricated grindstone is that of emptying out the water once the grinding is finished. The grindstone—whether it be natural quarried sandstone or artificial abrasive—is porous and will soften wherever the water soaks it and will wear out of shape in that spot. Therefore, the water and sludge residue must be drained out of the holding tank and emptied on waste ground.

The grindstone itself can be kept true and square by occasionally applying an iron pipe across the working edge.

The modern horizontal grindstone looks like a revolving turntable for playing records. The wheel is formed of artificial abrasive such as silicon carbide or aluminum oxide. Both materials are excellent for grinding and—having been produced in an electric furnace—have greater consistency of abrasive quality than do natural stones. These artificial stones use oil, rather than water, to wash off the grit and metal particles and to cool the grinding stone. A filter inside the machine traps all the metal particles after each cycle, returning only filtered oil for further lubrication. An excellent tool rest holds the blade at the precise angle desired and enables the craftsman to sharpen with greatest accuracy.

Maintaining the Oilstone

This sharpening stone may be cut of quarried stone—as the more expensive oilstones are—or it may be manufactured from an artificial abrasive, such as silicon carbide or aluminum oxide. If the oilstone is quarried, it is generally named for its place of origin—such as "Washita," or "Arkansas, USA." If it is manufactured, it may be called "Carborundum" or "India."

Whatever the abrasive material, oilstones are generally 8 in. × 2 in. × 1 in. in size—convenient for sharpening plane irons as well as chisels. Whether in use or in storage, the stone is always kept in a shallow tray and is buffered at either side by pieces of end-grain

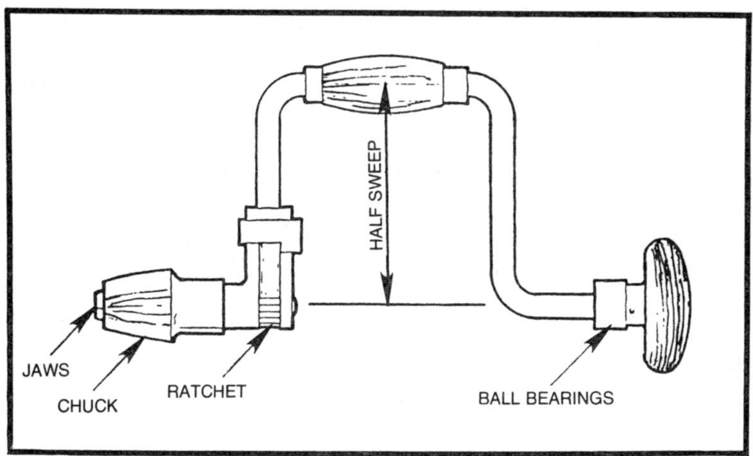

Fig. 3-51. Brace drill.

hardwood to prevent the tools sharpened on it from chipping its edges. A wooden cover protects the oilstone from dirt and dust when it is not in use.

As previously mentioned and as the name "oilstone" implies, this stone is lubricated with oil before being used as a sharpener. Neatsfoot oil—the sort of fine oil used for keeping saddles and hostlery tack soft and pliant—or bicycle oil is best for this purpose. Oils, like linseed oil, which dry up should not be used because they leave a gummy residue on the stone; whereas, oils which remain liquid wash the stone of metal particles, reduce friction and overheating when the stone is abraded, and produce a smoother, keener cutting edge on the blades honed on the stone's oiled surface.

If the stone gets dirty, or becomes coated with the wrong lubricant, it may be soaked in a bath of kerosene, which will clean it by absorbing the oil and soil.

An oilstone must be flat to sharpen correctly. When an oilstone develops hollow depressions in its center from hard usage, it may be flattened by rubbing it with a piece of glass liberally coated with abrasive carborundum paste—a long, tedious process, but effective.

Repairing Cramps

These holding tools are capable of performing yeoman service with a minimum of care; however, if they are neglected, they are virtually useless. Glue and moisture can rust the bar and prevent the shoes from sliding easily. The tail shoe chain can snap and break off the peg which anchors the shoe to the bar (see Fig. 3-50).

The bar should be cleaned after every use to remove any glue drips and should be polished with an oil-soaked cloth and powdered emery until the shoes—given a little push—slide easily back and forth along the bar. Screw threads should be oiled and the chain examined for breaks and replaced, if need be. The anchor peg should be secured in it socket. A nut and bolt fitted over the end of the bar will act as a stop and prevent the shoe on that side from sliding off the bar. The new cramps often come equipped with such bolts and care should be taken to replace them if they have been removed to extend the cramp.

Maintaining the Brace Drill

Give the brace drill a good cleaning from time to time, scouring the metal frame with steel wool or fine emergy cloth dipped in mineral oil, if it is unplated, or with a soft cloth soaked in mineral oil, if the frame is chromium-plated. The wooden handles will benefit from an oiling, too; however, remember to use mineral oil for metal parts and linseed oil for wooden parts. Linseed oil, being a vegetable oil, is a drying oil and metal parts need an oil which does not dry off to protect the metal from rust (see Fig. 3-51).

A few drops of oil in the bearings inside the head, and a little grease applied to the threads and the inside cone of the chuck, will make the brace operate more smoothly. Lubysil GPI, a soft silicon grease, works excellently on enclosed gear boxes and bearings. Take care not to overgrease, or future operations will be messy, to say the least.

Maintaining Gauges

The mortise, marking and cutting gauges should be oiled with light machine oil. The spurs on the mortise and marking gauges require sharpening with a file, as does the cutter on the cutting gauge which can be honed on an oilstone, following the sharpening pattern instituted by the manufacturer as closely as possible. Be sure to polish all wooden parts of the gauges with a few drops of linseed oil.

Maintaining Hammers

A hammer with a dirty face is a bane to the craftsman because it bends nails and slides off the work, marring it. Clean the hammer face of glue, paint and varnish, and polish the entire metal hammer head from poll to peen with emergy cloth and mineral oil. Rub a little linseed oil into the handle, inspecting it carefully for splits. If the hammer head shows too much play, tap the metal wedge more firmly into the eye.

Maintaining Mallets

Mallets require very little repair. An occasional polish with linseed oil will keep the wooden parts gleaming.

STORING CUTTING TOOLS

More tools with cutting edges are damaged by the way they are stored than are ever damaged by usage. Planes should be stored on their sides to protect the cutting edge, which always extends below the bottom of the plane and will be damaged if the plane is stored in the same position in which it is used.

Padding the drawer bottoms in which chisels, gouges, knives and cabinet scrapers are kept with a folded towel will prevent harm to the cutting edges of these tools when they are stored. Lay them in the drawers carefully and separately; never stack or bunch them. If storage space is limited, layer them with thickly folded towels between.

Because of their offset teeth, saws should be hung on a peg or nail rather than stored in a drawer. If drawer storage is a must, a bent strip of cardboard placed over the teeth and held in place by rubber bands or twine will save hours of sharpening.

Chapter 4 Fastening and Attaching Devices

Of the several means employed to join together two pieces of wood, the most unusual are nails, screws, wood joints and glue. Any or all of these fastenings are frequently used in making one object. We will discuss each method in this chapter.

NAILS

The nail is the quickest method of fastening two boards together. It is quicker to install than a screw; but it is not as strong, nor as easy to remove.

The forerunner of the nail was the wooden peg. With the coming of the steel age, the cut nail was introduced; then the wire nail, in many thicknesses and lengths, made its appearance. Today's innovation is the cartridge nail—a bullet-shaped nail designed for rapid-fire insertion with a power gun.

Since nails serve a variety of purposes, they are manufactured in many shapes and sizes (see Fig. 4-1) and the materials used in making them are varied. Nails in most common use are made of steel, iron, brass, copper and aluminum. Steel nails are blued, barged, have a galvanized finish and are coated with zinc, cement or tar to give them greater holding ability and to prevent corrosion. Some nails are twisted along the shaft for firmer anchorage. Brads, casing nails and finishing nails are the types used most often in furniture construction. Antiques are sometimes repaired with cut nails—modern-day manufactured copies of hand-forged nails with wedge-shaped shanks which give them better bind against the wood grain than wire nails and, therefore, greater holding power.

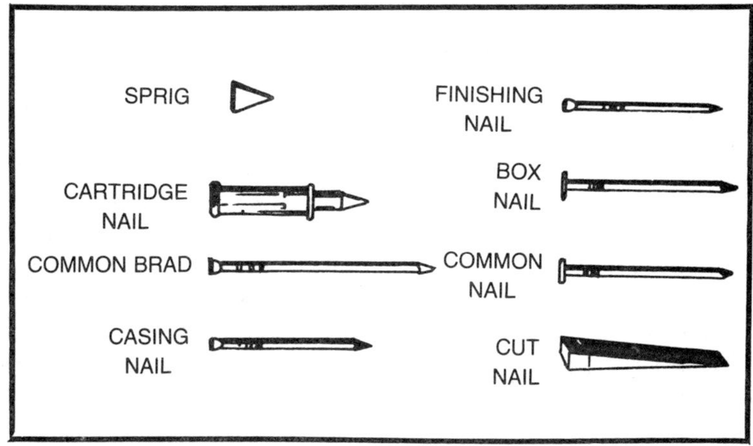

Fig. 4-1. Different kinds of nails.

Common Nail. The so-called "common nail" is available in lengths of 1 to 6 inches, with the gauge of wire increasing as the length increases. The common nail is very widely used in scaffolding, house-framing, making building forms and crates—in any construction, in fact, where speed of assembly is more important than appearance.

Box nail. This nail was designed, as its name suggests, for constructing boxes. It penetrates thin stock neatly and cleanly and is less likely than heavier nails to split the lumber. Box nails are not made in long lengths and have less holding power than common nails, although they are often coated with resin or cement to increase their abilities to hold and to resist corrosion.

Finishing Nail. This is a fine nail with a small, flat head and conical shaped sides sloping toward the point. These nails are driven flush with the wood, leaving no hole or depression around the head. A coat of paint makes the nail head invisible.

Casing Nail. This nail has the same head shape as a brad, but is made of heavier gauge steel. It is available in sizes ranging from 1 to 4 inches and is very useful in "casework," as cabinetwork is called. It is an excellent nail for fine work where a smoothly finished surface demands that the nail head be sunk into the wood and the resultant depression filled with stick shellac or wood dough.

Brad. This is a small finishing nail made of thin steel wire with a rounded head flattened on the top side. It is ¼ inch to 2 inches in length and very inconspicuous in usage. It is widely used in constructing furniture and in making small articles such as boxes, picture frames, lamp bases, serving trays, bookends, etc.

Sprig. This very small nail has no visible head and a tapered shaft. It is perfect for holding pictures in a frame, and is usually inserted with the side of a large chisel acting as a hammer.

Cartridge Nail. This bullet-shaped nail is fired by a special power gun into the material. The nail is classified, according to usage, by a system of color-coding which indicates whether it should be used for laminates, wood, steel, block or brick.

Cut Nail. This nail is a manufactured reproduction of the first soft steel nails which were forged by hand. It has a thick, tapering, rectangular shaft (almost square) and a large head. The wedge-shaped shaft binds against the wood fibers, instead of splitting them, and the nail's holding power is consequently enormous. In repairing antiques, one would have use for this nail—particularly on pieces where nails of this sort were originally used.

Corrugated Nail. This fastener is made of flat steel wire crimped lengthwise with a sharp point on the bottom of the long length. Because the corrugated nail is wider than it is long, it can be driven into the wood surface across a joint to its full length so that only a thin, wavy line shows. The corrugated nail is often used on butt or mitered joints where it will not be seen.

The varieties of nails are almost endless. Many are designed for use only on special materials. Masonry, flooring, roofing, lathes, shingles, felt, carpeting, upholstery, etc., all demand special nails to secure them. The nails we have mentioned here are frequently used in woodworking.

The length of nails is indicated by the word "penny" (sometimes designated by the letter "d.") The term "penny" refers to the weight of one thousands nails; thus, nails weighing six pounds per thousand are called "sixpenny nails."

However, the penny weight system of measurement is not accurate nowadays because, although the length per penny stays constant, the thickness (gauge) of nails varies so that the weight per thousand would not be the same for nails of the same length but a different gauge.

The following is a table of nail lengths of 1 inch to 6 inches—the lengths most commonly used. The letter "D" has been used throughout this table to indicate the word "penny."

2D—1″	7D—2¼″	16D—3½″
3D—1¼″	8D—2½″	20D—4″
4D—1½″	9D—2¾″	30D—4½″
5D—1¾″	10D—3″	40D—5″
6D—2″	12D—3¼″	50D—5½″
		60D—6″

Table 4-1. Nail Lengths.

Nails are usually sold in one hundred pound kegs, but they can also be purchased in smaller weights. Smaller sizes of brads are sold by length in little pasteboard boxes or plastic packages, rather than by penny size.

To determine the size of nails or brads needed for any given project, multiply the thickness of the lumber being nailed by 8, and add 1½ to the result. For example: If you wish to nail through a board measuring 9/16-inch in thickness, a 6D nail would best serve. Here is the mathematical computation by which one arrives at that conclusion:

$$9/16\text{-inch} \times 8 = 4\tfrac{1}{2}.\ 4\tfrac{1}{2} + 1\tfrac{1}{2} = 6$$

To determine the length in inches of a nail or brad from the given "penny" size, up to the penny size 10D, simply divide the penny size by 4 and add ½. For example, a 7D nail measures 2¼ inches.

$$7/4 + \tfrac{1}{2} = 2\tfrac{1}{4} \text{ inches}$$

APPLYING NAILS

1. Make sure before driving a nail that it is the proper type and size for the job.
2. Greater strength results if nails are driven at a slight angle.
3. Three precautions will prevent splitting the board:
   - Drilling a small pilot hole first,
   - Position the nails in a staggered pattern,
   - Use finishing nails wherever possible, for their small heads do not split the grain.
4. When setting nails below the surface of the work, always use a nail punch smaller than the head of the nail.
5. Take constant care not to strike the wood surface with a hammer. If the hammer slips and dents the wood, sponging with water will raise the grain. (Fig. 4-2 illustrates these suggestions.)

REPAIRING WITH NAILS

Using small-headed brads for repair and reinforcement is a time-honored practice, well known to all woodworkers. However, very few woodworkers are aware of the following innovative method of drilling the holes for setting these slender nails. This-method entails selecting a nail of the same size as those to be set in the drilled holes and removing the head. The beheaded nail will now serve as a bit for the actual drilling.

The advantages of using a beheaded nail in the drill chuck, rather than a bit, are many. Even if a twist drill bit were obtainable in the exact thickness of the nail used (to make a hole large enough so that the nail would not split the wood, yet not so large as to prove a sloppy fit), the nail would not bind so well in the hole as it does when the hole is drilled with a beheaded nail of the same size. The twist bit's fluted shaft reams out a differently shaped hole, even if it is precisely the same width. The beheaded nail bit, on the other hand, makes a hole which exactly fits the nail along its entire length and, thus, binds the sides of the nail shaft. Also, the fact that the bit used is a beheaded nail means that the hole drilled will not be as long as the whole nail and will, therefore, provide a strong, solid-wood anchor for the point of the nail when it is driven in.

Very thin brads are the most difficult nails to use as drill bits; but, by centering the beheaded brad carefully in the chuck and taking care to exert only minimum pressure in order not to bend the thin steel shank, the task can be accomplished. A small hand-drill is ideal for this work.

When fashioning jointures of any sort between two wooden parts, the woodworker should remember that small-headed, strategically placed nails will lend tremendous, yet inconspicuous, reinforcement. Slats, rungs, arm posts, stretchers, legs, spindles and bannisters are just a few of the furniture joints which can be so strengthened. All joints near an edge, or positioned where the nail can be driven in from an outside surface, can take this means of repair; however, the parts must be already assembled, and the glue thoroughly dry, before the nails are driven.

The procedure is as follows:

1. Choose a nail of the length and thickness best suited to the work. Cut the small head off and center the shaft in the chuck of a hand-drill (preferably one with a short bite), making sure that the nail is firmly secure.
2. Drill the hole, being careful to prevent the face of the chuck fom touching and marring the wood surface. Hold the drill straight, and steady to minimize the strain on the nail. If the nail is being placed into the edge of a thin board, take care to center the hole exactly and to keep the drilled depth of the hole parallel to the sides of the board.
3. Remove the bit slowly and carefully from the drilled hole.
4. With cautious taps of Warrington hammer, drive in a small-headed nail similar to that used in drilling the hole. Keep pounding until the head is flush with the surface.

Some types of joints are greatly strengthened by "toe-nailing"—a method of driving in a nail at an angle, making sure that it passes through one piece of the joint into the other in order to hold

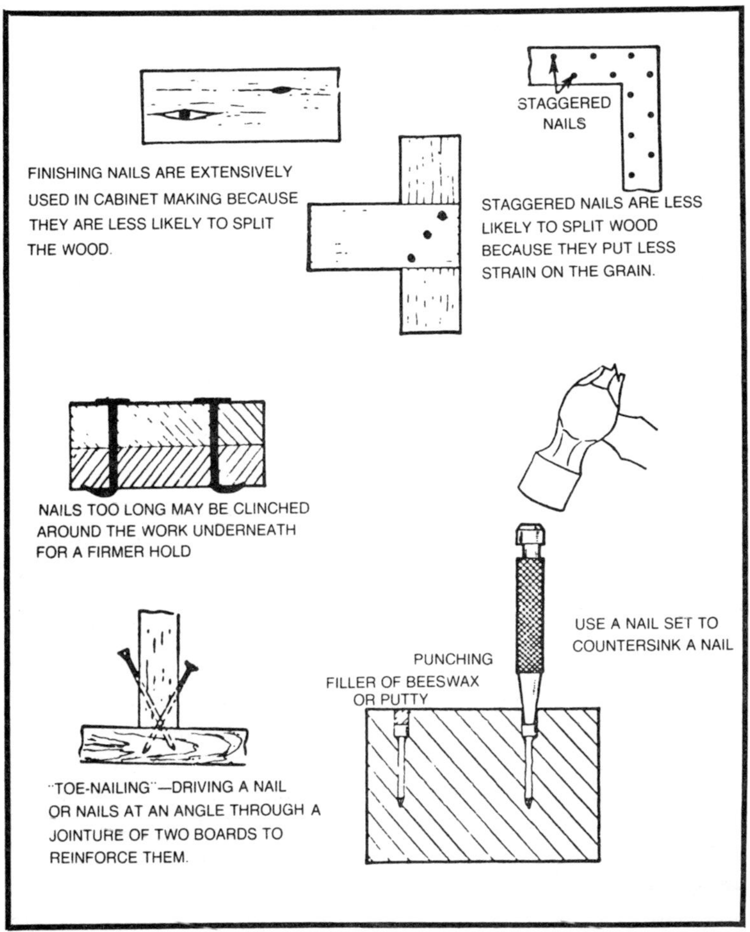

Fig. 4-2. Proper use of nails; nails that are too long may be clinched around the work underneath for a firmer hold; using a nail set to countersink a hole; toe-nailing is driving nails at an angle through a jointure of two boards to reinforce them.

them tightly together. This method of strengthening has a more professional appearance than the use of conspicuous hardware, such as corner braces or mending plates. In "toe-nailing," even the nail heads are hidden by sinking them with a nail set below the wood surface and filling the resultant hole with wood dough or stick shellac of the same color. With a knife and fine abrasive paper, the filler is then carefully smoothed to look like an undisturbed wood surface.

Using small-headed nails, "toe-nailing" is done in the same manner as that outlined above, except that the beheaded nail is used as a drill bit to drive a hole at an angle through both glued-together boards of the joint. The joint is secured in a vise during this operation so that the woodowrker can use both hands for the task. For added strength, the longest nail possible is used.

REMOVING NAILS

Before attempting to remove a nail with a large, embedded head, try to break the "bind" of the nail against the sides of the hole. To do this, hold a spike with the point sawed off, or other blunt tool, against the head and strike the spike one sharp blow with the hammer. This may not loosen the nail, but it is worth a try.

If the nail is situated where it can be raised by pounding the underside of the board, place a 6-inch block of wood as nearly as possible under the nail and pound this block with a hammer. If this action raises the nail head, place a thin metal plate under the inverted, curved crown of a claw hammer to protect the work and draw the nail upward with the claws. As the nail is withdrawn, substitute a block of wood for the thin metal plate under the hammer head. This block will elevate the hammer head, providing a fulcrum and giving greater leverage. Now the claws can exert almost perpendicular pull and may extract the nail completely.

If the nail to be withdrawn is holding together two pieces of wood, and a sharp hammer blow to the head fails to raise it, insert a hacksaw blade (removed from the frame) between the two pieces of wood; saw the nail through: and punch it out from the underside of the top board with a nail set. The piece of shank remaining in the bottom board may be unscrewed by holding it between the jaws of diagonal cutting pliers. Take care to protect the work from the scrape of the pliers with a piece of metal.

These same diagonal cutting pliers (sometimes called "side cutters") are very useful for nail extraction. First, the jaw points are forced under the stubborn nail head. Then a downward push is exerted on the pliers. Because the jaws of this tool are set at a slight angle from the handles, pushing downward will exert leverage which will prize the nail straight up. As the nail rises, a lower grip on the nail shaft is taken by the plier jaws, downward pressure is exerted, and the nail is raised a little more until it has been completely withdrawn.

SCREWS

Wood screws have greater holding power than do nails, with the added advantage of being more easily removable; therefore, they are excellent for making objects which may later need to be dismantled for storage or for shipping purposes. There are three basic types of wood screws, readily differentiated by the shapes of

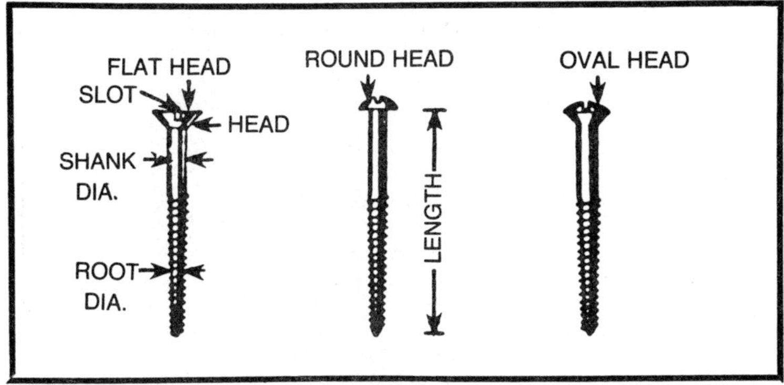

Fig. 4-3. Three basic types of woods screws.

the heads: the flat head, the rounded head, and the oval head (Fig. 4-3). Each of these three types comes in a variety of lengths and sockets (Fig. 4-4), each requiring a different screwdriver to install it. The various nail sockets available are called the Slotted, the Phillips, the Robertson and the Posidriv. The Robertson (which has a square, recessed anchor hole with crisscrossed slot lines centered in the screw head) and the Posidriv (which has crisscrossed slotting with a round recess where the two slots cross) are both gaining in popularity with woodworkers. Each holds the blade of the screwdriver securely in the anchor hole, preventing it from scoring the wood.

Screws come with two styles of threading: the conventional and the twinfast. The latter threading was developed for softwoods and new man-made wood products—low-density chipboard, blockboard and fiberboard This twinfast threading spirals up the shaft almost to the head, leaving just enough released shank to eliminate wedge action and minimize splitting. Its two-start thread bores into the hole with greater speed than does the conventional thread because it buries two thread pitches at each turning.

Screws come in a variety of metals—steel, brass, silicon bronze and aluminum alloy. Finishes include zinc, nickel, chrome and brass plate, bronze and antique copper. As much as possible, screws

Fig. 4-4. The four types of screw-head sockets available in flat, round and oval-head screws.

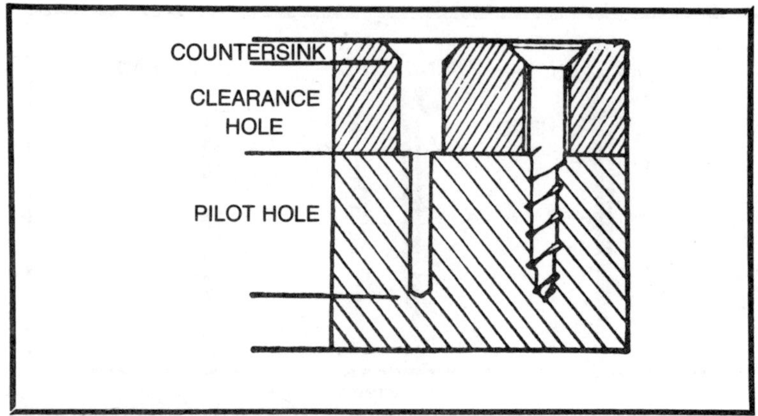

Fig. 4-5. Countersinking wood screws.

should match the metal and blend with the wood they fasten. Brass screws are not as strong as other screws, but they are less likely to corrode; therefore, they are often employed in oak which has a high acid content. Silicon bronze screws are used for marine application. Stainless steel screws are very popular because they have the best resistance to corrosion.

APPLYING SCREWS

Screws, because of their fluted shanks, cannot be set in either softwoods or hardwoods unless pilot holes are first drilled to accept the shanks. Most commercial charts suggest that the pilot holes drilled in hardwood be approximately 1/16-inch larger than those drilled in softwood. Regardless of the wood density, however, the drill selected to make the pilot hole should be just larger in diameter than the screw shank which will fill it.

In determining the position of the screw, always use a center punch to mark the insertion spot for the drill hole. The punch will leave a slight depression which will serve to anchor the rounded drill bit and prevent it from wandering.

Countersinking is a method of application used for both screws and nails. In the case of screws, countersinking is necessary only when working in hardwoods; no countersink is required in softwoods where the pilot hole, which is always drilled to take the screw, is sufficient to ease the screw's insertion. However, if—once the pilot hole has been drilled—the threading on the core of the screw balks at going in smoothly, greasing the shank with soap or vaseline will greatly facilitate insertion and will not impair the screw's holding power.

Both screws and flat-headed nails require countersinking into hardwoods or where they are being used to fasten two pieces of wood in a joint (see Fig. 4-5). First, a pilot hole is drilled completely through the *surface* board and at least halfway through the board beneath, using a drill bit slightly *larger* than the shaft if a screw is to be used and slightly *smaller* than the shaft if a nail is to be used.

When a flat-headed screw is employed, the pilot hole must be made larger at the top to accommodate the head of the screw. Using an 82-degree countersink drill bit, the pilot hole is counterboard to half its depth, and the screw head is sunk below the surface. To mask the screw head and fill the depression its countersinking has made, a wood plug is set above the screw head (Fig. 4-6). This plug should be of the same wood as the surface wood and the grains should match.

Nails are countersunk in exactly the same manner as are screws, except that the nail head is countersunk only until it is flush with the wood surface. Then a nail set and hammer are used to drive the nail head below the surface of the work. Because nail heads are not so conspicuously large as are screw heads, the depressions they leave in the surface when they are set below it are filled with shellac stick if the wood is to be stained, or with wood dough or wood putty if the work is to be painted.

Table 4-2 shows the diameter of the clearance hole and of the pilot hole which should be drilled in hardwood for countersinking various gauges of screws.

Wood screws vary in length from ¼-inch to 6 inches and in gauge sizes from 0 to 24. A wood screw gauge is useful in measuring the diameter of the shank just below the head. Wood screws are sold singly, by the dozen or by the gross . A box marked "'1' Gross. 1½, No. 8, F.H.B. screws" would contain 144 screws, each 1½-inch long with gauge 8 shanks and flat heads in bright steel.

The following is a handy reference table showing the various lengths in which wood screws are manufactured and their corresponding gauge size designations in both steel and brass. For example: Screws 1-inch long are made in steel from gauges sized 3 to 16, inclusive, and in brass from gauges sized 4 to 14, inclusive.

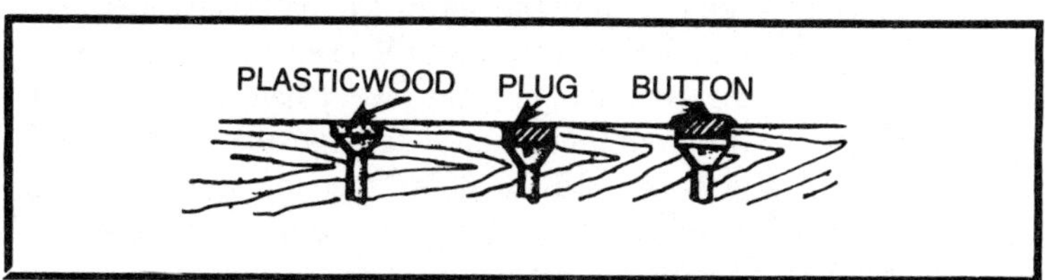

Fig. 4-6. Various types of plugs used over counterbored screws.

Table 4-2. Countersinking Screws in Hardwoods—Sizes of Screws and Drill Bits to Use.

Countersinking screws in hardwoods—sized or Screws and drill Bits to Use.			
Screw Number	Diameter of Screw Shaft	Size Drill For Pilot or Anchor Hole	Size Drill For Clearnace or Countersunk Hole
	Inch	Inch	Inch
0	1/16	1/32	1/16
1	5/64	1/32	3/32
2	3/32	1/32	3/32
3	7/64	1/16	⅛
4	⅛	1/16	⅛
5	⅛	1/16	⅛
6	9/64	3/32	5/32
7	5/32	3/32	5/32
8	11/64	3/32	3/16
9	3/16	3/32	3/16
10	13/64	⅛	7/32
11	13/64	⅛	7/32
12	7/32	⅛	7/32
14	¼	⅛	¼
16	9/32	5/32	5/16
18	5/16	3/16	5/16
20	21/64	3/16	⅜
24	⅜	7/32	⅜
Note: Should the pilot hole size be desired for softwoods, use a size smaller drill bit than that designated in this table. For example: for a No. 10 screw, use a 3/32-inch drill in place of a ⅛-inch drill.			

REMOVING SCREWS

Screws can be very difficult to remove, particularly if they have rusted in the hole or are very deeply buried. A few drops of kerosene applied to the screw head and allowed to soak into the wood will loosen a rusted shaft, but it will darken the wood (particularly if it is softwood). Therefore, unless the wood is to be finished with a dark stain or paint, the kerosene should be avoided.

Methods for extracting screws are as follows:

1. Select a screwdriver with a blade as wide as the slot to prevent damaging the slot and complicating the task.
2. If a hand-turned screwdriver will not budge the nail, use a brace with a screwdriver bit. Press down firmly on the brace to keep the bit in the screw slot and give the sweep handle a counter-clockwise turn to loosen the screw. If the screw refuses to move, give the sweep handle a quick turn clockwise, then another counter-clockwise, repeating until the screw is loosened in the hole. Once the screw is loose, it can be removed with a hand-operated screwdriver.
3. If the above methods will not start the screw, try jarring it loose by pounding sharply on its head. First, place a

screwdriver in the head slot, then strike the handle of the screwdriver a sound blow. Now attempt unscrewing with a hand screwdriver. If this fails, try the brace with the screwdriver bit.

4. A round-headed screw with a damaged slot poses a special problem. If the screw head is flush with the surface, the slot may often be widened and deepened with a hack saw blade removed from the frame. This repair to the screw head permits you to use the proper hand screwdriver, as suggested in Step One above, and to follow the procedure already described.
5. Flat-head screws with damaged slots are difficult to remove indeed, because the head is flush with, or buried below, the surface. Try the following suggestions in the order given:

Insert a nail set into the slot of the damaged screw at the extreme right end. Slanting the nail slot toward the board, but keeping its point firmly in the slot, strike it a good, firm blow with the hammer. Now try to turn the screw. If it fails to respond, strike it repeatedly with the hammer until it finally loosens or until the head is raised sufficiently to grip it with the jaws of the diagonal cutters. Held

Table 4-3. Wood Screw Lengths and Gauge Sizes.

	Made in Gauge Numbers: (Numbers Inclusive)	
Screw Lengths in Inches	Steel	Brass
1/4	0 to 4	0 to 4
3/8	0 to 8	0 to 6
1/2	1 to 10	1 to 8
5/8	2 to 12	2 to 10
3/4	2 to 14	2 to 12
7/8	3 to 14	4 to 12
1	3 to 16	4 to 14
1 1/4	4 to 18	6 to 14
1 1/2	4 to 20	6 to 14
1 3/4	6 to 20	8 to 14
2	6 to 20	8 to 18
2 1/4	6 to 20	10 to 18
2 1/2	6 to 20	10 to 18
2 3/4	8 to 20	None
3	8 to 24	12 to 18
3 1/2	10 to 24	12 to 18
4	12 to 24	None
4 1/2	14 to 24	None
5	14 to 24	None

fast by the cutters, it can generally be prized or unwound from the wood.

If this method proves ineffective, drill a shallow hole with a twist drill about half the diameter of the screw head through the center of the head. Select a screwdriver with a blade slightly wider than the drilled hole, and pound the blade into the hole, so that its greater width will create slots on both sides of the hole. With the screwdriver in the newly-made slot being pressed firmly down, turn the screw suddenly and decisively counter-clockwise. If greater leverage is needed use a monkey wrench on the flattened sides of the square screwdriver shaft and push the wrench as you would a brace while simultaneously exerting firm pressure on the screwdriver to keep it anchored in the screw slot.

Should both these methods prove ineffective, drill a deeper hole through the center of the screw head, deliberately severing the head from the shaft. Now the upper board can be lifted off the remaining screw stem and the severed screw head can be picked out of the upper board or pushed out from the underside with a nail set.

The remaining shaft of the screw is left protruding from the lower board. A pair of pliers can be used to unthread the shaft.

OTHER FASTENERS

In addition to nails and wood screws, many other types of hardware fasteners and assemblers are available in a variety of sizes and metals. Some of these are shown in Fig. 4-7.

Screw Eyes and Hooks

The eyes, in small sizes, are excellent for holding the hanging wire on picture and mirror frames or in forming a door or gate fastening when used with a hook-style catch. Screw hooks themselves are handy for holding suspended articles—cups in a cupboard, potted plants, the chains of hanging lamps, items on a wall rack, etc.

Plates

All shapes and sizes of metal plates are indispensible in reinforcing and repairing furniture. These reinforcements are particularly recommended for such projects as holding formerly warped boards in place, securing top pieces to frames, repairing loose joints or cracks, etc.

These metal plates come in several finishes. The galvanized finish is best to use when the plate reinforcement is to be hidden because it can be painted, if desired, and thus camouflaged. Plates made of brass are generally used where they must be exposed. All plates should be affixed with the length of nail which will not penetrate entirely through the wood to which the plate is fastened.

The following are the most common varieties of such reinforcement plates, with their common uses defined:

Corner Irons. These L-plates make reliable reinforcements for corners or places where a mitered joint has been used. Usually, they are applied to the underside of the work and thus hidden. However, the currently popular "captain's chest"—a present-day reproduction of the handsome, sturdy furniture used aboard sailing vessels in bygone times—features exposed ornamental corner brasses as part of its design.

Mending Plates. These plates (or "cleats," as they are sometimes called) are the perfect reinforcement to strengthen the glued jointure of two boards. Affixed to the underside across the jointure, they should be installed 12 to 24 inches apart for adequate strengthening.

T-plate. Where a vertical member meets a horizontal member in furniture design, a T-plate can be used to great advantage to strengthen the assembly.

Off-set Plates. This piece of hardware is designed to make blocked joints sturdier.

Supports

Desk Support. This type of supportive slide is almost always used in such furniture as the secretary-desk or breakfront, and in all other cabinetry where a shelf is pulled out to increase the surface space. This support slides out automatically when the extension is pulled out. The proper support of such extension shelves requires the application of two slides—one at each side—to prevent the extension shelf from tipping. The slides are always hidden under the shelf.

Lid Support. Furniture repair often calls for the installation of device to prop up and support the lids of chests, cabinets, desks or poudre tables so that when the top is lifted upward, it can be maintained in that almost vertical position without falling shut and splitting the wood or breaking the hinges. Such a lid support is installed inside the lid at one end; only one support is used. It is easy to install. The only problem is to keep it in alignment and be sure that it is properly adjusted.

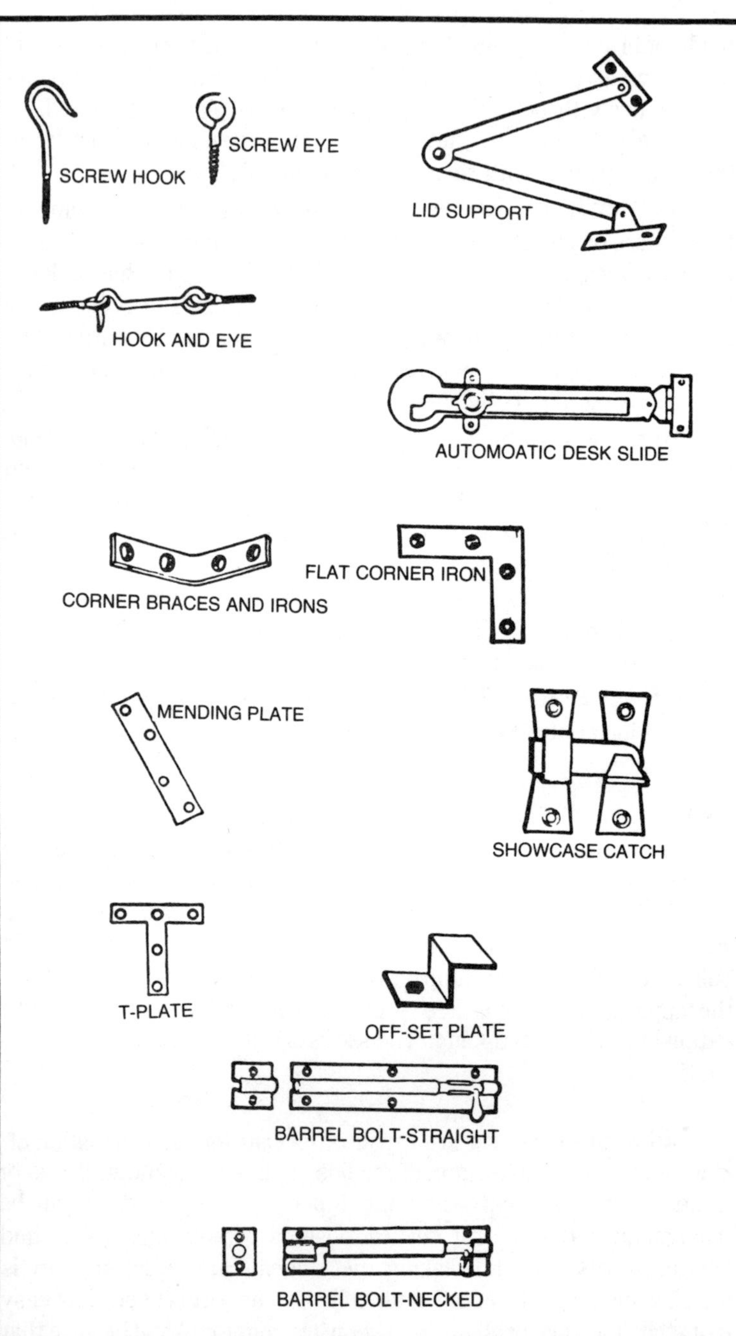

Fig. 4-7. Various types of hardware fasteners.

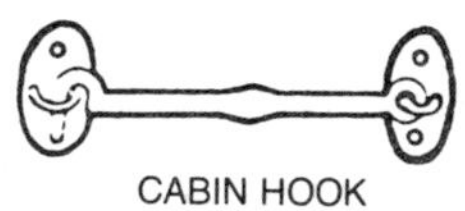
CABIN HOOK

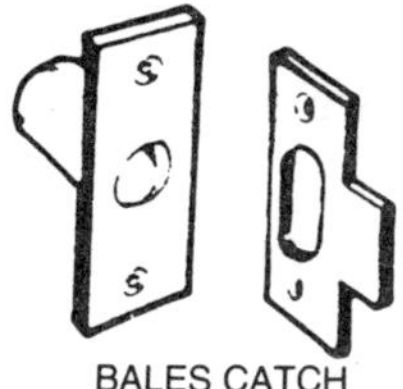
BALES CATCH

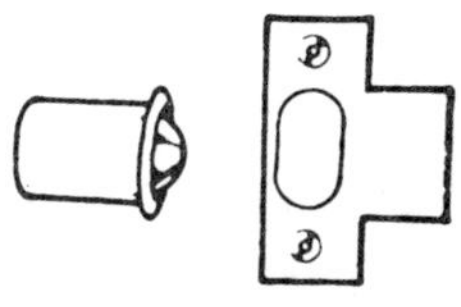
BALL CATCH

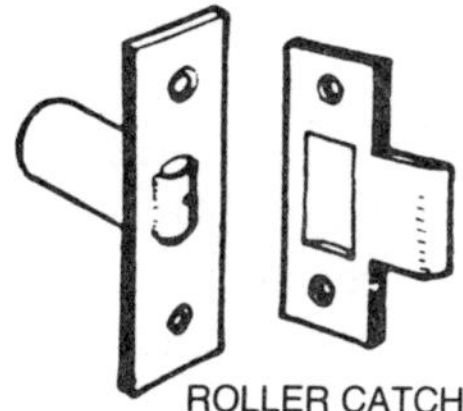
ROLLER CATCH

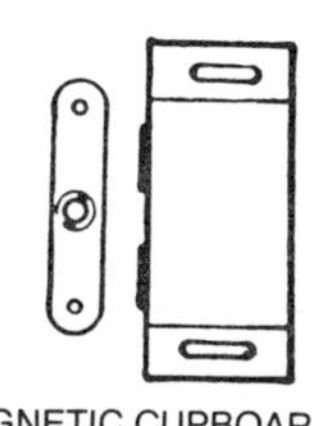
MAGNETIC CUPBOARD CATCH

CUPBOARD CATCH
SPRING AND WEDGE PATTERN

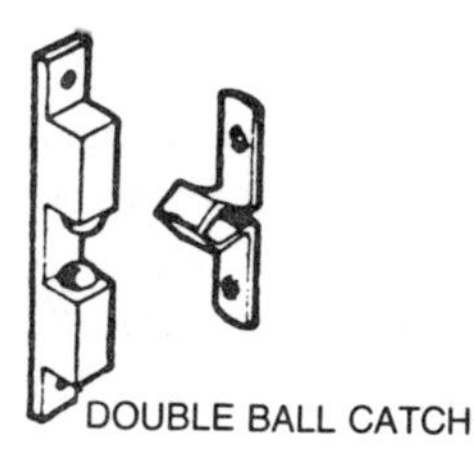
DOUBLE BALL CATCH

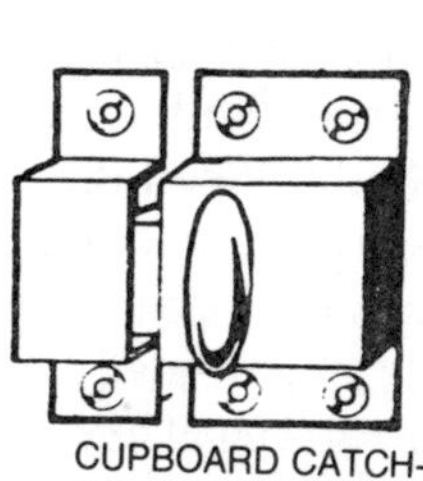
CUPBOARD CATCH-
OVAL KNOB PATTERN

Catches

Catches of all sorts are obtainable for cabinetry. The following are some of the most popular:

Draw Bolts. Among the ancient designs of drawer catches still in common usage is the draw bolt. It is widely available in both straight and bolt-necked styles. The cross-bar showcase latch is a variant of the bolt fastener.

Cabin Hooks. The hook-and-eye fastener is still widely used to fasten doors, gates, screen doors, shutters and louvered jalousies.

Spring Wedge Catch. This familiar catch secures a cupboard door by the tension between the metal wedge and the spring. The double ball catch is a smoother-functioning, more sophisticated version of the wedge fastener.

Bales Ball and Roller Catches. Each of these catches has a tongue which releases into a corresponding perforation in a plate inset into the door frame. These latches operate automatically—releasing when the door is pushed closed and retracting when the door is pulled open. On the other hand, *the oval knob cupboard catch* is designed on the same principle, but it demands a manual turning of the oval screw handle to engage or release the catch when closing or opening the door.

Magnetic Catches. These modern catches rely on the magnetic pull between the steel latch plate and the catch, which is studded with powerful magnets. These types of catches should never be used on antique furniture—the hardware for which should likewise be antique, if possible, or at least faithfully reproduced designs of the correct period.

Hinges

Butt Hinge. The hinge most frequently found on antique furniture is the butt hinge, with "fast" (permanent) pins through the knuckles rather than "loose" (removable) pins. With either kind of pin, these hinges are known as cabinet butts. When the flaps are shaped like the ornamental embossed hinge illustrated, the hinge is known as a "butterfly hinge." (Figure 4-8 shows a variety of hinges.)

The best quality butt hinge is made of extruded brass. The knuckles are solid and, consequently, very strong. They are always of an uneven number, generally five. For strongest assembly, the plate with three knuckles is fastened to the cabinet and the plate with two knuckles to the door. The pins in solid brass hinges are either

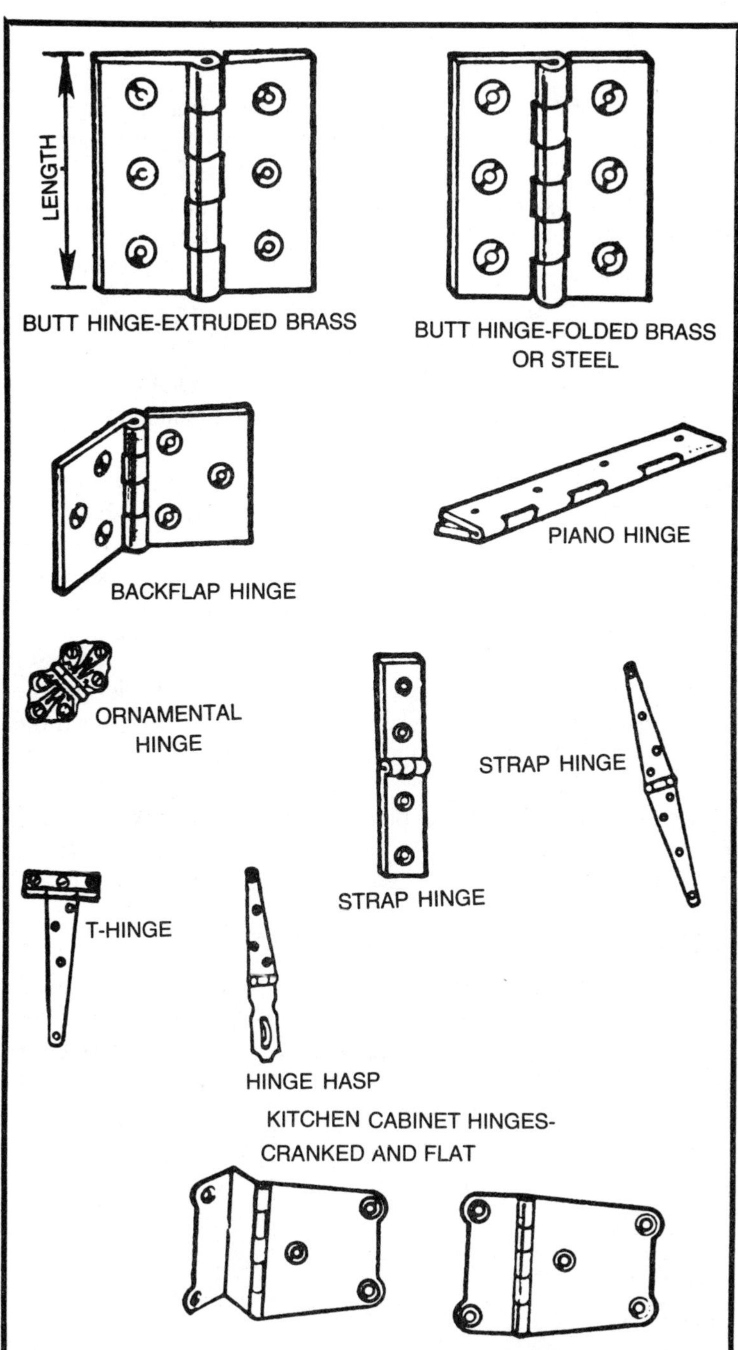

Fig. 4-8. A variety of hinges.

brass or steel and to mount such hinges, brass countersink screws are always used. These hinges are expensive, but their appearance and durability justify the cost.

The butt hinge is also available in folded brass. This hinge is less expensive, but not so strong, and can usually be distinguished from solid brass by the fact that it has an even number of knuckles.

Backflap Hinge. This hinge is designed for drop-leaf and gaming tables where panels are required to turn in wide arcs.

Piano Hinge. This is an extra long hinge designed for use on pianos and furniture pieces with similarily folding panels. The most common size is 36 inches.

Strap Hinges These hinges come in a vareity of styles, some highly ornamental, and are employed mainly on trunks, chests, etc. Strap hinges are made of natural brass with a steel pin. *The hasp hinge* is a variant of the strap hinge with a hole in one plate which fits over the keyhole of a lock or the eye of a padlock.

Kitchen Cabinet Hinges. These hinges have many uses besides that for which they are named. They are applied to the surface of a work and are available in two styles—the flat and the cranked—the latter being designed for a framed and rebated door.

Hinges come in a wide variety of metals and finishes—galvanized steel (for painted pieces), bright-finish and dull-finish brass, chromium plate, bronze, copper, nickel and dead black. Brass and dead black are the two recommended for antique restoration.

PULLS AND HANDLES

These necessary hardware items are available in such a wide variety of styles and finishes that their description would fill volumes. They vary from carefully reproduced classic period stylings to contemporary designs. The woodworker should have no difficulty in finding the exact hardware desired.

Chapter 5
Paint Brushes

A good brush is an absolute necessity for good work. Choose the best brush you can afford. When the bristles get old and begin to lose resilience, relegate the brush to those woodworking jobs which are less demanding—such as brushing on paint remover or paint filler. Conserve your best brushes for applying varnish, lacquer, shellac or enamel—all jobs where a poor brush can defeat your best efforts.

SELECTION

When buying a new brush, be selective. At first glance, one brush may appear to be almost identical to another; but, the actual differences are manifold and most important.

Some differences in brushes are readily apparent. Brushes differ in width, bristle length, shape of handle and type of bristles. The latter is the most important difference.

In days gone by, the most expensive brushes were made of natural hog bristles and were imported from China. Today, though natural bristle brushes are still obtainable, the stiffer ones are made of horse hair, rather than hog bristles, and the softer ones (which are best for varnish and shellac work) are made of goat, sable, badger and shunk hair, rather than fitch hair, as they once were.

However, nowadays the bristle which gets into more paint than any other—or than all other bristles combined—is one which is made of man-made nylon. Nylon paint brushes gained in popularity over natural-bristled brushes very slowly, but today even professional painters, refinishers and cabinetmakers endorse them. In appear-

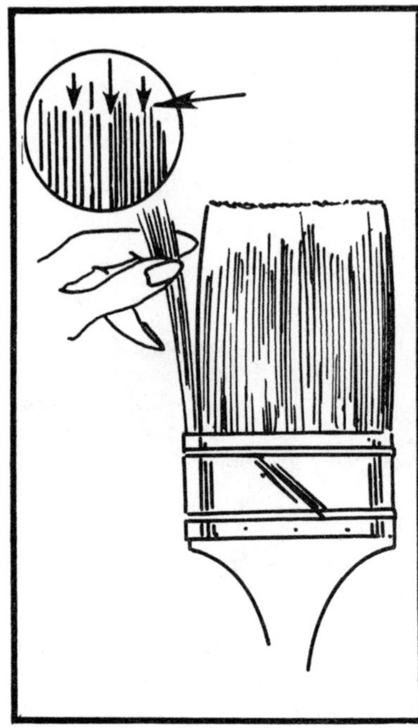

Fig. 5-1. Examining a paint brush for flatted tips—a good brush is well-endowed with these.

ance, nylon-bristled brushes look so like natural bristle brushes that only the label positively identifies them. More importantly, they perform just as satisfactorily in every way.

Whether you purchase nylon or natural bristled brushes, be sure to get enough bristles in the brush you buy. The bristle filling near the ferrule should be very compact and fully packed. Pinch the brush at this point to get a good indication of how generously bristled the brush actually is. Too much give indicates that the bristling is somewhat skimpy. A brush whose bristles are too sparse carries so little paint that the job takes twice as long. Nor will an insufficiently bristled brush apply a smooth finish.

Another important consideration is how carefully the bristles are tapered. A brush which has fully tapered bristles generally costs a little more, but the extra efficiency of such a brush is well worth the extra cost. A well-made brush will be tapered to a chisel edge so that most of the bristles touch the surface with every stroke. Sighting the bristled end while the brush is held in profile will quickly reveal this tapering, if it exists.

Also, the bristles should have bounce and resilience, and there are two ways of testing for this. The first is to touch the brush to the surface as though one were using it to apply paint. If the bristles fan out broadly and bend so pliantly that they appear almost broken at the center, the bristles are not springy enough. Another test for sufficient stiffness can be made by winnowing the bristles and separating them into small groups with your fingers. If the separated bristles do not act lively, resuming their place of their own accord, discard the brush and select a new one.

While you are separating the bristles to test their resilience, examine the ends for tiny splits or flags. Every good brush has a predominance of such split bristles. (See Fig. 5-1.) These hold the paint better and leave fewer brush marks than the blunt-cut bristles. One brush of the same brand may have many more split-end bristles than another; there is no fixed requirement for the number each brush must have. Just make sure that you choose one which is endowed with flagged-end bristles.

When you find a brush which meets all the foregoing requirements, and has as well a tightly secured ferrule and a handle which feels comfortable to the hand, buy it. The 2-inch sash brush and the 3-inch trim brush are the most practical sizes for most refinishing, although eventually you will want to acquire all sizes of brushes. (See Fig. 5-2.) Generally speaking, it is wisest to buy the widest brush which you can handle easily on the particular surface you are painting. It will finish the job quickly and will apply the paint with fewer stroke marks and streaks. Narrower brushes are reserved for narrow moldings, stripings, etc., where you would have to use a wider brush sidewise (a practice which is never recommended because it can damage the bristles of an expensive brush).

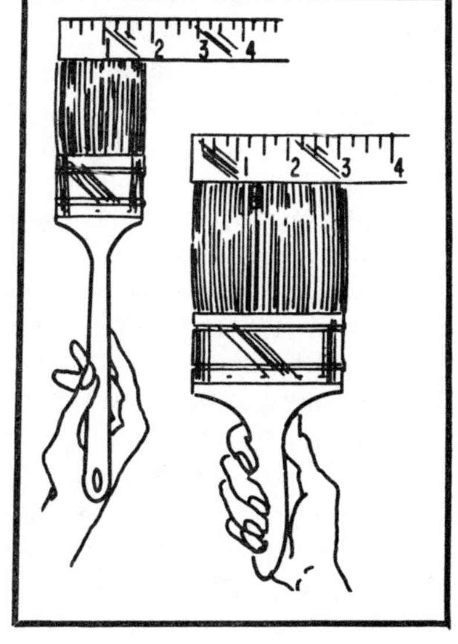

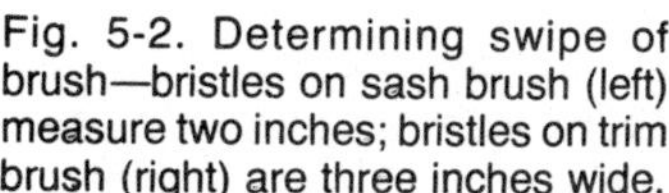
Fig. 5-2. Determining swipe of brush—bristles on sash brush (left) measure two inches; bristles on trim brush (right) are three inches wide.

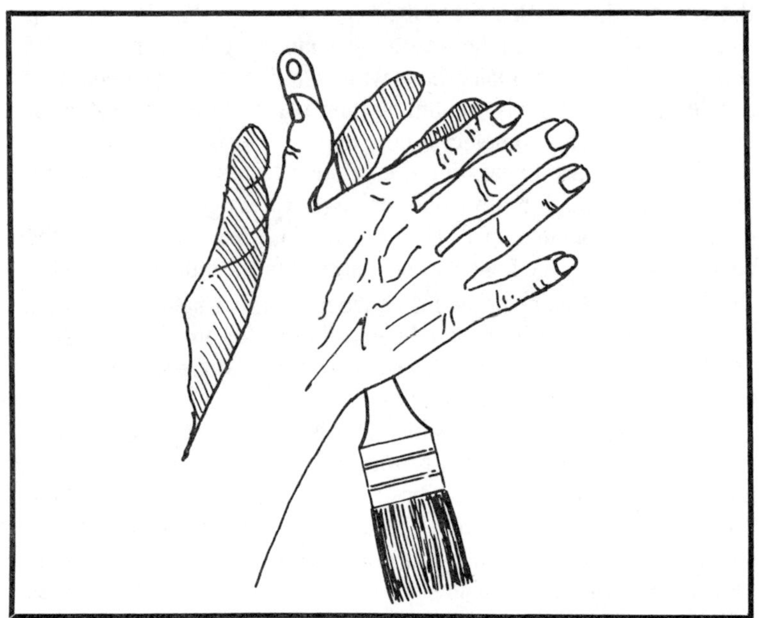

Fig. 5-3. Twirling the brush between the palms causes dust and loose bristles to fall out.

PREPARING A NEW BRUSH FOR PAINTING

Before using a new brush, stroke the brush across your fingers repeatedly to remove grit, dust and loose bristles. Then, holding the handle between the palms of both hands, twirl the brush rapidly and vigorously to spin out any loose dust or grit remaining (Fig. 5-3).

Some finishers soak a new brush overnight in linseed oil to condition it. However, brushes with synthetic bristles or those which are going to be used to apply shellac or lacquer should never be pre-treated with linseed oil. A good shampoo in warm, soapy water, followed by a thorough rinse and a combing to smooth the bristles, is all that is needed.

Brushes pre-treated with linseed oil must be flushed of all unabsorbed oil before using. This is accomplished by placing the brush on clean paper toweling on a flat surface and pressing out the oil with a piece of dowel. When most of the oil has been squeezed from the bristles in this manner, pull the brush through two dowels held tightly together—much as you might pull clothes through the rollers of a wringer—to press out every bit, then twirl the brush between your palms to shake off remaining drops. Submerge the bristles in turpentine for at least five minutes and comb them carefully with a hair comb. Test the brush for freedom from oil by dipping it in the paint you are going to use and making a few trial strokes on a clean surface to see how well the brush paints.

HOW TO USE A PAINT BRUSH

A brush should be held just like a pencil is held—the relaxed finger grip being on the ferrule and the handle resting against the forefinger (see Fig. 5-4). Painting is a very easy, pleasurable task if one follows a few simple rules. The brush should never be dipped further into the paint than one-third the depth of the bristles. Dipping the brush deeper only loads the working heel of the bristles with paint which will be hard to remove and may finally destroy the brush's working ability. The paint-freighted bristles should then be tapped against the inside of the can, not stroked over the rim, to remove excess paint before applying.

Since most paint cans come filled to the brim, with no room inside the can for stroking the excess off the brush, you may want to

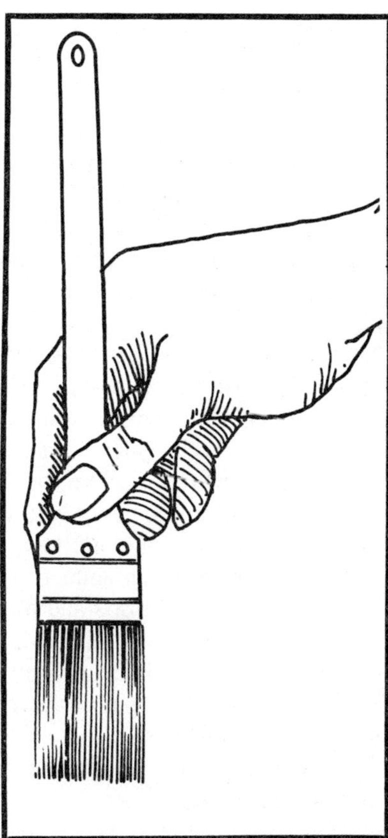

Fig. 5-4. The correct way to hold a paint brush—note how the handle of the brush rests against the forefinger, as would a pencil.

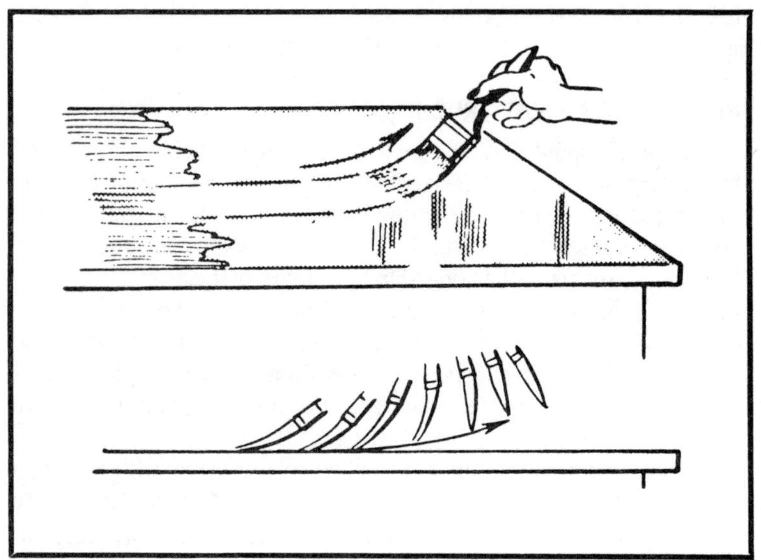

Fig. 5-5. The proper way to feather strokes is by lifting the brush gradually at the end of each stroke.

pour the paint out of the can into a larger disposable can or bucket (an old coffee can is ideal), saving the original paint can to store the unused paint in when the job is finished.

Apply the paint with a moderate amount of pressure, not as though you are pushing or scrubbing it in. Always paint from the dry, unpainted surface toward you into the surface already wet with paint. Lift the brush gradually as it comes to the end of the stroke and "feather" the painted surface, blending the brush marks into the still-wet paint (see Fig. 5-5).

Paint on a horizontal surface wherever possible. This prevents the paint from both running or sagging, and from loading the heel of the brush. However, when you are painting built-in furniture, or furniture too heavy to move, you will have to apply paint to perpendicular surfaces. Stroke on the paint vertically, from the bottom to the top. Then, with an almost dry brush, cross-brush the stroke lightly to discourage drips and obtain a smooth, overall coverage.

Carvings or elaborately sculptured moldings require an almost dry brush, also. A light application of paint on these places will prevent the paint from puddling in the crevices and obscuring the fine details of the carving.

Although you may often be tempted to do so, never stir the paint with a brush. Obtain a stirring stick from the paint store when you buy the paint and use this disposable stirrer instead.

Fig. 5-6. Method of temporarily storing paint brush by suspending it in container of solvent—bristles must not touch the bottom.

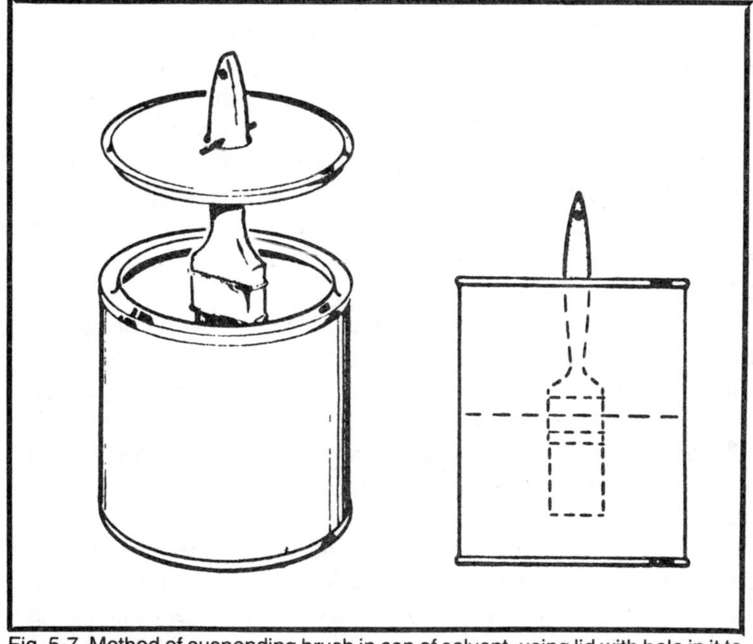

Fig. 5-7. Method of suspending brush in can of solvent, using lid with hole in it to keep brush upright—note wire through hole in handle which anchors brush in vertical position.

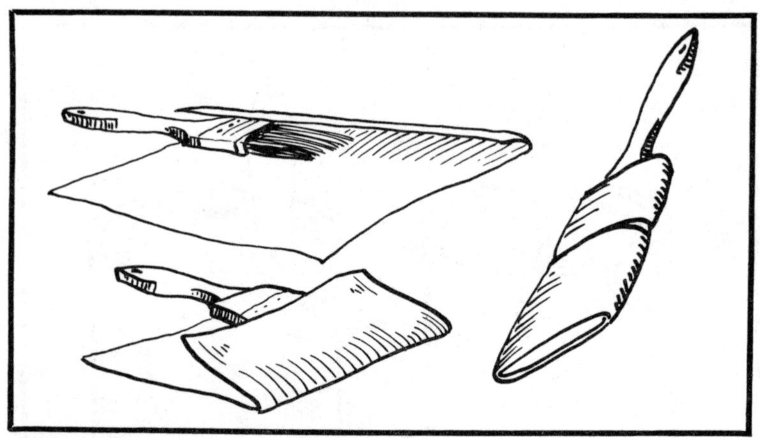

Fig. 5-8. When the job is finished, or suspended for more than several hours, brushes should be cleaned immediately and stored by wrapping in aluminum foil.

When you abandon the job for a few moments, be sure to suspend the brush on a wire threaded through the hole in the handle and suspended between two slots cut in the rim of a tall coffee or fruit juice can. The brush should dangle from the wire, suspended over the bottom of the can, so that its weight will not rest on the flagged bristles and destroy them (see Fig. 5-6).

If you are knocking off work for an hour or more, suspend the brush in a can of solvent. Be sure that there is enough solvent in the can to completely cover the bristles and part of the ferrule, so that the brush will be soaking clean as it hangs. To keep the brush from slumping down into the solvent and damaging the bristles, make a hole in the can lid. Insert the handle of the brush through this hole and secure it in an upright position by inserting a wire through the hole in the handle above the lid, as shown in Fig. 5-7.

CLEAN-UP

When you complete the job, you should clean the brush immediately. If varnish was the finish applied, you should use mineral spirits or turpentine. (The former is much cheaper and just as effective for this job as is the latter.) If shellac was used, the brush will clean-up easily in warm water and ammonia or by soaking it in alcohol. Lacquer thinner will effectively clean a lacquer-coated brush.

When a soak in the proper solvent has stripped the bristles clean, a wash in warm water and mild detergent is advisable. Rinse the brush well and hang it to dry. Then comb the bristles and wrap the brush for storage in aluminum foil. See Fig. 5-8 for the best method of wrapping a brush to keep all the air out.

Chapter 6
Abrasives

In woodworking, abrasives are a very vital aid to the finishing process. Choosing the proper abrasive for each job, and using it correctly, can mean the difference between a fine, professional finish on the work, and a poor, amateurish one. Because abrasives leave particles in the wood grain which will dull a sharp-edged tool, they should be used only after all the cutting has been done.

In preparing *nude* lumber for a flawless finish, it should be cleaned up first with a finely set smoothing plane (which will remove all tears better than long-term abrasion will) and with a scraper plane to handle the more difficult cross-grain smoothing. The resultant cut surface will be sheer; but it will have sparkle and crisper grain markings under transparent stain and varnish than an abrased surface, whose fibers have been scrubbed back and forth, will have!

However the refinishing process undertaken on wood which has been already finished demands sensitive sanding, particularly if the furniture being refinished is a valuable antique. Moreover, it is important to know which type of abrasive will do the best job best and most efficiently.

Abrasives rid the wood of any marks left by tools or by careless usage, as well as of natural wood blemishes, thus enabling the wood surfaces to reveal their full beauty under transparent, reflective finishes.

Of the many abrasives which have been mined and developed for modern-day usage, none of them are sand. Although "sanding" is still the term most commonly used to describe the smoothing process, so many superior abrasives have been discovered since sand was generally used that the term is now a misnomer.

SELECTION

Abrasive come in three basic forms: (1) bonded with glue to sheets of paper, (2) bonded with glue to canvas cloth, (3) or powdered. The principal abrasives in wide use today are flint, garnet, aluminum oxide, silicon carbide, emery, pumice and rottenstone.

Flint (or glass, as it is sometimes called) is made of crushed white Canadian quartz in grit sizes ranging from very fine to very coarse. It is the softest of all popular abrasives and is ideal for sanding exterior surfaces.

Garnet is a reddish-brown, semi-precious mineral found in Canada. It is medium hard, has a good cutting property and is more durable than flint, outlasting it five to one. Garnet papers are available in more grit sizes than flint-ranging from 3½ through 8/0, which is extremely fine. This abrasive is widely used in cabinetwork for smoothing, finishing and polishing wood surfaces.

Aluminum Oxide is a gray-brown abrasive which is extremely long-lasting and tough—the most wear-resistant of all abrasives. Close to a diamond in hardness, this abrasive can smooth metals and very hard woods. It will outlast flint ten to one and is often used on the belts and discs of machine sanders.

Silicon Carbide is black in color and very brittle, breaking into sharp slivers. It is used wet or dry on paints, lacquers, varnishes and synthetic coatings. Commonly called "carborundum," this abrasive is used in place of garnet papers by many cabinetmakers.

Emery is a dull black, mined material glued to cloth backing. The cutting edges of emery break down under pressure, so it is usually mixed with harder abrasives before being bonded to the backing. It is useful for smoothing turned posts, spindles and legs and in sanding carving. Because of its cloth backing, it is more pliant and flexible than many papers.

On paper backing, two densities of abrasive coating are available: close-coat (or close grain) papers, and open-coat (or grain) papers.

Close-coat abrasive papers are covered edge-to-edge with abrasive particles for greatest possible cutting action.

Open-Coat papers have abrasives less densely distributed, covering only 50 percent to 70 percent of the paper. These sheets do not clog as quickly with sawdust and are, therefore, more efficient and longer-lasting when smoothing resinous woods. Also, they are more pliable for use on carvings, turnings, etc.

Wet-and-dry papers, as the term implies, may be used dry, as other abrasives are, or may be soaked in water and used wet. The backing of these papers is waterproofed to withstand soaking. Only the finest grades of abrasives are so backed, because these papers are designed for final the sanding in finishing and for delicate sanding of all sorts. Dampened with water, gasoline or oil to raise the "whiskers" on the wood, they are used to give wood surfaces their final painstaking rub-down.

The papers and cloth backing on abrasives come in a choice of grades and weights. The "A" weight is a soft, pliable grade of paper used where flexibility is necessary; "C" and "D" weights are thicker, more wear resistant and designed to perform the more severe sanding jobs; "E" weight is the heaviest backing paper used and is primarily designed for machine sanding.

Some manufacturers tint the paper backing in different colors to distinguish the weight of the backing.

The cloth which backs abrasives comes in a choice of two grades, as follows:

Lightweight cloth, symbolized by the letter "J", is used for backing emery cloth and other finishing and polishing cloths.

Heavyweight cloth, marked "X", is used with power tools.

Lightweight papers and canvas are coated with fine abrasive grains, whereas heavyweight papers and canvas are coated with coarse grit abrasives.

The grit number given an abrasive paper is used to describe the density of abrasive grain on the working surface of the paper or canvas. This grit number refers to the actual number of openings per linear inch in a standard measuring screen such as those used by all manufacturers. For instance, "100 grit sandpaper" compares to an industrial screen having 100 grit openings per inch. The coarsest grit is the number 12; the finest, 600.

The grit number of an abrasive is sometimes symbolized by a grade number which indicates whether the abrasive is very fine, fine, medium, coarse or very coarse. The reverse sides of paper and cloth backings are usually printed with these designations: the "grit" or density of the abrasive coating, the grade symbol for the grit, the type of abrasive used and the weight of the paper or cloth backing. Usually, the information "wet-or-dry" or "waterproof" is also given (see Fig. 6-1). Here is an actual example of one such designation: *3/0–120 A*. Decoded, this designation means that a medium-grade abrasive with 120 grits, symbolized by the grade number 3/0, has been glued to A-grade (thinnest) paper. This designation does not reveal what abrasive was used, but usually the color of the abrasive

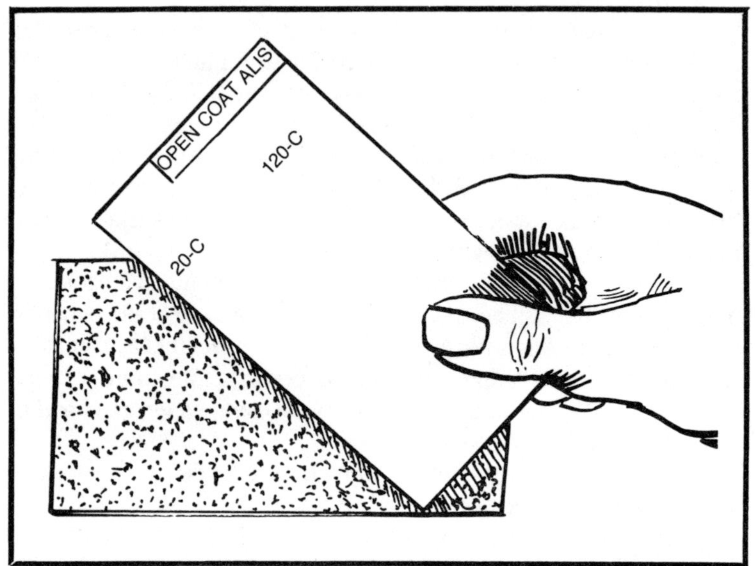

Fig. 6-1. Sandpaper identification.

will provide some clue. Although this designation describes one type of "finishing paper" (finishing paper being fine or extrafine grit abrasive on lightweight backing), it may not be marked as such on the back.

Granules of abrasive are applied to the backing by one of two methods. The first is electrocoating which embeds the particles evenly over the bonded backing surface with the sharpest edges impelled to stand on end, points upward. The second is the overhead hopper method in which the law of gravity distributes the sprinkled abrasive evenly over the glued surface. This last method coats the working side of the paper uniformly; but the roughest edges of the abrasive particles fall haphazardly and are not always uppermost, so they tend to wear more quickly and unevenly.

Abrasive papers are purchased in sheets from paint and hardware stores and are more economical when purchased in quantity than when purchased singly. The woodworker is wise to keep a good supply of the most commonly used grades on hand, since more than one grade is usually needed for a project and the papers wear out quickly. Nine inch × 11 inch sheets are the most practical size to purchase. These sheets may be folded into six even sections by creasing the backing paper and folding the abrasive surface to the inside. Once creased, they tear easily along a straight edge into sections which can be individually affixed to sanding blocks (Fig. 6-2).

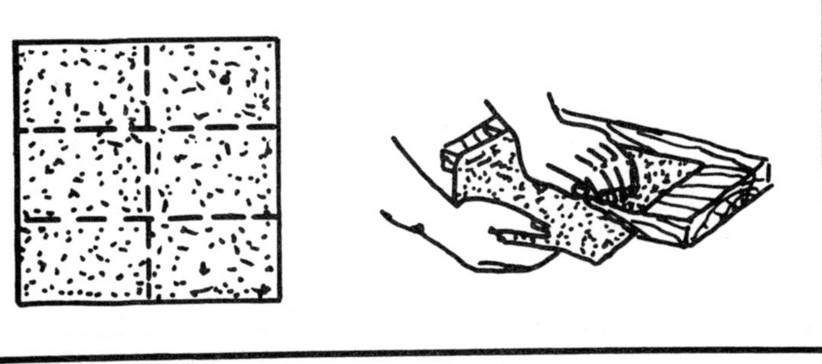

Fig. 6-2. How to tear abrasive sheets into more manageable pieces: 1. Fold the abrasive to the inside to obtain a straight crease; 2. tear the abrasive paper along a straight edge.

USE

Every woodworker needs a number of sanding blocks in various shapes and sizes, not only to reach every area of the work, but to rest his hand by a change of grip. We will discuss the skiwaxing cork, which makes such an excellent sander, in Appendix A. Now consider these other styles—each of which has special features:

Table 6-1. Comparison of Sanding Abrasive Grades.

COARSENESS EVALUATION	GRIT	GRADE	USAGE
	600	—	
	500	—	
Very fine	400	10/0	
	360	9/0	
	320	—	Polishing and finishing
	280	8/0	
	240	7/0	
	220	6/0	
	180	5/0	
Fine	150	4/0	
	120	3/0	Finishing
	100	2/0	
	80	0 or 1/0	
Medium	60	½	Cabinet
	50	1	
	40	1½	
Coarse	36	2	Rough Sanding
	30	2½	
	24	3	
Very coarse	20	3½	Coarse Sanding

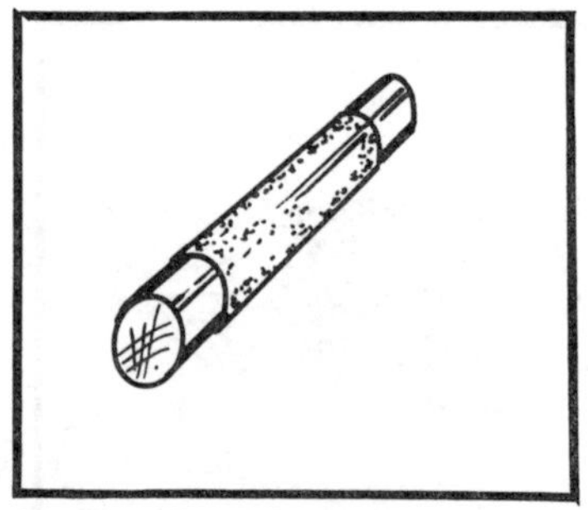

Fig. 6-3. Slotted wood cylinder for sanding irregular shapes.

Fig. 6-4. Molded rubber sanding block.

Cylindrical sanders—sloted segments of old broom handles wrapped with cement-on felt and then with disposable pieces of abrasive paper, the ends threaded into a slot in the wooden cylinder to help them stay smooth on the dowel and perform an efficient sanding job on curved openings, carvings and turned posts (Fig. 6-3).

Arched rubber sander—a molded rubber sanding block, slotted at both ends to hold the adhesive paper securely and arched to fit the arch of the woodworker's palm, which spells the muscles of the hand on lengthy sanding jobs (Fig. 6-4).

Wooden block sander shoed with metal plate—This rectangular wooden block sander is attached by a turnscrew to a metal plate, the bottom of which is padded by felt or cork. The efficient, practical design allows for speedy replacement of worn sandpaper. When the turnscrew is loosened, the metal bottom plate comes loose from the wooden block. A fresh piece of adhesive paper can be wrapped around the padded bottom and over the edges of the metal plate on both sides, the ends of the sandpaper being held securely by the bite between the metal plate and the wooden block when the turnscrew is tightened. When the felt or cork padding wears away, a new piece can be cemented on and the sander becomes as good as new (Fig. 6-5).

Block sander—a rectangular block of waste softwood with felt or cork cemented to the underside and abrasive paper enveloping it. The paper edges secured by drafting tape and the woodworker's hand when it grips the block make an excellent two-handed sander for edges or narrow boards (Fig. 6-6).

Blackboard eraser—The type of chalk blackboard eraser commonly found in schoolrooms makes an excellent sander. As the abrasive paper wrapped around its padded felt bottom wears thin, the paper may be shifted to make full use of the entire piece.

Cardboard—for sanding curved surfaces and tight, awkward spots, the sandpaper is best manipulated by the woodworker's hand, the paper backing being further reinforced by a strip of cardboard to temper the pressure and wear.

Although abrasives are most commonly backed with either cloth or paper for use in woodworking, there are two powdered abrasives which are frequently used to smooth and finish furniture.

Pumice—a light, porous or spongy lava of various colors powdered in four different grades—the finest being 4/0, the coarsest 0. Mixed with oil or water, pumice is a time-honored abrasive for fine cabinet work.

Rottenstone—although classed as an abrasive this is actually a polishing agent. Rottenstone is finely powdered limestone containing silica. Although its abrasive qualities are negligible, it imparts a fine polish to wood. It should always be used mixed with rubbing oil, after the pumice-and-oil mixture has been applied to impart a fine sheen to the work. Rottenstone is available at paint stores and drugstores in one grade only.

In using both pumice and rottenstone, it should be remembered that rubbing with oil is slower than rubbing with water, but it leaves a higher luster. Oil may also tend to darken the lighter woods. When oil is used with any rubbing abrasive, the surface should be cleaned thoroughly with benzine before the next coat of varnish is applied.

Some of the abrasives helpful in furniture refinishing are not of the gritty variety. Steel wool for example, is a pad about the size of the palm of the hand of interfolded filament-fine steel strands—a more delicate version of the "Brillo" pad used in scouring pots—which is available in several grades, and which is unsurpassed as a sanding agent for either smooth or carved surfaces (See Fig. 6-7).

A number of commercial finishing compounds are available. One which is excellent for rubbing down finished surfaces is automobile compound. Originally formulated for metal surfaces, this is

Fig. 6-5. Metal-plate with felt or cork pad.

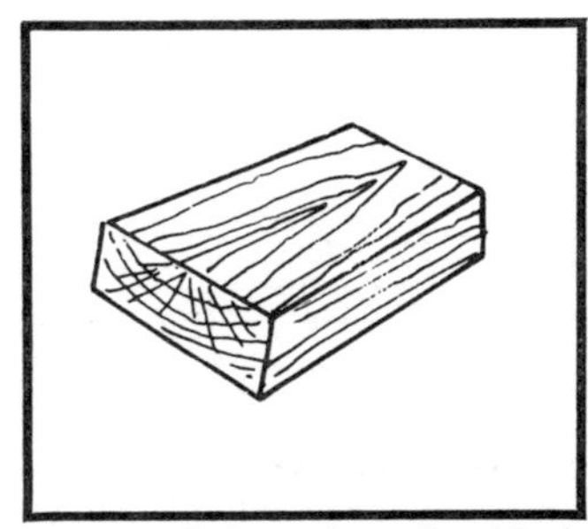

Fig. 6-6. Softwood sanding block.

Fig. 6-7. Sanding with steel wool pads.

a highly abrasive material and must be used with care. It is especially useful for sanding lacquers and enamels.

To obtain a glass-like smoothness on nude hardwood, sponging the surface with water and permitting it to dry will raise the ends of the wood fibers like so many wiry whiskers and make them easier to abrade away. Similarily, moisture is what makes pre-soaked wet-and-dry abrasives more effective at removing every last, almost-invisible splinter (Fig. 6-8).

CLEANING

Because abrasive papers are used constantly and in large quantity, they represent a fairly large expenditure in the woodworker's

Fig. 6-8. Using wet-and-dry abrasives with water for a smooth finish on hardwoods.

budget. Fortunately, there are many uses in every workshop for partly used abrasive papers. These may be cleaned of the sawdust and paint particles which clog the abrasive aide after usage. To renew them, clean them with the proper solvent for the type of residue clogging them and spread them out flat to dry. They may then be stored separately for future use.

For example, varnish-clogged papers may be cleaned with turpentine; papers used to smooth lacqured surfaces are renewed with lacquer thinner; shellac-coated papers are rendered reusable with alcohol. A small, stiff-bristled hand brush makes an excellent scrubbing tool.

Chapter 7 The Nature of Wood

Wood is a fibrous, organic vegetable material composed principally of two substances: cellulose and lignin. Natural wood is derived from trees, but not all trees produce timber. Those which do are called timber trees. The wood from these trees is of particular interest to cabinetmakers.

TREES

Trees consist of three principal parts: (1) the crown of leaves and branches, where the food of the tree is manufactured by the leaves from elements from the soil and air—the leaves must receive light and heat to produce this food; (2) the trunk with it's vascular system which transports the food elements to the leaves by way of the sap, and food to the branches, trunks and roots by way of the inner bark; (3) the root system which anchors the tree to the ground and absorbs water and minerals from the soil which the leaves use to make the tree's food (see Fig. 7-1).

The Tree Trunk

The cross section of a tree trunk contains a documented history of the tree. The various thicknesses of the annual rings indicate the changing climatic conditions during the lifetime of the tree. The number of annual rings is an indication of the age of the tree (see Fig. 7-2). The structure of the trunk is as follows:

Bark. The bark is a thick, rough textured tissue which acts as armour to shield the tree against bacteria, insects, injury and the

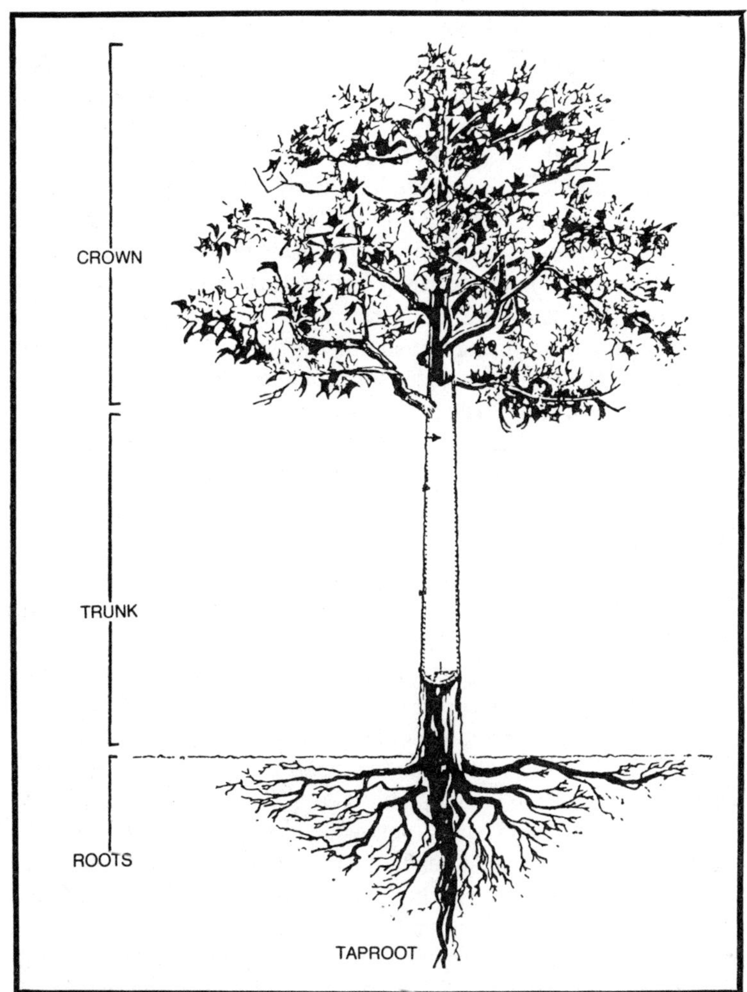

Fig. 7-1. Parts of a tree.

weather. Like the hide of an animal, it acts to insulate and protect the body of the tree. The inner back carries the food manufactured by the leaves to other parts of the tree.

Cambium Layer. The cambium layer is always growing, increasing the diameter of the trunk. It lies next to the inner bark and is constantly building new tissue within the tree.

Sapwood. The sapwood is a pale, soft porous layer which carries a great deal of sap—the moisture which causes the greatest shrinkage in lumber. This layer is prone to attack by beetles and fungi.

Heartwood. The heartwood is a layer rich in resins and harder than the other layers because it has been firmly compressed over the years. Heartwood is valued for its rich color, outstanding beauty and resistance to decay.

Pith. The pith is a soft center core, the oldest part of the tree.

Medullary Rays. The medullary rays are long cells growing radially from the pith center of the trunk. They cross and bind the annual rings. These rays are more noticeable in some woods than in others; in oak, for instance, they are particularly attractive.

Annual Rings. The annual rings are concentric formations of wood resulting from spring and summer growth. The rings of spring growth are light colored, wider, softer and more porous, reflecting the rapid growth of the tree after it's winter dormancy. The rings of summer growth are thinner and darker. By counting the annual rings, one can determine the age of the tree.

LUMBER

Commercially, lumber is divided into two main groups—hardwoods and softwoods. Within these two categories are open-grained and close-grained varieties.

Softwoods come from trees which produce cones and narrow, needle-like leaves which remain intact on the tree for several years. With certain unimportant exceptions, these trees are the evergreens. Most of the softwoods are used in building construction. Such woods as pines (chief among these, Scots pine), firs, cedars, spruce, hemlock, and red and yellow deal are widely used throughout the United States and Canada and throughout Europe for building construction. Most of the timber used in houses—the rafters, floorings, window frames and lathing—are of softwood. Softwoods, particularly spruce, are widely used for making paper pulp. Packing cases and crates are made of softwoods, which are strong and cheap. Commercially, softwoods are in far greater demand than are hardwoods; in fact, the trade in softwoods is about nine times greater than that in hardwoods although, comparatively, hardwoods are available in much greater variety.

Hardwoods are woods from "deciduous" trees, as trees with broad leaves are termed. The trees from which hardwoods come are grown in warmer climates than are softwood trees. Hardwoods are obtained from such trees as maple, birch, cherry, walnut teak and mahogany, to name but a few. Some hardwoods are close-grained; some are open-grained like ash, oak and hickory. Generally, hardwoods are more difficult to work with than softwoods—although this statement is somewhat misleading, since some hardwoods like

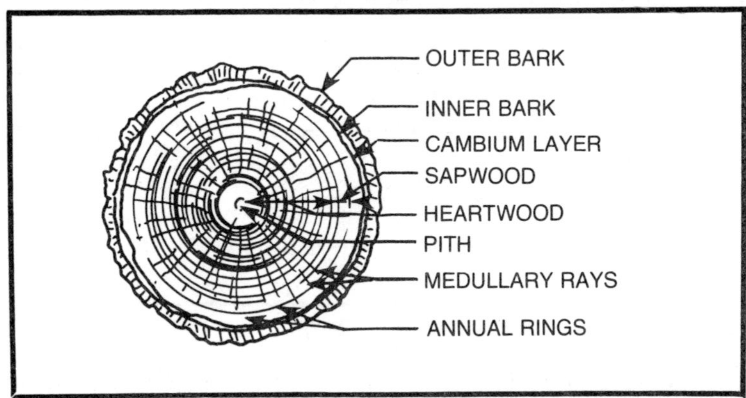

Fig. 7-2. Cross section of a log: outer bark shields the tree from injury and invasion by bacteria, insects, etc.; inner bark carries food manufactured by leaves to the branches, trunk and roots; cambium layer constantly grows in diameter, building outer bark tissue and inner wood tissue; sapwood carries sap from roots to leaves; heartwood is an inactive layer which imparts strength; the pith is the soft inner core of the tree trunk; the medullary rays are long radial cells growing from pith to bark; and the annual rings are formed by spring growth and summer growth forming one layer every year.

balsa are much "softer" to saw, nail and drill than some so-called softwoods like yew. However, hardwoods as a generic group possess greater durability, strength and hardness than do softwoods; they are less easily marred. Also, they display greater beauty of grain and are able to take a wide variety of finishes. Hardwoods, therefore, are used for better grade cabinetwork and fine paneling.

Conversion of Lumber

Conversion is the term used to describe the process of reducing a felled tree to lumber. Care must be taken in cutting a log into useful thicknesses of boards to obtain the greatest possible quantity of good quality lumber. The region of the tree from which the lumber is cut and the means by which it is seasoned are two of the factors which determine the grade of lumber obtained. Shrinkage is an important factor in quality lumber; because of the cell structure of wood, a board always shrinks more along its width than it does along its length. Also, a board which has been cut in part from the sapwood of a tree will have greater moisture in the sapwood portion than it has in the heartwood region. As it loses this moisture after cutting, shrinkage will take place in the sapwood areas of the board, causing the board to cup toward the bark (see Fig. 7-3). This fact must be considered when selecting this board assemblage with others in construction of a large surface.

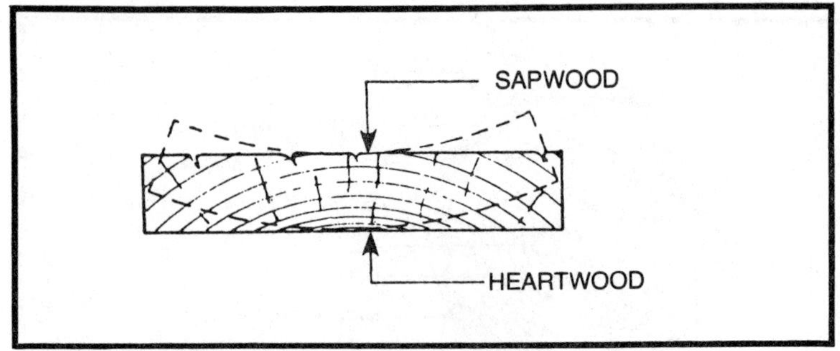

Fig. 7-3. Shrinkage in sapwood causes cupping.

Converting logs into lumber may be done in one of two ways: by plain cutting or by quarter cutting (see Fig. 7-4 A and B). Most softwoods are plain sawed. These plain cut boards are wider, have more color variation, and display a floral pattern in the graining; but, they are more likely to warp than quarter cut boards.

Most hardwoods are quarter sawed in a radial manner dictated by the medullary rays—a cut which produces spectacularly figured graining, but which is more wasteful than plain cutting since quarter cutting results in much narrower boards (see Fig. 7-5A). Radial quarter cutting requires more handling at the mill, but its straight-grained boards have less tendency to warp.

As the reader can see from Fig. 7-4A, some plain cut boards are sawed at a tangent to the annual rings rather than at right angles to them, as radially cut boards are sawed. The configuration of graining is different between one plain cut board and another, even though they are sawed from the same log. Tangentially sawed boards frequently have the moire-patterned graining configuration which so enhances any wood project, as is evident in Fig. 7-5A. Therefore,

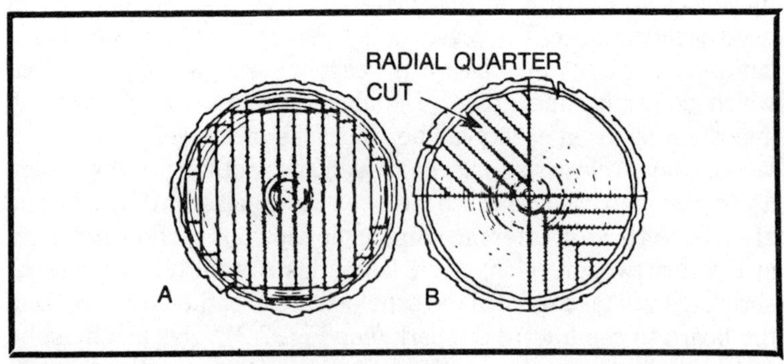

Fig. 7-4. Methods of sawing lumber: A) plain or slash cut; B) quarter cut, showing two methods—radial quarter cut and one more economical quarter cut.

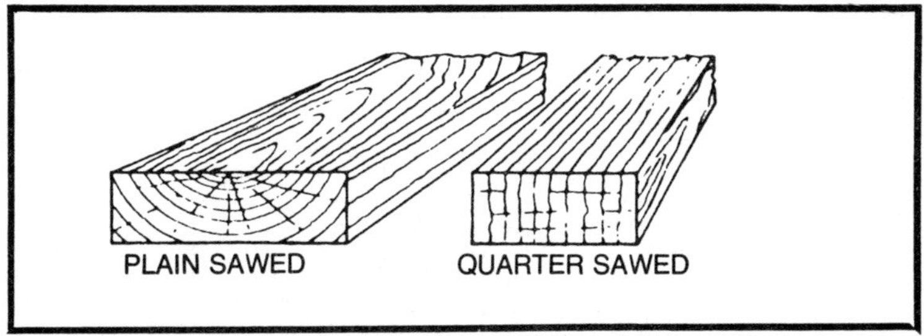

Fig. 7-5. Grain patterns on boards:plain sawed planks have a floral pattern and quarter sawed boards have a straight grain configuration.

the careful woodworker may want to examine the cut lumber to obtain exactly the configuration he desires, rather than simply ordering a job lot of lumber he has not first inspected.

Radial cutting of a log in the manner shown in Fig. 7-6A is the only method of conversion which will produce solely quarter sawed boards, but the reader will readily see how much waste lumber this method leaves. Consequently, alternate methods of quarter cutting are generally employed. Although these alternate methods, shown in Fig. 7-6B, produce random-sized boards rather than boards of matched size like those in Fig. 7-6A, they waste very little of the lumber. Boards cut in this more economical manner are not truly quarter cut, although they are so designated; but they are decoratively figured, very stable considering shrinkage and excellent for fine cabinetry.

Seasoning Lumber

Green lumber, when first cut from the log, contains a large proportion of water. This water content makes the lumber unfit for

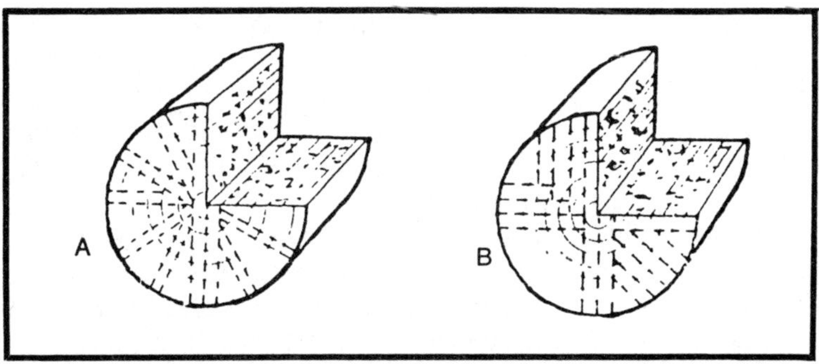

Fig. 7-6. Quarter sawing: (A) Illustrates the only method of conversion producing only quarter sawed boards of approximately the same size; (B) illustrates yet another less wasteful way of quarter sawing.

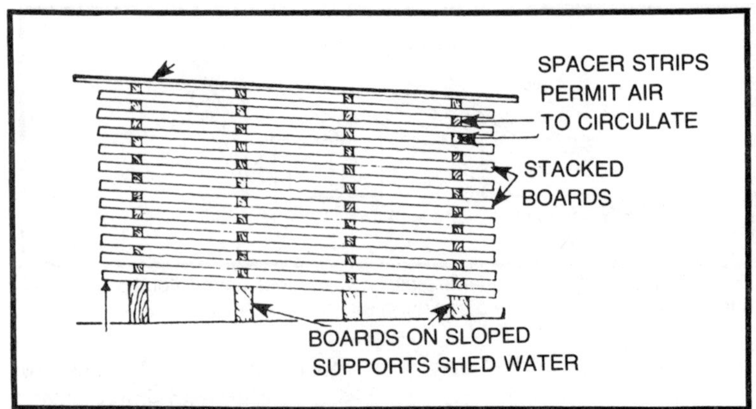

Fig. 7-7. Air-drying green lumber.

immediate commercial use. The lumber must first be dried out or "seasoned," as the drying out process is called. ("Curing" and "conditioning" are other terms used for this process.) Proper seasoning removes excess moisture and renders the lumber lighter to ship and handle, less likely to shrink and warp, much easier to plane and to paint or stain, and more resistant to fungi.

Seasoning is the exposure of freshly-sawed "green" lumber to specific conditions of temperature and relative humidity over a period of time to allow the sap to dry up and the lumber to acquire a moisture content consistent with these conditions. Seasoning is accomplished by one of two methods—by air drying and by kiln drying.

Air drying is the traditional method of seasoning lumber. The planks of wood are neatly stacked in the open air under shed roof, each plank separated from the next by strips of wood called "spacer strips" to allow the air to freely circulate (see Fig. 7-7). Care is taken to prevent the planks from drying out too rapidly. The roof of the drying shed protects them from the sun and a coating of paraffin or thick paint is given the plank ends to keep them from losing sap so rapidly that they crack. Using this seasoning method, a plank one inch thick takes a year to season, with every inch of additional thickness requiring another year.

Kiln drying is much faster. The control of heat and humidity possible in a kiln greatly speeds the seasoning process. Here, warm air and steam are circulated by fans to dry the green lumber which is stacked with spacer strips between each board in the same way as for air drying (see Fig. 7-8). Seasoning in the kiln takes about thirty days. Too rapid seasoning can result in loose knits, twisted timbers and a fuzzy grain which is difficult to plane.

Air-dried lumber is used in general construction work, whereas kiln-dried lumber is used for furniture, interior woodwork and trim, floors, and paneling.

MOISTURE IN WOOD

Wood will either absorb or give up moisture until the moisture content of the wood is in balance with that of the surrounding air. Seasoning in the kiln can extract all the moisture from wood. However, bone-dry timber—once out of the kiln—will immediately begin to gather moisture from the surrounding air. No amount of applied paint, varnish, wax or polish will prevent this. Everyone has dealt with window frames which absorb so much moisture on a rainy day that they cannot be opened; yet these same frames will rattle in their frames on a hot, dry day as though they were improperly sized.

The moisture content of wood is generally expressed as a percentage of the over-dried weight. A sample of green wood is first weighed and then kiln-dried to bone dryness to establish a comparison. The desirable moisture content of lumber for furniture making is 6 to 12 percent and this low degree of moisture is generally possible only in a kiln. Air-seasoned lumber usually has a moisture content of around 20 percent. At that degree of moisture, wood is fairly impervious to stain and decay and can be used for general construction work; but it is still not dry enough to take a good furniture finish.

GRADING OF LUMBER

Like most other products, lumber is quality-graded according to the number and extent of blemishes and defects. The following points serve as a general guide when purchasing lumber:

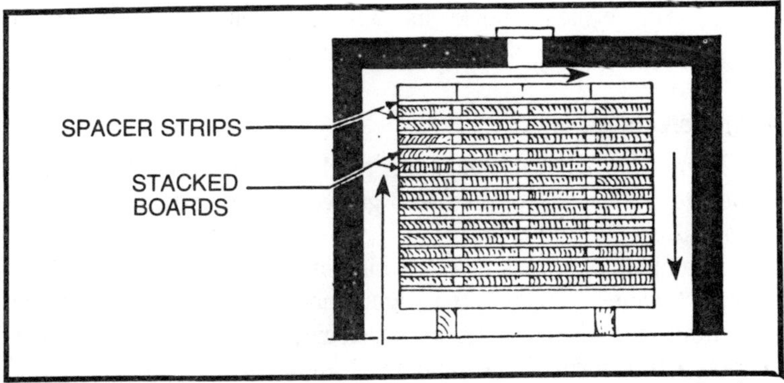

Fig. 7-8. Kiln drying green lumber—controlled forced hot air and humidity circulates through lumber stacked on spacer strips.

Hardwood Grades

- *First* are 91 percent clear.
- *Seconds* are 83 1/3 percent clear.
- *Selects* can be cut into 2-foot lengths that are 91 percent clear.
- *Number One* can be cut into 2-foot lengths that are 66 2/3 percent clear.
- *Number Two* can be cut into lengths that are 50 percent clear.

In hardwoods, most yards do not carry all grades, stocking only Firsts, Seconds (F.A.S as it is sometimes abbreviated), Number One and Number Two.

Softwood Grades

- *Select A, B, C, and D Grades*—Grades A is the highest quality in this group. Select grades are suitable for cabinetwork and for making patterns. They give a good appearance wherever used.
- *Numbers One and Two Common*—Boards with intact knots and with reasonably few checks and shakes are admitted to these grades, which are not as good in quality as selects, but are satisfactory for general construction work.
- *Number Three Common*—This grade may have numerous medium knots, worm holes, medium warp, shakes, hard rot and pith pockets. However, it will cut into sound small pieces which can be economically utilized.
- *Numbers Four and Five Common*—These grades are of poor quality, containing large knots, shakes, worm holes, rot, wanes, checks and stains. Their use is limited to low-cost construction where little strength is required.

Wood Defects

Numerous factors contribute to the defects found in wood. Some are the results of distorted growth, insect attack or timber diseases.

Examples of *growth defects* would include such things as resin pockets, wanes (which are irregular identations in the lumber, sometimes with the bark still on, which give the boards cut from that section a free-form shape) and dead knots. These latter are the cross-sections of branches which are sometimes dead and dry, so

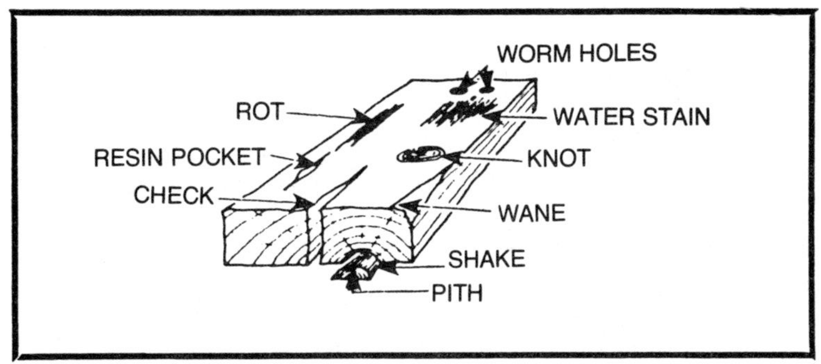

Fig. 7-9. Common defects in lumber.

that they readily fall out, leaving large holes. Wood is always weaker at a knot; but live, firm knots can be arranged most attractively to enhance cabinetry or paneling (see Fig. 7-9).

Cupshakes are also growth defects, caused by the spring wood growth in the annual rings shrinking from its surrounding layers. The phenomenon is often seen in pine and fir trees, but fortunately is usually small in area and without serious effect (see Fig. 7-10, A and B).

Insect attacks have often left their mark on wood, particularly in the sapwood which is prone to fungi. Rotted areas and worm holes are often evident in cut boards—the results of parasite invasion.

Excess moisture or excess dryness can do harm to wood. A board may retain water stains or sustain pithy fall-out in areas where too much moisture is retained. Conversely, over-seasoning can result in checks or small splits which occur at the ends of long boards which have been dried too rapidly in the seasoning process. Checking can usually be prevented by coating the board ends with paraffin or paint, as mentioned before. Star shakes (see Fig. 7-11) are caused by the log drying out more rapidly on the outside than at the heart. The resultant shrinkage in the dried-out area causes this type of splitting.

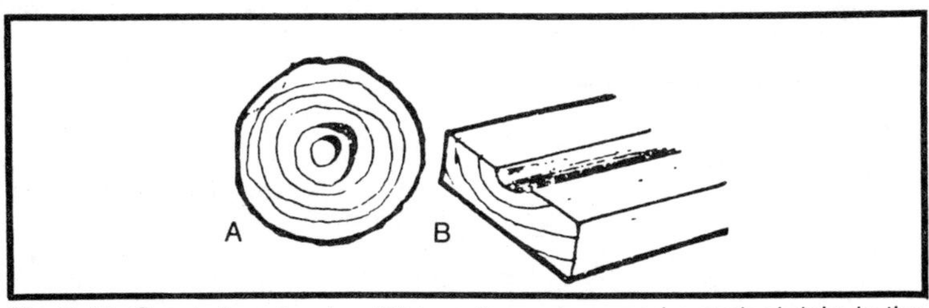

Fig. 7-10. Cupshake, showing (A) how the spring wood growth shrinks in the annual rings, leaving channels which look like (B) grooves in the sawed boards.

Fig. 7-11. Star shake, showing splits along the medullary rays.

Handling Defects

Methods of handling lumber can produce defects. Thundershakes across the grain (see Fig. 7-12), for instance, are frequently the result of improper felling. (African mahogany is very prone to this injury.) Heartshake—cracking which starts in the pithy center of the log and spreads along the medullary rays (see Fig. 7-13.)—happens when the felled log has been allowed to lay too long before processing.

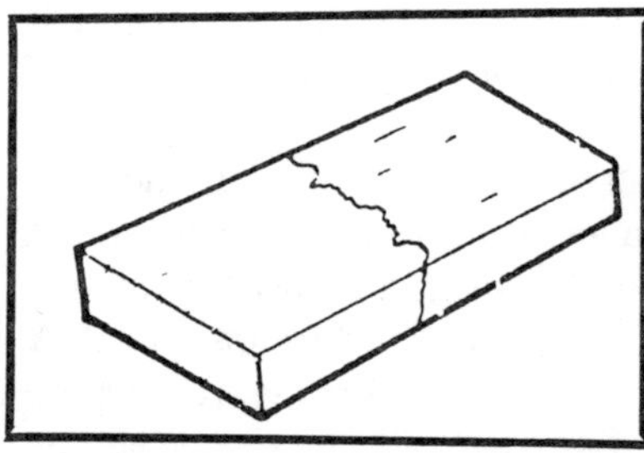

Fig. 7-12. Thundershakes are caused by improper felling.

Shrinkage

All lumber has a tendency to warp (see Fig. 7-14). Due to the region of the trunk from which it is cut, the way it is cut, and the means by which it is seasoned, one board may warp and shrink considerably more than another. As the wood dries, the loss of water will cause shrinkage, particularly in the sapwood areas where the wood will have a tendency to cup toward the bark. This cupping tendency can be prevented by stacking the lumber with risers (or

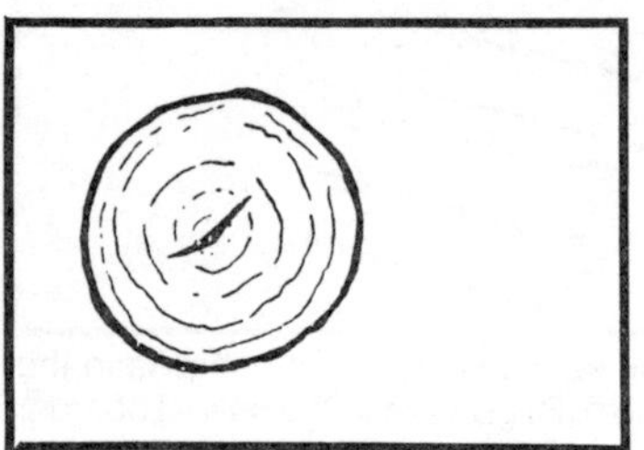

Fig. 7-13. Heartshakes start in pith section.

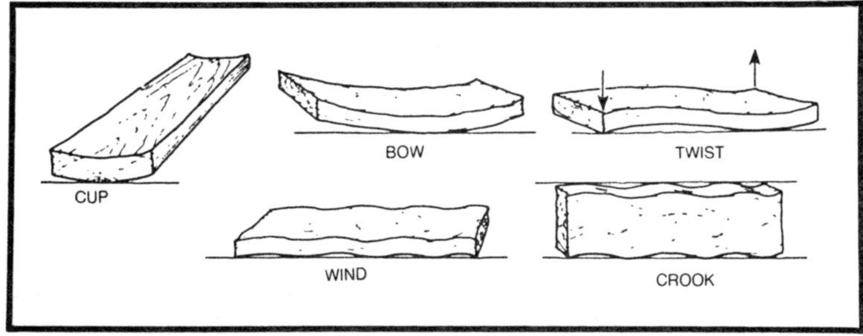

Fig. 7-14. Various forms of warping.

"stickers," as they are often called) between each piece. The weight of the stack will hold the boards flat.

In gluing several boards together to form a larger surface, arranging the end grain patterns as shown in Fig. 7-15 will minimize warping. Because boards shrink more along their width than along their length, the deliberate placement of grains with different warp directions next to one another makes one board's warping counteract against another's, keeping the glued assemblage straight.

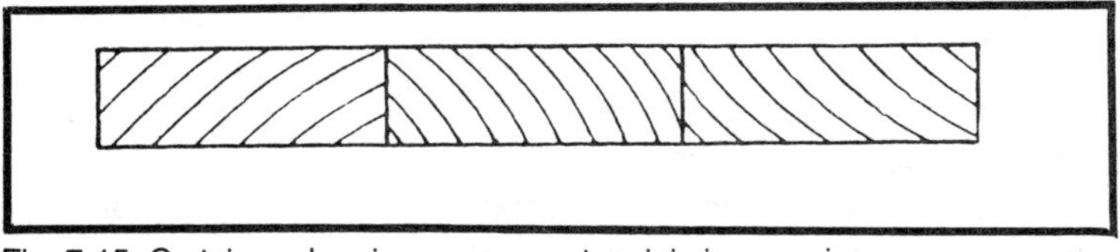
Fig. 7-15. Certain end grain arrangements minimize warping.

Dampening warped boards and keeping them under weights for a day or two will flatten them.

Figure 7-16 shows how certain cuts of boards change shape as they dry. Note that there is greater warpage in the tangential cuts

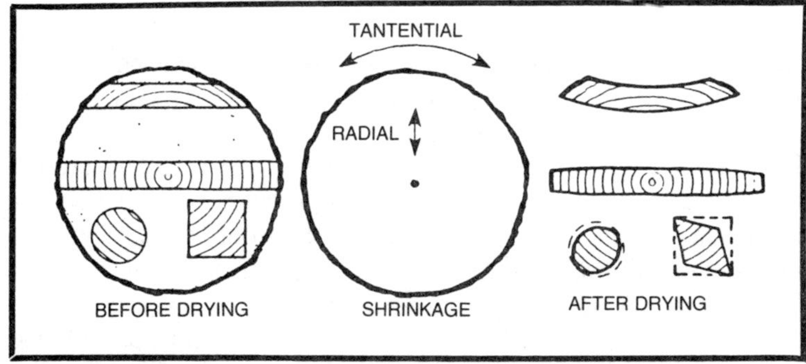

Fig. 7-16. How shrinkage changes the shapes of certain cuts.

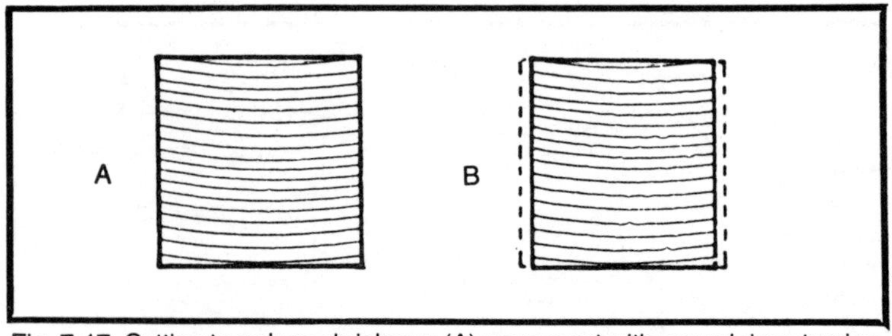

Fig. 7-17. Cutting to reduce shrinkage: (A) square cut with annual rings turning horizontally; (B) after seasoning, square cut retains its shape.

then in the radial cuts. The quarter-sawed plank holds stable. However, the round stock shrinks to an oval and the square stock shrinks to a diamond shape because both the square and the round cuts were made on the diagonal.

Figure 7-17 shows a square section cut with the annual rings running horizontally. Although such a square will shrink somewhat, as is evident in the second sketch, it will retain its square shape.

STORAGE

Improper storage can quickly reduce the quality of lumber. If handled incorrectly, the boards will decay, warp and split. Even well-seasoned lumber is unlikely to be sufficiently dry to withstand the temperature of a centrally heated shop. Therefore, it should be stored in a cool, dry place for a period of time before being brought into the workroom. If there is no room to stock the planks, they should be stored on end and upright. This position prevents their bowing lengthwise, although it cannot prevent cupping. Planks should never be left in an untidy heap or leaning against a wall where each will develop a permanent sag.

VENEERS

The practice of covering unattractive woods with veneers of rare, costly woods dates back to ancient Egyptian and Roman times, but the art of veneering probably reached its peak in the eighteenth century when such renowned cabinetmakers as Sheraton, Hepplewhite and Chippendale used veneers to great decorative advantage. Veneer is a thin layering of wood cut from a log. It varies in thickness, depending on the method of cutting. Generally, veneers range in thickness from 1/28 to 1/42 of an inch, but extremes of 1/500 to 1/4 of an inch are not uncommon.

Veneers are prized for their beauty of color, grain pattern and texture. Generally, they are applied to plainer wood surfaces by gluing, and the bonded parts are subjected to heavy pressure by large veneer presses.

A veneered piece of furniture has certain marked structural and picturesque advantages over a solid stock piece. It has less tendency to check or warp. It is an economical way of producing a piece of arresting beauty, for the exquisitely grained veneer can be used to cover cheaper wood of nondescript appearance. Veneer lends itself to intricate designs and parquet effects, many of which might be impossible to produce in solid wood. Moreover, it conserves rare, exotic show woods, making a little go a long way.

Veneers are cut from the holes of trees—from that area above the roots and below the first limb. Four different methods of cutting veneers are used commercially: sawing, slicing, rotary cutting and half-round cutting. Of the four, saw cutting is the most wasteful and is now reserved for extremely hard woods, woods with difficult grains such as curls, small diameter logs and where thick veneering is required.

Prior to knife cutting, a log has to be softened by steaming in a vat from a few hours to several weeks, depending on the hardness of the wood and the thickness of the cut required. Machinery which moves either the knife or the log is used for this cutting process.

Sawing with a segment saw is probably the oldest commercial method used (see Fig. 7-18). This method is especially wasteful when producing very thin veneers.

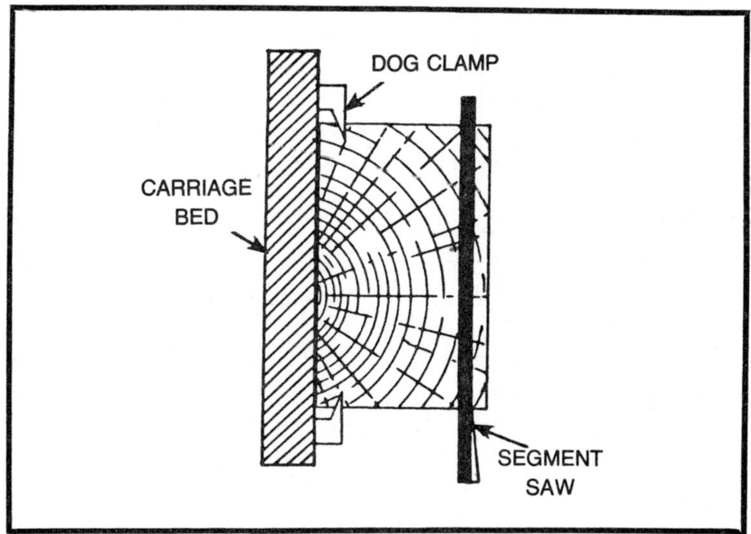

Fig. 7-18. Sawing veneers.

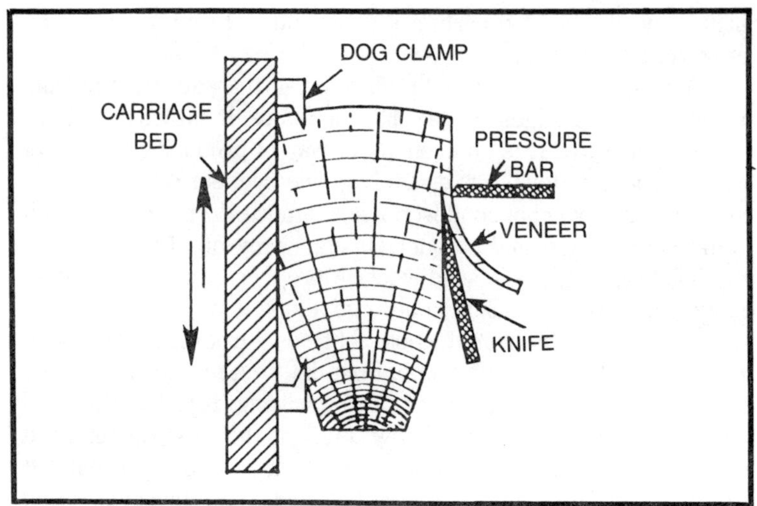

Fig. 7-19. Slicing veneers.

Slicing produces long, narrow sheets from logs 12 to 16 feet long. It is a particularly effective method of obtaining interestingly figured veneers for paneling and cabinetwork. By varying the angles of the cut, many distinctive grain patterns may be obtained (see Fig. 7-19).

Rotary Cutting is the most widely used method of cutting veneers for plywoods. The veneer is obtained by rotating the log (or "bolt," as it is called) against a stationary pressure bar and knife held against the side of the log (see Fig. 7-20).

Half-Round Cutting is a slight modification of rotary cutting used to obtain figured veneers from crotches, stumps and burs. The pre-steamed log pieces are rotated on eccentric chucks, producing a series of matched veneers (see Fig. 7-21).

MANUFACTURED BOARDS

All man-made lumber is manufactured in one of two main ways—by gluing together natural wood pieces and veneers (as in plywood, blockwood and laminboard), or by bonding together wood chips and wood and plant particles with glues under heat and pressure into boards of various thicknesses (as in platewood, particle board, chipboard, flaxboard and hardboard).

Plywood

Plywood is made from three or more odd numbers of veneers glued face-to-face with the grain of each layer of veneer running at

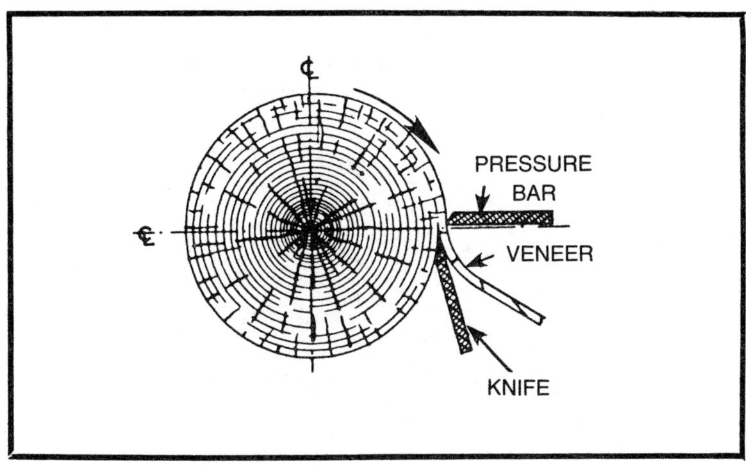

Fig. 7-20. Rotary cutting of veneers.

right, or 45-degree, angles to its neighbor. The resultant assembly is very much stronger in terms of bending strength than its equivalent in solid wood would be. It is lighter in weight, less likely to split and available in much larger sheets (see Fig. 7-22).

Its disadvantages are that it can warp, has an ugly edge and is stronger in one direction than another. It is very useful for building cheap furniture, for backing cabinets and for making drawer bottoms. A special kind of waterproof plywood is used for building marine craft, because it will withstand immersion in water and exposure to weather and is unaffected by microorganisms.

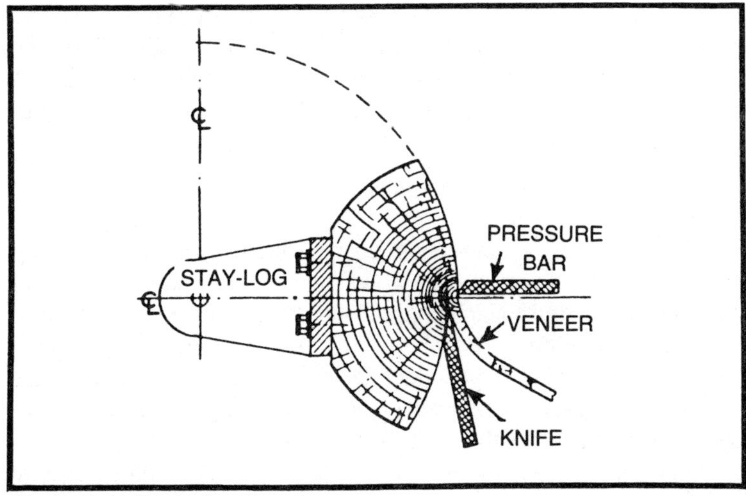

Fig. 7-21. Half-round cutting of veneers.

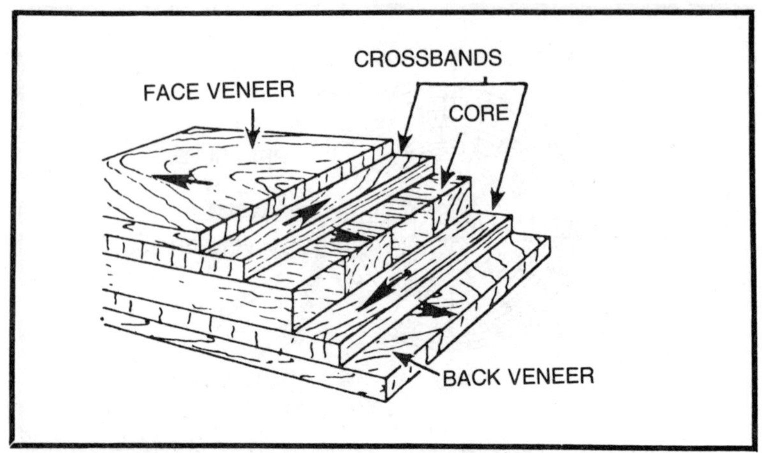

Fig. 7-22. Making plywood.

Some plywoods are made with a solid wood core, while others are made with a veneer core. The former is suitable for cabinetwork, where straight surfaces are put together with wood joints. The veneer core, however, gives the plywood more layers of crossbands to counteract warping and greater strength than the solid core type. The crossbands are generally 1/8 to 3/16 of an inch thick and the face veneers are about 1/28 of an inch thick.

Over recent years, many types of plywood have been developed for both interior and exterior use, with special waterproof glues being used in the exterior-use boards. The various types of plywood are labeled as to their construction content—"P.C." for platewood core, "F.C." for fire core, and "S.W." for softwood core. Exterior plywood carries the symbol "PMBC EXTERIOR" on the edge, which certifies that waterproofed glue has been used. Various surface patternings can be produced on plywood by routing, sandblasting or etching.

Platewood

Platewood is a man-made board which is manufactured by bonding chips and particles of wood together. Crushed sections of wood are subjected to high pressure and heat, and glue is added to bond them together. The platewood may later be surfaced with veneer on both sides to produce large, attractive boards that are highly water-resistant. Because the wood fibers have been completely reorganized by the mode of manufacturer, platewood shrinks only negligibly. When surfaced with arborite, it makes an extremely satisfactory material for countertops (see Fig. 7-23).

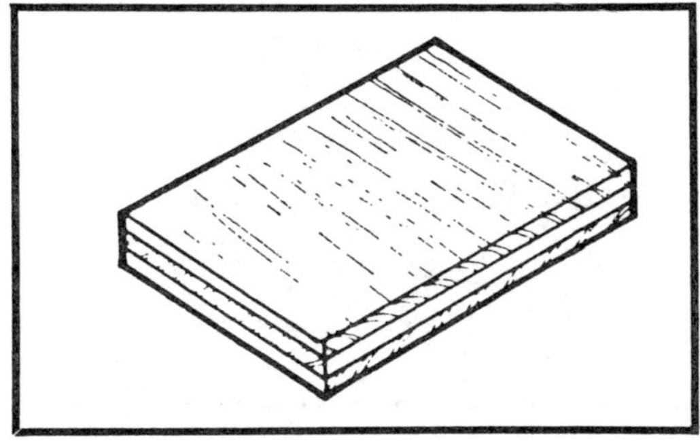

Fig. 7-23. Platewood.

Chipboard

Chipboard is another type of particle board made from wood chips dried to a constant moisture content and bonded together with synthetic resin under heat and pressure. It is available in various densities—the greater density being the better grade—and is available with either a plain or a veneered surface.

Chipboard is best adapted to solid construction and to mass production, rather than to crafted items. It is a fairly stable material, rather heavy and quite expensive—in fact, sometimes solid wood is the more economical buy. Although chipboard can be worked by hand, it is difficult to groove and rebate. Dowel joints are most practical for fastening chipboard, or a special coarse-threaded screw which is manufactured especially for this material can be used. Ordinary screws tend to lose their holding power in chipboard if they are over-tightened (see Fig. 7-24).

The craftsman should be cautioned about using chipboard in unsupported lengths because without sufficient support it will soon sag under its own weight.

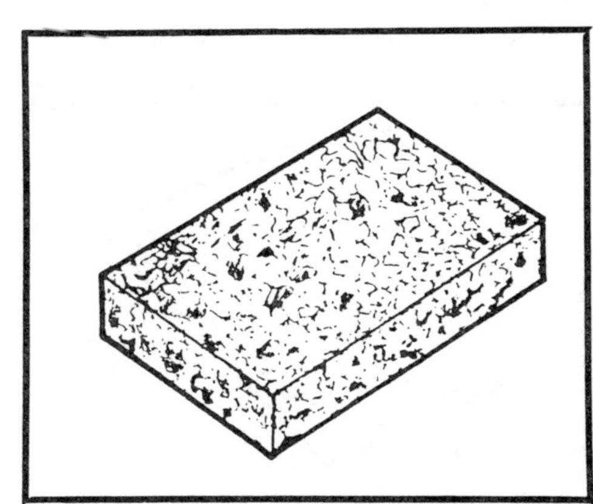

Fig. 7-24. Chipboard.

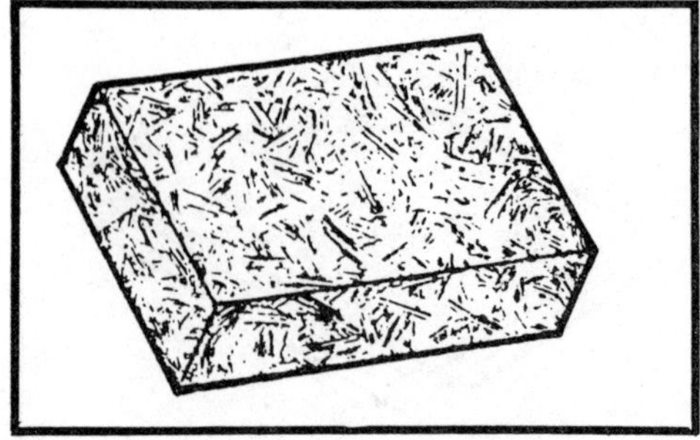

Fig. 7-25. Flaxboard.

Flaxboard

Flaxboard is manufactured from chemically treated flax shives, which are the chaff of the flax plant after the linen fibers have been removed. Mixed with synthetic resins and hot-pressed, this residue plant material becomes flaxboard. After the shives are scutched from the dried, soft fibers of the plant, they are graded. The long shives are used to make course linen, linen-content writing paper and cigarette paper. The less suitable, shorter fibers are made into flaxboard.

Flaxboard is gaining in importance commercially. It is lower in price and lighter in weight than chipboard—both advantages to the craftsman using it for cupboards and wardrobes where the doors, if overheavy, can cause the lightweight frame to over-balance (see Fig. 7-25)

Hardboard

Hardboard is a rugged, durable material manufactured from pine logs which have been chipped, defiberated and felted, by mechanical process, into rigid sheets of highly compressed material. Hardboard is an extremely smooth product—so smooth, in fact, that

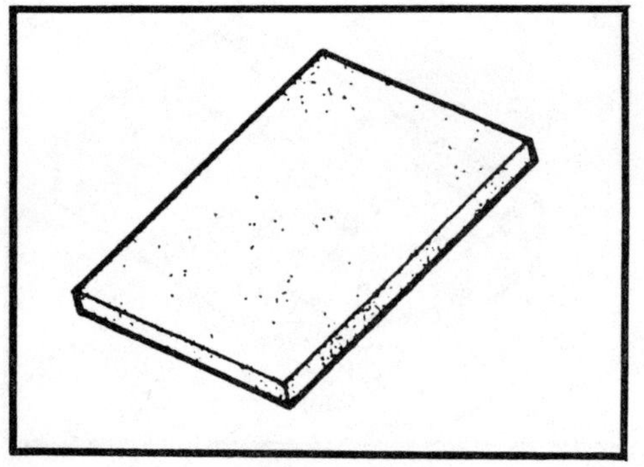

Fig. 7-26. Hardboard.

Fig. 7-27. Blockboard.

it can be painted without sanding. Its homogeneous construction keeps it from warping.

Hardboard is a highly utilitarian construction material. It is used for cladding, for backing framed cabinets and mirrors, for making picture frames and flush doors and for fashioning sturdy toys. It is widely used in exhibition pegboard stands for retail displays. The 1/8-inch thickness is most popular, but 1/4-inch thicknesses are also in demand (see Fig. 7-26).

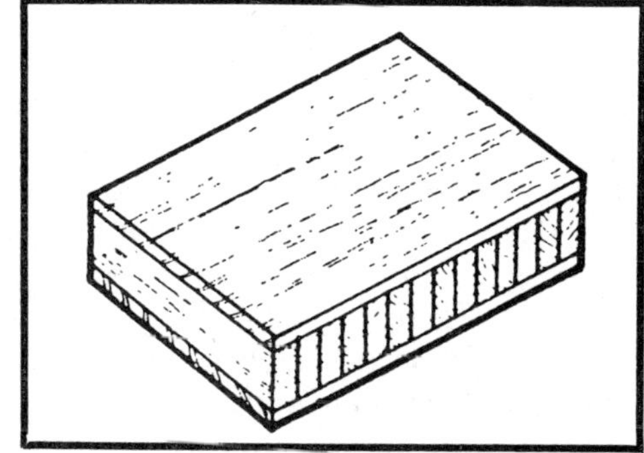

Fig. 7-28. Laminboard.

Blockwood and Laminwood

These materials (see Figs. 7-27 and 7-28) are both made similarly to the way in which plywood is made—of layers of natural wood veneers over a core (or center ply) of narrow wooden strips glued together to make up the necessary width, length and thickness of a given sheet. Laminwood is more expensive than blockwood, but it is more well made, more solid, stronger and takes veneering beautifully. The uses of both laminwood and blockwood are the same as those of plywood—for inner cabinetry construction and inexpensive furniture.

Chapter 8 Furniture Construction

A knowledge of the way furniture is constructed is as important to the person who is interested only in repair and refinishing as it is to the person who will undertake to make an entire piece of furniture. Before undertaking the repair of loose joints, legs drawers and table tops it is indispensible to know how they were assembled in the first place. There are many ways of joining two pieces of wood and each woodworker chooses the one he considers most suitable for the jointure he is fashioning. Knowing the various joining techniques and their relative merits will enable the woodworker to make an approp-riate selection of method in either an original construction or in a repair.

Equally important is the selection of the right type of wood for the particular application (see Table 8-1).

SELECTING THE CORRECT STOCK

Selecting the correct stock for a given project can be a highly complex problem. Prime consideration must be given to the function to which the object under construction will be put, and construction materials must be chosen which will be appropriate. If the wood-worker is an amateur, he would be wiser to select softwoods for his first projects, because hardwoods are harder to work with the more expensive to purchase.

The **hardness** of wood is not measured by weight, but by the amount of pressure necessary to sink an iron ball weighing twenty-five pounds halfway into the wood. Parodoxically, some woods designated as softwoods resist this testing better than some so-called hardwoods! Selecting a stock which works well and easily, therefore, is somewhat more difficult than it would appear at the outset.

The **finish** desired may suggest certain choices of stock. If the object is to be painted, a softwood of smooth texture such as basswood, poplar or pine would be very suitable. However, if a transparent finish is contemplated, a hardwood of interesting grain, color pattern and texture will be the selection, because such a wood has beautiful reflective qualities when enhanced with stain or varnish.

Other attributes such as strength, shrinkage potential and durability must be weighed as well. Certain woods, such as ponderosa or redwood, are hardy and weather-resistant for outdoor use, while oak, particularly white oak, gives its best service when used indoors in flooring, panels and wood trim.

The following is a table of woods, their attributes and their uses. Of the thousands of excellent construction woods which grow in the world, those mentioned are a few of the most widely used and highly prized. The woodworker need not limit his choice to those suggested. Loving the look and feel of this beautiful natural material as he does, he will be constantly discovering woods which inspire him to undertake ever more ambitious and rewarding woodworking projects.

LUMBER SIZES

Lumber as it comes from the saw mill is called *rough lumber*. After the rough boards are planed and seasoned ("dressed," as these combined processes are termed), they are smaller in size than when they left the sawmill because of the water lost in drying out and the dimension lost in planing. Planed or surfaced wood is designated by one of two terms: "S2S," meaning surfaced on two sides, or "S4S," meaning surfaced on four sides. Dressed lumber, therefore, is smaller than rough lumber in two dimensions only—width and thickness. The length of a board remains constant. Softwoods are generally bought dressed, although they can be purchased in a rough state.

Dressing 1 inch thick stock generally reduces it by ¼ of an inch in thickness and ⅜ of an inch in width on boards up to 6 inches wide. Boards wider than 6 inches are reduced by ½ an inch. As an example, a rough board 1 inch × 6 inches would be reduced to ¾ of an inch × 5⅝ inches.

Table 8-1. Characteristics of Furniture Woods (continued on pages 187 through 193).

Wood	Grain Texture	Hardness & Strength	Source	Color	Uses
Agba	Straight grained with close, even texture.	Durable, with resistance to decay	W. Africa	Light yellow	Same uses as oak; often used as a substitute for oak.
Ash	Straight, open grained.	Tough, hard, flexible. Very strong and heavy.	Europe and North America	Light brown to white.	Sports equipment, boats, boat parts, bent wood furniture, tool handles.
Basswood	Straight grained with fine texture.	Soft, medium strong, but light in weight.	Throughout U.S.	Light cream to white.	Painted furniture, picture frames, novelty wooden articles, boxes, etc.
Beech	Fine grained.	Extremely stonrg; works well on machine tools.	Europe	Pinkish red to yellow-brown.	Widely used for furniture, tools and tool handles, and—because it holds tacks well—for upholstered furniture.

Birch	Curly, close grained.	Hard, strong	World-wide.	White to reddish brown.	Furniture, interior trim, floors, dowels.
Butternut	Coarse-grained	Soft, medium heavy in weight.	U.S. and E. Canada	Pale gray to brown.	Millwork, interior trim, boats, scientific instruments.
Cedar	Coarse to close grained.	Similar to mahogany but lighter in weight. Very durable.	Canada, U.S. and British Honduras.	Light brown. deep reddish brown.	Chests, posts, lawn furniture, moth-proof closet linings, cigar boxes.
Cherry	Close, smooth end grained.	Medium weight, hard, durable and stable.	U.S. and E.Canada.	Reddish brown to white. Darkens with age.	Cabinet veneers.
Chestnut (Sweet)	Open grained. Sometimes used as a substitute for oak.	Rather soft, but works and finishes well.	Europe	Yellow brown.	Cabinet work.
Cypress	Open grained.	Lightweight, soft and weak, but decay-resistant.	Eastern U.S.	Pale brown to red	Fences, boats, crates,building consturction, caskets.

Table 8-1. Characteristics of Furniture Woods (continued from page 187 and continued on page 189).

Wood	Grain Texture	Hardness & Strength	Source	Color	Uses
Doussie, Afzelia	Close, smooth grained.	Strong and durable with low shrinkage factor.	W. Africa	Light brown.	Fine furniture, ships' decks, bench tops for laboratories, workrooms and garden furniture.
Ebony	Extremely fine grained.	Hard, heavy and stable.	Dutch East Indies.	Black	Cabinet work, inlays, black piano keys, flutes, knife handles.
Elm	Handsome, straight grained.	Water-resistant. Heavy, hard and strong; does not cleave easily.	W. Canada, Great Britain, Japan and Holland.	Reddish brown	Good for bending—as in upholstered furniture frames and boat hulls. Makes excellent flooring, wheels and coffins.
Guarea	Fine grained with a texture good for finishing. Similar to Cuban and Honduras Mahogany	Hard, stable and strong, but easy to work. Lacks dimensional movement; therefore, good for interior construction. Sawdust from this wood can be irritating.	W Africa.	Pinkish brown	Quality construction of all sorts, including fine furniture, paneling. Used for interior drawer sides.

Gumwood	Fine grained	Medium heavy, soft, fairly strong.	Australia and U.S.	Light to deep reddish brown.	Fine furniture, interior trim, musical instruments.
Iroko	Well-figured, handsome, open grained.	Strong as oak; resistant to fungi, insects, wear and acids.	W. Africa.	Light yellow when first cut, becoming rich, golden brown	Excellent for cabinetry, worktops, and for fine furniture.
Lauan	Open grained with ribbon striped configuration	Medium hard, medium weight and fairly strong.	Phillippines	White to reddish brown.	Plywood paneling.
Mahogany	Moderately open grained, attractively figurd. Takes finishes excellently.	Hard, stable, extremely strong and durable. Medium weight.	W. Africa and Britiish Honduras, Spain	Pink to medium red and reddish brown.	Fine furnture and high class construction, musical instruments and boats.

Table 8-1. Characteristics of Furniture Woods (continued from page 189 and continued on page 191).

Wood	Grain Texture	Hardness & Strength	Source	Color	Uses
Makore	Similar to close-grained mahongany. The attractive block-mottle veneer is called Figured African Cherry.	More dense, harder and heavier than mahogany	W. Africa.	Mahogany-like.	High Class work and furniture
Manšonia	Straight grained, smooth and fine textured.	Fairly hard and durable The dust can be very irritating.	W. Africa	Heartwood is purple brown.	Used as a substitute for walnut. For quality work, fine cabinetry.
Maple	Fine grained, figured (the birdseye configuration).	Hard and stiff.	E. Canada and U. S.	Cream, pink to reddish brown	Flooring, interior trim, musical instruments, school equipment, furniture.
Muniga	Pleasing grain. Good finishing properties. An excellent show wood.	Mild and stable; works well by hand or by machine.	E. Africa	Warm brown color	A versatile, multi-use wood. Its only drawback is that the quarter grained cuts show some white spotting which can be covered by finish.

Nanigon	Rather open grained.	Very durable; very hard.	W. Africa.	Reddish wood with dark flecks on the rays when quarter sawed.	Same uses as mahogany. Popular in the furniture trade.
Oak	Coarse and por-ous: open grained	Hard, touch, elastic and strong.	U.S. England, Canada, Australia, Europe, Japan, North America Yugoslavia.	Light grayish brown to red.	Furniture, flooring, ship building and church building. Yugoslavian oak is the finest—of slow, even growth, of uniform color and straight grain. Used for cathedral woodwork.
Obeche	Fine textured	Soft but firm. This large tree produces clean lumber of exceptional length, dimensional stability and reliable quality.	W. Africa	Creamy white to pale yellow.	Lower priced kitchen furinture and cabinetry.

Table 8-1. Characteristics of Furniture Woods (continued from page 191 and continued on page 193).

Wood	Grain Texture	Hardness & Strength	Source	Color	Uses
Paledo	Close, striaght grained with conspicuous figuration	Hard, strong	Indochina, Philippines	Gray-brown to red brown or black markings.	Contemporary furniture
Pine (Douglas Fir, Columbian Pine, Parana Pine, Scots Pine, Red and Yellow Deal, European Spruce)	Soft, fine-grained.	Soft to hard: medium to strong. Fir is highly water-resistant.	World-wide	White to reddish, depending on variety.	Building construction, window frames, doors, cupboards, docks.
Poplar	Close, straight grained	Soft: medium strength	North America	Yellow to brown	Used for plywoodcore, exterior trim, painted furniture.

Ramin	Very clean, straight grained	Similar to beech. Moderately hard, strong and heavy. Paints, varnishes andmachines well. Large sections tend to check.	Sarawak	Pale straw color	A principal wood for picture frames, mouldings, general utility work.
Redwood	Straight grained	Soft but fairly strong. Nails, works and finishe well. Impervious to weather, disease and insect invasion.	North America	Red or reddish brown	Usually given a clear finish rather than paint. Used for outdoor furniture, patio decks and cupboard lin-ings.
Rosewood	Close, figured grain	Hard, strong, eleastic. Purple dust will stain clothes, hands.	Brazil, India, Ceylon, Australia	Reddish to brown, streaked with dark grain lines.	Impressive furniture, in-lay, tool handles
Sapele	Marked, regular striped grain, particularly in quarter-sawed wood; interlocking grain is difficult to hand-plane.	Tough, resistant to decay, and hard—harder and heavier than mahogany	W. Africa	Similar to that of mahogany	Same uses as mahogany.

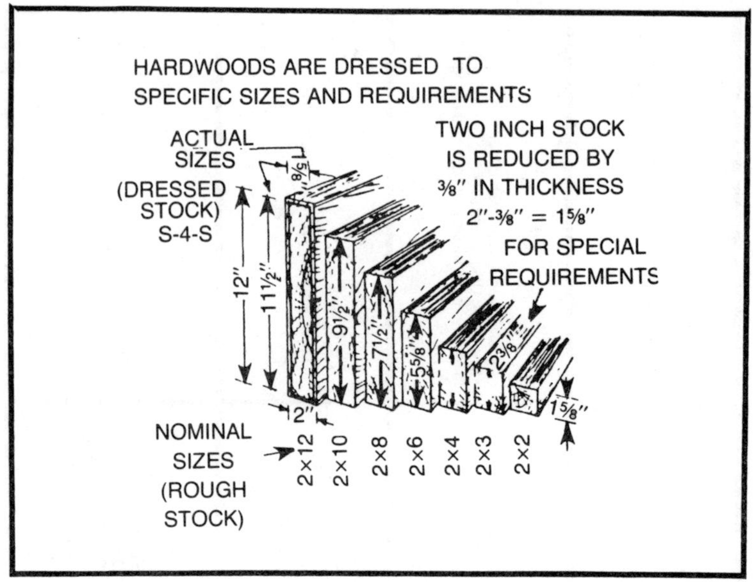

Fig. 8-1 "Dimensional" lumber (hardwood) comes in two inch stock, four to 20 inches long.

All 2 inch thick stock is reduced by ⅜ of an inch in thickness. A 2-inch × 4-inch piece is actually 1 ⅝ inches × 3 ⅝ inches. These actual measurements are important to keep in mind when calculating the amount of lumber required for any given project.

Special types of lumber, such as ship-lap or tongue-and-groove, may vary from the standard dressed size; but, most dressed lumber dimensions would be as described above.

Softwoods and hardwoods are two completely different departments in a large lumberyard; even the units of measurement are different. Hardwoods are bought by the cubic foot (see Fig. 8-1). Softwoods are purchased in "standards"—a standard being 165 cubic feet (see Fig. 8-2). Softwood standards are usually available in even widths—2, 4, 5, 8, 10 and 12 inches—and in even lengths, as well—6, 8, 10, 12, 14 and 16 feet.

Lumber materials are sold in three measures—by the linear foot, the square foot and the board foot. Doweling, carved trim and picture framing are sold by the linear foot. Plywood, masonite and platewood are sold by the square foot. Boards and planks are sold by the board foot.

A board foot is equivalent to a board which is 1 inch thick, 12 inches wide and 12 inches long. To ascertain the number of board feet in any piece of lumber, multiply the thickness *in inches by* the

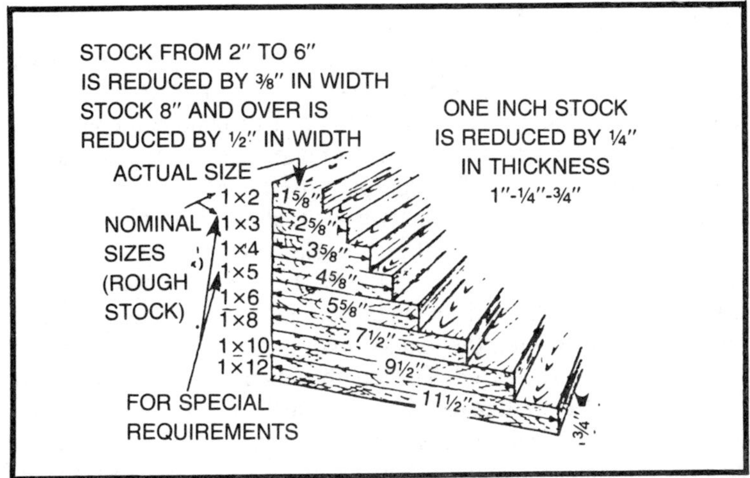

Fig. 8-2. "Board" lumber (Softwood) comes in one inch stock, four to 20 inches long.

width in feet and the length in feet. If width or length are expressed in inches, they must be converted to feet by dividing by 12.

For example, in a piece of lumber measuring 1 inch × 10 inches × 12 feet, you would multiply 1 × 10/12 × 12 = 120/12 = 10 board feet. If a piece of lumber were 1 inch × 12 inches × 48 inches, you would compute the number of board feet by multiplying 1 × 12/12 × 48/12 (see Fig. 8-3).

Although dressed lumber is actually less than rough lumber in size, the dressed lumber buyer is charged for the corresponding rough lumber sizes. Any shrinkage less than one inch is charged as one inch.

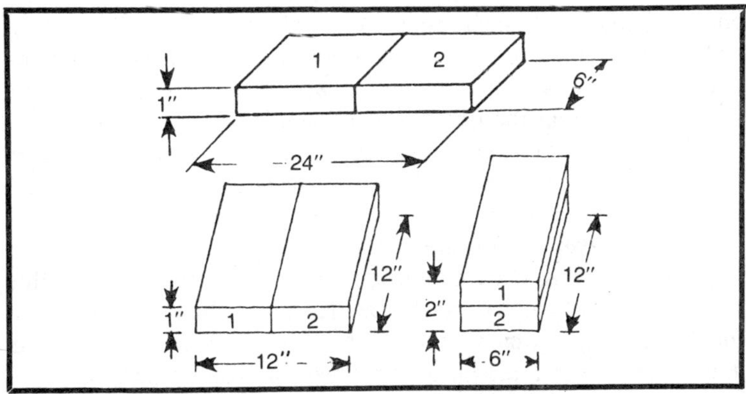

Fig. 8-3. Boards in various arrangements, each arrangement equivalent to one board foot.

PURCHASING LUMBER

In purchasing lumber for any given project, the craftsman should prepare a cutting list to present to the lumber merchant, along with the detailed drawings of the construction contemplated.

Most projects require more than one type of timber and the cutting list should carefully segregate the types under respective headings—such as American black walnut, plywood, chipboard, etc.

A further breakdown on the cutting list should be the qualities of similar items required—such as 4 legs, 2 side rails and 2 end rails. Dimensions for each item should be noted, always giving the length dimension first, even if the length is not the greatest dimension of the piece of wood required. The length is measured in the direction of the grain. The craftsman must add ½-inch (¼-inch extra on each end) to the length measurement as his allowance for sawing the ends square. He must remember that the lumber mill, in dressing the lumber, never alters the *length*, sheathing only the sides and edges. Therefore, he will have to square off the ends himself, and the ½-inch allowance is to give him waste margin for that purpose. However, in ordering from the mill, he should specify the length as "finished" (or "f"). The lumber mill may have to cut the length dimension from a much larger board, and the specification "finished" on the cutting order will insure their allowing him the ½-inch allowance he will need.

The second dimension given is the width. Here again, the craftsman should specify as to whether he wishes rough or finished lumber and should remember to calculate the *actual* size—with the ¼-inch required for planing (⅛-inch on each side) deducted—when making his measurements.

The third dimension given is the thickness. The thickness on finished lumber is ⅛-inch less than that of unplaned rough lumber, and this actual measurement should be considered by the craftsman in making his measurements and, in writing up his cutting list, he should specify that the *finished* dimension is being ordered.

Thus the cutting list for four legs of a stool which must stand 16 inches high when finished, with legs 1 ⅜ inches wide and 1 ¼ inches thick would read:

"4 legs teak 16 ½ inches f × 1 ⅜ in. f. × 1 ¼ in. f."

By specifying each dimension with an "f." for finished, the craftsman would receive exactly the dimensions he will use (except for the leg height which he must square off for himself, since the lumberyard never alters the length dimension in dressing lumber). If he does not specify "f." for finished, he will receive rough lumber in the sizes ordered, without allowances having been made for planing.

Even if he then dresses the lumber for himself, the resultant dimensions will be too small.

Since dressing lumber, which entails sheathing both sides and both edges with a plane takes a great deal of time and effort, most craftsmen order dressed lumber. Rough lumber is ordered only when it can be utilized "as is."

OTHER WOOD PRODUCTS

Wood represents one of the world's most plentiful natural resources; forests are well-distributed over the face of the earth, so that only a few areas are without trees. Trees are the largest and oldest of all living things. The banyon tree in Central America is the biggest tree in the world, but the Australian eucalyptus and the sequoia of California are both towering giants in their own right. Some sequoia trees are 35 centuries old, the bark layer on their trunks a foot thick—adequate protection against disease and fire, the tree's two most formidable enemies. The world's largest redwood is alive and well in Ureka, California. It measures 20 feet in diameter at the base and rises to a height of 264 feet.

Trees benefited the earth millions of years before anyone made use of the wood they produced. Trees provided a natural shelter for birds, animals and man himself. The Druids were still living in trees when the Romans invaded the territory later known as the British Isles. In addition to affording refuge, trees shaded and strengthened the sides of hills and mountains, checking floods and erosion.

Man's first adaptive use of trees was for food and later, after he had discovered fire, for fuel. With a sharp stone for a chisel, he fashioned wooden tools and weapons. As Man himself evolved, so did his use of wood. He utilized logs and, eventually, sawn planks for constructing shelters, building furniture and making transportation vehicles.

North America has been actively engaged in lumbering for almost 200 years. The heavily forested areas of the United States and Canada provide much of the world's lumber. This commodity accounts for about 80 percent of Canada's export trade and about 20 percent of U. S. exports. Readily available wood for constructing permanent homes, wagons, stage coaches, and sailing vessels and to use for fuel was an important factor in the successful colonization of America.

The economic importance of our forests has increased in direct proportion to the increase in the use of wood and wood products. Research and technology have uncovered and developed many new uses for wood and for derivatives of wood. Laminated wooden beams for large-span construction, plywood, masonite, wallboard, platewood and tentest are all new man-made building materials which are composites of wood. The packaging, disposable paper products and publishing industries demand more wood pulp every year.

A great number of products are presently being made of the two basic ingredients of wood—cellulose and lignin. Rayon, plastic, lacquer, alcohol, turpentine, resins, sugar, dyes, acetone, yeast, tanning agents and water softeners are just a few of the many by-products made from wood's two principal ingredients. As research moves us forward to make wood and wood products which are resistant to burning, shrinking, swelling, warping or decaying, more and more industries will spring up to manufacture such wood products. The tremendous commercial potential of wood has not yet been fully realized.

CONSTRUCTION SEQUENCE

The woodworker must pursue a certain seqence of operations in constructing any given item in order to insure maximum results with minimum effort, time and expense. A practical order of procedure is as follows:

1. Set out all parts, and, using a sharp pencil, number the joints adjacent to each part on the outside surface of the wood, marking even the face sides and edges, if necessary.
2. Using a marking knife, mark all pieces of wood to length. Later, these knife blade lines will act as guides for the saw. However, do not saw the wood as yet, until all dimensions have been checked and the joints have been cut.
3. Mark all the joints, indicating by penciled hatch marks all the waste areas in the pieces of stock from which the joints are to be cut, so that you will be readily able to distinguish the actual joint from the waste area once the joint is cut.
4. Make sure that all necessary marking is done before starting to cut. Choose the most important joint and cut it first, but only after you have rechecked your dimensions.
5. Fit the joints, using either a sash cramp or a hammer and block of wood to close the joint. Do not glue yet.
6. When all the joints have been cut and fitted, take each joint apart in turn and clean up the inside surfaces with a smoothing plane. Remove exactly two shavings and no more. Sand the surfaces which will eventually be glued together, but keep the sanding action to a minimum so as not to create a gap between the pieces of the joint.

7. Sand and wax the rest of the joint, since this area will be hard to reach once the joint is glued. Take care not to wax the surfaces which are to be coated with glue.
8. Cramp the pieces of the joint together without glue, using waste wood to prevent the cramp shoes from marking the work. Examine to see that the joints fit well. Check them for squareness and examine them for any twist before proceeding. This procedure will set the cramp shoes as to length, so that they will go on more readily once the glue is applied.
9. Check the number on each joint and be sure that it corresponds to the number on the wood part to which it will be glued.
10. Glue the joints in a warm room to prevent the glue from hardening too rapidly. Work quickly but carefully on this most important step. Apply glue evenly, but not too thickly, to both adhering surfaces. Wipe off any excess glue with a damp cloth before it hardens. Apply the cramps and be sure that they are tightened to exactly the right degree. Over-tightening could distort the work.
11. Make a careful check before leaving the work to set:
    - Insure squareness. Are the diagonals even and of equal length? If not, try moving the cramps slightly in the direction of the long diagonal.
    - Sight for twist. This can be corrected by moving the cramps or packing the end of one cramp off the bench with a piece of wood.
    - Check that all joints are closed and fitting tightly. Wipe off any excess glue. Leave joints to set.
12. The next day, or when glue is dry, slowly remove cramps and clean outside surfaces of work with a few passes of the smoothing plane to render all protruding parts of the joints flush.

AUXILIARY CONSTRUCTION

In furniture construction, wood cuts and joints are auxiliary construction pieces fashioned for one purpose—either as decorations to a piece of furniture, or to fit together parts of the furniture's structure. If made from a single piece of stock, such auxiliary pieces are called *cuts*. If styled from two pieces of wood and designed to fit together, such pieces are referred to as *joints*.

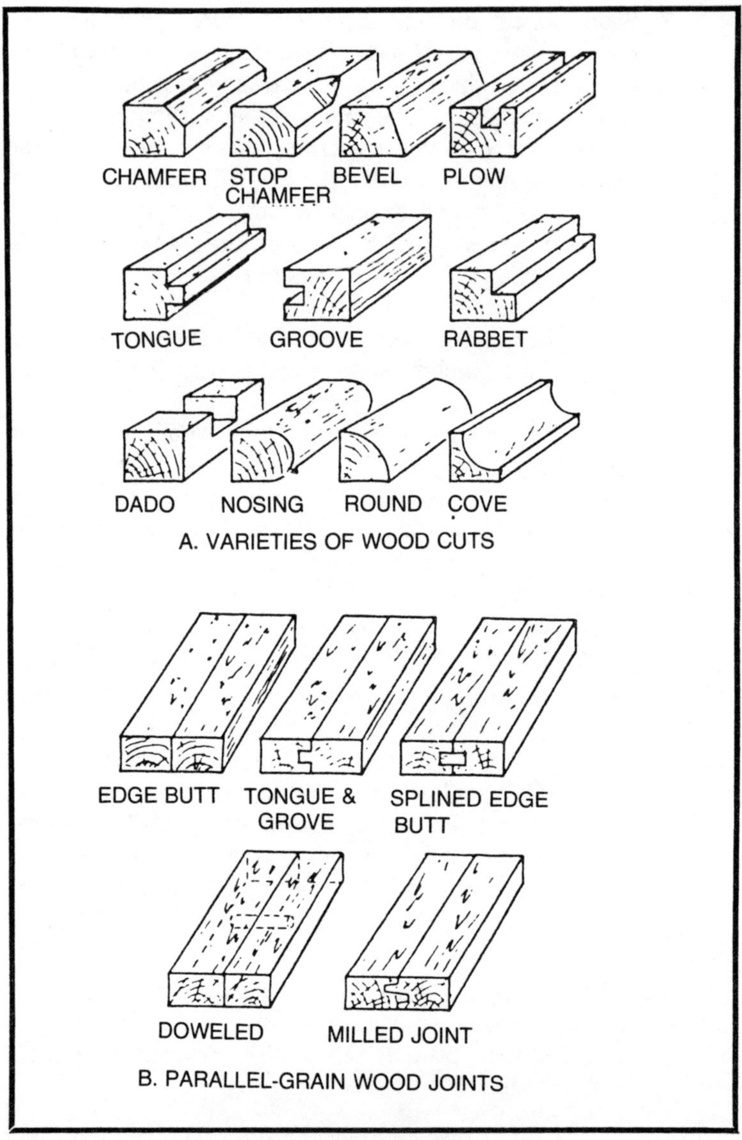

Fig. 8-4. Varieties of wood cuts and parallel-grain wood joints.

Wood Cuts. The woodworker must learn to recognize wood cuts so that he can use them effectively in furniture trim and moldings. They can be shaped by various hand tools—notably saws, planes, chisels, portable routers and shapers, and molding heads on a saw. Wood cuts include such decorative designs as the chamfer, stop chamfer, bevel, plow, tongue groove, rabbet, dado, nosing, round and cove (see Fig. 8-4 A).

Joints. These are essential in fastening two or more pieces of wood together. The basic types of joints used in cabinet work are the butt, rabbet, dado, miter, dovetail, mortise-and-tenon, dowel and lap. Countless variations of these basic stylings are in use, as well. Each joint is designed for a specific construction purpose, and it is important to choose the most suitable one for each particular job (see Fig. 8-4 B).

The holding power of any joint depends on a well constructed, accurate, snug fit. Poorly constructed joints make any structure of which they are a part look amateurish. To choose the right one for your job, consider these factors:

- Strength and durability of the object under construction—Which joint will give the most reliable, long range service?
- Ease of manufacture—Have you the tools and equipment to reproduce the selected joint?
- Angle of the grain—Is the joint to be cut with the grain, at right angles to the grain, or on a diagonal to the grain?
- Method of fastening—Will glue, nails, wood screws or other hardware be used in conjunction with the wood joint?

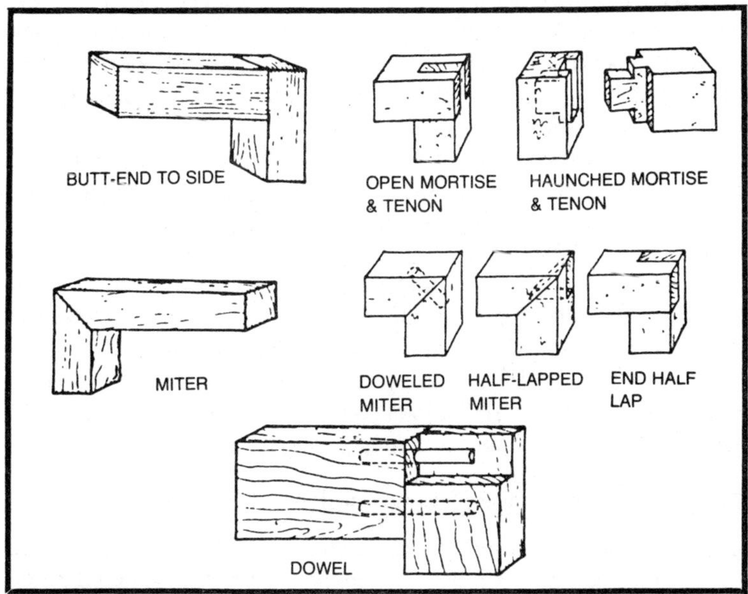

Fig. 8-5. Right angle joints with grain at right angles.

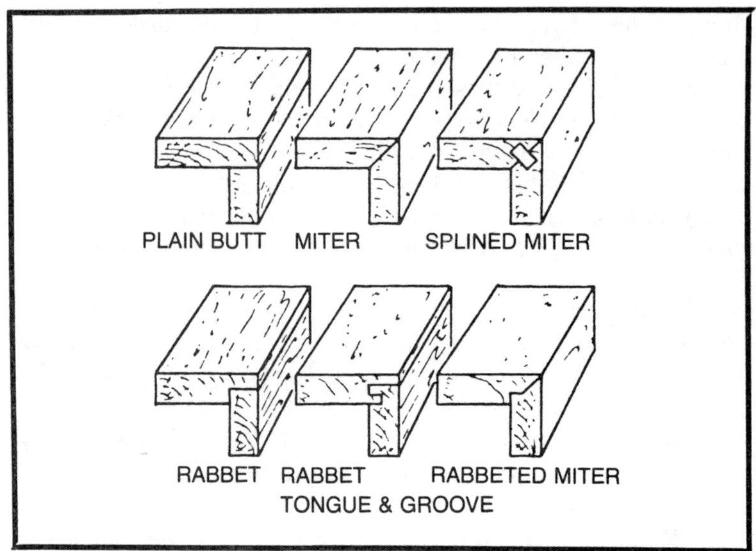

Fig. 8-6. Right angle joints with grains parallel.

Right Angle Grain Wood Joints. When two pieces of wood are joined with the grain of one section meeting the grain of the other at right angles, the resultant joint is called A "right angle grain wood joint" (see Fig. 8-5).

Right Angle Joints with Grain Parallel. When a right angle joint where the grain is parallel is used, greater strength comes from adding nails, screws, dowels, splines or blocks as reinforcement. The finish desired determines the reinforcement used. Dowels are inconspicuous, but splines are strong (see Fig. 8-6).

Whatever the joint used, the parts must be pre-fitted to insure a tight, smooth-fitting joint. This trail assembly, using cramps but no glue as yet, will point up any defect in the joint and enable the craftsman to rectify it then, before the glue is applied.

The tools necessary for the layout and construction of wood joints are the marking knife, marking gauge, try square, backsaw, chisel, auger bits, doweling jig and miter box. The hand router plane, the rabbet plane and the jointer plane are also used in the construction of certain joints. All the joints we will discuss can be made with hand tools, but machine tools may be used to speed production.

CONSTRUCTING A DOWELED EDGE JOINT

1. Arrange the wood for the two parts of the joint so that the surface grain on both pieces is running the same direction and the end grain on the two boards is alternated.

2. Mark the boards and number each, so they will not be interchanged.
3. Plane the edges to be joined using a hand plane or a machine jointer, and see that they fit together well.
4. Now clamp the boards together in a vise or cramps, making sure that they are both in correct position to one another as marked.
5. Mark lines across the adjacent edges of the two cramped together pieces at intervals of 6 inches, leaving a 3-inch margin on either end of the two boards.
6. Set the marking gauge to half the thickness of each board, and intersect the lines drawn by the try-square (see Fig. 8-7). These intersecting lines mark the position of the dowels. Before drilling at these designated spots, some craftsmen like to drive a panel nail into the wood, inserting it into each board to the same depth as the dowel will be set, and then withdraw it. The resultant nail hole acts as a guide for the drill bit.
7. Select the auger bit for the size of the dowel to be fitted (generally either 5/16-inch or ⅜-inch is used for this type of jointing, although commercially-cut dowels are available in thickness from ⅛-inch to 1 inch), and bore holes at the points marked by the intersecting lines on both boards. Dowels are usually 2 inches in depth; therefore, the hole

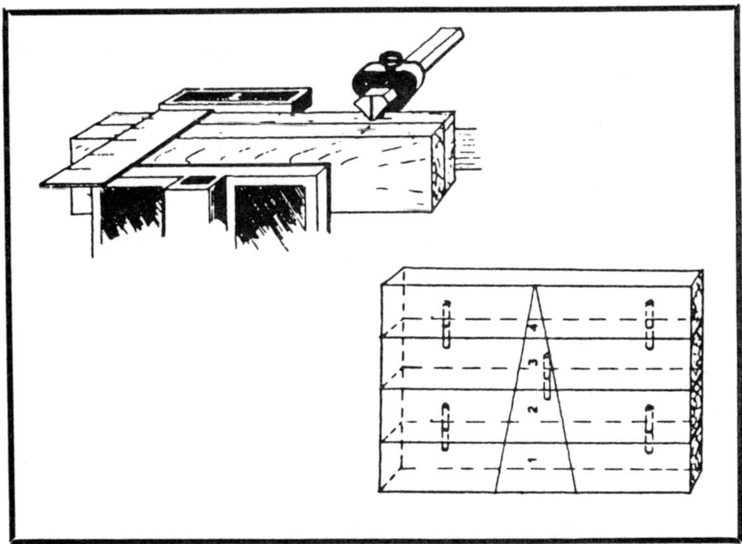

Fig. 8-7. Marking the position of dowels in constructing a doweled edge joint.

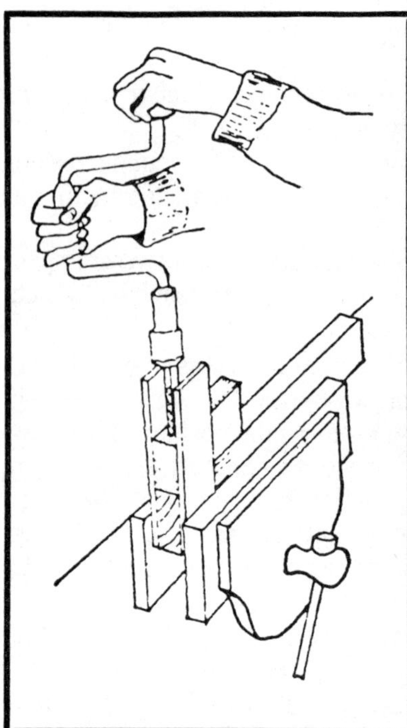

Fig. 8-5. Drilling the dowel holes in a section of a joint with the auger bit.

drilled into each board, which will eventually make up the doweled edge joint, will be a little over 1 inch in depth. (The reason for drilling a hole slightly deeper than the dowel actually requires in each board of the joint is to prevent the dowel from resting flush on the bottom of both holes when the pieces of the joint are fitted together and, thus, to prevent the joint from closing). A depth stop may be fastened to the auger bit to insure a uniform for all holes (see Fig. 8-8).

8. A segment of dowel of the proper diameter should be measured off and cut ready for insertion. To provide an escape for excess glue when the dowel is glued into the joint, the dowel should be beveled or grooved along its length (see Fig. 8-9). Otherwise, the hardening glue can burst the wood.
9. If a doweling jib (see Fig. 8-10) is used to position the dowels, it should be set up to accomodate the size of bit which will be used and the thickness of the stock.
10. Try the dowel segments in the drilled holes for size, to be sure they will fit snugly when glued.

Fig. 8-9. Preparing the dowel peg for the joint—note how the dowel is beveled or grooved to allow the glue to escape.

11. If the parts of the joint fit properly and the dowel pins are correctly sized, apply glue and secure the joint in clamps until it is thoroughly dry.

The dowel joint helps to align boards which are bowed and greatly reinforces an edge joint. For surfaces which support weight

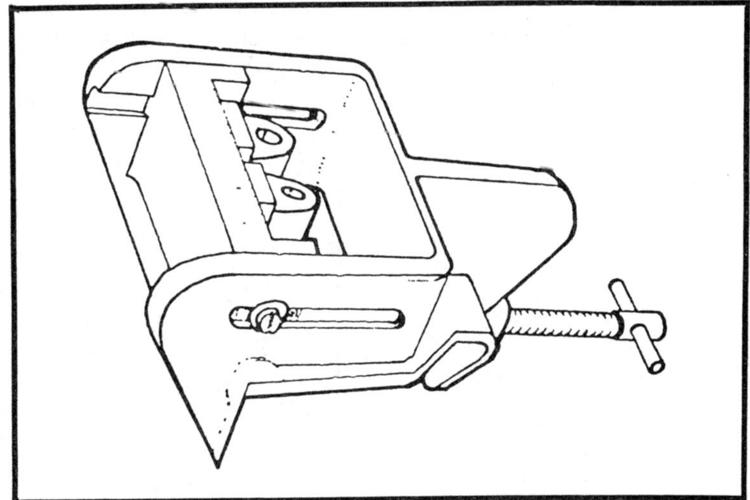

Fig. 8-10. Doweling jig.

Fig. 8-11. Selecting wood pieces for mortise-and-tenon joint.

and have no other reinforcement, bracing or rails, a dowel joint is advisable.

STUB MORTISE AND TENON JOINT

Using wood which has been planed to size and sawn to length (see Fig. 8-11).

1. Place the section in which the mortise is to be cut in the vise, and rest the tenon piece across it (see Fig. 8-12). Check the position of the top piece with a try-square and a steel rule, making sure that it is positioned at exact right angles to the lower piece in the vise.
2. Draw along both edges of the top piece with a pencil, and square these outlines with the upper surface of the mortise

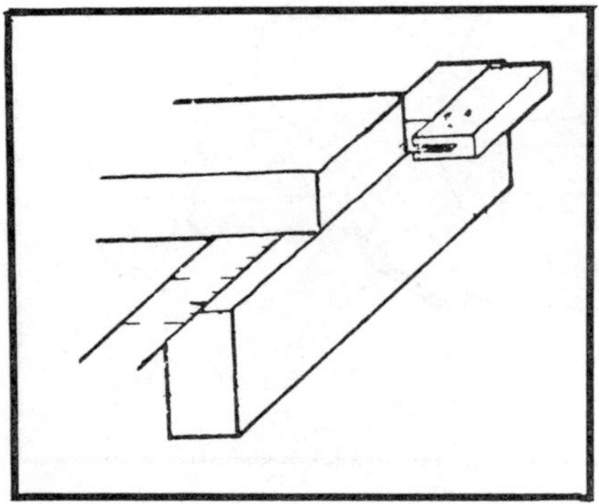

Fig. 8-12. Placing joint sections at right angles in vise.

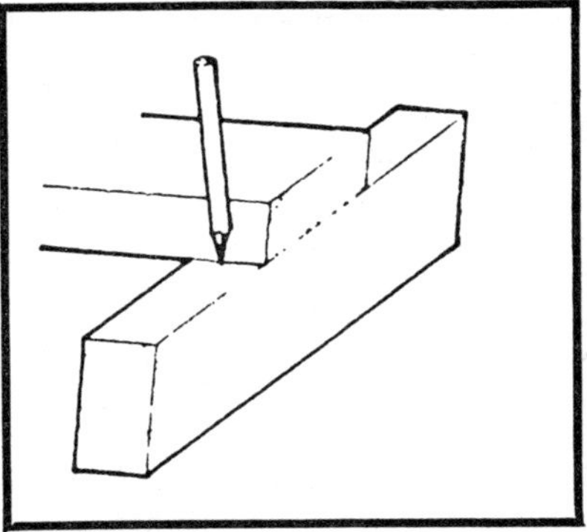

Fig. 8-13. Marking shoulder lines on mortise section shoulder.

piece. These lines are the shoulder lines for the mortise section of the joint (see Fig. 8-13).

3. If several similar joints are to be cut, mark the shoulder lines for all of the other mortise sections of the joints, as well (see Fig. 8-14).
4. Mark ⅛-inch inside the shoulder lines with a pencil, and square these across (see Fig. 8-15). These are the boundaries of the mortise incisions, the ⅛-inch margin providing a cover on the tenon to conceal the hollowed-out mortise.
5. On the tenon piece, mark a shoulder line for the tenon with a marking knife and check the knife line for squareness all around (see Fig. 8-16). The length of the tenon is usually ⅔ of the width of the mortise section.
6. Select a mortise chisel about the same thickness as ⅓ of the width of the mortise wood. Set it exactly in the center of the mortise, checking the marks on both edges to maker

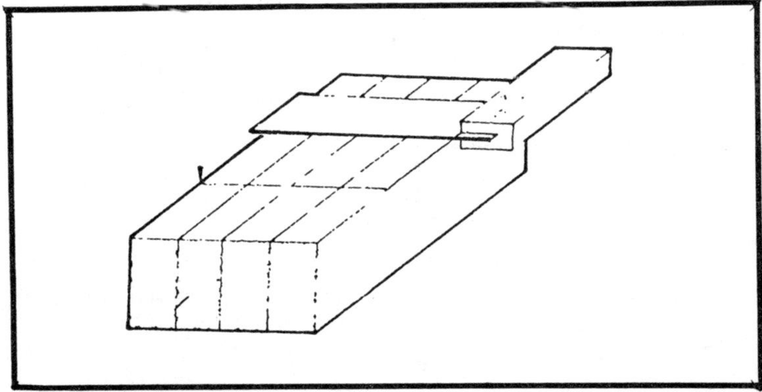

Fig. 8-14. Marking shoulder lines on all mortise sections when more than one mortise-and-tenon joint is required.

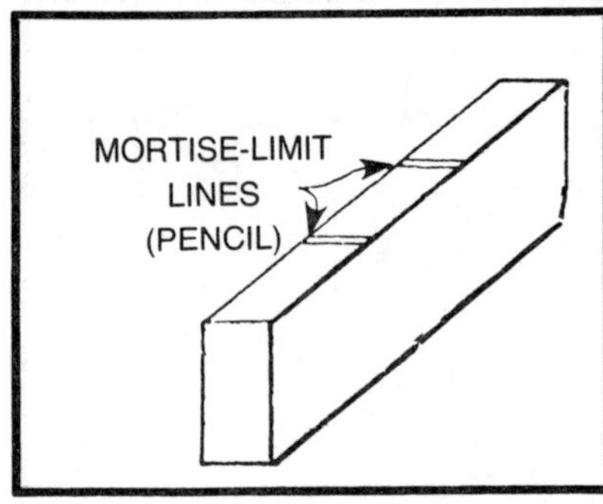

Fig. 8-15. Marking mortise limits ⅛-inch inside shoulder lines.

sure the chiseled-out area would be in the exact center (see Fig. 8-17).

7. With a gauge, mark the mortise and the tenon sections from the face side, dividing the width of each section into thirds (see Fig. 8-18).

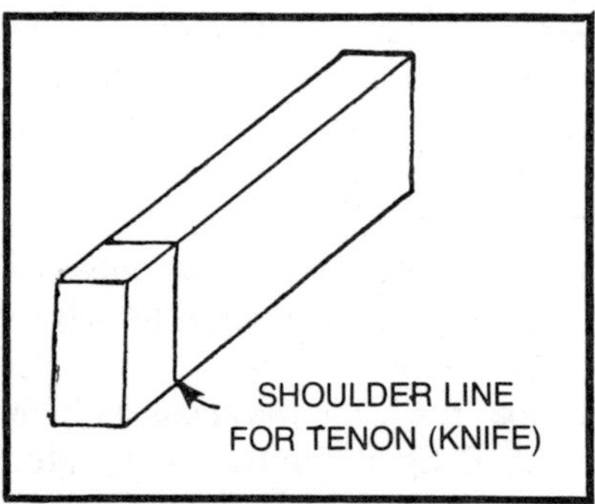

Fig. 8-16. Marking shoulder line for tenon section.

8. With a pencil, hatch mark the waste areas on the mortise section (see Fig. 8-19).
9. Again using penciled hatch marks as indications, mark the waste areas on the tendon section (see Fig. 8-20).

Fig. 8-17. Determining exact position of chiseled-out area.

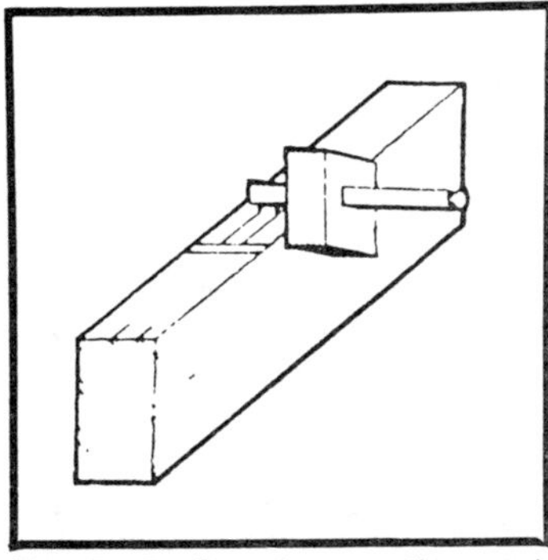
Fig. 8-18. Gauging mortise and tenon sections from face side.

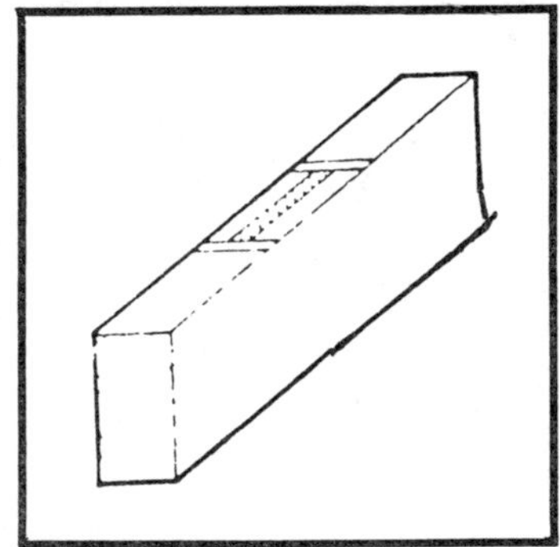
Fig. 8-19. Hatch-marking waste area of mortise section.

10. Using a G-cramp and some waste wood for buffering, secure the mortise section to the end of the bench.
11. Begin hollowing out the mortise by making two angle cuts with the chisel, as shown in Fig. 8-22, always working with the flat side of the chisel towards you. Remove the wood from the notch.

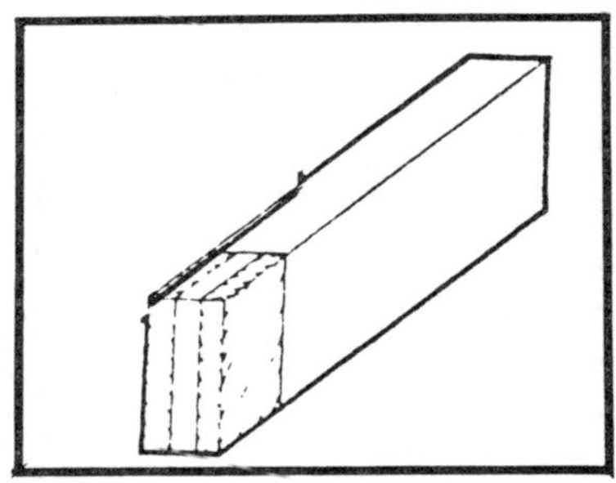
Fig. 8-20. Hatch-marking waste area of tenon section.

12. Now, using a mallet to drive the chisel in and first marking the depth of the cut on the chisel with chalk or colored tape to prevent driving it too deeply, work away from the notch. First, make angle cuts to widen the notch more and more

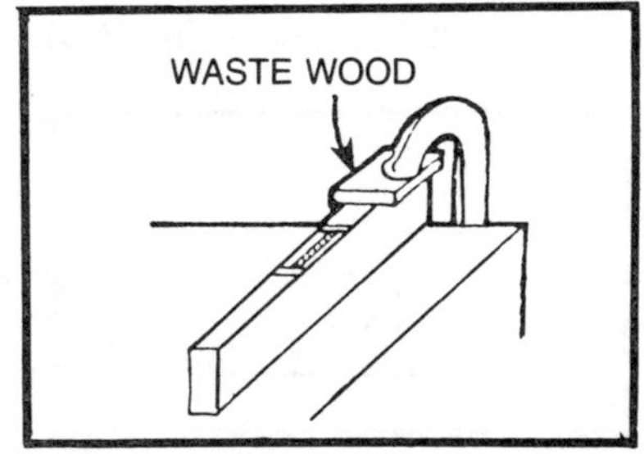

Fig. 8-21. Securing mortise section in cramp preparatory to chiseling.

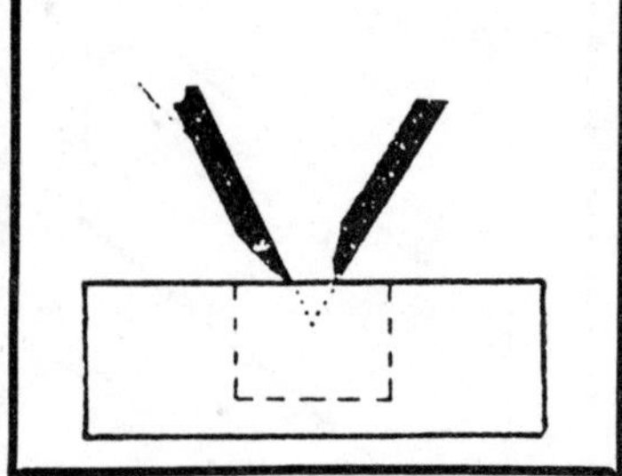

Fig. 8-22. How to direct and manipulate chisel.

on each side. Then, to remove the corner waste, make several perpendicular cuts on either side of the notch, working by cautious degrees and driving the chisel in cleanly, always on the waste side of the wood (see Fig. 8-23).

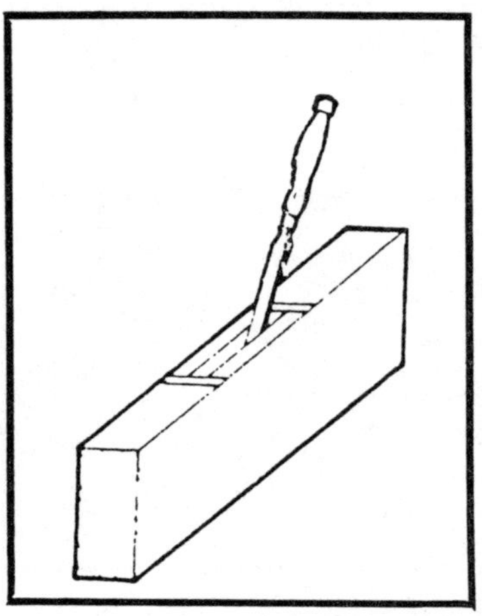

Fig. 8-23. Correct way to chisel angle cuts to widen notch.

13. Remove the wood from the G-cramp and put it into the vise. Carefully prize out the waste wood form the mortise section, levering it in chunks with the chisel. Do not use a mallet, and take care not to round the corners of the hollow mortise (see Fig. 8-24).

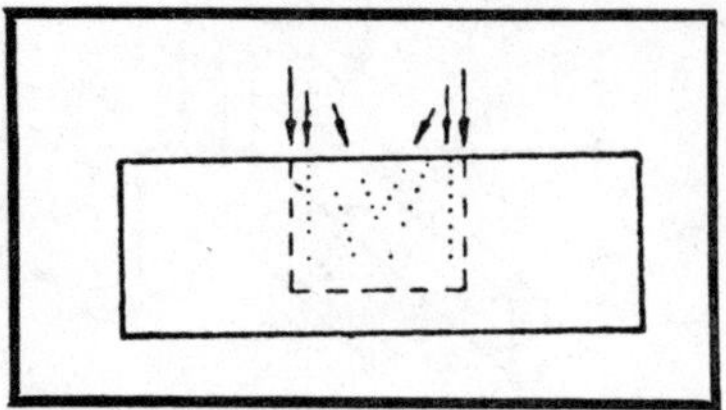

Fig. 8-24. Prizing out waste wood with chisel.

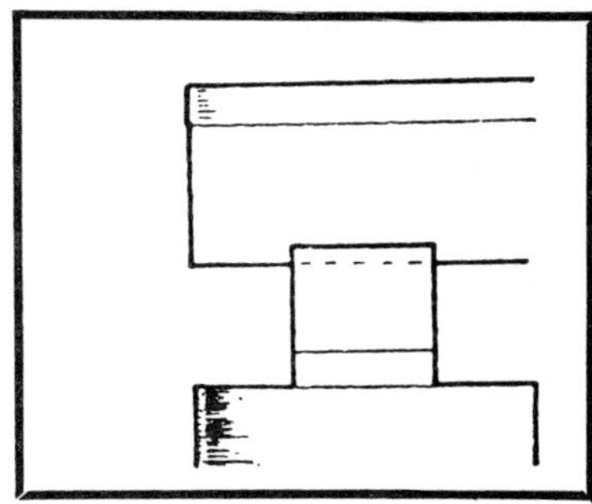

Fig. 8-25. Sawing initial shallow groove in tenon section with saw.

14. Place the tenon section upright in the vise and, with the tenon saw, cut a shallow horizontal groove on the waste wood side of the shoulder line on both sides of the tenon (see Fig. 8-25).

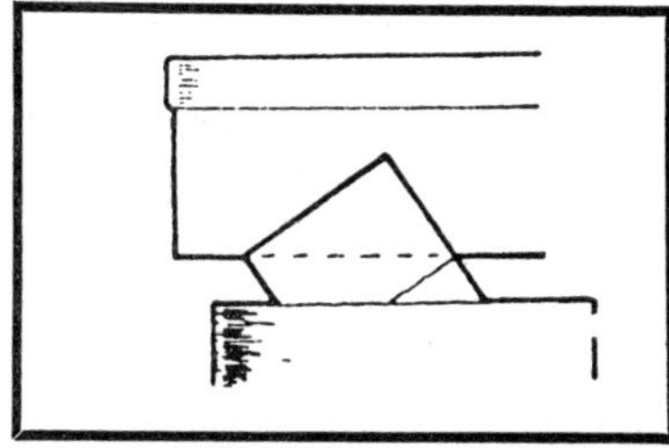

Fig. 8-26. Tilting wood in vise to enable saw to cut shoulder line.

15. Tilt the wood in the vise to a 45-degree angle, and saw down to the diagonals on both sides of the tenon (see Fig. 8-26).
16. Now straighten the wood upright in the vise, and saw straight down to the shoulder line on both sides of the tenon (see Fig. 8-27).
17. Now place the wood across a bench hook, table edge or a saw horse, as shown, and saw the shoulder line of the tenon on both sides, being careful to stay on the waste side

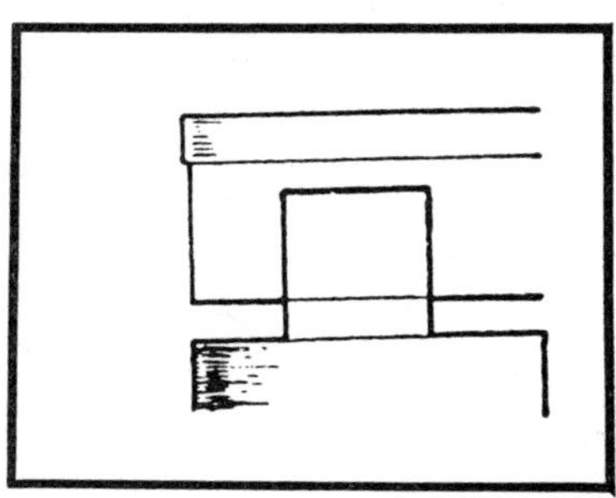

Fig. 8-27. Sawing straight down to shoulder line, with tenon section upright in vise.

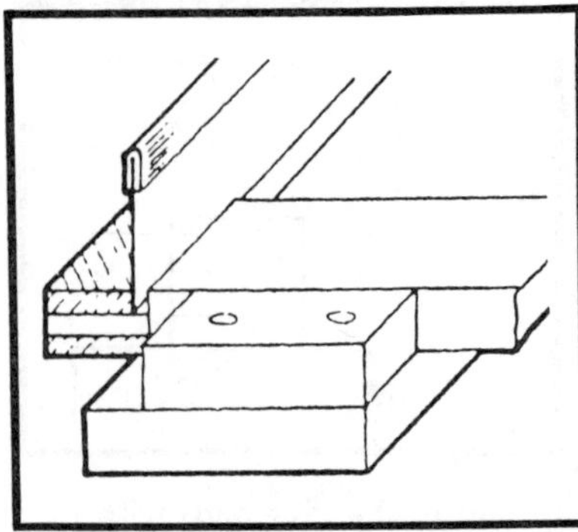

Fig. 8-28. Sawing shoulder line on tenon section with section lying across bench hook or saw horse.

of the line and not to cut into the tenon itself. Remove the cheek waste wood (see Fig. 8-28).

18. Finally mark off ⅛-inch on either end of the tenon and saw these pieces free by sawing down to the shoulder line first, and then across the shoulder to the tenon itself, as shown in Fig. 8-29.
19. The mortise and tenon joint is ready for gluing. The tenon will be glued into the mortise and the glued-together pieces placed in cramps until the glue dries (see Fig. 8-30).

LAPP BUTT JOINT

The making of a lap butt joint is somewhat simpler than the construction of other joints; but it, nevertheless, demands precision of measurement and crisp, accurately cut edges if it is to fulfill its purpose as a strong, durable furniture joint. Assuming that the wood has already been planed to size, sawed to length and squared up, here is the procedure:

1. Arrange the parts and number them in pairs, penciling the identification of each wood piece on its outside surface (see Fig. 8-31)

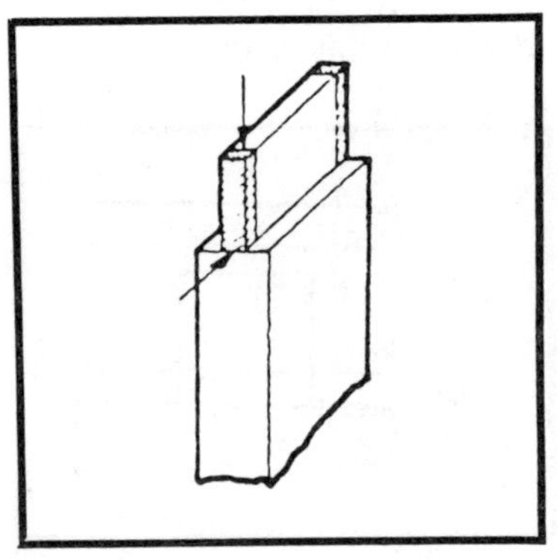

Fig. 8-29. Marking off margin of waste wood on sides of tenon section preparatory to sawing them off.

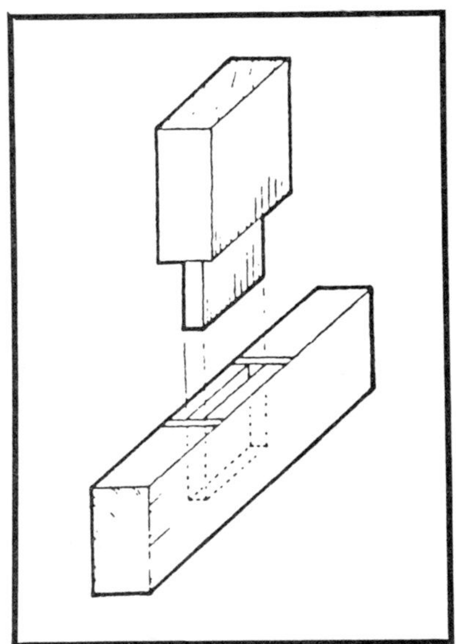

Fig. 8-30. The finished mortise and tenon joint, with diagram showing how it will fit when glued.

2. Set the cutting gauge to just over the thickness of the wood (see Fig. 8-32).
3. Using the cutting gauge spur to do the marking, score in the shoulder line across the inside surface and along one-third of each edge (see Fig. 8-33).
4. Reset the marking gauge to one-third the thickness of the wood. With the piece secured in a vise, score with the gauge across the end and down both sides to the shoulder line. Mark the waste section for removal with penciled hatch lines (see Fig. 8-34).

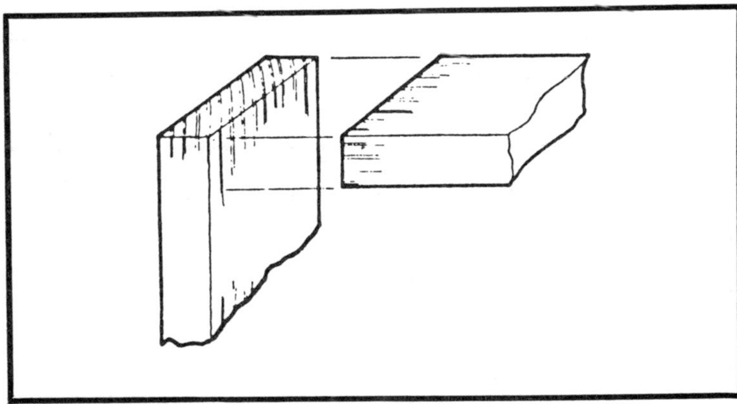

Fig. 8-31. Arranging the sections of the joints and numbering them in pairs.

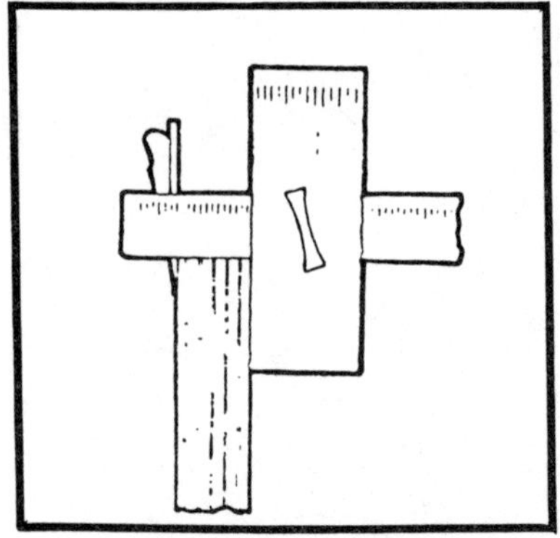

Fig. 8-32. Setting the cutting gauge to just over the thickness of the wood.

5. Place the work against the bench hook, or cramp the end opposite that on which you are working to a work table, and saw along the waste side of the shoulder line with a tenon saw (see Fig. 8-35).

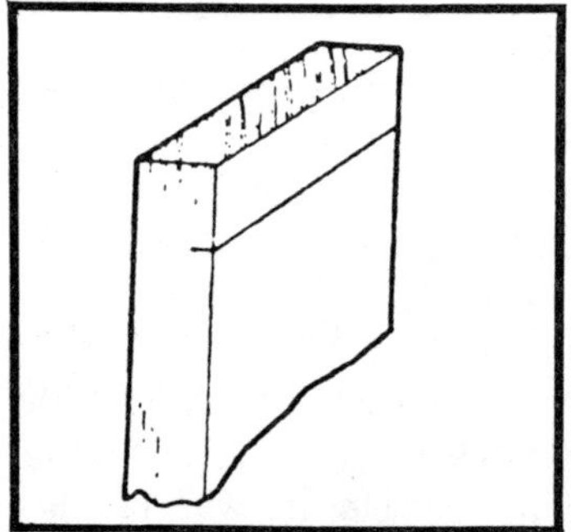

Fig. 8-33. Scoring shoulder line across inside surface and along one-third of each edge.

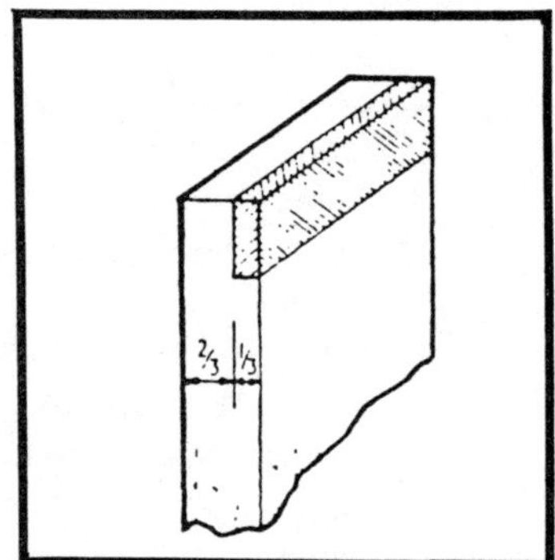

Fig. 8-34. Setting marking gauge to one-third the wood thickness.

6. Stand the wood upright in the vise and, with an inchwide chisel and mallet, clean away the waste in stages or use a tenon saw to incise off the waste. (see Fig. 8-36).

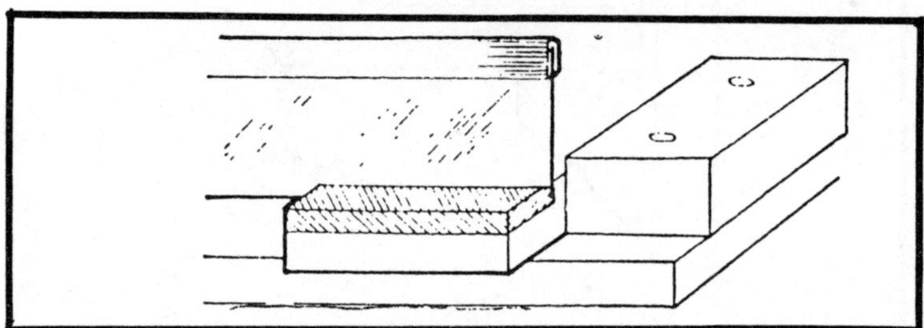

Fig. 8-35. Sawing off waste section at shoulder line.

Fig. 8-36. Chiseling away waste area with mallet and chisel.

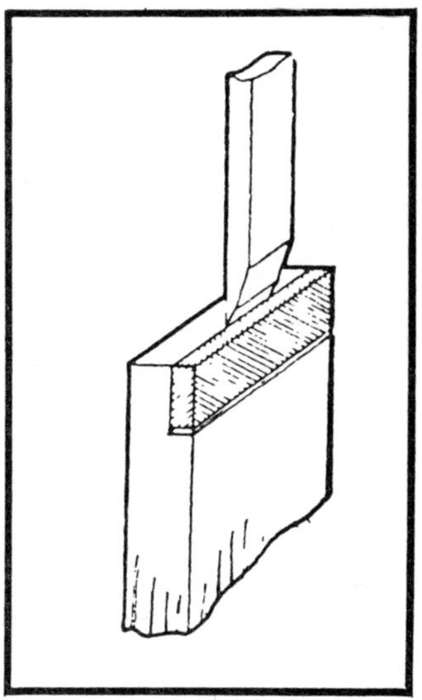

7. Try the two parts for fit and glue them up, cramping them together firmly until the glue dries (see Fig. 8-37).

THE THROUGH DOVETAIL JOINT

First, key each individual joint with a key *letter*, writing the letter on both sections of the joint. Next, number the two sections of each individual joint. Let numeral 1 stand for the section of the joint from which the pins are cut and numeral 2 indicate the section of the joint from which the tails are cut. Be sure that all letters and numbers identifying the joint sections are penciled on the *outside* surfaces, where they will be readily visible during the entire construction procedure.

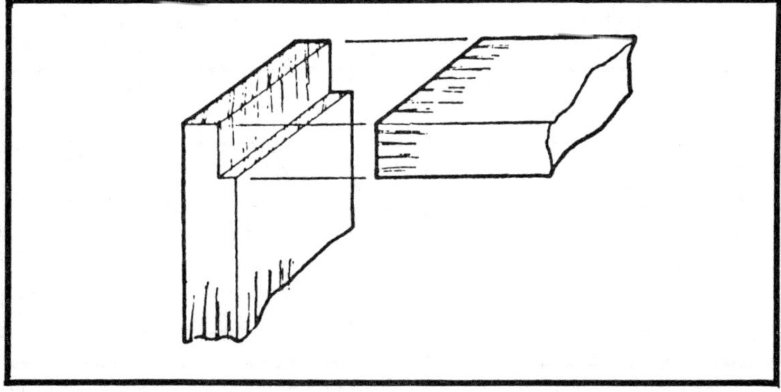

Fig. 8-37. Trying two sections of joint for fit before gluing them together.

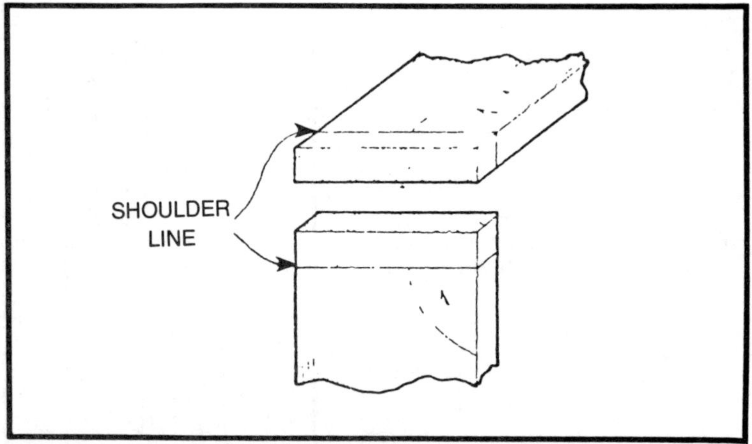

Fig. 8-38. Marking shoulder lines with a knife and numbering joints.

On all joint sections regardless of key or number, mark the shoulder line with a pencil (see Fig. 8-38).

Marking and Cutting the Tails

1. On the Number 2 pieces, mark out the tails on the shoulder line with a pencil (see Fig 8-39).
2. Use a dovetail template to complete the marking out. Hatch mark the waste with a pencil.
3. Position the wood for the tails low in the vise to prevent undue vibration, and slope the work so that the lines are vertical (see Figs. 8-40 and 8-41).
4. The waste margins may be removed from either side of the dovetails by placing the wood horizontally in the vise and sawing vertically on the waste side of the shoulder line (see Fig. 8-42).

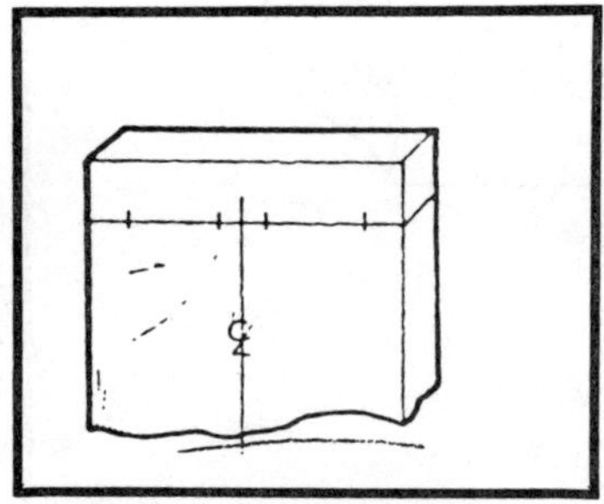

Fig. 8-39. Marking position of tails on shoulder line of proper section.

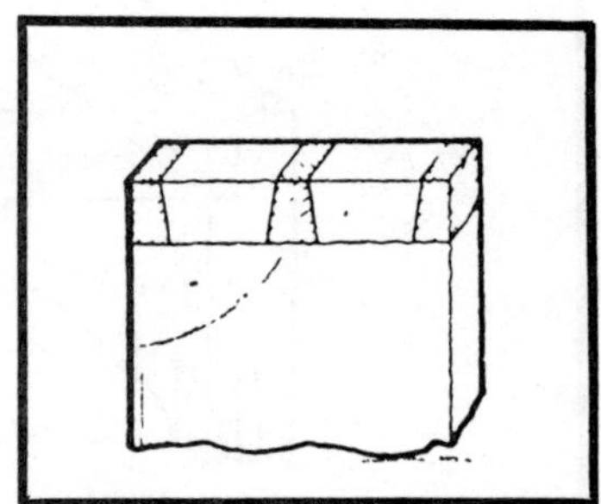

Fig. 8-40. Using a dovetail template to outline tails.

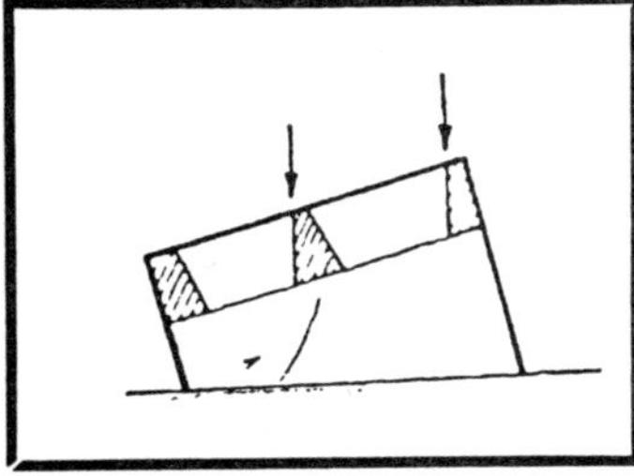

Fig. 8-41. Sloping wood in vise and sawing sloping lines indicated.

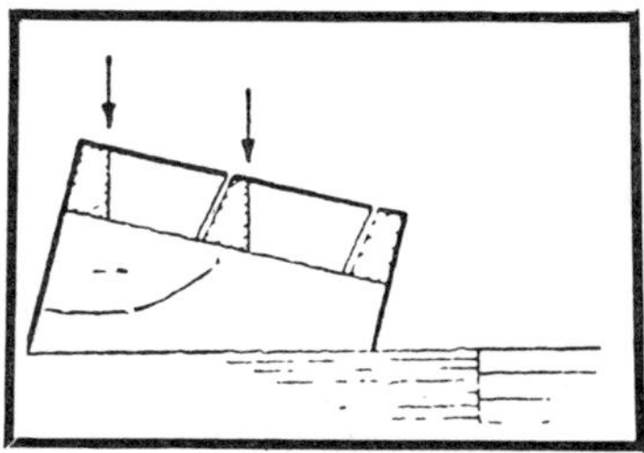

Fig. 8-42. Sloping wood in vise the opposite way and sawing sloping dovetail lines.

5. Most of the waste between the dovetails may be removed with a coping saw. The reminder may be chiseled out to the shoulder line with a beveled edge chisel (see Fig. 8-43). A flat, rectangular piece of metal makes an excellent chiseling board. It shields the workbench or work table from cuts and scratches and can be held in place by the same cramp which secures the joint section, with a wooden ruler acting as a buffer and gauge between the cramp jaws and the work (see Fig. 8-44).

Marking and Cutting the Pins

1. Place the Number 1 piece for each individual joint into the vise, and lay the Number 2 piece for that particular joint which has already been cut into dovetails across the Number 1 piece. Check the squareness of the assembled pieces with a try-square, and be sure that the tails are correctly in place, corner-to-corner over the unsawed wood for the pins. Mark around the tails with a pen knife. If it is difficult to see the knife marks, rub the end grain of the Number 1 piece with chalk before scoring with the knife.
2. Square the marks down the side of the Number 1 joint section to the shoulder line, using a pencil to indicate the sew lines. Hatch mark the waste areas.

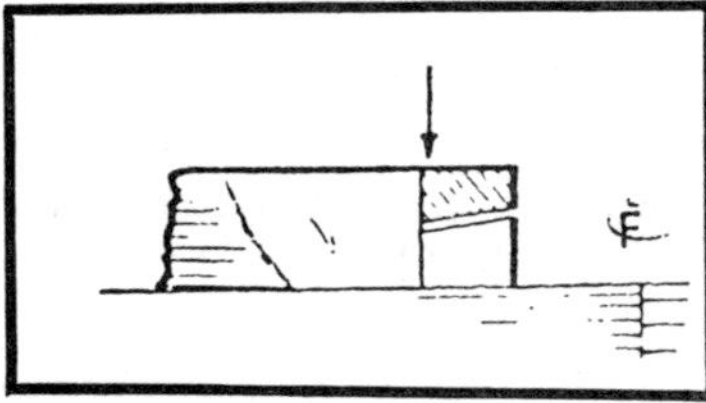

Fig. 8-43. Removing waste areas by sawing along shoulder line.

Fig. 8-44. Removing waste from between tails with saw and chisel.

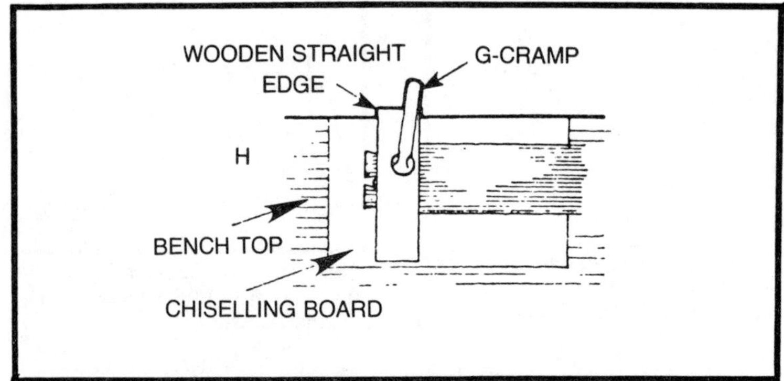

Fig. 8-45. Aerial view of work clamped to worktable or bench.

3. To cut the pins, the Number 1 section of the joint may be placed *upright* in the vise, not sloped as it was to cut the angles of the dovetails on the Number 2 piece. Using the dovetail saw, cut down the saw lines indicated to the shoulder line, always being sure to *cut on the waste side*.

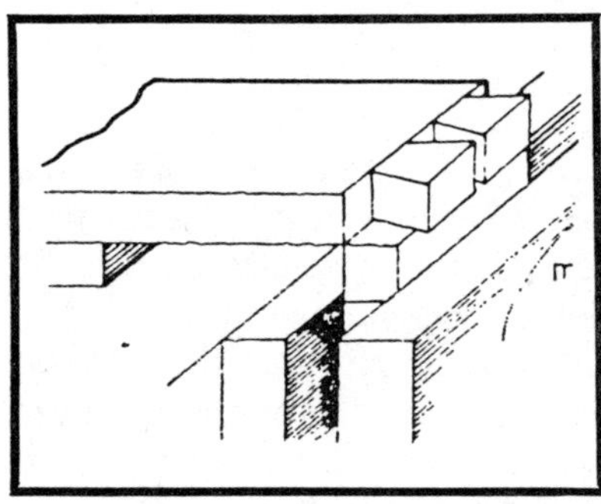
Fig. 8-46. Using the tail cuts as a pattern for the pins.

4 Remove most of the waste with a coping saw. Then pare away the remainder very carefully with a beveled-edge chisel, using/the same method used in cutting the tails.

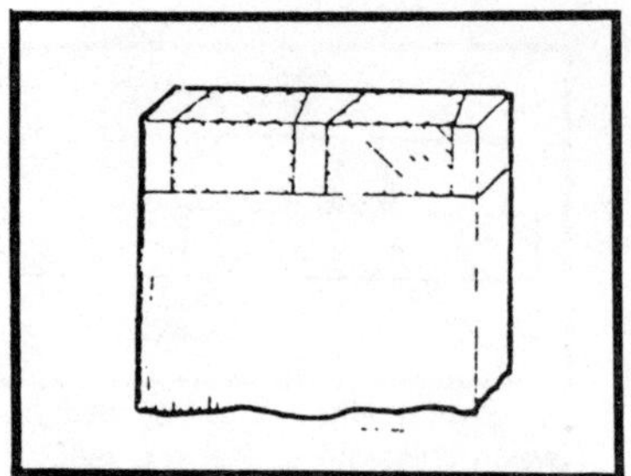
Fig. 8-47. Squaring the pins down to the shoulder line.

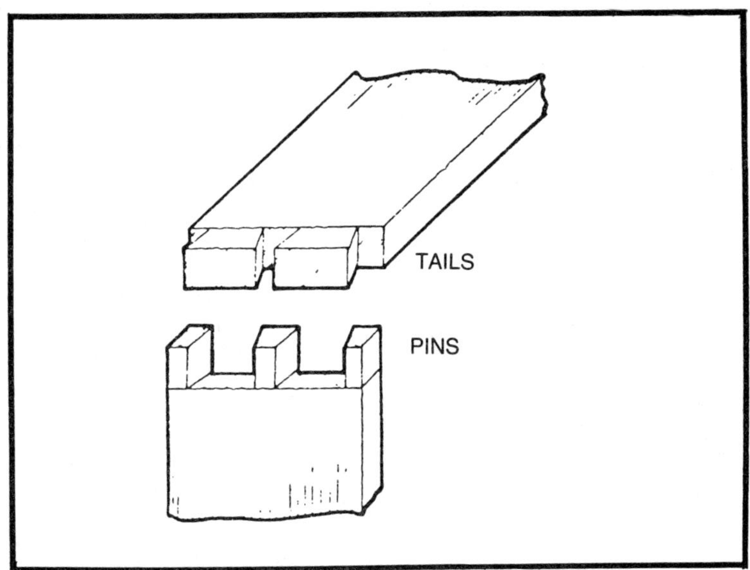

Fig. 8-48. Dovetail joint ready for gluing.

Remember that it is easier to chisel from both sides into the center of the wood, and then square off the corners.

5. The dovetail joint is now ready for gluing. Try to fit and maker any minor adjustments before applying the glue to both parts and joining them. Wipe off any excess glue and secure the two joined sections with a cramp until they are thoroughly dry (see Fig. 8-45).

We have now covered the construction of the most commonly used furniture joints. Shown in Fig. 8-46 are some joints uniting end-grain pieces to face stock. These are very useful on occasion. Figure 8-47 illustrates some types of reinforcing joints which brace, as well as join, two pieces. These are called for at points of stress in the production of furniture.

Chapter 9 Cabinet Structures

Cabinet structure is an integral part of furniture making, requiring specific techniques and knowledge. We will discuss both decorative and utilitarian furniture construction beginning with solid stock, which demands greater consideration and woodworking ability, but which produces the ultimate in appearance, adaptability and satisfaction. We will describe the making of tables, cabinet frames, draws, shelves and doors.

TABLES

Because table structure is the simplest and most basic form of cabinetry, the woodworker must first learn how to build a table. The surface of a table is its most important part so the table top will be our first consideration. There are various materials available for use in constructing this surface. The most elegant material for fine pieces is, of course, solid wood stock which is made from a series of carefully matched boards glued together and jointed to produce a surface of lasting beauty and durability.

However, some surfaces, particularly those used on counters, serve a strictly utilitarian need. They are designed as work areas for kitchens, nurseries, laundry rooms, laboratories or offices. They will be subjected to very hard wear, abrasion and scratching and will come in contact with damaging chemicals of all sorts. The skill, attention and expense necessary for their construction in fine woods would be a waste. Instead, they should be built of one of the modern man-made wood materials which is virtually water and stain-proof, or which is covered in a no-mar plastic.

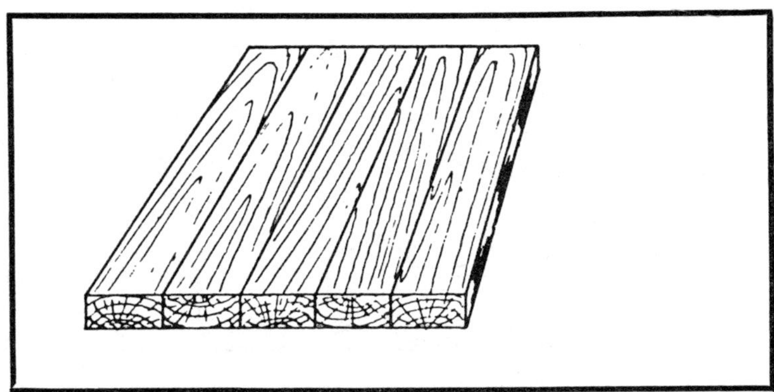

Fig. 9-1. Assembling boards correctly for solid stock top.

Solid stock is stable, reasonably strong and highly attractive. Because its entire thickness is one piece of wood, it can be refinished many times. Its edges can be readily shaped and finished without exposing unsightly grain. However, solid stock is responsive to changing atmospheric conditions and, if imperfectly assembled, can cup. Therefore, the woodworker, in constructing a solid stock panel, must be extremely careful to arrange the integral boards properly. Figure 9-1 illustrates the five steps he must remember:

1. To alternate the annual rings noticeable in the endgrain. See how they curve down at the end of one board and up on the end of the board adjoining.
2. To be sure that the surface grain on each board runs in the same direction. In the illustration, all surface grains run the length of each board.
3. Surface grain patterns must match in a way which is pleasing to the eye.
4. Color tones must blend throughout the assemblage of boards.
5. To form an attractive surface, boards should be 3 to 5 inches in width; all boards in any table top should be the same width.

To prevent cupping in a solid stock table top, straight saw cuts may be made on the undersurface. The cuts should run lengthwise and be spaced about 1½ inches apart, and should be half the depth of the stock. They should not run edge-to-edge, but should stop about 4 to 5 inches from the edge in order that a reinforcing batten can be added at both ends of the saw cuts for reinforcement. Staggering the placement of the screws which hold the batten will prevent undue damage to the wood fibers (see Fig. 9-2).

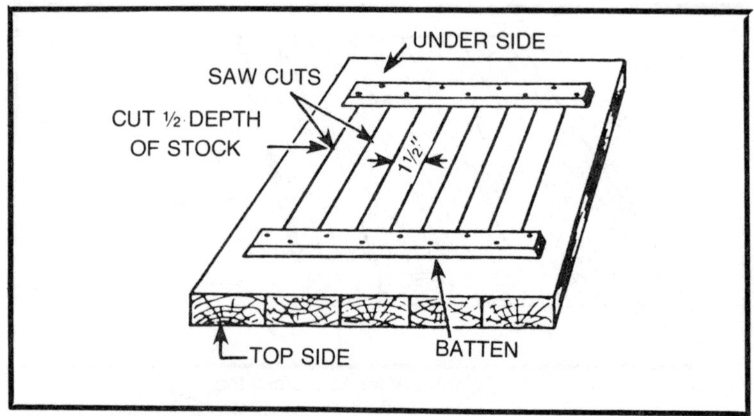

Fig. 9-2. Methods for overcoming warping in a solid stock top.

Plywood may be the next best choice if solid wood is not suitable for the surface you have in mind. Plywood has a veneer surfacing in a wide choice of wood grains, and it gives the same visual effect as solid wood. The veneer surface is more difficult to refinish than solid wood because it is very thin and cannot withstand much abrasion. However, plywood comes in very large sheets and can be easily constructed into a wide range of thicknesses. Because plywood is a laminated, multi-layered product, the raw edges are unsightly and must always be concealed in some fashion. Wood tape with a grained pattern similar to that used in the surface veneer is available. Aluminum stripping or ornamental wood moldings are two other edgings which attractively mask rough plywood edges (see Fig. 9-3).

Platewood and fiberboard are also available with surface veneering. The lack of any grain pattern in the core of either of these materials makes them highly stable. Because shrinkage is negligible,

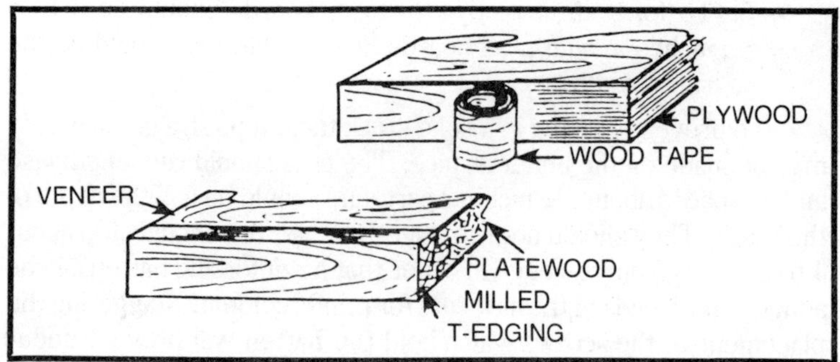

Fig. 9-3. Masking edges of plywood top with wood tape or veneer.

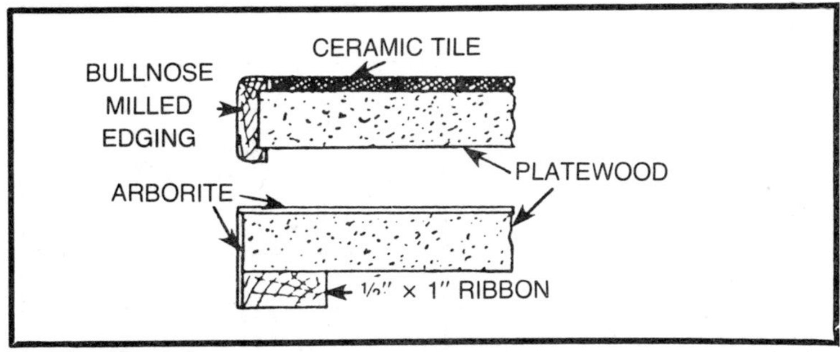

Fig. 9-4. Platewood and fiberboard tops masked with ceramic tile or arborite.

the table top may be fastened directly to the understructure. Platewood is not as strong as solid stock when used in joint construction or when fastened with nails or wood screws. It is highly water-resistant, however, and has good tensile strength. Like plywood, it has an unslightly edge which must be covered. Arborite, ceramic tile or glass tile used over a plain platewood core make attractive, practical countertops (see Fig. 9-4).

The tops of tables should be fastened to rails on the underside for reinforcement. These supports add greatly to the strength and solidarity of the piece. Different methods are used in fastening these rails, depending on the stock and construction involved. With solid stock tops, the wood button insert on a rabbeted block, or the offset metal plate and screw, are the methods generally used. To fasten either rabbeted block or offset metal plate to the table top, a plow must be cut on the inside of the rail before the pieces are assembled. See Fig. 9-5A showing rabbeted-block-and-wood-button assemblage and Fig. 9-5B showing the offset plate and wood screw assemblage. Note that either method allows a slight clearance space between the rabbeted black or the metal plate (whichever is used) and the rail to permit the table to expand or shrink.

If the platewood or plywood is being used in the table top, rails may be fastened directly to the top, since no provision for shrinkage or expansion is necessary with these materials. A wide variety of

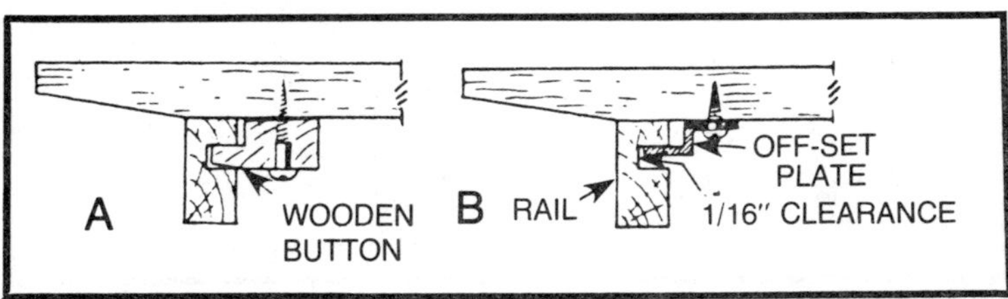

Fig. 9-5. Approved methods of fastening solid stock tops to rails.

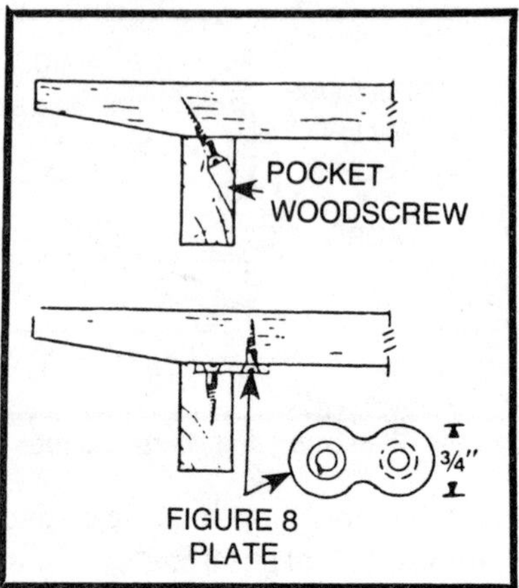

Fig. 9-6. Methods of fastening plywood and platewood tops.

brackets, blocks and wedged dowels may be used, combined with wood screws countersunk from the underside of the rail (see Fig. 9-6 and 9-7).

Legs are generally fastened directly to the rails using special lag screws and hardware plates if the legs are turned, or forked wooden joints if the legs are square. Figure 9-8 illustrates one method of securing a tapered turned leg to a platewood table top and reinforcement rail. A table leg bracket is fastened to the top of the leg with a lag screw bolt which requires a special T-wrench to sink it. Then the table leg and bracket are fastened with countersunk screws to the reinforcing rail strip. Figure 9-9 shows how securely a square tapered leg may be fastened to a rail by fashioning the top of the leg into a forked joint which fits over and around the rail, and then

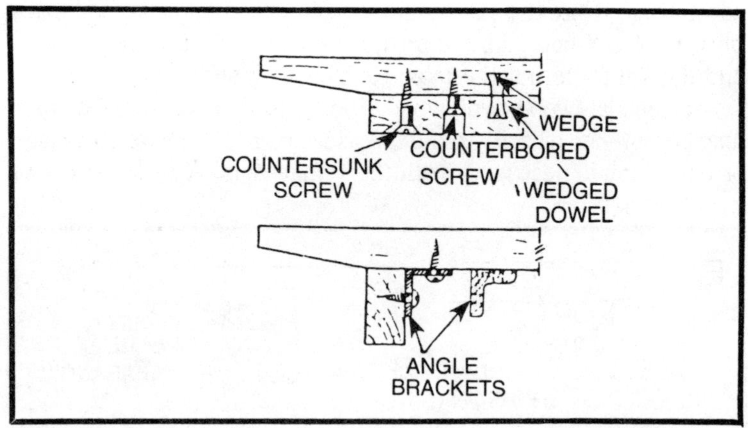

Fig. 9-7. Alternate methods for fastening plywood and platewood tops.

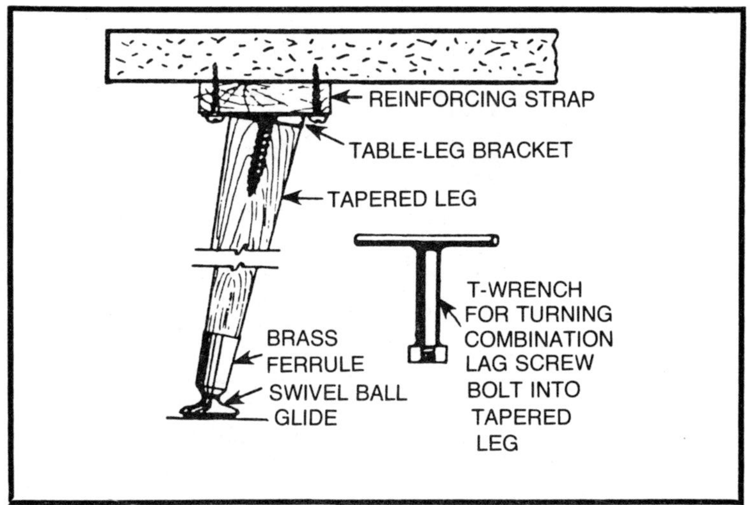

Fig. 9-8. Fastening turned legs to table top.

fastening both leg and rail as a unit to the table top using counterbored wood screws.

In Fig. 9-10 an ingenious design combines legs and rail in a single unified piece in the top tier of this step table. The unit is then secured with combination lag screws to its table top, and the assembled upper tier fastened to the lower tier table top by two more combination lag screws driven through the lower table top from underneath and into the legs of the upper table.

The hardware, wood screws, and combination lag screws used to fasten rails and legs are always deliberately chosen because they are removable and, therefore, may be dismantled for moving or storage.

DRAWERS

The making of workable drawers is one of the most difficult of all woodworking operations. Considerable skill and care must be exercised in fitting a drawer accurately enough so that it will close tightly without gaping and yet will glide easily when it is slid open or closed. The allowable amount of tolerance is small, particularly in fine furniture.

Drawers are basically one of two styles—the type with a front panel which closes flush with the gables of the cabinet, or the type with an overlapping front panel which extends beyond the actual drawer opening by a wide margin. The former drawer is often seen in dressers, desks and vanities; the latter style is popular for kitch-

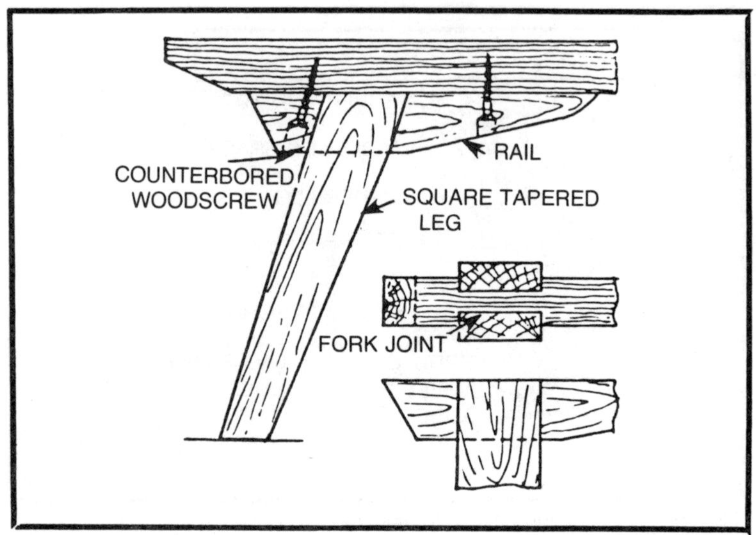

Fig. 9-9. Fastening square leg to table top.

ens, utility rooms and much built-in furniture where the fit is not so critical (see Figs. 9-11, A and B).

Drawers are suspended by different means, depending on their size and weight. Dadoed wooden strips may be used to support and guide the drawer. This type of drawer guide is glued to the inside of the casework gable or affixed across the bottom surface of the drawer from front to back with wood screws.

Metal drawer guides are available with either metal or plastic rollers. These are always attached to the sides of drawers, which

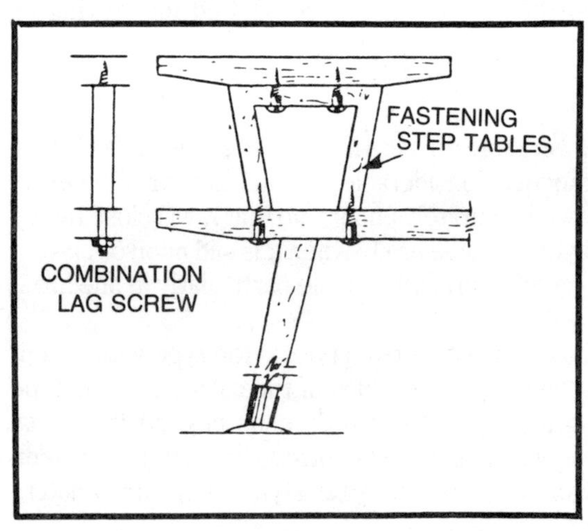

Fig. 9-10. Fastening step tables.

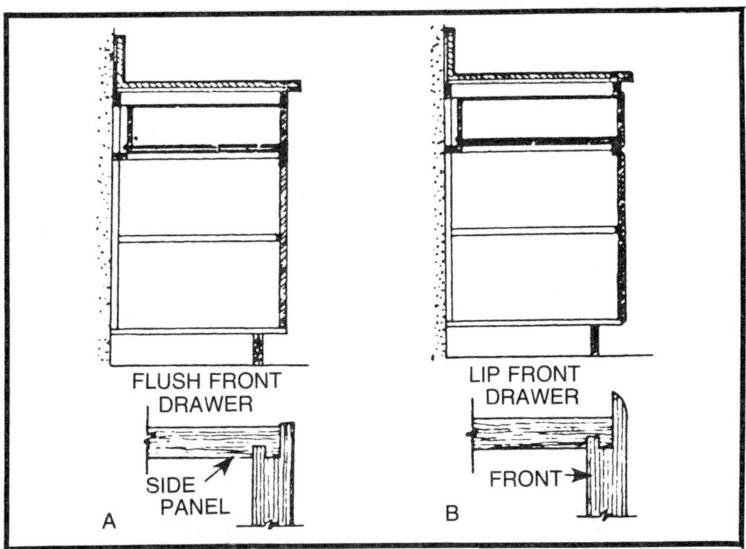

Fig. 9-11. Two basic drawer types and how each fits cabinet carcase.

means that their width dimension must be taken into consideration in calculating the thickness of the stock which will be used in making the drawer (see Fig. 9-12).

To construct a drawer which fits the cabinetry satisfactorily, yet glides in and out easily, take the following steps:

1. Study the working drawing of the drawer to be constructed to determine the exact dimensions required for its height, width and depth.
2. For the interior parts of the drawer use a softwood, such as pine or basswood, or a rugged wood material, such as plywood. For fine furniture, quarter-sawn oak is preferred for the back and side rails. Whatever the wood, the grain should run from the drawer front to the drawer back to make planing easier.
3. The front panel of the drawer should be made of the same wood as that used in color and graining if the proposed finish is clear stain and varnish.
4. Decide on the joint desired. For drawers, such joints as dado, rabbet, dovetail and a combination of dado and tongue-and-rabbet are generally used (see Fig. 9-13A). If top-quality furniture is the project, the drawers should have dovetail joints at the back corners and lap dovetail joints at the front corners where they will be concealed by the drawer front (see Fig. 9-13B).

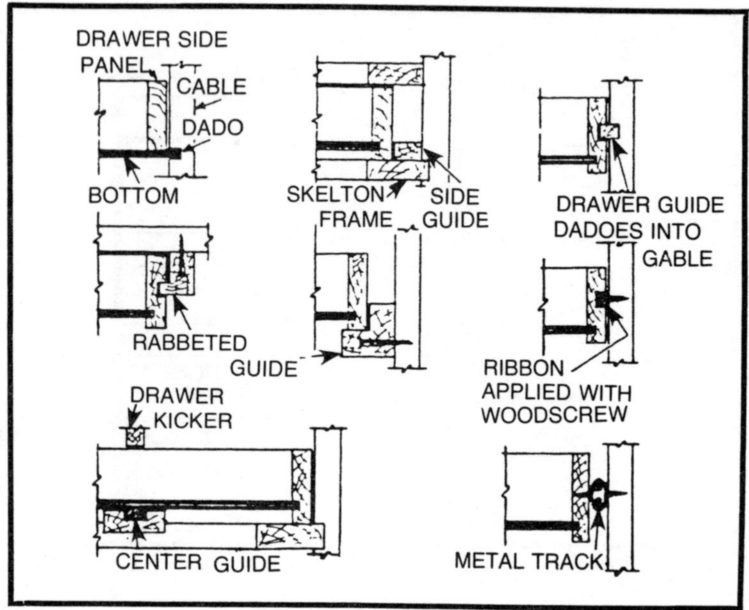

Fig. 9-12. Various methods of drawer suspension.

5. Now consider the layout for the drawer itself. Usually, the stock sizes for drawer construction are these: ¾-inch stock for the front panel, ⅜-inch stock for the left and right sides, ⅝-inch stock for the back panel, and ¼-inch wood for

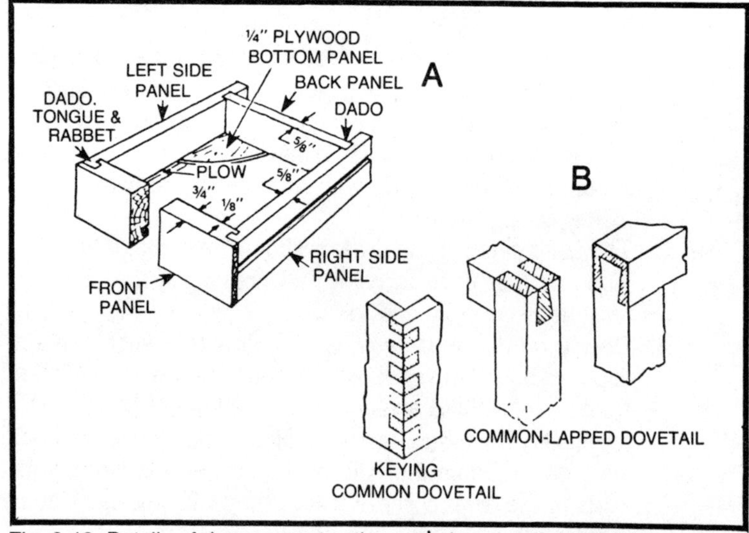

Fig. 9-13. Details of drawer construction and close-up of dovetail joints used.

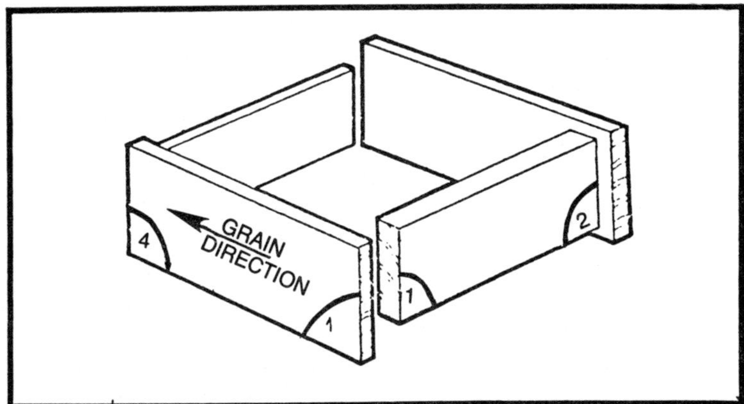

Fig. 9-14. Drawer rails marked for joint replacement.

the bottom. Tradition dictates that the bottom of a drawer be made of solid wood. However, plywood offers a good alternative. The grain of a drawer bottom must run from side to side, never from front to back. The bottom is fitted into a groove in the drawer front and both drawer sides and is, therefore, able to expand with amperage out the back of the drawer, where it extends beyond the back panel instead of being grooved into it.

6. After calculating the clearance required by the joint selected, cut the stock to size. Mark the lower outside corners of the side and back rails where the joints are to be made (see Fig. 9-14).
7. Lay out the joint on each panel, and cut each joint very carefully.
8. Plane the inside faces of the drawer with a trying plane.
9. Square the bottom edges of the side rails.
10. Plough a ⅛-inch groove in each drawer side, about ⅛-inch from the edge. This groove runs the length of the drawer side, from drawer front to drawer back. Mark a saw line parallel to the groove and about ⅛-inch from it. Saw off from each drawer side this grooved strip, which will be glued inside the finished drawer to act as a reinforcement and to hold the drawer bottom in its grooved slot (see Fig. 9-15).
11. Plane a face edge on the drawer sides.
12. Gauge and plane the drawer sides to width, so that they will fit just inside the carcase.
13. Plane the bottom edge of the front piece square to fit the carcase.

Fig. 9-15. Drawer rails plowed and marked for sawing side slips.

14. Plane both ends of the front piece to fit the carcase snugly lengthwise.
15. Now plane the top edge of the front piece to fit the carcase snugly in width. Make the rear half of the top edge of the front piece one shaving out of square, so that the drawer will enter the carcase for only half of its thickness.
16. Plow a groove on the lower inside of the front piece to receive the drawer bottom. Remember to allow at least ¼-inch underneath the bottom for drawer stops.
17. Plane the back rail to width. (The back rail is usually ½-inch narrower in width than the drawer sides.)
18. Plane the back rail to a tight fit lengthwise.
19. Gauge the back and front rails for length of pins for the dovetail joints. Remember that the side rails are presently thicker than they will be when planed, so set the gauge to the *eventual*, rather than the present, thickness.
20. Gauge for the length of the dovetail across the end grain of the drawer front (usually ⅔ of the thickness of the drawer front.)

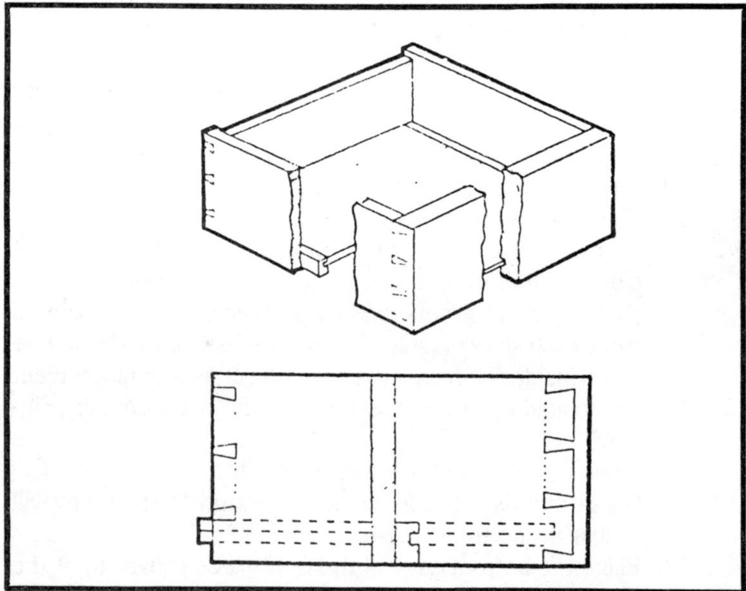

Fig. 9-16. Drawers marked at corners for dovetails.

Fig. 9-17. Sawing both dovetail sections as one unit.

21. Saw the sides to length (somewhat shorter than the depth of the carcase.) Place the side rails together in the vise and plane the ends square.
22. Gauge the length of the dovetails around both side pieces.
23. Mark out the dovetails, allowing for the groove in the drawer front and for the narrow width of the back rail (see Fig. 9-16).
24. Saw the joint sections marked for the dovetails together as though they were one piece (see Fig. 9-17), using cramps to secure them.
25. Separate the pieces and remove the waste from the tails.
26. Using the dovetail cuts as a pattern, mark the outlines of the pins with a scriber.
27. Cut the pins. The dovetail pins at the back of the drawer require only straightline sawing, but cutting the lap dovetail joint in front is more difficult. First, cramp the workflat on the edge of the bench. Now saw down the sides of the joint at an angle on the waste side of the lines, cutting as deeply as possible. The rest of the waste will have to be removed with a chisel, working downward the grain and then into the joint from the end. Make sure that the chiseled surfaces are vertically straight.
28. Before applying glue, make a trial assembly to see that all parts fit together properly and that the drawer fits the drawer opening in the carcase.
29. Glue up the joints. Use a hammer to close the joints, with a waste wood block buffering the hammer head. Squeeze the joints in cramps just tight enough to expell the excess glue. Wipe off this exuded glue and check to be sure the drawer is square and flat—not twisted. Allow glue to dry.
30. Now cut grooved drawer slips to length and glue them into place inside the drawer against the side rails with the groved slits facing the drawer interior. Cramp them snugly into place to dry.

31. Plane the drawer bottom to remove any saw marks. If it is necessary to glue more than one board together to make a large enough bottom, be sure that the grain on all boards is running horizontally across the drawer.
32. Rebate the ends of the drawer bottom to form a tongue which will fit the ⅛-inch groove in the drawer strips. Then slide the bottom into place and mark the front edge of the drawer on the drawer bottom. Plane this edge true, then rebate so that the bottom fits into the groove along the drawer front (see Figs. 9-18 and 9-19).
34. Plane down the sides to the end grain of the front and back pieces. Use a trying plane and shear from the front of the drawer to the back.
35. Place the drawer in position and plane the front level with the carcase. A little Ronuk rubbed into the drawer will make it work well.

SUSPENDING SHELVES IN CABINETS

The spacing of shelves in a cabinet is determined by three factors: (1) the overall design of the cabinet, (2) what is to be stored on the shelves, and (3) the constructional methods employed.

Suspending shelving by wood joints attached to the cabinet frame makes a sturdy, attractive piece of furniture (see Fig. 9-20). However, less flexibility of arrangement is possible inside the cabinet with such shelving than is possible with shelving supported on brackets, pins and clips. These hardware items allow for ease of adjustment within the storage space itself. Shelves can be removed

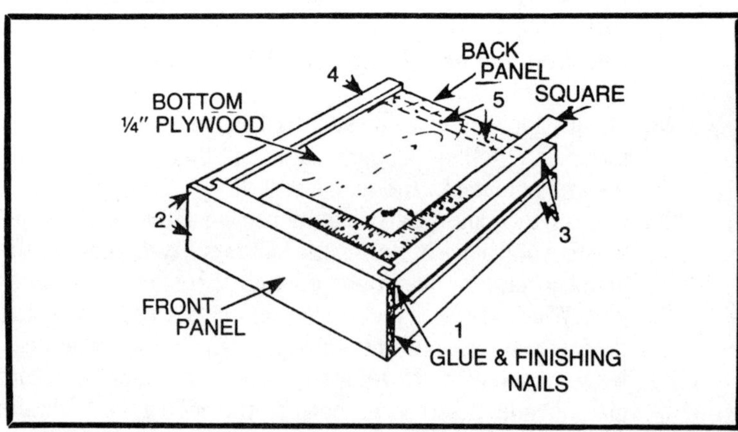

Fig. 9-18. Rebating drawer bottom to fit into slotted side slips and grooved drawer front.

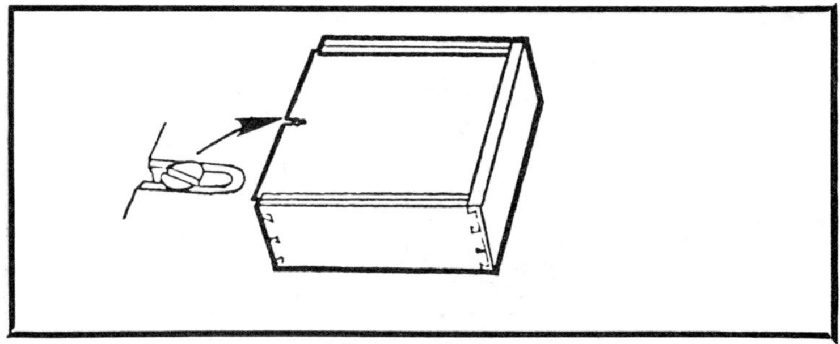

Fig. 9-19. Fitting underside of drawer with door stops.

for cleaning when not in use, and their spacing can be rearranged as necessary to accommodate the objects stored on them.

A variety of shelf support hardware is available—some props being designed to fit into holes or slots in upright rails installed in the corners of the cabinet, and some pegs and clip-ons being designed to insert into holes in the cabinet wall (see Fig. 9-21).

CABINET FRAMES

A finished cabinet is composed of several parts—the *carcase* or structural frame (See Fig. 9-22), to which the drawers are fitted or the doors hung to transform the basic carcase into a piece of *casework*, as the finished cabinet, complete with doors, drawers and ornamentation, is called.

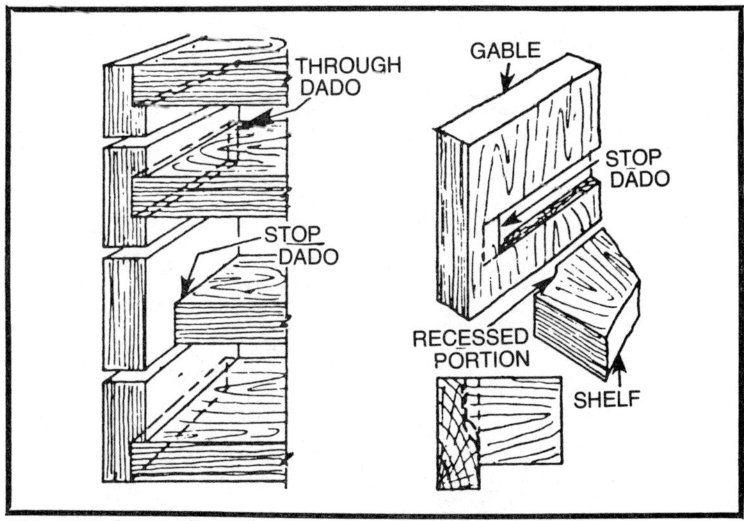

Fig. 9-20. Suspending cabinet shelves with wooden dado joints.

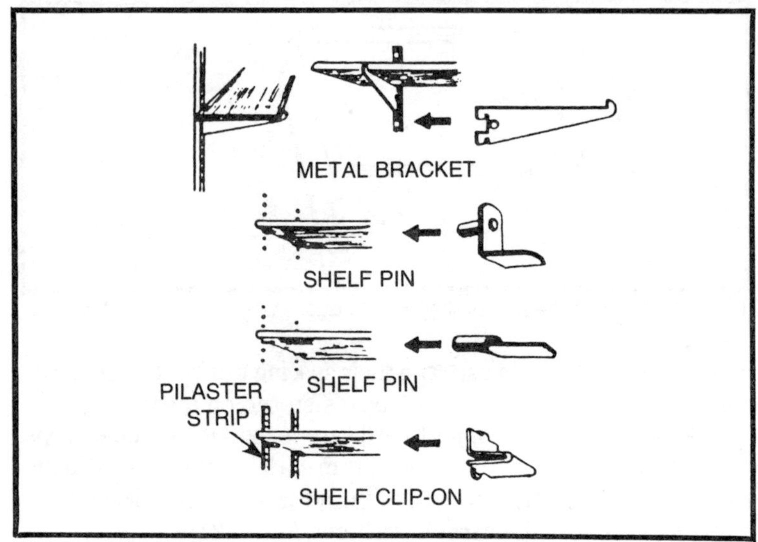

Fig. 9-21. Hardware for suspending adjustable shelves.

Cabinets may be produced in a wide variety of styles. The woodworker will be able to find working drawings and plans for the exact style he wishes. In addition to selecting the design which best suits his taste and decor, he should be influenced in his choice by the function he wishes the cabinet to perform, the availability of the materials he will need and the cost of construction. The working

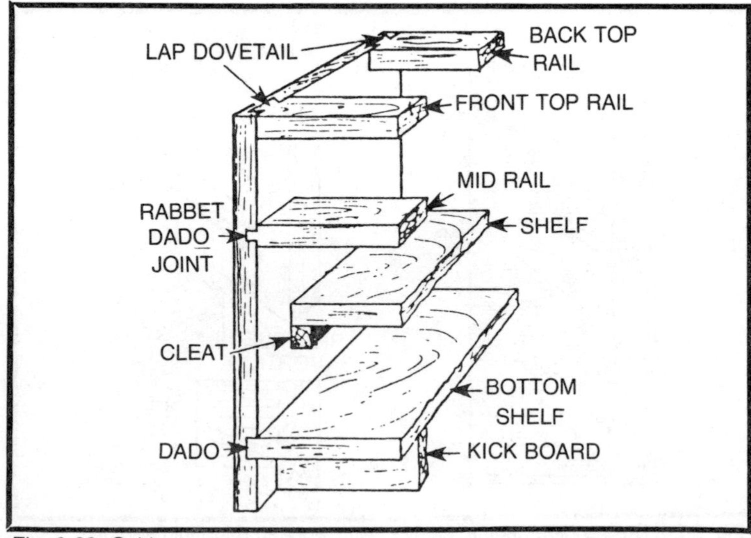

Fig. 9-22. Cabinet carcase.

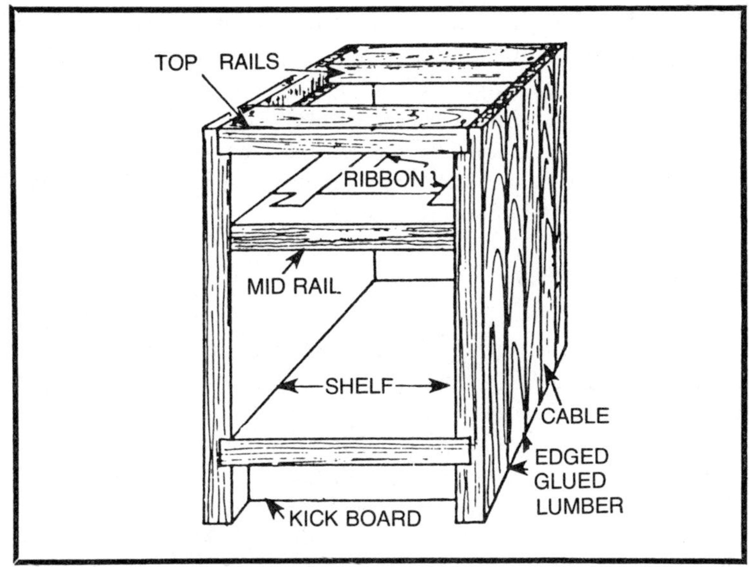

Fig. 9-23. Solid stock panel frame.

drawing he obtains may provide sufficient instructions for the cabinet's construction, as well as a list of materials needed. However, the woodworker often lacks the necessary tools to follow instructions exactly, or wishes to modify the specified design to more exactly suit his own purposes. Therefore, he needs to know the basics of construction in order to follow the instructions intelligently and to be able to incorporate his own ideas into his projects.

Solid Stock Panel Frames

Solid stock panel frames require high quality lumber and a number of glued joints; they present, therefore, a more extensive task to true-up, glue and sand. However, they provide a very strong, stable, attractive frames which takes a finish beautifully and which can be refinished again and again throughout a long and useful lifetime. Their only drawback, besides the greater labor involved in making them, is the fact that they may wrap in excessively humid surroundings (see Fig. 9-23).

Paneled Frame Construction

Panel frame construction is used for desks, wardrobes and chest-of-drawers. It consists of legs, a top and bottom rail, and a panel of thin stock or plywood (see Fig. 9-24). The legs are secured to the rails with a tenon or dowel joint. A groove is cut in both top and bottom rail into which the panel is inserted. A paneled frame will not shrink or warp, but must be kept precisely square when it is being glued. It is lightweight, yet sufficiently strong for the attachment of drawers and doors. Other carcase features—drawer guides, cleats, plowed thresholds for sliding doors, and dust bottoms—may be added to legs or rails of the frame as desired to support shelves, drawers and doors in the finished piece.

Solid Plywood Frame

The solid plywood frame is becoming very popular, even replacing the solid lumber frame because of the wide variety of face veneers and thicknesses in which plywood is available and because it is available in large sheets. The paramount drawback, however, is that the raw edges must be faced in some way; they cannot be sanded and finished as solid wood edges can be. Wood tape, ornamental moldings and aluminum stripping must be used to conceal the laminated layers visible at the edges (see Fig. 9-25).

Platewood and other composition woods are also used in cabinetry—especially in utility furniture and built-ins.

X-Frame Construction

The furniture frame easiest to construct is certainly the X-frame. This type of frame lends itself to such structures as benches, picnic tables, desks, counters, doors, etc., where the main

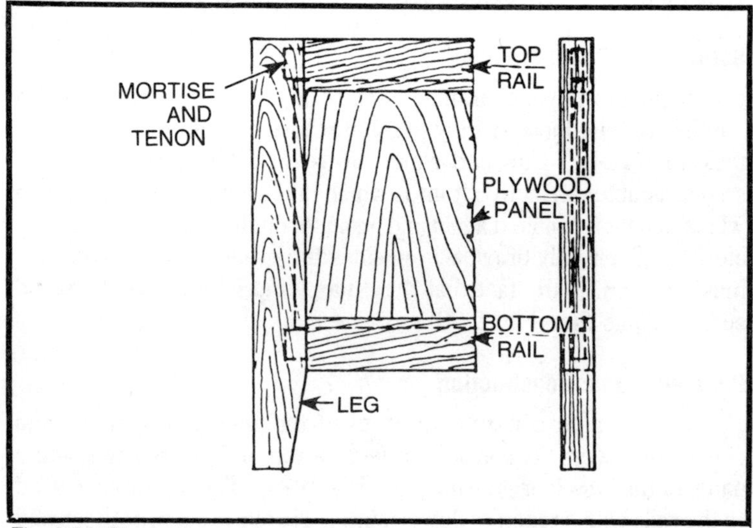

Fig. 9-24. Plywood panel frame.

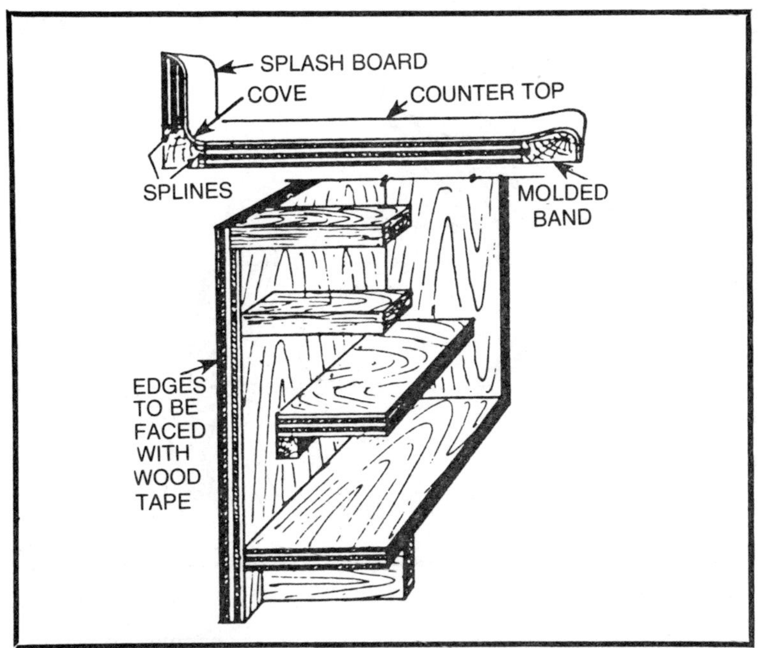

Fig. 9-25. Solid plywood frame.

function of the frame is to support a working or serving surface, rather than to enclose a storage space (see Fig. 9-26). An X-frame structure has a very airy appearance, and its exposed construction and clean, functional line go well with today's architecture with its so-called "cathedral" open-beamed ceilings, visibly displayed wall studding and open, lattice-work room dividers.

Despite its light appearance, the X-frame is very sturdy, particularly if properly reinforced. With the installation of the proper hardware fasteners, X-framed furniture may be folded for storage or shipping.

USE OF METALS

Such metals as wrought iron, steel, brass and aluminum in both sheet and tubular forms are used for building furniture. For office use, combinations of metal, wood, glass and fabric are currently being utilized in creating crisp, clean-lined furniture for places of business (see Fig. 9-27). Metal frames may be very delicate in appearance, yet they are strong and durable. Aluminum can be cast and anondized to create interesting colors, and the objects produced are most attractive, as well as light weight. The cobweb traceries of wrought iron have been utilized in furniture design for several

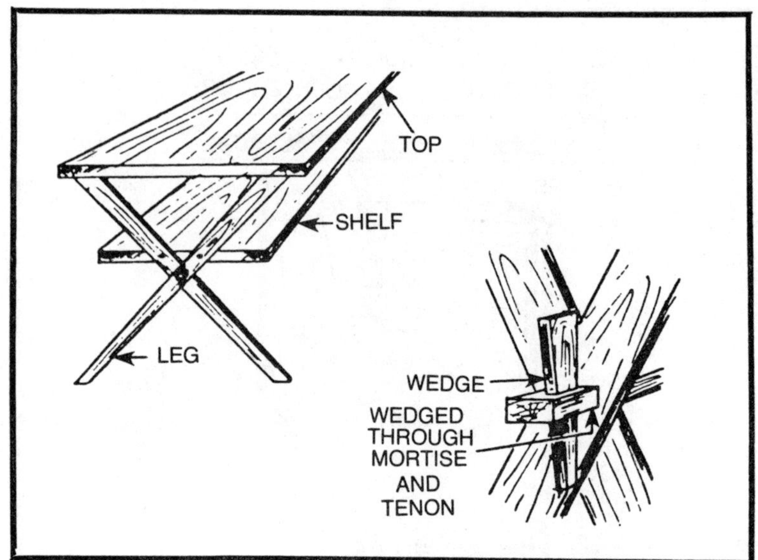

Fig. 9-26. "X" frame.

hundred years. Brass—in tubular form or in shimmering sheets further embellished by chased and embossed designs and hammered texturing—has lent its jeweler's finish to fine furniture and ornament since ancient times. Such recently developed materials as lucite, plexiglas and fiberglass are presently much in vogue. The furniture produced in these materials is outstanding for its exquisite purity of line and remarkable range of colors.

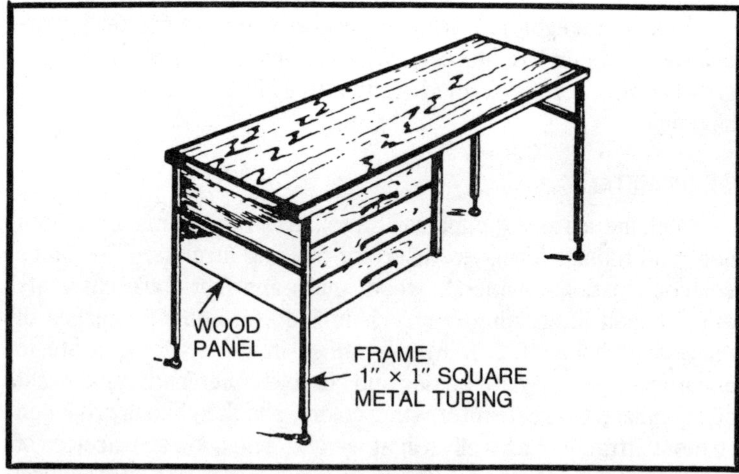

Fig. 9-27. Combination metal and wood frame.

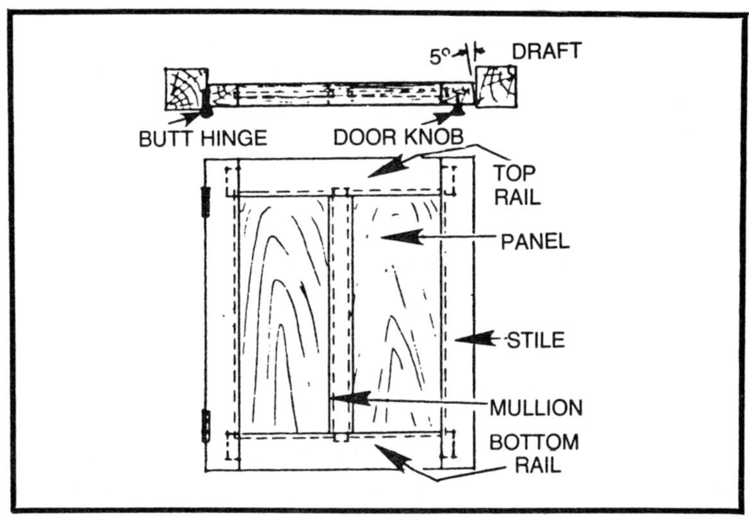

Fig. 9-28. Panel door.

The design and materials for any project in furniture craftsmanship should be selected for appropriateness to the lifestyle the furniture piece will augment, the decor in which it will appear, and the purpose it is to fulfill. Other important considerations would be those of practicality, availability of materials and ease of execution.

DOOR CONSTRUCTION AND SUSPENSION

In furniture design and construction, the doors most frequently encountered are cupboard doors. Cupboards vary widely in design, subject to the arrangement of their component parts and to their overall size. Such features as stiles, rails, panels, moldings, glass, fabrics and ornamentation all dictate subtle modifications of the basic box design (see Fig. 9-28).

Dimensions

The dimensions of a cupboard door are designated as width, height and thickness. Doors may be suspended on hinges to swing in one direction, or may be double-hinged to permit their folding accordion-fashion.

The door must be pre-fit to the door frame opening. The stile, which is the edge to which the hinge will be affixed, is trued first. The top is then squared with the true edge, and checked against the opening of the cabinet. Next, the door is planed to width, allowing 1/16-inch clearance on each side for expansion and to accommodate the thickness of the finished material (see Fig. 9-29).

The next consideration is the height of the door, which must be very carefully measured, allowing 1/16-inch at the top and 1/16-inch at the bottom for a door designed to fit within the door frame on all four sides.

Hinges

Once the door exactly fits the opening, it is ready for hinges. The butt hinge is generally used, but many other hinges are available for specific uses, as discussed in the section on hardware. The size of the hinge chosen depends on the weight and size of the door. Sizes range from 1 inch × ½ inch to 4 inches × 2⅜ inches, depending on the quality of metal used and whether the hinge has an even or an uneven number of knuckles.

Hinges should be positioned at a reasonable distance from the top and bottom of a door. If the door is paneled, the hinges should be positioned within the inner edge of each rail. After selecting the type of hinge desired, locate its position on the door and on the door frame, using the working drawing as a guide.

If a butt hinge with an uneven number of knuckles is used, the side with the most knuckles is fastened to the cabinet, and the side with the fewer knuckles is fastened to the door.

There are two ways of attaching a hinge. The first is to position each of the flaps an equal distance from the edge—one from the edge of the door, and one from the edge of the frame (see Fig. 9-30). The other method is to position the side of the hinge with the fewest

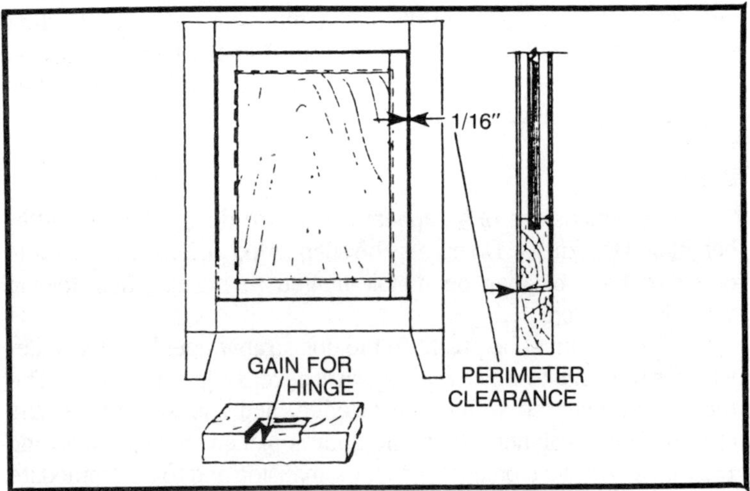

Fig. 9-29. Installing a hinged door.

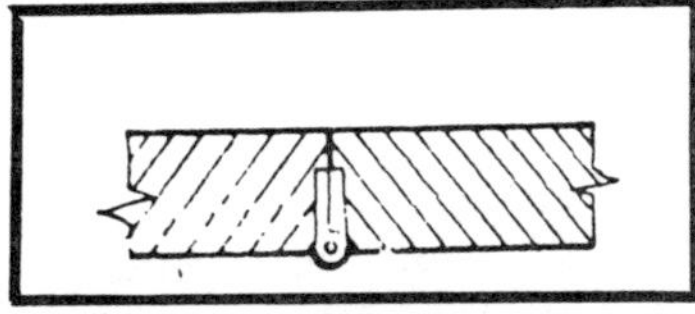

Fig. 9-30. Showing hinge set equally into both door and frame.

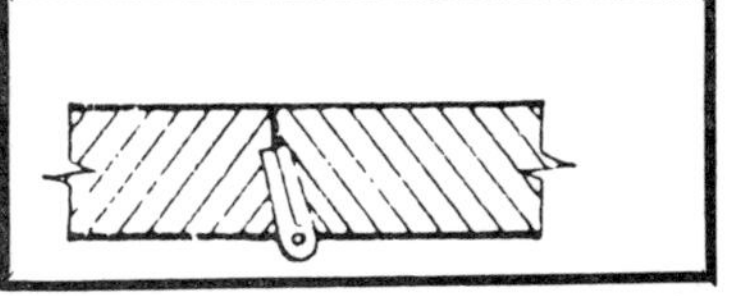

Fig. 9-31. Showing hinge and knuckle set entirely into moving part.

knuckles (if the knuckles are of uneven number) to the door, placing the hinge far enough from the door edge so that the knuckle is also covered by the edge of the door (see Fig. 9-31). This second method, with the hinge flap and its knuckles both let into the moving parts, is the application method generally used for cabinetry because the hinge is less conspicuous when attached in this fashion. Whatever the method used, the procedural steps for attaching hinges are as follows:

1. Depending on the method used, set the marking gauge to either (A) one-half the width of the hinge (see Fig. 9-32A), or (B) one-half the width of the hinge plus the width of the knuckle (see Fig. 9-32B).
2. Transfer the gauge measurement to the wood (see Fig. 9-33).
3. After making sure that the position marked is square with the door side, hatch-mark with a pencil the area to be gouged out of the door to accommodate the hinge flap (see Fig. 9-34).

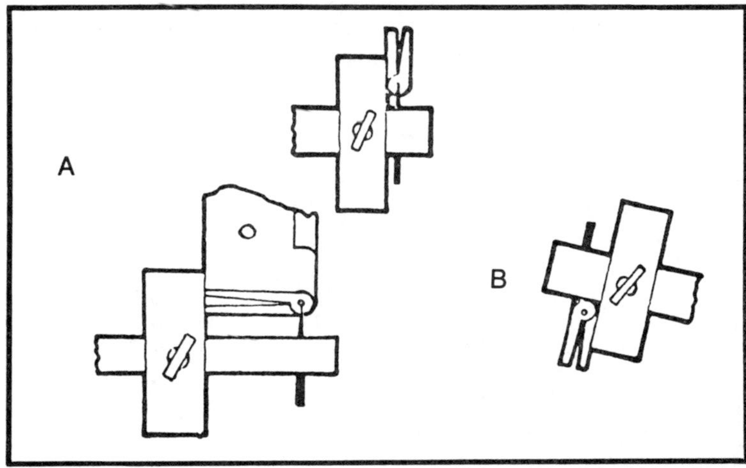

Fig. 9-32. Setting marking gauge: A) for one-half the width of the hinge; B) for one-half of the hinge plus the width of the knuckle.

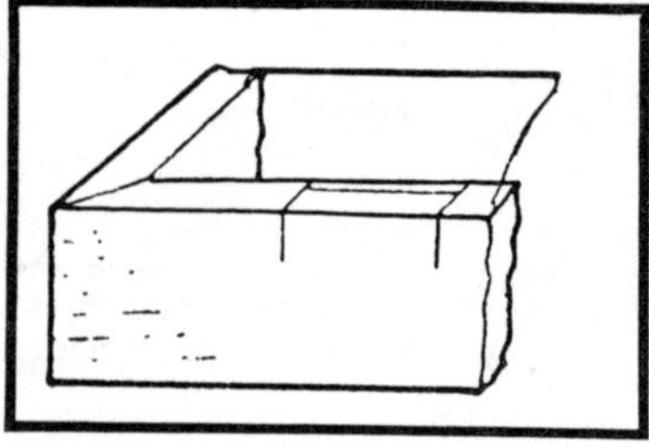

Fig. 9-33. Transferring the measure of the hinge to wood.

4. To make the depression (or "gain," as it is sometimes called) for the hinge flap, first saw across the hatch-marked area, penetrating as deeply as possible (see Fig. 9-35), and remove the waste with a chisel. The base of this recess should slope slightly to make room for the hinge.

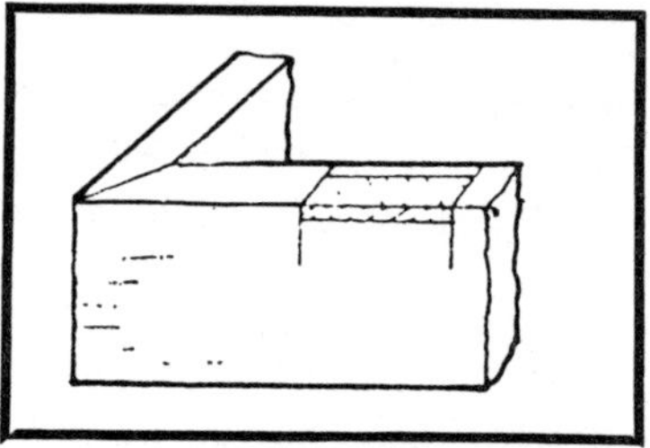

Fig. 9-34. Waste area hatch-marked with pencil.

5. Fit the hinge carefully into the depression, and mark the hole for the center screw with a nail punch. Adjust the fit of the hinge into the recess by "pelleting" the hole mark (that is, levering the fibers across the hole mark with a bradawl). Using the proper size bit, drill a pilot hole for the center screw and fit the hinge flap over it. Insert the center wood screw, then the other screws, and tighten them.

Fig. 9-35. Sawing hatch-marked gain for hinge flap preparatory to removing waste wood with chisel.

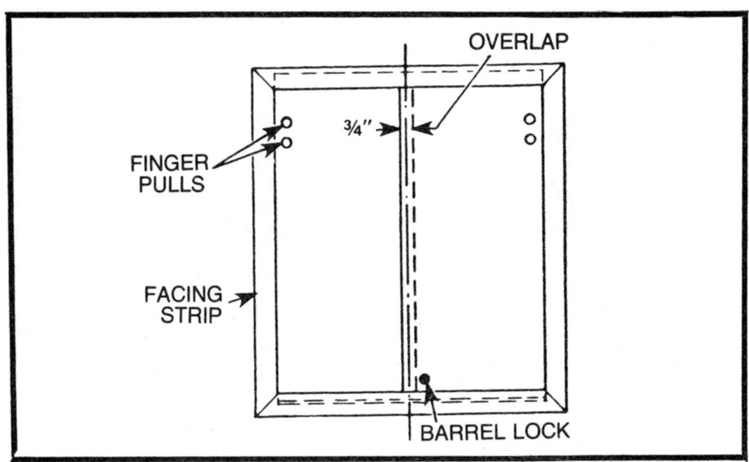

Fig. 9-36. Sliding door, showing finger pulls and lock.

6. Test the door for clearance, and make any necessary adjustments.

SLIDING DOORS

Where there is a limited space to swing a door open, a sliding door is the only answer. An almost endless variety of glides, tracks and hardware are currently being manufactured for stock-size sliding doors; the proper fittings are readily available even for unusually large, heavy doors. Roll-away style closet doors find great favor with

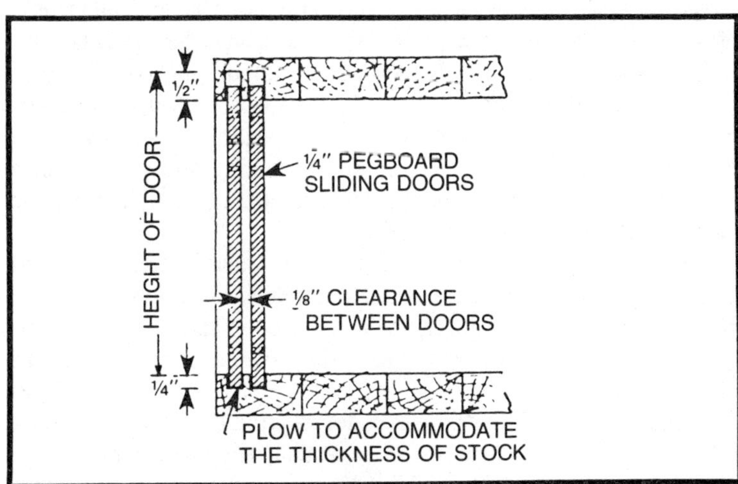

Fig. 9-37. Basic construction of sliding doors.

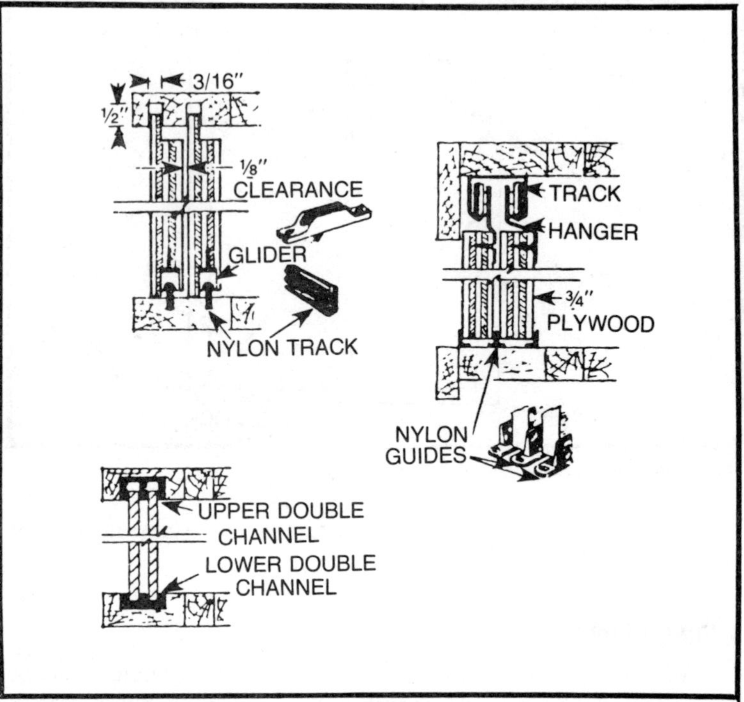

Fig. 9-38. Various tracks available for sliding doors.

modern architects and homeowners because sliding doors do not encroach on the room space; therefore, they permit the placement of furniture next to the door openings. However, sliding doors do curtail the spaces inside closets, where the door hanging and tracking mechanisms cut down on the space available for shelves, etc. Sliding doors should be fashioned of very stable material, such as plywood, platewood, fiberglass and plate glass, because the clearance between the two sliding panels is necessarily small. However, these panels are not affected by the shrinking and swelling of a frame, as are hinge-hung doors, and are popular for this reason in cabinetry as well as home building.

Sliding doors may be removed from the track for refinishing and cleaning by lifting up on each panel and pulling out the bottom end. Recessed finger pulls make them easier to open and close. A barrel-type lock may be inserted through the bottom of both panels as shown in Fig. 9-36.

The size of the door panels is determined by the kind of stock and the sliding mechanism used. Essentially the same construction techniques are used for all sliding doors whether they are closet doors in architectural structures or cabinet doors in casework (see

Fig. 9-37). However, the methods of hanging and tracking them differ with the particular mechanism used (see Fig. 9-38). Consequently, the woodworker or carpenter must follow the manufacturer's directions precisely in installing the doors. A worthwhile precaution would be to check and recheck the layout before cutting the panels or rabbetting the doors for various glides.

Chapter 10 Finishes

The application of finishes to new or old furniture can be, of itself, an interesting and thoroughly fascinating occupation. The proper choice and application of an appropriate finish can enhance an otherwise drab piece of furniture or exploit to the fullest the inherent elegance of a classical period piece. Although modern materials can make possible the application of excellent finishes with less work and effort than some of the older methods, the serious woodworker will want to emulate the work of the old masters. This will be particularly true when restoring valuable older pieces of furniture.

The secret of a good finish is in the meticulous preparation of the wood and this will be discussed in detail before delving into the many interesting and exciting types of finishing techniques that are the subject of this chapter.

REMOVING DISCOLORATIONS

Before applying any finish whatsoever, the craftsman may wish to freshen the color of stripped wood. He can successfully restore color to gray and faded wood with detergent soap powder and very hot water, vigorously applied with a scrub brush. When the wood is thoroughly clean, the soap is rinsed off with hot water, and the wood is towel-dried with a soft cloth. While the wood is still wet, a hot solution of oxalic acid is applied and allowed to remain on the wood for ten minutes. Then it is washed off with hot water, and its action is neutralized with an application of household ammonia or white vinegar. The action of the oxalic acid solution (mixed by adding two ounces of oxalic acid crystals or one ounce of oxalic acid powder to a pint of hot water) will be halted by the neutralizer. When the neutralizer is removed and the wood is wiped dry, the surfaces are allowed to dry thoroughly. An even mellowness of color tone will be evident, and the grain raised by the wet applications is easily smoothed by sanding.

Grease Stains

Grease stains of animal origin are removable with the same sort of solvents which eradicate such stains from clothing. Vegetable origin grease stains yield to acetone. Apply either preparation with a small artist's brush, working the solvent well into the spot until the spot has been removed, then wiping it dry with a cleansing tissue.

SANDING

No finish is any smoother than is the wood beneath it, so the craftsman's first consideration before applying a new finish is to sand the wood which is to receive it to a satin sleekness.

Use garnet or aluminum oxide abrasive papers for this task. Start with a 3/0 grade used over a sanding block. Sand with careful uniformity of pressure and brush the surface frequently to remove sanding dust. Following the initial sanding with 3/0 papers, continue sanding with finer and finer grades—particularly if the piece is of hardwood and you are applying a transparent finish. Six/0 papers are usually the finest abrasive needed for softwood, and 4/0 the finest for painted wood. However, fine transparent finishes require that you dampen the surface to raise the grain whiskers and then sand the surface with fine wet-or-dry abrasive papers until no further whiskers can be raised when the surface is dampened.

This wet surface sanding treatment leaves the surface ready for final sanding with steel wool. But before this step, you will want to make a wet test for color by rubbing a little water into one section of the abraded surface to see how much grain and color will show under the layers of transparent finish. You may find that the grain markings are so pale that even when stained they will not reach the intensity of color configuration you desire. If so, now is the time to apply a mixture of pure linseed oil and pure turpentine in equal parts with a soft cloth to all exposed surfaces, rubbing in the application until the wood takes on an even color, and then carefully wiping off any surplus. Allow the piece to dry for 24 hours until the turpentine odor is completely gone. Then give the surfaces a thorough rub-down with steel wool.

Remember that the undersides of the piece, as well as the visible surfaces, require protection if they are to withstand moisture absorption and warpage. The application of linseed oil and turpentine to these areas will prevent a host of future problems, and it takes but a few minutes to perform. Therefore, the underside and unexposed areas should be given the treatment at this juncture, regardless of the finish contemplated for the exposed surfaces.

WASH COAT

The purpose of this application is to seal the pores of the wood so that the old stain which still colors it will not bleed into the new application and so that the new stain will not penetrate too deeply. There is some difference of opinion among experts as to the merits and efficacy of a wash coat because some stains (water based and spirit stains) need to penetrate more fully and because varnish stains and penetrating stains are supposedly so formulated as to contain a sealer.

The antique furniture restorer, however, will be wise to use a wash coat. He is working with old, dry wood which will benefit from this application and which will acquire a smoother color coat because of it.

Mix one part of white shellac with five parts of denatured alcohol. Apply with three strokes of a 2½-inch brush—one stroke each way to apply the wash coat and one stroke to tip it off and spread the excess. Proceed quickly until the surface is covered. Allow to dry. Smooth the surface with 4/0 steel wool, and wipe clean.

VARNISH OR ENAMEL

The preliminary steps thus far delineated are essential for the preparation of either opague or clear finishes. At this juncture, the woodworker must decide as to whether the wood on which he is working has sufficient character and beauty of grain to warrant a transparent finish, or whether the grain is so unpreposessing or so badly matched that it is best hidden.

Should he decide on a transparent finish, he may want to deepen the rich coloration of the wood by staining it before applying the reflective, transparent finish. The application of the clear finish will darken the wood somewhat, and perhaps the graining is such that the woodworker feels this would be sufficient. If so, he will omit staining as part of the finishing process. Such woods as cherry, walnut, pine, maple and mahogany are often finished without staining.

If, however, the grain is interesting but indistinct, and the piece would look richer if darkened, he will apply stain.

If the wood is ugly or so innocuous as to lack any character whatsoever, he would be wise to finish it with enamel.

Each of these finishes is applied in a somewhat different manner. Therefore, we will deal with each finish separately.

Enamel Finish

Enamel is made with a varnish base to which pigment has been added for color. Enamels come in flat (or matte), high gloss and semi-gloss (or satin-finish) lusters. Flat finishes are fine for picture frames, decorative items, walls, ceilings—things which will not be required to withstand heavy usage. Flat enamels are not rugged enough for furniture refinishing. High gloss enamel may be too garish in effect, because its luster is almost mirror-bright. Semi-gloss enamel—with its somewhat muted sheen—is the type most frequently recommended for furniture.

Enamel is an impenetrable cover for a multitude of wood flaws as well as for an old finish. If you are planning to apply enamel over an old finish which is itself intact, and not crazed or peeling, simply wash the piece down with detergent and water to remove wax and polish, and sand the finish to glossy smoothness just as though it were stripped wood. The wet-and-dry sanding may be omitted, but the piece should be given a wash coat like that described for other finishes, followed by a buffing with 4/0 steel wool, and a wipe-off with water to clean the surface.

At this juncture, all refinishing experts agree that enamel should be given an undercoat. However, they disagree as to what such a coat should be. Some prefer thinned enamel itself to an especially formulated commercial undercoat. We recommend using three parts commercial undercoat mixed with one part colored enamel. Whichever you decide to use, brush it on very carefully and smoothly, covering every square inch of surface. Be careful of sags and runs, and smooth them into the surface immediately before they have time to set. Allow the undercoat to dry at least 48 hours. When it is dry, smooth it lightly with 4/0 sand paper wrapped around a felt-padded sanding block. Wipe off the dust and begin applying the enamel, limiting the application to small areas. Your first brush strokes should always be with the grain. This action levels the paint and eradicates brush marks. Before moving to an adjacent area, hold the brush perpendicular to the surface and use only the very tips of the bristles to stroke the paint with the grain. This "tipping off" proceedure should leave the paint smooth as glass.

Although one coat may be sufficient for many purposes, two coats will give a much more lasting cover and impart greater beauty to the price. First, sand the dry first coat lightly to make the second coat cling better. Then apply the second coat exactly as you did the first.

If you used high gloss enamel, you may wish to rub down the surface. Use slightly worn, dry 6/0 garnet paper for this. Wrap the abrasive paper around a sanding block and sand carefully with the grain until the surface is level and completely dull. Wipe with water and rags to clean off the abrasive dust, and rub with FF pumice and water, using a felt-padded sanding block.

When the pumice and water are washed away, the surface will be smooth as fine ceramic, but very dull. To restore exactly the degree of luster you desire, rub the surface with the grain using rottenstone and water. A folded pad of felt makes an excellent polisher. Rottenstone is a fine polishing agent rather than a an abrasive. It will impart to the piece that mellow glow you admire, and the more you rub, the more it will polish. When you finally have the surface to your liking, wash off all vestiges of the rottenstone, and wipe the surface with benzine as a final cleanup. Wax and buff the surface to a glowing shine.

The glaring, hard brilliance of the high-gloss enamel finish will have been tempered to a rich, lustrous burnish.

ANTIQUE ENAMEL FINISH

The unique method of finishing wood which is known as "antiquing," and which for many years has rightly been considered an art form in itself, is basically the application of a colored glaze (or two differently colored glazes) over an enameled piece. At one time, the artisans of this craft guarded as secret the formulas for the colored glazes and the methods employed in wiping them to achieve the antique effect. Nowadays, however, you can buy kits for antiquing at every craft and paint store. Usually these kits include a can of base semigloss enamel, one or two cans of glaze (the one glaze differing in color, if there are two, and being designed to serve as a top coat, highlighting the underglaze), a can of clear varnish, two paint brushes, sandpaper, steel wool and cheesecloth for wiping the glaze. Even more important from the novice's point of view is the fact that the paint supply and hobby shops carry a complete line of wood chips showing exactly how the individual kits look when applied—a reassuring display indeed for those who are dubious about what color to choose, or concerned with what the final effect will be.

Probably for your first attempt at antiquing you will want to work from one of these antiquing kits. The amount of paint they contain is exactly right for one piece or project. There is very little wasted surplus to dispose of in the event that you are only undertaking the one antiquing project. However, if you decide to finish several pieces in the same manner, you will want to know how to mix the glaze yourself, since buying it in the kits—each of which supplies less than a pint of glaze—is much too expensive a way to secure enough glaze for a set of furniture or an armoire.

Here is the formula for antiquing glaze, the proportions of which can be doubled or tripled to make the amount you need:

- ¼ cup of paint thinner or turpentine.
- ¼ teaspoon of *boiled* linseed oil.
- ½ to 1 inch of artist's oil color squeezed from a tube.
- ½ to ¾ teaspoon of bronzing liquid or varnish. (If varnish is used, a little more oil should be added.)

To mix these ingredients, first thoroughly blend the concentrated oil color (½ inch) with the boiled linseed oil. Add the colored oil to the paint thinner or turpentine, and stir until completely dissolved. Add the varnish or bronzing liquid. Test the colored glaze on a scrap of lumber painted with the enamel base coat to see how the colors blend. If the glaze color is too light, mix more of the artist's oil color with the boiled linseed oil, and add it to the mixture until the depth of color desired is obtained. If the glaze color is too deep, add more thinner and linseed oil in proportion until the right color is obtained. Keep a careful record of any extra amounts added to the basic formula so that you will know how to duplicate it if you need to make more.

Burnt umber is the artist's oil color most frequently used to color the glaze. It creates an effective and beautiful tone over almost any base coat. A gold-color glaze is also very beautiful, and can be made simply by adding gold-colored artist's oil or bronzing powder to the mixture. Introduce only small amounts of color to the liquids at a time, and test on waste wood scraps after each color addition to see if you have reached the desired tone.

Surplus color glaze can be safely stored for later use in a jar with a tight-fitting lid.

Applying the Glaze

The distinctive beauty of antiqued furniture is the direct result of the way in which the glaze is applied. This thin, translucent color coat is brushed or wiped on over the base color of satin-finish enamel. Then after the glaze has set, but before it is dry, it is wiped away in spots, revealing the base coat and producing a unique aged effect which is completely charming.

This aged effect can be greatly enhanced by *not* removing the scars and scratches which wear has left on the surface. Therefore, is you so desire, you can *omit* the "Sanding Before Refinishing Steps" we have just described as a preliminary to applying a finish. Instead, use Liquid Sandpaper or some other sanding formula on the old finish you are going to transform with an antiqued finish. Be careful to follow the manufacturer's directions exactly for applying the sanding formula. Some sanding preparations demand that the application be applied over the entire piece and left on a few minutes, while others ask that you work on one surface at a time, wiping off the sanding preparation immediately, and applying the base paint.

From the application of the base coat to the application of the second coat of enamel, the antiquing procedure follows the regular steps in applying enamel. When the second coat of enamel is fully dry, the glaze is applied to one surface of the piece and allowed to "set up" for about 15 minutes. When the glaze begins to dull, it is ready for wiping. Now the actual process of antiquing begins.

With a clean piece of cheesecloth, remove *only the glaxe* and remove it only from those areas where you want the base color to be more prominent. If you have observed how wear affects an old piece, you will know that the centers of doors, the centers of work surfaces and the centers of shelves where candlesticks or kerosene lamps were placed are generally worn to a lighter color than the surrounding wood. Emulate this wear pattern in removing the glaze. Wipe it away from the high spots of bas-relief carving, but leave it in the grooves. Wipe it off the knees of carbriole legs and the curved surfaces of serpentine fronts, but leave the rest covered. Spindles tend to wear where they bulge most, or at the knobbly points of the turnings, so wipe off the glaze there. Panels and doors wear light at the center; the sides and corners are darker. The areas around handles where hands have touched them are lighter from wear.

Keep stepping back to look at your work. When you visualize the overall effect, you can make the shading more symmetrical. Note how the glaze fills and colors any nicks and cracks in the surface and the charming distressed look these cracks give the piece.

The wiping effect will be different if you use carpet scraps or burlap rather than cheesecloth. You may wish to experiment with such textured wiping cloths. The aim is to produce an overall ombre effect—the color gently and subtly deepening from the lighter worn areas to the darker and darker tones at the corners and edges.

When the piece is as you desire it, allow it to dry. If you later feel that more glaze should be added, or that another color of glaze would enhance the effect, apply it. On the other hand, if you feel that the glaze is too prominent, overshadowing the base color, a light rubdown on the overglazed areas with 4/0 steel wool will reveal more color.

When you have the piece exactly as you like it, allow it to dry thoroughly before applying a coat of clear varnish (satin-finish polyurethane varnish is best, if none was provided with the kit). Allow the piece to dry for several days.

SPECIAL ANTIQUE EFFECTS

These are further enhancements or embellishments to the art of antiquing which you may wish to use on certain projects or in antiquing certain materials for unusual effects.

Striping

Painting a fine line of gold, silver or deepertoned contrasting color along beveled edges, in grooves, moldings or crevices will add just the right accent to certain pieces.

Splattering

Dotting the glazed surface with black flat paint, a contrasting shade of glaze, or gold may produce an interesting effect. To apply, use a very stiff-bristled brush across the wet bristles to splatter the color at random over the surface.

Graining

A very effective way of imparting a stained wood appearance to a painted surface is that of applying the glaze, and then simulating wood-grain markings through it with a stiff-bristled brush or a piece of carpet scrap. To make this mock graining look genuine, start every time at the same edge and proceed in one long stroke across the surface to the other edge. Grain the edges themselves, as well. Use random strokes, and do not wipe off the glaze. Simply drag the brush or carpet scrap through it. The applicator will become filled with glaze; it must be wiped clean after almost every stroke so that it will make well-defined marks. Good graining effects demand a minimum of brushwork. Using a few strokes, go over the entire surface. Then stop, and let the work dry.

Tortoise-shell Effect

Over a warm brown base coat which has been allowed to dry, apply an orange tinted glaze. Brush it on liberally. As soon as the glaze has had time to "set up," start tipping the surface with your fingertips, much as you do in finger-painting, to create a random pattern which exposes the base coat in spots. Allow the glaze coat to dry. Then spot the surface with coin-sized dots of gold glaze, made by adding metallic artist's oil paint to the glaze. "Track" the gold puddles over the already dry orange-and-brown surface until sufficient gold accent color has been introduced. Allow the gold coat to dry several days before varnishing.

Stippling

A softly mottled appearance can be given an object by blotting the color glaze with a scrap of turkish toweling a sponge or crumpled tissue paper. Pat the surface, don't rub it, and let the wrinkles and sponge pore marks remain in the glaze. Don't smear them or try to obliterate them. When the mottled glaze is thoroughly dry, apply varnish.

Weathering

A dry-brush coat of color contrasting to that of the base color coat, can produce a most interesting weathered effect, especially if the second color is stroked on in a random way with a very dry brush, so that it merely streaks the surface without covering it. When the second color coat is dry, rub it down with steel wool to reveal even more of the base coat. Then apply a colored glaze. The effect can be atonishingly beautiful. This is a particularly interesting treatment for a furniture piece which has first been stained in a wood tone, and is eventually to be given an antiquing glaze finish coat. The introduction of a second color in the dry-brush coat described, before the antiquing glaze is applied, will give the piece a simulated appearance of age which is like a patina and most interesting to behold.

Marbleizing

A glaze of dramatically different color to that of the base coat—a white glaze over a black enamel base coat, for example—can create a stunning marbleized effect if the wet glaze is patted with crumpled sheets of plastic wrap. Do not wipe the glaze. Simply press it while wet with the plastic, and peel the plastic off carefully to avoid smudging or smearing the interesting wrinkles. When it has thoroughly dried and the varnish has been applied, the piece will be a real attention-getter.

Marbleizing may also be done over a base coat of white enamel to accurately simulate genuine marble. For this effect, unless you have a very well-developed color sense, you will want to purchase one of the commercially prepared kits, in which the colors have been blended by experts. By all means, examine a piece of genuine marble before you begin to see how the colors fuse and blend. Here are some beautiful color formulas which will give a plain wooden table top the elegant appearance of marble.

White Marble Formula:

- White enamel base coat
- Tint one: mixture of raw umber and white enamel
- Tint Two: mixture of raw umber, Thalo blue, violet and white enamel
- Black enamel for accent

Pink Marble Formula:

- White enamel base coat
- Tint One: mixture of cadmium red, Alizarin crimson, orange and white enamel
- Tint Two: violet, Thalo blue and raw umber with white enamel
- Black enamel for accent

Cream Marble Formula:

- White enamel base coat
- Tint One: mixture of raw sienna, raw umber, and white enamel.
- Tint Two: mixture of raw sienna, cadmium red, raw umber and white enamel
- Black enamel for accent

Black Marble Formula:

- White enamel base
- Tint One: mixture of raw umber and white enamel
- Tint Two: mixture of cadium red, raw sienna, raw umber and white enamel
- Black enamel for accent

Whichever marble effect you choose, the marble effect is obtained by following these simple steps:

1. Paint on a base coat of white enamel and allow it to dry until it begins to get tacky.
2. Apply Tint One over the base coat by dribbling it on unevenly with a craft stick.
3. Apply Tint Two in the same manner, but only use about half as much of this color as you need of Tint One.

4. With crumpled newspaper pads, daub the surface lightly, following the track of the dribbled colors. Continue to cover the entire surface, including all edges, until the desired marble-like effect is obtained. Discard saturated newspaper pads for dry ones as you proceed.
5. For accent, dribble on very small amounts of black enamel and work these into the colors by patting with newspaper pads.
6. A few veins in the table top will add realism. These veins may be made by dribbling on a hairline stream of white enamel and allowing it to dry in a barely noticeable, uneven line.
7. Let the table top dry for at least 24 hours before applying varnish.

Note: A glass table top may be marbleized in the same way. However, this project requires that the tints be applied to the *underside* of the glass after cleaning the glass itself with ammonia. Apply the darkest tint first by splattering it lightly over the surface in random pattern and then patting it lightly over the surface in random and then patting it with newspaper pads to spread it. When all the tints have been applied by letting each tint dry before applying the next, splatter on clear turpentine, and allow the top thoroughly. Next, apply a coat of clear varnish and let it dry thoroughly. Then apply gold leaf size and gold leaf. No/red undercoat is necessary in this instance; the color tints act as an undercoat. When the gold leaf has been allowed to dry, varnish it well and let it dry thoroughly for about a week. Then the glass may be replaced on the table top, color side down, so that the surface of the table top may be wiped clean without disturbing the undercolor.

Frosted Antique Finish

A really unusual effect may be obtained by covering opague, pastel base coats with glaze mixed with white primer or white enamel as a coloring agent, instead of with artist's oils. This sparkling, frosty glaze is applied and wiped off just as any tinted glaze would be. When the desired ombre effect has been achieved, the piece is varnished.

White Lime Finish for Knotty Pine

Glaze with flat white tinted to desired shade. Use extra-thin and wipe glaze from knots only. This is very dramatic used over a honey-toned stain undercoat.

Pickled Pine Finish

Use either dark green or gray stain as the undercoat. Then glaze with raw umber and black. Do not wipe glaze too smoothly, allowing a lot of undercoat to show at random.

Dusty Antique Finish

Add about 1½ ounces of rottenstone to a quart of glaze mixture. This combination will make the glaze take on a dull sheen when dry.

Worn Gold Finish

Apply a glaze colored with metallic gold artist's oil over an undercoat of dark wood stain. Wipe stain to simulate wear, and let dry. Apply a second coat of pale cream glaze to which rottenstone has been added in the proportions given above. Wipe to highlight undercoat and gold glaze. Let dry and varnish.

Streaked Gold Effect

Over white enamel undercoat, apply a glaze of metallic gold, using artist's oils to color the glaze. Wipe to simulate wear. Apply second glaze colored with raw umber or sienna. Then wipe to highlight, leaving dark pigmented glaze in crevices and gold showing through on raised areas. When dry, apply clear varnish as a finish coat, followed by an application of well-buffed furniture wax.

Antique Effect on Stained Furniture

Apply glaze to piece over an undercoat of wood-tone stain. However, instead of wiping glaze off evenly, wipe it off most in those areas which would receive most wear. The result accurately simuates a patina of wear.

STAINING

Stains are always used as undercoats. They emphasize and enhance the beauty and color of the natural wood. They are generally a blend of tones matched as exactly as possible to the wood being covered. They are applied by wiping in multiple coats over the preliminary wash coat already described.

Stains are available in three basic formulas: Pigmented Oil Stains, Water Stains and Non-Grain-Raising Stains.

Pigmented Oil Stains

These are oil-based stains, variously packaged in cans, tubes or containers with built-in applicators. The particular colors are identified by wood names such as "maple," "walnut," etc. However, these names are no indication that the contents will in any match the furniture being stained. Therefore, the wise woodworker buys stains in small quantities and in a variety of wood tones, with the intent of experimenting with various shades. He applies one tone of stain over the other until he arrives at the exact shade which matches the furniture he is finishing. Pigmented stains may be lightened considerably by wiping them as soon as they are applied. Conversely, they may be darkened by allowing them to penetrate before wiping, or by adding a coat of darker stain.

Pigmented stains in can containers must be carefully stirred before and during use to distribute the coloring matter which has settled in the bottom of the can. Pigmented stains in tubes are paste-like in consistency and are so formulated that they may be wiped, rather than brushed, on. Those put up in bottles with a built-in applicator need a thorough shaking before using.

Pigmented stains—even the liquid, oil-based varieties—may be wiped onto the wood, or they may be applied with a brush. The former method is preferable because it gives the worker greater control over the coloring process and insures an even coat. He must work on one surface at a time and he must apply the wiping stain across the grain at right angles to the grain lines. After a wait of several minutes, he should wipe off the stain, working with the grain to remove it. He must keep refolding his cloth applicator so that he is always wiping with a relatively clean surface. If he is blending more than one wood tone, he should do so by applying the various colors in individual coats, always keeping in mind the formula for the final color which he has previously worked out on a scrap of waste wood—two coats of cherry, one coat of mahogany, one coat of walnut, or whatever. On each surface of the piece, he must be sure to apply the stains being blended in the order and the number of coats which prior experimentation has assured him will produce the exact match he is seeking.

As previously stated, these coats of pigmented stain should be applied over a preliminary wash coat, which prevents the stain from penetrating the wood too deeply and producing too dark a tone. After the coats of stain are applied and dry, you will want to apply a sealer coat to the stain and a coat of filler. The mixing and application of filler will be covered later.

Water Stains

These are packaged in dry powder form, ready for dissolving in very hot water. They are much less expensive than pigmented stains, do not require constant stirring while they are being used, and they penetrate the wood without leaving any residue—unlike pigmented oil stains, which leave a film of residue pigment on the wood.

Water stains should be applied with a brush, using long, rapid strokes, working with the grain. The surface being worked on should be positioned so as to be horizontal, if at all possible.

The choice of brush is important because too small a brush will slow the work so considerably that each brush stroke will be overlapping one which has partially dried, and these overlapping areas will produce streaks. The brush must be cleaned, and of a 2-inch size or larger, to do a complete surface before any drying takes place. If the water stain is too light, it can be darkened by adding a small amount of black water stain to the wood-tone color. If the stain is darker than desired, it can be lightened by adding more water. As with any stain, test samples of the stain color should be made on waste wood before applying it to the work.

Wiping each coat immediately after application will spread the stain more evenly and avoid the lap marks which amateurs find hard to avoid when using water stain. With experience, the wiping may be eliminated, but this step certainly aids the novice in obtaining a smooth, streak-free finish every time1

Sufficent coats should be applied to produce a smooth, even surface.

This type of stain, like all others, is applied over a preliminary wash coat and followed by a sealer coat and a filler coat.

Non-Grain-Raising Stains

These are sold in concentrated liquid form and are thinned with denatured alcohol or special thinner. This type of stain contains little or no water and, therefore, does not raise or roughen the grain. However, as the vehicle in this type of stain is instantly evaporated, the stain dries unusually rapidly and, therefore, lap marks where one stroke overlaps another which has partially dried pose an even more serious problem with non-grain raising stains than they do with water stains. One way of eliminating this problem is to mix the concentrated color stain with an equal amount of thinner. The individual coats of stain will be lighter, of course, if the stain is so heavily diluted, but since each coat dries very rapidly, three or four coats may be applied in a single day, so no time is actually wasted. Also, wiping each coat as soon as it is applied will spread the stain evenly and avoid streaking. Using these two precautions, even an inexperienced worker can obtain a smooth, even finish the first time.

Non-grain-raising stains (or "NGR" stains, as they are often termed) are applied over a preliminary wash coat, and are followed by a coat of sealer and one of filler.

Sealing the Stain

Just as the wood is sealed against the applications of stain with a shellac wash coat to prevent the stain from penetrating the wood too deeply, so the coats of stain are protected by a wash coat from the coat of filler, which will be the next coat applied. This sealer coat will prevent the filler solvents from penetrating the coats of stain and causing them to bleed through. Although sealer coats may seem like a lot of needless efforts, they actually save time in the long run because each insures such a smooth surface for the next coat. To mix a wash coat, use white shellac over pale wood-tone stains, and orange shellac over dark wood-tone stains. To mix this wash coat, thin 3-pound-cut shellac with denatured alcohol-one part shellac to seven parts alcohol. To speed the drying, add this mixture to an equal quantity of mixing lacquer. Thoroughly cover the surface with one thin coat of this solution, and allow it to dry.

Wood-Filler Coat

Wood filler is available in both liquid and paste forms, but the latter is best for most furniture jobs. It fills and hides the wood pores, and produces a flat glass-smooth surface. It is composed of linseed oil, silex and a drier. It is available in natural wood tones or in natural cream color-tinted to match the wood with oil stain. Making the filler ever so slightly darker than the wood enriches the effect.

Filler is usually mixed in one of three consistencies: thick (six ounces of turpentine to 12 ounces of 16-pound filler paste); medium (eight ounces of turpentine to 12 ounces of 12-pound filler paste); and thin (eight ounces of turpentine to eight ounces of eight-pound filler paste.) None of these three consistencies is so thick that it cannot be applied with a brush. The pint formula given here will cover 35 square feet. Merely double the quantites to make a quart, except in the case of the medium consistency, which requires 13 ounces of thinner to 1 ½ pounds of 12-pound filler paste.

All open-grained woods must be filled unless the woodworker desires a natural, textured appearance with obvious grain. All woods which are being given the sleek, richly colored and glowingly reflective finish of quality furniture must be given a filler coat—otherwise the desirable characteristic finish isn't possible. The only woods not requiring any form of filler are the following: basswood, red cedar, white cedar, cypress, fir, holly, magnolia, white pine, yellow pine, poplar, spruce and willow. All other woods should receive a filler similar in consistency to the grain of the wood—that is, thin filler for fine-grain woods, medium filler for medium-grain woods and thick filler for coarse-grained woods.

A stiff, short-bristled brush is best for applying filler. Brush the filler on with the grain, making sure to generously cover the entire surface. After spreading the paste over the surface, work it in with cross-grain strokes. When you see dull spots forming, that's your signal to put down the brush and pick up the board-blade scraper. Working across the grain, shovel up the filler and remove it, wiping the blade constantly before beginning to scrape again. After you have scraped off as much as possible, take a square of burlap or some other coarse material and wipe across the grain, removing every possible particle of excess filler. Do not wipe with the grain, because to do so would be to remove the wood filler from the wood pores where you want it to remain.

If you wait too long to begin wiping, or wipe too slowly, the filler may harden and resist your efforts. When that happens, moistening the wiping cloth with turpentine will speed the work. Work on a single surface or a section of surface at a time—applying the filler, then scraping and wiping to remove it before proceeding to an adjacent surface. For carvings and moldings, a scrub brush, toothbrush or picking stick may be necessary to remove the crusted filler. In any case, keep at the task until you have removed all excess. Otherwise, the final finish will show streaks.

The filler coat, when dry, will need the same sort of sealer coat as was applied previously. However, proportions differ for this particular sealer coat. Using 3-pound-cut shellac, combine one part of the shellac to four parts thinner, mixing the two well before pouring the mixture into an equal quantity of mixing lacquer. Brush on a thin but complete coat and let dry. The project is now ready for the transparent top coats.

TRANSPARENT FINISHES

For furniture made of fine wood whose intricate graining deserves display, the most appropriate and desirable finish is a transparent one. Transparent finishes are of three basic types—varnish, lacquer and shellac. Each of these three has its own peculiar properties, some of which are assets and some liabilities. Each is applied in a different way.

Varnish

Varnish is a popular, durable, protective finish for fine wood, imparting the appearance of depth and exquisite color gradation to the grain. Modern varnishes, because they are manufactured rather than natural, are much easier and more satisfactory to use than were the old-time varnishes.

Varnish is always labeled to indicate the type of resin contained: phenolic, alkyd and urethane being the most usual ones. Any of these resins produces superb results. Alkyd varnishes are usually a little cheaper than urethanes, but they aren't as durable. Phenolic varnishes stand up admirably to weather and are, therefore, best for outdoor use. Urethane varnishes are crystal-clear; they do not have the yellow cast of other varnishes. For fine furniture, no varnish is more satisfactory than urethane varnish. Its slightly higher price is more than justified by its performance.

The room in which varnish is applied is as important to the outcome of the job as is the workman himself. The atmosphere and surroundings must be as free from dust as is possible, because dust is the greatest single enemy to a flawless varnish finish. The tiny motes of dust adhere readily to the sticky varnish surface and each seems magnified by the reflective qualities of the varnish.

Therefore, clean, dust-free surroundings are essential. Outdoors is a poor choice because there pollen and insects are additional hazards. The best choice is a spare room indoors which can be dedicated temporarily to the task of varnishing. Be sure that everything used in performing the job is as clean and dust-free as the room itself. Even the clothing worn by the workman must be free of fuzz or lint. Dampening or scrubbing the floor first is a wise precaution, if at all possible.

Before beginning to apply the varnish, sand the work surface lightly with fine sandpaper, wipe off the abrasive particles, and wash off the surface with mineral spirits.

Just before applying the varnish, wipe the surface very carefully with a tack cloth. A tack cloth is a clean square of lintless cloth which has been soaked in warm water, and then wrung out and saturated with turpentine. The turpentine is distrubuted all through the cloth, then wrung out, and a tablespoon of varnish is added to the cloth and kneaded all through it until evenly distributed, folding and refolding the cloth differently to insure that every corner of the cloth is covered. This cloth is kept just tacky enough by sprinkling it with turpentine and water as it is used, and storing it when not in use in a clean jar with a tight lid. Always use this to wipe any dry surface to which you are about to apply the first coat, or subsequent coats, of varnish. The tack cloth will collect every particle of dust and render the surface immaculately clean for varnishing.

You will require a 2-inch varnish brush of good quality with firmly rooted bristles and a strike wire can into which a small amount of varnish has been poured and allowed to settle, so that all the froth and bubbles have disappeared. Never work from the varnish can itself. Instead, keep it tightly sealed and work from the strike wire can, where you can wipe off all excess varnish on the strike wire, and thus obtain a more even coat.

Varnishing Vertical Surfaces

Brushwork plays a highly important part in determining the appearance of a varnish finish. On vertical panels or sections, the first brush strokes are used for "cutting in"—that is, outlining the area to be varnished.

To "cut-in," you begin stroking at the corners, and stroke to the center of the panel. When you have the entire panel outlined in this way, you then brush across the grain. Work from both sides inward to the middle, lifting the brush as you approach the meeting of the strokes to prevent the varnish from piling up in the center. Then with a nearly dry brush, stroke lightly *with the grain* from top and from bottom inward to the center. These brush tip strokes are very important. The brush should be held at right angles to the work, and only the tips of the bristles should graze the stain. If at all possible, the surface being varnished should be placed in a horizontal position to prevent runs.

Varnishing Horizontal Surfaces

For table tops and other flat surfaces, the staining technique varies. Here, the brushwork is with the grain, starting at the center and brushing to the ends. As the brush reaches the end, it must be lifted to preent varnish from collecting on the edges of the piece.

The edges themselves should be done with a brush small enough so that the bristles don't come in contact with the wet varnish on the top surface.

Turnings such as chair legs, stretchers and spindles, should be varnished across their width, rather than lengthwise. Tipping off should be performed only where turnings are not too intricate. If the varnish is not being applied over a penetrating oil stain or a shellac wash coat, the first coat should be thinned with one part turpentine to five parts varnish. This mixture should be made a day in advance of use, and thoroughly stirred to give the varnish sufficient opportunity to absorb the turpentine. Subsequent coats (or coats not applied over penetrating oil stain or shellac wash coat) need not be thinned.

If any tiny dust particles appear on the wet varnish surface, remove them at once before the varnish dries. Use the handle tip of a size 0 brush or a finely pointed stick of wood to lift the dust mote. Even more effective at this clean-up task is the powered resin ball which professionals make for themselves. They first melt the powdered resin in a small pan placed in a pan of water over low heat. When the resin liquifies, they mix it with a little varnish—six parts of resin to one part of varnish. The mixture should be kneaded into a ball with wet fingers. To remove particles of dust, a bit of the resin ball is picked up on a sharp stick which refinishers call a "picking stick," and touched very lightly to the particle being removed, not to the surface. The dust will stick tight to the resin and come away from the varnished surface without leaving a mark. All dust particles should be kneaded back into the ball with moistened fingers as they are picked off.

Varnish cannot be re-touched after it has been applied. Whatever the defects, it must be left to dry thoroughly and absolutely before sandpapering it for the next coat. Drying a single coat may take as long as two days in humid weather.

The first coat is sanded with slightly worn garnet paper—the 5/0 grade—working with the grain. No water should be used.

All subsequent coats should be wet sanded with 6/0 garnet paper used over a sanding block. The sanding must be sufficient to level the surface and dull it completely. After the final coat, a rubdown with FF pumice and water, using a felt-padded block will give the surface a satin sleekness. The pumice should be washed off with water and the surface dried with clean rags. The surface will be smooth and even, but very dull. To restore the luster, rub with rottenstone and water, using a felt-padded sanding block. Rottenstone is a polish, not an abrasive, and the luster it imparts to wood increases with every rub. When the surface is as burnished as you want it, wash off all particles of rottenstone with water, and dry with clean cloths. Then wax and buff the dry surface to a high polish.

Note: Varnish may be applied over unstained wood for a beautiful natural finish. Pigmented varnishes are available which greatly enhance the natural wood tone. The process is the same as that just described.

VARNISH AND OIL FINISH

Here is a finish which is not well known to many finishers, but which will give a beautiful, lasting sheen and color, particularly to open-grained woods (such as oak, walnut, mahogany and chestnut), but which will enhance close-grained woods as well. When the finish is applied over a paste filler and varnish-and-turpentine sealer coat as directed, using quality materials and allowing sufficient drying time between coats, the results are invariably successful. Moreover, the varnish and oil mixture lessens the risk of damage from many acids, alcohol, heat and water.

Apply a sealer coat of 50 percent spar varnish and 50 percent pure turpentine, using a rag to stroke on the mixture and allowing it to dry thoroughly. Lightly smooth the surface with worn abrasive paper.

In a container, mix 25 percent spar varnish, 25 percent boiled linseed oil and 50 percent turpentine. Apply this mixture generously to the surface using a rag as applicator, and rub it well in until the turpentine starts to evaporate, but before the surface becomes sticky. Wipe the surface thoroughly with a clean, dry rag. Continue the same procedure on another surface.

After moistening the applicator rag in the mixture, always replace the top loosely to prevent evaporation. When the whole piece has been coated, rubbed and dried, wipe off the threads of the container cap and the container mouth, place the rag in the remaining mixture and seal tight until the next using. Store in a cool place.

Allow the furniture piece to dry in a dust-free atmosphere for 48 hours. Smooth the surface with No. 00 steel wool until all dust particles and tiny bumps have been removed. Apply at least three more coats, allowing each to dry thoroughly, and buff each coat with No. 00 steel wool before applying the next coat. When the last coat is applied and dry, rub it with No. 8 open-coat garnet paper dipped in lukewarm water. Clean and dry the piece well. Wax and buff to a high burnish.

LACQUER FINISH

This transparent top coat is more difficult to use than either varnish or shellac, just because it has the wonderful attribute of drying quickly. In less than fifteen minutes, a coat of lacquer has dried dust-free. But the rapidity with which it dries means that the finisher must work very swiftly in brushing it on.

Lacquer must never be applied over a surface which has not been first given a sealer coat. The properties of lacquer have a softening solvent effect on paint, varnish, fillers and some stains which create disastrous results unless the surface is first stripped bare or well-protected by a shellac sealer.

Lacquer may be applied in two ways: by brushing or by spraying. The former is really much the best method, but lacquer may be purchased in aerosol cans for those finishers who do not have a spray gun. Spraying demands a certain technique of its own, but a few minutes of practice should be enough to train a novice in the fundementals. Too liberal an application will produce sags and runs. Spraying over a coat which has not been allowed to dry sufficiently results in a surface pockmarked by pinholes. Spraying from too great a distance causes a bumpy surface not unlike orange peel. Spraying lacquer is even faster drying than brush lacquer, and cannot be applied with a brush. However, brushing lacquer may be used to load a spray gun with no adverse effects.

To apply lacquer by brushing, one must use a much broader brush than that used for varnish. The lacquer is "flowed" on in the same manner as varnish, but the strokes are all with the grain and much longer than the strokes used in varnishing. Lacquer is most successfully applied with a minimum of brushwork, so that—if at all possible—the finisher should never cover the same area with a second brush stroke. Instead, he should flow on the lacquer with one swift stroke across the entire surface, refill the brush and lay on the second stroke barely overlapping the first while the edges of the first stroke are still wet. Be sure that the strokes overlap to avoid those bare spots between strokes which finishers call "holidays." Runs and sags must be immediately smoothed out as soon as they occur. Once the lacquer begins to set, it cannot be touched without great damage to the finish.

Lacquer is best applied in several (at least two) thin coats, and should be thinned with one part of lacquer thinner to three parts of lacquer before applying. About eight hours drying time should be given between coats, followed by dry (never wet) sanding to smooth any tiny defects noticeable in the prior coat.

When the last coat is thoroughly dry, the surface should be given an abrasive rub with pumice and oil, followed by a polish with rottenstone and oil.

Note: Lacquer is to be avoided in refinishing antiques because of its disastrously solvent effect on most other stains and paints. Lacquer requires a special filler coat over either water stain or spirit stain (powdered stain mixed with lacquer thinner). Furthermore, it must be applied only over a shellac sealer coat. Since the underlayers of paint on antique furniture are generally unknown, using lacquer as a transparent top coat might damage the entire piece.

Another very valid prejudice against lacquers—shared by furniture finishers and discriminating collectors alike—is that lacquer imparts a hard gloss to furniture, unlike the softer sheens which characterize varnish or shellac and which are identifiable with the genuine antique.

The only antique furniture traditionally finished in lacquer is the Chinese. In the Orient, colored and clear lacquers have been used for centuries. Some antique pieces are covered by as many as 300 opague coats, giving them a durability and indefinite imperviousness to blemishes.

SHELLAC FINISH

Here is a transparent top coat which answers many an amateur finisher's anxious prayers. It is easier to apply than any other finish; it dries dust-free in less than 30 minutes. Its only shortcoming is that it damages when touched by alcohol or water, unless kept very highly waxed. However, it is a great finish for articles which are never going to be used as serving pieces—such as screens, picture frames, chairs, beds, armoirs, etc.

Shellac needs at least a two-coat application to cover adequately. However, only a four-hour time lapse is necessary between coats, so that even a multicoat job may be completed in less than two days. Finishers who have trouble brushing on lacquer or varnish will be happily surprised at the ease they expereince in applying shellac. Taking only moderate care, they can achieve a surface free of all brush marks, bubbles, sags, runs, build-up or other defects.

A point to be considered in buying shellac is the relatively short shelf life of the product. Buy only as much, therefore, as you will use immediately, and try to buy a brand which prints an expiration date on the can. If you cannot find a dated can, buy from a busy store where the turnover insures a fresh stock. If the shellac is not fresh, the drying time will be considerably longer than if the shellac was recently canned. The label should state that the shellac is pure, and the amount (or "cut") of denatured alcohol which has been added as thinner.

Shellac comes in two colors—clear shellac, which is commonly called "white," and orange shellac, which greatly enhances some dark hardwood finishes. Your own preference, or the type of wood being finished, will dictate the color chosen.

Shellac is a natural product, the secretion of a small parasitic insect which lives on the sap of the lac trees which grow in India. The resin secreted by the insects forms a crust over the twigs which is washed off a sifted free of dirt, bark and leaves. The pure orange gum shellac into flakes and shipped in this form to all parts of the world. The shellac manufacturers further process the shellac by bleaching some of it white by a complicated chemical process. The flaked shellac—both white and orage—is then subjected to a process known as "Cutting," which means dissolving given amounts of flaked shellac in given measures of denatured alcohol. The dissolved shellac is then poured into cans, labeled with the proportion of resin to alcohol and shipped to the retail dealers for sale to consumers.

Shellac is purchased in basic "cuts"—a "cut" being the number of pounds of flaked shellac dissolved in one gallon of denatured alcohol to make this particular solution. Manufacturers recommend that a 3-pound cut be used for most purposes, but beginners will have greater success with a 1-pound or a 2-pound cut. The thinner cuts dry more quickly, are easier to brush on smoothly, and are more self-leveling than the thicker cuts.

Although shellac is always cut by the manufacturer in dissolving the shellac flakes into liquid shellac, it is always cut even further by the finishing before using. The amount of denatured alcohol added should be carefully measured and mixed before applying. Here are some measurement tables for reducing various manufacturers' cuts of shellac to the 1-pound and 2-pound cuts needed for furniture refinishing.

Shellac should be flowed on in full, wet coats using with-the-grain strokes and minimum brushing. Between coats, the surface is leveled and smoothed with an open-coat paper and sanding block. After the final coat, sand again with abrasive paper and then 4/0 steel wool to dull the surface. Protect the shellac with at least two coats of paste wax, rubbed in well and thoroughly "buffed."

Note: A shellac and wax finish like the one just described is a popular and beautiful finish for *unstained* woods—particularly pine. If white and orange shellac are mixed before cutting with alcohol to a shade most complimentary to the wood, the natural wood tones are beautifully intensified.

FRENCH POLISH FINISH

This is a classic traditional finish, long extolled by finishers and antique collectors alike for the incomparable beauty it imparts to wood. This high-grade finish has been used for more than three centuries, and is still unsurpassed by any finishes since developed. Furniture which is to receive this type of finish should first be thoroughly sanded, stained with a water or nongrain-raising stain, filled and sealed. The surface must be thoroughly dry.

The shellac used should be white shellac, thinned to a watery 1-pound cut. A piece of silk stocking made into a ball makes the best applicator. The pad is dipped into the shellac and applied with straight, fast strokes, using moderate pressure. When the wood is dry, it is sanded lightly with 6/0 paper,and another coat is applied. Approximately six coats are applied in this fashion, drying and

Table 10-1. Thinning Manufacturer's Shellac for Furniture Refinishing.

MANUFACTURER'S CUT	NEEDED CUT	ALCOHOL ADDED PER QUART OF SHELLAC
5 pound	3 pound	7/8 pint
5 pound	2 pound	1 quart
5 pound	1 pound	2/3 gallon
4 pound	3 pound	1/2 pint
4 pound	2 pound	3/4 quart
4 pound	1 pound	2 quarts
3 pound	2 pound	3/4 pint
3 pound	1 pound	3 pints

sanding between each coat. Any cracks which might appear are sprinkled with a little pumice and covered with another application of shellac until the cracks are filled.

When a light glow appears, a cone-shaped muslin pad is constructed and saturated with shellac. Over this pad, a cover of soft lint-free linen is wrapped. This outer cover has been moistened with a few drops of boiled linseed oil. Now the strokes are rotary in nature starting in the center and working to the edges. The boiled linseed oil is added a little at a time until a deep, glowing finish is obtained. This requires about six more coats. When twelve coats in all have been applied, remove the oil-moistened outer cover from the pad, and continue rubbing with the shellac-saturated inner pad until the piece is dry. Let the entire piece dry thoroughly. Protect the finish with two coats of paste wax, thoroughly buffed.

BLOND FINISH

The bleaching required to lighten the color of wood is not recommended for antique furniture, but for refinishing furniture of the 1940's and 1950's, when such pale wood finishes were in vogue. The so-called "modern" furniture of that period used these bleached finishes to emphasize the pure, streamlined designs.

Basically, the finish consists of first bleaching the stripped wood (or nude wood) with a very strong two-formula wood bleach available in paint stores in bottles marked No. 1 and No. 2. Rubber gloves, goggles and old clothes are the required uniform for the finisher who undertakes to bleach wood. He must apply the bleach according to the manufacturer's instructions with a long-handled cotton dish mop, washing it off with a hose while he scrubs the surface with a scrub brush. When applications of bleach have lightened the wood sufficiently, the finisher washes it completely with the hose and wipes it dry with towels. After the wood has been allowed to dry for at least 48 hours, he smooths all surfaces with fine abrasive papers.

When the piece is glassy smooth, he applies clear urethane varnish coat by coat, drying and sanding the piece between applications until a sufficiently reflective finish has been attained. Then he gives a final rubdown with 4/0 steel wool, followed by a coat of wax, buffed to a high luster.

PICKLED FINISH

We have already discussed a special pickled finish for pine, applied over a green or gray stain. But blond woods of all sorts may be dramatically accented by a pickled finish. This finish requires that the piece be bleached in exactly the same manner as for a blond finish. When the wood is as light as desired, it is rinsed with the hose and dried for 48 hours. Then a sealer coat of one part clear spar varnish and one part pure turpentine is applied. Once it is thoroughly dry, the sealer coat is smoothed with Grade 00 steel wool or worn 6/0 to 8/0 garnet paper.

After wiping the surface free of abrasive particles, the finisher now applies white paint to the surface with a pad of folded rag, rubbing the paint crosswise against the grain of the wood. Keep the pad only moderately coated with paint by removing the excess on the can rim, and apply only enough to the wood to fill the grain. Allow the white paint to dry. Now rub the surface crosswise to the grain with steel wool until all paint has been removed from the surface except that which remains in the wood grain. Apply successive coats of clear urethane varnish to finish the piece, allowing each coat to dry thoroughly and sanding lightly between coats. When sufficient luster has been given the surface, allow the last coat to dry completely. Then etch it lightly with No. 00 steel wool, apply wax and buff to a high luster.

OIL FINISH

If you have the time, patience and willingness to perform the rubbing necessary for this type of finish, it is a time honored method for producing a rich, glowing color on the wood. This finish renders the impervious to water, heat, scratches and most stains. The furniture will require no waxing.

This finish should not be used on carved pieces, because the convolutions of carving make the finish too difficult to polish. This finish does not look well on cherry, and will turn walnut black.

The finish is made by mixing 66 percent boiled linseed oil with 33 percent turpentine. Have plenty of soft, lint-free cloths on hand and some hard-woven pieces of cloth, such as pieces of man's suits.

The wood must be free of finish, repaired, sanded and dusted.

Apply the mixture (hot or cold) generously with a rag pad, and rub into a limited surface for 15 to 30 minutes. The mixture will be absorbed more readily if hot, but care must be taken not to ignite the mixture while heating it. Warming it over a very low flame in a double boiler is the best way. Wipe off the surface after the oil application with a soft cloth, making sure to remove it from carvings and grooves where it would harden quickly. Then rub the oiled area with a hard-surface rag. Use vigorous pressure and keep polishing the surface for about 20 minutes. The heat developed from this friction will engender a luster which is the exceptional beauty of this finish. Repeat this process over the entire surface of the piece until five to 25 coats of oil have been applied and no dull spots remain. After the application of five coats, the remaining coats, if necessary, may be applied while the piece is being used, for regular applications of the linseed oil and turpentine mixture are necessary to the upkeep of this finish. Two or three times a year, the piece must be given another complete coat. However, if this restorative work is faithfully performed, the piece will never show scratches and will never require refinishing.

FLAME FINISH

This is a spectacular finish for nude wood which is extremely unconventional but strikingly attractive—often transforming an inconsequential piece of furniture into one of remarkable charm. The only tools needed are a propane torch and a stiff-bristled scrubbing brush. If you have never tackled this sort of task before, you will want to experiment first on waste wood before putting the furniture piece itself to the torch.

The primary aim of this method is to char the bare wood surfaces as evenly as possible. The propane torch should be kept moving over the entire surface at a speed fast enough to prevent any part of the surface from catching fire. Special care must be taken at the edges where the cross grain tends to break into flame very easily.

Once the entire surface is evenly charred, scrub the surface with the stiff-bristled brush, working with the grain and brushing off all the loose, charred material. When you have removed every possible particle of char, apply carnauba paste wax and buff with a soft cloth to a very high luster. No other finish need to be used. The piece will have a most novel appearance, obtainable in no other way, and is sure to be a conversation piece.

Needless to say, this is no way to treat a fine antique. But as an arresting finish for an undistinguished piece of unfinished furniture, it has no peer.

Chapter 11
Furniture Restoration

The most difficult phase of restoration is repair. If the craftsman believes from past experience that he lacks the knowledge, skill and patience—or the necessary tools—to do a good job, he is best advised to take the work to a professional. Even then, he should be highly selective as to the caliber or repairman he hires to do the work, because not all professionals are worthy of the name. The value of an antique can be greatly altered by the quality of repair given it; only top quality artisans should be employed.

However, if a series of botched jobs has not convinced the amateur craftsman of his ineptitude, he should certainly attempt repairing for himself. He may discover to his delight that he possesses a remarkable aptitude for the work and that the task, though tedious, is so rewarding as to more than compensate for the effort expended.

This section will cover furniture repair in detail, carefully outlining the steps for accomplishing each task successfully. If the reader can follow directions and will give the project an honest try, he will be astounded with the ease with which he succeeds.

To restore any piece to salon condition, the craftsman must first examine it carefully and make a list of what needs to be done. He should search the surface for cracks, dents, gouges or small holes which must be filled and refinished. He may discover bruises which need attention. Veneers may be blistered, wavy or cracked, with loose edges and missing pieces. Any parts which are missing or broken should always be replaced. Drawers which are balky must be made to glide smoothly. Joints may be gapping for want of glue.

Working from the list of repairs needed, the craftsman then plans a step-by-step procedure for rectifying each impairment. He begins by repairing the structural damages, inside and out, because these repairs restore the piece to its usefulness. When all parts are again in alignment, intact and functioning correctly, he then begins to remove surface scars.

If the piece on which he is working is a genuine antique, he must take care not to carry his surface repairs past a certain point. Although every repair should be done thoroughly, the worker must not overdo to the extent of removing all signs of age and wear from the piece. Much fine old furniture has lost its charm, beauty and much of its value as an antique because of the over-zealous manner in which it was "restored."

GLUES AND ADHESIVES

Glue is one of the oldest of furniture fasteners. Museums are full of early Egyptian and Roman furniture which is still in one firm piece after many centuries because it was fastened with glue. Glue has always been used as an adhesive for veneers, but its primary use in furniture construction is to cement joints. Although nails, wedges, dowels and pegs were used to reinforce joints in ancient times just as they are used today, it was the addition of glue which permanently cemented the joint. Properly glued joints have greater strength than the natural strength of the wood itself. Wood is quite porous and when glue is applied over a wood surface, it seeps into the pores. When applied to both parts of a joint, the glue maintains a good grip on the adjacent surface and produces a bond which holds the two pieces together indefinitely. A glued joint is neat-appearing, incomparably strong and extremely durable.

Many kinds of glue have been developed, and are currently being developed, for gluing wood. Each has specific properties and characteristics which determine where and how it is applied. The glues most commonly used in woodworking are of the following types: animal (flaked and liquid), casein, (synthetic resins formula which include urea formaldehyde and resorcinol formaldehyde adhesives), contact cement, epoxy cement, white glue and vegetable glue.

Animal Glue

Animal glue is made from abbatoir waste—the hides, horns, hoofs, bones and sinews of animals. This traditional adhesive for furniture is available in two forms—old fashioned flaked form (sometimes called Scotch glue) and ready-to-use liquid form. The flaked variety is made by boiling the animal parts down to a gelatin-like consistency and allowing this gelatine to harden into sheets. Before being sold, these sheets are broken into flakes or "pearls." The woodworker dissolves these flakes in boiling water as needed, using one part flakes to two parts water, and heating the mixture to 145 degrees Fahrenheit until the hard, brown flakes liquefy. The craftsman may use either a cast-iron glue pot or an enameled double boiler. The latter will not burn the glue and is much easier to clean. Also, since the glue is not likely to stick in such a pot, it may be left in the upper section of the double boiler while the gluing-up takes place, the steaming water beneath keeping the glue from chilling and having to be reheated.

While the flakes are liquefying in the boiling water, the craftsman must stir the mixture to avoid lumps.

Liquid type animal glue comes ready to apply and spreads best in a temperature above 70 degrees Fahrenheit. It is light in color and does a very good job of gap filling.

Either type of animal glue requires at least 24 hours to dry firmly, depending on the quality of the glue, the room temperature and the amount of moisture in the wood itself. This factor is an advantage if the project is a large one, or if the repositioning of parts is necessary. However, although it is slow to dry, this type of glue sets quickly because it penetrates the pores of wooden parts, forming little dowels of glue which hold securely, are fairly flexible and do not disintegrate into powder. Because this particular adhesive must penetrate to hold, it will not work on glass, metal or plastic, although it holds leather very satisfactorily.

Because animal glue is fast-setting, a trial assembly should be made before gluing up to be certain that all parts fit correctly, so that once the glue is applied, the work may be immediately secured in clamps without further alteration or adjustment.

Casein Glue

Casein glue is a powdered glue manufactured from skim milk, hydrated lime and other chemicals. It must be stored dry and sealed against the carbon dioxide in the air to retain its efficacy. It is mixed with water before using, in proportions of one part powder to two parts water to weight. The mixture is allowed to cure six or eight hours before using. The alkalinity of casein glue makes it ideal for gluing oily woods such as teak and pitch pine. Its gap-filling properties are good, but not quite equal to those of other glues. It does not require heating and works excellently in low temperatures; this fact and its low cost make it popular with the building industry. It will bond linoleum, Formica, cardboard, paper, cloth, cork and leather; it is best at bonding similar, rather than different, materials. It is water-resistant, but not waterproof; it will not permanently bond outdoor furniture.

Casein glue allows the woodworker 15 to 45 minutes for gluing up, and requires about the same amount of clamping time as animal glue.

Synthetic Resin Glue

Synthetic Resin Glues were developed fairly recently and are products of research for adhesives which would be relatively resistant to moisture and to bacterial attack. Some of these synthetic resin glues are water-resistant; others are virtually waterproof. Waterproof glues may be subjected to water or wet weather and still remain unaffected even by prolonged exposure. Water-resistant glues are capable of withstanding high humidity and sporadic exposure to wet weather if the periods of exposure are not of long duration. Such glues must be stored in a cool, dry place because heat and moisture cause them to polymerize (that is, change into other compounds). Freezing affects their bonding ability. The room temperature at which they are applied and left to dry likewise affects their efficacy. No other types of glue are quite so sensitive.

Among the synthetic resin glues now on the market are Casco PVA, Cascomite, Aerolite 300, Extra Bond, Resin W. and PVA—as well as many others of the resorcinol formaldehyde variety. PVA—called merely by the initials for polyvinyl acetate emulsion glue—is one of the most effective of the synthetic resin glues. It is a composite of coke and lime obtained in an emulsion form. In the liquid, minute particles of PVA are dispensed in water. When the glue is applied, the water is absorbed, and this has the effect of forcing the particles of resin together and uniting them in a firm bond. This glue is swift-gripping, especially of porous materials, fairly waterproof, colorless and possessed of a certain flexibility. This last is a great attribute, since many glues become brittle when dry. Also, it requires no mixing. PVA glues everything except rubber, polyvinyl and polythene.

Urea Formaldehyde

Urea Formaldehyde Glue is produced by the reaction of ammonia to carbon dioxide and formaldehyde. Continued to saturation, the process would produce a glass-like solid. However, the process is only partly completed in the manufacture of this glue. A hardener is added to act as a catalyst and the final reaction takes place in the joint, making a bond which is very firm, long lasting, and highly resistant to moisture, heat and bacteria. This is an admirable glue for all outside work, boat building and Formica.

Urea formaldehyde adhesive is available in two forms: resin and hardener in separate tubes, or powder form with hardener already added. The cold-setting variety can be applied at room temperature, has a setting time of five to 20 minutes, and bonds in cramps in two to six hours. The other type requires a temperature of 200 to 260 degrees to polymerize the resin. The cold-setting type is extensively used for marine construction and edge gluing.

Resorcinol Formaldehyde Glue

Resorcinol Formaldehyde Glue is another form of synthetic resin glue. Phenol is combined chemically with formaldehyde to produce a glue which sets at high temperature. Phenolic-resin glues are widely used in producing weatherproof plywood because resorcinol formaldehyde glues are completely water-resistant and will hold even in moist or humid conditions. This glue is impervious to alcohol, gasoline and wood preservatives—to mention just a few of many chemicals which do not affect its efficacy. Assembly time is about ten minutes; cramping time can vary from two to ten hours.

Contact Cement

Contact Cement is especially valuable to the woodworking hobbyist who may be short on cramps. It bonds immediately, on contact. No clamps are needed. It is first applied to the surfaces of both pieces being joined and allowed to cure, a reaction which takes about half an hour. After the cement is properly set, the two sections of the work and joined in a permanent bond. Contact cement is ideal for wall paneling and for affixing porous and non-porous laminates to floors and counters. It works very satisfactorily on wood veneers, leather, fabric and hardboard. This effective adhesive adhesive is available in one of two types: rapid-drying which is highly flammable, and water-based which contains no ignitable vapors but which costs about one-third more.

Epoxy Cement

Epoxy Cement is one of the most versatile adhesives. It produces very staunch joints and is frequently used industrially to join materials which would otherwise require welding or brazing. Although it is more expensive than other adhesives, it is a bargain at any price because of the work it can do. Usually, it is packaged in two half-ounce tubes—one containing the resin or adhesive, and one containing the hardening agent. The contents of both tubes must be mixed before applying. Simply squeeze an equal-length segment of the contents of each tube into an old saucer and stir with a match stick until the colors are well blended. Then apply a thin layer to both surfaces which are to be bonded, clamp them firmly together (but not so firmly as to cause the epoxy to leak out of the joint and weaken it.) Chemical reaction, rather than exposure to air, will cause the glue to harden. So reliable is this hardening process that if the tops are inadvertently switched on the tubes, you may never again be able to remove them. Enough alternate material may be present in the tube caps to seal them tight forever!

Basically a multi-resin adhesive, epoxy glue will even bond materials of different porosities and shrinkage rates, such as wood and metal.

White Glue

White Glue is the handiest all-around glue for household use. It will secure wood, cloth, leather, paper and many other materials, as long as at least one of the materials to be joined is porous. White glue has a very short setting time, usually about 20 to 30 minutes. It is not waterproof; in fact, if it hardens it can be rendered usable by adding a little water and, if dripped or spilled, can be washed off. However, white glue has one unique attribute. Although milky looking when applied, it is transparent when dry. Thus, glued repairs are rendered completely inconspicious—an advantage every repairman appreciates.

For best results, white glue should be applied to only one surface being joined. However, on uneven jointures, both surfaces may need gluing. For fabrics, a thin coat is sufficient. On wood joints, a generous application is necessary.

Vegetable Glues

There are two types available: the starch type, derived from cereals and potatoes, and the protein type, derived from legumes (mainly soy beans). Such vegetable glues are very inexpensive, allow the woodworker a long assembly time and are very durable. The major drawback to their use is their tendency to stain light-colored wood. Commerically, they are widely used in the manufacture of veneered pieces.

REGLUING JOINTS

Repairing and regluing joints is of primary importance in furniture repair. Where the original adhesive has finally lost its grip, the particles of dried glue must be completely removed from the wood before fresh glue is applied. The following methods are best:

1. Scrape or sand off all the old glue, paint, oil, wax, grease and dirt, pursuing this task until the old joint is as clean and dry as if it has just been cut from new wood.
2. Many old glues prove highly resistant to removal, in which case try softening them with hot vinegar and scrubbing them vigorously with an old toothbrush.
3. Sponge joints made from oily wood with lacquer thinner to give them a better gripping power when the new adhesive is applied.
4. Uneven or worn surfaces must be planed, sanded or scraped so that the two parts of the joint fit perfectly and make complete surface contact. Otherwise the glue will not hold.
5. When possible, slightly roughen or slash the surfaces to be glued. In this way, the surfaces are given so-called "tooth," which increases their holding power and makes them more receptive to the adhesive when it is applied.
6. Be sure that all parts of the joint contact one another and that they touch one another closely, so that there is no gaping. One should never try to make up for a bad fit by applying a lot of glue. A thin, even coat—correctly applied—will hold better and longer than a thick, lumpy coat.
7. Spread glue on both parts of the joint and assemble the parts. Always spread newspaper over the work surface to catch drips and spills before applying glue.
8. Next, put the work in cramps to set and dry. Be sure to buffer the work from the bite of the cramp jaws with pieces of waste wood, folded newspaper or cardboard. Because repairs are generally undertaken on an already-constructed piece of furniture, tourniquets may work better than cramps. Also, you will want to spread waxed paper, which moisture cannot penetrate, wherever glue drips might occur to prevent exuding glue from defacing the finish. Check the cramped work from time to time and wipe off any glue seepages with a damp cloth.
9. Before the glue has a chance to set firmly, check the piece on which you are working for alignment by seeing if it sits

firmly on a flat surface without wobbling. Should the piece be out of alignment, its squareness would be impossible to establish once the glue was dry.

10. Allow at least 24 hours in a warm room for the glue to dry. Then carefully remove the cramps or tourniquet, and allow the piece another 24 hours of drying time before further working on or using the parts glued.
11. The cramps or tourniquets are certain to be concealing places where the glue has been squeezed out by pressure and which must be removed. Cut or scrape off the glue carefully in these parts, taking care not to harm the finish. Any glue remaining will show through a clear finish.

REGLUING OLD FURNITURE

One aspect of gluing up which must be considered in restoring old pieces is that of renewing the adhesive without dismantling the furniture. This is a skill which the furniture constructor never needs to acquire because he is assembling new furniture from custom-cut nude wood parts. Not so with the furniture restorer, however, who must find ways of applying new glue to an old joint without first taking the joint apart which he would hesitate to do, since the soundness of any old piece is, in part, the result of its reaction over the years to wear, warping and shrinking. Age—with its manifold, unpredictable effects—has subtly altered and modified the original structural design. To dismantle it now might forever destroy the cohesive harmony of the many parts.

Before undertaking the regluing of a ready-made piece, examine it carefully to ascertain if there are any parts needing replacement or if, perhaps, countersunk screws, hidden nails, dowels or braces might not be added to give greater reinforcement than regluing would give. Place the piece on a flat surface and study its alignment before making any other repairs; the correct alignment influences the holding ability of every joint in the piece.

Rickety, palsied joints in antique furniture must be reglued without removing a single piece. The first step is to make sure that the joint is clean and that as much of the old glue as possible has been prized out and scraped away. Where the joint fits too closely to permit the glue to be applied with a brush, use a toothpick to insert the glue into the joint, applying small amounts at a time until enough has been inserted to hold the joint firmly. Rock the piece back and forth to spread the glue evenly. Wherever possible, turn the piece until the joint will automatically flow downward into the joint.

An old joint which must be glued without dismantling may not fit as precisely as it did when it was new. The small discrepancy in fit may be rectified by inserting glue into all areas of the joint abutment with toothpicks, pushing the toothpicks well into the crevices of the joint and leaving them there to act as wedges. The ends of the toothpicks should be sheared off with knife flush with the edge of the joint. Toothpicks are preferable to match sticks because they are made of hard wood.

To prevent the glue from running out of the joint when the work is turned to glue another area, wrap the jointure crack tightly with string, and leave the string tied around the crack until the glue is firmly set, but not dry. When the string is removed, any crystalized glue which has escaped from the crack may be cut off with a knife without doing harm to the finish.

Available commercially are several specialized products such as Devcon Grip-Wood which do a superb job of snugging up loose joints. Grip-Wood has both adhesive and wood-fiber-swelling properties. The adhesive itself comes in a squeeze tube which allows it to be easily applied to both surfaces. In addition, the manufacturer makes a large plastic syringe by which the adhesive may be inserted into tight places where the joint is wobbly, but not removable.

DISMANTLING OLD FURNITURE

Sometimes a joint has been so badly damaged or is so choked with old glue and dirt that there is no alternative to dismantling it in order to repair it. If more than one joint must be taken apart, be sure to mark both parts of each joint and key the respective joints with a letter, so that later they may be reassembled with the same joint sections for which they were originally cut. Matching them up again as they were originally is the only way to get an accurate fit, since joint sections all differ slightly from one another, especially if they are hand-crafted, as antique joints always were. If the ends of the inserted sections and the insides of the receptive sections are marked, using a marking knife instead of a pencil or chalk, there is little chance that the marks will be obliterated when the joints are cleaned. Another excellent way to avoid mismatching parts is to remove only one joint at a time, clean it, apply new glue and replace it before going on to another.

To prepare pieces for regluing, clean each part of the joint thoroughly, scraping off the dirt and old glue with a knife blade, and actually cleaning the joint sections with solvent or hot vinegar as described earlier in the section on regluing joints in old furniture. When the joint surfaces have been smoothed and sanded until they adhere to one another evenly and tightly, apply the glue and reassemble them as they were originally.

In general, the waterproof synthetic resin glues are the best to use because they have the greatest strength and tenacity. However, the wise craftsman will not depend entirely on glue to hold the furniture piece together, but will employ nails, screws, dowels and hardware reinforcements to augment the efficacy of the glue.

There are many old pieces of furniture which should never be dismantled because they cannot be taken apart without damage. This is especially true of old chairs, the stretchers of which were shaped out of dry wood with a ball on either end. Rungs of this type were then inserted into legs made of green lumber which gradually dried, shrinking around the bulb end of the stretcher, holding the ball fast. Even though in time the rung may begin to move and rattle in the socket of the leg, it cannot be removed for repair without destroying both the chair and the stretcher.

Similarly, glued joints which have been further reinforced by wooden pegs or wedges cannot be dismantled without doing irreparable damage to the joint itself and to the surrounding wood.

Probably more loose joints are found in chairs and sofas than in any other furniture, with stands and tables having nearly as many. Most of these loose joints are either mortise-and-tenon or doweled joints, and are located (on chairs) where the back splat fits into the back post, or (on chairs and tables) where the stretcher fits into the legs. Perhaps the wood itself has suffered shrinkage or has been kept in a room where there was insufficient moisture. Perhaps the piece has suffered hard usage and abuse. In any event, the loose joint must be tightened and the woodworker has a number of reliable methods of repair:

Tightening Joints with Wedges

To make this repair, cut a slot in the end of the piece which will finally be inserted into the hole—that is, the tenon piece, rung, stretcher or spindle—using a hacksaw. Into the slot just cut, pound a wedge made of hardwood. The wedge should be as long as the hole into which it is to be inserted, but not quite so wide. Apply glue to the wedge and the slotted end of the insertion piece, and drive the wedge-widened section into the hole. If the hole goes all the way through the piece, and the wedge end protrudes from the hole, it can be trimmed off flush with the hole and sanded smooth once the glue is dry.

Tightening Square Joints with Shims

A hardwood shim as wide as the hole into which it is to be driven, but with a tapering edge, will tighten a square-sided joint admirably. Simply apply glue to the joint hole, and drive the shim in.

Reinforcing Joints and Screws

Stretchers or mortise-and-tenon joints which do not go all the way through the furniture part into which they are inserted may be greatly strengthened by inserting a screw through the joint from the outside in such a manner that the screw penetrates both the base of the hole into which the insertion section of the joint is fitted and the insertion section itself (tenon, stretcher, spindle, or whatever it may be). In such cases, a hole large enough for the screw head should be drilled through the receptive member; a smaller hole to accommodate the screw shank and thread should be continued through so that when the screw is in place, its head will be recessed in the wood surface and can later be covered by a glued-in plug of dowel, sanded smooth and finished to match the wood surface.

Making a Round Hole Smaller

When a rounded end of a furniture joint is loose in the round hole designed for it, the hole should be completely plugged with a section of dowel the same size as the hole. The piece of dowel should be grooved along its length to allow excess glue to escape, and then glued securely into the oversize hole. Once the glue is dried, a new hole can be drilled in the dowel to fit the rounded end of the insertion piece, and the insertion piece glued snugly into the new hole. This is an excellent method for tightening loose chair rungs, spindles, etc.

Tightening a Joint with Cloth

A round or square joint section which fits sloppily into the hole prepared for it may require a flexible material to enlarge it for better fit. In such a case, strips of cloth narrower than the insertion point should be cut and glued criss-cross over the protruding end of the joint section. These crossed strips should be trimmed to ¾ of the depth of the joint (longer strips may show when the joint is assembled) and glued to the sides of projecting section of the joint. After the glue on the cloth strips is dry, glue the entire projection end and insert it into the glued socket hole to dry. Should the cloth wrapping show around the edges of the hole, it can be trimmed off with a razor blade after the glue is dry.

Tightening Joints with String

Another flexible padding for loose joints is string. Lengths of cord or twine may be wrapped around a loose rung end or spindle tip which has been coated with glue to prevent the cord from slipping. When the string-wrapped end is dry, glue is applied to the socket hole into which the spindle or chair rung will fit, and the twine-wrapped end is driven into the hole.

INSTALLING NEW JOINTS

In performing restoration repair, the craftsman will occasionally be faced with the problem of installing new joints in an old piece either because the original joint is missing or badly damaged or because he feels that the wrong joint was used in the first place. Often "provincial" antiques, hand-made in the villages by amateur craftsmen, manifest these interesting fallacies in design. One must bear in mind that these early amateur craftsmen were necessarily limited by the lack of proper tools, and by their lack of experience and exposure to fine craftsmanship. Skilled only in the rough, crude construction of farming implements, animal shelters and rustic dwellings, their artistry in cabinetmaking was severely limited. Although such homemade, country-style furniture has great interest for the antique collector, it often requires extensive structural repair to render it serviceable and practical again. The decrepit state in which many such pieces are found is not so much from hard usage as simply proof that they were poorly constructed in the first place.

Fortunately, there are any number of stalwart joints which can impart great structural strength to such old pieces. But which joint to use? The craftsman must be fully knowledgeable of the peculiar merits and drawbacks of each type of joint, so that he will employ them intelligently and to the best advantage in restoring and repairing old pieces.

A discussion of each of the joints most frequently used, describing its design, the kind of structural support each gives, and the further reinforcement each should have, may help the novice craftsman to determine which joint to cut for a specific job.

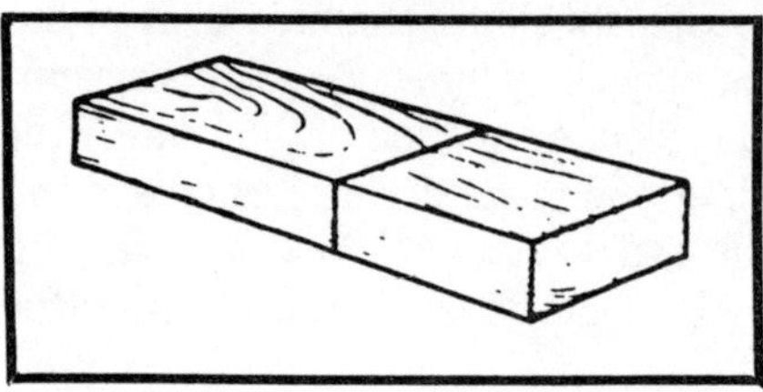

Fig. 11-1. End-to-end butt joint.

Fig. 11-2. Scarf joint.

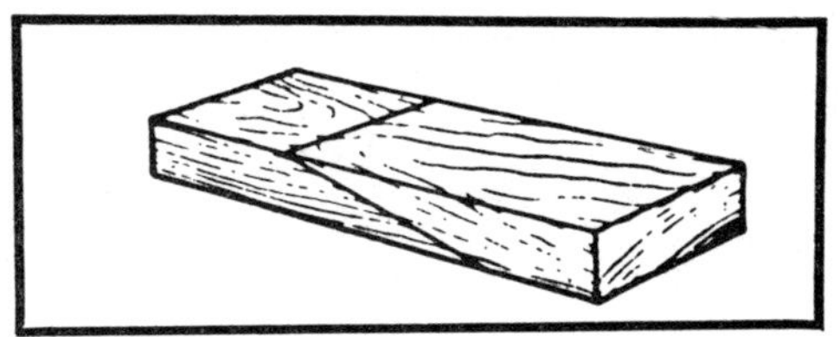

End-To-End Butt Joint

One of the simplest joint types; effective if plates are used to support it, or if dowels are set into the edge of one section, and holes are drilled into the edge of the other section to receive the dowel pegs (see Fig. 11-1).

Scarf Joint

A speedy, effective way of repairing broken or split boards—by cutting off each of the broken ends at an angle and gluing the bias cuts together, one over the other, making a joint of the same thickness as the original board. This joint may be strengthened by staggered screws—each screw sunk below the board surface—and the resultant depression filled with plugs of dowel or of wood dough (see Fig. 11-2).

Serrate or Finger Joint

More complex way of repairing split or broken boards. Needs the support of mending plates on the edges, on both edges of the joined boards (see Fig. 11-3).

Butt Joint

A simple butt joint, made by gluing a horizontal wood piece to a vertical wood piece. Must be reinforced, however. The abutted surface of each piece may be bored with two opposite horizontal holes and a segment of dowel glued into each hole to peg the pieces together. This is the best and most inconspicuous reinforcement for such a joint; however, L-shaped corner braces or angle irons may be used, if desired (see Fig. 11-4).

Fig. 11-3. Serrate or finger joint.

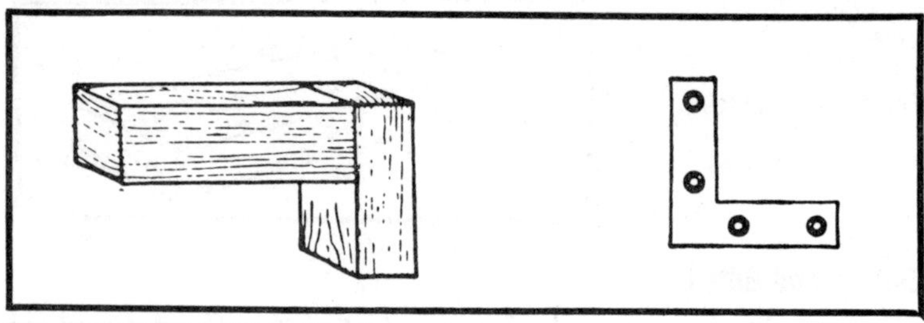

Fig. 11-4. End-to-side butt joint.

Miter Butt Joint

A corner joint like the Butt Joint just described. May be inconspicuously reinforced with wood nails driven into the edges vertically and to sufficient depth to penetrate both sections of the joint. The nail heads are driven below the surface of the wood, and the resultant holes are filled with plugs made of dowel segments or with wood dough. This would be the least noticeable and most professional way of reinforcing this joint, but L-shaped corner braces or angle irons may be used if desired (see Fig. 11-5).

Dowel Joint

One of the best and most inconspicuous of joints—very much used by early craftsmen and, therefore, an ideal joint for use in restoring old furniture. In Fig. 11-6, a portion of the joint has been cut away to permit the reader to observe the construction. Dowel joints of this type may be reinforced by mending plates.

Mortise-and-Tenon

Another hidden joint like the Dowel Joint, often found in quality furniture. The illustration shows the corner of the upright piece cut away so that the reader may see how the tenon, which is an integral part of the *horizontal* joint section, fits closely into the mortise (the rectangular recess) cut into the upright piece. Another design of a

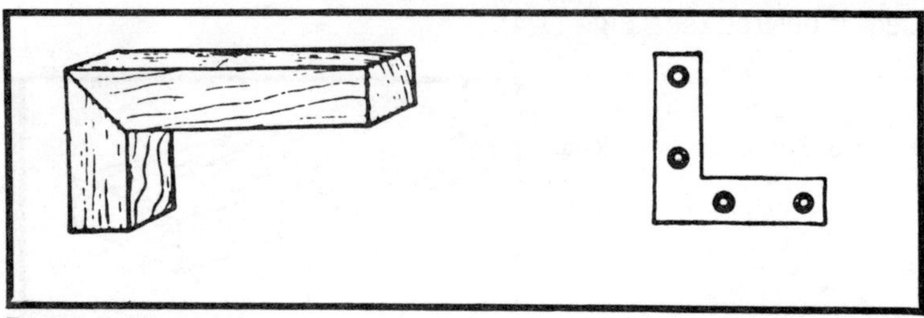

Fig. 11-5. Miter joint.

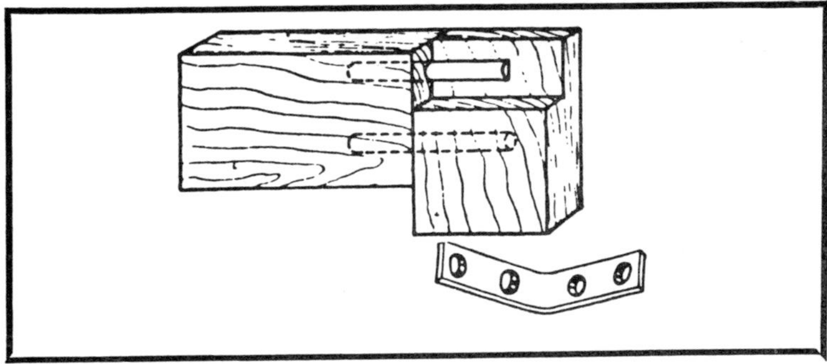

Fig. 11-6. Dowel joint.

mortise-and-tenon joint has an even longer tenon, one which fully penetrates the upright piece. Either type of mortise-and-tenon joint is reliably secure; but, should reinforcement be necessary, two horizontal dowels driven completely through both joint pieces so that they penetrate the joint at the place where the tenon is driven tight into the glue-coated recess of the mortise will produce a joint of outstanding strength. As an alternative to dowel reinforcements, mending plates may be used (see Fig. 11-7).

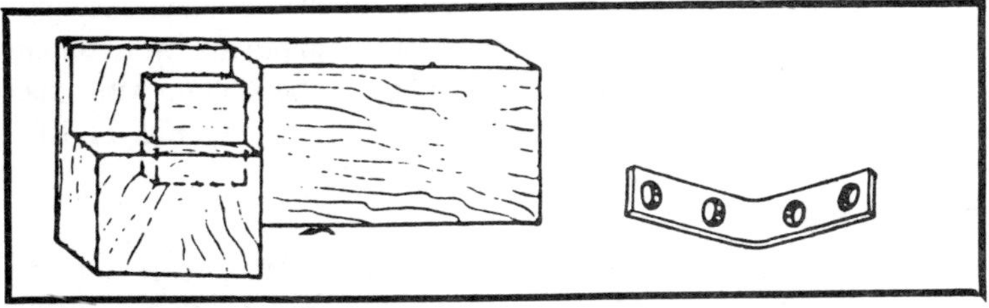

Fig. 11-7. Mortise and tenon joint.

Dado Tongue and Rabbet Joint

The modifications of this type of joint are virtually endless. Here we show one where both horizontal and vertical joint sections have a projection which extends into the other section. When glued, this is a relatively strong joint. Should it require reinforcement, mending plates are recommended (see Fig. 11-8).

Fig. 11-8. Dado tongue and rabbet.

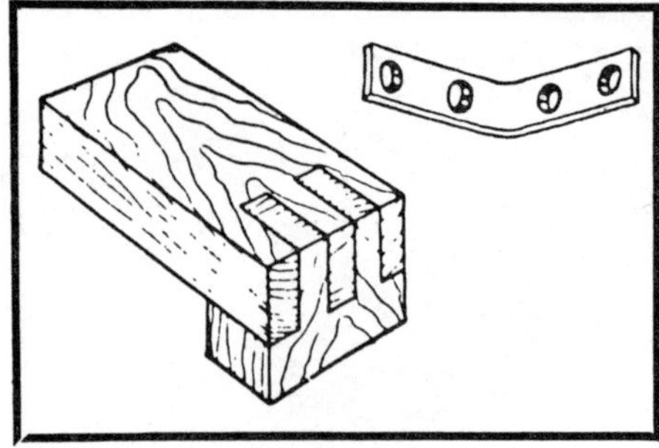

Fig. 11-9. Slip or lock corner.

Slip and Lock Corner Joint

This joint is a simpler, less effective version of the dovetail. This type of joint is usable at the back corners of drawers, but it is not so secure a joint as the true dovetail. Corner braces may be used as reinforcements (see Fig. 11-9).

Dovetail Joints

The true dovetail design, often called a "cistern" dovetail joint, has many modifications, some of which call for complicated cabinetwork. The dovetail joint is often used in fine furniture. If these joints are well made and properly glued, they require no additional support. However, in old furniture many of the joints are worn and in need of repair. In that case, each dovetail may be built up with small shims or the entire joint secured by corner angles (see Fig. 11-10).

Blocked Joint

The primary use for the blocked joint is to secure tops to frames. If securely glued, the blocked joint is outstandingly sturdy, especially if holes are drilled through the joint in two directions to permit screws to go through the block and penetrate both the frame and the top. Fashioned in this manner, the blocked joint will give more strength and hold better than corner angles (see Fig. 11-11).

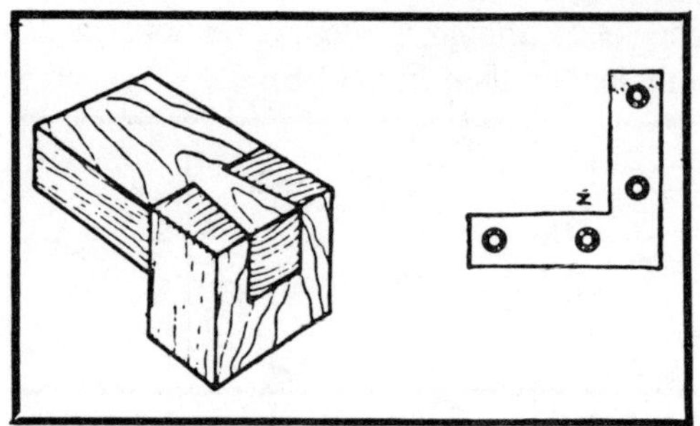

Fig. 11-10. Dovetail joint.

Fig. 11-11. Blocked joint.

Tongue and Groove Joint

Used only in cheaper furniture, but a favorite joint flooring. This joint may be strengthened with mending plates (see Fig. 11-12).

Fig. 11-12. Tongue and groove joint.

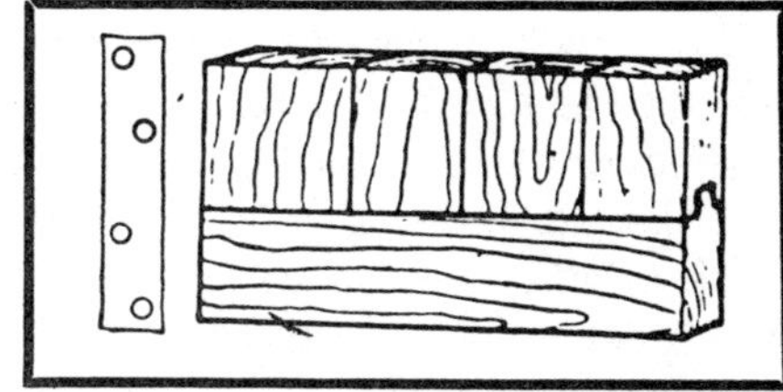

Plain Edge Joint

The joint most commonly used in both old and new furniture construction in securing tops, etc., made of several boards. If the individual boards to be assembled are thick enough, the best reinforcement is with dowels. Blocked joints and corner angles may be used to hold the boards to the frame. The individual boards may be held to one another with mending plates (see Fig. 11-13).

Fig. 11-13. Plain edge joint.

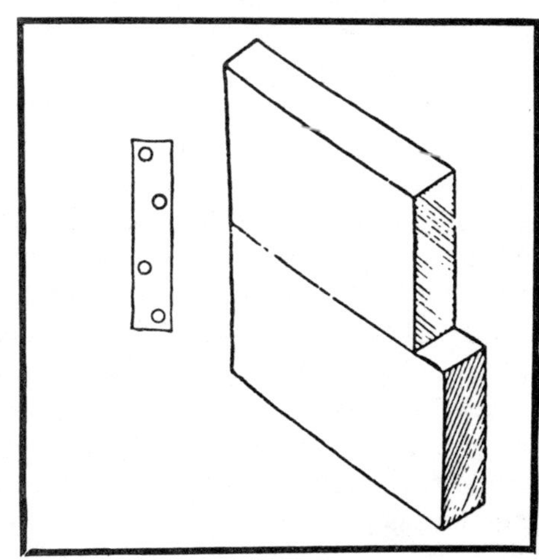

Splined Joint

A rigid, strong joint between two boards often encountered in antique furniture. This joint is made by cutting identical grooves in the abutted edges of both joint sections, and then inserting a wood slat between both grooves to act as a connector between the joint sections. This slat is cut to the same thickness as the grooves and is the same width as the combined depth of both grooves. Glued firmly between the abutted boards, it forms a full-length jointure of great supportive strength. In the illustration, a part of one section of the joint has been cut away so that the reader may see how firmly and fully joined the two abutted joint edges are. If necessary, this joint may be reinforced with mending plates (see Fig. 11-14).

Any badly damaged joints encountered in inspecting old furniture must be replaced. Such replacements—like any other patches, additions or substitutions made in restoring old furniture—should be cut from old, rather than new, wood—especially if they are in a visible position. A surface patch of new wood is so conspicuous and such a detraction from the beauty of an antique piece that it can actually decrease its value. Any part to be replaced or added must be matched carefully with the rest of the piece in texture and color. New wood, even when stained and finished in the same tones as old wood, seldom resembles old wood exactly. Those differences in grain and texture which only age produces are lacking in new wood. No matter how skillful the craftsman is, he will have difficulty in duplicating the exact color because old wood—being drier and more porous than new wood—has gradually absorbed the color of the original finish. When a transparent finish of varnish or shellac is applied, these differences in color become startlingly obvious. The old wood will be strikingly darker in tone than the new.

So necessary is it to find old wood for patching—particularly surface patching—that the careful craftsman will sometimes purchase a decrepit piece of similar wood and like age and cannibalize it for repairs and patches. However, there is another means of obtaining suitable old wood which he should try first. Often, if he carefully examines the piece he is repairing, he will find the proper wood being utilized as a block reinforcement to a frame, a drawer stop or a parting rail between drawers. Such pieces he may safely utilize for surface patching and repair, replacing them with custom-cut pieces of new wood without detracting in any way from the value of the antique. Before removing the old part, however, he should scrutinize it carefully to make sure that it is the proper species and grain for his purpose.

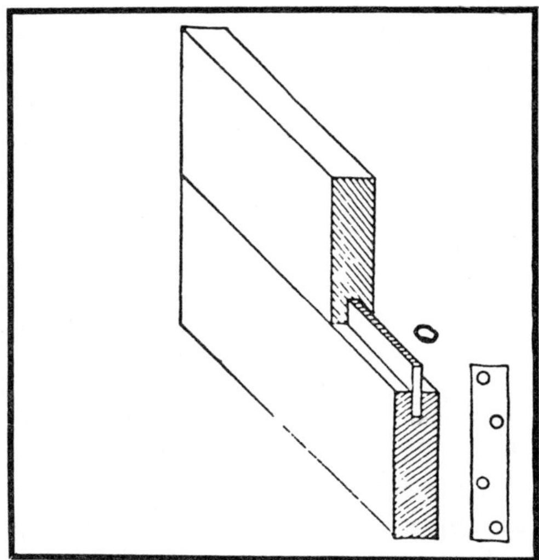

Fig. 11-14. Splined joint.

Craftsmen who plan to do an extensive amount of antique repair will be wise to buy up junk parts of old furniture—table tops, head boards, bed side rails and foot rails—in oak, mahogany and walnut and keep them on hand for future need. Such scrap items may be obtained for very little money, especially if they are in irreparable condition, from junk yards, Salvation Army and Good Will outlets and from cabinetmakers. They may then be stored carefully in a special place for future use and will prove priceless indeed when the need for old wood arises. Even small pieces are reusable, so save every precious scrap!

REPAIRING CHAIRS

If an amateur craftsman has an antique chair to repair whose restoration demands the exact duplication of a certain piece, or if the installation of missing parts is unusually difficult, he would be wise to take the chair to a professional cabinetmaker. The shaping of arms, the rendering of carvings, the designing of bowed or comb backs, ornate splats, intricate turnings, etc. are best left to a well-qualified shop. The proper tools and equipment are as necessary to a satisfactory job as is the expertise. In this text, we will limit our discussion to those repairs which can be effectively accomplished by a craftsman of limited ability, using the tools normally found in home workshops.

Shaping and Installing Rungs

Rungs of large diameter may be made from an old rake or hoe handle. Those of smaller diameter should be made of a hardwood which properly matches that used in the chair.

Replacement rungs should not be tapered for any great length at the ends. Instead, they should be reduced rather abruptly at the ends to fit the hole, with a slight swelling (or "shoulder") just outside the narrowed projection designed to penetrate the hole. The joint end must have a snug, drive fit, with the shoulder, which is of larger diameter, helping to plug fast the tapered joint.

Simply shaped rungs may be whittled with a penknife. Measure the diameter of the hole to be plugged with inside calipers and transfer the measure to the end of the new rung. Whittle the new rung end to this measure, and try it for size in the hole, turning the rung in the hole to see if further whittling is necessary. If the rung is a slender one, it may be bent slightly like a bow in installing it and so released that both ends will spring straight into the joint holes which have been coated with glue to receive them. If the rung is thicker in diameter, it will have to be anchored deep in one glue-coated hole, and then bent slightly to spring straight into the other. A tourniquet or clamp should be applied until the glue dries.

Shaping and Installing Spindles

Complicated, intricately turned spindles should be copied by woodworking professionals, but simpler spindles—such as the style with central bulb and tapered ends often found on Windsor chairs—are relatively easy to reproduce using a draw knife or penknife and a spokeshave or short block plane.

First, a rough version of the spindle is whittled with the knife. This rough-hewn version is then secured in a vise and smoothed carefully with the spokeshave. As the work progresses, the outside calipers are constantly used to test measurements. A similar length spindle still intact in the chair serves as a pattern for the new spindle. The outside calipers are set to the various gradations of the egg-shaped bulb and the tapered ends, and these dimensions are transferred to the new spindle to insure that the replacement spindle will copy the original spindle as closely as possible. As he works, the woodworker should constantly compare the two spindles to insure that the dimensions of the swelling and tapering are the same and are in the same relative positions on the new spindle as they were on the old.

If a block plane is used to shear the spindle, the spindle is not secured in a vise. Instead, it is held in the hand, its opposite end placed against a very thin block of waste wood nailed to the bench. By exerting pressure with his hand, the woodworker can bend the slender spindle slightly outward while the hand holding the plane shears off this outward bulge to create the tapering effect from the egg-shaped bulb which characterizes this style of spindle.

The final consideration in creating a new spindle is the shaping of the ends which will be inserted into the existing holes in the chair back, top rail and seat. When these are whittled sufficiently to fit exactly, glue is applied to both holes, and the new spindle is installed by driving the end of the spindle as deeply as possible into the top rail, then bending it slightly and allowing it to straighten into the hole in the seat. A spindle too thick to bend may need a slightly deeper hole drilled in the top rail to allow the upper end of the spindle to be driven in more deeply, so that the bottom end of the spindle can be more easily let down into the hole in the chair seat.

Replacing Back Splats

Many back splats are very simple in design and can be reproduced by any woodworker who is handy with tools. However, such splats as the bannister back, which is first turned and then sawed in half lengthwise, or a contoured back splat similar to those used in Queen Anne or Chippendale chairs, often embellished with carving or with fretwork, should be made and installed by a professional. If the splats themselves are intact, but they wobble in the rail grooves, they can be rendered rigid with Devon Grip-Wood, which contains both adhesive and wood swelling properties and which comes with a syringe applicator capable of penetrating even tight, narrow jointures to apply the glue.

Repairing Broken Turnings

Any part—such as a stretcher, rung, spindle, splat or arm rest—which shows only minor damage should be repaired rather than replaced. Repair is always the approved means of restoration where antiques are concerned; replacements are undertaken only when absolutely necessary. To repair a minor crack or split in a part, simply pry it far enough open to insert glue on a toothpick, and hold the crack closed with cramps until the glue dries.

However, if the split is a wide one and close to the end of the member, more complicated repairs may be required, such as the glue-and-dowel repair. This method entails drilling a hole crossways through the split, using a drill bit one size larger than the dowel which is to be inserted. Next, a dowel peg slightly shorter than the depth of the drilled hole is cut, the hole being deliberately left empty on both ends to allow the excess glue a place to escape when the joint is glued. The dowel peg is grooved by squeezing its sides hard between the serrated jaws of a pair of pliers so that it will have a roughened surface, or "tooth," to hold the glue. Now glue is applied to both sides of the split, to the hole and to the length of the dowel peg. The length of the dowel peg is countersunk in the hole so that it acts as a bridge joining the two split sections. The assembly is secured in clamps to dry. When the clamps are removed, the glued dowel will have joined the two sides of the split and made them one piece again. The drill hole into which the dowel was countersunk can be filled with wood dough or wood putty and refinished to match the rest of the member.

If a member has completely broken in two, a glue-and-dowel repair similar to the one described may be used. However, instead of cross-drilling through the split, the broken ends of both pieces are individually drilled so that a common dowel peg can be inserted to join them. To ascertain the accurate alignment of the dowel which will join the broken parts, a brad may be driven part way into the exact center of one broken part, and the other broken part pressed hard against the head of the brad to mark the wood. Then the brad is withdrawn and a hole one size larger than the dowel to be inserted is drilled at the place where the brad was inserted on the one piece and at the mark of the brad head on the other piece. The dowel segment which will join the two pieces is now cut. It must be a little shorter than the *sum* of the two holes drilled to hold each end of it, so that when it is installed it will have room to recede sufficiently into the hole to allow the two broken pieces to come together snugly. The segment of dowel used must be grooved by squeezing its sides between the serrated jaws of a pair of pliers, as described. Now glue is applied to the holes in both pieces and to the dowel ends. The dowel is tapped into the hole in one broken piece until half of its length is driven in. Then the hole of the other broken piece is fitted over the protruding section of dowel and tapped into place against the first broken piece, so that the two pieces are joined just as they were before they broke apart. A folded pad of cloth should be used to buffer the mallet blows and protect the finish.

Lengthening Legs

Antique chairs are sometimes sadly crippled because the bottom of a leg has worn away to such an extent that the chair wobbles and lists to one side. If this condition exists, a piece must be added to the bottom of the leg to correct this wobble.

If the leg is a square or round one with straight sides and no shaping, the simplest method of elongating it is to cut the leg off squarely and drill the center of the leg bottom for the insertion of a dowel. An extension piece may then be cut which is a little thicker and larger than the original, and a peg hole drilled in its center for the dowel. When the leg and its slightly larger extension are glued to a common dowel and to each other, and the glue is thoroughly dry, the new extension can then be filed and sanded down to the exact size of the original leg to which it is attached, and the leg cut off to the exact measurement of the opposite leg which sits flat and firmly on the floor.

A note of caution: The craftsman should make sure that the floor on which he tests for wobble is truly level. With a spirit level, he should check the flatness of the floor before sawing off the leg extension to measure.

If the leg is a turned style, the extension will have to match the turnings exactly. However, the extension should be made slightly wider and longer than is finally desired, so that final adjustments can be made after the extension has been glued on. A dowel-shaped button may be cut on the center of the top surface of the extension, and this button used like a dowel to penetrate a hole drilled in the leg bottom. If some discrepancies are noted when the two are joined—such as the button being slightly off-center or the turnings not exactly aligned with those on the chair leg—these variances can be rectified when the extension is sanded down to size.

The wobble-producing variance in the length of the leg may be such a slight one that a felt chair tip which screws into place, or a metal chair guide (which is dome-shaped and has claws underneath to penetrate the leg bottom when pounded into place) will adjust the variance.

Correcting Unbalance

Sometimes the reason why furniture cants to one corner or another is more involved than merely lengthening one leg. Sometimes all four legs are so rounded on the bottoms that none are sitting squarely, with one leg noticeably shorter than all the others. If the application of felt chair tips or metal guides does not instantly correct this crippled condition, here is a procedure which will rectify it:

1. Move the piece to an area of the floor which is confirmed as absolutely flat by testing it with the spirit level.
2. Pare a small block of wood thinner and thin until, by trial and error, you arrive at the exact thickness to elevate the short leg to the place where it will sit squarely even with the rest.
3. Remove the block from under the short leg just long enough to cut a duplicate to the identical thickness. Glue

the first block under the short leg, and place the other block flat on the floor close against one of the longer legs. Move the measuring block carefully around each of the longer legs in turn, marking off the height of the measuring block around the circumference of each of the longer legs with a sharp pencil. Check your measurements carefully.

4. Using a tenon saw, cut off the longer legs on the waste side of the pencil mark, leaving the pencil line itself. After the legs are sawed off to an even length, test the surface of the piece, if any, with a spirit level to be sure all is in alignment. If necessary, file down the minimal variance which would render each leg the same length and the piece squarely level.

Altering Leg Styles

Sometimes the craftsman wishes to transform a small dining or game table into a coffee table, or convert a high seated chair into a slipper chair—projects which require that he shorten the legs considerably, yet produce new leg bottoms which rest flat on the floor. The method is as follows:

1. With the spirit level, the worker tests the floor on which the piece stands for absolute flatness, and the surface of the piece (the table top or the chair seat) for levelness.
2. When he is sure all is in alignment, he measures one leg from the floor to the place where he plans to cut off the leg, and marks the proposed leg end with a pencil line. Noting on the ruler the number of inches which will be cut off each leg, he uses the ruler to mark the other legs with a similar pencil line.
3. Next he chooses a block of wood to use as a gauge. He places the end of the block precisely on the waste side of the pencil line, and marks the place on the leg to which the extremity of the block extends with a chisel cut, using the back of the chisel to make a sharp score. Carefully, he moves the block around the entire circumference of the leg, always placing one end of the gauge block just against the pencil line, and marking the place where the opposite end touches the leg with a chisel cut.
4. He repeats the measurements with the gauge block on all four legs.
5. Making sure that the saw kerk is on the waste side of the chisel line, he now saws off all four legs, angling the cut slightly, if this is necessary to insure a flat leg leg bottom.

6. If his measurements were accurately done, all four shortened legs will now rest on the floor, flush and square. A test with the spirit level will indicate any slight divergence which must be filed down.
7. With the wood block resting on the floor and butted against the leg, he now goes completely around each leg, scoring with the chisel where the top of the wood block touches the leg. This score mark should come very close to the pencil line which indicated how short the legs were finally to be. However, he will saw off the legs at the *chisel* line, rather than the *pencil* line, correct any slight error in balance, taper the bottom edges of the legs with a file, and finish the raw wood bottoms with a coat of stain.

Strengthening Chair Structure

In rendering chairs more serviceable, the craftsman must consider that such chairs as dining chairs, occassional chairs, and overstuffed easy chairs and sofas—all of which have padded seats with no underbracing—put much greater strain on the chair frames than do wooden-seated chairs. These chairs are only as strong as the joints in the frames and often are discovered to have insecure front rails or side rails which are loose at their juncture with the back rail and legs.

One of the best ways of repairing such sitting pieces is by adding triangular corner blocks, preferably of birch, to the corners of the

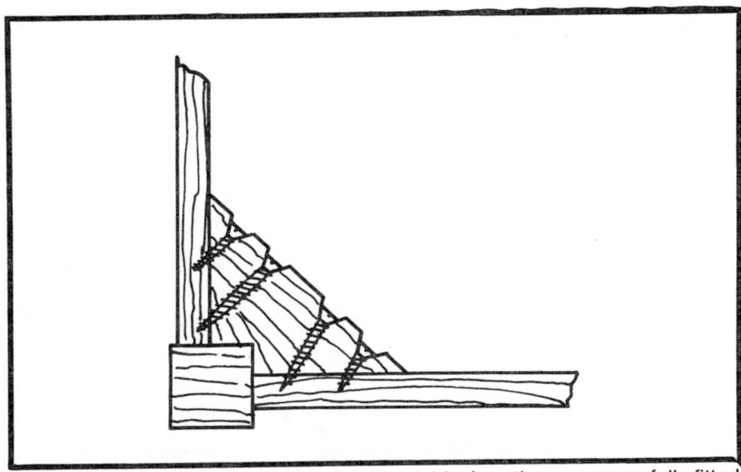

Fig. 11-15. Triangular wooden reinforcement blocks—these are carefully fitted into the corners of the chair seat frame and secured by four countersunk screws (positioned so that two are on either side of the leg) driven in at an angle from the hypotenuse of the triangular block to the seat frame.

frame, securing them with glue and with four countersunk screws—two on either side of the corner—which are driven through the hypotenuse of the triangular reinforcement block into the chair frame (see Fig. 11-15). These blocks should be at least 3 inches long on the 90-degree angle sides and at least 1½ inches thick. The point of the 90-degree angle must fit exactly into the corner, and the two abutting sides must firmly meet the frame.

To prevent the screws from binding in their holes, a drill bit one size larger than the screws is used. Then four holes are drilled through the triangular reinforcement to penetrate the square chair frame. These holes are not straight, but angled outward like the spokes of a fan for better support. Each hole will probably require a screw of a slightly different length, because the holes are differently slanted, but none of the screws should be as long as the hole it is chosen to fill because the heads are to be sunk into the wood edge and the holes plugged with dowel segments or wood putty. Finally, glue is applied to the holes and the screws are threaded in. When the glue dries, plugs of dowel are glued over the countersunk screw heads.

Care must be taken in removing the padded seat, usually fastened with screws on the underside. In some upholstered pieces, padding and even springs must be removed as well. If the craftsman feels that he is not qualified to replace them correctly, he should relegate the work to an upholsterer.

REPAIRING FLAT SURFACES

Next to table tops, the antique furniture most likely to show serious warpage are such items as drop-leaf tables, desk tops which drop down to form a writing surface, and hinged chest tops. Because these pieces have large surfaces which are not supported by a rigid frame, they are prone to warpage.

Surfaces of dressers, chests and stands often show warpage as well, especially when these surfaces have not been sufficiently fastened to the frames on the underside with an adequate number of glued blocks and screws.

Another frequent cause of warpage is the failure on the part of the cabinet maker to apply a proper finish to the undersurface of a drop-leaf table or a fold-down desk top. Unless the same amount of varnish, shellac or linseed oil has been applied as was applied to the top surface, the moisture in the atmosphere will penetrate the wood from the underside and cause warpage.

Unfortunately for the home woodworker, the equipment with which professional shops are equipped—such as steam boxes—is not available to him. He must substitute home methods which are neither as fast nor as efficient. Nevertheless, with reasonable care, he can perform this difficult repair with admirable success.

When boards twist, they do so on the *lengthwise* of the grain; when they warp, the unevenness is *across* the grain only. Also, the board edges in furniture tend to warp upward toward the finished side. The top side has the concave (depression-shaped) warp; the under side bulges in a convex curve. In an antique, some warpage is forgivable; in fact, some collectors regard a slight warpage as an authentic evidence of age and, therefore find its presence charming. However, serious warpage which distorts the line and renders the surfaces lumpy is impractical and should be rectified.

If a one-piece-wide-board furniture top is not too badly warped, it may often be straightened by clamps and secured more firmly in place than before to prevent it from bulging again. However, the tension must be very slowly and carefully applied by tightening the clamps a little at a time and allowing the wood to adjust to that amount of tension for a considerable period before tightening them again—otherwise, disastrous cracks will occur.

Before repairing any warp, major or minor, the frame should be carefully examined for structural rigidity, soundness and alignment, and all necessary repairs made on it first. Then the warped area itself should be examined, and a method of eradicating the warpage determined. Consideration should be given the degree of warpage, the thickness of the boards affected and their location in the piece. The entire repair procedure should be carefully planned; every item necessary to carrying it out should be readily at hand so that the moment the warp is removed by steam or moisture, the cramps with their buffers of waste wood or folded cloth may be immediately applied, before the boards can spring back into the uneven state in which they were found. Immediate action is the only way to achieve satisfactory results.

Wet Pack Method

The direct application of moisture to wood is the simplest of all methods for eradicating warpage. It sometimes does not work if the wood is not sufficiently porous or if heavy coats of paint keep the wood from absorbing moisture. This method requires that the wet pack be applied to the underside of the wood where, generally speaking, no paint has been applied. However, if the board being straightened is the lid of a desk or the drop-leaf of a table, the underside to which the moisture is applied will, of course, have been finished. The finish may suffer sadly in the process or may have to be stripped off entirely to promote absorption of the moisture.

Also to be considered is the fact that the glues used in old pieces is not waterproof; waterproof glues were unknown when such pieces were made. The application of moisture may loosen the adhesive and necessitate regluing the entire assembly.

This method of wet-packing warpage works best on surfaces which can be cleated on the underside to keep them flat once the warpage is removed. Table tops and drop leaves are frequently reinforced with cleats. The procedural steps are as follows:

1. Fill any screw holes on the underside of the piece with wood dough. Pack in firmly and allow to dry.
2. Lay the boards on a freshly watered lawn in the bright sunlight or near a heated cookstove on wet blankets wrung out of hot water or on pads of wet burlap. Allow the boards to lie there several hours until they have absorbed sufficient moisture to flatten out. Keep renewing the wet packs, always using hot water.
3. Once the boards are straightened and before they dry, secure them to the frame in their original positions. If the boards were held with screws, replace these. The newly straighened boards should be reinforced with corner irons and with mending plates screwed into the underside wherever possible to prevent their warping again. If the underside is sometimes visible—as in a drop-leaf table—use inconspicuous wooden cleats rather than hardware. These must be applied as soon as the boards are flat, for the boards will tend to spring back the moment they are dry.

Steam Method

This method is best for stubborn warpage, because the live steam fully penetrates the wood and wood so treated is much less likely to resume its previously buckled shape, once straightened and its flatness reinforced. The steps are these:

1. Remove all finish from the warped boards to permit the moisture to fully permeate the wood.
2. Have the boards steam-treated in a commercial steam box. Although such facilities may be somewhat hard to find, inquiring for their whereabouts at lumberyards and cabinet shops should locate one.
3. Before steaming the wood, all nail holes on the underside of the boards should be fully packed with wood dough and allowed to dry thoroughly.

4. If the wood is exceptionally dried out, or of the type which has very open pores, an even coat of 50 percent denatured alcohol mixed with 50 percent denatured alcohol mixed with 50 percent white shellac will prevent the moisture from being absorbed too rapidly. Before applying, however, ask at the steaming shop if such a treatment is necessary.
5. If it is necessary to secure a board in a flat position for a temporary period while you transport if from the steaming shop to your workshop where you can apply reinforcements, cramp rigid strips of wood on both sides near the ends and in the center. Remove these only after you have drilled holes for cleats or other reinforcements and are immediately reassembling the boards.

Grooving To Remove Warpage

This method of straightening warpage is necessarily limited to those boards which are not visible on both sides (as drop-leaves of tables are) and which may be removed for sawing. It involves cutting lengthwise grooves with a power saw on the reverse sides of the boards. The method is as follows:

1. Remove the warped surface from the piece and turn it over. On the reverse side, where the wood swells outward convexly, saw the wood lengthwise with the grain in grooves about three inches apart and as deep as ¾ of the board width. A power saw should be used for this job. The grooves should run almost full length, stopping just short of the ends of the boards so that the grooves will not be visible on the end surface.
2. If the boards are not too thick or too badly warped, they may be reassembled immediately and secured to the frame by screws and corner irons. Otherwise, the boards should be placed, grooved side down, on blankets or burlap wet with hot water near a heated stove until they are straight, and then immediately replaced on the frame.

Sawing Boards to Remove Warpage

This method of removing warpage must be done in a professional shop equipped with large power tools. The boards cut must be one inch or more in thickness since the boards will have to be planed as a final operation and boards much thinner than one inch would not allow for much shearing. Drop table leaves straightened by this method are smooth-finished on both the surface and the underside. When further reinforced with wooden cleats, they remain straight permanently. In fact, the only objection to this method is that it removes all evidence of age and wear, leaving boards which are thinner than the original boards and of a different color tone, which may prove difficult to stain to the same shade as the rest of the table. The method is as follows:

1. The board is cut lengthwise with a ripsaw into strips about three to four inches wide.
2. The cut edges are smoothed on a joiner and alternate boards in the assembly are turned upside down so that when assembled the end grain of the boards will cup in alternate directions, thus offsetting warpage.
3. The boards are glued together and firmly cramped along their length to secure them throughout the glue to dry. When dry, the now-straightened boards are put through a planer and sanded on both sides, ready for refinishing. The saw marks where the boards are newly glued will be virtually invisible. Note: Another little-used method for eliminating warpage is to insert and glue dowels through the entire width of a board, once the board has been steamed straight. The drilling is most accurately done with a power tool. If the board is not too wide or too thin, this method works admirably.

Installing Cleats

This type of reinforcement must be undertaken immediately after the boards are straightened, by any of the foregoing methods, and before the board surfaces have had a chance to resume their former concave condition.

Cleats are installed on the underside of the leaves and across the grain of the boards. They are positioned eight to ten inches from the end of the leaf at a place where they will not be conspicuous from the ends and will not interfere with the frame or the legs. If at all possible, a third cleat may be installed across the center of the leaf as well, providing it does not interfere with the gate-leg, frame arm or brace which swings outward from the frame to support the leaf in horizontal position when the table is open. The support furnished by such a center cleat is highly desirable. The method for applying cleats is as follows:

1. For greatest effectiveness, cleats should be of hardwood, such as oak. If the leaves to be reinforced are of medium

width, the cleats should be ¾-inch thick, and from 1-inch to 1½-inch wide. In length, they are about 1-inch less than the width of the leaf.

2. Cleats are installed with the *narrow* width placed across the boards and the *wider* dimension extending vertically outward from the board.
3. For proper resistance to bend, cleats must be sawed lengthwise from a board of the desired thickness. Thus the narrow dimension of the cleat (the ¾-inch aforementioned) is the width of the board from which the cleats are cut, and the strips are measured to the 1-inch or 1 ½-inch width desired.
4. To fasten cleats, flat-headed steel screws of a length which will penetrate the cleat plus half the width of the table leaf should be used. (Brass screws would not be practical because brass is too soft a metal to take the strain of such deep penetration without breaking off.) The screw holes should be drilled about six inches apart, with a drill bit one size larger than the screw being used, so that the shank of the screws will have free clearance through the cleat. All screws are countersunk with a rose bit until the heads are flush with the surface.
5. The edges of the cleats should be rounded with a file and sanded to prevent their catching on napery or clothing when the table is used for dining. Sand the surfaces to be glued so that they are flat and smooth to adhere better.
6. If the table is not too large, it should be turned upside-down on spread newspapers and accurate measurements made of all four corners from the edge of the leaf to the leg in ascertaining where the cleats should be positioned. Enough clearance must be left so that the cleat does not interfere with the legs when the leaf is dropped and hanging. The lines indicating the placement of the cleats must be parallel to the board ends.
7. When the measurements have been double-checked and the position of the cleats outlined with a drawing knife, the finish must be removed from the place where the cleat will be positioned so that the glue will hold the cleat.
8. Now fairly thick waterproof glue is mixed and spread on the position the cleat will occupy and on the cleat itself. The two glued pieces are abutted, and the cleat is secured with screws driven fully in with a drill bit and brace. As mentioned in Step 4, the screws should be spaced about six inches apart along the cleat.

9. All excess glue is wiped off and cramps are applied to hold the cleats rigidly in place until the glue dries—about 48 hours since the steamed boards are probably still moist.
10. The cleats are stained to match the table underside and, after the stain dries, a coat of 75 percent boiled linseed oil and 25 percent pure turpentine (or a coat of varnish or shellac) is brushed on the entire underside to prevent the moisture from penetrating the insufficiently treated wood and causing warpage, as it did before.

Cleats may be used on the undersides of hinged desk and chest tops after the warpage is removed. In such cases, they are installed at the extreme ends of the top, if space permits.

REPAIRING DRAWERS

Cabinet and dresser drawers subjected to long-term, hard usage often develop loose joints. The most efficient way to repair them is to take them completely apart. Step-by-step instructions are as follows:

1. First, remove the drawer bottom. Usually this piece is held in place by a small nail driven through the bottom and into the end rail.
2. Next, loosen the dovetail joints at the corners. Care must be taken in so doing. Place a small board next to the dovetail joints and pound the small board with a hammer to relax the grip of the dovetails and loosen them.
3. Clean all the old glue thoroughly from the joints and the grooves in the side rail which holds the drawer bottom. Apply heavy glue to both members of the dovetail joints and reassemble them. A small brad driven into both members of the joint will effectively reinforce them.
4. Remove all old glue from the drawer bottom itself and from the groove in the drawer front into which the drawer bottom fits. Apply new glue to the grooves in the side rails and in the drawer front, and to the drawer bottom itself, and slide it into place. Before the glue sets, try the drawer assembly in the drawer opening to be sure it fits satisfactorily. Slide the drawer back and forth a few times to test the ease with which it moves.
5. If the drawer drags along its sides, it may have to be planed and sanded after the glue dries. Slight dragging may be quickly relieved by applying a little talcum powder, soap or soapstone to the sides.

6. If the drawer drags on the bottom slides, an application of furniture wax to the slide will make it glide easily. If this does not help, the slide may have to be planed or sanded and then waxed to enable the drawer to move slickly back and forth.
7. If the drawer is too loose vertically in the drawer opening, a thin strip of wood may be glued into the drawer slide to raise the drawer. To test for what thickness of wood strip is needed, push a few thumb tacks into the trough of the drawer slide and try sliding the drawer in and out over the elevation of the tacks. Then remove the tacks, noting how deeply they had to be driven to accommodate the drawer, and make the wood strip as thick as the head and shank portion of the tack which protruded.

WASHING SOILED FURNITURE

When the necessary structural repairs to the furniture piece have been completed, the furniture should be given a thorough washing with a soft, clean cloth and warm water to which a small amount of mild soap flakes such as Lux or Ivory has been added. If the piece has been very heavily waxed, a thorough preliminary wiping with a cloth dampened with turpentine will remove the buildup of old wax, after which the piece should be carefully and completely washed, inside and out, with the mild soap solution described above. Wash a small section of the piece at a time, going over it as often as necessary to remove the grime. Then dry the area thoroughly with soft cloths or disposable household towels and proceed to the next section. Special care should be taken with veneered areas, which should be dried very thoroughly the moment they are clean so that the water will not penetrate and dissolve the glue with which the veneer is fastened. If the veneer is badly cracked or broken, a commercial product used for cleaning veneer or a cloth moistened in turpentine should be substituted for the water wash.

If stubborn stains such as finger marks, syrup, butter, etc., refuse to yield to the mild soap bath, the U.S. Department of Commerce book entitled *Furniture, Its Selection And Use* suggests that powdered green soap, available at the drugstore, be used. A teaspoon, worked into a lather on a soft wet cloth, and then massaged into the stubborn spots with a circular motion until the surface is covered with lather will generally remove oily or sticky stains. When the stains have yielded to this concentrated cleansing, the cloth is washed out and all the soap is thoroughly rinsed off. Then, using a soft, dry cloth and rubbing with the wood grain, the piece is waxed and polished.

When washing furniture, the carcase of the piece should not be forgotten. Drawers should be pulled out and washed both inside and outside. Dust covers, if any, should be washed free of dirt and the cabinet framework should be cleaned with a damp, soapy cloth. The amount of dirt thus removed will astound you. Many marks which you will have believed to be serious blemishes will be found to be merely dirt. Only after the soil of years is removed will you be able to assess the surface repair needed with any sort of accuracy.

REMOVING DENTS AND BRUISES

On almost every hardwood or softwood, except for rock maple, blemishes in the finish may be removed by the use of water alone, or by water and heat in combination. (Rock maple requires sanding.)

For example, softwoods often need only water to raise a dent. Simply apply water to the depression with your finger tip until the water level is above the surrounding surface. As soon as the wood has absorbed this amount of water, add more, and keep doing so until the bruise has been raised a little higher than the surface around it. Allow the bruised area to dry thoroughly. In so doing, it will lose some of its excess moisture, and will shrink to the same level as the wood around it.

If the water is being absorbed more slowly than it should be, prick the depressed area with a very fine needle. The water absorption will be speeded up, and the needle holes will close up and become invisible.

Usually, hardwoods require the application of heat to bruised and dented areas because these woods are generally closer pored than softwoods and, therefore, not so readily absorbent. To raise a depression in hardwood, fill the depression with water as described for softwoods. Heat the tip of an old metal spike—a knife blade, screwdriver, or ice-pick—and insert the hot tip in the water, being careful not to touch or burn the wood. The water will steam away, and more water will constantly have to be applied. Keep up this process until the wood fibers beneath the dent have sufficiently expanded with heat and moisture to raise the dented area higher than the area around it. Then allow the bruise to dry. It will resume the same level as the rest of the surface.

Depressions near a glued joint have to be handled with special care because the water used in raising the bruise may dissolve the glue. However, here is a method to raise the dent without imperiling the structural fastenings.

First, the depression is filled with water and a clean piece of blotting paper is placed over the puddle to float on the wet spot. An electric steam iron set at a moderate heat ("silk" or "rayon" on the fabric scale) and is allowed to get as warm as that thermostat setting permits. A metal thimble from the sewing basket is pressed into the now-moist blotting paper, rounded head down, and positioned in the depressed area. The warm iron is placed against the top of the thimble. Soon the metal thimble has warmed the blotting paper poultice to the place where it is steaming the wood fibers and causing them to expand and push upward. As the water evaporates and more and more water is added, there is ample opportunity to examine the condition of the bruise before continuing the treatment. When the dented area is as high as or higher than the surface surrounding it, the treatment may be discontinued and the wood permitted to dry.

A damp woolen cloth or a piece of wet woolen blanket may be substituted for the blotting paper. Again, the moderately-heated steam iron is employed to raise the wood fibers. By placing the warm iron over the bruised area with the moist blanket between the sole of the iron and the wood, enough steam is generated to slowly raise the wood fibers to normal level. If the craftsman is vigilant during any of the steaming processes just described, there should be little or no damage to the finish. However, if the finish is of a non-waterproof variety, white spots may result and the finish will have to be revived. If heat and moisture have only slightly dulled the finish and there are no white spots, a rub with linseed oil and rottenstone will restore the glow.

Should the wood being treated be nude wood, without any finish whatsoever, the surface must be sanded smooth in the area where the bruise was raised. Fine abrasive papers in grades from 6/0 to 8/0 will shear off the wood fiber "whiskers" raised by the steaming.

REPAIRING AND PATCHING GOUGES

Small gouges of holes in a wood surface are very quickly and inconspicuously repaired by filling them thoroughly with stick shellac of the proper color or with stain-matched wood dough. However, when the surface patch is large enough to show some graining, the repair must be accomplished by actually inlaying a piece of wood of a specific grain, texture, age and color so that, when finished, the patch will blend virtually invisibly with the surrounding wood.

The wood chosen must be thoroughly seasoned (or the color will lighten as it dries out), cleaned thoroughly of dirt and grime and of any former finish, and smoothly sanded with fine and extra fine abrasive papers and steel wool.

Essentially, there are two types of patches—the *shallow* patch which fits into a trough or "grave," filling a hollow with vertical sides and flat bottom, and the *plug* patch which fits a hole cut completely through the board. The shallow patch is used to fill places where rot has partially destroyed the wood, where deep troughs such as those left by cigarette burns are present, or where gouging has badly mashed and splintered the surface. The plug patch is used to replace injured or rotted wood which extends completely, or almost completely, through the board.

Shaping the Patch

The shape given the patch is all important to the appearance of the repaired area. The grain of the patch must match the grain it replaces as nearly as possible. The end of the patch must be joined to the board being patched at an angle of 45 degrees, otherwise the place where the patch joins the edge of the board being repaired will be very noticeable.

The shapes recommended for skillful surface patching are the square, the diamond, the double arrow patch, the reverse arrow patch and the parallelogram patch. Consideration must be given to the direction of the grain on the surface of the patch; it must go the same way as the grain on the board it is patching. Where the edges of the patch cross the surface grain, they do so at an angle of 45 degrees wherever possible (except for the diamond patch, which inscribes a 30-degree angle with the grain).

- A **Square Patch** is inserted with the grain to cover holes, pitting or large nicks (see Fig. 11-16).
- The **Diamond Patch** repairs long gouges or narrow, lengthwise holes in wood with a subtle, indistinct grain (see Fig. 11-17).
- The **Reverse Arrow Patch** is useful as a patch between two members. The grain of the patch runs the same way as the surface grain (see Fig. 11-18).
- The **Double Arrow Patch** is excellent as a repair device for damage close to a corner and is inserted so that the

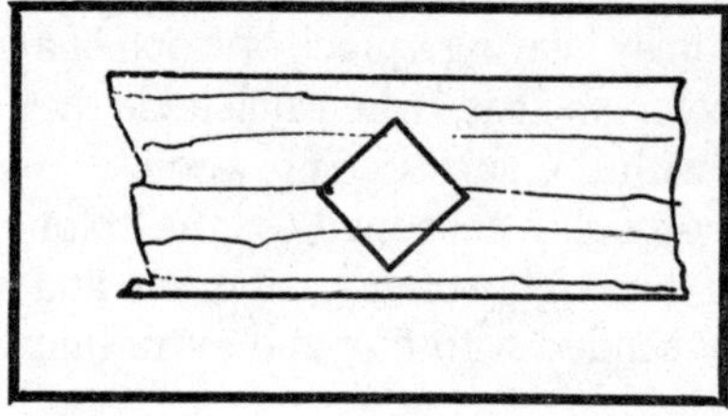

Fig. 11-16. The square patch—note how it is cut with the grain crossing it from the upper left-hand corner (as you view it) and how it is inserted on an angle to match the surface grain of the wood being repaired.

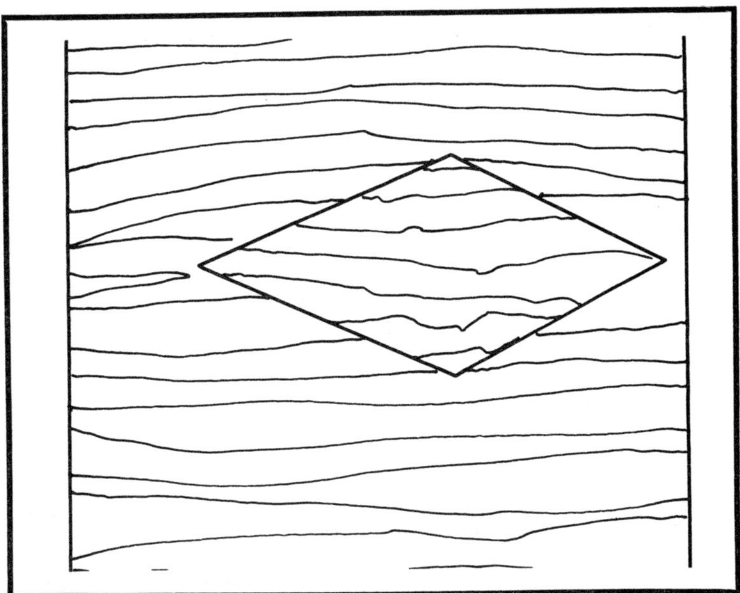

Fig. 11-17. The diamond patch is an excellent patch for smooth surfaces.

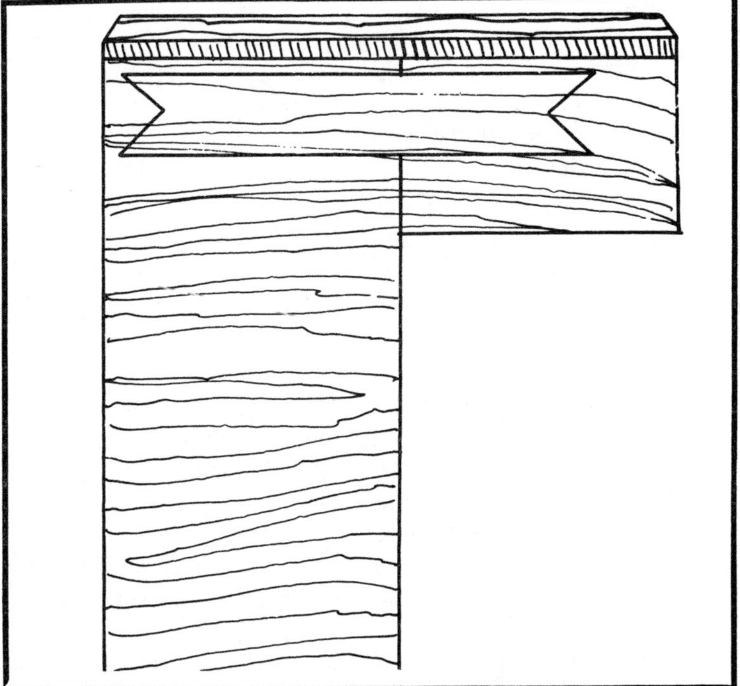

Fig. 11-18. The double arrow patch is ideal for patching corners and should always be cut and inserted on the lengthwise grain.

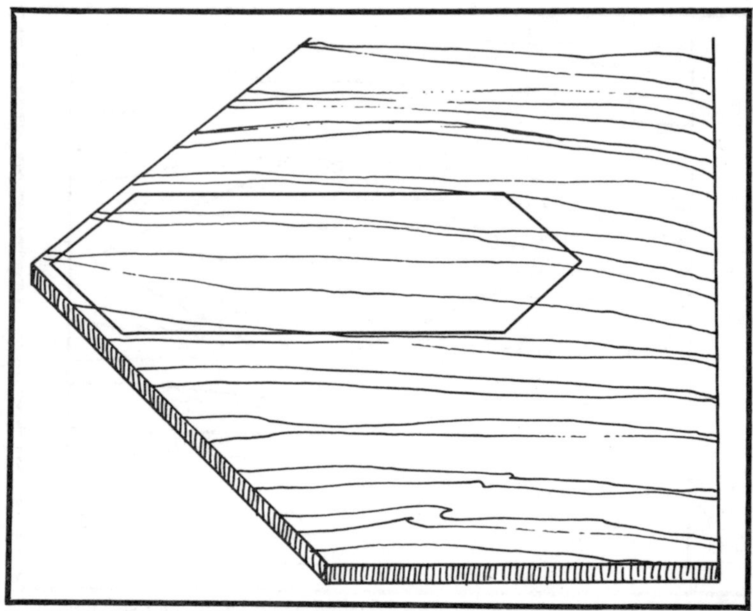

Fig. 11-19. The reverse arrow patch is especially useful where a patch is needed between two level parts of an object.

patch grain runs parallel to the surface grain (see Fig. 11-19).

- The **Parallelogram Patch** is a good edge patch because it angles in from the edge and, thus, inserts no conspicuously unmatched grain in the board edge (see Fig. 11-20).

The ultimate aim in this type of surface repair is a patch which so precisely fits the grave dug for it that when the patch is glued in place and refinished, it looks like part of an untouched board. This achievement is not nearly as difficult as it sounds, if you follow these directions:

1. The damaged area must be carefully measured in length (the dimension *with* the grain) and in width (the dimension *across* the grain). Remember that every bit of hurt wood must be fully covered by a patch of sound wood, so do not skimp on the dimensions.
2. Choose the type and shape of patch best suited to the size and shape of the damaged area and the position of repair.
3. Make a cardboard template (pattern) in the shape chosen to the measurements of the damaged area. Use straight lines drawn with a ruler to mark the outline of

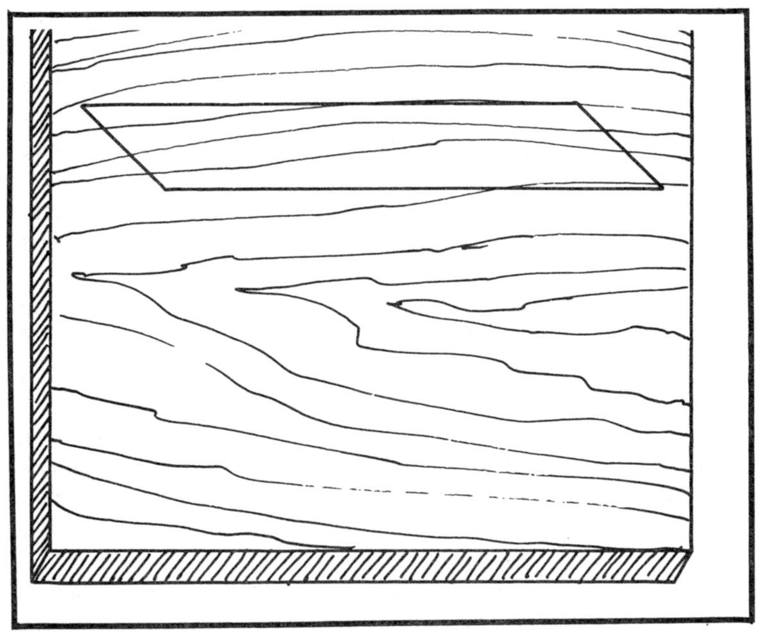

Fig. 11-20. The parallogram patch makes an excellent edge patch because it covers the split or crack without introducing much non-matching end grain into the grain of the edge.

the sides. Measure the angles of the end points with a T-bevel and protractor (see Fig. 11-21).

4. Cut out the template with an X-acto knife or a sharp razor blade. Lay the template carefully over the damaged area, making sure that it covers the hurt wood. Hold the template firmly against the surface while you score around it with a drawing knife or penknife.

5. Select a sharp chisel with deeply beveled blade and beveled sides. Place the chisel on the waste side of the outline, perpendicular with the surface, and with the beveled edge turned inward toward the center of the

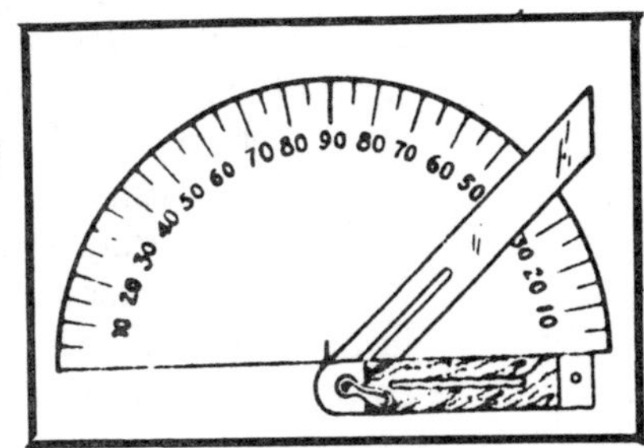

Fig. 11-21. Method of measuring angles with t-bevel and protractor.

outline. With light blows from a mallet, drive the chisel into the surface all around the outline. Make the corners crisply square and keep the side incisions as straight as possible. Do not drive the chisel too deeply at this point; you will clear the "grave" to the proper depth in the next step.

6. After the outline of the "grave" has been cut out completely with the chisel, the surface in the center must be lowered to the correct depth by chiseling out the damaged wood which the patch will replace. Start the depth chiseling about one-half inch from the far end of the grave and work backward toward yourself, holding the chisel blade at right angles to the grain at an angle of 45 degrees with the surface. Pound the chisel in lightly with the mallet to raise the chips. Then move the chisel back towards you about one-quarter inch and continue raising chips until you have worked the length of the patch to the end nearest you.
7. Keep chiseling out the grave pit until you have removed all the damaged or rotted wood. Then level off the bottom, making it uniform in depth on all sides. The grave is now ready to receive the shallow patch, when the patch has been cut to fit.

Plug Patches

If the board you are patching is damaged clear through, you will want to install a plug patch rather than a shallow patch. To do this you will drill a hole of the size required completely *through* the board, proceeding as follows:

1. After scoring the outline of the template on the damaged area as you would for a shallow patch, use a brace drill and a ¾-inch auger bit to bore holes at the corners of the outline and within its boundaries. Drill the holes close to the outline, but not touching it.
2. Wherever possible, secure a piece of waste wood against the place on the underside of the board where the bit will emerge. This will provide the drill bit with waste wood it can penetrate, thus, preventing its tearing up or splintering the undersurface of the work itself. If this precautionary measure is not possible, reduce the pressure on the brace drill and slow its revolutions as you penetrate the underside.

3. Using the bored holes as a starting point, thread the blade of a keyhole saw through the opening and carefully cut around the inside of the outline, keeping the saw cuts straight and on the waste side of the scored lines.
4. With a wood file, remove the slight margin of waste wood exactly to the lines. Be sure that the corners are true 90-degree angles and sharply cut.
5. The hole is now ready to receive the plug patch, once it is cut.

Whether the patch is a shallow patch or a plug patch, it is cut after the hole to receive it is made in the board surface. The reasons for this order of proceeding are two: (1) More rot or damage may be discovered when the board is cut open which might necessitate making of a new template and starting afresh, and (2) the patch must fit the hole exactly, so the opening into which the patch fits must be made in advance in order that an accurate measurement for the patch may be made.

Cutting the Patch

Whether the work requires a shallow patch or a plug patch, the steps for making a patch which fits snugly and smoothly are these:

1. Lay the template on the wood chosen for the patch, making sure that the long dimension of the template is positioned lengthwise on the grain. In depth, the patch should be very slightly deeper than the depth of the depression it covers, so that when it is sanded, it will be exactly level. Outline the template with a sharp pencil.
2. Saw or cut the patch carefully, keeping the kerfs or knife cuts on the waste side of the penciled line.
3. Test the patch for size in the depression into which it will fit.
4. Trim the patch to an exact fit with a file or knife. Rub the edges square and smooth with medium-fine abrasive paper. When the patch fits flush with the surface, you are ready to apply glue.
5. Apply glue fairly thickly to the sides and bottom of the depression and the patch.
6. Place the patch in the depression, holding the patch at surface level by inserting a small pin or brad in the depression on each side and allowing the side of the patch to rest against the shaft of the pin until the glue

dries and the pin can be removed. Using this method, you can be sure that the patch dries in place *and ever so slightly higher* than the surrounding surface so that when it is sanded for refinishing, it will be precisely even with the surface all around.

7. Wipe off the excess glue and allow the patch to dry for at least 24 hours. If the glue has exuded to the surface of the crack around the patch, scrape it out with a pin before it hardens. Otherwise, this visible glue will be doubly visible when the finish is applied because it will not take a stain. The crack around the patch may be filled at the srface level with wood dough or with stick shellac of the proper color before refinishing, if necessary. These fillers take a stain admirably and will render the patch truly inconspicuous. However, before applying the stain, the patch must first be sanded level with the surrounding surface, using extra fine sandpaper and steel wool. If the texture is found to be different from that of the surrounding surface, a paste filler is applied and sanded smooth, followed by a sealer coat. After the sealer coat is dry, the stain is applied.

If the patch is made of wood similar to the wood used in the furniture being repaired, an application of 50 percent linseed oil and 50 percent turpentine (applied generously and rubbed in very well until the color of the wood takes on an even tone; then wiped off completely with a clean, dry cloth) will sometimes leave the patch wood the same color as the surface wood. The knowing craftsman will use a part of the furniture piece itself for patching. Usually, it will match exactly, once the same finish is applied.

Since furniture which has suffered damage to require patching generally needs refinishing as well, the task of duplicating the old finish as to type and tone is not necessary because the entire wood is to be stripped clean an refinished. However, should spot finishing be necessary, the craftsman should first experiment on waste wood with first one stain and then another to find the combination of colors which most closely approximates the color of the original finish.

REPAIRING VENEER

Spot damage repairs to veneer may be undertaken in the home workshop. However, if the veneered surface is large or contoured, it should be repaired by a commercial cabinetmaker who will have the special molds and cramps to handle such repairs.

If the veneer is not loose, but is scratched or split, it may be repaired with stick shellac, unless the defect is on an edge or a corner. In that case wood dough will do a better job because it is not as brittle as the stick shellac and is less likely to break off under strain.

Bruises and Dents

Bruises and dents usually yield to the following moisture treatment: With a sharp, slender needle, prick the bruise along its outer edges and use a sharp knife point to make tiny cuts in its center. Wet the area with water applied with the fingertips to the perforations and when the water disappears, repeat the process several times. Next, heat a soldering iron and hold its hot tip over the holes, being careful not to actually touch the wood with the iron. The steam engendered will lift the bruised or dented area to its former level. However, steaming will have raised the surface fibers as well and when the area is dry, it will be necessary to sand the veneer lightly with fine abrasives paper or steel wool to smooth the surface.

Blisters and Waves

Blisters and waves, which are the result of moisture beneath the veneer just as a blister is the result of water beneath the skin, may be repaired in one of several ways described below:

- If the veneer is unbroken, the method is simple. Place a moderately hot flat rion gently on the raised veneer surface and keep a sharp eye on the result. The heat of the iron should draw out the moisture without damaging or burning the veneer. Also, it will soften the old glue so that the now-flat veneer will adhere more evenly. When the blister has been eliminated, unplug the iron and allow it to remain on the spot for 24 hours, until the glue dries.
- If the wavy, blistered veneer is also cracked, or a piece is missing, it is unusually wisest to cut out the defective piece, flatten it with a moderately hot flatiron, and reglue it in such a way as to show no edge lines. Put wax paper over the glued piece and weight it or clamp it for 24 hours.
- If the veneer is cracked and there is no dirt under the surface, the old glue may merely need reactivating. Fill the air pocket with hot vinegar, and position the piece to retain the liquid. Wait eight to 12 hours. Drain off any vinegar not yet absorbed, and dry the area with a moderately heated household iron placed over dry blotting paper. The heat

will shrink the blistered or wave veneer and flatten it; the blotting paper will absorb the moisture.

Now, lift the edge of the crack with a knife point and insert glue underneath the veneer with an eye dropper. Be sure there is glue on both surfaces of the crack—the underside and the overflap. Rub the surface, first away from the crack and then towards it, to spread the glue. Wipe off any escaping glue with a damp cloth. Cover the wax paper and weight or cramp for 24 hours.

- If the veneer is cracked and there is dirt under the surface, make a cut with a razor blade across the crack to the non-blistered area on both sides. The blistered area is now divided by the crack and is cross cut into four attached flaps. Lift each of these flaps in turn, being very careful not to bend or crack the veneer. (A wet cloth compress applied to the veneer will make it more pliant.) With a penknife, scratch all the old glue from the area beneath the veneer and the underside of the veneer itself. Be sure that the edges of the flaps are free of glue so that they can lie flat when reglued. When the surface is as free of old glue as you can get it, insert new glue under the veneer and press the flaps down in place. Wipe off excess glue with a damp cloth, and put a sheet of wax paper over the veneer before weighting it flat to dry for at least 24 hours.
- If the veneer is cracked and there is dirt under it, cut a "door" flap in the veneer, incising two cuts with the grain and one cut across the grain in the area where the veneer is buckled. Raise the flap as though opening a tiny door, and clean off the dirt and glue on the area covered by the veneer and on the underside of the veneer itself. Spread new glue under the veneer, press flat, wipe off excess glue with a damp cloth, cover with wax paper and weight down until thoroughly dry—about 24 hours.

Replacing Veneer Inlays

If any of the veneer is missing, it will have to be replaced with an inlay of the same thickness and grain pattern and of the same wood as the original piece.

If the missing veneer is part of the overall surfacing of a furniture piece, it is simpler to repair than if it is a part of an inlaid veneered design—such as a parquet patterning or a fruit or floral design composed of varied woods of free-form shapes representing leaves, petals, stems, butterflies, etc. Whether the veneer is a surfacing veneer is a surfacing or part of a design, the method of repairing it is the same. However, free-from patches, amoeba-like in shape, are somewhat harder to cut and fit than are the diamond shaped patches used to repair surfaces entirely covered by veneer.

The overall surface only is patched by first cutting new straight edges for the raggedly-shaped veneer-stripped area where the patch is needed. A ruler and a razor blade are used to incise a crisply-shaped diamond pattern around the ragged stripped area. This pattern will increase the size of the patch needed, but make the patch easier to install because of its regular shape. Two lines of the new "grave" should run parallel to the grain; two should run across the grain at an angle to it. The size of the new grave will depend on the conspicuousness of the grain to be matched and on how closely the grain must blend with the sound veneer. With a penknife, the waste wood between the ragged boundaries of the damaged area and the newly cut boundaries is lifted and removed,and the old glue and dirt are cleaned out of the fresh grave.

The next step is to place thin paper over the grave. Holding the paper in place with one hand depress the paper into the new grave with the fingertips of the other, and outline the depression until the paper takes the impression of its shape. This impressed paper is the pattern for the new patch. Cut out the impression carefully and fit it into the new grave to be sure it is accurate. If it fits precisely, lay the pattern on the new veneer and draw around it carefully with a sharp pencil. Cut the new veneer patch out with scissors; glue it carefully into place, using animal glue or plastic-resin glue which will not stain.

Repairing a Veneer Edge

Edges of veneered pieces are particularly prone to damage and when they come loose, they are rather tricky to repair. If, in order to get under the loose edge and scrape out the glue, you lift the veneer too high, a piece will snap off. The wisest coarse in instances of edge repair is to have someone else elevate the brittle veneer, lifting it just high enough so that it can be safely held open, while you caustiously clean out the old glue underneath it with a round-tipped palette knife. This tool will dig out the old glue without penetrating the veneer itself. When the underside of the veneer and the surface it covers are both clear of old glue,reglue both sides with plastic-resin glue, using the palette knife to apply it, and press the veneer to the surface carefully, wiping off any glue which may exude. Apply moderate pressure with a C-cramp padded with waste wood. After a few minutes, loosen the cramp and wipe away any glue which may have oozed out. Wrap the glued edge in aluminum foil and refasten the cramp and the waste wood buffer. Allow the edge to dry at least 24 hours.

Making New Veneer

If the broken piece of veneer has been lost, or is too damaged to re-use, the craftsman may have to visit a cabinetmaking shop to obtain a scrap for making repairs. These professional shops are often very cooperative in assisting you to find suitable veneer for your project. Choose with care, however. Try to find as accurate a grain and color match as possible, or the patch will be conspicuous.

If you are unsuccessful at finding any scraps to buy, you may have to make your own. The lumber yard will probably be able to supply you with a board or block of the same wood species. Using a plane, shave a thin slice from the edge of the board or from an area of similar grain. If a thicker piece is required, vary the blade adjustment of the plane to obtain it.

Some woodworking and craft suppliers sell veneer sample kits containing pieces which would be very adequate for small repairs. H.L. Wild, 510 East Eleventh Street, New York City, New York 10009, puts out an excellent catalogue listing a wide variety of cabinet woods and veneers. And, of course, every woodworker, professional and amateur knows of Constantine & Son, 2050 Eastchester Road, Bronx, New York 10461, whose extensive catalogue carries hundreds of items which the well-equipped workshop needs, including veneers of all sorts.

Collecting Old Veneer

This is a most profitable pursuit for the prolific woodworker, providing him with a ready source of suitable veneer for restoration work. If he keeps a vigilant lookout for derelict pieces in second-hand stores, trash collection heaps, salvage businesses, swap meets and thrift stores, he will soon have an enviable supply on hand which he has purchased for a few dollars. To best utilize this old veneer, he should remove the old finish and sand the veneer surface with fine abrasive paper to open the grain. Then he should apply a wet cloth poultice, leaving it on and keeping it moist for at least 12 hours or until the veneer is loose enough to lift off with a palette knife.

Turning the still-damp veneer upside-down on a flat surface, he should then scrape away all the old dirt and glue with a knife blade. When the veneer dries, he should give it a careful sanding to further clean it, and store it flat in a drawer under weights to prevent its curling.

REPAIRING CRACKS

When juxtaposed boards on any piece of furniture shrink across the grain, a crack will appear between them. These cracks may run the full length of the board, as sometimes seen in dressers, desks, cabinets and tables. If the cracked surface is not removable, the best method of repair is as follows:

1. With a thin knife blade, remove the old paint or old glue, plugging the crack.
2. Fill the entire crack with stick shellac of the right color—a time-consuming job, to be sure, but one which will obliterate the crack completely.

If the top is removable, the crack may be handled in a more professional manner as follows:

1. After the top is removed from the frame, it is completely dismantled. The boards are separated from one another, and the edges of each board are cleared of dirt, paint and glue. A rough sanding is given the edges to detach any crusted dirt and to give the new glue a "tooth" to which it can cling. Next, the boards are placed together as they were before the top was taken apart, and are critically examined to see how closely in contact they are. The edges are planed, if necessary, to bring them into closer contact.
2. Any screw holes made by the screws which held the boards in place are packed firmly with wood dough. Once the boards are reassembled, the screws will not be replaced in the same positions as before, and plugging the gaping screw holes renders the entire job neater and more professional looking.
3. On the level surface where the boards will be reassembled, wax paper is spread; the boards are reassembled on these papers in the order in which they will be permanently attached. Waterproof glue is applied to the board edges and the boards are joined together, the edges being carefully lined up so as to absolutely even, and the entire assembly being pulled together and secured at either end with a bar cramp.
4. Excess glue is removed with a damp cloth, and the cramps are kept in place for a minimum of 24 hours. After the cramps are removed, the boards must not be handled for two days.

5. When the boards are thoroughly dry, the newly repaired surface of which they are a part is replaced on the frame and fastened with screws in the same manner as before. Because the assembly is now tighter and firmer, and fits the base differently, new holes will have to be drilled for the screws. The boards should be reinforced with mending plates or angle irons, if there is any way to attach them inconspicuously underneath.
6. "Toenail" the boards at the ends by driving countersunk nails slantwise from the edge of one board across the glued crack into the second board, while the nail from the second board is driven on a reverse slant across the same crack into the first board, the two nails crossing each other in an "X" formation to reinforce the surface edge and prevent future cracks.

Repairing Cracks Near an Edge

One of the most obvious flaws in any furniture piece is a crack near the edge. If not properly repaired, it can mar the appearance of the finest piece. However, a few simple steps will mend it completely.

The primary difficulty in the successful repair of such an injury is in inserting the glue. To apply sufficient adhesive, the initial crack has to be opened more widely. This is accomplished by gently inserting numerous small softwood wedges into the crack until the crack is forced open to receive the glue. Spread the glue into the crack as deeply as possible, using any tool thin enough and long enough to reach every segment of the crack. When sufficient glue has been applied, remove the wedges and apply cramps, placing flat sticks under the jaws to prevent them from biting the work. After the cramps have been in place a few minutes, carefully wipe off the glue which their pressure has forced out of the crack. Use a damp cloth and clean off every drop. Then put wax paper over the crack in the edge, and allow the crack to dry in the cramps at least 24 hours.

A tourniquet may be used, rather than a cramp, if it is able to exert sufficient pressure. Be sure to put pads under the rope wherever it touches the work, to prevent its marring the wood.

Repairing Interior Cracks

Such cracks in furniture must be either glued or filled. Since the former is generally the easiest method of repair, and the least noticeable, let us discuss it first.

To repair a crack by gluing, simply clean it out thoroughly to be sure that no foreign material is present to prevent its joining along its entire length when glued. Apply a tight-gripping bar cramp (with buffers of waste wood under the jaws) and see if the crack can be made to close fully under pressure. If this is possible, apply sufficient glue with a toothpick, knife blade, spatula or any tool thin enough to penetrate, and cramp the crack firmly, leaving the cramp on until the glue has thoroughly dried.

Using Stick Shellac

If a crack will not draw together when cramped, it must be filled. If the crack is a surface one, easily visible, no other filler except stick shellac should be used. It is simple to use and capable of repairing holes, cracks and dents so inconspicuously that they are virtually invisible.

This product is available at large paint stores in both transparent and opaque styles, and in a great variety of shades and colors, ranging from light buff through brown to deep red. The color chart may reveal a shade which exactly matches the wood on which you are working.

Stick shellac, as its name implies, is produced in stick form, very like the form used to produce sealing wax. In fact, stick shellac resembles sealing wax in texture and brittleness and, like sealing wax, must be heated before using. The method of using stick shellac is as follows:

1. Select a stick of the correct color and shade. Use an opaque shellac if the crack is a deep one which is exposing the wood. Use a transparent stick if the crack is a shallow one which has not bared the wood.
2. If the crack to be repaired must be stained, the stain should be applied first, and allowed to dry thoroughly. It will change color when dry, and this alteration may affect the color of the stick shellac chosen.
3. Fill your homemade spirit lamp with alcohol or canned heat, and light it.
4. Heat an old table knife with a rounded blade over the flame, positioning the knife blade so that the flame strikes it in the middle. Hold the stick shellac near the blade's tip so that, as the shellac melts on the blade, the melting shellac will be easier to spread. As any melted shellac accumulates, apply it to the crack at once. The shellac penetrates best when it is warm and liquid. To prevent the hot shellac from falling

on the finish surrounding the crack, the adjacent area should be covered with masking tape.

5. The shellac should be smoothed into the crack with a clean artist's spatula held at a 45-degree angle. The worker should do the smoothing while the shellac is warm and malleable, adding enough shellac to the crack so that the crack filling rises slightly above the surrounding surface. When the worker judges that sufficient shellac has been applied, he heats the spatula blade over the spirit lamp and smooths the surface without leveling it—much as you would smooth icing on a cake. Then the shellac is allowed to thoroughly dry.
6. When the shellac is hard and brittle, it is carefully scraped with a single-edged razor blade or with a chisel laid flat on the table with the beveled side up. After scraping, light rubbing with dampened wet-or-dry 6/0 abrasive paper will smooth the repair. A final buffing with 4/0 steel wool will effectively dull the sheen of the shellac and blend it impreceptibility with the wood.

Note: If the exact shade of stick shellac is not obtainable, a slightly lighter color may be used and darkened after applying by touching it up with stain.

Using Wood Putty

"Wood Putty" is the name we are giving to the commercial simulated wood products (Durhan's is one brand) which are available in powder form and to which dry colors and cold water must be added to convert the powder into a heavy putty which can be used to patch small holes and cracks in obscure areas where the repair is not readily visible. Wood putty enjoys several advantages over Wood Dough. It hardens more rapidly and with less shrinkage and results in a smooth, flat finish. However, this smooth, flat finish has no grain whatsoever, nor does it resemble wood in any way, even though it may be colored to match the wood it repairs. Consequently, Wood Putty is most useful for repairs on surfaces which are going to be painted or given some other sort of non-transparent finish. On clear varnished surfaces, Wood Putty is very conspicuous. Nor is it useful for re-building broken-off parts. That job is best done by Wood Dough.

However, Wood Putty has a definite, irreplaceable function in furniture repair, and every woodworker should know these simple directions for its use:

1. Make only as much Wood Putty as you will use immediately because this product cannot be reactivated by adding more water once it had hardened.
2. Use a rinsed-out tin can or a paper cup to hold the mix.
3. First, mix the dry Wood Putty powder with one of the dry colors available at paint shops. Usually, one of the following basic colors—or a combination of them—will exactly match antique furniture: raw sienna (yellow), burnt sienna (red), raw umber (light brown), or burnt umber (dark brown). Mix the powdered color by the teaspoonful with the Wood Putty powder until you believe you have produced the color desired.
4. You can test the color by adding a few drops of turpentine to a pinch of the powdered color, mixing powder and liquid, and wiping the resultant stain on a piece of waste wood. Wipe off the surplus stain immediately and let the stain dry. In a few moments, it will give you a very positive test of the color, shade and tone which the stain will leave on the surface under repair.
5. When you have blended the powdered color to your liking, mix it thoroughly and add a small quantity of water to make a very heavy, thick, putty-like mix.
6. Dampen the crack or hole to be filled and the surface immediately surrounding it, and apply the Wood Putty to the crack or hole, taking care to keep it from contacting the surrounding surface. Pack it down with a dampened finger until it is just above the desired level.
7. Wipe away any bits which have fallen on the surrounding surface, using a damp cloth stretched over your finger.
8. Allow to dry, and shave off the surplus with a knife or single-edged razor blade. Sand the spot and apply varnish.

Using Wood Dough

"Wood Dough" is the name given to the ready-to-use product—sold under such trademarks as "plastic Wood" or "Duratite"—composed of finely ground wood mixed with a binder and kept pliant and soft by the addition of quickly evaporating solvents. Wood Dough is available in tubes and cans; either container must be kept tightly closed to prevent the dough from hardening as the solvent evaporates. Additional solvent may be purchased for softening Wood Dough or a high-grade lacquer thinner may be substituted, if the proper thinner is not available.

Wood Dough is highly useful to fill cracks, holes, knot holes—even to sculpt and shape broken parts. It may be sanded, planed, drilled or carved. It will hold nails and screws. It will withstand shock without chipping. Quickly and cheaply, Wood Dough can effect a strong, permanent repair, but it has one drawback. No matter how well it accepts the staining, smoothing and finishing necessary to render it part of the repaired object, it has no grain—a fact which makes it contrast noticeably with the wood on which it has been used.

Wood Dough is available in five wood colors. Two or more colors of Wood Dough may be mixed, if necessary, to attain the color desired. Also, a penetrating oil stain may be used to touch up the repair. .The directions for its use are as follows:

1. Inspect the place where the Wood Dough is to be applied to be sure it is free of dust and dirt. If the Wood Dough is being applied to an already finished surface, roughen the area slightly with sandpaper.
2. Apply the Wood Dough to the spot to be filled or added to, being very careful to avoid dropping any on the surrounding surface, which should be further protected with masking tape. Should Wood Dough fall on the surrounding surface, it will so deeply fill the pores of the wood that it will be difficult to remove by sanding. Instead, use a lacquer thinner if the surface is not finished in lacquer. This solvent will remove the Wood Dough without affecting the finish.
3. Pack in the Wood Dough, pressing it firmly into the holes with a wet finger. Allow it to dry thoroughly.
4. Slice off the surplus Wood Dough with a sharp knife or chisel, and *sand the Wood Dough only* with 7/0 to 8/0 abrasive paper. Avoid sanding the surrounding area.
5. Wood Dough shrinks slightly in drying. Should the repair be an extensive one, allow each application of Wood Dough to dry thoroughly before adding another, always building up the final cost to be slightly higher than the desired level, in order to provide a margin for smoothing it down.
6. When the repair is of extensive depth, fill up a part of the hole and then drive two screws into the dry Wood Dough repair; leaving the heads exposed, but beneath the repaired surface. Pack the next layer of Wood Dough tightly around the screws and continue building—layer after layer—until the proper level for finishing or carving is obtained. The hidden screws will give strength to the newly constructed part.

7. Before staining Wood Dough, put a coat on a piece of scrap wood, allow it to dry and apply a coat of stain. When the stain is dry, check the color to see that it matches the surface under repair. Stain usually lightens somewhat in drying. If it dries too dark, however, it cannot be removed. A single coat of one-quarter white shellac mixed with three-quarters denatured alcohol may be applied carefully to the sanded surface of the Wood Dough to lessen the absorption of stain.

Note: Although each has its own necessary and valid place in furniture repair, neither Wood Putty nor Wood Dough is as good for *visible surface repair* as is stick shelac. This material is nearly perfect for eradicating wood blemishes. The successful furniture repairman places more reliance in stick shellac then all other surface-restoring materials.

CORRECTING CRAZED FINISHES

Furniture which has been allowed to dry out, or which has been overexposed to sun or central heating, may develop a crazed finish not unlike that seen in porcelain where the surface glaze has taken on a crackled appearance. In furniture, this myriad cracking is called "checked" if the lines are small and shallow, or "alligatored" if the lines are deep grooves. Although such damage is often considered to be irreparable, it is sometimes healed quite satisfactorily when the right treatment is applied. Certainly the effort is worth expending; if it fails, nothing has been lost. The process may even aid in removing the old finish preparatory to applying a new one.

Correcting a Checked Finish

Make a pad of a piece of closely woven, smooth, clean cloth about 11 inches × 15 inches square. Use this pad with benzol or any other commercial solvent which may be used as an amalgamator. Rub the amalgamator into a small area, working with the wood grain. Observe the effect. If the benzol has smoothed away some of the lines, wet the cloth and rub the same area even more lightly a second time. Keep the cloth applicator wet at all times. Do not allow natural evaporation to dry it out. When the finish starts to smooth out, permit yourself only one more very light rubbing. Too heavy a hand may roll up the softened finish. Permit the smoothed finish to dry overnight. Then apply paste wax or furniture polish and rub to a glow.

Correcting an Alligatored Finish

There are two methods for eradicating an alligatored finish. One is harder to successfully perform than the other, but both can produce satisfactorily smooth surfaces under certain circumstances.

Method One—This method is especially effective on varnished surfaces. Apply benzol or a commercial amalgamator to the alligatored surface by spreading it on with a paint brush in generous amounts. Wet the surface very thoroughly until the finish begins to melt and become liquid. At that juncture, allow the surface to get completely dry. Then, with a pad, smooth the finish with Grade F pumice stone. Use water to lubricate the abrasive if you plan to varnish the surface. If you plan to use shellac, lubricate the pumice stone with oil (paraffin is best.)

Method Two—The second method is the more tedious one, but it is often highly successful in restoring alligatored finishes produced by heat and sun exposure.

Apply a small amount of commercial paint remover to a small area with a soft, lint-free cloth. Rub lightly to dissolve and spread the finish. When the cracks are filled, stop the finish from dissolving further by wiping the surface with a soft, lint-free cloth saturated with turpentine. Repeat the process on an adjacent alligatored area, overlapping the two areas slightly and always exerting light rubbing action so as not to roll up the finish.

Caution: Paint and varnish removers are highly volatile and inflammable. Be sure you are working in a well-ventilated room where there is no flame of any sort and no spark.

REMOVING WORN-BARE SPOTS

This particular repair is one of the most tedious and exacting of all those necessary to the restoration of furniture. However, with care, the following process will repair a most unsightly blemish and, perhaps, save the woodworker the task of refinishing the entire piece.

The most difficult factor in this repair is that of finding a colored stain, or a combination of colored stains, which matches the already-finished surface. Many stains change color radically as they dry, so the woodworker must allow his experimental color swatches—made on waste wood chips—to dry before comparing them to the original finish.

Commercial touch-up kits are available at many paint and hardware stores. Some of these would be too far from the desired shade to be helpful, others may at least provide a basic color which you can tone with other colors to obtain the shade desired. Or you may prefer mixing your own color match using artist's oils and turpentine, or combining several prepared wood stains. Try the color you believe to be a good match on an inconspicuous area on the piece to be repaired, and allow it to dry. When the swatch of new color matches the old as precisely as desired, you are ready to proceed.

Prepare the edges of the bare spot by feathering them lightly and carefully with No. 400 wet-or-dry finishing paper. Use paraffin oil with the abrasive paper if you plan to finish with shellac. Use light paraffin oil with the abrasive paper if you plan to finish with shellac. Use clear water if you contemplate finishing with varnish. Clean off the abraded area and allow it to dry completely.

If the bare spot is a conspicuous one and you have doubts about how well the refinishing color will match the original finish, apply a wash coat of one part white shellac to six or eight parts of denatured alcohol. This will somewhat retard the absorption of the stain by the wood, so that it may be removed more easily if the color is wrong.

When the wash coat has dried and the area has been lightly sanded with fine, worn sandpaper, the stain may be applied. Apply the stain with a piece of soft cloth, rather than a brush. Make each application a thin one, and allow each coat to dry before applying the next. This method allows you to control the color more exactly. Sand very lightly with used 7/0 or 8/0 garnet finishing paper between coats. When the exact color tone has been obtained, allow the spot to dry thoroughly before applying several finishing coats of varnish or shellac, whichever was originally used on the piece.

The several layers of varnish will build up the area of the spot to be slightly higher than the surrounding surface. You will want to use the correct abrasive in sanding the spot to the level of the surrounding surface so that the spot will match in texture, as well as color. For an ordinary semi-gloss finish, Grade 00 or 000 steel wool, rubbed carefully with the grain, will produce the same texture. For a smoother semi-gloss or high gloss finish, No. 400 wet-or-dry sandpaper (using water as a lubricant, if varnish was the finish agent and paraffin oil as a lubricant, if shellac was the finishing agent) will produce a similar look. For a polish-rubbed finish, FFF pumice stone should be rubbed into the wood with a moist pad (moistened with water for varnish and with paraffin oil for shellac) to produce a good match.

Finally, dust the surface well and apply furniture wax or polish, buffing the wood to a soft glow.

REVIVING OLD FINISHES

The woodworker faced with the refurbishing of an old piece of furniture has one primary decision to make at the outset which, even at best, is a dilemma of pros and cons. To restore or to re-finish, that is the question. And the answer is not so pat as one might first suppose.

If the amount of labor involved is the consideration on which the woodworker bases his decision, he is still at a loss. Where surface repairs are obviously extensive, complete refinishing represents no more—and perhaps even less—time and effort than does restoration.

However, the old finish may be so unattractive and so badly worn that it really does not justify further effort. If the finish is many layers of paint, the woodworker is certainly wisest to totally strip off the accumulated applications of many years. However, in so doing, he must be prepared for disappointment, if he is contemplating a transparent finish for the piece. He may discover, to his sorrow, that the reason for using paint rather than clear finish in the first place was a valid one—that the wood is of a cheap sort, of very indifferent or ugly grain, and not really worthy of display. In that case, he may have to repaint the piece himself or make it the subject for decoupage, gold leafing, etc.

If the piece on which he is working has a finish which was attractive when new, but which is now so obscured by damage and time that restoring it seems an impractical impossibility, he may see eradicating it as the only sensible procedure. However, in so doing, he must forfeit the patina and softly blended coloration which only age produces and which adds immeasurably to the value of the antique.

The best advice is, therefore, this: *do not condemn an old finish too hastily*. Try, at least, to *revive* by the methods we will now cover. Only if these are unsuccessful should you strip away the old finish and reconstruct a new one. *Restoration, not refinishing, should be the primary aim in rehabilitating antiques*.

Determining the Original Finish

Knowing the type of finish originally used on an antique is essential to the process of restoring it. If one wishes to revive the old finish, rather than remove it completely, one must first ascertain whether the final transparent coat was lacquer, varnish or shellac. Anyone who values the patina which only time can give old wood will certainly wish to preserve as much of it as possible, and making surface repairs with the right materials is essential to preserving it, because unless one recognizes and works with the original finish, these necessary repairs may prove such a defacement that the original finish will have to be stripped off to salvage the piece.

The type of finish employed originally may be easily determined. On a hidden surface of the piece, where the wax has been completely removed, rub on a little lacquer thinner with a soft cloth. If the finish is unaffected by this test, you can be sure that it is either varnish or shellac. If it is lacquer, the thinner would remove it.

Next, test with alcohol on a soft cloth. If the alcohol melts away the transparent outer coat, you will know the coat was shellac, for alcohol is the agent used to thin and remove shellac.

Now, try turpentine. If the surface gloss begins to disappear from the wood and shows on the cloth, you can be certain that the final coat is varnish.

Using the same finishing coat as that used for the original finish when you perform spot repairs will assure more professional results.

Reviving Cloudy or Faded Finishes

Often the finish of an old piece will have an unattractive, fogged-over appearance which destroys the beauty of the wood entirely. However, the craftsman must not conclude from this condition that complete refinishing is his only recourse. First, he should try to revive the finish by one of several methods, depending on the type of finish. If he suceeds, he will have preserved a most valuable attribute his antique. If he fails, all he has expanded is time and effort.

Removing Wax. Wax is an agent which often clouds the surface, especially if it has built up over a period of years and is the result of many layers applied over a dirty surface. Use a cloth saturated with turpentine to clean it off. You may be pleasantly surprised at how much clearer the old finish instantly appears.

Reviving a Shellac Finish.

Rubbing the surface with a mixture of two parts of paraffin oil and part of white shellac, applied with a soft cloth if the surface is only slightly clouded, will do wonders to brighten the finish. If the surface is badly clouded, a pad of No. 000 steel wool should be used instead of a cloth. Always, the application should be made in the direction of the grain.

Reviving a Varnish Finish

A mixture of equal parts of linseed oil and turpentine will often completely remove the fogged-over look which old varnished surfaces sometimes have. A varnished finish also responds beautifully to a rubdown with a quart of clear water to which one or two tablespoons of vinegar has been added. The solution is stroked on with a cloth, in the direction of the grain.

The milky look which varnish acquires—especially in damp or humid atmospheres—indicates that the varnish is poor quality. A good rub with a half-and-half mixture of raw linseed oil and turpentine will often erase it entirely. Use a firm-textured, closely woven cloth and rub briskly. If the marred surface does not improve, the piece will have to be refinished.

Reviving a Lacquer Finish

Sometimes an old finish can be marvelously beautified by giving it a single coat of the finishing material originally used. This method of restoration is certainly easier than stripping off the entire finish, and refinishing the naked wood. In addition, it preserves the patina of age and the mellow tones which the old finish has acquired from years of good care.

When the piece is clean and dry, sand it lightly, wipe off all abrasive particles and apply the finish material—lacquer, varnish or shellac (whichever was originally used on the piece). Apply more than one coat if desired, /allowing each coat to dry, and sanding with steel wool between coats. When the finish is at last to your liking, allow the final coat to dry thoroughly and give the entire surface a radiant glow with paste wax.

Reviving a Clear Finish on Carving

First, rub the carving with one gallon of hot water to which two heaping tablespoons of sal soda have been added. This will remove all grease and grime. If the carving is waxy, give it a wash with turpentine. Now, rinse the carving with clear water, and allow to dry thoroughly. Then, using the same clear finish as was originally used, apply with an orange stick wrapped in a cloth or with a soft brush, carefully covering every nook and cranny of the carving. Allow the finish coat to dry and apply a thin coat of paste wax or furniture polish.

REVIVING STAINED MARBLE AND TILE

If you own or acquire an antique piece with a badly-stained marble top, deal with the problem of removing these stains before attempting any other repairs. Both marble and tile are highly porous, and the grouting around tile is probably the most porous of the three.

Consequently, every stain threatens to become permanent unless quickly eradicated. Some experimentation may be necessary to find the proper solvent to remove the particular stain, unless the cause of the stain is known. But the task should be pursued diligently to a successful conclusion or the surfacing may be permanently defaced.

First, assume that the stain is soluble,and apply a mild solvent such as trisodium phosphate (or a commercial cleanser containing it, such as "Spic 'N Span"). If this solvent does not prove strong enough, use ammonia. If the stain still resists, try turpentine or white vinegar. Stubborn stains may require bleaching. Laundry bleach is a safe, mild bleach to start with; but, you may have to resort to hydrogen peroxide (20 volume) to get results. Whatever the chemical eradicator used, allow about 30 minutes for the reaction to take effect. Then wash off the chemical with hot water and dry the surface carefully. Always wear rubber gloves because these chemicals can prove irritating to skin.

For stains which defy both solvents and bleaches, you may have to resort to abrasives. Again, it is wisest to begin with a mild scouring powder and steel wool. If this has no effect, switch to fine wet-or-dry sandpaper, if the surface is marble. Never use sandpaper on glazed tile, however; it is sure to score the surface.

If the stain can be readily identified, the task is much easier. For coffee, tea, food and fruit stains, trisodium phosphate is generally highly effective. Should any slight stain remain, however, laundry bleach will eradicate it. Fingernail polish is best removed with amyl acetate, or nail polish remover. Trisodium phosphate and cold water should erase bloodstain; if they prove obdurate, try hydrogen peroxide. Grease marks give way to a scrub composed of one part sal soda and nine parts water. Ink stains will resist solvents, but they usually yield to peroxide or laundry bleach.

The foregoing alternatives may make the task of cleaning stained marble or tile seem much to complex and risky to undertake. However, the successfully restored marble or tile surface has such enduring loveliness and lends such enhancement to the antique piece of which it is a part that the endeavor necessary to revive its inherent beauty is well rewarded.

SPOT REMOVAL

Under normal circumstances almost all furniture will collect numerous scars such as dents, scratches and spots. In most cases these scars of age add to the charm and character of the piece. There are certain types of spots, however, that will detract from the esthetic appearance to the extent that removal becomes necessary.

Spots left by liquids, particularly water and alcohol, are especially unsightly, probably because they are associated with slovenliness. The following instructions will help in the removal of these and other annoying blemishes.

Removing Water Rings

The leper's spot, as regards lovely furniture, is the water mark. Fortunately, these hideous eyesores, produced by carelessly leaving a wet glass on a finished wood surface or on failing to wipe away spilled water, are not the incurable blights they appear to be. They are removable, but only if they have not penetrated too deeply, and only if the woodworker uses the proven method of repair for that particular finish. Here we list the various restorative procedures for this defacement, starting with the mildest and working up to the most powerful. All of the methods employ some sort of abrasive; all must be carefully applied with the wood grain.

1. First, try liquid furniture wax rubbed in with No. 0000 steel wool. Work with the grain, using light, gentle pressure. If the ring is still visible, rub a little butter into a soft cloth and use the lubricated cloth to massage cigar or cigarette ashes into the white ring.
2. Apply butter to a cloth and use the buttered cloth to rub sufficient rottenstone into the watermark to make a paste. Rub into wood, working with the grain. Sewing machine oil, Grade 10 motor oil or raw linseed oil may be substituted for the butter. If the ring refuses to fade away, put a thick blotter over it, and press with a warm iron. Keep the warm iron application brief, but frequent, until the spot is steamed out.
3. Dampen a piece of flannel with spirits of camphor, a few drops of ammonia or essence of peppermint. This treatment is particularly efficacious on varnished surfaces.
4. Work up a thick paste of FFF pumice stone and raw linseed oil. Apply paste to the ring with a soft rag. Keep wiping the area from time to time to observe the progress of the cure. When the ring disappears, clean off the abrasive paste with a cloth moistened with turpentine. This method is especially suitable for varnished surfaces.

When you have banished the white water ring forever, celebrate your victory by applying a good coat of paste wax to the piece. Rub the wax well in, and polish it to a high burnish. Wax may not prevent white rings where the water remains on the surface indefinitely, but it can surely retard the absorption of water by wood and give you some time to clean it up.

Removing Ink Spots

"The writing finger writes, and having writ, moves on"—leaving ink spots which are often almost impossible to remove. If the ink spots were not expunged the moment the inkwell tipped by blotting up all the spilled ink and then removing the stain immediately with a wax similar to Johnson's "Jubilee"—the woodworker may have to resign himself to a complete refinishing job. However, there are some alternatives you may try first. Sometimes ink stains will yield to a solution of pure household ammonia (the Double X Type available at paint and hardware stores), or a hot solution of oxalic acid. Even these strong agents must be used in repeated applications to remove the spot.

If the ink spot is only on the surface, a paste made of pumice stone or rottenstone and light oil, rubbed into the wood grain with a soft cloth and then cleaned off with turpentine on a clean cloth, may erase it forever.

If an ink spot resists all other efforts to erase it, you may have to resort to scraping it off. This method is invariably successful, except on bare wood, which is so vulnerable to stain and so porous that stains are quickly absorbed, becoming too ingrained to be easily removed. Scraping the spot with a single razor blade will usually completely remove an ink stain on finished wood. If the wood is nude, you will have to use a cabinet scraper. If the scraping is not excessive, the spot may be revived with furniture polish or wax. However, if a wide area has to be scraped, or the scraping is deep, the piece will have to be completely refinished.

Removing Burned Spots

Using a new single edged razor blade which is held perpendicular to the burned surface, the craftsman scrapes away every particle of charred wood. Clean the damaged area well, using a cotton swab dipped in naptha.

The damaged area will look rough and uneven, and must be carefully smoothed with extra-fine sandpaper; it must feel sleek to the touch.

Using an old white saucer or small plate on which the color is clearly visible, mix one or more shades of penetrating oil stain until you have as exact a color match as possible to that of the original surface. Apply this compound color to the burned area with a thin, pointed artist's brush. Wipe off the excess. If the stain is too light, add another coat. Allow the color to dry overnight, then seal the burned area with matching stick shellac until the burned area is filled in level with the surface. Scrape off the extra shellac with a razor blade, then sand the repaired area with extra-fine sandpaper. If sanding has left a bare area around the repair, stain it to match the surface. Finish by rubbing with rottenstone and oil. Then apply wax to the entire surface, and buff to a high luster.

Removing Alcohol Spots

Liquor, perfumes or medicines must be wiped away immediately if they spill on finished wood. Otherwise they may leave a very unsightly stain. To remove such damage, apply silver polish, linseed oil or car cleaner with your fingertips and rub in well. If the stain is still evident, moisten cigarette ashes and massage them into the spot; or put a few drops of ammonia on a damp cloth and rub the spot with the wood grain. If the spot fades away, wax the surface immediately.

However, if the spot resists removal, experiment with a paste made with rottenstone and oil, using a soft cloth and rubbing with the grain. Quicker results may be obtained by using FFF powdered pumice and oil; but rottenstone and oil should be the last application, in any case. After finishing with rottenstone and oil, give the surface a good waxing.

Removing Milk Stains

The lactic acid in milk is a mild, but very efficient, paint remover. Consequently, when milk or any food containing milk, such as ice cream, custard or pudding, is left for any length of time on a finished surface, it will leave a stain exactly like that left by alcohol. If you discover such a stain, clean off the foodstuff with water, wax the entire surface to remove dust and grime and proceed to eradicate the spot, using the same procedure as that given for removing alcohol spots.

Removing Candle Wax Stains

If you use candles as decorative accents on dining tables and other surfaces, you are sure to discover some candle wax drippings on your furniture which will require removal. Fortunately, unless the wax is dripped on boiling hot, there will be little, if any, permanent damage. If the wax is still liquid, harden it quickly by applying an ice cube. Then scrape as much of it off the surface as you can with your finger nails and a dull dinner knife. When every visible particle of wax has been removed, rub the surface briskly with furniture wax, using a dry cloth to work up a shine.

Removing Heat Marks

The hideous white marks left by hot plates on furniture may require a complete refinishing job. They are among the most difficult stains to eradicate. However, before resigning yourself to removing the old finish completely, try lightly rubbing the spot with camphorated oil, using a lint-free cloth which will not leave fuzz on the wood. Wipe off the oil immediately after applying with a dry cloth. If the surface of the white mark feels rough, make it silken-smooth by rubbing in paraffin oil with No. 0000 steel wool.

If the white spot has resisted all these blandishments, try rottenstone and oil. If the finish is varnish or shellac, the white spot may fade away like Marly's ghost when spirits of camphor or essence of peppermint is dabbed on. Leave either application untouched for about half an hour to perform its magic. Then wipe it off, and give the area a final rub with rottenstone and paraffin oil.

Minor Scratches

The etch mark of some scratches is so slight that it requires only a rubbing with the oily meat of a nut to color the scratch and render it invisible. The world-famous almond stick, which can be purchased from any paint or hardware store, is formulated on the same nut-oil principle and it does a superb job of covering light scratches. Before coloring any scratch with nut oil, however, the surface should be cleaned of wax with a naptha-saturated cloth. Then a nutmeat, chosen for its similarity in coloring to the wood it is to finish, should be broken in half and rubbed well into the scratch. The nuts offering the largest amounts of oil are walnuts, pecans, brazil nuts, black walnuts, almonds and butternuts.

If this treatment fails to camouflage the scratch, try a brown coloring crayon or one of the similarly formulated wax sticks especially made for furniture touch-ups which may be purchased at a hardware or paint store in a variety of wood tones. These handy scratch fillers are even softer than crayons and, therefore, easier to use. They almost liquefy when you apply them, and the scratch they cover needs only to be massaged with your finger and buffed with a soft cloth to disappear.

If the surface under repair was lightly distressed originally to give it an authentically antique look, you might be able to disguise the new scratches as further distressing by rubbing into them the burnt sienna or raw umber oil colors used to highlight the original finish.

Paste shoe polish in a color which matches the wood makes an excellent scratch eradicator. Apply it to the scratch with a cotton swab or a toothpick end wrapped in cotton, and buff dry. If the color is too dark, simply wipe it off with naptha and try another shade. For ebony or black lacquered surfaces, black shoe polish is the best possible scratch eliminator, unless the black surface has a non-glossy matte finish—in which case the shine of the polish, when buffed, may make the repair noticeable.

Scratches on red mahogany should be given first aid with iodine. Use a thin-tipped Size 0 artist's brush to fill in the small scratch. Allow the iodine to dry, then buff the area well.

On brown mahogany, use old iodine which has turned dark brown. It is an exact color match.

To accurately reproduce the tone of red maple, dilute old iodine half and half with denatured alcohol. Apply with a brush and let dry to be sure the color is exact before waxing.

One of the best commercial scratch eradicators for fine to medium scratches on dark finishes is Old English Scratch Remover Polish. So remarkably efficacious is this product that many funriture refinishers never fail to rub in a good coat of this product just prior to waxing a repaired antique. It covers and fills all those infinitesimal scratches too tiny to be seen by the naked eye, and it restores the color and nourishes the condition of the old wood. Allow the application to remain an hour or so before wiping it off to apply the wax. The thirsty wood will have absorbed a great deal fo the polish in that time, and when you wipe away the rest, you will be pleasantly surprised at how much better the wood looks.

If you encounter a scratch which fails to yield to any of these remedies, resort to tried-and-true rottenstone and oil, applied a you would to remove water marks.

Deep Scratches

Deep scratches cannot be suitably camouflaged by the methods used for minor scratches; they must be filled with stick shellac, using the same procedure as that described for filling cracks. Old wax and oil must first be removed with a rag saturated with naptha.

If you are unsuccessful at finding stick shellac in the color required, you can always resort to staining the crack first to match the original surface, and then filling it with white shellac. The method is this:

After cleaning the surface thoroughly with a naptha-soaked rag, select a penetrating oil stain which matches the original finish as closely as possible. Mix several stains together, if necessary, to get the color desired. If the hue is right but the tone too deep, lighten it with turpentine.

For some rare, distinctive colors, you may have to resort to artist's oils—the kinds which are obtainable in tubes at an art supply store. These are very highly concentrated, so start your blending with about one-sixteenth of an inch of each color squeezed from the tube. Use a white plate for a palette, and mix in sufficient turpentine to lighten the color to the degree desired.

When the color is as exact as you can get it, apply it to the deep crack with a fine-pointed artist's brush. Allow it to dry. If the color is not deep enough, apply another coat, and then another until the match is perfect. Allow the color to dry overnight.

Next, seal and fill the crack with white shellac, applying as many coats as necessary to fill the crack completely, and allowing five to six hours between each coat for the shellac to dry. Build up the crack with the shellac until it is higher than the surrounding surface. Then smooth it to a glassy smoothness and to the same level as the surrounding surface with extra-fine sandpaper wrapped around a sanding block. As a finishing touch, rub the area with rottenstone and oil, followed by a brisk burnish with paste wax.

This method works extremely well in removing scratches in unusual and exotically tinted wood finishes—such as "driftwood" "weathered oak" and "fuedal oak"—or in painted finishes which can only be duplicated by a blend of artist's oils—such as the celedon greens and salmon-pink-beiges found so frequently in 18th century French furniture.

REMOVING AN OLD FINISH

Methods of removing an old finish fall into three categories: mechanical (by sanding or scraping), thermal (by applying a blow torch or torch lamp), and chemical (by using paint and varnish solvents). Each method will strip the furniture piece of its old finish. However, some methods are so excessively harmful to the wood itself that they create more problems than they solve. We will discuss the advantages and disadvantages of each method in detail.

Sanding

If the woodworker is patient and will limit himself to hand (rather than power) sanding, this method is a highly acceptable one.

It eliminates the old finish without harming the wood. Its only negative aspect is the fact that it works best on flat surfaces. If the piece has many spindles or elaborate carving, the most patient woodworker may wish he had never begun. Also, because very coarse paper must be used at first to abrade away the worst of the old paint, the surfaces may become so badly scored that almost endless hand-sanding with even finer abrasive papers will be necessary to smooth the wood sufficiently for a new finish.

Power sanding, on the other hand, although much tidier than hand-sanding if the power sander is equipped with a dust-collector bag, is so efficient that it completely removes all the patina and texture with which age has endowed the piece, and (as with hand-sanding) often leaves the surface so abraded that it creates more work than it saves.

Scraping

Using a cabinet scraper requires consummate skill; otherwise, the sharp scraper will gouge out dents and valleys which are hard to repair. Also, the cabinet scraper—like the power sander—tends to eliminate all evidence of age. The cabinet scraper is an invaluable implement for removing small areas of paint from tight corners, joints and angles, but to use it to remove all paint from a piece is decidedly impractical—unless one is a professional with years of experience in using this tool. Even after softening the finish with chemical paint remover, some professionals decline to use a hand or cabinet scraper. Instead, they make a beveled wooden scraper to clear the stripped surface, rather than trusting themselves to scrape it with the sharp scraper blade.

Thermal Methods

Thermal methods are more likely to destroy the antique than to aid in restoring it. Burning off the finish with a blow-torch, or softening the old paint for scraping with a heat lamp, certainly effectively removes the finish. In fact, these same intense heat generators sometimes remove the woodworking shop and the woodworker himself, as well! So drastic are the effects of these two appliances, even in the hands of persons skilled in their use, that—in our opinion—they should be reserved for the steel surfaces of water craft or automobiles. Even if the wood is not scorched or burned in the process, all evidence of antiquity is completely obliterated from it.

If the woodworker faces a situation where nothing else will work—such as layers of paint so obdurate that they refuse to yield to any other method of removal—he should remember that a torch lamp is somewhat safer than a blow torch. However, even a torch lamp is very prone to burn the wood if it is not kept constantly in motion over the surface. The slightest pause can result in a blackened or blistered area which can permanently deface the piece.

Chemical Removers

Lye has probably removed more paint than any other chemical agent. However, its action on wood is so corrosive that it not only harms the work, but can also act adversely on the new finish once that has been applied. For these reasons, lye should be avoided whenever possible.

The commercial paint and varnish removers, on the other hand, are *solvents* rather than *corrosives.* They will react more slowly on old paint than on the new paints for which they were formulated, but they are the only chemical formulas which will remove paint, varnish, shellac and lacquer safely. If used as directed, they are never too caustic for the priceless wood surfaces. They do not leave marks on it, nor do they raise the grain. Because they contain no water and are highly volatile, they evaporate before they can soften the glue on veneered pieces. They are scientifically formulated to attack and dissolve the vehicles in which the coloring agents are based—the linseed oil in paints and the resins in shellac, varnish and lacquer. When properly applied, and then washed or wiped off, they leave the surface clean. Although they cost more than lye, they are equally efficient yet much more gentle at paint removal and, because they consistently give excellent results, are usually more economical in the end. The woodworker need only abide by the manufacturer's directions in applying them for very satisfactory results.

Commercial paint and varnish removers differ as to content and are sold under many brand names. Some contain paraffin or wax, which is added to prevent the volatile ingredients from evaporating too rapidly. These paint and varnish removers may act faster than the other kinds because the waxes act as air barriers, retarding evaporation, but the waxes themselves may cling as stubbornly to the wood as did the original finish. If you use such a remover, you must be prepared to go over the bare wood thoroughly with sufficient turpentine or other solvent to thoroughly clean off every particle of wax. Otherwise, the new finish may never adhere properly and may never dry completely.

Some woodworkers prefer the liquid removers to be thin; but, the thicker, more molasses-like liquids adhere to the surface better, thus, speeding the removal process considerably. For very large

Fig. 11-22. Lining drawers with heavy wrapping paper or newspaper to protect them from inadvertent splattering with paint remover.

furniture pieces which are too heavy or cumbersome to turn on their sides so that the woodworker can work on a horizontal surface, paste style removers are obtainable. These stick to the sides of furniture, making paint removal easier on vertical surfaces.

Among the higher priced paint removers are those which wash off with water; no scraping is needed. The crackled old finish is wiped off the piece first. Then the wood is scrubbed with a scrub brush and water to loosen and remove every vestige of paint, after which the piece is rinsed clean with clear water and dried well to await the application of a new finish.

Another important feature of the more expensive paint removers is the substitution of methylene chloride for benzol or any other inflammable ingredient. The difference this factor makes in the safety of using such a product more than justifies the difference in price. Benzol is not only highly inflammable; it also has highly toxic effects on the woodworker. *All paint removers, however, should be used outdoors or in a very well-ventilated atmosphere, with all windows open.* Also, the woodworker should wear rubber gloves, since these agents are highly irritating to the skin. Any such solution should be washed off immediately if accidentally spilled on skin or clothing.

Before paint remover is applied to a piece of furniture, all hardware such as drawer pulls, escutcheons, or hinges must be removed. Any surfaces which are not to be removed must be covered with masking tape to protect them from solvent. Such areas as the interiors of drawers, insides of doors or shelves should be covered with newspapers to prevent their being splattered (see Fig. 11-22).

The floor on which the work takes place should be covered with at least one layer of corrugated cardboard (sections of old boxes are ideal) and many layers of newspaper to prevent the dripped solvent from soaking through and damaging the floor. If the weather permits, the work can be done outdoors in a shady spot where the direct sun will not speed evaporation.

Paint remover should be applied generously either by pouring it on or by brushing it on with an old brush. If a brush is used, apply the remover with a single stroke, if possible. Don't brush it to an even thin surface, as you do paint, because a thin application will dry too quickly to do any good and the brushing itself will introduce air into the remover. Also, the film which forms on the surface of many paint removers to retard evaporation will be destroyed by repeated brushing (see Fig. 11-23).

Limit yourself to small areas—three or four square feet. After applying the remover to this area, wait for indications that it has loosened the paint before scraping. Although different removers vary as to the amount of time required to soften paint, ten to 20 minutes is generally long enough. By that time, painted surfaces should be very wrinkled and varnished surfaces should be covered with a slushy mush indicating that the remover has penetrated and is lifting the layers of surface finish. Before the area has a chance to

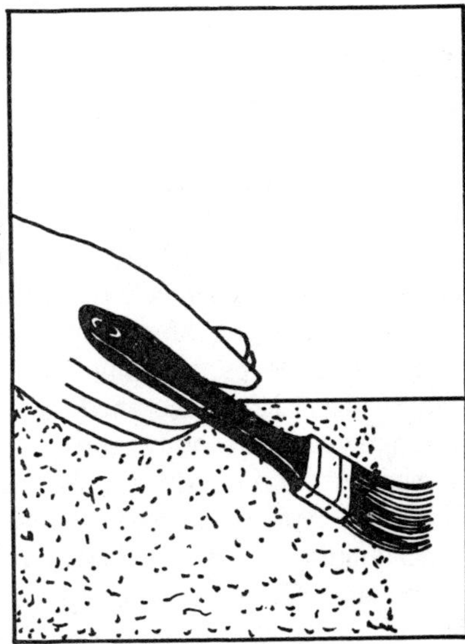

Fig. 11-23. Wearing rubber gloves, the woodworker gives the old finish a generous, single-stroke application of paint remover.

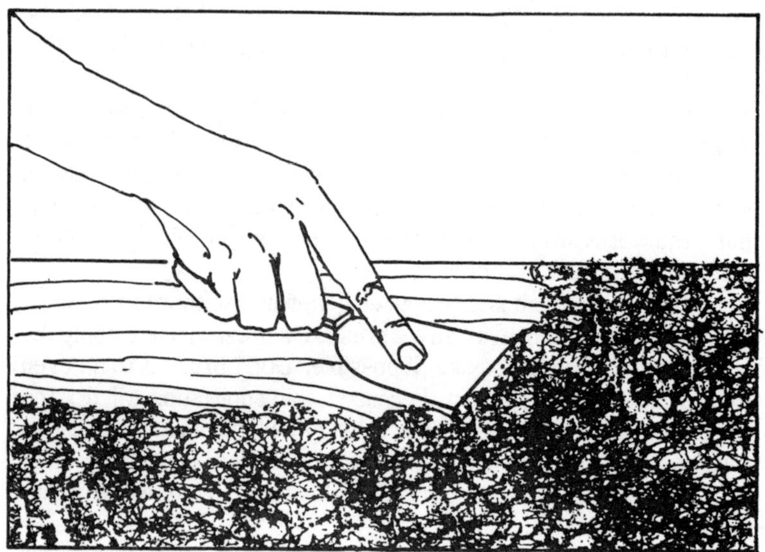

Fig. 11-24. With a broad, pliant scraper, the chemically softened old finish is removed from the surface.

dry, you should begin scraping. With a broad-bladed scraper, try to gently remove the softened finish (see Fig. 11-24). If the old paint does not scrape off readily, apply more solvent and wait a few minutes longer.

The type of scraper used to shovel off the gooey paint is most important. Often new scrapers or putty knives purchased for the job have blades which are too sharp and corners which are too pointed. These tend to gouge and score the softened wood. Blunt these sharp edges with a file before using and be sure that the scraper used has no burr (see Fig. 11-25).

The very safest tool for paint removal is a homemade maple scraper about 8 inches long, with a wedge-shaped beveled blade and a rounded, easily-gripped handle. This wooden tool is safest for scraping fine wood. Doweling of different diameters which has been cut on one end to a 45-degree angle makes a great tool for removing paint from grooves, moldings and carvings. Such implements as orange sticks, like those used for manicuring finger nails, wooden meat skewers, old toothbrushes, and steel wood are all excellent for cleaning out carving, penetrating corners, grooves and reeding (see Fig. 11-26). Spindles and stretchers can be scraped clean with an old dinner knife or artist's spatula (see Fig. 11-27).

Scrape off all the softened paint you can possibly remove. Then wipe off the surface with crumpled paper and apply another coat of

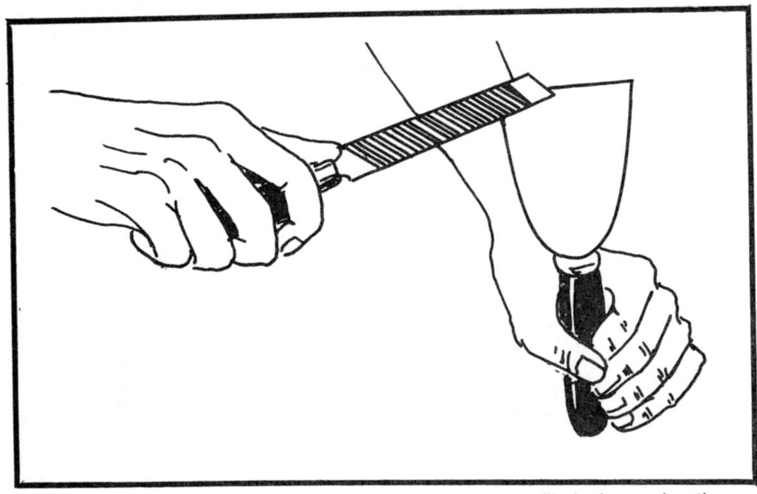

Fig. 11-25. Round the corners of a paint scraper with a file before using them.

paint remover. Wait until it has reacted on the residue. Then, using clean cloths (burlap is best), clean off the remaining paint as completely as possible.

If the manufacturer of the remover you are using recommends a scrub with denatured alcohol at this juncture, be sure to follow his

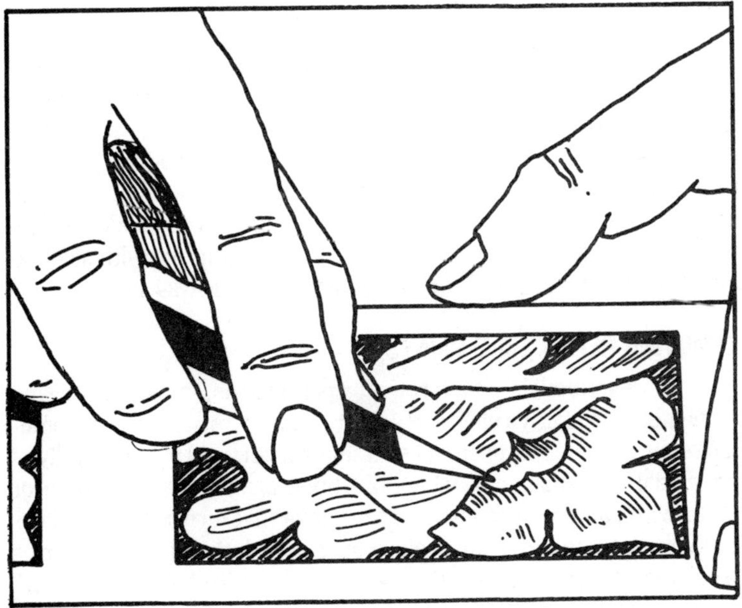

Fig. 11-26. Using an orange stick to clean old paint from carving.

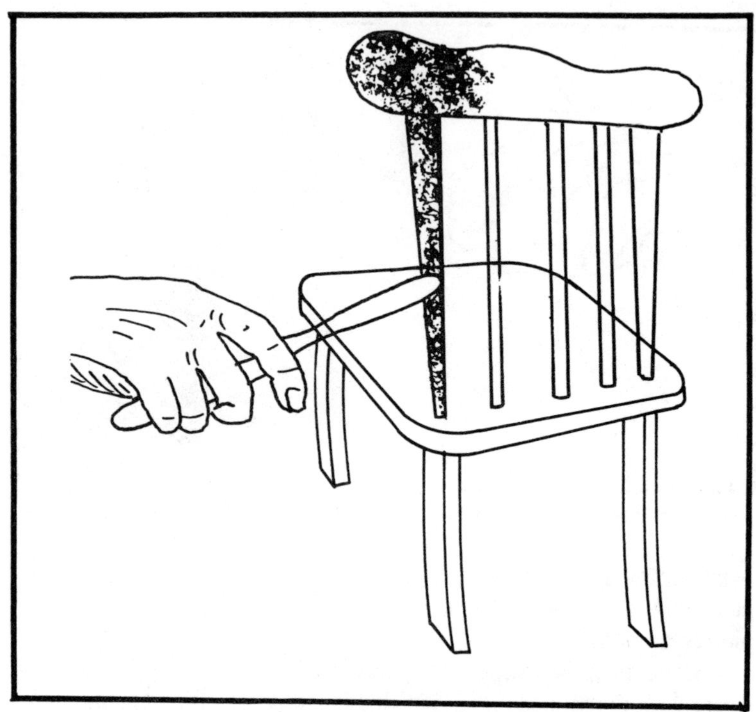

Fig. 11-27. The paint scraper used to remove softened paint from spindles should be blunt and flexible, like an artist's palette knife.

instructions (see Fig. 11-28). The alcohol will not only clean off the residue of paint and the traces of paint remover, but will neutralize the surface against further action from the remover. Some professionals use benzine, turpentine or gasoline—not the ethyl type—for this purpose.) Use a 4-inch scrub brush dipped into alcohol to clean up the place. Then wipe off the soil and repeat the rubdown with more alcohol and steel wool, wiping the entire surface with alcohol-moistened rags. Allow to dry thoroughly, at least 24 hours.

REMOVING REFRACTORY PAINTS

As described in the foregoing paragraphs, most paints and varnishes yield fairly readily to solvent removers. However, sometimes the antique restorer will encounter a very old piece, usually of provincial craftsmanship, which has been painted at some time or other with paint so stubborn and tenacious that furniture refinishers have given them the name "refractory," which the dictionary terms "resistant to ordinary treatment, difficult to reduce, obstinate." These refractory paints were homemade and were generally formulated of skim milk or buttermilk to which pigments, such as sooty lamp-black, or earth colors, such as red iron oxide or brown sienna, were added. These opague paints were generally used on such woods as knotty pine to hide the imperfections in the wood. Certainly they made cheap woods appear more beautiful, but they are almost as difficult to remove as the leopard's spots. If refractory paint is only one layer of many layers in the build-up of old paint coats, the task is somewhat easier. But if this type of paint is the only paint used on the antique, it has sunk well into the pores over the years and the task of removing it will be a difficult one. We can recommend three methods. We suggest that you try them in the order in which they are discussed in the text, starting with the mildest and working up to the strongest.

1. Moisten the surface with denatured alcohol. Using steel wool (Grade 2/0 or finer) or garnet abrasive paper (Grade 6/0 or finer), rub the alcohol into the wood grain, wiping the surface frequently with a soft cloth; then apply more alcohol and rub again. If this method fails to remove the paint buried in the wood grain, make a mixture of 65 percent high grade white shellac and 35 percent denatured alcohol. Using a clean 2-inch paint brush, paint a liberal coat on the surface where the paint is deeply imbedded and allow it to dry for at

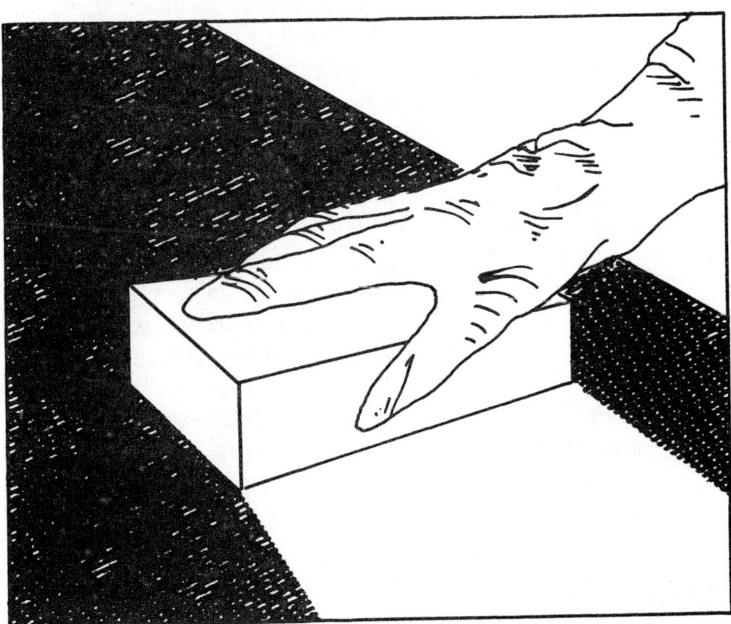

Fig. 11-28. Cleansing the newly stripped surface with alcohol.

least 24 hours. When it has dried, remove it using a good commercial paint and varnish remover. All or part of the deeply buried paint may come off with the shellac.

Note: The above method is an excellent way for removing any imbedded paint, whether refractory or not. It rarely fails to pull the old, unwanted paint out of the wood pores.

2. This second method for removing refractory paint cannot be used on veneered surfaces because it is a water soak which would loosen the glue. It should be used directly following the application of a commercial paint and varnish remover, while the work is still wet. This method is best undertaken out of doors, in a shady spot convenient to a faucet-attached garden hose. Both goggles and rubber gloves should be worn to prevent eye and skin damage from splatters.

   A solution of one pound of sal soda or trisodium phosphate is dissolved in an enameled or galvanized pail containing five quarts of hot water. Another pail of hot water only is needed for rinsing. Using a cotton dish mop with a large handle, the hot solution is applied sparingly on the painted surface—which is positioned horizontally, if possible, to make the solution easier to apply. After about one minute, the surface is scrubbed vigorously with a brush. Then the scrubbing brush is rinsed in the clear water pail and used to wash off the surface. The scrubbing process is continued until sufficient paint has been removed. The piece is then rinsed with cold water, using the garden hose and scrubbing every corner and cranny vigorously while the water is sprayed on. If the cleaned surface meets with your approval, dry it off carefully and proceed to adjacent surfaces, turning the piece so that each surface in turn is horizontal.

3. The third method used to eradicate refractory paints is that of applying a mixture of 50 percent household ammonia and 50 percent turpentine to the painted surface with steel wool. Keep turning the steel wool pad as it collects the paint and discard it when clogged for a new one. This method is one used by many experts to good avail and certainly is one of the easiest to apply, albeit one of the most powerful.

REMOVING VARNISH

Sometimes the antique restorer might wish to remove only the varnish on a piece, leaving the old finish intact to be protected later by coats of new varnish. Fortunately, varnish is somewhat easier to remove than is paint, provided very delicate handling is exercised and the woodworker knows when to stop. Applying denatured alcohol on wads of cotton waste to small areas may effectively remove the varnish. If it fails to do so, try equal parts of benzine and alcohol. If this does not remove the glossy varnish, try equal parts of pure turpentine and alcohol. If the varnish stands up to off of these ingredients, a light coat of commercial paint and varnish remover, carefully monitored until it begins to "lift" the varnish and then halted in its action by a thorough wiping with alcohol, may penetrate the varnish and make it more vulnerable to continued alcohol applications on wads of cotton. If another application of paint and varnish remover is necessary, use it; but carefully examine the results of each step, and quit when you are ahead.

Chapter 12
Antiquing Furniture

Antiquing furniture is the art of transforming an old piece (or a raw wood piece) by opague paint and glaze, or clear stain and varnish, to resemble a genuine antique. For hard-used, battered furniture it offers a skillful face-lift. Because the appearance of antiquity is the goal of this achievement, reconstruction or extensive repair of the piece is not the concern. In fact, the signs of usage and wear are carefully preserved, if possible, to give the item the look of great age. Only when decoupage is contemplated are surface dents or gouges given consideration. Because decoupage involves the application of paper prints, embossed paper lace, or gold and silver leaf to furniture, the surface of the piece must be as smooth as silk. Even coarse graining will show. Therefore, great care and attention are expended on preparing the surface for decoration. Sprackling paste is frequently used as an overall filler because it can be sanded to a sleek surface and completely camouflaged by coats of paint.

METHODS

Basically, there are two methods of antiquing. The first is clear finishing with see-through stain, shellac and varnish—allowing the wood grain to show through. The second is opague finishing, with gloss or semi-gloss enamels and pigmented glazes, obscuring the wood grain completely. Either imparts to the object being antiqued an elegance and distinction which makes it stand out dramatically in any decor.

The tools and materials used in producing these masterpieces are manifold—for antiquing is an art in which individual imagination plays an all important role and may be given free reign. In the eighteenth century, when antiquing reached a peak of artistry hitherto unequaled, each artisan guarded the secrets of his trade jealously, refusing to reveal the personal techniques of design and finishing which kept his works in popular demand.

However, the technological age in which we live has tended to substitute scientific formula for the artistic, highly personalized methodologies of old-time craftsmen. Now, antiquing stains, paints and glazes are packaged in ready-made kits, available at every paint store and hobby shop. These antiquing kits will put the patina of age on any piece you choose in jig time and with a process so simple and easy that perfect results can virtually be guaranteed. How the eighteenth century artist, painstakingly grinding lapis lazuli with mortar and pestle to produce the exact shade of blue for his palette would marvel at this sterotyped technological solution to the mystique of antiquing! Yet today's reliable antiquing kit has enabled thousands of people devoid of artistic talent to produce beautiful masterpieces and to experience a personal thrill in the creation which otherwise they might never have known.

TOOLS AND MATERIALS

Some of the tools and materials used in the art of antiquing are curious indeed (see Fig. 12-1). Many of them are utilitarian household items having no other association with furniture finishing and design—such as carpet scraps, to produce the effect of wood graining; household sponges, to create mottled finishes and to remove glue; and crumpled wrapping paper, tissue paper, plastic wrap or paper toweling to create the look of veined and dappled marble. Cotton pads are used as pouncers and burnishers to smooth, blend and highlight the finish. Cheesecloth is a primary necessity; pads of this soft, thin material are used to apply paint. A small porcelain roller (see Fig. 12-2)—the type with a handle used in smoothing wallpaper—can serve the same purpose in smoothing decoupage appliques. Cotton swabs, tweezers and orange sticks, usually found on the dressing table, perform scores of chores for the antiquer.

At the end of this chapter is a complete list of all the tools and materials required for each of the following finishing methods. This list should be consulted before actually starting on the application of any of these techniques.

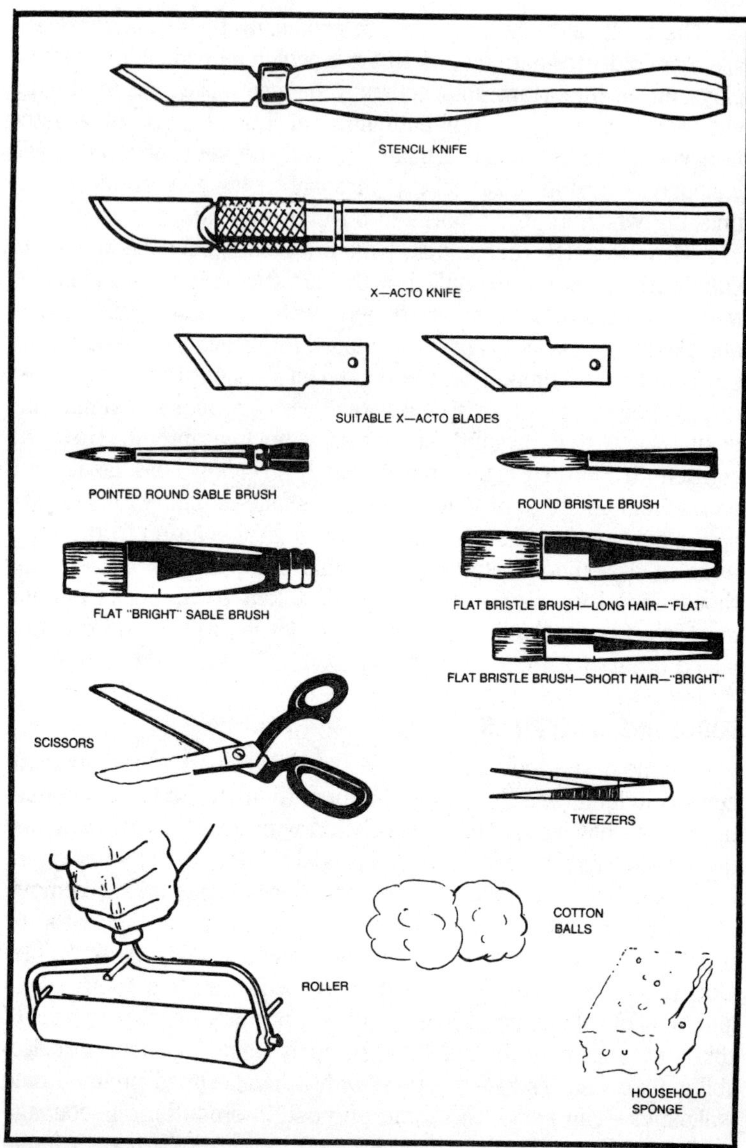

Fig. 12-1. Furniture antiquing tools.

DISTRESSING

The art of antiquing breaks all the rules laid down for other types of furniture finishing. On contemporary pieces, the finish is prized for its flawless perfection, and any refinishing is done to restore this perfection. Not so in antiquing. Here, every effort is made to preserve and to simulate the appearance of age and wear. Even the dirt in the pores and cracks of a piece is considered a valued asset, and many professionals actually rub handfuls of dirt into the piece to increase its look of antiquity. Some finishers use garden soil for this effect; others prefer workshop sweepings. Many cannot bring themselves to add this touch of realism, and use burnt umber in the cracks and crevices instead. Such synthetic age signs must only be employed if the piece is to be stained, not painted, since paint adheres only to a dirt- and oil-free surface.

To create the small nicks, scratches and gouges found in real antiques, a distressing tool can be employed. Here again, the best of these are found or made at home. A ring of keys, or a homemade mace with nails protruding at random from the striking end (see

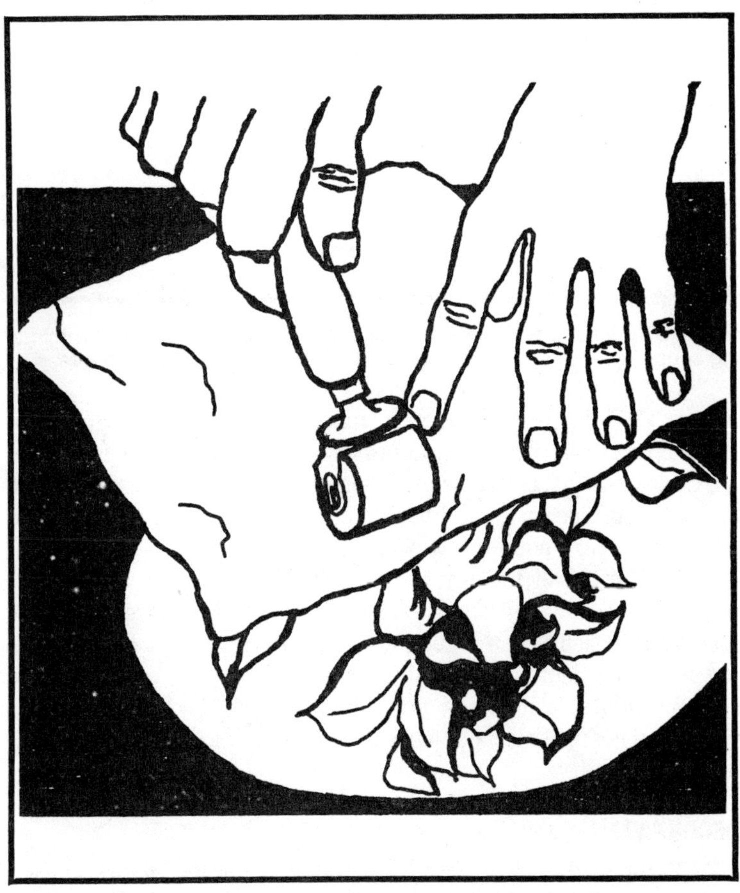

Fig. 12-2. Small porcelain roller used to smooth down glued print—a cloth between roller and print pads the pressure action.

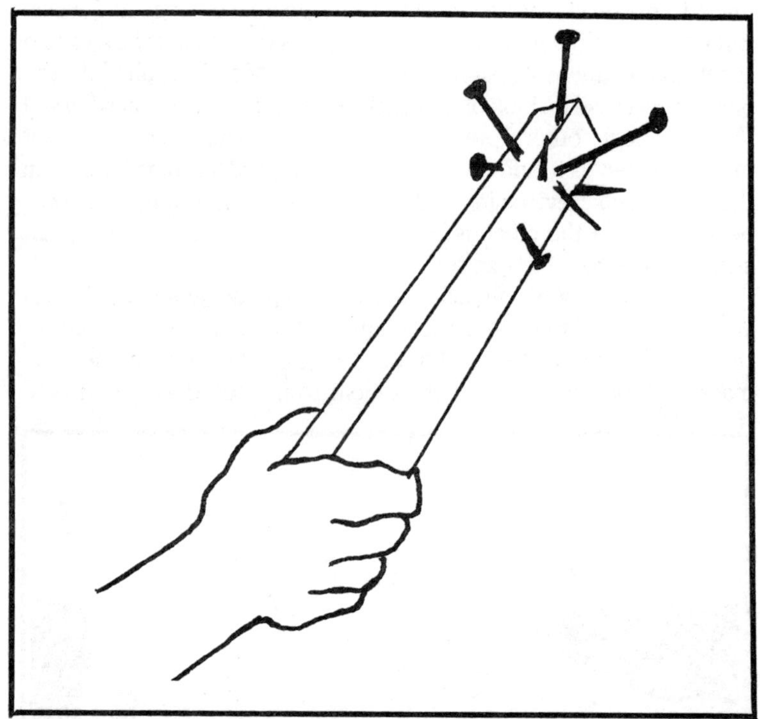

Fig. 12-3. A homemade mace—made of a scrap stick with random nails protruding at one end—can simulate age and wear with scratches and gouges.

Figure 12-3), a small ballpeen hammer—any of these can produce some interesting scratches, dents and gouges, giving a surface the appearance of hard, protracted usuage. A length of chain slapped against a surface or tugged back and forth over a too-perfect edge produces a very authentic worn, battered aspect.

The hurts inflicted in such latter-day distressing look genuinely old, once the piece has been carefully refinished with fresh coats of stain and varnish. Then detecting which marring is new and which is old is virtually impossible. All sorts of additives are used in the stains, paints, varnishes and glazes—and in the techniques employed in applying these various coats—to increase this appearance of antiquity.

DECOUPAGE

Through the ages, one tried-and-true method for producing beautiful furniture has been that of appliqueing various other materials to the surface. This resurfacing of the piece is an excellent expedient when the original wood is too nondescript to warrant a fine stain-and-varnish finish or so battered that restoration is not feasible. We will cover several such applied surfaces in this chapter, starting with the one which is the most ingenious and elegant of all—decoupage.

Decoupage—used over an antique finish or over gold and silver leaf—can turn a derelict, drab, damaged old piece of furniture into an object of astounding beauty (see Figs. 12-4 and 12-5). If antiquing itself can be said to give old furniture a face lift, decoupage is the magic wand which transforms a shabby Cinderella into a splendid princess.

What is even more important to the craftsman is the fact that decoupage obliterates a multitude of sins, camouflaging them in such

Fig. 12-4. Decoupage treatment on the wood portion of an upholstered classic chair.

Fig. 12-5. Decoupage renews the life of an old silver chest.

a charming and graceful fashion as to make their existence a matter of good fortune. Decoupage is particularly useful in refinishing the antique object which has seen such yeoman service through the years that it literally defies anyone to rehabilitate it. Utilitarian objects often fall into this category. Indifferently made originally, of cheap ugly wood they are now so battle-scarred and decrepit as to possess no virtue save the fact that they are genuinely old. However, with decoupage the dented milk can (Fig. 12-6), broken churn, grievously-used kitchen table, dingy kitchen cabinet, stained dough box, or all-but destroyed horseshoe bench or cobbler's bench can take on greater beauty than they ever had when they were new. Casualities can be turned into assets; disasters become delights. For the antique furniture refinisher, decoupage represents the "when all else fails" method which never fails.

The use of decoupage adds an array of interesting and beautiful materials to furniture refinishing. Since decoupage is actually a combination of three art forms—*collage, montage* and *assemblage*—it naturally utilizes many of the same materials as these other three.

COLLAGE

For instance, collage is a twentieth cenury technique involving paper cutouts, fabric stencils and embossed cardboard artwork or artifacts in a pleasing design. The mounting of these objects may be flat or repousse, with the cutouts overlapping one another in part to create a bas-relief effect. The background to the collage—like that of decoupage—is often painted, generally with oil, casein or acrylic paint. Decoupage often employs precisely the same techinque—using a hand-rendered oil painting of a landscape as a background and superimposing scaled-down thin paper cutouts of human figures and objects against the background and embossed pictures of castles, chateaux and gazebos cut from heavier greeting card stock in the foreground to create an effect of perspective and dimension.

Fig. 12-6. A milk can decorated by means of decoupage becomes an attractive ornament.

Fig. 12-7. A gold-footed cigarette box covered in silver tea paper and decoupaged in rocaille design of scrolls, shells, ribbons and flowers—the shadowbox top features a hand-colored bouquet of flowers, strawberries, butterflies, bees and a fly on a pale blue silk ground—a charming montage grouping under glass.

MONTAGE

Montage is another art form akin to decoupage. Here, all manner of three-dimensional objects, scraps of wood, pieces of cork, metal shavings and small objects of all sorts are glued to a common background; the overall design expresses the whimsical imagination of the artist. Decoupage often employs many of the same textural contrasts—a scrap of real feather and woven straw to fashion a lady's bonnet, an appliqued rose with furled satin petals, a bit of real lace used as a shawl, the entire portrait framed in an appliqued rococo wooden molding. Garden scenes are sometimes depicted with real pressed dried ferns, flowers and grasses gracefully arranged, with perhaps a real butterfly, fabric bumble bee or feathered hummingbird hovering above. This bas-relief work is another form of decoupage (see Fig. 12-7).

ASSEMBLAGE

Assemblage is another art departure similar to montage which has been in existence for hundreds of years before the twentieth century, but which had no classification or definition as a specific art form earlier. Assemblage is a representation in high relief shown under glass or mounted to a panel. The domain of this craft comprises the many types of representation enclosed in a curio table top of a shadow box—miniture room scenes and street scenes in which open windows and doors reveal glimpses of other vistas. Other examples would be all sorts of objects artistically mounted on a panel. Collections of shells, for instance, are sometimes displayed in this way, or are used as integral parts of an underwater scene depicting marine life, or a representation of a beach using sand, bits of driftwood and seawood. Such three-dimensional settings are assemblages. Decoupage sometimes draws inspiration from this intriguing art form (see Fig. 12-8).

This discussion of the many forms of decoupage will alert the reader to the infinite variety of tools and materials used in this complex art. The true enthusiast spares no effort in the execution of a project. Decoupage is exquisite in expression, requiring perfection of execution even in the smallest detail. Because decoupage offers such scope and range to its creator, the dedicated decoupeur finds opportunity for endlessly expanding his creativity.

Fig. 12-8. Shadowbox assemblages, as the one above, sometimes used real fabrics and jewels in the gowns and real brocade on the walls.

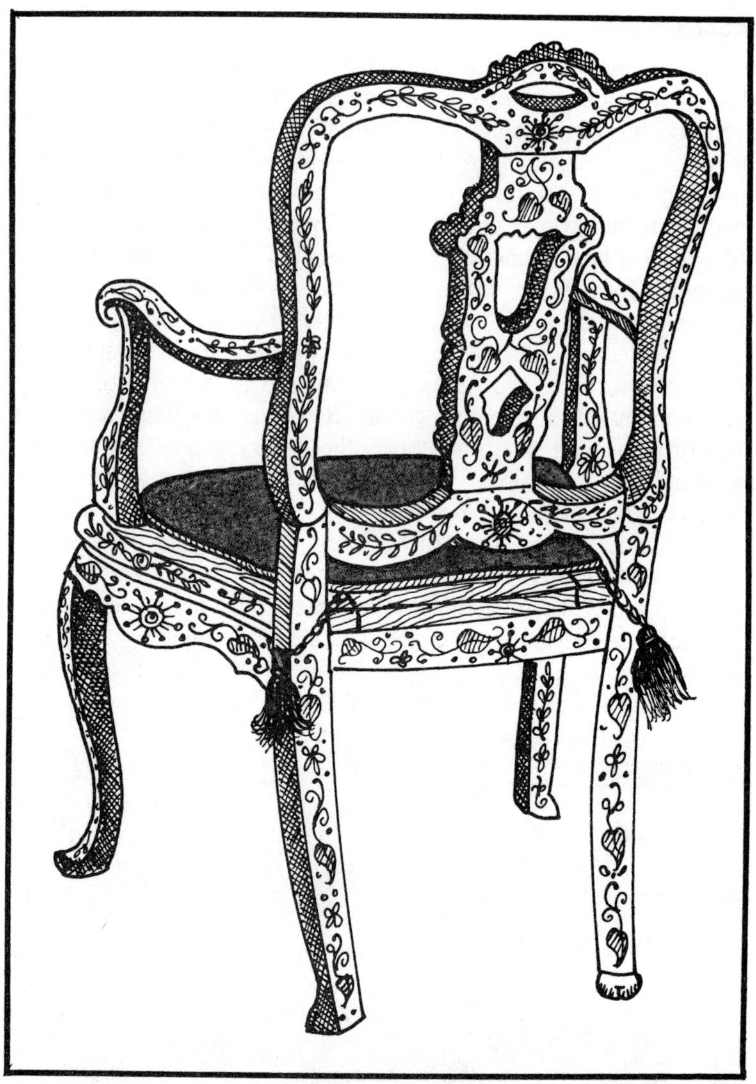

Fig. 12-9. Beautiful example of decoupage decorated French chair of the Renaissance period.

HISTORY

Decoupage is a relatively old art—one which has been in existence for many centuries. In its long history, however, it has enjoyed several distinct renaissances, the most important of which occurred in France in the eighteenth century. The leisurely life of the aristocracy during this golden period, and the reverence with which art in any of its forms was regarded by the French court, provided an excellent climate for the flourishing of this complex handicraft.

Actually, the French had first observed the art in Italy and in Italian imports. Commerce between France and the art centers of Venice, Florence and Rome was brisk and vigorous. This interchange introduced decoupage into Paris, along with many other cultural expressions reawakened to new eloquence by the Italian Renaissance (see Fig. 12-9). Ladies of the French court began to commission Italian artisans to fashion for them secretaries and dressing tables ornamented in decoupage; soon they were attempting the art themselves, their eager, if inept, scissors cutting out motifs and scenes from fine engravings. The number of priceless engravings wantonly destroyed in such experimentations is deplorable to contemplate. Although craftsmen today are as fond of famous masterpieces as were their predecessors, they use scaled-to-size prints, not original works, as was the practice in the extravagant days of yore.

Fig. 12-10. Use of gold braid as a border in decoupage.

In order to create decoupage typical of the eighteenth century, the modern craftsman needs to study the kind of engravings and paintings which were employed. The chinoiserie engravings of Jean Pillement were in great demand for decoupage. In fact, so inspiring to the craftsmen of the period were the works of this extraordinary illustrator that he is often called "The Father of Decoupage." Other artists of the period whose paintings were also popular were Antoine Watteau, Francois Boucher and Pierre Joseph Redoute. All of these artists were consummate colorists and the decoupeur of today will do well to study their canvases which reflect so accurately the color schemes typical of the decors, ornaments and fashions of the period.

After the eighteenth century, the next revival of the art ot decoupage occurred in the Victorian Period. The forms and departures taken by the art during this period were vastly different from those of its former hey-day. Gold braid and lace paper were widely used in borders and filigree effects. Imported German cutouts were used which required very little trimming. Scissors were employed only for splicing and matching. These cutouts were lithographed in bright colors and hand-colored prints ceased to be the vogue. Even when engravings were used, as they frequently were, they were appliqued as complete pictures in the original black and white (see Figs. 12-10 and 12-11).

Now decoupage is once again tremendously popular. Modern decoupage, however, is radically different from the rich, fabric-dressed portraits of the Italian Renaissance, the graceful self-expressions of the French Golden Age, and the charming sentiments of the Victorian Period. Reflecting our life and times, decoupage now makes use of present-day artifacts—theatre tickets, dance programs, menus, souvenirs, fabric swatches, wood appliques, and cutouts from newsprint, greeting cards and gift wrap. The results are often highly dramatic, interesting and even amusing. The differences in the textures employed and the impact of the subject matter makes them exciting, treasurable art pieces.

The hand-coloring of prints was traditional with craftsmen in the eighteenth century. Then, as now, engravings provided ideal compositions for decoupage because their crisply explicit rendition of light and shadow indicated to the colorist exactly where and how intensely the tones should be applied. In the eighteenth century, oils, watercolors and pastels were all employed for hand-coloring. Watercolors and pastels were the media generally used on paper; oils were reserved for the wood itself, the landscapes, architectural studies, street scenes and interiors being used as background for decoupage cutouts of figures, boats, carriages and statuary.

Fig. 12-11. Use of lace paper and hand-colored print in decoupage.

MODERN TECHNIQUES

Today, most decoupeurs use oil pencils. These are easier to manipulate than a brush; will not blister the paper, as will watercolors; or thicken it, as will oils. Moreover, if errors are made, the colors may be erased, using a soft eraser. The colors are elegant, subtle, typical of the period of the furniture piece itself, and very easy to apply smoothly and to blend. In addition, the oil pencil is a much neater medium for applying color than is the brush. The colors need no pre-mixing, do not drip or splatter and require no cleaning of the coloring implement once the job is done.

The choice of available colors in oil pencils is virtually endless. The artist should attempt to confine those used on a particular project to the period of the piece being ornamented, studying paintings and artifacts of the period to ascertain what colors were in vogue (see Fig. 12-12).

Once the artist has arrived at a palette, he should carefully work out a color scheme for his project, first deciding on the background color which the entire object is to be painted; then choosing the

Fig. 12-12. A museum piece such as this will provide clues to the popular colors of the period.

accent colors in which the appliqued prints are to be rendered. He must keep in mind that any color scheme he chooses will be covered with at least 20 coats of varnish. These coats will "tame" the colors dramatically. To better visualize the final effect, he can test the colors chosen under a 4-inch × 6-inch piece of glass which has been varnished with 20 coats. He will soon see that the colors must be carnival-bright if they are to retain the tonal values desired when fully varnished (see Fig. 12-13).

Once the color scheme is determined, the craftsman should make a tracing of the actual decorative motif; then color the tracing in the color scheme selected. Any necessary modifications as to hue and tone would be instantly apparent and the colored tracing would, thus, serve to direct the application of color on the actual prints themselves. These should always be colored and given a coat of sealer before they are cut out.

The colorist should keep a piece of scratch paper handy beside the print on which he is working, where he can test for the color blending desired. When he finally arrives at the exact shade for which he is striving, he should jot down the names and/or numbers of the pencils used to produce it so that he can reproduce it at will.

In coloring the actual print, the artist begins by coloring all the shadows one basic color, his pencil following the lines of the engraving (see Fig. 12-14). This basic color underlying the shadowed areas (each of which, when finished, is a blend of different overlying tones) is what gives the finished print coherence, unity and dimension. Next, he gently adds light green to the tops of trees, shrubs and grasses, blending to darker and still darker greens on the lower branches where the wash of sunlight does not penetrate so strongly. Trees and grasses as observed in nature have accents and highlights of blue, yellow, straw, pink and red. These accents the artist should add to his rendition. Brown, pink and yellow highlights will depict tree trunks.

Now he is ready to color the figures. Flesh tones are among the hardest tones to reproduce accurately. Starting very lightly, the artist applies a tint of pink, accenting this base tone with fragile shadows of yellow-green sometimes mixed with pale blue. The clothing of the figures should be rendered in colors which harmonize with those in the landscape. Lastly, the shadows should be crisply accented with the darkest color in the palette to give dimension and vibrancy to the finished work.

All prints, whether colored or uncolored, must be given a coat of sealer before cutting (see Fig. 12-15). The sealer coat serves three purposes: (1) it stiffens the paper and makes precision cutting

Fig. 12-13. Start out with bright colors, as they will be subdued by the many coats of varnish required.

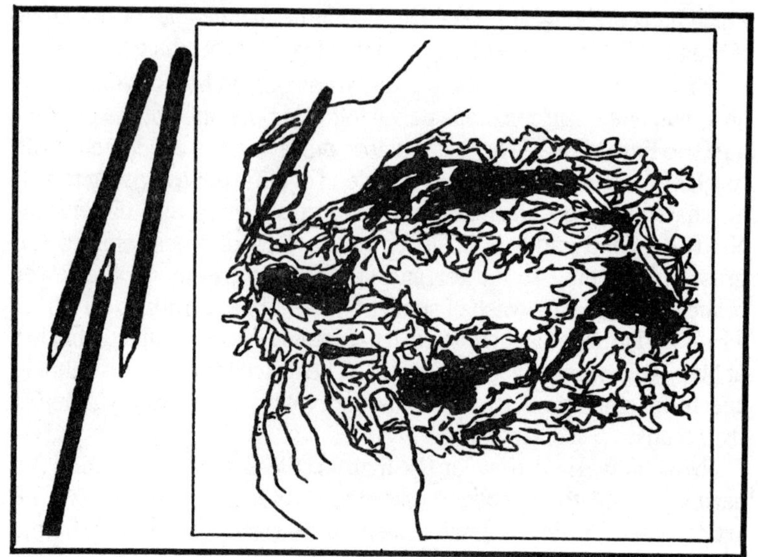

Fig. 12-14. Applying color to the print—all shadow areas are the same basic color.

easier; (2) it prevents the print from shedding apart when it is wet with paste and is being manipulated into position by the fingers; (3) it prevents the many coats of varnish from penetrating and discoloring the print.

Clear plastic sealer should be carefully brushed or gently sprayed onto the face of the print, moving the brush or spray can in one direction only so as not to cause the colors to run. The excess is then blotted off carefully with paper towels. Two coats are better than one. The print must be allowed to dry thoroughly between coats. The colors will blend subtly as soon as the sealing process is begun.

When the print is thoroughly dry, it may be cut out. Straight-blade scissors are used to trim away the excess paper surrounding the citout; then the special curved decoupage scissors are employed to do the trimming. This trimming step is probably the most important in successful decoupage, so it must be very carefully executed. First, a bright-colored pencil is used to draw in the joining strips needed to keep the print intact until it is pasted. All portions of the print which are weak or isolated on a long stem should be joined to the main body by narrow strips of paper which can later be snipped away when the print is being pasted to the object it is to decorate, but which meanwhile will prevent the appendage pieces in the design from getting crumpled, torn or lost. When all these joinings have been penciled in on the waste paper areas between the main body of the design and the appendages, the print is ready for trimming.

The decoupage scissors are small German steel cuticle or surgical scissors with curved blades. They should be held in a relaxed manner, with the blades curved away from the person cutting. The thumb and third finger are slipped through the handle rings, allowing the blades to rest on the index finger. The hand holding the scissors remains almost stationary during the cutting, while the other hand moves and turns the print (Fig. 12-16) continuously feeding the paper into the scissors blades so that the cutting may be done close to the blades' pivot point. The tip of the blade is called into play only when absolutely necessary—for cutting into a corner or snipping away minute bits of waste paper in the design.

The reason for holding the blades curved *away* from the person cutting is a scientific one. This position of the scissors blades actually produces a bevel cut along the edges of the print, so that none of the white paper underneath will show. When properly cut in this fashion, the printed surface of the paper is actually a fraction larger than the

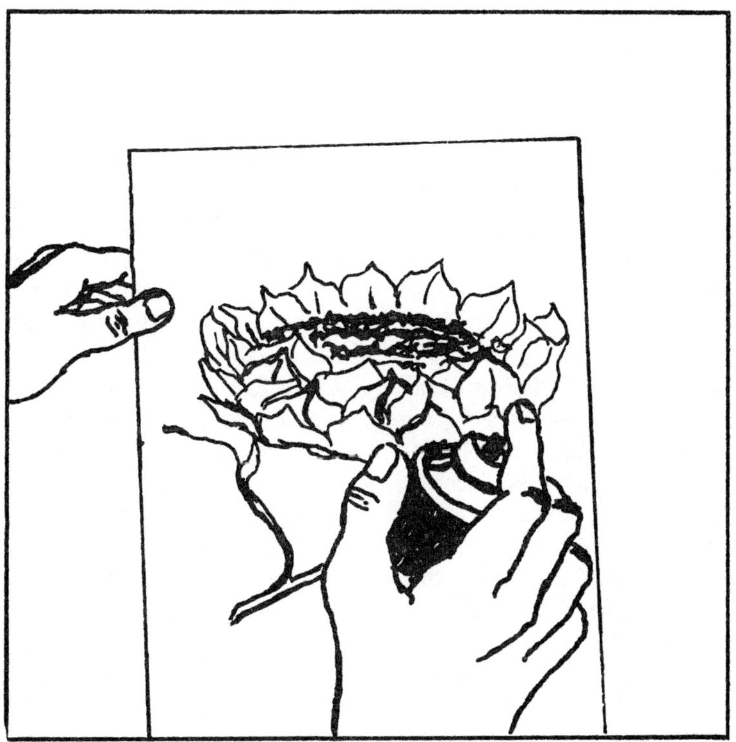

Fig. 12-15. Sealer is applied before cutting out the print.

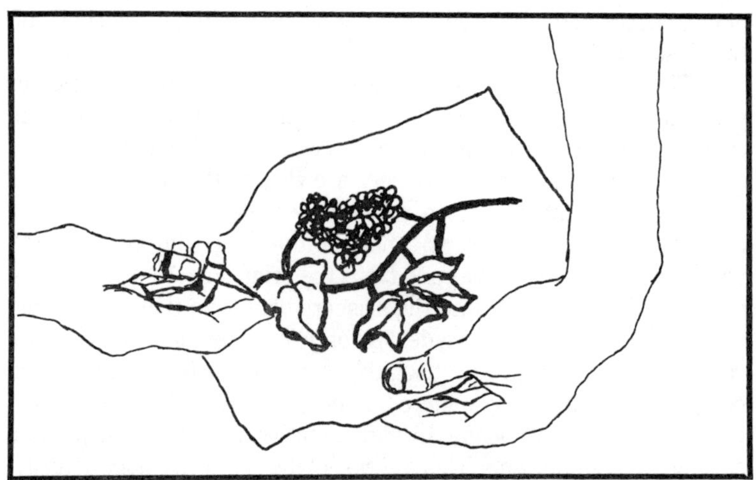

Fig. 12-16. Cutting out the print—the hand holding the scissors remains stationary while the other hand moves and turns the print.

underside. This bevel cut gives the print a neat, clean, crisp edge when it is glued flat, so learning to hold the scissors properly is well worth any effort it takes.

Trimming with the decoupage scissors should begin in the center of the print (see Fig. 12-17). To remove this excess paper first minimizes the risk of tearing. All joining strips formerly indicated in bright pencil should be left intact. The trimming should be very meticulously done, with no rounded or indefinite edges and with crisp corner cuts. The scissors should contour the figures of the print to give them dimension and indentity. Any very long, straight-line cutting should be avoided. Instead, when such a cutting is called for, the paper should be wiggled back and forth during the cutting to produce a softer edge for blending (see Fig. 12-18). The comparison of a straight cut with a feathered, serrated edge will immediately demonstrate the merit of this method.

The furniture or decorative item which is to receive the decoupage must be satin-smooth, free of dents and scratches, with the various coats of primer, enamel and glaze (if the piece is antiqued) already applied and thoroughly dry. All hardware must have been removed (see Fig. 12-19).

Decoupage has been fittingly described as "painting with scissors." The very name, translated from the French, means "to cut out." Dorothy Harrower once spoke of the art as a "limitless world of decoration." And so it is. Tastefully chosen cutouts, artistically arranged and smoothly appliqued, can add immeasurable style and

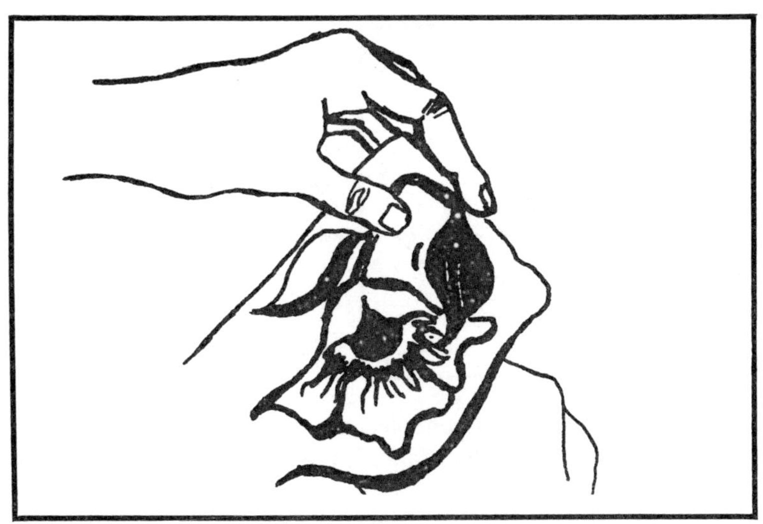

Fig. 12-17. Trimming begins in the center of the print.

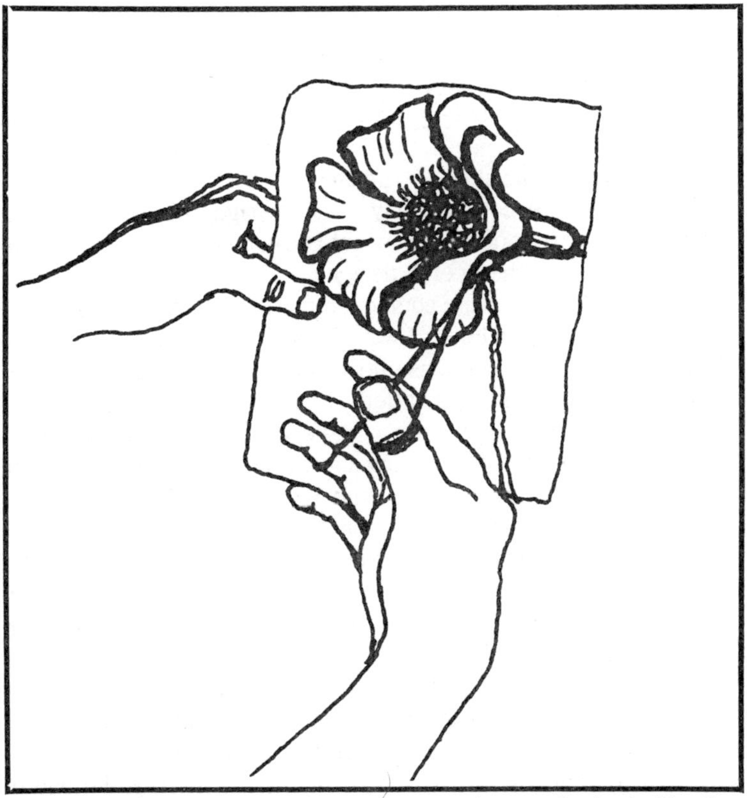

Fig. 12-18. Wiggle the paper back and forth to produce a soft edge for blending.

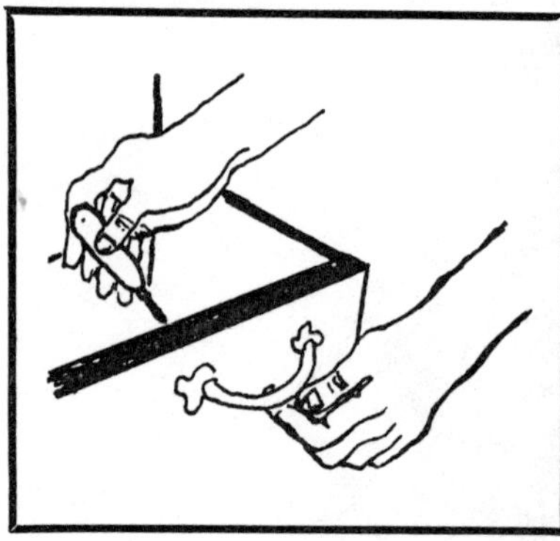

Fig. 12-19. Before attempting decoupage, all hardware must be removed and carefully stored with the fastening screws for remounting when the piece is finished.

charm to furniture and accent pieces. The positioning and arrangement of the individual cutouts affords the artist tremendous creative opportunity (see Fig. 12-20).

Now that the component pieces have been carefully trimmed, the artist will want to arrange them on the article or furniture piece which they are to decorate to see if they will produce the composition which he conceives. When they are finally positioned exactly as he wants them, he will use bits of drafting tape to hold them in place for pasting. As the paste-up proceeds, this tape can be removed without damaging the paper. The artist may find that certain cutouts need trimming in one area, and adding to in another. Such "pruning" and "grafting" are possible only in decoupage, where a segment taken from one part of the composition can be utilized in another to the betterment of the overall design.

The pasting-up of the component parts is the next step. First, the artist gets a small bowl of water, a slightly damp sponge, and a small cloth. Next, he opens the paste, which should be of the non-staining, water-soluble variety—like Sobo or Elmer's Glue-All. Using two fingers to apply the paste, he spreads a thin, even film on the underside of each print, using a few drops of water if necessary to keep the paste from drying (see Fig. 12-22). As each print is placed in the position designated for it, the drafting tape is removed and the print is stroked outward from the center in all directions, the ball of the fingers rolling and pressing the paste outward and a small cloth pad acting as a burnisher. Should the paste seep out from beneath the edges of the print, it is immediately removed with the dampened sponge. The paste-up is performed as quickly as possible to prevent the glue from hardening. If the pasted surface seems too dry, a few drops of water are smoothed over it with the fingers. After each cutout is smoothed as flat as possible with the pad of cloth, the damp sponge is used to press the print very firmly into the paste (see Fig. 12-23). The sponge should be thoroughly rinsed in the bowl of water every time it is used to lift a bit of excess paste to prevent its carrying the paste to the print surface. Then the sponge is wrung out until it is barely damp before using it again. A too-damp

Fig. 12-20. The positioning and arrangement of the original cutouts affords the artist tremendous creative opportunity.

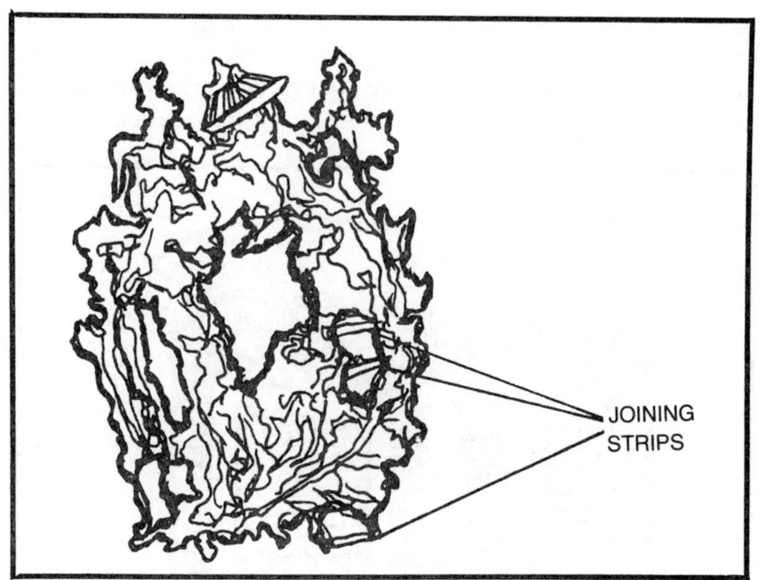

Fig. 12-21. The print is held together with drafting tape until positioned in place.

sponge can dissolve the paste under the end of the cutouts. The paste-up must be constantly examined to detect any paste oozing out from behind the prints which should be blotted instantly with the sponge. The clean-up must be thorough; the slightest bit of glue which is allowed to remain will become obvious when the varnish is applied.

With the cushion of a finger operating like a roller, the craftsman works every puddle or blister of paste detected under the print to the edge for quick pick-up. If the trapped paste resists all efforts to evict it, a small pin hole should be punched into the print at the place where the paste makes a bulge, and the paste gently expressed through this hole.

To avoid creating air bubbles and paste traps, many artists choose to use a roller, rather than a pad of cloth and their fingers, as described above. This smoothing tool is the same as that which wallpaper hangers use and is available at any paint or wallpaper store. The roller works efficiently in producing a firm, flat bond between the paper and the surface of the object being appliqued. However, great care must be taken to prevent the tool's marring the fragile cutout or the furniture surface. Always use the roller over several layers of the cloth pad and work from the center of the print to the edges, going slowly and applying pressure to assure complete adhesion.

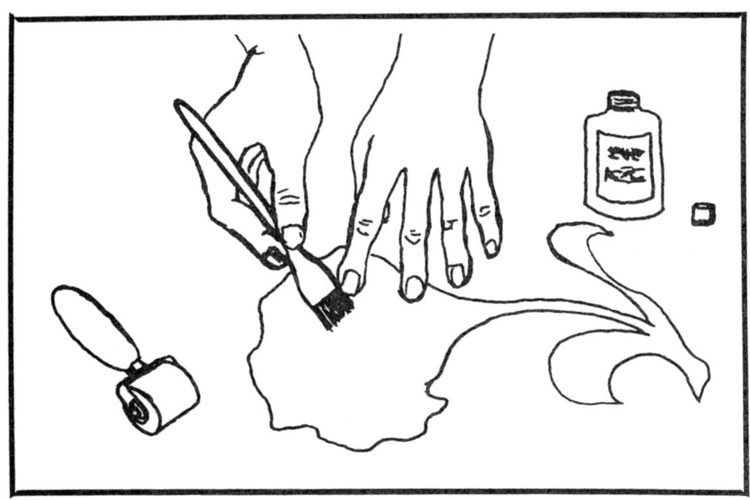

Fig. 12-22. A thin film of paste is applied to the underside of the print.

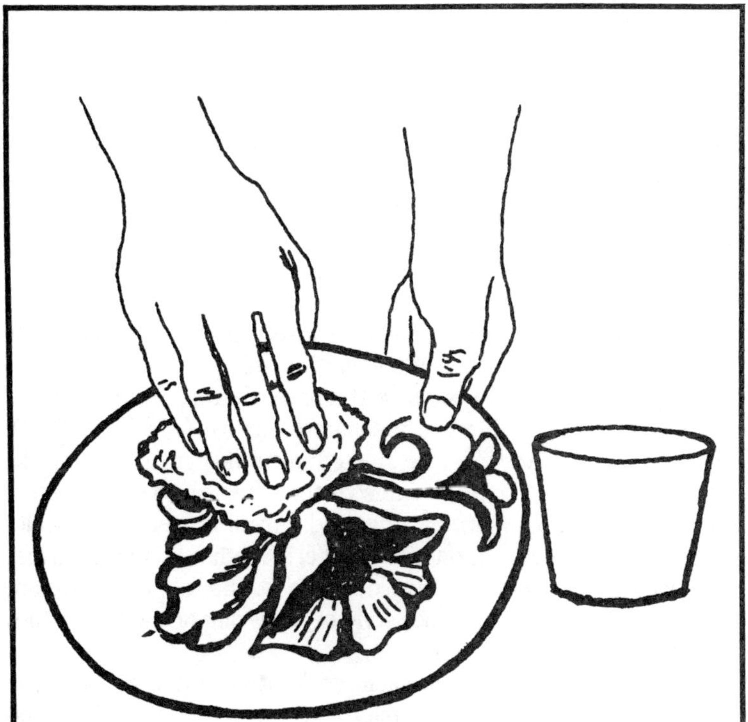

Fig. 12-23. A damp sponge, thoroughly cleaned of paste, is used to press the print firmly in place.

Sometimes, regardless of the care taken in applying paste to the entire backside of the cutouts, a spot is missed. This oversight produces an air bubble under the print when paste-up is attempted. To introduce paste into this area, make a small incision in the bubble with a razar blade and insert a drop of glue into the slit with a toothpick. Complete the repair by pressing the paper down firmly with the cloth pad or the roller buffered by the cloth, and use the dampened sponge to tap up any oozing paste.

As we have mentioned before, only non-staining, water-soluble paste is used as an adhesive for the paper cutouts. However, if cloth braid or fabric applique are used in the design, these must be secured to the surface with glue, which does not stain and is not water-soluble or removable. For instance, glue—not paste—is employed to install fabric linings or to hold thread-woven gold braid in place. Frequently, such accents are used in decoupage; but, they are generally applied last, as accents, when the print is thoroughly dry.

In applying pasted cutouts to a surface, do not overlap the edges. Overlapped layers must be given numerous coats of varnish in order to finally acquire an even, smooth surface. Moreover, in sanding layered treatments between coats, there is too much danger of sanding too deeply on the built-up areas and, thus, removing the varnish and harming the print. Layering of prints is properly reserved for collage, which is usually hung like a picture and, therefore, need not present the glossy, smooth surface required of fine furniture.

For the same reasons as those just mentioned, all edges must be tightly fixed to the surface. If the slightest looseness is noted, a toothpick laden with paste should be inserted under the edge and pressure exerted to produce a smooth bond.

Apply the prints to one side at a time, treating each surface of the piece as though it were a separate picture (see Fig. 12-24). However, each side must be related in its design to that on the adjoining side and top. Sometimes you may be using a design where the interrelation is expressed by tendrils and flower stems which actually trail from one surface to another. Another composition may employ different prints for the sides than for the top, related to one another only by color scheme, style of rendering or the period they illustrate.

However it is achieved, each article ornamented with decoupage should convey a certain unity and coherence of design. This attribute makes it arresting as a whole and interesting as to details.

After the pasted decoupage is thoroughly dry, successive coats of varnish must be applied. These coats of varnish give the finished

Fig. 12-24. Although each surface is treated as a separate picture, each must be related in its design to that on the adjoining sides and top.

Fig. 12-25. A strike-wire can is used to remove excess varnish from the brush.

piece its characteristic three-dimensional quality and luminosity. Many coats are better than few for producing these effects—how many coats is a matter of judgement. The number can never be too many, only too few. Thirty coats may seem like a lot of work, but actually that is not the case. The brush work takes only minutes for each coat. What takes the time is the drying, for each coat must dry at least 24 hours before another is applied.

For a flawless finish, the designs are given a first coat of an equal mixture of shellac and alcohol. This coat is allowed to dry for 24 hours. Then the surface is buffed very lightly with 4/0 steel wood and carefully wiped clean with a damp sponge. Next, the first coat of varnish is applied, using long, flowing strokes—not short, choppy ones. The varnish is applied generously, but never with so full a brush as to produce sags or runs. Using a strike-wire can to smooth excess varnish from the brush each time it is applied can help in producing a more even coat (see Fig. 12-25).

The varnish should be flowed on with the brush in long, gliding, even strokes all going in one direction. Brush marks and bubbles should be avoided and instantly removed by the brush if they occur. If any bristles fall on the surface, these should be picked off instantly with the edge of the brush.

In applying varnish, care must be taken to lift the brush every time it reaches an edge and feather it back into the wet varnish area. This action blends all strokes and prevents the varnish from accumulating against the edges, where otherwise it might roll over, producing unsightly sags and drips. Constant vigilance must be maintained to smooth away any such uneven places the moment they occur, before they have a chance to harden. If a drip is detected anywhere after the varnish dries, it can be sliced off to the varnish level with an x-acto knife and allowed to dry before sanding and revarnishing.

After each coat, the brush must be thoroughly cleaned in solvent, and suspended in a baby bottle one-third full of solvent. Clipping the nipple from the rubber cap and inserting the brush handle into the resultant hole before putting the rubber top on again will keep the brush upright in the bottle, supported in that position by the nipple (see Fig. 12-26).

When a sufficient number of coats of varnish have been applied to produce a glass-like surface where no print edges can be detected by feeling the varnished area, the work is ready for its first sanding. Usually, 20 coats are enough to produce the "glazed porcelain" smoothness desired. However, the thickness of the paper may

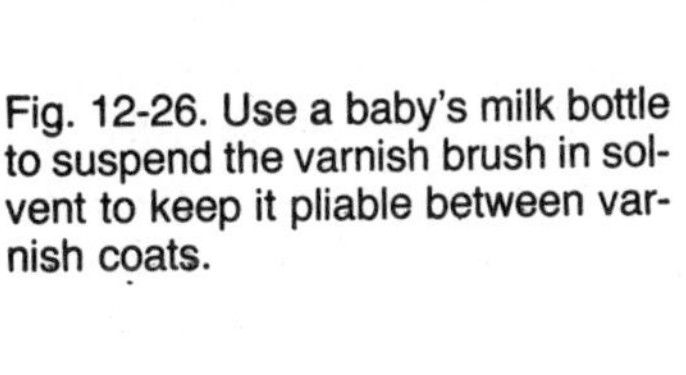

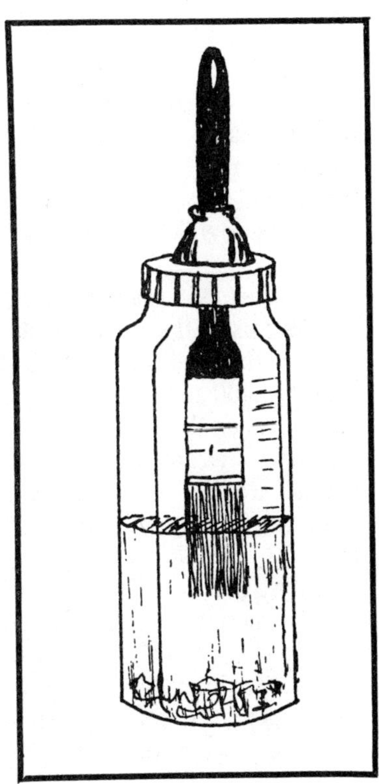

Fig. 12-26. Use a baby's milk bottle to suspend the varnish brush in solvent to keep it pliable between varnish coats.

Fig. 12-27. The rubbing-down agents for decoupage are sandpaper in successively finer grits, steel wool and soft cheesecloth pads.

require more; if the prints were cut from heavier quality paper, such as wallpaper, they will require more coats to cover them.

Once this stage has been reached, the work is sanded lightly with a circular motion, using No. 400 silicon-carbide sandpaper soaked in water. Black wet-or-dry Tri-M-Ite or wet-or-dry Minnesota Mining & Manufacturing sandpaper is a suitable abrasive for this task and, because the paper and the surface are sopping-wet when sanded, less dust is generated to cause sneezing. Moreover, the abrasive action of these sandpapers demonstrate unusual endurance.

To keep the surface of the sandpaper level, it may be backed up by a felt-padded sanding block. A thorough, but gentle, sanding is given with three successively finer grades: 280 (coarse) for first sanding, 400 for second sanding and 600 for polishing (see Fig. 12-27). Then the surface is wiped off with tissues or paper towels, cleaned with a damp sponge and allowed to dry. Then more coats of varnish are applied. A total of 24 to 30 coats is generally sufficient; often fewer may be enough, depending on the judgement of the artist.

As a finishing touch, the thoroughly dry varnish is rubbed in a circular motion with 4/0 (No. 0000) steel wool or with a soft cloth treated with a mixture of pumice and Valspar furniture oil. Then the surface is wiped with tissues and paper napkins and cleaned with a damp sponge. A gentle polishing with a soft cloth and the surface is ready for waxing (see Fig. 12-28).

An alternate finishing touch to the oil and pumice treatment is the matte finish much favored by decoupage guilds in olden times. This finish entails the application of three creamy-smooth, swansdown-light coats after the steel wool buffing just described. One coat is applied every day for three days. For these coats, use one-half inch soft, flat brush strokes on the matte finish in one direction only, pulling horizontally across and then down on the sides, but not back up again. The piece is allowed to dry thoroughly and *lightly* sanded with *wet* No. 600 sandpaper, using small circular motions. Next, the surface is wiped off with tissues, rinsed with a damp sponge and buffed very lightly in a circular motion with *dry* No. 0000 steel wool. The resultant particles are wiped off with tissues, the surface washed with a damp sponge and polished with the heel of the hand. An incredibly smooth surface, similar to that of polished

Fig. 12-28. A soft cloth treated with a mixture of pumice and Valspar furniture oil gives a glowing finish to decoupage.

ivory, is now ready for waxing. However, before describing the method used in waxing, we will discuss one last problem in varnishing which deserves special mention—that of varnishing a box.

VARNISHING

Varnishing a split box requires a certain order of procedure to insure that the varnish will dry smoothly. First, the rims (or top edges) of the box are varnished—the part where the hinges go, and the parts where the lid meets the box bottom. When the edges are coated, the box is turned upside down, and —holding it with his left hand inside the box—the artist varnishes its top section (lid) or the bottom of the box proper, depending on which of the two box sections he wishes to start on. (The hinges have been removed at this point, so each of the two box sections is separate from the other.)

After putting the first coat on the section, the craftsman then varnishes the sides, holding each side as horizontal as possible while he works on it, applying the varnish first horizontally and then vertically (from tip to bottom edge of the box section), lightly pulling the varnish down with each stoke. He uses a strike-wire can to keep the brush from carrying too much varnish. When a side is completely varnished with strokes from top to bottom, the craftsman applies a second coat to the varnished side, but this time his brush strokes are from bottom to top, gently pulling the varnish up. He wipes off any drips which may have accumulated on the bottom edge and repeats the same procedure on another side until he has gone completely around the box or lid.

When the entire box section has been varnished, he places it upside-down on a flat-top which will support it until it is dry (see Fig. 12-29). Since the can touches only the unpainted interior of the box section, the varnish coat is not subjected to marring contact with anything. The varnished piece is allowed to dry in this position for 24 hours and, even then, the surface should be pressed hard with a finger to insure that it is dry enough for another coat. If no finger print remains after so pressing, another coat is applied until a minimum of 20 coats has been given both sections of the box. If the varnishing is skimped, sanding will abrade away part of the print. The print should be submerged so deeply in varnish that sanding only smooths the gleaming surface, leaving the print beneath intact.

If the varnish crazes, simply allow the wrinkles to dry. Then continue varnishing and the wrinkles will eventually disappear as you add more coats. Mache varnish is the type of varnish we recommend for use on decoupage because it is specifically formulated for use over paper, but any good varnish will do.

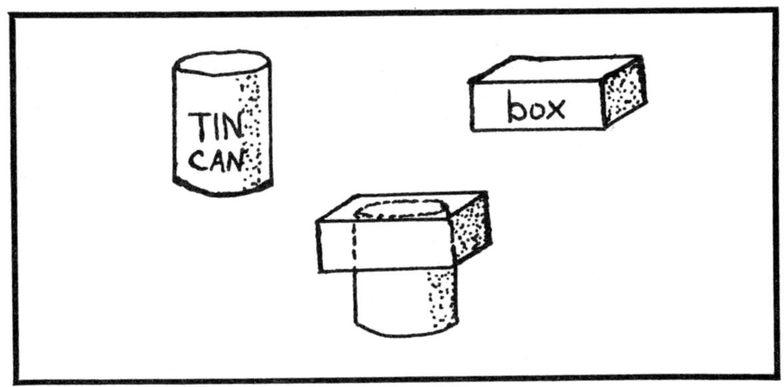

Fig. 12-29. Method of drying half section of split box over a tin can.

When all exterior coats of varnish are thoroughly dry, the box sections—both bottom and top —are given a coat of sealer inside, preparatory to installing a lining.

Waxing the Varnished Decoupage

A single coat of wax produces a marvelous transformation. The slightly etched, dusty-looking finish takes on the translucent brilliance of a porcelain glaze. When the piece is buffed to a high polish, the depth and richness revealed are like that observed in a polished gem. This dimensional effect can only be produced by the classical method of many coats of varnish.

There is a wax unlike all others which has been especially formulated for decoupage, although it can also be used for other fine furniture pieces. This unique wax is called Parquet Royal Wax and can be purchased by mail order from the Patricia Nimocks Studios, P.O. Box 7187, Louisville, Kentucky 40207. However, any good-quality, colorless paste wax may be used. Goddard's English Paste Wax is a traditional favorite. Butcher's Bowling Alley Wax produces a fine, luminous polish.

The wax is applied with a damp piece of cheesecloth which has first been soaked in water and then wrung out. Using just a little of the wax at a time, the varnished surface is completely covered and allowed to dry for approximately ten minutes. Then it is polished to a lasting, lustrous sheen with a dry piece of cheesecloth.

COVERING AND LINING

The less obvious finishing touches given any piece of furniture or ornament should be done with the same care as that lavished on its surface. No detail should be shirked. For instance, the finish given the underside of an ornament or box, the lining installed in an article, the way in which the interior is finished—all of these details make important contributions to overall elegance. All bottoms of boxes should be smoothly varnished. If desired, small decorative brass feet may be installed and a border dado pasted around the bottom to trim that area, with at least four coats of varnish applied to protect the applique (see Fig. 12-30). If the box is a heavy one, or is designed to rest directly on the table, a colored felt or natural cork covering on the bottom will prevent the box from scratching the surface on which it rests.

The interior of the piece itself offers yet another area for decoration, particularly if the piece is a vitrine, china cabinet, bookcase or display table. A decoupaged box might carry out the same designs inside or use a related print in correlated colors. Paper is a favorite furniture liner. Silver or gold tea paper; silver, gold or metal leaf; or plain wallpaper in a contrasting color to the outside finish—all these impart a warm glow to the interior of a display cabinet, particularly when it is lighted. Textured papers and papers in correlated prints are often used to line decoupaged furniture. Marbleized bookbinding paper is an appropriate tailored lining for a bookcase.

Cloth linings are very popular. Velvets, brocades and silks are widely employed in this way—the latter two fabrics being lined or padded, the velvet used without padding. These linings are particularly effective in antique virtrines and curio tables with display-case tops in which collections of precious coins, snuffboxes and antique jewelry are displayed. Boxes in which precious jewelry is to be kept are frequently fabric-lined.

Frequently, the craftsman will want to cover and line ornamental boxes with the same paper inside and out; for this reason and because the processes care similar, we will discuss cover and lining together. As an example, we will use a box, since this is an article often covered and lined with paper and since the box structure—whatever its dimensions—is the structure with which the craftsman will generally be dealing.

Because the paste used on paper is water-based, the artist will need to use sealer on the front and the back of the paper and let it dry throroughly before beginning. If gold or silver tea paper is the choice, a generous coating of mache varnish should then be applied to the underside of the paper and wiped off with paper towels and tissues until it is dry. Then the tea paper is turned over, and the thinnest possible coat of mache varnish applied evenly over the gold or silver side, and allowed to dry.

Fig. 12-30. Border dados should be protected by at least four coats of varnish.

Gold and silver leaf requires specific handling. For directions on how to surface a box in leaf, please refer to the section later in this chapter under the heading "Applying Gold and Silver Leaf."

While the lining paper is drying, the craftsman will remove the hardware from the box and put it away with the screws which secure it for remounting when the box is finally finished—covered, varnished, rubbed smooth, waxed and lined. The box is now in two pieces: lid and bottom. Whether the wood is new wood or old wood stripped of its former finish, it must now be given an all over coat of protective sealer, inside and out.

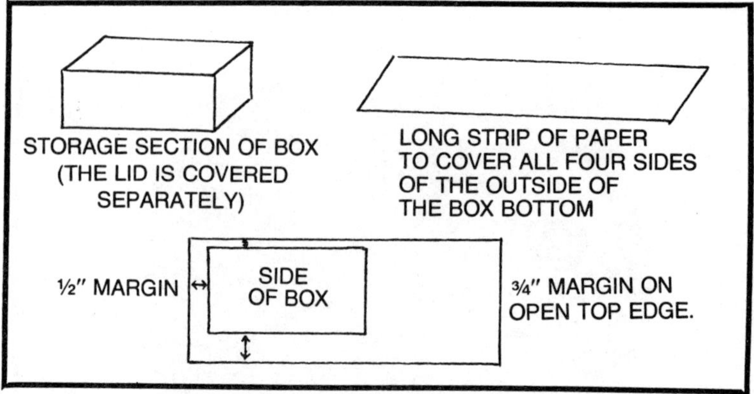

Fig. 12-31. Covering the four sides of the box bottom.

The Covering

The first step in covering a box with paper is to cut out the pattern. The best place to begin is with the *sides* of the upper section and the *sides* of the bottom. The depth of the upper section and the depth of the bottom are measured and one inch is added to those figures. The circumference is measured and one inch is added to those figures. Two strips of the sealed paper are then cut to these dimensions, the measurements being marked off in pencil on the backside of the paper. The excess inch in both depth and circumference is to allow for the stretch or shrinkage of the paper when wet with paste. Better to have some excess to trim off than to have to rip off a too-small piece and start again.

Using his fingers, the artist spreads the glue evenly all over one side of the box, working it in well. Then he wets his fingers and works in one or two dips of water until the water and paste mixture feels like olive oil or melted butter. To insure a firm bond, the paste and water must never be mixed beforehand, but only after the glue has had a chance to grip the wood.

Now the strip of paper already cut to cover the side of the box is positioned on the paper with the opening toward the artist. A margin of ½-inch is left at the box end, ¼-inch along the box bottom, and ¾-inch along the open top edge (See Fig. 12-31). Now the artist places his hand inside the box near the corner and uses his thumb to press and roll the side of the box against the paper. This anchors the paper and prevents it from sliding or shifting.

Next the artist turns the box with the paper adhering toward him, so that the unadhered end is opposite him and ahead of his hands. Using only the ball of his thumb or finger, he presses and rolls the paste forward toward the unadhered end, always looking from inside the box. He takes care not to push, rumple or stretch the paper, and he makes sure that the paper is firmly and smoothly down by constantly examining the right side of the work. When he reaches the corner opposite his starting point, he stops smoothing and "butters" the next side of the box with glue and water. Then he stretches the paper strip smoothly and tightly around the corner, creasing the corner edge between thumb and finger and proceeds as before—rolling and pressing from inside the box, keeping the unpressed glue ahead of his working fingers until he has completely circumvented three sides of the box. When he reaches the last uncovered side, he tears the original projecting margin along its edge (to deckle the edge slightly and avoid a sharp-edged underlayer) and folds this overlap around the corner at which he started to the uncovered side facing him, pasting it firmly down (see Fig. 12-32). Then he smooths glue and water on the unfinished fourth side *and* on the pasted-down overlap and covers the side—overlap and all—with paper to the corner where he started. He cuts his paper flush with the original corner, leaving an almost invisible seam.

Now, using his curved cuticle scissors, he trims the bottom edge of the paper flush with the bottom box edge, crispy and neatly removing the ¼-inch margin he has left there. Then he stands the box section on its bottom and carefully covers the top edges with glue, using no water this time. He rolls and presses with his fingers. working the glue upward from the sides and over the narrow edge, leaving the corners loose and folded together, standing erect like a kitten's ears. Using this two thumbnails pressed together, he creases these four corner points sharply. When all the box edges are firmly and smoothly glued, with no bubbles or bumps of glue anywhere, he takes the tips of his cuticle scissors and cuts diagonally from the outside corner to the inside corner, severing the pointed pieces and leaving a mitered corner. This he presses flat with a moistened thumbnail (see Fig. 12-33). If he is planning to paint or

Fig. 12-32. Tearing a paper edge for deckled effect—hold it firmly against the box side with one hand and, with the thumb and index finger of the other hand, tear toward you, making a wider, softer edge, less conspicuous when underlying a covering layer which must look smooth.

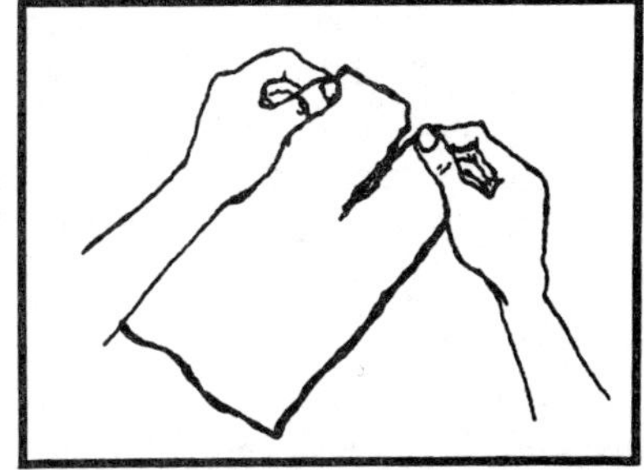

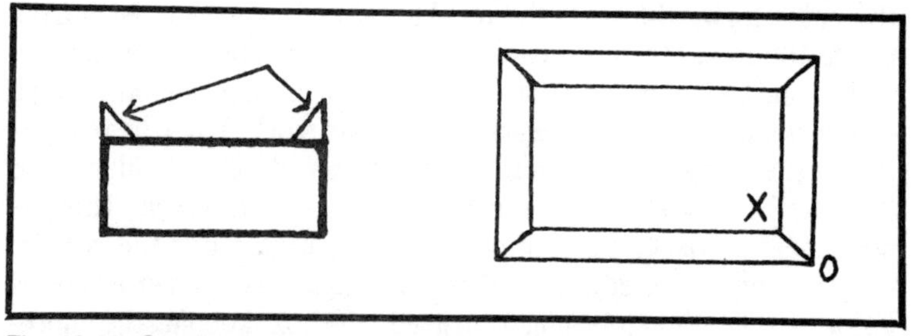

Fig. 12-33. Completing the box coverage.

decoupage the inside of the box, he trims off the remaining margin of paper at the box edges, making it flush and neat with the inside of the box edge. If he plans to line the box with fabric, he turns the remaining margin over the box edge, and glues it to the inside of the box, where the fabric lining will hide it, once it is installed.

The craftsman is now ready to butter the underside of the box with glue mixed with a dab or two of water. When the mixture feels like oil to his fingers, he puts the paper cut to fit the bottom on the glue-coated bottom of the box and, starting at the center, works it free of all bumps and bubbles by pressing and rolling it with his thumb. When the bottom is smoothly, flatly down, and all the edges neatly met, a margin of ¼-inch will be left all around, protruding beyond the edge of the box. Using the curved scissors, this margin is trimmed away flush with the box.

To more firmly seal the rim edges of the box, the paper covering the bottom is now peeled slightly back and an extra bit of undiluted glue worked in all around the outside rim. Using thumb and forefinger as a wedge, the two edges are pressed firmly together and allowed to dry as is, without removing the excess glue (the removal of which might cause the rim to come loose and pop up again).

The work is allowed to dry naturally, without using heat to accelerate it. When properly dry, the craftsman uses a piece of kitchen sponge about 1½-inch × 1½-inch, wrung out of hot water to wipe *along* the edges, never against or over them, until all glue is removed. Any dull spots on the paper surface can be removed in the same manner. The bottom storage section of the box is now covered with paper, ready to decoupage or varnish.

Exactly the same steps are followed in covering the lid.

Lining

The paper lining is installed in exactly the same manner as that just described for covering the box with paper, except for these two vital differences: (1) The lining paper is cut out differently, after being carefully coated front and back with sealer (and with mache varnish if the paper used is gold or silver tea paper) and allowed to dry; (2) The pieces of lining paper, cut out according to the pattern, are applied in a different order that that used in covering the box with paper. To line the box and lid, the pieces cut to fit the box bottom and the box lid are glued inside first —*before* the lining around the sides is applied, rather than after, as is the procedure for covering the outside of the box with paper.

The difference in cutting out the pattern are as follows: Turning the sealer-treated paper face down, the artist places the box bottom flat on the paper and outlines it exactly with a sharp pencil. Then, using dividers, he precisely measures the width of the box edge (the thickness of the wood used in making the box bottom), making sure to place one point of the dividers exactly on the pencilled line, and marking the width of the wood all around the four sides of the paper outline's inside area. With a sharp pencil and steel straight edge, he connects the prick marks left by the divider points. This inner penciled line is the one he trims, cutting around it carefully with his curved scissors. When tested inside the box bottom, this lining piece should fit perfectly. Both box bottom and box top (lid) liners are tailored to fit in the same way, and they are the first pieces glued down in mounting the liner paper on the box (see Fig. 12-34).

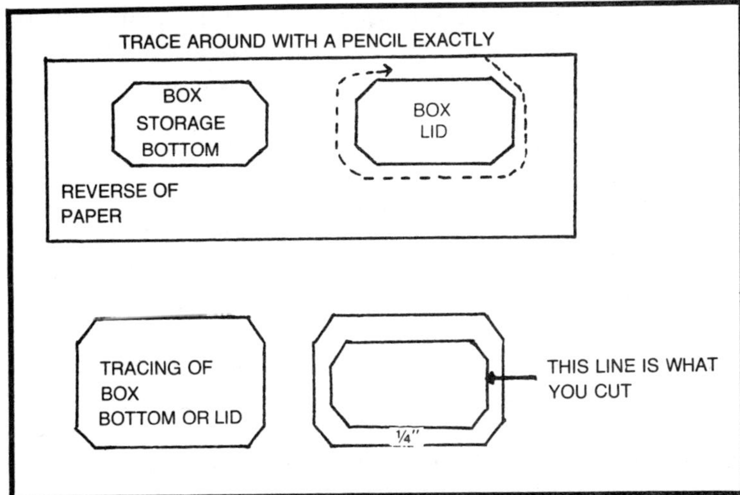

Fig. 12-34. The line between the two "0's" is the width of the wood used in constructing the box as measured with the dividers and transferred to the exact outline made above. Using the prick marks of the dividers as a guide, the inner outline is drawn and this inner outline is the one cut out to line the box bottom and the lid.

The box liner side pieces are cut out exactly as the box covering side pieces were cut, with the same two margins—a-inch for over lap at the end of the strip and 1-inch safety allowance at the top edge of the strip. (Be sure to use a straight paper edge as the bottom edge of the side strips.) Starting with a corner—any corner—the side lining strips are glued on in exactly the same manner as the side covering strips were glued on, with only one exception: the top margin of ½-inch is trimmed off flush with the top edges of the box. It is not turned over the box edge, as the covering paper was turned.

The lining strips for the sides must firmly, squarely and neatly cover every corner. An orange stick is helpful in working the paper well into the corner to fit the 90-degree angle. The craftsman will find that pre-creasing the corner line on the unglued/side lining strips will help immeasurably in insuring a crisp corner. Therefore, when approaching a corner in the gluing-down process and before the corner lining paper has been pressed against the glue-coated box side, fit the loose paper carefully into the corner, marking the corner line with a fingernail. On the backside of the paper, crease the exact line indicated between thumb and forefinger. The paper lining should then fit the corner angle perfectly and be easier to glue down (see Fig. 12-35).

Lining With Fabric

These same instructions may be used in lining china cabinets, curios, display cases, etc. The dimensions will be larger, of course, but the technique is the same because the basic structure is essentially that of a box.

The box is placed facedown on the tin, white cardbaord which will be used as a backing for the fabric lining. Using a sharp pencil, the box bottom is outlined. The thickness of the wood is measured between the points of the divider and the thickness is marked off inside the box outline, making sure to place one point of the divider exactly on the outline and indicating the measure with a prick mark. By connecting these prick marks with a pencil line, a new outline is drawn inside the original outline. This subtracted cardboard outline is cut out with straight scissors and placed inside the box to test for size; it is trimmed until it fits just loosely enough to drop out when the box is turned upside-down. The top of the box (lid) liner is fashioned in precisely the same way.

Next, the inside height (depth) of the box section and the inside height (depth) of the lid section are measured from bottom to top and two strips of cardboard are measured off to line the sides. For purposes of this text, let's say that the inside height of the box is

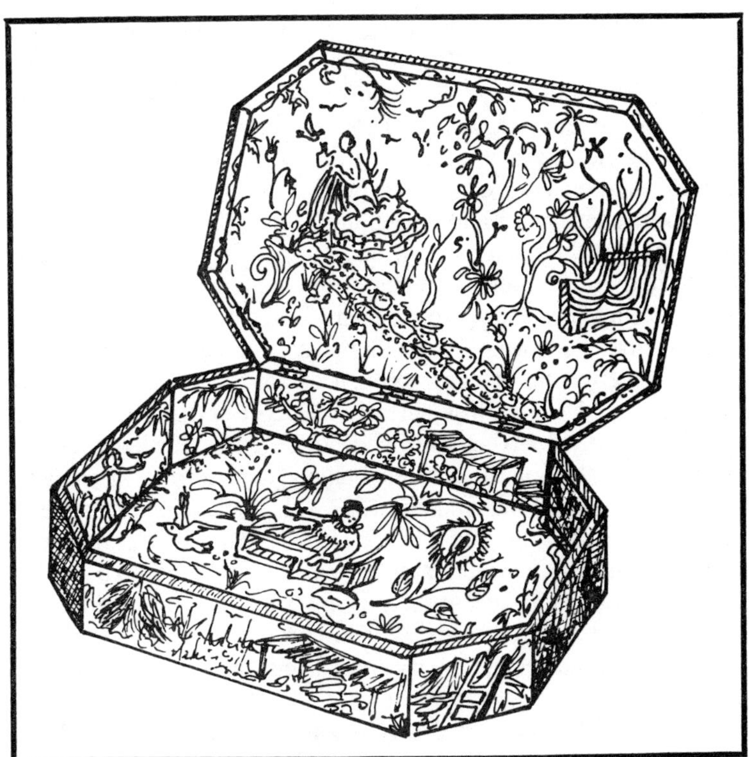

Fig. 12-35. A neatly lined box.

1-inch and that of the lid is ½-inch. Long strips of cardboard would be cut in each of these widths. With a pencil, the sides of the box were square: the sides would be numbered 1, 2, 3, and 4 in the box bottom, and 5, 6, 7, and 8 in the box top (lid). The 1-inch strip of cardboard would be measured off into sections by placing it along the inside edge of the box above the side numbered "1," and marking it with a pencil at the inside corners. Using the straightedge to insure a 90-degree angle cut, the artist would then cut off a section of the cardboard with the straight scissors and number it "1." In like manner, he would number all sides from 1 through 8.

The numbered sides of the cardboard will be the sides finally glued to the wooden box itself; the other side will be glued to the fabric. Now the artist has eight strips of cardboard, all measured and cut, and he is ready to applique the fabric. Before doing so, he brushes protective sealer on the unmarked sides of the cardboard, and allows it to dry. Then he spreads his fabric facedown on the table, being sure it is smooth and uncreased, (the creases may be pressed or steamed out with an iron if it is not) and places the ten cardboards on the fabric. The patterns must be so placed that the 1-inch widths (depths) of the side pieces are on the lengthwise threads of the fabric. The lid and bottom liner patterns must be so placed that the lengthwise thread of the fabric crosses them either exactly horizontally or exactly vertically.

With a sharp pencil and a ruler, the artist outlines each of the ten pieces an cuts them out with the straight-bladed shears, allowing a ¼-inch margin all around. He marks the number of the cardboard pattern from which it was cut on each of the pieces of fabric. Using applique cloth glue, he now applies a thin coat to the entire unmarked (sealer-coated) side of each cardboard, applying enough glue to produce a tacky, but not wet, surface. This type of glue dries rapidly, so he works rapidly. When the glued cardboard is sufficiently tacky, he presses the back of the correspondingly numbered fabric piece to the glued cardboard and smooths it flat with his fingertips to effect a strong bond. When the glue is dry, he trims the lid and bottom liners flush with the cardboard all around. On the eight side pieces, he leaves a margin of ¼-inch at the top and trims only the bottom and edges flush with the cardboard. The ¼-inch margin at the top will be folded over to the back of the cardboard and glued down to give the lining a finished look at the box edge.

Now he fits all the pieces back into the box, and trims each piece with the straight scissors to make them fit exactly. He cuts through fabric and cardboard, trimming the side liner pieces along the bottom edges until the pieces are absolutely flush with the top edge of the box or lid. If they stick up, they will prevent the box from closing. The ends of the side liner pieces may also have to be trimmed ever so slightly to fit perfectly at the corners—without buckling or (worse yet) without gaping.

When all pieces finally fit flawlessly, the lining pieces are removed and applique glue is applied generously to the wooden bottom of the box. The glue is spread almost—but not quite—to the edges, leaving a slight margin so that it will not exude around the edges of the fabric lining when it is installed. The cloth-covered bottom lining piece is placed in the box first and pressed gently and firmly into the glue with the balls of the fingers. Care is exercised to keep from touching the fabric with the fingernails for fear of scoring it. Next, each side liner piece is glued into place, one at a time, matching each numbered lining piece to the corresponding number pencilled on the box side. If more glue is needed, it may be inserted with a toothpick under the lining piece. Care must be taken not to drip any glue on the fabric front, because it cannot be removed.

Note: The lining must never be applied until the box is completely finished—decoupaged, varnished, sanded and waxed. The same procedure is used for lining the shadow box lid as for lining the box bottom, except that the lid is lined *first*.

APPLYING GOLD AND SILVER LEAF

Another pasted-on surface covering quite prevalently used is that of gold leaf and silver leaf. This type of finishing is used to cover entire pieces, as well as for accent on pieces which have been painted or stained. Like decoupage, this form of furniture surfacing and decoration has a rich traditional history. Ancient civilizations produced ornaments and artifacts finished in this manner, using gold leaf in their architecture to gild domes, pillars, ceilings, etc. The eighteenth century saw this opulent surfacing used lavishly. Louis XIV commissioned splendid silver furniture for his palaces, starting a vogue much imitated in England in both gold and silver (gold being a substitute). One of the most magnificent surviving silver suites of furniture was made in Augsburg for the court of Hanover in 1720.

There are two basic methods used in leafing a surface—oil gilding and water gilding. We shall discuss them both, beginning with oil gilding, which is a simpler but not quite so smooth finish as water gilding. It is very beautiful in its own way.

For either oil or water gilding, the thin sheets of beaten gold are purchased in 4-inch squares, a handy size with which to work. Dutch Metal, which is a synthetic gold leaf, is available in the same size sheets. Real gold leaf comes in many grades, colors and prices—depending on the quality of the gold used. The individual 4-inch × 4-inch sheets are sold in packets of 25 sheets. The packets are of two types: (1) looseleaf and (2) with attached paper backing for

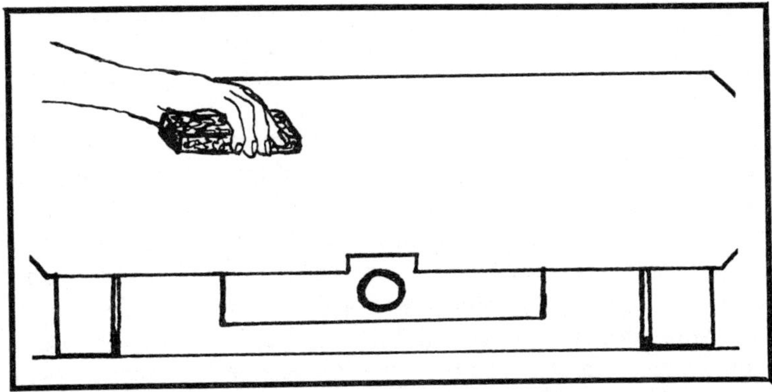

Fig. 12-36. Before applying gold or silver leaf, the surface must be satin-smooth.

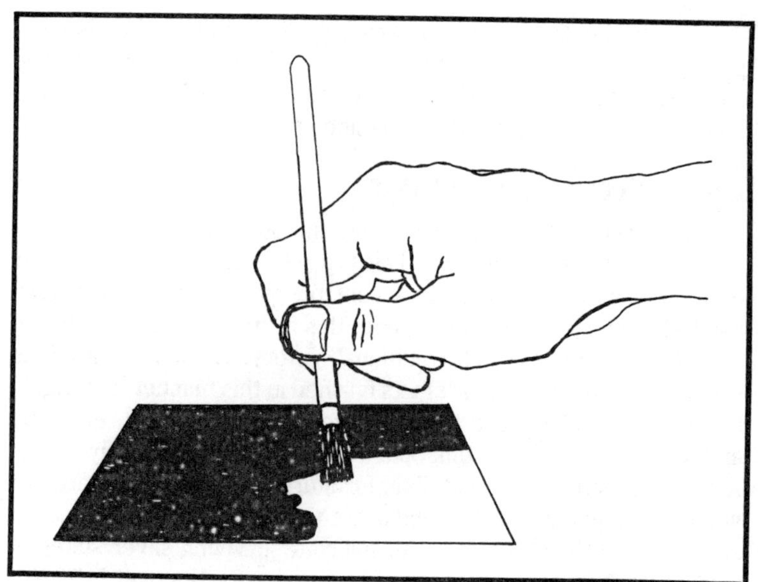

Fig. 12-37. Red oil-based paint is traditionally used under gold leaf.

"gilding in the wind," as projects such as gilding domes or letters on signs are termed. The looseleaf style is best for decoupage. Gold leaf is available in a number of colors: pale, yellow, rich, lemon and white. Rich gold is the color used most prevalently.

For leafing, as for decoupage, the surface covered must be satin-smooth. Therefore, the first step is the proper preparation of the work surface (see Fig. 12-36). All holes and dents must be filled with gesso or sprackle paste and allowed to dry. Sprackle paste, prepared as the directions on the package indicate, is rubbed well into an already finished piece to fill any dents, gouges, scratches of chips and to fill every depression. It is applied wet and, when dry, is sanded to satin-smoothness, using fine and extra-fine sandpapers and finishing the buffing with steel wool in preparation for a coat of sealer.

New wood and stripped wood, however, are best smoothed with gesso. This mixture of bolted whiting, rabbitskin glue and cold water may be purchased already mixed at most art stores. Care must be taken, however, to use only those gesso preparations which do not contain plastic. The gesso and plastic mix is ideal for sizing canvases, but resists sanding as would armour plating.

Gesso hides the seams, grain, knots and pores in nude wood as nothing else can. To open the pores of the wood to receive gesso, paint the wood with a solution of 50 percent clear ammonia (not the sudsy kind) and 50 percent denatured alcohol. Allow this coat to dry and then paint the wood with gesso as though you were icing a cake—flowing it on and avoiding drips and brush marks as much as possible. Allow each coat to dry before applying the next one. Four to five hours should be sufficient drying time. When the third coat is thoroughly dry, sand with No. 280 wet-or-dry sandpaper, and polish with No. 0000 steel wool until the wood feels like polished alabaster.

In preparation for the gold leaf, a coat of sealer is applied. If sprackle paste was used to fill and smooth the wood, a coat of acrylic will fill all the pores and prepare the surface for an undercoat of paint. Shellac should not be used. The waxes in shellac do not bond with oils. If gesso was used, the acrylic sealer must be thinned half-and-half with denatured alcohol and two coats applied. When the final coat dries, the gesso will be smooth and shining all over. Red oil-based paint is traditionally used under gold leaf because it adds warmth and glow to the leaf applied over it. Use a flat enamel and give the surface one coat (see Fig. 12-37). Allow it to dry and apply another coat of the sealer. When the sealer is dry, the surface is covered with a special gold leaf adherent called Japan gold size. This adhesive is applied evenly over the entire work surface, using a flat brush power. When the size is dry enough that the knuckles of a hand placed lightly on the surface do not stick, but only pull slightly and

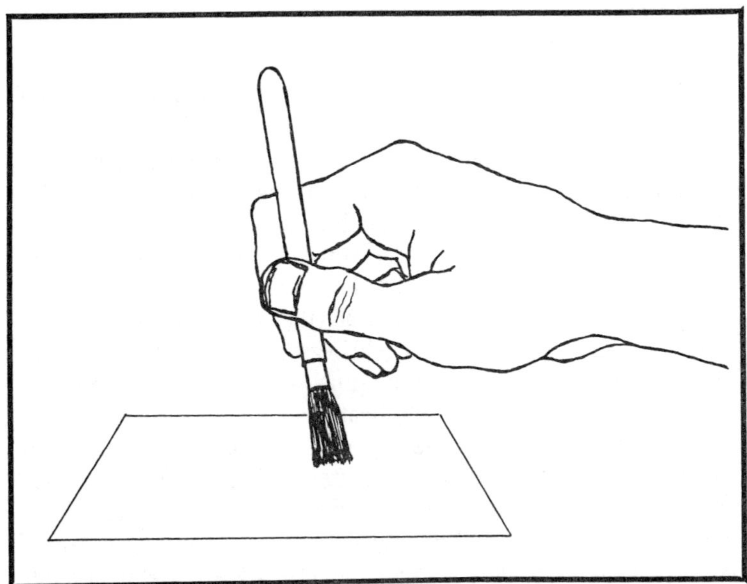

Fig. 12-38. The gold or silver leaf is held in place by a special adhesive called Japan gold size.

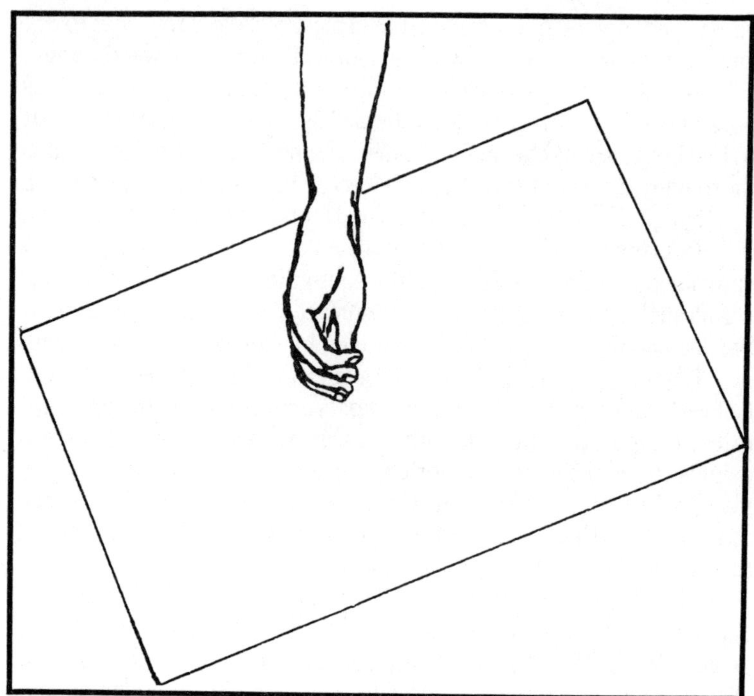

Fig. 12-39. Make sure the adhesive is ready for the leaf application. The knuckles of the hand are placed lightly on the surface and should come away with a soft snap.

come free with a soft snap, the size is exactly right to receive the leaf (see Fig. 12-39).

Gold or silver leaf is very fragile. The thin sheets look like foil, but are much thinner, and infinite care must be taken not to touch the gold leaf with the fingers or expose it to drafts because it will blow away at either contact like milkweed down. The leaf is made of gold or silver beaten to the desired thickness. Artisans who make leaf are called gold beaters, and the skin in which they put the gold to pound it into tissue-thin sheets is called a gold beater's skin. The skin used is the outer coat of the caecum (intestinal pouch) of an ox, specially prepared for the use of the gold beater.

Each sheet of gold leaf is approximately 4-inches square. In applying the leaf, these squares are lifted with the protective paper which is used to separate them in the packet or by sliding a similarly sized piece of cardboard beneath each square, leaving a 1-inch margin hanging free from the edge (see Fig. 12-40). The overhanging margin is placed carefully in position on the size and the paper, or the cardboard, is slowly withdrawn, lowering the entire square to

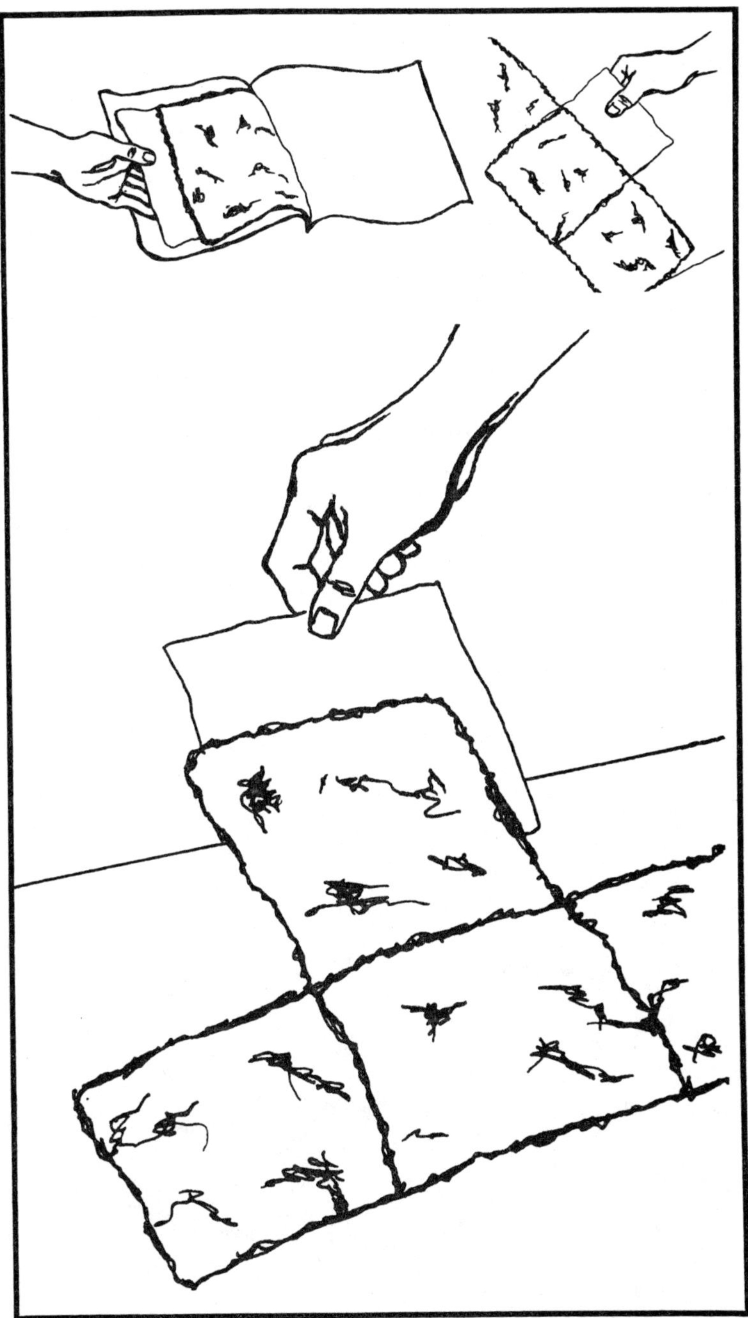

Fig. 12-40. Maneuvering gold or silver leaf into position with the aid of cardboard squares.

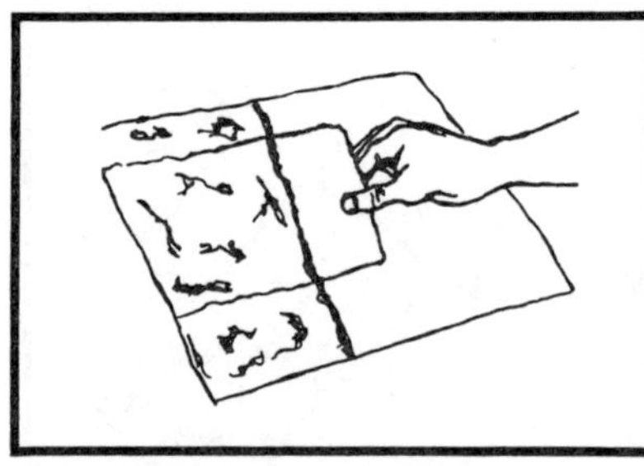

Fig. 12-41. Lowering a square into position.

the sized surface (see Fig. 12-41). To assist in laying the leaf, a clean, dry, flat brush similar to that used to apply the Japan size or a gilder's tip is very helpful when used in the following way; the brush is flicked back and forth through the artist's hair at the nape of his neck to generate static electricity. When held over the gold leaf, it will attract the leaf like a magnet. Twisting the brush gently will free a small piece of the foil from the sheet and this piece can be shaken gently off the brush and floated onto the sized surface, the brush may be pulled gently away after smoothing the piece with thistledown lightness by touching it briefly with the bristles of the brush.

Fig. 12-42. The pieces of leaf overlap one another slightly.

Fig. 12-43. With a cheesecloth pad, the gold leaf is pressed firmly into the glue. Work from the center of each square outward to the edges in all directions.

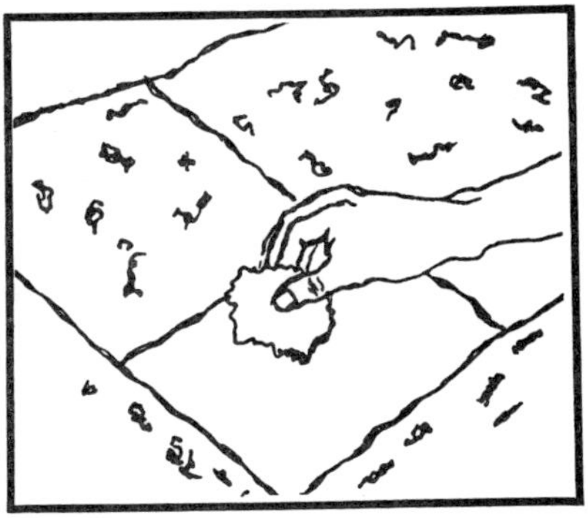

When the entire surface is covered with leaf, using either brush and/or cardboard (the pieces of leaf being so placed that they overlap one another slightly), the surface is allowed to dry thoroughly (see Fig. 12-42). It will not be smooth; the gold leaf will be standing up like scales on a fish. After it is dry, a cheesecloth pad is used to smooth it (see Fig. 12-43). Working from the center of each square outward to the edges in all directions, the artist now presses the leaf firmly and smoothly into the glue. When each sheet has been pressed down in this manner, the entire surface is burnished to ultimate smoothness with a pad of cheesecloth (see Fig. 12-44).

Some professionals recommend a swatch of pure silk velvet instead of cotton for smoothing and burnishing. Rayon or cotton velvet will scratch, so delicate is the surface. In any case, the burnishing must be done very gently, much as one would touch a baby's face, with absolutely no scrubbing action. Small spots needing retouching maybe dabbed with Japan size on a small, pointed brush, allowed to get tacky, and patched with a bit of gold leaf. These patches should be allowed to dry before smoothing.

To prevent discoloration of the metal, the surface must be covered with a protective coat. Good grade varnish of any type or

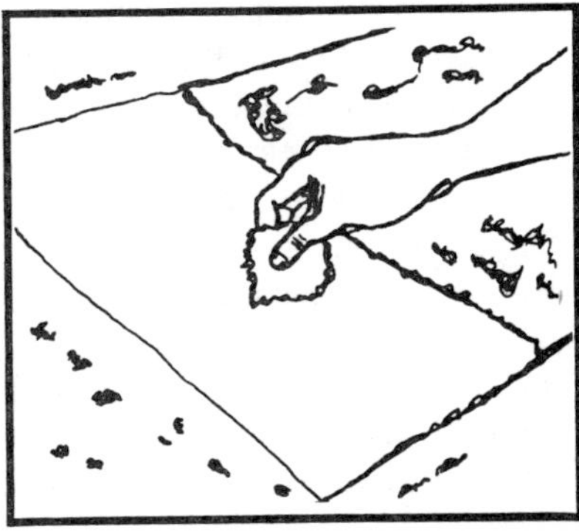

Fig. 12-44. After each sheet has been pressed down, the entire surface is burnished to ultimate smoothness with a pad of cheesecloth.

special gold leaf sealer is ideal for this purpose (see Fig. 12-45). Do not use acrylic over gold leaf because it may turn the leaf black. Lacquers may lift the leaf and shellac may turn orange and streak. Over the coat of special gold leaf sealer, use a coat of good synethic varnish and a soft brush that won't lose its hairs. Try to keep the coat even. If you do not wish to antique or marbleize the gold leaf, or to apply decoupage, the surface is now finished.

The oil-gilding method described above is one of two methods for applying gold leaf. The other, as we mentioned earlier, is water-gilding.

Water-Gilding Gold and Silver Leaf

This method of gold leafing must be applied over gesso and over a gesso surface which has *not* had an application of sealer, but which has been sanded and steel wooled until it is smooth as face powder. Acrylic sealer is applied *under* oil gilding but never *over*. However, the same acrylic sealer *is* applied over water-gilding, but never under. An excellent protective sealer for both purposes is available by mail order from Manning Studios in Boston.

To commence water-gilding, two heat-proof ovenware bowls are assembled and a candle warmer or Salton hot tray is heated. A mixture of rabbitskin glue (obtainable at the paint store) and water are muddled together with an orange stick or pencil stub in one of the heat-proof dishes (an individual baking ramekin is excellent for this purpose). The proportions of the mixture are these; a scant quarter-teaspoon of rabbit glue to three-quarters of an ounce of hot water. The water level should be carefully noted and more water added when that which is in the rameskin steams away. When the glue is dissolved and the water steaming over the warmer, a tablespoon of Hasting's red burnishing clay is placed in the other rameskin and enough of the hot glue and water mixture added to produce the consisitency of heavy cream. By stirring and adding the hot water and glue mixture to the burnishing clay as the work proceeds, the artist can maintain this consistency.

The gesso surface is painted with this mixture, which is red and which will not go on smoothly as the oil-based paint does in the oil-gilding method. In fact, this first coat is sure to look patchy and to let the white gesso show through. Nevertheless, the hot mixture is flowed on as smoothly as possible, avoiding brush marks and drips, and is allowed to dry a few hours before the second coat is applied. Now the surface should be red all over, with no white showing, and should be allowed to dry thoroughly before proceeding.

Fig. 12-45. To prevent discoloration, the surface is covered with a protective coat of high grade varnish or special gold leaf sealer.

Water-gilding is just what the name implies—applying gold leaf with water, as the next step demonstrates. Have the necessary tools and materials at hand (Fig. 12-46). First, to the hot mixture of rabbitskin glue and water, sufficient alcohol is added to make the mixture swirl around in the rameskin and turn cloudy. The mixture is then applied to the dried work surface—not by brushing it on, which would wet the water-soluble clay too much, but by tamping the surface with a wet brush. When the surface is partially dry, it is wetted again with the mixture. Using a dry, flat brush, the artist "floats" a piece of gold on the thoroughly wet surface. The alcohol grabs the piece, and floats it flat to the wet surface. Quickly, the artist offers another piece of gold leaf on the dry brush, allowing it to slightly overlap the first piece. He never touches the gold leaf, never

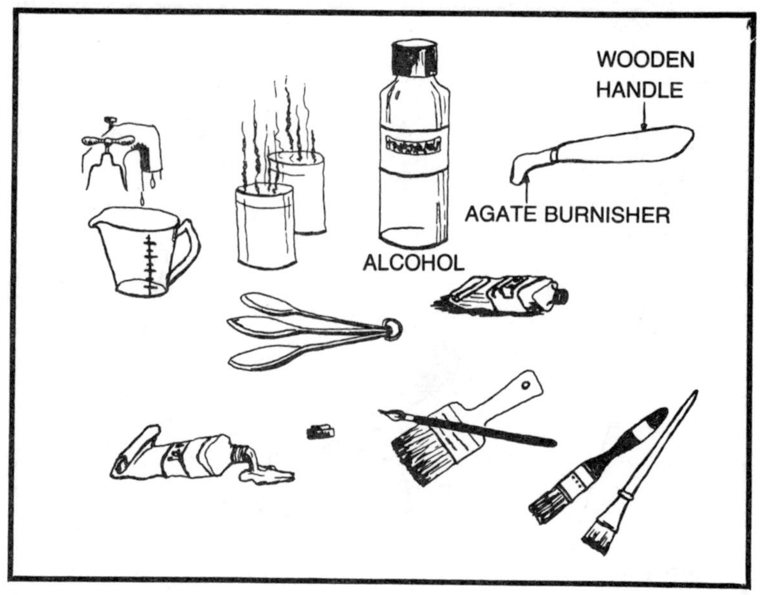

Fig. 12-46. Tools and materials used in water-gilding.

brushes it. He keeps applying the leaf to the surface close at hand, keeping all areas not yet leafed thoroughly wet. He takes great care not to allow the glue, alcohol and water mixture to flood back on the previously applied gold leaf. The mixture would permanently spot the gold leaf, and render it impossible to burnish. The gold leaf should be laid only on a thoroughly wet surface. If the wet surface refuses to grab the gold leaf, the mixture cloud and swirl again.

When gold leaf has been applied to the entire surface, it must be allowed to dry overnight. However, if the artist stops in the middle of a surface, the stop and go marks will be all too visible. So, each surface must be finished in a single work period.

When dry, the leaf will look ragged, the many overlaps loose as a lot of hangnails. But the agate burnisher rectifies all that. The artist—still without touching the gold leaf with his hand—employs the agate burnisher to smooth the surface. He exerts only light to medium pressure on the burnisher, and he strokes it back and forth, never round and round. Working on one small section at a time, he makes certain to cover every particle of the surface. The dull, patchy-looking surface with its many loose ends (the overlaps) will begin to look smooth and shining as a gypsy's earring. If the artist does his job thoroughly, but cautiously, not a single dull spot will remain, and the effect will be as rich-looking as the jeweler's finish on a gold wedding ring.

However, if he exerts too much pressure, or uses circular strokes on the leaf, it will blister and bits of gold and red burnishing clay will snap off the gesso ground, leaving the artist no alternative but to repeat the red clay, hot water and alcohol applications again.

The burnished gold surface is brushed with a thin coat of protective sealer, and it is ready to decoupage or varnish.

ANTIQUING GOLD AND SILVER LEAF

Gold and silver leaf may be antiqued to impart a patina of age to the gleaming surfaces. The artist's colors available for this antiquing are of two types—water-based casein colors and oil-based colors. Either is applied over the final coat of varnish given the gold leaf, so that the antiquing will not harm the gold leaf itself.

If water-based casein paint is the type chosen, the artist simply chooses the color he desires, squeezes a small amount of it out of a tube into a small bowl and carefully mixes it with water until a thin consistency is achieved (one inch of paint to ¼ cup of water, approximately).

If the oil-based artist's paint is the type chosen, about ½ to 1-inch of the color is squeezed from the tube and mixed with ¼ teaspoon of boiled linseed oil until blended; then this is thinned with turpentine (about ¼ cup) until the color is dissolved and thoroughly mixed. If the color is too deep, when tested on a piece of scrap, more thinner and linseed oil are added in proportion. If the tone is too light, a dab of color is added from the tube (see Fig. 12-47).

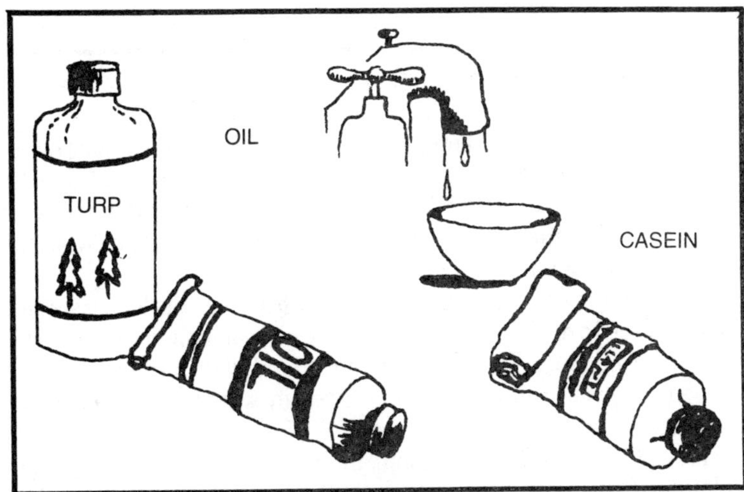

Fig. 12-47. Two types of paint which may be used in antiquing gold leaf: artist's oil paint thinned with turpentine or artist's casein paint thinned with water.

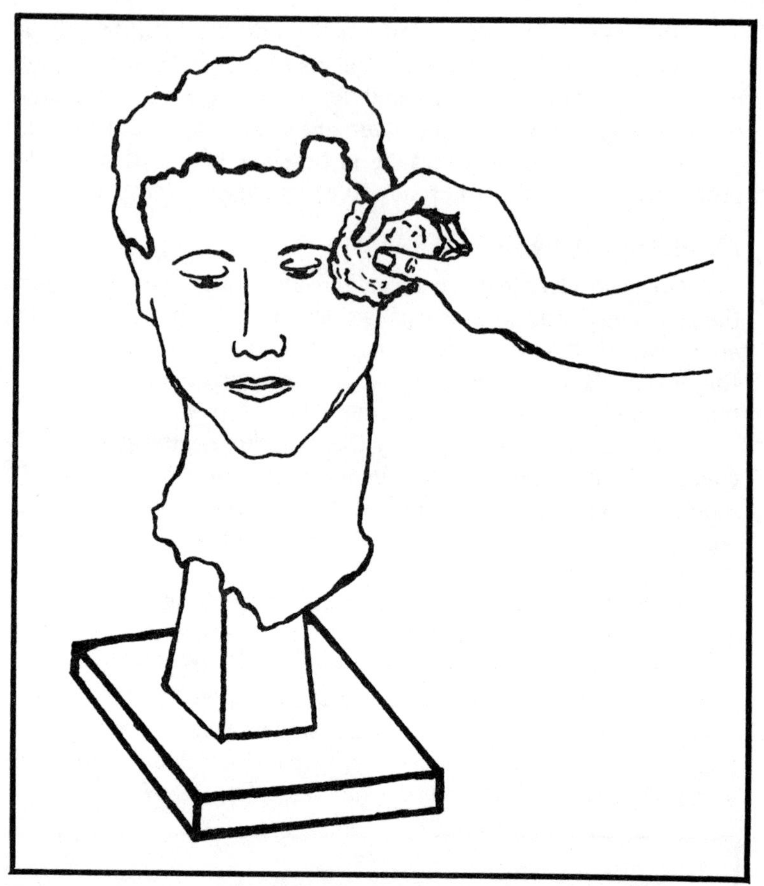

Fig. 12-48. The surface is lightly polished to a soft luster before applying varnish.

The colors used in antiquing leaf are a matter of personal taste. Ochres, siennas, burnt umbers, grays and off-whites are popular with gold leaf; blues, lavenders, greens and pinks are attractive with silver leaf. But the choice is not confined to these. Any color in the artist's paint box may be employed.

Next, the color mixture is brushed on all over the leafed surface and allowed to dry. Then, using cheesecloth dampened with water (if water-based color was used) or moistened with turpentine (if oil-based color was used), the paint is carefully wiped off, leaving it only on edges, in cracks and in the crevices of carvings. When the effect achieved is to the artist's liking, the piece is allowed to dry completely. Then, using a dry, clean cloth, the surface is gently, lightly polished to a soft luster as a prelude to applying varnish (see Fig. 12-48).

MARBLEIZING GOLD AND SILVER LEAF

Contemporary decoration has introduced a new finish for metal leaf—one which in former times was the natural result of age. We refer to the marbleized finish which is currently popular on furniture, screens, statuary, and room accessories. Here again, as in the antiquing process just described, oil colors in tubes, like those found in an artist's paint box, are used. For antiquing gold leaf, shades of blue, green, red, yellow and orange are usually chosen; for silver leaf, cool pastel shades such as lime green, pink, lavender, grey, pale blue and white provide beautiful contrast. The best marble effects are created by employing three complimentary colors—one dark, one medium dark and one pale. For discussion purposes, we

Fig. 12-49. Mixing the oil paints for marbleizing: three complementary colors are chosen from the artist's palette and are each mixed separately with turpentine to a runny consistency.

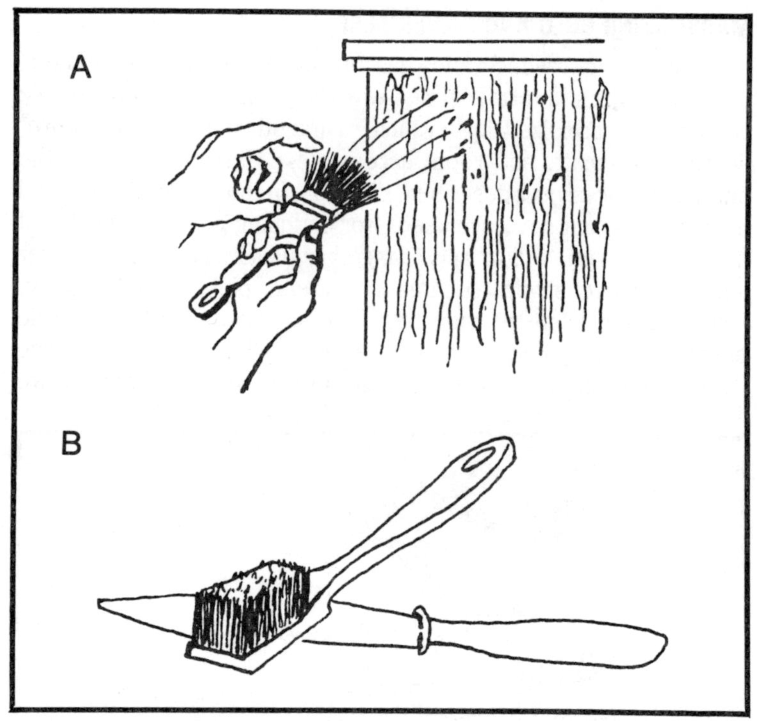

Fig. 12-50. Splattering on the colors may be done in two ways: a) by loading a broad paint brush with paint and flicking the bristles with a finger, or b) by filling an old toothbrush with color and scraping the bristles with an old dinner knife.

will assume that we are applying Yellow Ochre, Burnt Sienna and Burnt Umber to gold leaf.

Marbleizing is done only after the last coat of varnish or antique top coat has dried on the applied gold leaf. To marbleize this finished surface, the artist squeezes a small amount of each of the three desired colors from their tubes into three small bowls and thins each to runny consistency with turpentine (Fig. 12-49). Dipping a brush in the darkest color, he splatters the gold-leafed surface at random. Allowing a few minutes for this to dry, he then applies the medium tone color over the first color—again in a random, haphazard pattern, allowing the two shades to run together or to form overlapping blots. Then he applies the lightest tone color for accent in the same manner as he applied the other two (Fig. 12-50).

Finally, he fills his brush with clear turpentine and flicks it over the paint to cause the colors to blend and run together, producing a mottled, veined effect similar to that observed in genuine marble. What the artist has done is apply splashes of thin color over the top of color which has partially dried and is, therefore, thicker. The difference in viscosities makes the colors mottle and dapple. As each wet color strikes the drier colors, it slightly melts and smudges the edges, allowing a soft, misty blending of colors (Fig. 12-51).

When he has succeeded in producing the finish he desires, he allows the paint to thoroughly dry, waiting at least 24 hours before applying the clear antique top coat (sealer) and varnish which will impart to the finished gold leaf surface a lustrous, permanent color accent.

WOOD APPLIQUES

Another time-honored means of enhancing furniture by applique is that of gluing on carved wooden motifs and moldings as decoration. Adornments of this sort were used by many distinguished cabinetmakers in the past—notably the Adams brothers, eighteenth century Scottish architects whose insistance of a chaste, formal classicism in every aspect of the Palladium-style homes they created led to their designing the furniture contained in those elegant dwellings, as well as the dwellings themselves. They favored furniture design whose ornamentation repeated the motifs employed in the architectural detailing. Each piece of furniture was created for a specific position in the overall decor where it could best display its affinity of design with that of the room it appointed.

For example, the urns and garlands inlaid or painted on the doors of a cabinet would be repeated exactly in the cornices over the doorways between which the cabinet stood and in the ceiling molding above it. This meticulous repetitive detail often necessitated the

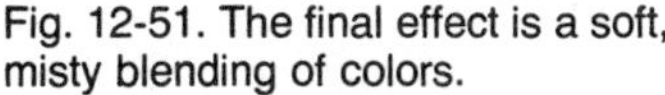
Fig. 12-51. The final effect is a soft, misty blending of colors.

Fig. 12-52. Examples of Compo molding—when applied to a picture frame and painted, the result is a hand-carved effect.

carving of a predominantly featured motif in the same wood as that used in the house structure. This wood carving would then be appliqued in a strategic place on the furniture item, so that the beholder's eye might notice and appreciate the artistic unity thus achieved.

Today, decorative carvings and moldings add the richness of carved sculpture to chests, cabinets, chair backs, picture frames, mirrors, doors, ceiling and walls. A variety of motifs to suit any decorating need are stocked by frame shops, hobby shops and building supply stores. They are available in both wood and plastic; the wood, of course, is infinitely preferable.

Wood moldings and bas-relief appliques of all sorts—finials, medallions, escutcheons, fretwork, filigree, decorative corner pieces and handles—can be obtained in the same wood as the piece they are to decorate, or in a constrasting wood. Dimensional decorations made from other materials are also available. Manufactured moldings made of polyester resins are available in six-foot lengths. Decorative corners, filagree and medallions are available in molded styrene. Compo is another plastic substance which has long been on the market and which affords the home decorator a wide variety of moldings. Compo becomes pliable when it is exposed to heat. When pieces of it are applied to a picture frame and the surface painted, the result is a handcarved effect (see Fig. 12-52).

These wooden or plastic appliques may be stained, painted or gold leafed to match or contrast with the surface they are to decorate. However, the base coats of the finish desired—stain, paint of metal leaf—should be applied to both the applique and the object it will decorate before the applique is glued into place. Once the glue is dry, the final varnish or glaze coats may then be added to the already assmbled piece (see Fig. 12-53).

A wealth of interest and elegance can be given the plainest piece of furniture with bas-relief carvings and moldings. Stark, unfinished furniture can thus acquire the detailing of a period piece to fit more gracefully into the decor in which it will be displayed (see Fig. 12-54).

APPLYING PLASTIC LAMINATES

Occasionally, a table is reclaimed from an attic or junkyard which has attributes meriting its salvation, but whose top is so

Fig. 12-53. A plain box is given greater ornamental interest with appliqued wood carvings.

scratched and gouged that enormous effort would be required to refinish it. In such instances, laminating a woodgrained plastic to the damaged top may be the most practical course. Although such surfaces can never compare in beauty to the surfaces of wood, they are astonishingly realistic as a coloration and graining. Moreover, they are highly utilitarian—usually guaranteed not to mar, scratch or stain and to require minimum upkeep. They can be purchased at lumberyards and building supply stores in a wide variety of wood patterns and in high gloss or satin finishes. Satin finishes are preferable for furniture.

Manufacturers of such laminates advise that the old finish be removed before the laminate is applied to assure that the contact cement used to bond the laminate to the surface will hold securely. A belt-sander will remove the old finish with speed and ease. Such a tool may be rented from the lumberyard or the hardware store for the purpose.

When the old finish is stripped off, any gouges are filled with plastic wood and sanded until smooth.

Before cutting the laminate, a pattern must be made of the table top. An actual outline may be made on brown paper. However, the simplest method of making a pattern is to outline the table itself directly on the laminate. Lay the laminate out flat, invert the table, and place it face down on the plastic. Whether the outline is made on the face of the laminate or on the back depends on the type of saw which will be used to trim the outline. If a crosscut saw will be used, the top is outlined on the *face* of the laminate to avoid the laminate's chipping when the fine-toothed crosscut saw incises it. However, if a saber saw is the tool selected, the outline of the table top must be drawn on the *underside* of the laminate and the sawing done from the back. The best blade for sawing plastic laminate is that used in a saber saw for metal cutting. This blade has 32 fine teeth to the inch and is capable of cutting the laminate cleanly and quickly.

A special snips designed to cut laminate may be rented at the lumberyard, if you prefer. However, regardless of the tool used, the material must be cut 1/16-inch larger all around than the pattern indicates.

Next, a liberal coat of cement is applied to both the surface of the table and the surface of the laminate, using a brush or a special toothed applicator. The cement must be allowed to dry for some time before bonding the laminate to the surface. Depending on the type of adhesive used, this drying period can be as long as 45 minutes. The degree of dryness must be tested by pressing a scrap of wrapping paper against the cemented surface. If traces of cement adhere to the paper, more drying time is necessary.

When the cement is sufficiently dry, one edge of the plastic is aligned with the table edge and the plastic is brought down into

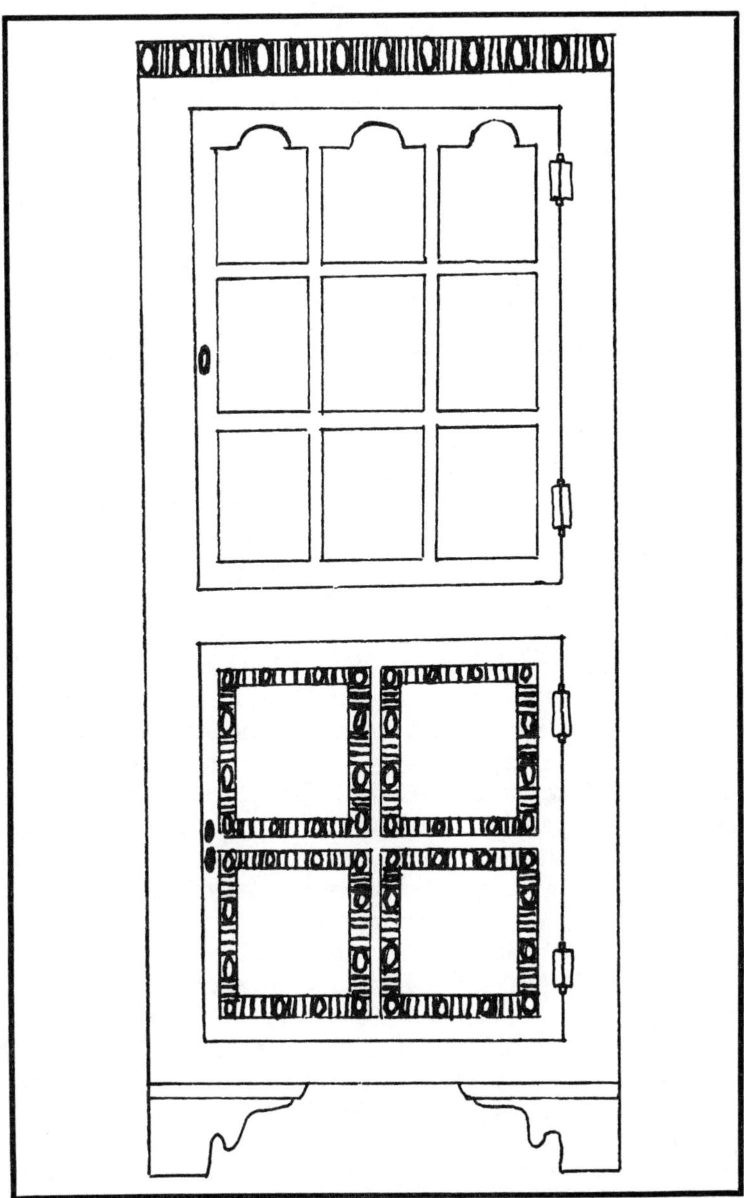

Fig. 12-54. A plain bookcase achieves a more elegant look with applied molding.

position on the surface. Great caution must be taken with this step because the contact cement has a very tenacious grip which makes repositioning the laminate impossible once it is down. The workman is advised to proceed slowly because the positioning must be right the first time.

Once the laminate is in position, the entire surface is gone over with a roller, working from the center to the edges to press the cemented surfaces together more firmly and to make sure that they establish contact at every point. If no roller is available (of the sort recommended for decoupage) a rubber mallet or a hammer with a small block of wood to pad the surface will perform the same task to satisfaction.

Finally, the edges of the laminate must be trimmed to exactly coincide with the table edge. A flat file does a smooth job. So does a block plane, except that the blade dulls quickly. If a very large surface must be trimmed, it may be covered with a matching strip of laminate or a decorative strip of ornamental molding.

APPLYING CERAMIC MOSAIC TILE

This form of applied surfacing can give a table top, antique wash stand or server a completely different appearance and is a very practical renovation where the original wood surface is so badly damaged or of such indifferent or unnattractive grain that refinishing with stain would be a labor lost.

The surface to which ceramic tile is applied should be clean and level. Paint should be removed, preferably with a power sander, so that the tile adhesive can bond properly to the bare wood.

A graph-paper pattern makes an excellent guide to laying tile, particularly if more than one color of tile is being used or if ornamental tiles are being interspersed with plain tiles. Each of the squares on the graph paper can represent one tile and can be filled in with colored pencil in the color patterning contemplated for the table top. Next, following the graph paper pattern, the actual tile should be positioned on the surface. This procedure will indicate which tiles must be cut to fit. An ordinary glass cutter may be used to score the faces of the tile at the cutting line and two pairs of pliers-each pair holding one side of the tile—can snap the tile at the score line. To make the job easier, a plier-like tool known as a "tile-nipper" may be purchased or rented at any tile supply house.

Free-form tile can usually be so arranged that cutting can be avoided. However, these tile should be experimentally positioned on the table top before being cemented down and the graph paper pattern modified, if need be, to insure that no trimming will be necessary.

Cut tile edges are extremely rough and must be smoothed on an oilstone. So very hard and brittle are their edges, however, that they may groove a grinding wheel or expensive oilstone and render it useless for sharpening. Therefore, to buy an inexpensive oilstone just for this task is wiser from the sandpoint of economy.

A notched trowel is used to apply the ceramic tile adhesive to the table top. The adhesive may be spread in any direction, so long as the entire surface is coated. However, if the table top is very large, only one section at a time should be spread with adhesive and immediately tiled so that the adhesive doesn't set too firmly before the tile is applied.

The teeth of the trowel can act as a guide as to the thickness of the adhesive coating. If the trowel teeth are kept in contact with the surface throughout each stroke, the trowel itself will serve as a gauge as to the thickness of the adhesive application.

Ceramic tile adhesives are highly flammable. Even the vapors are dangerous. Therefore, they should be used only in a well-ventilated room in which all electric fans, motors, heaters, pilot lights, etc., have been turned off; all cigarettes extinguished; and all windows opened. The can containing the adhesive should be kept tightly closed, except when the adhesive is actually being applied.

Each tile is individually set into the adhesive and pressed firmly to form a strong bond. Excess adhesive is immediately removed by scraping with a single-edge razor blade. When the table top is entirely covered with tile, a period of four to 24 hours (depending on the type of adhesive used) must elapse to allow the adhesive to dry thoroughly.

The final step in tiling is the application of grouting, which fills the joints between the tiles. Grouting comes in powder form and must be mixed with water to a creamy consistency. Normally grouting is white, but it may be colored if desired by thoroughly mixing the powdered grout with powdered grout color before the water is added. The proportions of powdered grout and water are indicated in the grout manufacturer's instructions.

A trowel or squeegee is used to apply the grouting, which is spread evenly over the entire surface. The grouting is then worked into the joints between the tiles with a sponge. The grouting must be almost (but not completely) dry before the excess is wiped from the faces of the tile with a clean, damp sponge. This clean-up must be performed very thoroughly, indeed; hardened grout cannot be removed. When the surface is completely dry, buff with wax to a high luster.

TOOLS AND MATERIALS GUIDE LIST

To summarize the tools and materials used in applying surface appliques to wood, the following checklist has been compiled. Since the use of these items has already been described in detail where they pertain, this listing will merely serve to assist the reader contemplating such projects in assembling the necessary implements and materials before beginning.

Distressing Wood

- Garden soil
- Burnt umber oil paint (available at art supply stores)
- Ring of keys
- Homemade mace with projecting nails
- Ball peen hammer
- Length of link chain

Decoupage

Materials and Tools for Coloring and Positioning Prints

- Colored oil pencils (Prismacolor, Derwent or Colorama)
- Soft gum eraser
- Pencil sharpener
- Smooth cardboard or pad to work on
- Prints, engravings, magazine cutouts, newspaper cutouts selected for the project at hand
- Varnished testing glass, 4-inches × 6-inches.
- Tracing paper
- Flat brush, half-inch width.
- Clear plastic sealer

Materials and Tools for Cutting Out Prints

- German steel cuticle scissors or surgery scissors (available at drug stores and at surgery supply houses)
- Straight-blade scissors—the 6-inch size
- Drafting tape
- Oil pencil of brilliant hue to act as marker

Materials for Decoupage Paste-Up

- Bowl of water
- Household sponge
- Pad of sheesecloth
- Water-soluble paste (Sobo or Elmer's Glue-All
- Straight pin

- Single-edged razor blade
- Small porcelain roller
- Toothpicks
- Glue (not water soluble or removable—for affixing woven gold braids or fabrics, if any)

Materials and Tools for Varnishing Prints

- Mache varnish (obtainable by mail order from Manning Studios in Boston, Mass.)
- Soft brushes (½-inch size made of squirrel, sable or badger)
- Flat brush for most pieces
- Brush for large pieces, 2-inches.
- Flat-topped jars or cans to support print during drying period
- Newspaper to protect worktable and floor from drips and splatters
- X-acto knife for slicing off drips, if any form

Materials and Tools for Varnishing Boxes

- Screwdriver to remove hardware
- Mache varnish
- Flat brush, half-inch width.
- Strike-wire can
- Flat-topped cans to support box and lid while drying
- X-acto knife to slice off varnish drips, if any form
- Newspaper to protect worktable and floor from drips

Materials for Sanding Decoupage

- Wet-or-dry sandpaper in three grades: No. 200 A (coarsest) for first sanding, No. 400 for second sanding and No. 600 for polishing (Black Tri-M-Ite or Minnesota Mining abrasive papers recommended)
- Steel wool No. 0000 for buffing
- Bowl of water for wetting sandpaper
- Paper napkins and tissues for wiping up sanded surface
- Household sponge for washing off surface

Materials for Applying the Final Finish to Decoupage

Finish No. 1:

- No. 0000 steel wool
- Cheesecloth treated with pumice and Valspar furniture oil
- Tissues for wiping surface
- Household sponge for washing surface
- Dry soft cloth (cheesecloth is best) for buffing

Finish No. 2:

- No. 0000 steel wool
- One bottle matte final finish
- Soft, flat brush; half-inch wide.
- No. 600 wet-or-dry sandpaper
- Bowl of water for wetting sandpaper
- Paper napkins or tissues

Materials for Final Waxing of Decoupage

- Good grade of paste wax
- Small 3-inch × 3-inch soft cloth for applying wax
- Bowl of cold water for wetting cloth
- Soft, dry cloth for polishing

Materials for Applying Paper Covering and Lining to a Box

- Paper cut as per instructions
- Protective sealer and brush
- Mache varnish and brush for gold or silver tea paper
- Divider and ruler for measuring
- All-purpose glue
- Cuticle scissors
- Bowl of water
- Small piece of kitchen sponge, 1½-inches square
- Paper towels
- Orange Stick

Materials for Applying Fabric Lining to Box

- Thin white cardboard (the kind used to stiffen men's shirts available at art stores)
- Cloth (velvet, brocade, etc.)
- Straight, sharp scissors
- Applique cloth glue
- Soft lead pencil for marking
- Ruler and dividers
- Bowl of water and paper towels for cleaning hands

Preparing an Old Piece of Furniture for Gold Leafing

- Sprackle Paste
- Water
- Sheets of fine and extra fine wet-or-dry sandpaper
- Water for wetting sandpaper
- Steel wool No. 0000

Preparing New Unfinished Furniture for Gold Leafing

- Dry, cold water gesso which does not require cooking (available at any art store)
- Clear ammonia (not the sudsy type)
- Denatured alcohol
- Soft, flat ½-inch brush
- Tri-M-Ite wet-or-dry sandpaper No. 200-A
- Water for wetting sandpaper
- No. 0000 steel wool

Materials for Applying Undercoats to Old and New Wood Before Gilding

- Flat enamel paint with a Japan oil base to use as undercoat to the leaf—enough for two coats (Traditionally, flat red enamel is used under rich gold leaf to give it a flow; yellow or green is used under lemon-colored gold leaf; and blue under silver leaf.)
- Protective sealer—use full strength on sprackle paste, if sprackle paste was the filler used
- Denatured alcohol—used to dilute the sealer half-and-half, if gesso was the filler used
- Tri-M-Ite wet-or-dry sandpaper No. 200-A
- No. 0000 steel wool

Materials for Oil-Gilding

- Book of gold leaf—the looseleaf kind not attached to backing paper
- Bottle of Japan gold size
- Two *flat*, soft brushes with bristle area ½-inch wide and ½-inch long
- Cardboard square about 4-inches × 4-inches
- Cotton balls
- Silk-velvet pads (optional)
- Agate burnisher (available at fine art stores)

Materials for Water-Gilding

- Hasting's red burnishing clay (available at art stores)
- Rabbitskin glue (obtainable at paint stores)
- Grain alcohol (not denatured—at drugstore with doctor's prescription, if necessary)
- Hot water
- Candle warmer or Salton hot tray
- Soft brushes (flat or round, depending on project)

- Gilder's tip (special brush for applying gold leaf, obtainable at art store)
- Two small heat-proof containers (one to hold glue and burnishing clay, one to hold glue-alcohol-water mixture)
- Orange stick or pencil stub for stirring mixtures

Materials for Antiquing Gold or Silver Leaf

Using Water-Base Casein Colors:

- Small bowl to mix color
- Tube of artist's casein paint in color chosen
- Water to thin color
- Orange stick or pencil stub to stir color
- Cheesecloth for wiping off and polishing
- Varnish

Using Oil-Based Colors

- Small bowl to mix color
- Tube of artist's oil-base paint in shade desired
- Turpentine to thin paint
- Pencil stub or orange stick to stir color
- Flat brush, half-inch width.
- Cheesecloth for wiping off and polishing
- Varnish

Materials for Marbleizing Gold Leaf and Silver Leaf

- Three small bowls in which to mix light, medium and dark colors
- Three tubes of artist's oil paints in chosen shades
- Turpentine
- Flat brush for splattering, two-inch width.
- Brush for applying sealer, half-inch width.
- Cheesecloth for wiping brushes
- Clear antique top coat for sealing (available where antiquing kits are sold, at paint stores and hobby shops)

Materials for Applying Plastic Laminates

- Satin-finish wood laminate—enough to cover table top
- Rented belt-sander to remove finish
- Plastic wood
- Sandpaper—coarse to fine
- Brown paper to cut pattern for laminate (optional)
- Sharp pencil for drawing pattern

- Crosscut or saber saw
- Rented laminate snips (optional)
- Special laminating cement
- Brush or applicator for applying cement
- Roller, rubber mallet or hammer (the latter used with wood block to buffer blows) used to smooth cemented laminate
- Flat file, block plane or rented router to trim edge of laminate
- Decorative molding to cover edge (optional)

Materials for Applying Ceramic Tile

- Rented power sander for removing paint
- Graph paper and colored pencils for making pattern
- Glass cutter and two pairs of pliers for severing tile
- Tile nipper (used instead of glass cutter and pliers) rented or purchased from tile supply store
- Inexpensive oilstone for smoothing tile edges
- Tiles—enough to cover surface
- Tile adhesive (purchasable at tile supply store)
- Notched trowel for applying adhesive
- Single-edged razor blade
- Powdered grouting
- Powdered grout color (optional)
- Water to make grouting
- Trowel or squeegee for applying grout
- Two household sponges—one for working grout into crevices, one for wiping off tile
- Water to clean sponge for repeated wiping
- Tile wax
- Dry, soft cheesecloth for applying wax

Appendix A
Special Tools for Furniture Refinishing

At one time or another, all the tools listed here are vitally needed in refinishing furniture but, there are certain specialized tools and materials which are undoubtedly more useful in refinishing than anywhere else.

For instance, such miscellany as cotton swabs, orange sticks, toothpicks and hairline brushes are tremendously important to furniture refinishing, where they are used to apply glue, sealer and stain to minute cracks; to probe carved surfaces in paint removing, etc. Candle stubs are excellent for lubricating drawer guides to make them slide easily and quietly.

Clothespins are an excellent wedge to expand a loose rung or leg. If the looseness in a chair stretcher or spindle is only minimal, string saturated with glue and wound around the loose end will insure a snug fit. Shoe polish of the proper color applied to a scratch can render it almost invisible. Iodine camouflages scratches in mahogany and walnut shells, steeped in boiling water until wood touch-ups. The list of such homeopathic cures for hurt furniture is virtually endless. In addition, there are many tools—some of them homemade—which are exactly right for certain tasks. We will name a few.

Tools for Surface Preparation

A Spirit Lamp is very useful for melting the stick shellac used to fill scratches and cracks on old furniture. Such a lamp is easily made from a small empty jam jar with a twist-on metal lid. Simply bore a hole in the center of the metal lid and solder a 2-inch piece of narrow metal piping into the hole. Thread a length of cotton wick through the tube. This spirit lamp should be fueled only with Sterno. Any other source of heat leaves soot on the shellac, which must be heated over the lamp to melting temperature.

Artist's Palette Knife. This springy spatula in a 3-inch length is ideal to catch the liquefying shellac as it melts from the stick and for applying it to the scratch or crack.

X-Acto Saw and X-Acto Knife. These sharp-bladed tools are accurate means of cutting and sizing very thin pieces of veneer.

Pop Riveter. This automatic rivet driver does a fast, easy job of overhauling metal furniture. The tool should be used with rivets of a similar metal to the metal furniture being repaired. To hold firmly, these rivets should be ⅛-inch longer than the thickness of the work. They can be applied very quickly and neatly with this tool; but, of course, nuts and bolts or self-tapping screws may be used instead, if desired.

Glue Gun. This electric tool may be loaded with a cartridge of rapid-bonding, polyethylene-base glue. A touch of the gun's nozzle to the loose piece, the application of pressure insure a durable, waterproof bond.

Ski-Waxing Cork. This item makes the best sander obtainable and is available in any sporting goods store. It is wasted at the sides to fit the hand, so that the woodworker can use it a long while without tiring. If the face of the cork is padded with felt before the sandpaper is pasted on, there is very little danger of scratching the wood surface when the sandpaper begins to wear away.

Propane Torch. A propane torch equipped with a flattened tip called a flame spreader, may be used to burn off the old finish or to produce an attractive charred finish on new wood. Either is a decidely hazardous process, and great care must be taken in execution. The chances of starting a fire are obvious. Hot embers may rain down on sawdust before bursting into flame. Before beginning such a project, all combustibles, such as paint and turpentine, should be removed from the shop and, if possible, the floor should be wet down. A bucket full of water and a connected hose should be kept handy.

To take off layers of old paint, hold the torch in one hand and a paint scraper in the other. To prevent burning the wood, keep the torch moving slowly, but continuously, following the blistered path it leaves with the paint scraper and removing the charred paint as soon as it yields to the torch.

Although this method is too drastic for use on fine furniture (being more suited to removing paint from battleships, bomb shelters and barns), it is undeniably an easy, fast way to remove old paint. If you decide that it is the best way to eliminate the finish you are trying to remove, please consider the use of an *electric* paint-removing appliance, such as the Smith-Victor Torchlamp; such a heat source does not rely on an open flame so the fire hazard is minimized, and the paint is softened for removal just as rapidly.

The propane torch, however, is the only appliance which will produce a charred finish.

Paint Scrapers. By far the safest tool to use as a paint scraper is a homemade one of maple or some other hardwood. It should be about eight inches long with a wedge-shaped blade and a comfortable, rounded handle whittled to the right size for the hand which is going to wield it and smoothed with a rasp.

If the project being worked on has carvings, turned legs and spindles or deep grooving, a paint scraper is too large and clumsy for the job. Use, instead, an old toothbrush to clean the paint from the carvings, an orange stick for removing paint from grooves, and a wad of steel to strip turned spindles and stretchers.

If the piece is a fine antique, avoid using any kind of paint scraper. Rely on burlap rags, steel wool and patient wiping to remove the paint remover. These are the only "paint scrapers" which will not leave scratches on the wood.

If you use a conventional paint scraper or a putty knife, be sure that its edge is dull, free of burrs and its corners rounded so that it can lift the softened paint without damage to the under surface.

Molding and Patching Tool. This plastering tool is most efficient at applying glue or wood dough. It is made with two offset blades—one pointed and one square—and can be purchased at low cost at paint stores, although it is sometimes hard to find.

Varnishing Aids

Strike-Wire Can. This is a homemade remedy for a thick, uneven coat of varnish. A clean tin can about 4 inches in diameter, with its lid removed, is used to hold the varnish. About 1½-inches from the can top, two holes are punched in either side of the can opposite one another, and a wire is stretched between the two holes across the open can with the two ends twisted together on the outside to hold the wire taut. Every time the brush is dipped into the varnish in the can, it is stroked free of excess against the wire, thus preventing a thick, uneven coat from being applied.

Tack Cloth. To remove every particle of dust from a surface just before varnishing it, finishers use a tack cloth. Such a cloth can be purchased ready-made at any paint store or one can be prepared at the workbench. As its name implies, it is a tacky cloth kept sticky by being moistened with varnish. Its sticky surface picks up every mote of dust. To prepare such a cloth, take a clean square of old cotton—one with hemmed edges, to avoid raveling—and soak it in warm water. Wring it well, fold it into fourths, and pour turpentine on it. Work the cloth well to distribute the turpentine, then wring it once again. Now pour a tablespoon of varnish into the cloth and twist and fold the cloth until the varnish is evenly distributed. Continue working the turpentine in until the cloth is nearly dry. To revive its tacky action, you will have to sprinkle the cloth with turpentine and water before using it and before string it away. The cloth should be kept in a clean, closed jar when not in use. To clean a surface before varnishing, simply fold the cloth into a convenient size and dust the surface carefully.

Picking Stick. Professional finishers use a special tool for picking up the tiny particles which sometimes drop on the surface while the varnish is being applied. Sometimes this tool is a delicate Size 0 brush; sometimes it is a finely pointed piece of wood known as a picking stick. To make such a stick yourself, melt powdered resin in a pan placed in boiling water (a double boiler retired from kitchen use will do nicely). When the resin has melted, mix six parts of resin with one part of varnish and knead the mixture into a ball with moistened fingers. Pick up a small piece of the mixture on the end of a pointed stick. Working very carefully so as not to touch the varnished surface, use the sticky end to pick up the dust particles before the varnish can dry and trap them on the surface.

Appendix B
Bending Wood Into Curved Shapes

Wood contouring can be accomplished by a number of methods—notably steaming, making relief cuts and laminating. In each of these methods, how the wood is held in the clamps is all-important. The natural elasticity of the lumber employed and its graining must be carefully considered. Such woods as ash, mahogany and oak are ideal choices for such a project.

In designing and cutting the piece to be contoured, one must consider the fact that wood bends more easily if the annual rings in the lumber are parallel to the radius of the curve. Also, the thinner the stock used, the less the fiber stress in a given radius.

Jointing or drilling contoured wood should be done only after the piece has been formed to shape.

Steaming. This is a tried-and-true method for making wood more pliable. Any means of exposing the wood may be used, so long as the condensed steam does not directly touch the wood. The form to which the steamed wood is shaped should be slightly smaller as to the radius of its curves than is desired in the finished piece, because the wood will spring back slightly when it is released from the cramps. Once the steamed wood is cramped to the form, it must be allowed to dry thoroughly or it will not retain the contouring.

Relief Cutting. This is an expedient method for rendering the wood more pliable. When time is of the essence, it is an excellent method to use—especially when the wood being curved is not essential to a strong structure. At given intervals, depending on the radius of the curve, the wood is cut with a saw. These relief cuts are

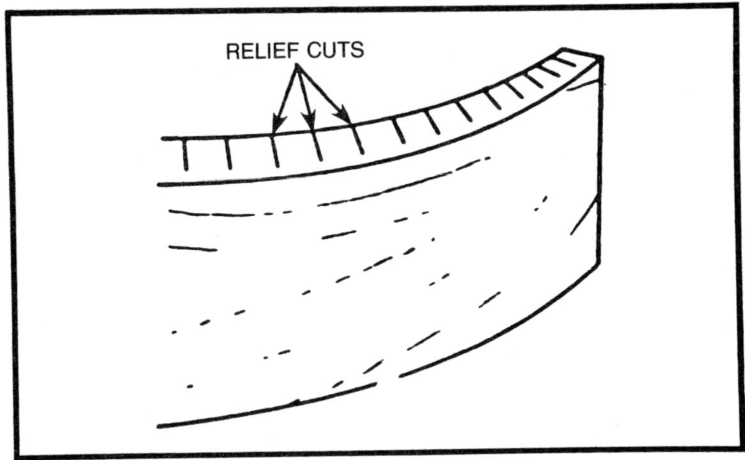

Fig. B-1. Relief cutting—when contoured wood is thoroughly dried, glue is inserted into the cuts to strengthen the piece.

uniform in size—about two-thirds of the wood thickness—and they are closer together and relatively deeper where the bend is sharpest (Fig. B-1). Soaking the wood in warm water after the cuts are made renders it much easier to bend. If necessary to the strength of the curved piece, glue may be applied between the saw cuts, or a very thin strip of wood may be glued to the inside of the curve for reinforcement. However, none of these steps can be taken until the wood has been curved to the desired shape in the cramps, press or jig, and until it is thoroughly dry. Greatest care must be taken in removing the curved piece from the cramping devices, lest the release in tension cause it to spring back to original shape. The tension of the restraints should be lessened slowly, gradually easing the pressure on the curved piece.

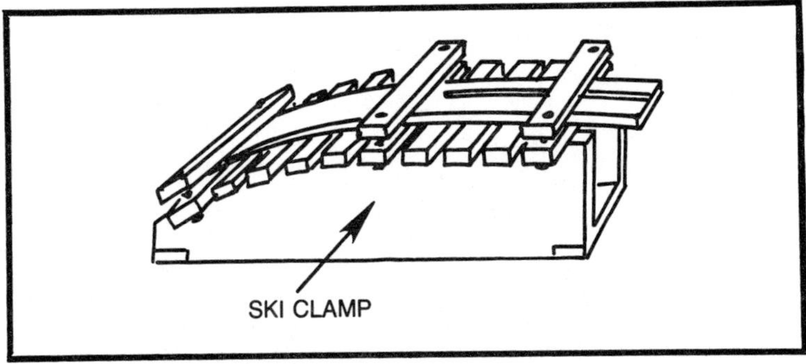

Fig. B-2. Laminated layers of wood are bent as a unit on a form like this one constructed for bending skiis. (Note the special ski clamp.)

Laminating Wood. In laminating wood, forms are built on which a number of sections are placed, one on top of the other, and bent as one unit (Fig. B-2). Laminated sections—such as plywood—have much greater strength than solid stock of comparable size. All sizes of articles, from small cases to large beams and arches, may be formed by this process.

Appendix C
Truing-up Lumber

Before any construction can begin, each board which is to be used in the project must be smooth, flat, square and correctly sized. Planes play a paramount role in preparing the lumber.

The truing-up process is a meticulous one, and a systematic procedure must be followed to expedite the work and eliminate mistakes. The next paragraphs contain some practical suggestions.

If all six sides of a piece of lumber are to be planed, start with a large surface first—that is, with one side of a board. Place the board flat on a workbench, or similar support, with the grain pointing away from you. Keep the board from sliding by placing heavy weights in a bookend-fashion against both ends. Adjust your plane to cut a thin, uniform chip and begin planing with long, even strokes, keeping the bed of the plane against the lumber and applying pressure evenly. When the surface has been smoothed all over, check it with a straightedge (Fig. C-1) to detect any cups of windings, mark the high spots and plane them again, using a very fine setting. (Very hard woods or difficult graining may come smoother if you hold the plane at a slight angle to the edge of the board.)

Now turn the board and place one of the long, narrow edges upright in a vise with the grain pointing away from you. (Wood nomenclature in shown in Fig. C-2.) Repeat the same smoothing procedure on the edge, using a jointer plane with a long bed which will shear off—rather than follow—every rise and fall, like a shorter plane will do (Fig. C-3). Take care not to tilt or dip the plane on the narrow surface. When finished, check the surface for flatness with

Fig. C-1. Checking planing for even smoothness and squareness—place the try-square stock against a side of the wood which has just been planed (called the face side) and hold the board edge on which the try-square blade rests up to the light to see if any discrepancies exist. Mark with a pencil and move plane as shown to smooth them away.

the steel straightedge (Fig. C-4) and, using a try-square, check the edge with the previously smoothed side for squareness, testing at both corners and at regular intervals along the length of the board.

Now you are ready to plane one end of the board (Fig. C-5). The end presents the greatest challenge in truing-up because it must

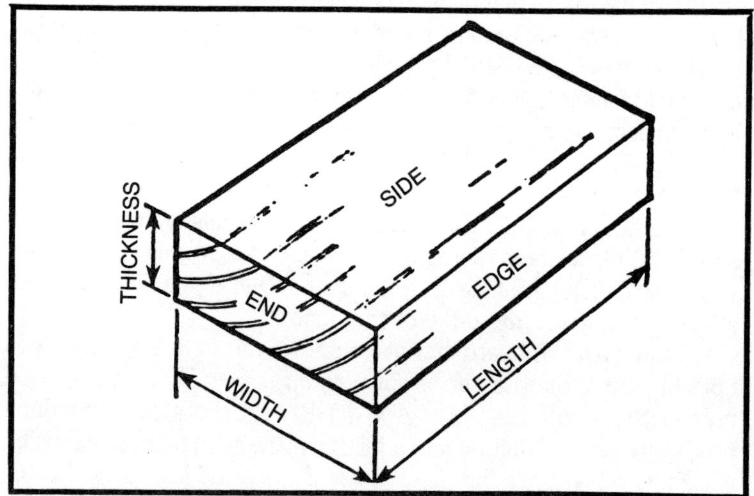

Fig. C-2. Names of the various surfaces of a piece of lumber—note grain direction.

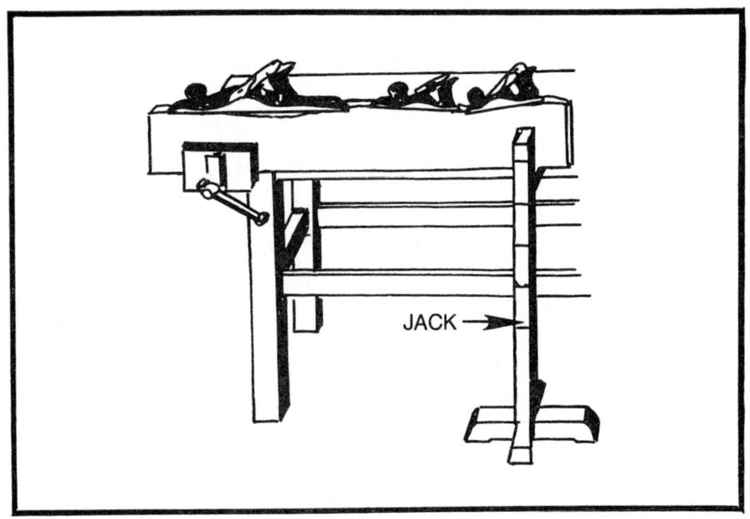

Fig. C-3. Planing the edge of lumber with too short a plane—note how the short plane tends to rise and fall with the ripples in the board edge, while a longer plane would shear them off.

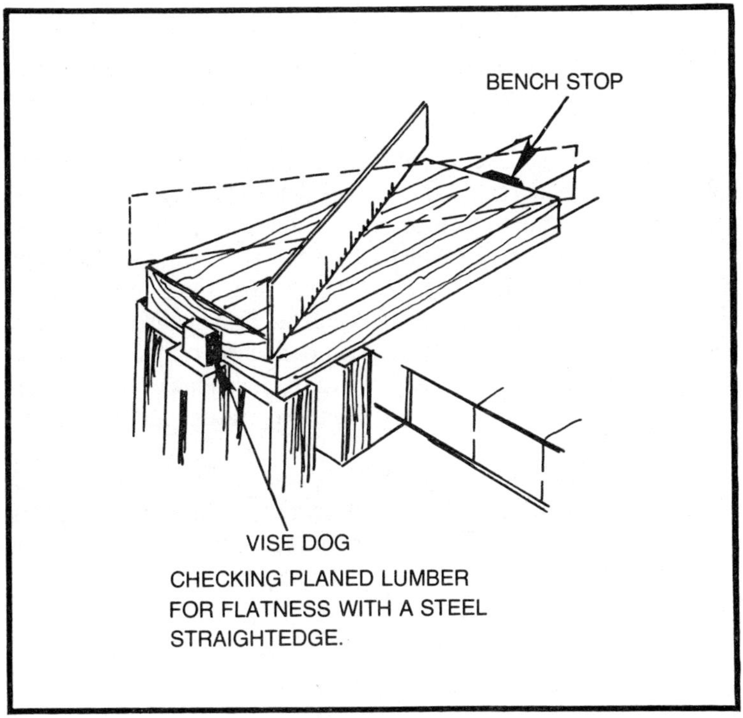

BENCH STOP

VISE DOG

CHECKING PLANED LUMBER FOR FLATNESS WITH A STEEL STRAIGHTEDGE.

Fig. C-4. Checking planed lumber for flatness with a steel straightedge.

Fig. C-5. Methods of planing end grain to prevent split edges: 1) Plane from the edges toward the middle, 2) deliberately chamfer the edges, and 3) buffer the edge with waste wood which will take the splitting, leaving the work unharmed.

square-up to two surfaces—the side and the edge. To complicate matters, the crossgrain is more difficult to smooth, requiring a sharp cutting edge and fine adjustment.

After securing the board end-up in a vise, shear the end smooth holding the plane at a slight angle to the side. This angle will produce an effective shearing cut across the end fibers and enable you to hold the plane parallel to the end surface for the remainder of your planing. To avoid chipping the end fibers near the opposite edge, plane from all edges toward the center. Test frequently with a try-square to ascertain that the end is precisely at right angles to the side and the edge already planed. Mark the locations of any indentations or elevations which the try-square indicates, and re-plane to render them smooth.

Having established a level surface and square corners on *one* side, *one* edge and *one* end, you will now repeat the same processes on the *opposite* side, the *opposite* edge and the *opposite* end. The stock is then ready for sizing.

Appendix D
Measuring Stock

Measurements must be made with extreme care. A drawing knife or pencil should be used to mark the saw lines which will trim the lumber to the length and width desired. The try-square is most useful in indicating waste margins; however, the edges of boards—because of their narrowness—are especially difficult to measure unless the woodworker has a measuring gauge at his disposal. A measuring gauge features a gauge-ruled beam on which is threaded a headpiece shaped like a large washer. When the thumbscew on the

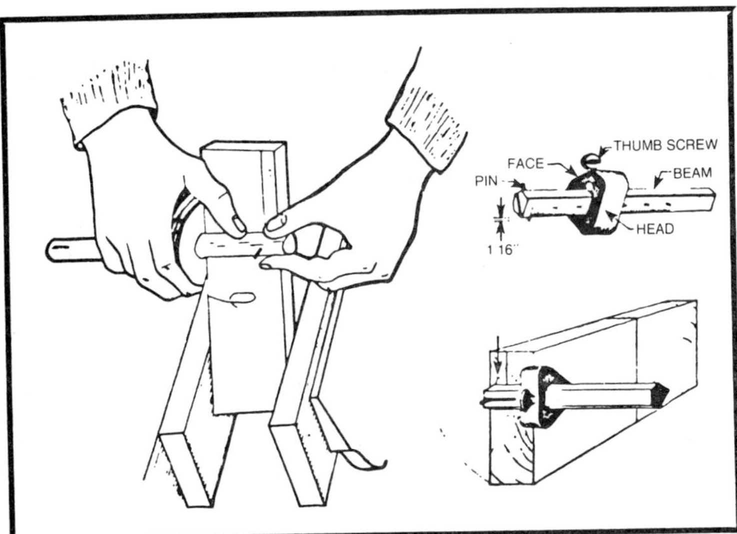

Fig. D-1. Using a marking gauge, work is secured in a vise. Both hands press the gauge against the lumber and keeping the head piece firmly against the planed board edge, push the beam along the lumber with the grain. The spur will score the saw line.

headpiece is loosened, the headpiece can slide along the ruled beam to mark one perimeter of the measure desired. On the end of the beam, a sharp spur marks the other perimeter. To score the lumber to this measure, the flat face of the head is held tightly against the vertical edge of the board and the thumbscrew tightened to fix its position (Fig. D-1). Then, while one hand holds the headpiece against the edge of the board, the other hand pushes the beam along the board with the grain, the spur scoring the lumber to mark the measure. Since both hands are needed for this task, the wood must first be secured in a vise with the sides of the board held vertically between the jaws and the edge to be measured fully exposed.

After lumber is sized by sawing or planing, it must be rechecked for squareness at the corners and for flatnesses on all surfaces. Any deviations from smoothness can be planed away.

Index

R

S